OPERA CARAVAN

OPERA CARAVAN

Adventures of the Metropolitan on Tour
1883-1956

BY QUAINTANCE EATON

WITH A FOREWORD BY RUDOLF BING

Layout of Illustrations by Jean Morris

and a New Introduction by the Author

A DA CAPO PAPERBACK

Library of Congress Cataloging in Publication Data

Eaton, Quaintance.
    Opera caravan.

    (A Da Capo paperback)
    Reprint of the ed. published by Farrar, Straus and
Cudahy, New York, for the Metropolitan Opera Guild.
    Includes index.
    1. New York. Metropolitan Opera. 2. Opera—
United States. I. Title.
[ML1711.8.N3M425 1978b]   782.1′06′27471   78-9128
ISBN 0-306-80089-6

ISBN: 0-306-80089-6

First Paperback Edition 1978

This Da Capo Press paperback edition of *Opera Caravan*
is an unabridged republication, plus a number of corrections
by the author and her new introduction for this edition, of
the first edition published in New York and Toronto in 1957.
It is reprinted by arrangement with the author, with
the permission of the Metropolitan Opera Guild.

Published by Da Capo Press, Inc.
A Subsidiary of Plenum Publishing Corporation
227 West 17th Street
New York, New York 10011

AUTHOR'S INTRODUCTION TO THE 1978 EDITION

Twenty-two years is veritably a whole generation—especially in these fast-moving times. The gap between 1956 (when *Opera Caravan* was completed) and 1978 in Metropolitan Opera tours has brought about some changes, but essentially the impact is the same. The marvelous repertory company still takes to the road 375 strong, its glories transferred from Lincoln Center for the past dozen years instead of from the dingy yellow-brick building on West 39th Street. And to the eager cities throughout the country, they "take everything along except the opera house," in the words of Francis Robinson, that urbane gentleman of many parts, who first masterminded the tours in 1945 and has been in one or more important Met posts ever since. As the tour director today, he has the facts, figures—and fancies—of the annual treks at his fingertips.

The greatest change is of course that air travel has replaced the train for the personnel for the past ten years. People go by plane; scenery, props, and costumes by truck. If this arrangement is more efficient and time-saving, the tour has nevertheless become less of a "family" matter than when the many-linked special trains brought the company close together. And—as Francis Robinson reminisces—"those poker games never ended!"

The route has contracted in recent years—no such sprawling adventures as described in the earlier seasons. Only seven cities retain the honor as hosts in 1978, and two of them split the week's visit that is otherwise obligatory.

The one-night stands are a thing of the past. Though there are many requests from other cities—especially as the Met's national prestige grows through the legendary Texaco radio broadcasts and now television—few can afford an entire week.

Costs have, it goes without saying, mounted geometrically. When the Met loses $50,000 every time the curtain goes up at home (compare this with the $5,000 it cost to get the curtain up in the first days), what can the figure be when you add transportation, per diems, and the special sets that must be built to fit smaller stages? The answer is staggering. The tours have never been profitable, in spite of early bookkeeping that made them seem so by attributing all their expense to the home stand.

The Met is international as well. To the ventures described in *Caravan* have been added a rather ill-fated Paris jaunt in 1966 (related in this author's *The Miracle of the Met*), and a highly successful visit to Japan in the spring of 1975.

For the sake of its image, thus reflected world-wide, there will no doubt continue to be an opera caravan attached to the home body by an umbilical cord. As each decade produces new and glamorous singers, fresh and provocative productions, and (it is always hoped) great conductors, the Met will wish to share its treasures with the world.

For the record, the 1978 tour goes to Cleveland, Boston, Atlanta (still noted for the rich and rare parties recounted lovingly in *Caravan*), Memphis and Dallas (sharing the week), Minneapolis, and Detroit. A June week was recently added in

Wolf Trap Farm near Washington, D.C., and Philadelphia's splendid new Robin Hood Dell will have the honor of three June performances as well, with the hope of extending them to a week.

As for the annals of the tour years in the "Generation Gap," you will find them from 1966 to 1977 in the Met's own Annals volumes, this latest decade now available. And they will catch up with the years 1956-66 when the Met's centenary is celebrated in a sumptuous volume supervised by Gerald Fitzgerald of *Opera News* and Mary Ellis Peltz, this author's own editor for *Opera Caravan*.

So, once again, *Bon Voyage,* dear Metropolitan. Happy landings!

QUAINTANCE EATON

New York, 1978

CONTENTS

OPERA CARAVAN

*This book is dedicated
to the wonderful people in fifty-six cities
who made it possible*

To begin at home, my profound gratitude to The Metropolitan Opera Guild, which boldly commissioned the project. To Richard P. Leach, director of the Guild, and to Mary Ellis Peltz, editor of *Opera News,* who unfailingly offered encouragement, the one with wise counsel, the other with vast knowledge and keen editorial eye. To Mrs. August Belmont, whose enthusiasm was a constant inspiration.

The Metropolitan administration freely cooperated in allowing the author to join "Opera Caravan, 1955" for a glimpse of the enchantment of the road. In addition to those people named in the text (omitted from these credits for lack of space), my thanks to Anne Gordon and Louis Snyder, of the press department; Irene Barry and Winifred Short, patient guardians of the trunk lines; and Reginald S. Tonry, House manager, who made tour programs available.

"Operation Magic Carpet," a six-month flying tour of thirty-five cities, was materially aided by John Mezzatesta of Columbia Artists Management, while Manila O'Neal acted as friendly pilot driving through New York and into Canada.

Without a hundred others, *Opera Caravan* could not have taken to the road. Charles Menees of the St. Louis *Post-Dispatch,* Michael Canepa of San Francisco, and Manuel Aguilar, Jr., of Mexico, D.F., collected vital material. Unpublished notes or manuscripts came from William Glasgow Bruce Carson of St. Louis, Mrs. Louis Shouse of Kansas City, Edward Alexander Parsons of New Orleans, Helen Tvrdy of Omaha, and Maria de Segurola of Beverly Hills. Theses on local opera and theatre history were made available by Eldin Burton (Atlanta), Robert P. Nesbitt (Syracuse), and Donald Z. Woods (Minneapolis).

Old programs were shared by dozens of collectors, from Mrs. Bert H. Printz of Youngstown, Ohio, to Mrs. Peter B. Nelson of Kamloops, British Columbia. Among helpful members of the National Council of the Metropolitan Opera Association were Mrs. John Wells Heard of San Antonio, Mrs. Allen G. Oliphant of Tulsa, Elsie I. Sweeney of Columbus, Ind., Mrs. Frederick R. Weyerhaeuser of St. Paul, and Robert H. Tannahill of Detroit. In New York, Mrs, Norris Darrell and Marguerite Wickersham were unfailingly helpful.

"In the order of their appearance," scores of other individuals provided information or hospitality: Virginia Polak, Mildred C. Busby, Blanche C. Haas, Mrs. W. Wailes Thomas, Mr. and Mrs. Richard Glass, Mrs. Phinizy

vii

Calhoun, Mrs. William A. Parker, Mrs. Henry P. Johnston, Mrs. L. K. Thompson, Mr. and Mrs. Floyd S. Chalmers, Mr. and Mrs. Richard Johnston, J. Herman Thuman, Mrs. Mary Leighton, Mrs. Jesse Hawkins, Richard Wangerin, Ernst C. Krohn, Louise Mercer, Muriel Francis, Lionel Adams, Mrs. Edward B. Ludwig, Albert Voss, Mrs. James A. Lewis, Mrs. Bartram Kelley, Mrs. Ben Foster, Rosalie Talbott, Howard Skinner, Mrs. Carl Livingston, James Schwabacher, Wanda Krasoff, Dorothy Huttenback, Alice Taylor, Mrs. Edmund Gale, Mrs. Robert Machamer, Naomi Reynolds, Mrs. Frank A. Johnson, Helen Black, Blanche Lederman, Mr. and Mrs. Ronald A. Dougan, Mr. and Mrs. A. Beverly Barksdale, Mr. and Mrs. Gordon Saunders, William Martin, William Benswanger, John S. Edwards, Harold Mason, Hugh Miller, Mr. and Mrs. Henry S. Drinker, Irene Kahn, Sam Berkman, Elizabeth Howry, Marie Bourbeau and Murray R. Chipman.

For "services beyond the call of duty" in libraries from coast to coast I cite Philip Miller and his staff (music) and Archibald De Wees (reference) of New York; John W. Bonner of the University of Georgia; Mrs. Jacob Plaut (Cincinnati), James Cleghorn (San Francisco), Barbara Penyak (Cleveland), Irene Millen (Pittsburgh), Bernice Larrabee (Philadelphia), and Daniel J. Koury (Boston), as well as Harold Spivacke and Paul L. Berry of the Library of Congress, and Charles van Ravenswaay of Missouri's Historical Society. Also Mrs. Philip Miller, Sirvart Poladian, Mrs. Fanny Spearman, Josephine Cleveland, Mary Davant, Wendell Arnote, Mason Tolman, Dorothy Brown, Mae Walton, Ruth Wanatabe, Berna Bergholtz, Ellen Kenny, Charlotte Shockley, Alice P. Hook, Mabel Sprong, Carey Bliss, Ina Aulis, Louise Wells, Leah Riedesel, Mrs. Gladys Wilson, Robert E. Hoag, Wallace Harmer, Bess Finn, Elizabeth Ohr, Kurt Myers, Geraldine Rowley, James Dixon, Fred Lane, Alberta Kneeland, Zoltán Haraszti, Stanley Weinberg, Ethelyn Aldrich, Doris E. Cook and Charles W. Crosby.

Newspaper offices were uniformly cordial; radio and television stations helped to publicize the project; music critics, past and present, showed lively interest. Many contemporary writers appear in the narrative; others especially helpful include Edgar S. Van Olinda of the Albany *Times-Union,* Charlotte Phelan of the Houston *Post,* Marjory M. Fisher of the San Francisco *News,* Cyrus Durgin of the Boston *Globe,* and Warren Story Smith, formerly of the Boston *Post.*

The roll of scribes also includes Sam Kahn, Ben S. Parker, Louise N. Ahrens, Harry Martin, Sydney Dalton, Harold Henderson, Keith Marvin, Emma Van Wormer, William Fleming, Kenneth Gill, Theodolinda Boris, Harvey Southgate, Marshall F. Bryant, Arthur Darack, Eleanor Bell, Frederick Yeiser, William Mootz, Dwight Anderson, Thomas B. Sherman, Francis A. Klein, Ed Brooks, Gerald Ashford, Ann Holmes, Jack Frederick Kilpatrick, Maurice da Venna, Alexander Fried, Alfred Frankenstein, Conrad B. Harrison, Alex Murphree, Emmy Brady Rogers, Clyde Neibarger, Genevieve Robertson, Helen Mary Hayes, Martin W. Bush, Roger Dettmer, Walter Monfried, Edward P. Halline, Julian Seaman, J. Fred Lissfelt, Ralph

Lewando, Donald Steinfirst, Paul Hume, H. Earle Johnson and Carl E. Lindstrom.

During the collation of the statistical material and the writing of the text, the valuable assistance of Donald H. White proved essential. I am also indebted to Fred V. Grunfeld and Mary Jane Matz for necessary pruning, and to Gerald Fitzgerald for preparing the index. All photographs are from the files of the Publications Department of The Metropolitan Opera Guild unless otherwise specified.

Last, and lovingly, I dedicate *Opera Caravan* to Julie and Alec Templeton, who provided in their Connecticut home an ideal refuge for the writer.

QUAINTANCE EATON

New York
November, 1956

FOREWORD

One fine Saturday evening in April, the famous gold curtain comes down at the Metropolitan Opera House in New York for a last time: another season has become history. But no sooner has silence fallen on the old Broadway theatre than our orchestra tunes up, come Monday, in some other city: another Metropolitan tour is under way.

I am often asked how I feel about going on tour after the strenuous months of the New York season. By April we have grown so tired that we can hardly keep our eyes open after eleven. But once the tour starts, with all those delectable midnight suppers, we manage to feel chipper and gay until morning.

This is by way of saying that the tour is one of the most cherished events in our operatic lives. It is wonderful to feel the excitement and sense the affection generated by the Metropolitan in all those far-flung cities.

The fabulous cavalcade, history relates, started in the very first season. We constantly encounter citizens with keen memories who leave us in no doubt as to how long they have supported the Metropolitan. They tell us how Caruso did this and Pinza that; how the most thrilling pages of operatic history were written, if we but knew it, in their particular bailiwick.

In order to reveal the full story, much of it for the first time, The Metropolitan Opera Guild had the excellent idea of asking an experienced and enthusiastic journalist, Quaintance Eaton, to do the job. A splendid thought! I have made up my mind to read the book from beginning to end, but I also plan to consult the record of each city before visiting it again. Fair warning: next time I may know even more fantastic stories than the local citizenry! So may you!

RUDOLF BING

DRESS REHEARSAL

On the Fortieth Street side of the huge stage, which echoed to shouts of "Gangway!" "Watch it!" "Coming out!" and the hurrying footfalls of heavily laden men, falling scenery flats slapped the dust into whirlwinds. Battens and groundcloths and platforms were being taken down the ramps to the street to be loaded on the trucks under the supervision of Johnnie Flood, at his post for twenty years.

Louis Edson, young master mechanic, moved about, presiding over the dismantling of *Fledermaus,* the last show to be packed for travel. His father, Ralph, wearing the largest and gaudiest in his collection of caps to celebrate his eleventh tour as "prop" master, helped a crew store the properties in variegated boxes, hampers, chests and crates.

Jennie Cervini, wardrobe mistress, tucked away the last flounce of Adele's saucy ball dress as Rose Calamari bent her shoulder under a dozen hangers holding costumes to be packed. Rosina Cassamassa scurried away for a fresh load and May Cervini, Jennie's sister-in-law, pasted *Fledermaus* labels on the tall chests marked "SL (Solo Lady)."

On the other side of the House, Jennie's brother Angelo locked a trunk stenciled with the notice, "Wanted Every Day—Place on Stage," while William H. Zauder darted into the men's dressing rooms, collecting wigs.

Rudolph Kuntner finished stowing away a jungle of electrical paraphernalia in 150 assorted rust-colored boxes. Herman Krawitz, administrator of stage departments, checked his master records.

At last the loaded truck drove off to the railroad yards with Harold Hyde at the same wheel his father swung before him.

In his office on the Thirty-ninth Street side, Frank Paola mulled over a hundred details. Although his work of routing the tour and assigning Pullman space and tickets to every member of the company had long been accomplished, the musical secretary and company manager concentrated like a general before battle.

Content that these experts had the job well in hand, Rudolf Bing and his administrative assistants went home for a few hours' sleep. Mr. Bing, Max Rudolf and Francis Robinson, who had planned all the booking and repertory, would be on the special train when it pulled out of Grand Central Station Monday morning. So would Henry A. Fischer, assistant comptroller, Harry G. Schumer, librarian, and Florence Guarino, secretary *extraordinaire* to the administrators. Only Assistant Managers John Gutman and Reginald Allen would remain behind with the regular staff to keep them company for the next seven weeks.

The Metropolitan Opera, on the eve of its sixty-eighth national tour, remained true to its slogan, "Take everything along but the Opera House."

Francis Robinson, who adds public relations to administrative duties, has described the yearly migration as "the biggest thing that moves except the circus."

It was never simple to get the show on the road. But current logistics of moving a troupe of 325, with scenery for sixteen operas, 400 trunks and 150 musical instruments, in two special passenger trains with nineteen sleepers, plus the baggage train of twenty-nine cars, through the network of American and Canadian railroads to reach sixteen cities in twelve states, would have confounded the masterminds of earlier days.

The resourcefulness of the expert showman has always been a must on tour. Trains can always be late. Bugs can always lodge in delicate throats and upset an entire opera schedule. Difficulties magnify thousandfold away from home base.

America's most famous and most durable opera company has been a "traipsin' woman" throughout sixty-seven of its first seventy-two years. Of the seven so-called "German" seasons, 1884-85 through 1890-91, Manager Edmund C. Stanton and Conductors Anton Seidl and Walter Damrosch evidently kept their flock close to home in three—1886-87, 1887-88 and 1890-91. No resident company played in the season 1892-93 after the fire in the House, and none called the Metropolitan its home in 1897-98. In those five seasons the "provinces" had to be content with tourists under other banners, or with none.

How can one define what constituted a touring "Metropolitan Opera Company"? In earlier days, the traveling unit may have been called Henry E. Abbey's Italian Grand Opera, Maurice Grau's Italian Grand Opera, or merely Italian Grand Opera "under the direction of" one of these impresarios who leased the theatre. But the words "from the Metropolitan Opera House" were invariably appended.

In the German years, the wording was also varied: German Grand Opera, Grand German Opera or Damrosch's Grand Opera, again with the designation "from the Metropolitan Opera House."

The word "Metropolitan" first appears in an official title in Heinrich Conried's regime, still with the impresario's name prefixed. Only with Giulio Gatti-Casazza's advent in 1908 did the magic brevet, "Metropolitan Opera Company," emerge for the performing groups at home and abroad.

From the beginning, nevertheless, all safaris from the House were in fact if not in title Metropolitan Opera companies, and only once did a troupe go out without home sanction. Edmund C. Stanton, in his first year as manager, disapproved a proposed tour, but the "insurgents" were essentially Metropolitan and therefore belong in the record.

No documentation of tours in the German era can be found in New York. Official tour programs are missing altogether until 1898-99, and are incomplete until 1917.

Abbey's exploits may be spied in a crumbling ledger known in the comptroller's office as "The Bible." On long, narrow pages the fortunes of Mary Anderson, Lily Langtry, Lillian Russell and other Abbey protégées are totted up in flowing script filling the years when the manager was exiled from the Metropolitan. The opera account resumes when he returned in 1891 and continues with Maurice Grau's record and on to the present.

No similar accounting has come to light for Stanton's incumbency in the House. If Damrosch stored away any memorabilia of the four tours that have been certified in those seven years, the malevolent god Loge had the last word. A warehouse fire destroyed all these records.

After Abbey's fiasco in 1883-84, the American impresario kept Italian opera alive with a company headed by Adelina Patti. Its activities do not properly come under the aegis of the Metropolitan, although Abbey twice rented the House from Stanton for a short spring season. But because he was so soon to take up the managerial reins again, the most spectacular of his tours—that of 1889-90, when Patti, Tamagno and Nordica dedicated the Chicago Auditorium and journeyed to Mexico—is embraced in Metropolitan records as a courtesy.

Mexican data for this pilgrimage are difficult to verify because the most important newspaper of the day, *Monitor Republicano,* published only brief, incomplete accounts of the performances. In Paris, too, where the company paid its only visit outside our borders in 1910, reporting was more impressionistic than inclusive.

Two neighbors that are not generally considered as "touring cities" are included if for no other reason than their absence from all other accountings. Brooklyn, although a borough of Greater New York, is not a part of the Metropolitan's local annals. Furthermore the Metropolitan began its visits there when Brooklyn was still an independent city. Philadelphia in the early days constituted a part of the spring tour, before the practice of performances during the season was adopted.

City by city the scroll unwinds. Metropolitan tour history is sometimes hidden in huge, dusty, unwieldy bound volumes of newspapers that shred at the touch, leaving a pitiful fall of saffron confetti around the chair of the careful researcher. Sometimes neat small rolls of microfilm in the nation's libraries yield operatic secrets that are all but forgotten.

The cities that have played host to our illustrious and resilient lyric company—fifty-one in the United States, two in Canada and one in Europe (Paris)—are inextricably bound into its history, even though their names have not all survived in today's route book.

Travel patterns shift and change. Halls once suitable for the dazzling panoply of grand opera fall into decrepitude; new halls are built in other towns. Zealous individuals die; others beckon from other longitudes. New companies spring up in the tour's path and absorb local attention; the Metropolitan goes where it is needed more urgently.

And always, packed in the wardrobe trunks, in the scenery cars, in the Pullmans with their cargo of specially blessed human beings, goes that indefinable ingredient, glamor—immemorial handmaiden and inseparable traveling companion of grand opera.

Part I

ABBEY'S ADVENTURERS

1. OVERTURE

"The house was crowded as one rarely sees it. . . . The performance was noteworthy in several ways, first and foremost for a real orchestra, upwards of seventy. . . .

"Vianesi conducted with skill and authority. But we cannot congratulate him on finding a bass tuba part in the score of *Faust,* the most serious blemish in the orchestra. . . . The too, too ambitious person who played, or rather snorted, on the instrument was getting his—or Abbey's—full money's worth. Let him go play on the Common. . . ."

Thus the *Boston Evening Transcript's* William Foster Apthorp welcomed the "Company from the Metropolitan Opera House" in its first appearance away from home.

The scene was the Boston Theatre; the date: December 26, 1883. The opera was *Faust,* which had opened the new house in New York on October 22 and would enjoy a similar privilege several times on the tour.

The impresario was Henry Eugene Abbey, whose motto, "When in doubt, take to the road," christened the long trail.

This man, "a traveler equaled by no theatrical manager living," as the *New York Times* characterized him, dreamed that El Dorado lay just around the corner in the theatres and "Op'ry Houses" of the country.

The necessity of applying his formula to opera on a grand scale arose at the end of his first season as lessee of the Metropolitan Opera House. In two brilliant months at the new theatre, Abbey had staged opera in a more elaborate style than New York had ever witnessed, but the $1,000 allowed by the stockholders for each performance had melted away in the consuming demands of stage designers, costumers and high-salaried singers. The distraught manager was forced to dig cruelly into the layer of profit secreted by his previous forays with Bernhardt, Booth and Irving.

As 1883 drew to a close, contracts with his costly artists still remained unfulfilled. Abbey must give opera somewhere, and the New York vein was running out. The conclusion was obvious. Packing up his galaxy, he steamed off in the "railroad cars" to recoup his losses on the circuit that had seldom failed him.

1

When the directors of the new temple of lyric art at Thirty-ninth Street and Broadway beckoned Henry Abbey to the most challenging job in the American entertainment world, he was thirty-seven. Associated with him were great names in the theatre and the two reigning prima donnas, Adelina Patti and Christine Nilsson, although he had temporarily lost Patti to his archrival, Colonel James H. Mapleson.

Abbey had stepped in to rescue Patti midway in her 1881-82 tour, her first in America since girlhood. He immediately halved the $10 ticket price that had been urged by her Italian agent, Franchi. Nobody wanted to pay $10 to hear *anybody* sing, according to H. E. Krehbiel, *New York Tribune* critic. Abbey also persuaded the diva to include operatic excerpts on her concert programs, and arranged a short opera season in New York. Hastily prepared, these performances fell short of success, so that Patti was receptive to Mapleson's advances that autumn. The colonel's prize was dearly won, for Abbey forced the bidding to the unprecedented figure of $5,000 for each performance by the "divine Adelina."

Was it the link with Patti and Nilsson that prompted James A. Roosevelt and the directors of the Metropolitan Opera House Company to choose a man of theatrical stamp to head their operatic enterprise? Abbey's only other musical qualification was a boyhood struggle with a cornet in a school band, his only contact with opera, the management of a summer troupe in his home town, Akron, Ohio.

Experienced opera *generalissimi* came as scarce then as now, and candidates were quickly exhausted. Mapleson was bound by the New York Academy of Music, with which the Metropolitan had just broken; the London impresario, Ernest Gye, was a favorite contender until the New York directors decided against any possibility of domination by Covent Garden. The honor fell to Abbey.

He controlled the only artists who might dethrone Patti, now Mapleson's queen, and Etelka Gerster, Mapleson's princess. Abbey's dynasty began with the sovereign Christine Nilsson and Marcella Sembrich, heiress apparent.

Recognizing his own limitations, Abbey wisely engaged as second-in-command the experienced Maurice Grau, who had piloted several of his Uncle Jacob's opera companies, and also managed a French light opera troupe starring the beguiling Aimée. Abbey was inclined to be short with gentlemen of the press, who found him "reserved in manner and difficult of approach." Grau, on the other hand, was invariably amiable to newspaper men and believed in winning them over to his side.

Abbey impressed the Metropolitan directors by the very habits that were to ruin him: the "large purposes and princely generosity" attributed to him by *Music and Drama,* a contemporary journal.

No matter how prudent the counsel of John B. Schoeffel, Abbey's partner since 1876, and Maurice Grau, whom he took into active partnership after his first year in grand opera, Abbey never throttled his impulse toward largesse.

Grau provided the successes, it was said, Abbey provided the losses and Schoeffel did the grumbling.

Animated by a genuine ambition to revitalize Italian opera, which seemed to be fading into a Victorian "decline," Abbey was determined to equip his musical company with the same finesse he had bestowed on his theatrical troupes.

Alone in the field outside New York, he might have restored his own bank-roll to health and administered a necessary transfusion to Italian opera. But the wily Mapleson beleaguered him every step of the way.

War between the two, beginning with skirmishes over Patti's contracts, had assumed the status of a pitched battle as Mapleson, from his stronghold in the New York Academy of Music, fought Abbey, performance by performance, from the simultaneous opening nights of the two houses. Now the conflict spread to half a dozen fronts.

2. "RITORNA VINCITOR!"

Leaving three New York subscription performances dangling unconsummated, the manager led the first Metropolitan caravan forth on the day after Christmas to display its glittering wares in the capital of New England culture. Logically Boston was Abbey's first port of call. Four years previously he and his partner, John B. Schoeffel, had obtained a long lease on Beethoven Hall, ripped out its interior and reopened it as the new Boston Park Theatre.

Its stage could not, however, accommodate an operatic invasion of 250, so Abbey was obliged to rent Eugene Tompkins' Boston Theatre, which had housed visiting opera troupes for thirty years.

Mapleson had played the Boston Theatre regularly since his first tour in 1878, but his eagerness to anticipate Abbey had forced him into the less commodious Globe the week before the Metropolitan company arrived.

Curiosity brought out a huge first-night audience for *Faust* in the mellow old theatre. Unhappily, The Hub was not to see such a crowd again during the two-week engagement.

Abbey's conservative repertory could hardly have accounted for public indifference although it did provoke a critical outbreak. After the visit was three days spent, a Boston newspaper asked: "When will managers learn to turn the barrel over and give the old favorites a rest for a change?"

Abbey might have answered, "Never!" in defense of the operas that had induced the critic's ennui. They were Verdi's *Il Trovatore* and Donizetti's *Lucia di Lammermoor*, which had been pointed to the warehouse from time to time by critics of two decades, always to emerge fresh and appealing to less blasé audiences.

A glance at what Abbey had in store—*Mignon, La Sonnambula, La Traviata, Il Barbiere di Siviglia, Lohengrin, Martha and Carmen*—and with only *La Gioconda* as an unknown quantity, suggests that the manager was obviously trying to "meet the desires of the great public." Like Mapleson and others before and after him, he recognized the object of those desires— the one immutable element of grand opera, the singing star.

This "magnificent and honorable gambler in stars," as Walter Damrosch ungrudgingly termed Abbey, was the first to gather so large a galaxy under one system and to design a national showcase for his attractions. It mattered to no one but Mapleson that the peerless cast for *Faust* was almost entirely pirated from the Academy treasure house, for Abbey, like other entrepreneurs of the day, showed no hesitation in raiding the ranks of the opposition.

His prizes were Italo Campanini, the most admired Faust of the time; Sofia Scalchi, a Siébel unrivaled; Giuseppe del Puente, who was willing to pay 15,000 francs (about $3,000) to abrogate his Mapleson contract; Franco Novara, the bass whose real name was Frank Nash, and Mme. Emily Lablache, who, though legally prevented from singing on New York's opening night, proved to Bostonians that she "lacked nothing of perfection."

The five joined Nilsson, who shone unquestioned as the world standard for Marguerite, having created the part when Gounod revised his masterpiece for the Paris Opéra in 1869.

Nilsson's vogue in America had barely dipped from its zenith. She had returned two years previously after a long absence, beginning her concerts in The Hub; then "gave her attention to the spokes such as New York, Cincinnati and other outlying provinces," as a Boston correspondent condescendingly remarked.

She had always been a favorite, "especially with the ladies, because of the purity of her character and the tragedy that brought her marriage to a close." Her first husband, Auguste Rouzeaud, had died on February 22, 1882, "from insanity, caused by mental worry over business reverses," as Lahee put it in his *Famous Singers.*

Auguste Charles Léonard François Vianesi, Abbey's chief conductor, had functioned under Mapleson's standard as early as 1858, when he was paid eight pounds a month in London.

Fondness for the singers, all well liked in Boston, inspired enthusiasm for *Faust,* but it remained for a new star in *Lucia di Lammermoor* to sweep the proper Bostonians into what for them constituted a "frenzy."

Praxide Marcellina Kochanska, as Marcella Sembrich was known in her native Poland, darted into Metropolitan history like a humming bird. Her effect on Boston was instantaneous.

Audiences in that discriminating city have always been hard to please, both by temperament and taste. The *Lucia* enthusiasts on Abbey's second night recognized the soprano's quality from the start, cheering before she finished her first aria.

"Even the most jaded experienced a new sensation," confessed the *Transcript's* critic, Apthorp, who wondered "that a voice having the peculiar vibratory, nervous quality custom has taught us to believe is absolutely essential in singers who hope to command our emotions, should also be so flexible, so clear and so true."

Now that Boston had spoken, a new princess was crowned. It seemed a little late in the day, and a little ungenerous, to proclaim that the queen could do some wrong. Though the *Globe* critic still thought Nilsson an ideal Elsa and found her Gioconda magnificent, Apthorp's dissatisfaction with her "elementary sins" and "self-conscious" acting amounted to *lèse majesté:*

"Nilsson has so much innate power and personal magnetism that she cannot but be great at moments. She has an incomparable physique, superb voice, admirable carriage and habitual intensity of facial expression . . . but she has faults. . . . In rising above the rudiments, she has left the rudiments almost completely out of sight. . . . Her acting continually slights the ABC's. . . . Shut your eyes and you hear a completely beautiful interpretation. Open them and you see 100 departures from the truth."

Nor did the beloved Scalchi—she of "a dozen voices, each in a different register"—escape entirely unscathed, for her Siébel was questioned seriously, one of the few derogatory comments she ever received on this role. Apthorp said peevishly:

"The music is too high for her and a coarseness of accent marred otherwise fine singing in the Flower Song."

He was almost alone in resisting the lure of the shapely limbs whose tights seemed worn more becomingly than those of any other female on the stage.

Del Puente, the handsome, curly-haired Spaniard, retained his place as Boston's preferred baritone. After he was replaced on New Year's Eve as Germont by Achille Augier, a bass whose fortes lay among the Zunigas, the Ferrandos and the Raimondos, and whose *fortes* were practically inaudible, the *Globe* declared bluntly that Del Puente's illness was only temporary, fortunately for the patrons of the lyric season.

One singer who pleased everybody was the stern-lipped but sweet-voiced Alwina Valleria, another recruit from Mapleson's ranks. This Baltimore girl, who changed her name from Schoening to make her debut in Russia, was the first American to sing on the Metropolitan stage.

Aside from Sembrich, newcomers found no green pastures though Roberto Stagno had every right to regard Boston as the one oasis in a desert full of gritty encounters with the American press. Then Apthorp spoiled his compliments with a final barb: "His Lionel was a triumph aside from his customary exasperating tremolo."

Giuseppe Kaschmann, after singing the Count di Luna, was taken to task for the same fault: "A vicious style . . . aptly described as a 'wobble.!'" Giovanni Mirabella, a bass with a "powerful voice and good method," made his first appearance as Don Basilio in *Barbiere*.

Carmen, with which Abbey closed his Boston season, had not yet been given in New York. Thus Boston had the first opportunity to enjoy Zelia Trebelli's phenomenal voice, a rich contralto. Her Card Scene was "stronger than any in memory," in the *Globe's* opinion, although she did not quite dispel memories of Minnie Hauk's witchery.

Mme. Trebelli was regarded as a debutante throughout Abbey's tour, although listed with Mapleson's first American company in 1878. She had, indeed, sung under the colonel's management as early as 1862. A slim, dark Parisienne, Mme. Trebelli, nee Gilbert, evolved her stage name in a manner presaging advertising slogans of today. She spelled it backward, then Italianized the result.

Sophisticated as Boston claimed to be about its opera (it had enjoyed all the wayfarers from Grisi to Kellogg), Abbey introduced one feature that astonished and delighted the cognoscenti.

This was the orchestra, the largest ever to travel with an opera company. Apthorp's esteem for it was tempered by the offending "snorts" of the bass tuba, which, as he claimed, has no part in the *Faust* orchestra, though a proper denizen of the stage band.

Boston carefully weighed the merits of Abbey's two conductors. Vianesi's mastery was unquestioned, though the *Transcript* deplored his impetuosity. The young assistant, Cleofonte Campanini, was already beginning to show the talent that later made him a commanding figure.

In the pit for *La Sonnambula,* "that delightful idyl . . . of . . . Bellini's genius," the youth of twenty-four received many warmly approving glances across the footlights from the *tenore primo.* Italo Campanini was said to be responsible for his brother's engagement, and always sang more freely under Cleofonte's baton.

In *Sonnambula* he relaxed the tension that often gripped him on the stage and surprised everyone by his light comedy sense. The brothers were in high fettle for *Carmen* as well. Italo always acted with conviction, especially in the last scene. This evening he surpassed himself, said the *Globe,* and Cleofonte led the orchestra admirably.

Although his ledgers showed only three-fourths of what Abbey might have expected from the fortnight, he gambled on another Boston visit and signed for a week in March. Then he rounded up his songbirds for the trip home.

Pausing only a few days in his travels, Abbey showed New York the *Carmen* he had introduced in Boston, then added a *Gioconda* and a concert to complete the subscription season. During the week he found time to treat the "borough across the river" to three performances, which did not financially justify the hauls across the new Brooklyn Bridge, though they established the Brooklyn Academy of Music as an outpost for Metropolitan visits.

Then the entire company reembarked on January 14, not to return until March, with Philadelphia as their first objective. In the next five days Abbey laid the pattern of a lifetime habit for Philadelphia, which already thought proudly of itself as an "opera town." Whatever company went out from the Metropolitan in the years to follow—Italian, German or polylingual—it was certain to visit "Old Faithful."

The momentousness of the first invasion was recognized only in retrospect. "All Philadelphia knew about Abbey was the advertisements in the newspapers," according to a local historian, John Curtis. As late as January 1, the Quaker City felt scarcely a tremor of anticipation. The advertisements did not even appear every day as the engagement drew near. Several times only one line, "Next Week, Abbey Grand Opera," was squeezed in at the bottom of the Chestnut Street Opera House announcement of its current road show, Jos. K. Emmett in *Unser Fritz.*

Mapleson, however, daily proclaimed in bold type that Mme. Patti would sing her first *Aida* in Philadelphia, and Mme. Gerster her first Adina in *L'Elisir d'Amore,* opening just two days after Abbey's departure. The colonel had secured the only suitable auditorium, Philadelphia's already venerable Academy of Music, where his December engagement had already distracted attention from the new company.

The Metropolitan's repertory was not announced until January 10, and no casts were published. To learn "who sings who," the customer was obliged to call at the box office, a miscalculation hardly guaranteed to stimulate the largest possible interest.

Still the word spread, at least to the newspapers. The *Evening Bulletin* reporter advanced the theory that this would be *the* musical event of the season. Sales were said to be the largest ever recorded for grand opera in the city. In the days when the visitors proceeded at their own risk, impresarios depended on the good will of newspapers to stimulate patronage by advance trumpetings.

Abbey's first night seemed to bear out the oracles. The old Chestnut Street Opera House was jammed. "Hundreds were huddled together in a dense and confused mass, about ten out of a hundred of those that stood up being able to see the stage," the *Inquirer* reported. "No such throng has been seen in Philadelphia for years"—another remark regularly dusted off for use on every gala occasion, revealing that memory is short and civic pride is long.

Again, the opera was *Faust.* The next day, rosy prognostications had faded into the cool comment that Philadelphia had seen better performances.

"But never a more brilliant, enthusiastic, sympathetic audience," repeated the loyal scribe.

Had Sembrich been at her best, this Philadelphia story might have had a happy ending. But the prima donna became suddenly ill after the second act of *Lucia.* Both *Traviata* and *Barbiere,* scheduled for her, had to be canceled. The *Don Giovanni* that replaced *Barbiere* provoked unkind remarks from the *Bulletin:*

"Kaschmann is one of the dullest lady-killers ever, and Trebelli looked old enough to be Zerlina's grandmother." At forty-six the fact that she sang Zerlina at all speaks for her courage and versatility. The part was transposed for her deep voice.

The remainder of the week held few attractions for Philadelphians. In *Trovatore,* the Metropolitan thunders proved too Jovian for the small house, but the press blamed the conductor for the noise. When the company returned to the spacious Academy, Vianesi's refined ways with the orchestra became apparent for the first time.

La Gioconda commanded an audience comparable to that which crowded *Faust.* With Ponchielli's tunes, the "exceedingly graceful groupings" of the ballet and the delectable ballerina, Malvina Cavalazzi, the outlook brightened, but *Martha* and *Carmen* let the box office down sharply.

C. H. Matthews, treasurer of the company, reflected that pitifully few customers enjoyed Trebelli's "voluptuous but wily and cold-hearted" Carmen, and, sadly totaling the Philadelphia ledger column in red, inscribed the head of a new page:

"Chicago."

3. "GUERRA! GUERRA!"

In Chicago, omens were favorable for Abbey and the two-week season of his "cosmopolitan operatic army." Marching into the arena a week ahead of Mapleson, he counted on winning the allegiance of Chicago opera lovers before his enemy arrived for what was to be their first head-on collision outside of New York.

Abbey's local reputation was enhanced by the success of Henry Irving, who was then playing a brilliant season in the Loop, and whose prestige caused Chicago to look kindly upon the actor's manager.

"Irving theatre parties are sure to be followed by Abbey opera parties," the *Tribune* remarked ingenuously. "Society will consider it a duty to shine at Haverly's Theatre as long as the subtle influence of Abbey continues.

"Mapleson, on the other hand, is supported by the prestige of Patti's name and the charm which an extraordinarily expensive amusement possesses for a large class of persons."

Opera was a costly pastime for the average citizen even then. Both managers were asking $42 for subscriptions to twelve performances, but Mapleson promoted single seats for "Patti Nights" to $6, "Gerster Nights" to $5, while Abbey maintained a top price of $4 throughout, except for a "Grand Combination" of Nilsson and Sembrich.

Abbey desperately wanted to believe the usual promise of "the grandest and most brilliant season ever," held out by the *Tribune* on the day of the opening. The comfortable remark of next day's *Inter-Ocean* that it had been "an elegant evening," combined with the equally comfortable box office of $5500, supported him.

The *Tribune* found no fault with the musical performance. Nilsson's Marguerite was still irresistible, and Victor Capoul, substituting for Campanini, surprised everyone by the excellence of his Faust. His voice belonged to the past, but he still cherished a reputation as "the most ardent and fascinating lover known to opera in America." Scalchi sang gloriously in the seldom-heard third-act Romanza, restored at some performances.

The flaw in the picture was visual. The *Inter-Ocean's* casual comment that the scenery was tawdry passed unheard in the volley of the *Tribune's* invective.

Abbey had been betrayed by his own high standards. A few days later in Cincinnati, where he had gone to supervise the advance sale, he was still talking publicly about success in Chicago, but dropped a clue to his real state of mind in an interview with a Cincinnati *Enquirer* reporter:

"True, they have been giving us fits about the mounting of the plays [Abbey still thought in theatrical terms], but it is not our fault. In all Chicago there does not exist an opera house. In my company are eighty choristers, twenty-two ballet dancers, twenty-five in the military band, besides the supers, so that there may be 150 to 250 performers on stage at one time. You cannot do this in Chicago.

"So tonight thirty of my singers, twelve of my ballet and twenty of my military band are walking the streets of Chicago with nothing to do. I could not employ my own sets, but had to be content with stock scenery. Cincinnati is the only place we can mount the Metropolitan scenery."

As this interview was published on January 29, the opera in Chicago to which Abbey referred must have been *La Sonnambula*. The previous evening, *La Gioconda* had been credited with a *tout ensemble* the strongest and most effective of any. Only ten coryphees in the Dance of the Hours would have been unthinkable!

Like many another thrifty road manager of the century, Abbey counted on local theatres to supply the fittings for his conventional operas, even though at home the warehouse was crammed with his new settings. He was prepared with elaborate investitures for *La Gioconda, Don Giovanni, Mignon, Robert le Diable* and *Mefistofele,* but none of these could be made to fit the stage of Haverly's Theatre in Chicago.

The *Tribune* remained petulant about *mise-en-scène* throughout the fortnight. Its critic, first and most vigorous of contemporary reviewers, was George Putnam Upton, a hardy perennial who flourished for sixty years. In the light of his knowledge of the circumstances, his surprise at Abbey's "neglect of this important factor of scenery" seems overdone; his violence at the "unworthiness," "outrageous shabbiness" and "clumsiness" suggests an aftermath of disappointed expectations.

It would have been a waste of money to surround Sembrich with gorgeous trappings in the second night's opera, for the audience, meager as it was, could see and hear nothing but the Lucia. It comported itself, according to Upton, in a vociferous manner totally unlike Chicago.

"Without exception, this is the most pronounced and spontaneous success ever achieved by a newcomer . . . Gerster's voice is more wonderful, with a flute-like roundness the other lacks; [Emma] Abbott's natural gifts are not below Sembrich's; Litta is in some points superior; Patti, Nilsson and Albani most impressive and musical. But Sembrich captivates not only the mere senses but appeals also to the highest feeling. . . . It is the musician, not only the singer, who predominates in her."

Faust had satisfied the ear if not the eye, and Sembrich's *succès fou* had galvanized the press to a missionary effort that often helped populate the house for her next appearance. Chicago, however, was anticipating *Lohengrin* with the eagerness of a child!

Nine years before, on January 21, Albani, Carpi, Cary and Del Puente had introduced the opera to Chicago, and in 1879 Eugenie Pappenheim and Charles R. Adams enacted the Elsa and Lohengrin of Freyer's German Opera Company. Since then, Italian troupes had pre-empted the calendar and snubbed the Swan Knight. Chicago showed its eagerness to renew the acquaintance by buying $5,217 worth of tickets for Abbey's performance on January 23.

The crowd buzzed with excitement as it filled the theatre that night. Dismal weather had kept no one at home. Full dress was the rule in spite of the threat of pneumonia noted by the press:

"For a man, only a width of four-ply linen and a square foot of silk undershirt lie between the bare breast and icy blasts. Women, with bare heads, bare arms, bare necks and occasionally bare bosoms, apparently do not suffer as much. We just cannot understand it."

Thus bravely began the night that was destined to be a turning point in Abbey's Chicago fortunes. A notice in the program begging indulgence for Campanini and Novara aroused a murmur of consternation as programs rustled open, but the euphoria of the crowd persisted. Even the scenery did not offend the *Tribune,* for Upton conceded that the first act brought its magic picture, "brilliantly costumed, highly colored, the Herald in dazzling armor."

This happy state of affairs lasted about one minute. The chorus dropped below key; no two bars were correct, the critic insisted, and, warming to his task:

"A worse butchery cannot be imagined . . . [Vianesi] let the orchestra players go on in hand-organ style with no attempt at shading. In La Scala or other Italian theatres, the chorus and orchestra would be mobbed if they dared to treat a popular work in the same brutal manner."

Upton spluttered on, performing "a duty no critic can shirk." He savagely demanded that Abbey admit frankly he was unable to secure a chorus and orchestra capable of doing justice to Wagner's work. He even berated Nilsson and the other singers for not forcing Abbey to abandon *Lohengrin* when its inadequacies were first revealed.

Eventually he wrote the spleen out of his system and calmed down enough to give Nilsson her due as an artist. By the time he reached the climax of the evening, Upton was for treating it tolerantly, even humorously.

"When sweet words of love were issuing from Elsa's lips . . . and Lohengrin sat down beside her, the couch tipped. The situation was so irresistibly ridiculous that Nilsson lost her composure and burst out laughing. Then she regained it and the scene carried through in grand style."

Campanini, who had been singing fairly well in spite of his indisposition, was unnerved by the episode and the unabashed snickers from the audience. He refused to go on, and the final scene was omitted.

The *Tribune* put it astringently at the end of the week:

"Campanini was a very sick Lohengrin, indeed. The public is indebted that he prevented the finale from being murdered."

Abbey never recovered ground in Chicago. The performances were termed listless, and the shadow of approaching battle fell over the incumbents all too soon. The morning after *Lohengrin,* Abbey's ruffled spirits were scarcely soothed when he read that the crowd at Mapleson's advance sale had become almost unmanageable.

At the end of the week, Abbey felt something close to despair. Only two out of seven operas were in the black. *Don Giovanni* had been criticized as "mediocre" except for the women. Sembrich's Rosina had attracted a representative but comparatively unremunerative audience. The orchestra was splendid, if one account was to be believed; it broke down in *Barbiere,* claimed another. Evidence that something untoward had happened was provided by a letter from Vianesi to the *Tribune,* protesting that the contre-temps was not his fault; an artist had changed key and the orchestra had to wait for him to get back on it.

Rossini's *Stabat Mater* at the Sunday night concert had further depressed the management and singers. The *Inter-Ocean* critic said flatly that it was a question whether any worse performance of the work had ever been given in Chicago. Furthermore, the two feminine soloists, Emmy Fursch-Madi and Trebelli—though the former's singing was "glorious and inspired"—offended by their gay modishness. (Fursch-Madi, a plump, bright-eyed little French-woman, had joined Mapleson's American company in 1882 after singing with him several seasons in England. Her defection to Abbey further em-bittered the colonel.)

"It is the custom to be attired in black," the fussy arbiter of fashion and art complained. "Fursch-Madi was adorned with an abundance of artificial violets, which robbed her toilet of the required effect. Trebelli was in a princesse robe of cream-colored silk, the skirt pleated with light red silk."

Mapleson, meanwhile, was having his own troubles. The news broke in Chicago on January 25 in a front-page headline:

"OPERA SENSATION! Gerster Becomes Enraged at Baltimore's Marked Preference for Patti. Leaves for New York after Stormy Interview with Colonel Mapleson."

The colonel, acting promptly with the assistance of a railroad official, tele-graphed Gerster's train and the express from New York to stop at Wilming-ton as they passed each other. Gerster could, if her resolve had softened, re-turn at once.

She had, indeed, repented her hasty action, and gladly boarded the express to Baltimore. But before the train got under way, she saw the detested Patti in the only drawing room. Offended at the necessity of once more playing second fiddle, Gerster resumed her tantrum and her flight.

The grievance of the junior goddess embraced both personal jealousy and a very real sense of injustice at not being regularly paid. Mapleson had promised her $1,000 a performance; she had sung sixteen, but received only $6,000.

Her husband, Dr. Gardini, called on Mapleson to demand his wife's back salary. Mapleson turned him down in his own inimitable manner:

"Not a penny, dear boy; that wretch Franchi has taken it all—every cent—for Patti. We make no money the Gerster nights, and if I don't pay Patti she will stop. Then we shall have a jolly time and all starve together."

Gardini changed his ground of attack, the Chicago account continued, and asked for a private car for Gerster, similar to the boudoir car, with its silver ornaments, velvet carpets and bathrooms that Mapleson was reputedly building for Patti, at a cost of $60,000. Mapleson again evaded, giving as an excuse the glass-blowers' strike.

Abbey could smile ironically as he remembered that the luxurious private car was one of the inducements he had held out to Patti to return to him. Now Mapleson was paying.

On Monday night, January 28, the combat was squarely joined. Abbey led with *La Gioconda,* his only new opera; Mapleson resorted to a quasi-novelty of his own, *Crispino e la Comare (The Cobbler and the Fairy),* which had not been heard since the final days of Crosby's Opera House before the fire, when Minnie Hauk sang it "in a glad mood."

Abbey's protagonists were formidable: Nilsson, Fursch-Madi, Scalchi, Stagno, Del Puente, Novara; Mapleson's campaigners seemed less a brigade than a comet, its incandescent head the Queen of Song.

Chicago was stirred to its depths. The *Inter-Ocean* commented breathlessly:

"Our condition of mind is not unlike bewilderment at being confronted by the most famed of the world's sopranos. . . . The occasion was a triumph of music over every other consideration."

Gioconda's attractiveness as a stage piece ranked high, but "its musical effects failed to excite any furor of applause. Nilsson did not partake of that deep and soulful earnestness she can stimulate so well. . . . Stagno occasionally congratulated himself by holding favorite notes, but his triumph was not sustained by the unfeeling public."

Honors in the second attempt went to Mapleson. Gerster had repented her "huff" and had returned to Chicago, where she was well loved. The disagreeable weather was courteously cited as an excuse for the frighteningly low attendance at Sembrich's *La Sonnambula.*

The third round brought a rally for both sides, although Mapleson's entry, *Les Huguenots,* could be said to have the edge on Abbey's *Mignon,* calling forth "Chicago's flower of fashion and cream of chivalry" to revel in the bedazzlement of Patti and Gerster in the same cast. The diva's acting had developed "wonderful strength and intensity."

Mapleson brought up fresh troops in *La Favorita* to meet Sembrich's *La Traviata,* which played before a corporal's guard. Even Mapleson's second team in *Linda di Chamounix* prevailed over the satanic Meyerbeerian, *Robert le Diable,* whom Abbey was forced to throw into the fray as a substitute for *Le Prophète.* This was Abbey's lowest box office for an opera in Chicago: a scant $1,015.

When the fierce tournament ended, both weary contenders had won, both had lost. Patti had been wildly acclaimed as a matter of course, and Gerster's welcome was only slightly less effusive; still the pleasure afforded by great artists did not atone for the weakness of Mapleson's ensembles. Abbey had taught that lesson.

But his own company was top-heavy with expensive artists, and, in the *Tribune's* view, "the development of the musical taste, the musical education of the American people, has not gained a farthing.

"It is about time," continued the censorious critic, "that an earnest protest were entered against the policy of using great names as a cover for shabbily mounted and carelessly produced worn-out operas."

Not only were the impresarios finding life treacherous and difficult, but seven prima donnas spent that week in Chicago under exceptional tension. The top hierarchy in both companies was quartered in the same hotel. The ladies, in fact, occupied the same corridor. Mesdames Patti, Gerster, Nilsson, Fursch-Madi, Sembrich, Trebelli and Scalchi were near neighbors for better or worse. No one dared plead illness that week.

4. "LA CALUNNIA"

"Both Abbey and Mapleson are losing money, but Abbey has the worst of the battle. He pays no attention but keeps on giving the country better opera than it ever had before. . . . It will cost fully $30,000 to give seven performances here, and the local manager estimates the advance sale at only $8,000."

John W. Norton, lessee of the Olympic Theatre in St. Louis, was the authority for these figures, published in the *Globe-Democrat* on February 3, the day before the Metropolitan's first engagement in Missouri. He had contracted for the appearances of both rival companies, Mapleson being expected on February 18.

Mapleson's advance juggling of repertory irritated Norton and confused the subscribers, but although the colonel remained culpable in this matter throughout his career, he never again matched his 1882 record of six opera substitutions in one evening.

Abbey was equally guilty of shifting his repertory before the St. Louis season began. Taking advantage of "opening night fever," he passed over *Faust* and *Lucia* as possible gambits and eventually settled on *Trovatore*.

Trebelli, Valleria and Kaschmann did their best, but Abbey lost his first-night gamble. Wretched weather and the absence of first-line stars kept his audience at home. The house was about two-thirds full, and described as "a wilderness of vacancy upstairs," by the *Post-Dispatch*.

"Society crowded the Nilsson nights and gave Sembrich the cold shoulder, and so missed the best of the season," the *Globe-Democrat* concluded.

Sembrich's limited audiences had ceded her a total victory; still St. Louis was proud of discovering another heroine for itself. A replacement became necessary for Fursch-Madi, who had contracted an illness in Chicago but had not dared to give way to it. She succumbed at last on the eve of the *Gioconda* performance in St. Louis.

The day of several "covers" for one role was far in the future, and Abbey and Grau sought frantically for a Laura. At last, with some misgivings, they decided to give young Louise Lablache the assignment. Beyond replacing her mother as Marthe in *Faust* at the historic New York opening, she had been limited to concerts and participation in the *Carmen* smugglers' quintet. Because she was barely eighteen, her mother's formal consent was necessary.

Emily freely gave it. Then, all through the performance, the devoted mother stood in the wings, mouthing the words at Louise, calling out directions, even singing along with her daughter.

When Fursch-Madi remained ill the next day, one of the Lablaches was called on to meet an even more severe test. Whether Emily or Louise was chosen to sing Donna Anna is not clear, but it seems likely that the mother assumed this task. Versatile and obliging, the contralto had come to the rescue in a similar emergency years before, as Luigi Arditi relates in his memoirs.

Extravagant clothes were Emily's weakness. When she stepped into the earlier *Don Giovanni* performance, she wore her own costly dress. As her scenes with Don Ottavio progressed, she felt grave anxiety for the fate of her gown, for Brignoli, the tenor, afflicted his colleagues with his habit of constant expectoration. During the trio of the maskers, Emily was heard to say:

"Voyons, mon cher ami, ne pourriez-vous pas, une fois par hazard, cracher sur la robe de Donna Elvira?"

All through the week, while sober colleagues wrote judicious estimates of the performances, the mischievous *Globe-Democrat* "Notes" distilled drops of venom for visitors and natives alike.

Campanini, the favorite target in St. Louis as he had been in Chicago, must have smarted under the unfair treatment. He would have been justified in launching a dozen libel suits, for no *Globe-Democrat* issue went without at least one thrust at his weakest points. Several shafts were directed at what Krehbiel had euphemized as the tenor's "careless way of life."

The Midwest had not yet acquired that respect for "the noble ruin" that Philip Hale of Boston, in writing about Campanini, claimed was "of more value from an artistic standpoint than a new, cheap and cockney villa, freshly and hideously painted."

Abbey's other *tenore robusto,* Stagno, got off lightly with a bare mention in "Notes" of his collection of swords and a phonetic pronunciation of his name, but Signor Stagi, who was substituted for Capoul in *Barbiere,* received his critical baptism here as

". . . a second tenor, with a voice of poor quality, whose abominable efforts at acting nearly ruined the performance. He was a member of the orchestra before and had . . . better get under the stage again or get a hand organ and a monkey or an old hat to catch nickels in."

Comment on Abbey's solvency struck a tender nerve: "Abbey may lose money but he seems to pay salaries. Scalchi bought $1,000 worth of diamonds. . . . Traveling expenses for several voiceless wives and husbands of prima donne are laid out by Abbey. . . . He furnishs every piece of wardrobe. One man is paid to look after 300 wigs."

And perhaps the most ironic "Note" of all:

"Ticket speculation is a lost art this season."

Abbey often complained that it cost him $7,000 every time he raised the curtain. If this were true, not one audience so far on his tour had paid its way. Only seven out of forty-five had realized more than $5,000 in the box office. St. Louis requited him least, with an average of a petty $2,333 for each performance.

Turning his back on his losses, Abbey rested all his hopes on Cincinnati.

5. DELUGE AND DENOUEMENT

Unlike other cities where theatre managers controlled production and sales for Abbey's huge aggregation, Cincinnati offered a well organized civic committee, and a $50,000 guarantee. It also boasted a high degree of culture. A present-day historian, Alvin F. Harlow, has called attention in his *Serene Cincinnatians* to the "striking parallel between Cincinnati and the Renaissance, in that each developed a remarkable culture amidst dirt, disorder and public corruption."

When Abbey took up his stand early in 1884, the city was yet to go through its worst crime wave, which followed on the heels of the epochal flood. Cincinnati's artistic element remained undaunted by both phenomena.

Grau, always the suave propagandist, complimented local taste by remarking that "Cincinnati numbers more lovers of classical music in her population than many cities twice her size."

Singing societies had flourished since 1816; the Cincinnati Conservatory was founded in 1867; an orchestra had existed for twelve years when Grau presented his bouquet. The festival idea that took firm hold in many places had its American genesis in the Ohio city.

Music Hall, with its auditorium of graceful proportions and remarkable acoustics, has been the Cincinnati May Festival's home since 1878 and also housed the Opera Festivals produced by Colonel Mapleson's company under the sponsorship of the Cincinnati College of Music. It was the scene of almost every Metropolitan Opera visit, and still continues its useful life. Reuben R. Springer, banker, contributed half of its total cost of $405,000.

Popular demand for Patti in 1882 forced Mapleson to introduce his hated rival, Abbey, into the Cincinnati operatic scene, a fateful move for both men. Mapleson stole Patti from Abbey, but Abbey confiscated the Cincinnati Opera Festival. The colonel did not admit defeat until the flood of 1884 undermined the foundations of both operatic castles.

Baleful weather had been a continuous deterrent to the health and affluence of Abbey's company: a severe snowstorm in Philadelphia; sleet-burdened winds in Chicago; drenching rains in St. Louis. For several days before the advent of the travelers, Cincinnatians had been reading the ominous headlines spotting the front page of the *Enquirer*:

"WASTEFUL WATERS: La Belle Rivière on Its Annual Big Tear. . . . THE MAD RIVER . . . STILL SURGING," and, on February 10, the one word, "GLOOM!" in fat, black type.

The impact of these laconic bulletins on the opera adventurers must have been shattering.

We can almost see the two men reading the newspaper by the pale gaslight flickering in their temporary office in Music Hall that dreary morning: Grau, darkly-bearded, haggard after his overnight trip from St. Louis, his forehead carved by a frown of worry; Abbey, naturally pale, his large black eyes shadowed by strain, his habitually drooping black mustache concealing the firm set of his mouth, yet still sanguine, looking for the miracle.

He must have thought the miracle had arrived as he picked his way through the small print of the *Enquirer*. Though the distress of the upper Ohio Valley monopolized the first three pages, galvanic news exploded on the fourth:

"MAPLESON'S BREAK! Colonel Abruptly Cancels Cincinnati Contract. Gives No Reason for Extraordinary Conduct. Henck and Fennessy Thunderstruck by Queer Move. What Will Be the Outcome?"

Henck and Fennessy, who controlled a new opera house, had gone to considerable expense in the colonel's behalf, paying out nearly $3,000 for advertising, tickets and fixtures, which included a gas machine and additional electric lights for use in the impending emergency.

Music Hall had also been readied for any contingency by linking its gas system to the City Hospital supply. If that failed, no real harm done: Cincinnati would have its first electric light festival. "The main hall now has seven electric lights," the *Enquirer* marveled, "and eighteen locomotive headlights are available for corridors and the stage entrance."

From comparatively dry Chicago, Mapleson offered to organize a "grand benefit for the flood sufferers," but even this gesture could not placate the Cincinnati public, in whose eyes, the *Enquirer* decreed, "Mapleson will be eternally damned."

The situation still held perils for Abbey, even without his rival. The flood had amputated out-of-town sales, vital to the success of any operatic stand. Though faced with the prospect of a limited public, Abbey's gambling blood was aroused. He prepared to carry out his Cincinnati commitments with every resource at his command.

Flood superseded Festival in the city's attention all during the engagement, as was to be expected. Even the review of the first-night *Faust* was relegated to an inner page in the *Enquirer*. The audience, unwontedly sober in dress, filled Music Hall's 3,000 seats. Faces looked pale in the "uneven illumination" of the auditorium, murky with smoke from the incandescent lamps.

In the midst of his description of the unusual scene, the reporter found space to pronounce an astonishing verdict on the opera: "*Faust* affords little to catch the popular ear, but much to awaken thought and delight."

Nilsson was "the same brilliant, fascinating woman . . . the ill-natured remark that she is growing in flesh has no foundation in fact." The "short, curly and stylish silver-gray hair, parted on the side," that St. Louis had admired, also won Cincinnati's approval. "It was the opposite of masculinity." Campanini was appreciated at last: "Some have said the tenor is dead, but Cincinnati atmosphere must agree with him."

Most of the audience left before the fifth act of *Le Prophète* on February 12. "If this thing goes on, we shall have an opera like a Chinese play, which begins on Monday and winds up on Saturday."

The *Times-Star* reviewed the *Prophète* scenery and little else, with some justification. Investiture for the Meyerbeer "novelty," comprising six set pieces, ten wings and six full drops—Abbey's "heaviest show"—had been constructed and painted in Cincinnati by Charles Fox, Abbey's scenic artist. It would be shipped back to New York to be seen for the first time on March 21 in the spring season.

On February 13, the flood peak was reached: 70 feet 9¼ inches. Sembrich added Cincinnati to her chaplet of conquered cities. The only adverse comment on her Lucia was an indulgent one:

"The diva sacrificed truth to display and appeared in the rugged forest attired in a gorgeous dress with a long train which must have suffered among the rocks, while its brilliancy would have drawn the attention of Henry Ashton and the chorus of hunters to the forbidden tryst she was so anxious to conceal. But then, nothing is absurd in opera."

La Gioconda brought the festival peak, reminding the critic of one of the "old time nights." Nilsson, Fursch-Madi, Scalchi and Campanini were all on the stage; the electric lights behaved; the audience gleamed with cloaks and headdresses—"or better still, no headdress but the graceful one nature gave our common mother."

Now the flood waters were abating. On February 18, the *Times-Star's* dramatic headline was "ARARAT." The *Enquirer* flung a banner across four columns: "SINGING FOR CHARITY." Abbey had organized a benefit of his own.

Hundreds who could not go to the operas, and many who ordinarily would not permit themselves to attend Sunday entertainments but made an exception in so good a cause, were rewarded by a program of sixteen numbers. All the prima donnas collected money during intermission. Nilsson, "in a walking dress of plain black, but blazing with diamonds," kissed a child; the audience loved it. She kissed another, and still another, who "covered her mouth and sat with hanging head as though afraid the essence would evaporate."

For a climax, the entire company assembled on the stage to sing the finale from *Lohengrin:* three or four stars for each leading role, a chorus of 150 and full military band and orchestra.

To hear Scalchi, Lablache and Trebelli, with their different timbres, aiming in unison at Ortrud's half-dozen high A's, should have been worth the $6,250.30 raised.

The final burst of enthusiasm was expended on February 19, when Sembrich's sleepwalking Amina generated such excitement that "if it does not stop soon, Cincinnati music circles will be guilty of something extravagant." Unfortunately for Abbey, "it stopped" all too soon. As flood headlines at last disappeared from the front pages, interest in the festival began a decrescendo, never to rise again. Even *Mefistofele* and *Hamlet,* given for the first time on tour, failed to stir Cincinnati, and only *Martha* called out an audience of paying proportions.

The engagement came too late. It was a radical mistake to place the festival in flood jeopardy. Two weeks had proved too long, even for Cincinnati's educated public. Fortunately, the college had a surplus to meet the deficit.

"But will there be another festival?" the *Enquirer* asked.

The answer was, "No." M. E. Ingalls, president of the committee, consulted his board and decided to ring down the curtain.

Cincinnati would play host in the next few years to opera—Italian, German and English—but not again on a guarantee basis. The *Times-Star* had put a brave face on the inadequate advance sales by claiming that more latitude remained for single sales, and so "all the better for a 'people's opera.'"

"Very well," said the Festival Committee in effect, "let the people have it."

The *Enquirer* pronounced the decisive epitaph:

"Italian opera does not pay and cannot be made to pay in America!"

If cordiality could have saved the day, Washington would have redeemed the entire tour for Abbey, especially after a performance of *Don Giovanni* which, according to the *Post,* "those present hardly hope to witness again."

Scalchi had to repeat all her solos, indeed, nearly every concerted number; Kaschmann was praised for his engaging abandon and easy gallantry. Giovanni Mirabella, who had been cited in Chicago as the only newcomer of value except Sembrich, earned another line he could paste in his scrapbook as a Leporello of "rare power and capital comedy."

Still, Washington's public thought the ticket prices too high, and did not respond generously to four performances, so Abbey took advantage of an invitation from Baltimore. Cutting the week short in the capital, he led the company north to Baltimore's Academy of Music, only to meet another disappointment.

Sembrich created the usual furor, but only Nilsson brought out an audience. Backstage flurries disturbed the smooth surface of the engagement, according to the *Sun.*

"Scalchi took herself away to New York with her costumes, saying that she had a reputation in Baltimore and was not going to sing any such picayune role as Siébel." A rather unlikely excuse in view of the number of times she had sung it elsewhere. Louise Lablache was called on once again.

Sembrich, owing to a misunderstanding about transportation, was said to have sent Abbey a card reading: "At last my disappointments and annoyances in this country are at an end. I am done. I sing no more here."

"She will have to be pacified," the *Sun* prophesied darkly.

Abbey evidently mollified his princess, for she reappeared in Boston "as charming, unaffected and gloriously endowed vocally as ever," according to the *Globe,* which welcomed the company on its return in March.

Aside from *Don Giovanni* and *Barbiere,* Sembrich's two triumphs, Boston received Abbey's return coolly. The critics who had demanded novelties now spoke slightingly of *Hamlet* and *Le Prophète.* The excision of Bertha's suicide scene in the latter provoked the *Globe* to wrath: "The knife was put in [the work] and turned in a scarcely skillful manner, the edges left being exceedingly ragged." *Mefistofele* was "memorable" but poorly attended; *Robert le Diable* drew even less.

Deeply disturbed, Abbey tried yet once more, signing a contract with Nixon and Zimmerman for a return week in Philadelphia. In the congenial surroundings of the Academy of Music, the operas took on a new sheen for the critical hearers, but after the initial *Les Huguenots,* given for the only time on the road, business fell off alarmingly.

Robert earned the sad distinction of the lowest record on tour: $700.72. *Prophète* was little better; *Roméo et Juliette,* which Abbey never gave at the Metropolitan although he announced it three times, was played by Sembrich and Campanini for a scattering of patrons and a few enthusiastic critics.

Abbey's debts by now were estimated at half a million dollars; Schoeffel later confided to Krehbiel that the figure was $600,000. His offer to continue with the Metropolitan without salary if the directors would pay his losses was, understandably, refused. Not only were his profits from other ventures sacrificed to this reckoning of one season, but Abbey mortgaged his future. As late as January 18, 1888, the *Musical Courier* was to comment:

"Last Tuesday was a red-letter day for H. E. Abbey. In the afternoon he wiped out the last $2,000 of the debt he incurred in his disastrous first season. . . ."

Abbey might have lived to be an octogenarian, magnate of a chain of theatres from Boston to Omaha, if he had not become fatally addicted to grand opera. Even after his first failure, he did not abstain from the heady brew, particularly lethal to impresarios of the nineteenth century, which was to kill him at fifty, with a "hemorrhage of the stomach."

When the American manager returned to the Metropolitan in 1891, his timing was improved, his experience deepened and his partnership with Grau solidified. Of Abbey's first adventurers, only seven were to tour again with the Metropolitan during his lifetime—Campanini, Capoul, Del Puente, Novara, Scalchi, Kaschmann and Vianesi.

Meanwhile, the Metropolitan turned its back on Italian opera and entered on an experiment that was to reshape the tastes of the entire nation.

Part II

WESTWARD HO-YO-TO-HO!

1. DAMROSCH DARES

Damrosch's "German Grand Opera company from the Metropolitan Opera House" nearly missed its first engagement out of town. The audience in Chicago's Columbia Theatre waited, gossiping and laughing, that night of February 23, 1885. An hour had gone by since the doors had opened, but the good-natured crowd was behaving as if it were all a lark. They had come to hear *Tannhäuser,* and hear *Tannhäuser* they would, if it took all night.

Most people had seen the notices posted beside the paintings of Romeo, Juliet and Francesca da Rimini in the lobby, handsomely printed placards that read:

"On account of a snow blockade which may retard the company, the audience is asked to excuse a possible delay in the raising of the curtain."

One "well-informed" person circulated the story that the company had wanted to save $200 by taking the West Shore Railroad instead of the New York Central. This, unhappily, was the case.

Many times since his departure from New York on Saturday night, twenty-three-year-old Walter Damrosch had repented the decision to bring the German Company to its first tour engagement by a railroad that he admitted was a "rather lame rival of the New York Central."

All trains were delayed by "terrific snows" in upstate New York and the Midwest, but the opera special carried an extra jinx in its "palace cars." Even before the company reached Albany, heavy drifts had overwhelmed the two coaches, four sleepers, two baggage cars and diner. After many weary hours they were shoveled out. Then couplings broke; cars had to be chained together. The "worst wreck since 1883 when the road was opened" held up the troubadours outside of Canajoharie. They crawled into Buffalo; dropped one Pullman in Detroit; finally limped into Chicago one half-hour past the advertised curtain time.

Shortly before 9 o'clock the doors from the lobby were thrown open and into the auditorium and down the aisle hurried a man and a woman. Heads craned, voices lifted from whispers to audible comments as the portly, heavily-clad woman was recognized as Amalia Materna. Close behind her came Damrosch.

"It was [Manager] William J. Davis' idea," Damrosch said later, "to give ocular demonstration of our presence." The stunt produced the desired effect. Carrying their traveling bags, the famous singer and the young conductor mounted the stage, where they bowed in response to a ripple of applause and laughter, then disappeared behind the curtain.

A few moments later, a familiar figure appeared. Chicago's sociable Mayor Harrison asked patience for the troupe, which had been forty-nine hours on the road. Their diner had long since run out of warm food. Though hungry, they had hurried directly to the theatre from the station.

The gallery proposed three cheers for the mayor; the parquet hissed them down.

"The more refined and elegant were surprised, by no means pleasantly, to find the mayor thrust into conspicuous notice as apologist," criticized the *Inter-Ocean*. The *Tribune's* acid comment: "He didn't mention the $200."

At 10 o'clock Damrosch raised his baton. Perhaps for the first (and last) time in Chicago operatic history, an Overture was heard from the beginning; latecomers had long since become old settlers and everyone was in his seat.

After another wait of twenty minutes, the curtain went up at exactly 10:30.

Three hours later, the patrons were still seated and still enthusiastic. Materna, returning to a city where she had triumphed in concert, won a genuine ovation as Elisabeth. Anton Schott was an admirable Tannhäuser, Anna Slach a pleasing and artistic Venus and Adolf Robinson was hailed as the "singer of the evening," in the part of Wolfram. The crowd demanded the "Evening Star" three times.

The fear expressed in a dispatch to the *New York Times* that the contretemps might affect the success of the entire engagement seemed unfounded. Approval for the gallantry of the company outweighed the charge of inexperience and parsimony leveled at Damrosch. The Potter Palmers, John T. Lester, Sam W. Allerton, O. W. Potter and Marshall Field were in their boxes. All turned out well that had started badly.

Walter Damrosch, beginning a long career before the public, betrayed his naïveté by spreading the word of a possible return before his two weeks were sold out in Chicago.

Walter had been learning fast all through that fateful time. On February 15, the sudden tragic death of his father from pneumonia brought on by overwork and exposure, had precipitated a professional and personal crisis for the Damrosch family just when affairs seemed to be moving smoothly.

New York had accepted the new Teutonic features so carefully molded on the Metropolitan's countenance by Abbey's successor, Leopold Damrosch. No doubt all of the opera's box-holders did not understand or enjoy the "music of the future," but they appreciated a regime that asked only a fraction of the subsidy poured into the Italian operas. Houses were full nightly and newspaper reviewers were cordial, especially the *Tribune's* Krehbiel, who constituted himself the evangel of the new musical religion.

Leopold Damrosch's appointment in August, 1884, astonished a public conditioned to believing that opera was an untranslatable Italian word. Negotiations with Ernest Gye had once again broken down, possibly because the Londoner was married to a prima donna for whom he would expect preferential treatment. Even for Emma Albani, the illustrious lady in question, the New York stockholders were reluctant to dispossess Christine Nilsson—at least until it became apparent that the Metropolitan would no longer shelter Italian opera.

Damrosch offered ready-made orchestral and choral forces in his New York Symphony and Oratorio Society, singers marked with competence rather than high price tags and a repertory that had as its nucleus the neglected works of the Bayreuth genius. Satisfied that the Metropolitan Opera House would be kept alight for a second season, and trusting to their new shepherd to cope with Mapleson's annual threat, the directors signed the contract that was to bring seven years of German opera to the Metropolitan.

Out of the turmoil resulting from the elder Damrosch's untimely death, one clear course eventually emerged. Rejecting an unseemly bid for leadership by the tenor Anton Schott, which split the company into two factions, the board voted to allow Walter Damrosch to carry on his father's mission.

He had proved himself a capable conductor in the final days of his father's illness, when he had taken over the performances of *Tannhäuser* on February 11, *Walküre* on February 12 and *Prophète,* on February 14. An assistant, John Lund, finished the season, and was available to alternate with the young man on the road. The dates in the western cities would be filled. The New York papers mentioned several possibilities for the touring company; these narrowed down to three: Chicago, Cincinnati and Boston.

The German "non-star" policy was wisely timed by Damrosch, the *Chicago Tribune* admitted. Such care for ensemble, such "masterly interpretation of an instrumental score," had truly never before been witnessed in Chicago. Damrosch's orchestra, even when augmented to fifty-six for *Walküre,* fell short of Abbey's seventy-five, but the rich scores of Wagner, Weber and Beethoven may have accounted for the impression of fullness.

"What seemed to have contributed most to the success was the orchestration [sic], which appeared the more wonderful as young Mr. Damrosch was called to the conductor's choir [sic] so sadly and suddenly," according to a dispatch from Chicago in the news columns of the *New York Times* for March 15.

One or two die-hards missed "that pure sweet tone that forms the leading element among artists of the Italian school. It is difficult for some to accept the declamatory German style," the *Chicago Tribune* confessed.

New York believed that Chicago was seeing *Tannhäuser* for the first time, but the *Chicago Tribune* vouched for an earlier performance by Leonard Grover's German Opera Company in Crosby's Opera House in 1865. After twenty years Chicago revisited the Wartburg Valley with pleasure, but the extraordinary excitements of an opening night usurped the critics' attention; *Tannhäuser* stepped unchallenged into the fortnight's repertory.

Chicago boasted the out-of-town premiere of *Die Walküre* on March 10, and two repetitions, which prompted the *Tribune* (Upton still holding the reins) to proclaim: "Wagner is a genius, everyone knows. *Walküre* may become as popular as *Lohengrin* and *Tannhäuser*. After the second performance people hummed the love motive—but it needs singers with large voices, an extended and perfect orchestra . . . the cost will limit it . . . it will not hold the stage except at intervals."

Upton preferred to pass lightly over the *Walküre* scenery and the *Inter-Ocean* excused it while approving the lighting effects and deploring the introduction of a real horse.

For *Freischütz,* stock scenery produced the inevitable anachronism: "a libelous portrait of Mayor Harrison in the seventeenth century interior, although the mechanical devices of flitting bats, winking owls and slithering serpents were well contrived."

The *Cincinnati Enquirer,* presumably reflecting the tastes of a large German population, predicted:

"At last the Dream of the Faithful is realized." But next night it was obvious that the Teutonic influence was not powerful enough after all. A note of surrender crept in:

"*Lohengrin* was universally acceptable to open the season in a city the inhabitants of which, though essentially musical, are still prone, as Berlioz once wrote of a specific class, to 'hunt for a tune.' "

Cincinnati was not put to the ultimate test with *Walküre. Tannhäuser* marked the limit to what her audiences were asked to accept. The opera's "near-perfect stage representation" insured its success.

The city had never enjoyed opera before when "all parts were so well rendered . . . when there was no indecision and the attack was prompt and the harmony well preserved."

Boston, too, took its chief pleasure in the qualities of ensemble stressed by the new company. Stars there might be—Materna, Brandt, Slach, Schott and Robinson were illustrious enough for any opera house; but these five and all the others behaved like members of a stock company, accustomed to pull together.

Their acting was "pure delight" to Apthorp, who, however, could not speak "so sweepingly of singers . . . a sound vocal method is rare with Germans."

Tannhäuser was admitted to the list of works Boston termed "unhackneyed," *Fidelio, Orfeo* and *La Juive* among them; yet of more moment than the music itself was the presence in the cast of Charles R. Adams, the celebrated American tenor, who carried on a distinguished teaching career in Boston. Rejoining Materna in an opera they had often sung together in Vienna, he exemplified his own precepts when he "never lost his grip on a phrase, never miscalculated breath, never blurred musical rhythm."

"One thing must be beat into the heads of singers—and the public, too [the *Transcript* continued]—Wagner's voice parts *must be sung, must not be shouted or screamed.* . . . From the first note in *Rienzi* to the last in *Parsifal,* this is of primary importance."

Apthorp had been aroused two nights previously by the first performance in Boston of the mighty first segment of the Trilogy. *"Die Walküre* surpassed even sanguine expectations! . . . a red-letter night! An example of how vigorous, sincere and well-directed artistic effort can overcome imperfect material conditions."

Certain details of *mise-en-scène* were judged superior to New York. The firelight and sword business was artistic and intelligent, Fricka no longer appeared in a "ridiculous little go-cart—pardon, a goat chariot!" and Siegmund's death had been stripped of its ludicrousness. The closing fire scene "hung fire" and had been more effective in the Metropolitan. The Valkyries, who had displayed a "lamentable lack of time" in Chicago, kept on beat and pitch in Boston.

All of the singers won glowing words from Apthorp, with a special accolade to Materna for "1,000 delicate touches." Her Brünnhilde "lost none of sublimity by being taken on a plane of purely human emotion and pathos." The whole performance added up to an "aggregation of fine details, surpassingly good in totality. It was grand!"

Chicago and Cincinnati at least were spared blunders in stage management. In the Ohio city, Damrosch availed himself of Henck's new Grand Opera House shunned by Mapleson the year before. But gremlins joined the stage crews in Boston.

In the first *Tannhäuser* on April 7, Apthorp reported an "odd hitch in the transformation scene: Venus (Slach) stood faithfully over the trap, but it did not work, so she had to walk off up the valley and get back to Hörselberg as best she could. I fear she never did. When the transformation curtain rose we still saw her, not in the bowels of the mountain, but again in the valley. Poor goddess! Tramping about alone like a vagrant through Thuringia!"

Damrosch relates in his autobiography that while he was conducting the "beautiful monotony of the last E major chords of the Fire Charm" at the second evening performance of *Walküre*, he noticed the grass mat under Brünnhilde (Materna) had actually caught fire. Quick and discreet action on the part of a Boston fireman, who poured water from his bucket on the burning turf, prevented a more serious emergency. Damrosch, already showing his talent for capitalizing on the moment, insisted that the fireman share a curtain call.

Just before the final matinee, also *Walküre*, the orchestra went on strike. In another attempt to cut corners on the expense sheet, Damrosch had engaged steamship passage back to New York on the Fall River Line. The men balked, and demanded rail transportation for the return trip. Damrosch threatened to get along with two pianos. Fortunately for the sensibilities of the *Walküre* audience, the strikers yielded.

Damrosch rehearsed and performed two operas for the first time on the road. Neither saw the light in New York under the German regime.

La Dame Blanche was first produced by the Metropolitan company in Chicago on March 12, and provided for one critic "a melodious bagatelle . . . pleasing and successful variation from the [heretofore] heavy caliber." A Metropolitan audience heard it first in 1903-04.

Boston felt flattered to hear the first German performance in America, and the only performance of the season, of *Orfeo ed Euridice* on April 11.

Damrosch had planned the premiere of the Gluck work in Chicago, but had substituted *Fidelio*. One of the artistic successes of the season, *Orfeo* did not seem "grand," but its "direct simplicity, pure melody and beauty of dramatic expression went straight to people's hearts."

The only faults lay in the realm of the visual conception, which, for a "scenic opera," was insignificant. The critic chafed at the absence of choric dances, and at the "ill-judged costumes of the Furies and Blessed Spirits" who "looked like charity-school inhabitants."

With few worries about heavy scenes to transport in his two baggage cars, Damrosch could give single performances here and there, rigging them out of stock. Three in Chicago undoubtedly wore borrowed finery—*Guillaume Tell* (still known by its French title though it was, of course, sung in German); *Masaniello* (called by the name of its hero instead of *La Muette de Portici—The Dumb Girl of Portici*—as Auber's opera had been known at the Metropolitan), and *Don Giovanni*.

Hardly an opera escaped the tailor on the road. Wagner's Valhalla-like lengths inevitably came under the shears, not only *Walküre* but *Tannhäuser* as well. Apthorp mentioned that Materna sang a "somewhat cut" prayer, that Tannhäuser's first reply to Wolfram was never heard, and that the last Pilgrim's Chorus was omitted entirely, so that "poor Tannhäuser got beyond the powers of salvation after all."

Lying helpless under the knife, Meyerbeer's operas were whittled down each season. *Le Prophète* was a favorite victim. Under Abbey's management, the *Boston Globe* had complained; now the *Transcript* took up the crusade against Damrosch.

"Of course, *Le Prophète* must be cut," Apthorp ceded. "It is a perfect sea-serpent in length, and would last till nearly breakfast time. . . . But in music, nothing suffers by not being given at all; music *suffers* by being given piecemeal. Cut out the whole skating scene and ballet, cut out Fidès' *O gebt*—but cut whole numbers. If Walter Damrosch wishes to leave an immortal name . . . the opportunity is ready for him—let him revise the abominable system of cutting." That Damrosch did not heed this good advice was apparent throughout his touring career, but Apthorp admitted later, "it was probably not Damrosch's fault. No doubt the cuts were already traditional." On the other hand, Cincinnati heartily approved the shrinkage in *Prophète;* the *Enquirer* registered only one objection: the opera was still too long.

The German opera singers probably set a record for endurance and fortitude in the course of forty-two performances. On the distaff side, Anna Slach performed twenty-nine times in leading roles, and once five days in sequence. On February 28 she sang Venus at the matinee and Marzelline in *Fidelio* in the evening.

Appearing twice in the same day was almost a commonplace for Josef Staudigl, son of a famous father by the same name and himself also a "nobly expressive" bass by Apthorp's standards. To follow King Henry in *Lohengrin* by the Hermit in *Freischütz,* as he twice did, was perhaps not too strenuous, but even for a strong voice and constitution Wotan in the afternoon and

Leporello at night is something of a marathon. His list of twenty-nine appearances matches Slach's.

Next in the endurance contest came Marianne Brandt, with twenty-seven performances. She never sang more than three days in succession, but one of these was a matinee day, and Brandt made her own record by singing three roles within twenty-four hours: Fricka and Gerhilde in *Walküre* and Donna Elvira in *Don Giovanni*. Another day she paired Ortrud and Leonore in *Fidelio*. The passion and malignance of her Ortrud, the consummate vocalism of her Fidès, the tragic force of her portrayals proved her truly great, a "real chanteuse," said Apthorp.

Nor was the first tenor spared arduous duties. Anton Schott, determined to make up for earlier fractious behavior by performing faithfully and admirably—"he had come down off his high horse," Boston was told—was called on twenty-five times, although usually with a day between appearances.

Adolf Robinson owed his lesser record of nineteen performances to at least two indispositions which added to Staudigl's total. These and the replacement of *Huguenots* by *Fidelio* in Chicago because of Materna's illness apparently completed the list of major substitutions. Considerable crowing arose in the ranks of adherents to the new German regime, who delighted in pointing out the fallibility of the Italians under similar circumstances.

The prima donna of the company, if Materna may be so designated, restrained herself from more than seventeen performances, at intervals of from one to three days. Almost two weeks elapsed between Elisabeths in Cincinnati and Boston, during which she may have given a concert or two.

In spite of a few inadequacies and compromises, the company won its way into the good books of the three cities. Chicago gave it full marks for the best Wagner presentations ever seen there, Cincinnati considered that without pretensions it was quite as good as the Opera Festival and Boston remarked that it possessed more artistic grit than any troupe in years.

Walter Damrosch enjoyed his first sample of operatic life on the road. He had won "golden opinions" in Cincinnati, in addition to a description in one of the dailies as "a manly man, whose splendid physique and earnest blue eyes and frank countenance combine to form a pleasant picture." Chicago had forgiven him his informal arrival and Boston's bouquet contained few thorns.

2. STEPCHILD

"It is now definitely settled that the greater part of the Metropolitan Opera House artists and orchestra will go on a *tournée*," the *Musical Courier* reported in February, 1886. "The Metropolitan Opera House management wish it to be understood that they are in no wise connected with this affair, the financial arrangements of which are backed by Messrs. Rice, Friend and Bijoux, while management will be in the experienced hands of Mr. Herman Grau. Adolf Neuendorff will conduct. Lehmann, Brandt and Stritt have positively declined. . . ."

Against the handicap of disavowal by the Opera House, Herman Grau, an uncle of the better known Maurice, set out to keep his first engagement on March 15 with sixteen solo singers, a chorus of fifty and orchestra of fifty-five. His original ambitious blueprint of a coast-to-coast *tournée à la* Mapleson shrank until only four cities remained on his itinerary: Chicago, St. Louis, Cincinnati and Cleveland. Advance reports indicated that sympathy rested with his venture, rather than with the restrictive home management that had branded him a wildcatter.

Grau's German wayfarers stand unique in Metropolitan history, for never again would a road company be disowned by the House and allowed to entrain with an outsider.

Responsibility for the decision fell on Edmund C. Stanton, an elegant young man who enjoyed the favor of the directors as the relative of a member and as recording secretary to the board. With their decision to extend the life of a German regime for another season, he had been thrust into the managerial post. He was thirty-one, and confessed in a Philadelphia interview that he "did not know one side of the stage from another, or a wing from a fly."

By consensus the "most gentlemanly manager" the Metropolitan ever knew, Stanton has perhaps been described most clearly—if not entirely without malice—by Walter Damrosch in his memoirs:

"Tall, good-looking, with gentle brown eyes, always well groomed, of kindly disposition and most perfect and courtly manners, which indeed never failed him and which were about all he had left at the end of seven years' incumbency—at which time German opera crumbled to dust as a natural result of his curious ignorance and incompetency in matters operatic."

Lilli Lehmann's opinion, quoted in Chicago, lends itself to various interpretations:

"Stanton is a gentleman all over. . . . He loves and understands art and is at the same time a merchant and worth three million."

Fraulein Lehmann, who liked to take charge of affairs herself if not satisfied that all was going smoothly, remembered that Stanton, in that pre-union era, "shook all the wings in his white gloves" to see if the scenery the prima donna had set in place with her own hands would hold solidly.

Stanton's repugnance to touring was probably engendered by a Philadelphia visit which is said to have lost $15,000 for the stockholders—more than half of the total deficit for the season. Only Philadelphia received this accolade—a Christmas present of a two-week engagement by Stanton's entire company.

The choice of the holiday fortnight militated against a representative attendance; patrons were "scattered like righteous citizens of Sodom" in the expanses of the Academy of Music for the majority of the performances. At a top price of $2.50, Stanton failed to make expenses by half, and the taste of defeat embittered his view of the world outside New York.

Five of the six operas already heard at home were wrapped in the gift package; *Die Königin von Saba,* too ponderous to move, stayed behind. The premiere of *Die Walküre,* the sumptuous art of Lilli Lehmann and the mastery of Seidl overshadowed all other gratifications for Philadelphia's public and press.

Seidl's advent marked a new standard of musical perfection for the young company; his inability to tour deprived the nation for a few years of the finished performances that enriched New York and Philadelphia.

Lehmann, introduced to Philadelphia as to New York in *Carmen,* seemed different from all others in that "she both acted and sang," but her full magnificence was apparent only in *Walküre.* Her Brünnhilde seemed to the *Press* "worthy of the goddess in Keats' *Hyperion.*"

Albert Stritt, one of several important singers who abstained from the western tour, was never to return to the Metropolitan; hence Philadelphia enjoyed his only tour performances.

When Grau proposed a tour it was in Stanton's power to forbid the artists from following, as the *New York Times* carefully pointed out. The principal and almost the only objection was the fear that the tour would not heap credit on the Opera House. Not only were artistic values at stake, but financial security, since in an unauthorized company salaries might not be paid regularly and artists might be left stranded!

"To preclude such a possibility it is stipulated in contracts that two weeks' salaries are to be paid before the company leaves New York and after that the salaries will be paid in advance each week. As none of the singers has been heard anywhere in this country except in Philadelphia, where the brief season did not prove as remunerative as had been hoped, it will readily be seen that Mr. Grau is taking a good many chances."

Taking chances was any impresario's daily lot. Herman Grau was brought up in the proper atmosphere. With his brother, Jacob (the popular J. Grau of many opera troupes), he managed the Stadt Theatre on the Bowery and was associated with the Castle Square Opera Company and Terrace Garden. In appearance he did not resemble his famous nephew, Maurice; Herman moved more slowly, wore a heavy mustache and spade beard, and looked at the world through soft, kindly eyes.

Stanton's opposition did not cease with the withholding of a blessing, although the *New York Times* charitably stated that he did not attempt to throw any obstacles in Grau's way. The *Chicago News* told another story. This paper was authority for the statement that Stanton threatened to "give the cold shoulder next year to any artists who went with Grau." No reprisals were forthcoming, however, but "spiteful little paragraphs" were circulated, tending to injure Grau's prestige by disclaiming connection with the Metropolitan Opera House.

"The public need not take this into account," the reporter assured his readers. "The company is not equal in splendor to New York, of course. Only two operas can be called elaborate—*Rienzi* and *Die Königin von Saba.*

But even the others are splendid in comparison to slipshod Italian operas."

Further reassurance was offered by Theodore Habelmann, the stage manager, who brought news that the company would leave New York earlier so that the perplexing delay of the previous year should not be repeated.

Fourteen of the Metropolitan's singers had agreed to join the impresario, including Max Alvary, the tall, graceful tenor who had made his Metropolitan debut with Lilli Lehmann in *Carmen*, and Eloi Sylva, whose "glorious tenor voice and marvelous staying powers" had aroused the admiration of Anton Seidl, the Metropolitan's new musical director.

Lehmann, who had stirred New York in successive appearances, particularly with her first *Walküre* Brünnhilde, declined to share the venture. In her place Grau counted on Marie Krämer-Wiedl, wife of the tenor August Krämer, the first to sing Goldmark's Queen of Sheba, and on Auguste Seidl-Kraus, who had prefixed her husband's distinguished name to her own. Frau Seidl had been a member of Leopold Damrosch's company, but had not accompanied Walter on tour.

Seidl could diplomatically plead European engagements as a reason for not heading Grau's insurgents. Neuendorff, an admirable veteran of German opera, known favorably in Boston and New York for two decades, replaced him. Grau was also pleased to engage Georgine von Januschowsky, Neuendorff's wife, who would be invited to the Metropolitan the following year. Two additional married couples added a domestic note to the touring company. Frau Staudigl, whose husband Josef remained the stalwart among bass-baritones, came to Grau's assistance although she had never before sung in America, while Otto and Frau Kemlitz, both on the home roster, joined the expedition.

Emil Fischer had to omit his famous Hans Sachs on the road, for *Meistersinger* posed insoluble problems of transportation, but brought his noble voice and art to Wotan, King Henry, the Landgraf and even Méphistophélès. Adolf Robinson, whose "large, flowing voice, manly and powerful," had captured Chicago and the other two cities on Damrosch's route, promised to be an equally potent drawing card.

In Chicago the *Tribune* became a partisan of the company and remained staunch to the end. *Rienzi* indicated "the hand of genius" with a cast "strong enough for any stage." The second performance was termed without qualification "the most complete and satisfactory of any grand opera in Chicago, not excepting the *Tannhäuser* last year." *Lohengrin* showed Wagner "for the first time in a true light." *Faust* offered "agreeable relief from the seriousness of Wagner." *Die Königin von Saba* proved most brilliant of all.

The *Inter-Ocean* looked at the whole affair with distaste. Its reviewer dismissed *Rienzi* as "about as near a Metropolitan production as a crayon drawing is to a portrait." The brilliance of *The Queen of Sheba* arose from the scenery, "which reflects most creditably upon the generosity of the house management." The opera's "antiquated style of recitatives, cavatinas and concerted finales recalls *Aida* and *L'Africaine*. . . . The last act shows about the same relative weakness as *Manon*, the latest novelty presented by Mapleson." His final judgment: "This company is to the Metropolitan as a gas burner to electric light."

Grau was apparently fortunate to be able to produce Goldmark's opera at all. Rumors of an injunction against him continued to circulate until after the first performance. Three subsequent hearings supplied Chicago with a hoard of memories that would suffice for a good many years. When Walter Damrosch escorted Sheba's Queen to the Chicago stage again in 1890, she ranked lowest in popularity among opera heroines.

Grau's report card at the end of the fortnight bore an "F" for financial loss. Mary Anderson, the American actress, traveling under Abbey's management, and Mapleson, who had paraded his company through the Columbia Theatre in February, had drained Chicago's pockets.

Still, an "E" for effort and an "A" for artistry were freely granted Grau. Marshall Field headed a committee that organized a benefit for the company, which took the form of an extra performance of *Rienzi* on Saturday night, March 27.

Audiences had increased slowly during the last few days, and a third week might have turned the wheel in Grau's favor. But he was due in St. Louis on Monday.

This year no impudences from "Notes" pricked at the German singers' sensibilities, for the *Globe-Democrat's* columnist confined himself (or herself) to innocuous tracery of society's complicated patterns. Music criticism was also emasculated; an exponent of the "moonlight and roses" school had taken over.

"Beside the stately marches and grand choral effects of *The Queen of Sheba,* Goldmark has run a thread of soft, delicate and insidious music that seems to sigh through moonlit gardens and thrill the silver waters that ripple" on and on and on.

Unfortunately these raptures did not serve to entice an audience of fashion —or even of numbers—after opening night. The *Post-Dispatch* attributed the shortage to fear. "The popular impression is that German music, particularly Wagner, is too heavy. The bulk of the audience was German. The Americans avoided the Olympic Theatre."

Tannhäuser, indeed, had proved a "test of endurance, not only for the tenor but people in the audience"—and the *Globe-Democrat* oracle as well.

Lohengrin was rewarded with the largest crowd of the week, because of the presence in its cast of a home-town girl. The event of the evening was the presentation of a huge floral tribute, six feet high, tagged "Our Carrie," to the Ortrud, Carrie Goldsticker. Impressionable scribes failed to state how the lady sang.

For a final extra performance of *Fidelio,* Grau moved from the Olympic to the Grand Opera House. Next day, a small paragraph noted that the house had been full and that "tonight, Lizzie May Ulmer appears in *Dad's Girl.*"

German opera still failed to cut deeply into St. Louis' consciousness, so Grau, like Abbey before him, set his sights hopefully on Cincinnati. The warm approbation of the city must have soothed and pleased the company.

Who could fail to respond to such praise as *Die Königin von Saba* elicited from the *Commercial Gazette?*

"A performance of such magnificence and splendor, so gratifying in every respect, with such magic of spectacular exhibition, has never been equaled in this city."

The *Enquirer* counted Cincinnati "heavily in debt to the enterprise and skill of the company, which paved the way to a wider dissemination of present-day knowledge." Even the swollen Ohio River, flooding its banks again at opera time, did not perturb the company's spirits.

One additional triumph lay in store, in a city honored for the first time by a Metropolitan incursion. Grand opera visitors to Cleveland had been few and scattered; now the metropolis looked eagerly toward a future in which the lyric theatre would become a leading citizen. Spokesmen ventured to hope that even at a $3 top, the Opera House would be flatteringly populated for the Germans' four performances—which would cost Grau $8,000 to produce.

Once again the enthusiasm of the votaries failed to stimulate the ticket-buying public, though the newspapers suffered from hypertension all week. Almost every review blared with the opening announcement:

"Never before in Cleveland . . . !"

Rienzi? "Memorable! Nothing like it ever heard here!"

Queen of Sheba? "Splendid! Gave entire satisfaction!"

Lohengrin? "A rare treat to all able to appreciate the highest reaches in the art of music and poetry combined!"

Because *Tannhäuser* fell on a Saturday night after the *Lohengrin* matinee, reporters had no extravagant adjectives left. The opera "was very much enjoyed, and everybody was equal to the demands."

The *Plain Dealer* reporter roamed happily among the unintentional delights of the performances, witnessing an unusual scene backstage. Supers had become a nuisance by crowding on a bench near the first right entrance. To get rid of them, an electrician had fixed an electric battery under the seat. They learned their lesson. But on Saturday:

"Neuendorff, weary of so much Wagner, went backstage to rest [in intermission]. The fatal bench was convenient. He dropped down. In another second he was sailing in the direction of the flies, pronouncing the name of one of Wagner's operas. Those in authority say it was *Götterdämmerung.* Someone finally quieted his ruffled temper. The above accounts for the unusually long wait between the first and second acts."

Grau's German singers returned to New York, several of them to rejoin the Metropolitan next season. By the time the Metropolitan company again took to the road, Wagner would be a deity and Seidl his acknowledged prophet in America.

Mapleson's dynasty had collapsed at last. Even the indestructible colonel had succumbed to a disastrous season. Patti had absented herself. Sick, rebellious or capricious prima donnas of both sexes bedeviled him on the road; he scraped up money here to pay debts there; the Academy of Music directors made activity so difficult for him that he was forced to give up; London had severed connections.

The entrepreneur, still jaunty but shaken, evaded process servers by journeying to his steamer on a health officers' tug. How sharp a contrast from the tugs following his ship up the bay in other years with a band of music to serenade the colonel as he sat in his flower-crammed stateroom! He would try once more in 1896, but his reputation would have been less tarnished if the health officers had seen him off for good!

3. *RING* AROUND THE CIRCUIT

In his fourth season as manager of the Metropolitan Opera, Edmund C. Stanton changed his mind. He could no longer ignore the call of the road and the demands for the new music which had incited New York to wild enthusiasm. The reports had percolated as far as St. Louis that even tenors had been hugged and kissed by strangers, so great was the furor over Wagner's music dramas in the metropolis.

Walter Damrosch had been invited in 1887 to bring the singers to Chicago for a week's performances of *Die Königin von Saba,* but could not assemble the double cast imperative for nightly performances. Other bids had been pressing but Stanton had remained obdurate.

Only three important itinerant organizations had materialized during his tenure: Abbey's, which had fallen out of action in 1888-89 because Patti was touring South America; the American (later National) Opera Company, an elaborate concoction of Jeanette Thurber's which, despite the wealthy singer's beneficence, was soon to come to grief through alleged rascally management, and a troupe headed by Italo and Cleofonte Campanini, who had introduced Verdi's *Otello* to America the previous year.

Now Stanton decided it was time to take the Metropolitan touring again, and under its own management. Five cities were to hear the entire Tetralogy for the first time. Each reacted in a highly individual manner.

Philadelphia admitted only a budding acquaintance with the later Wagner and humbly awaited its dispensation. Boston's *Transcript* published an editorial on "Wagner's Great Theme," interpreting the Master to himself:

"The *Ring* is not based on the German *Nibelungenlied.* . . . Wagner decided that the pure soul of humanity was to be found in the realm of myth alone. He was somewhat influenced by Schopenhauer . . . yet commentators will probably try to unravel philosophic mysteries of which the author had not the least concept."

Milwaukee, chosen for its large German population as well as its proximity to Chicago, sent a request sponsored by numbers of prominent citizens that *Götterdämmerung* not be given on Good Friday. The opera was transferred to Saturday night. Attendance at other performances during Holy Week was condoned on the ground that Wagner "cannot be placed under an 'Amusement' heading, side by side with farces and comedies; it is therefore appropriate for the Holy Season."

Chicago, even after long indoctrination by Theodore Thomas, displayed a touch of apprehension in the face of "A Whole Wagner Week."

St. Louis, whose reviewers had received *Lohengrin* and *Tannhäuser* in 1886 with more gush than gumption, now prepared for *Der Ring des Nibelungen* with proper seriousness. *The Spectator,* a weekly, observed that "Browning and Wagner are for educated tastes, and for each a special kind of education is needed."

Such education lay opportunely at hand in the guise of "illustrated" lectures on the *Ring* dramas by a member of the company. The irrepressible Walter Damrosch, if he was not allowed to conduct more than a few performances of the beloved music, could at least talk about it. He consented eagerly to act as harbinger for the Nibelungs, Gibichungs and Valhalla-ites, and thus opened new vistas for America and a new career for himself.

In Milwaukee he donated a "specimen lecture" to an invited audience as an inducement to attend the series. The *Sentinel* reporter, who evidently did not take the bait, nevertheless admired the sample:

"Although sketchy, it was hugely entertaining and instructive, and brought out with much force the sublime poetry that pervades the works of the great composer."

Anton Seidl freed himself of European commitments in order to tour, and the effulgent Lilli Lehmann agreed to sing Brünnhilde to Max Alvary's young Siegfried if her own bridegroom of a year, Paul Kalisch, might fall heir to the *Götterdämmerung* heroes. Alvary possessed his share of temper and capriciousness in spite of the gallantry and gentlemanly bearing that had so impressed Chicago in 1886, and a feud sprang up between him and the Junoesque soprano with her husband as bone of contention, which titillated the public in several western cities.

Twenty-seven singers of the company, exactly the number Abbey had gathered under his wing for flight, undertook the missionary trip. To these Stanton added three: a heroic tenor named Jäger to replace Julius Perotti; a soprano variously named Triloff or Baumann-Triloff to sing an occasional Brünnhilde in place of Fanny Moran-Olden, and a comprimario, Heinrich Bartels, for the single role of Zorn in *Die Meistersinger.* The orchestra numbered sixty, still shy of Abbey's record.

The appellation "entire *Ring*" as applied to the truncated versions of the time was a misnomer, and yet no one questioned the feasibility—even the desirability—of radical cuts. Following New York's lead, although he would have resented the imputation, even Apthorp approved the mutilation of *Götterdämmerung.*

Shorn of five characters, the "twilight of the gods" fell earlier and more economically in those days. Not for ten years was the country to glimpse a Norn, Waltraute or Alberich in the final strophe of the cycle.

Though the *Chicago Tribune* critic regretted the absence of Waltraute, he did not miss the three fateful sisters: "The whole idea of the Norns is charmingly poetic but difficult in presenting the ideal of thread in material form, even though golden. Even in Bayreuth it seemed commonplace, and must always distract from the effect."

Alberich, too, represented no loss to an *Inter-Ocean* writer. The scene with Hagen was called "sinister and bloodcurdling—happily omitted."

Seidl, though he deplored the elision of a single measure, fell in with the requirements of the period and contented himself with giving orchestral "accompaniments" that had never been equaled in the memories of the five cities. He allowed himself only one indulgence: "some of the Norn music" as a prelude to *Götterdämmerung,* at least in Boston.

The extent of mayhem committed on *Siegfried* varied from place to place. Erda appears in the Philadelphia cast but nowhere else. The bear was "excellent" in Boston; non-existent in Chicago—"just as well, as it adds nothing to the drama and under ordinary circumstances could only be tiresome." Other excisions, not catalogued, telescoped the Chicago performance until it ended at 11 o'clock.

Many daily paper scribes showed themselves unable to cope with the intricacies of Wagner's musical structures, though they struggled manfully with what one Chicagoan called "lieb motives," and chromatic sequences. These novices tended to a coloratura style such as "This wondrous piece of music writing [The Ride of the Valkyries] o'ershadows and outleaps similar compositions akin to Titians' [sic] play with pygmies."

The pundits confidently aired their analyses and dissertations well in advance of the performances, along with properly reverent blueprints of the plots. This left the staging and performances as review material.

Rheingold offered uncommonly meaty stuff for descriptive pens. Its swimming Rhinemaidens, Nibelheim caves and rainbow bridge aroused universal curiosity and interest. Philadelphia found the staging clumsy, but Boston and Chicago compared it favorably to Munich and Bayreuth respectively. In Boston "the gauze curtain that simulated water acted as a terrible *sordino* on the Rhine daughters," however. "Even knowing the music by heart," wrote Apthorp complacently, "it was impossible to grasp the melodic outlines."

The river maidens were strapped to a wheel, rising and falling as the music flowed and ebbed, according to the *Chicago Tribune* newsman, who added a bit of criticism to his account:

"Who else but Wagner could write music which could be sung by girls borne head downward across the stage?"

Less attention had been paid to the tour scenery for the three later music-dramas, which had been longer in the Metropolitan's repertory.

"Walküre's scenic effects are the chaff of Wagner's wheat," Apthorp remarked scornfully, while the *Boston Globe's* Howard Malcolm Tucker spoke of "contemptible magic lantern images."

Siegfried, new to all of the cities, created the keenest appreciation. "Its signal departure from all pre-established custom is almost audacious," Apthorp opined, marveling at "its simplicity of plot, paucity of incident, and almost total lack of dramatic interest. Hardly ever more than two people appear on stage at the same time." And, regretfully, "There is no love-making."

Götterdämmerung's trappings disillusioned a Chicago girl reporter for the *Tribune,* who may have written the first "back-stage" chronicle in the annals of opera. This is what "Nora Marks" observed in the wings:

"Kalisch seemed mild and trivial in spite of his warlike accouterments. He smiled, and his rosy face beamed with good nature and idle interest in a lady who wore street costume and braved dragons and spells. . . . Lehmann, like a goddess in her dressing room, rose and swept her majestic figure across to Siegfried. After she had gone, he pulled his mustaches and skipped airily across to the Rhinemaidens, a modest Siegfried calculated to slay other than dragons. He flashed a German witticism, laid a detaining hand on the waist of one maiden and passed a caressing hand over the hair of another. He joked. What a comedian!

"Hagen [Emil Fischer] came off the stage in a rage, then wheezed over [to talk]. His Canton flannel draperies, in classical folds held by a safety pin, were redolent of cigar smoke. His wig looked like Nebuchadnezzar after his vow was fulfilled. The vassals strolled around in coffee sacks.

"The Rhinemaidens explained their costumes—bodices of net, brass or steel [breast] plates, skirts of gauze with a fringe of muslin grasses at the waist, artificial flowers on shoulders. Falling water was simulated by streamers of tinsel, and water plants rode in their hair."

The jibes at Kalisch further evidenced Chicago's absorption with the Lehmann-Alvary conflict. The *Tribune* published interviews with both the disputants, loaded in favor of Alvary.

Lehmann arrived a day later than "the charming tenor with whom she is at odds." Confronted with Alvary's alleged statement that Kalisch "cannot sing," the prima donna, "womanlike, declared she had nothing to say and proceeded to score Alvary unmercifully.

" 'Oh, he talk, talk, talk. . . . I will tell now. Chicago shall hear them sing, both, and see. . . . I never quarrel before mit no one.' "

It was fortunate that the two were thrown together only in *Siegfried,* for, fine artists though they were, a trace of dissension might have seeped into their performances. Indeed, Apthorp accused Alvary of lacking a "certain emotional energy" in the scene with Brünnhilde, but this may have been only another example of his gaucherie in love scenes.

Though continually at odds, Lehmann and Alvary lent the highest distinction to the season. If Alvary had sung no role but Loge, his reputation would have remained forever lofty.

"Loge to the life, the whole Loge and nothing but Loge," Apthorp cheered, citing "that bright, sly face, now and then tartened by a little sardonic fold around the mouth, usually full of laughing good humor—Loge, like Becky Sharp, is a good-natured schemer and really enjoys seeing people make fools of themselves."

Alvary commanded such respect in Boston that a lesser tenor, Jäger, was withdrawn from a *Meistersinger* cast to make room for the favorite.

Lehmann's Brünnhilde in *Walküre* was spoken of as "her crowning triumph"; yet her *Götterdämmerung* Valkyrie "surpassed everything she has ever done." She was "magnificent," she was "grand"; it was "difficult to praise her too highly." If only her adored spouse could have lived up to her advance billing, she might have been a thoroughly happy woman.

Kalisch, however, impressed few reviewers as the ideal *Heldentenor*. Only Philadelphia tendered unqualified praise for him while St. Louis spoke of his "verve and fire" in *Götterdämmerung*. Boston enjoyed his Siegmund chiefly because his wife played opposite him. As Sieglinde, she was a "wonderful revelation of dramatic truth and power." It was the teamwork that counted. "Not often does one see a couple who know so well how to play into each other's hands, both in acting and singing." Otherwise, the tenor was rated as fair.

Lehmann never became accustomed to singing at matinees, harnessing her mood to the "sober afternoon period that worked contrary to all the charm of an evening performance." She was called on for none during this tour. But other discomforts plagued her. Each town offered a different Grane—here a pony, there a drayhorse, as she recounts in her memoirs. Rats gnawed the feathers on the Valkyries' helmets.

Kalisch, on Siegfried's bier one night, whispered in agony to her that he was afire with itching and begged her to scratch. Surreptitiously, whenever she could spare a moment in the Immolation Scene, Brünnhilde applied a soothing finger to her spouse's epidermis. The exterminator was sent for the next day to fumigate the fur covering of the bier.

Though other singers tended to be shadowed by the two avowed leaders, their achievements were not less real. Memories remained in Chicago of Fischer's Hagen, "grim, dark and repellent," and his "stately, dignified and resonant Wotan"; of Beck's powerful Alberich; of Mödlinger's superb Beckmesser; of Traubmann's polished Elisabeth.

Boston would not soon forget Sedlmayer's capital Mime; Kaschowska's "delicious little Eva" and her Sieglinde of "excellent acting and singing, with an artistic devotion and painstaking truth of perception and beauty of effect."

The premiere of *Die Meistersinger* lost nothing of luster by the close association with the mighty *Ring*—on the contrary, its utterly surprising and adorable music came closest to the heart of the public. Apthorp again may be spokesman:

"The music and text are alike admirable. Wagner here is not only strong and skillful, but also thoroughly genial and charming. Sachs is the finest instance of a true gentleman in all opera."

This time the company had traveled not only under the benison of the New York House, but also with the good wishes of the chatelaine of Bayreuth. Seidl happily published in advance of the Chicago visit a letter from Cosima herself, hoping that the Trilogy (it was still the fashion to regard *Rheingold* as a mere prologue, in Bayreuth tradition) would be as successful in the west as in the east.

"America is a great field for his work," Wagner's widow wrote. "It must not be misunderstood or half understood. I do not think it can fail to grow."

But by the most generous estimates, it appeared that Wagner's time had not yet come in our outlying cities. The music dramas made slow headway against public apathy in spite of critical hullabaloo and cult-like devotion.

Stanton had succeeded in obtaining guarantees in Chicago and St. Louis and a special subscription in Philadelphia. The St. Louis *Spectator* declared at the end of the engagement that the Exposition director (the opera played for the first time in the huge Exposition Music Hall) took the risk up to about $18,000 and "it looks like a deficiency." On a guarantee of $36,000 for two weeks in Chicago, a loss of $6,000 was expected, the journal added.

The St. Louis *Republic* added that George Mills of the Exposition had worked hard but taken in only about $17,500 and would lose the balance. Before the engagement was one day old, large advertisements assured the public of reduced seat prices, and the *Republic* repented its original pronouncement that all four *Ring* operas *must* be seen if the full benefit were to accrue to the novice.

Milwaukee (sponsor, if any, unknown) lost $4,000; Chicago's loss was estimated at only $2,500.

Once again Stanton let discouragement overwhelm him. Although he gave permission for Damrosch to take the company to Chicago and Boston the following season, there was no attempt at a widespread tour. Furthermore, Wagner counted for only one-sixth of the repertory, and a single performance of *Walküre* in Chicago represented the *Ring*. The repertory was in fact a potpourri, the *Tribune* commented.

"It looks as if the managers were in a panic and prepared to make concessions to the ghosts of Italian opera. If so, it is one of the surest methods of reviving Italian opera."

The *Tribune* was right. Italian opera pranced back into the scene as though it had never been reported dead.

Part III

INTERLUDE WITH SWEET ADELINA

Adelina Patti, the greatest singer of them all, never became a member of the company at the Metropolitan Opera House although she sang there occasionally. In 1887, when her manager, Henry E. Abbey, rented the premises to show her off in New York, she braved the vast stage and formidable audience chamber. In 1892 she accepted an invitation as honored guest in a supplementary spring season after Abbey had returned to the stewardship of the House he had inaugurated in 1883.

And the diva made one tour with a company that belongs, if only by courtesy, in the Metropolitan's history books. In December 1889, when she was approaching forty-seven, Abbey lured her back to this continent for her first *tournée* in three seasons.

By then Patti's "farewell" tours had become classic. A *Brooklyn Eagle* statistician estimated that she had made her "last appearance" twenty-seven times; her "positively last appearance" nine times; had "permanently retired from the stage" seven times; had "retired to spend her days in her castle" three times and is "now getting ready to take another hack at the public and retire again."

The Divine Adelina had enchanted audiences since 1850. In a career unparalleled in musical annals, she would continue to arouse the public's delight —increasingly mixed with disillusion—until 1906: an incredible span of fifty-six years.

Perhaps the strongest appeal of this unforgettable prima donna for the public lay in that indefinable element, personality. Patti very well knew what people wanted: colorful incident and plenty of it. Her jewels, her three marriages, two to noblemen, with a distinguished tenor between, her castle, her private railroad car, the wardrobe that dazzled on stage and off, her black-eyed beauty and trim figure—she lacked no attribute to commend her to the heart of the world.

In 1886-87 Abbey had persuaded Patti to leave Craig-y-Nos, her halcyon castle retreat in Wales, under the pretext of an "official" farewell to America. She had willingly spent the intervening years under his management, twice journeying to South America, where the word "farewell" was presumably never mentioned. By now, surely, the singer would have liked to see it expunged from the language.

Patti needed no further excuse for the excursion in 1889-90 than her own professional spirit, which constantly reasserted itself. The ineffable sound of thousands of hands beating together in adulation never lost its power to intoxicate her. Her treasury could always stand replenishment, since the prima donna's tastes in living, dress and entertainment were as regal as her mastery of her art.

Abbey offered additional bait on a three-pronged hook: an invitation to dedicate Chicago's magnificent new Auditorium, and incidentally to earn several thousand dollars for a single song; another chance to visit San Francisco, where a "Patti epidemic" recurred annually; and the opportunity to sing opera in Mexico, where she had been tumultuously received in the concert tour of 1887.

Patti could not resist. She was content to trust herself to Abbey again, especially remembering several wild seasons with Colonel James H. Mapleson, the most talkative, temperamental and flamboyant impresario of the nineteenth century.

Whatever Abbey's magic, the diva was bewitched into reducing her fees for the 1889-90 tour. Celebrated around the globe for her exaction of $5,000 —payable in advance—every time she set foot on a stage, plus a percentage of the box office over $7,500, Patti graciously lowered her basic fee to $3,500. Still, her share of the 1890 tour was estimated at $160,000.

If Patti could only have sung every night, the claim of her biographer Herman Klein that she invariably brought profit to her managers might have held water. But the dainty diva bestowed her benisons only when she pleased, and she pleased only thrice weekly at a maximum, leaving hiatuses known as "off nights."

Klein rather high-handedly maintained that managers incurred losses "because they were so foolish as to persist in charging the same high prices when inferior artists sang."

Abbey's 1890 caravan of twelve cars seems like a toy train beside today's behemoths. Yet it was the wonder of the 'nineties, with four baggage cars containing "wardrobes" for eighteen operas (scenery remained chiefly a local affair); a diner; Pullmans; "tourist" sleepers and a coach. Bringing up smartly in caboose position rolled the elaborate home on wheels that bore the name "Adelina Patti."

The diva had traveled for several years in luxurious seclusion, though hardly in total solitude. Indeed, she required an entourage of a dozen or so, all of whose fares constituted an obligation of the management—including a personal chef.

At the head of the retinue marched Madame's second husband, the handsome, mustachioed Ernest Nicolini, himself a singer of some repute in London and his native Paris. America had admired him as a skilled tenor and a polished actor—with strong reservations about an incurable vibrato—until the suspicion arose that with Patti it was a case of "love me love my consort." Her package deal soon met strong objections in spite of its bargain value at $4,500 for the pair.

When the "Adelina Patti" was new and first attached to Mapleson's train, the specially built car had opened provincial eyes wide with excitement and curiosity. The company arrived in Omaha, Nebraska, one bright April night in 1884 on the eve of a *Lucia* performance.

The presence in their midst of an aviary of gilded songbirds in Mann Boudoir cars exotically labeled *"La Traviata," "Sonnambula"*—and above all the $65,000 traveling palace named for the peerless diva—left a lasting impression on many Omaha citizens, among them a representative of the *Bee,* who noted every public detail of that sojourn.

The diva invited a party to supper in her car and left the blinds open so that the crowd on the station platform could watch every mouthful.

"The curtains are of heavy damask silk," explained the reporter, "the walls and ceiling of gilded leather tapestry, the lamps of rolled gold. A grand piano of carved wood cost $2,500. Ship springs cause it to remain constantly balanced.

"Two valuable pictures from the easels of famous Italian artists [unnamed] are worth $2,000. All appliances for eating, cooking and the toilette are present."

Such opulence filled the lay beholder with awe and at least one prima donna with the pangs of envy, according to the company's conductor, Luigi Arditi, who credited Lillian Nordica, the rising young American soprano, with a smoldering anger at Patti's privileges, and quoted Abbey's comment:

"She can have an entire train if she will pay for it."

The presence of Nordica in Abbey's troupe provided an example of the impresario's belief that the "star system" should penetrate as deeply into his roster as the budget would permit. Klein's deprecating term, "inferior artists" had no place in Abbey's vocabulary.

Patti's pennant fluttered supreme, but on pinnacles slightly below her eminence the manager placed three powerful attractions.

Francesco Tamagno, the stalwart tenor who had created the title role in Verdi's *Otello* two years before, boasted a trumpet voice which was said to cause shivers in human spines and chandeliers alike. Emma Albani, a Canadian who had Italianized her girlhood home, Albany, for a stage name, once elicited Queen Victoria's tears (later crystallized into a diamond keepsake) by her soulful rendition of *The Blue Bells of Scotland.* Married to Covent Garden's former impresario, Ernest Gye, she often visited her native continent as a musical tourist. Both Albani and Tamagno would later spend a single season apiece as members of the resident Metropolitan Opera Company.

Abbey's third additional magnet, Lillian Nordica, had been making her way from "Down-East Maine" through Europe and America with the steadiness and willingness to learn that impelled her ever upward toward a brilliant career. Before Abbey engaged her, the soprano had won plaudits from French, Italian, Russian and British audiences and had completed several American sorties with Mapleson, in Italian roles exclusively. Her first appearance at the Metropolitan came at the end of this 1890 tour in Abbey's "rented" spring season; she would become a regular in 1893. Her later incursion into Wagnerian realms was responsible for her most impressive victories.

One of the four names was emblazoned on every bill: Patti with nine florid heroines, among them Lucia, Violetta, Rosina and Lakmé; Tamagno with seven roles including the touted Otello; Albani with Marguerite and *Otello's* Desdemona ("in which I am always at my best," she admitted), and Nordica, who was limited chiefly to *Aida, Trovatore* and *Africaine*.

This company had tapped a rich vein of tenors. In addition to Tamagno, Luigi Ravelli and Enrico Vicini stood ready to sing lyric roles, or even to substitute for the lion on occasion. Ravelli had acted the "bad boy" of Mapleson's troupes, but Abbey gently tamed him to good behavior—or at least kept any ruckuses out of the newspapers.

Additional value—and startling contrast—lay in Maria Pettigiani, a light soprano, "neatly nimble in florid work," and the uncomely but powerful contralto, Guerrina Fabbri, who struck various reviewers as ideal for "trouser" roles—the pages in *Huguenots* and *Roméo et Juliette*—a great Azucena in *Trovatore* but not feminine enough for Nancy in *Martha*.

An American rose, blossoming a trifle more sweetly under a foreign nomenclature, Giulia Valda, nee Julia Wheelock, claimed to be the only other American citizen except Nordica, who had been born Lilly Norton.

Musical director of the company, the genial, sharp-eyed, indefatigable Luigi Arditi was already a veteran with American experience since 1853. He combined shrewdness with a warm heart, was called by his colleagues "the pleasantest of men, frank, lighthearted, happy as a boy."

Audiences recognized him immediately by the "glorious bald knob so dear to their hearts." The diminutive Arditi fell in love with a Richmond girl appropriately named Virginia; Mrs. Arditi accompanied her husband on all his tours.

Rounding up his flock with such dependables as Del Puente, Marcassa, Castelmary, Novara and Vanni, Abbey sallied forth to Chicago.

A suspicion of Nordica's grievance must have trickled through to the press. One of Patti's champions, feeling that the American prima donna was giving herself airs, declared:

"Patti is bringing her voice and Nordica her wardrobe."

This seemed unfair on both counts; vocally to Nordica, sartorially to Patti. Although it was rumored that Nordica had spent £2,000 at Worth's in Paris, the diva outstripped—or rather, outdressed—her without half trying. Patti always traveled with an average of forty-four stage trunks containing principal robes, each described as a masterpiece. Her three *robes de style* for *Traviata* alone cost £1,000.

She arrived in Chicago with four new gowns for *Roméo et Juliette*—they could hardly be called costumes, as Patti's stage accouterment was designed less to show the character of a role than to enhance Patti's own charms.

For the Capulet ball she donned white satin with pink ribbons and pearls; for the secret marriage, gray and pink satin (the pink a shade so new that no name had yet been found for it). The bedroom scene called for a white gauze tunic over deep blue. Juliet died in her wedding gown, white satin embroidered with silver, orange blossoms and diamonds.

Only Chicago witnessed these confections, for *Roméo* received no further representation on the tour. Patti must have felt grievous disappointment, not only for the immobilization of the delectable wardrobe, but also because she had taken a drastic step expressly to appear as Juliette. The headlines soon found her out.

"Patti is a Blonde!" they shrieked.

The diva's raven tresses, indeed, glowed many shades brighter, although "auburn" perhaps described the degree with accuracy. In the days before ladies of the theatre and elsewhere changed hair tints at the drop of a whim, Patti's metamorphosis was revolutionary.

Chicago waited in the throes of a delicious delirium to set both the president of the United States and the world's favorite prima donna on the stage of its "Parthenon of modern civilization," as one newspaper termed the new quarter-billion Auditorium.

The great dedication night of December 9, 1889, passed "in a blaze of glory." Eight thousand persons crowded in somehow, and 30,000 milled about in the streets until midnight. The stage was cleared of scenery and 1,000 fortunate seatholders, tier above tier, looked out at the vast multitude in the auditorium.

"In such a place," the *Chicago Times* reverently breathed, "the heroes and the triumphs of all ages must come into a new existence for the gratification and elevation of modern society."

On this high plane the ceremony proceeded. Orations from local dignitaries reached a climax: the introduction of the president of the United States. Fittingly, Benjamin Harrison laid his tribute at the feet of the Muse and her acolyte, the diva:

"Only the voice of the immortal singer can bring from these arches those echoes which will tell us the true purpose of their construction."

Patti was led forth in the midst of a tumult. Her gown of richest white brocade, with black satin stripes, was trimmed with steel spangles and the corsage looped and gemmed with pearls and diamonds. The blending of black and white delicately albeit sumptuously signified a "second mourning" for the singer's sister, Carlotta, who had died in June.

The ensuing moments were captured for posterity by a sensitive writer for the *Herald:*

"The mellow notes of a flute came with delicious sweetness. A harp, played by a woman's hand, joined in. . . . Then came the song, beginning so faintly yet so clearly that it sounded like the warble of a bird concealed among the flowers on the stage. . . . Afterward, there was only a blushing, bright-eyed woman, bowing with crossed arms."

People rose to their feet, shouting and waving handkerchiefs. Patti was not to be let off merely with *Home Sweet Home* after all. Graciously, she sang Eckert's *Echo Song*. Now the applause assumed the fierceness of a tornado, said the *Herald,* but the diva's contribution was ended. For brevity and costliness it probably set an all-time record.

The three weeks in Chicago brought gratifying moments to other leading singers, as well.

Tamagno emerged as a "king among tenors," a "name to conjure with." Purity and lyric sweetness were not at his command but "audiences sat half-bewildered at the notes hurled from his deep, prodigious chest like missiles from a catapult."

Tamagno took his honors modestly. An extremely pleasant and cheerful man, according to Mrs. Arditi, the tenor showed courtesy even on the stage, subordinating himself when not in the limelight. Large of frame, with a short neck, a round head covered with brown curly hair, he turned a good-natured face to the world.

Tamagno was far from naïve, however, in business matters. Marcus Mayer, Abbey's advance man, looked up the tenor in South America on Patti's advice.

"He didn't exactly want the earth, but just about all there was on the surface," Mayer commented wryly. "Yet when the contract was finally signed, he was perfectly content and gave no more trouble."

Over a complex of railroads the special train headed south on January 5, its destination Mexico.

Just after crossing the border, the train was held up by a wrecked bridge at Torreon. The passengers discovered to their horror that an engine and "goods" train had gone down with the bridge.

"It might have been our fate," said Mrs. Arditi. "Everybody is so thankful for the lucky escape there has been no grumbling."

The accident delayed the arrival and opening by one day; the eager Mexicans could hardly wait. A local ruling prescribed that a portion of the house must be saved for single sales, but Mayer got a dispensation from his friend the governor; the embargo was raised and practically every seat was sold in advance. Several fanatical opera lovers pawned their jewelry to buy tickets.

Forgotten was the scandal of 1887, when a man representing himself as Marcus Mayer sold tickets for Patti in advance and absconded with the proceeds.

The first-night house for *Semiramide* displayed "such wealth, dresses and diamonds, such a galaxy of beauty and such an appreciative though exacting audience as one seldom sees," wrote Virginia Arditi. "I heard of a lady who positively paid £30 for a box and £14 for two seats in the gallery for her maid and her husband's valet!

"It is a perfect paradise of a place," exclaimed the conductor's wife. "The hotel, formerly a convent, was built around a garden of orange trees. . . . Before our arrival the best rooms were denuded to add to the elegance of Patti's apartments. As a special compliment to the company in general every servant *was ordered to have a bath"*—a directive that suggests the habitual level of local cleanliness.

Every one of the singers became indisposed at one juncture or another, possibly from the contagion that seemed to pervade the air. An epidemic of *la grippe* did not keep people at home; they merely joined in the music with robust sneezes and melancholy coughs. Tamagno's high notes elicited sympathetic wails from auditors and sneezes and barks punctuated Patti's arias.

This audience possessed something even more frightening than germs. It proved "more exigent than even the Italians, *et c'est tout dire,"* wrote Mrs. Arditi. "At the first *Faust,* Ravelli, not in good voice, was simply *hissed.*

Novara, the Méphistophélès, never had a hand the whole evening, and Albani, the Marguerite, was only applauded when she sang alone—a novel experience for the artists. The audience very soon lets them know when they sing out of tune."

Estimates varied about the final "take" in this rich season. Mayer let it be known that the company left with $225,000 in gold for fifteen scheduled and six extra performances. The "bible" in the Metropolitan's offices shows something less for a total: $187,071, and in Mexican currency. But whatever the profit to the management, the singers went away happy, as Albani, quoted later in the *New York Tribune,* admitted after a little preliminary grumbling:

"We have been roasted in Mexico, drenched to the skin in San Francisco, frozen to death in the western cities. We spent six days in the cars without stopping from Chicago to Mexico. It was simply horrid.

"But three weeks in Mexico were ample compensation for all discomfort. Mexicans do not see good opera very often and will cheerfully pay $12 a ticket and live on bread and water."

In 1890 Abbey barely missed the worst weather blockade in northern California history. All traffic in and out of San Francisco lay paralyzed by landslides, washouts and heavy snows. The city suffered isolation for seventeen days. On January 31, only ten days before Abbey's first curtain, the blockade loosened, but the damage already had been done to San Francisco's zest for opera.

Patti, however, found the city as lovable and almost as loving as before. The crank who threw the bomb on stage behind her in 1887 had long been incarcerated or had at least disappeared.

The diva could hardly have failed to relish this tour. She showed herself at each appearance *"plus Patti que jamais,"* as the *San Francisco Examiner* said quaintly. "Even the Philistines got their money's worth and honestly enjoyed themselves. The house for *Semiramide* was not only filled, but with the right people," a reference to the painful "tiers of solemn vacancy" that had greeted Tamagno the night before.

Denver, Omaha and Louisville maintained the chorus of paeans at full strength.

Nordica's presence made up for the shortcomings of *Trovatore* in the Omaha Coliseum which, in spite of strenuous carpentering and masking, still showed all too plainly its everyday use as a skating rink. Signs proclaimed: "No one allowed on the floor—only skates," and the chill of the ice still pervaded the air. Waiting while the orchestra "dawdled about in picturesque commonplaceness," the audience of 5,000 shivered in coats and mufflers and wondered if the kettledrummer's antics were part of the show.

But when Nordica appeared all troubles were forgotten, and the barnlike hall, with its glaring light and uncomfortable temperature, took on life, color and interest. "Her charming face and manner won the hearts of hundreds. . . . Her costumes by Worth offset any deficiencies. She dared to wear red hair and a pink gown and dared to look pretty with the daring combination."

Denver and Louisville also supplied weather problems: in Colorado the audience sat in overcoats and ear muffs for *"Faust en Frappé";* while in Kentucky a sudden cold spell reduced the audience for *Otello*—but not the enthusiasm for Albani and Tamagno.

Abbey would have been wiser not to have returned to Chicago for an extra series. The fickle public was already looking forward to the advent of Walter Damrosch and the German troupe from the Metropolitan (although their audiences shrank as usual after initial curiosity had been satisfied) and not even Patti could inflame Chicago's spring lethargy.

One week in Boston remained before Abbey hurled his challenge at New York. Passing over the Boston Theatre, traditional home for opera, Abbey engaged Mechanics Hall, a cavernous auditorium which housed conventions and exhibitions. Because the Hall would hold 7,000 it was Abbey's choice for the next few seasons, although Grau returned to the Boston Theatre in 1899.

Boston's critics without exception despised Mechanics Hall.

"The seats are as penitential as ever," wrote Louis C. Elson in the *Advertiser.*

"Those who sat in the gallery should have had spyglasses and ear trumpets," said the *Globe* man.

To the redoubtable Philip Hale, who had recently come to Boston from Albany and who would enrich the Hub's critical scene until 1934, "Mechanics Institute proved singularly well arranged for the exhibition of steam ploughs and fertilizers but not a place for opera."

Unhappily calling in his *bête noir,* Wagner, as a frame of reference, Mr. Hale admitted that "Patti is still the greatest singer, pure and simple, of the world. I confess that a scale by her is more pleasing than a half-hour of gutteral declamation emitted from the steam clouds in the face of an orchestral storm."

The critic knew how to appreciate a supreme artist, even if she had passed her prime, and stressed his predilection for "noble ruins" in 1893, after she had sung in the world premiere of *Gabriella.*

Of the final tour in 1903-04, even though Patti was ill but once and carried home a nugget of $250,000, the kindest comment is silence.

Part IV

FABULOUS 'NINETIES—
THE GREAT GAMBLE

1. FIRST POKER HAND: FULL HOUSE, KINGS AND QUEENS

"He swept into view in a swan-drawn boat, tall and fair as a Viking, the light playing on his shining armor . . . with a rarely fine physique, broad-shouldered and commanding, and a face strong yet fair, manly yet mild. . . . A strange audience in a strange land hailed him as king of the night."

On November 9, 1891, in Chicago's Auditorium, the American reign of Jean de Reszke began, and with it the Metropolitan Opera's fabulous 'nineties, the era that most accurately, perhaps, deserves to be called the "Metropolitan's Golden Age." Even those who maintain that a golden age always lies just twenty years ago sigh with nostalgia for the galaxy that Abbey and Grau summoned up on their return to the Metropolitan.

The peerless De Reszkes, the quintet of prima donnas most intimately associated with them—Eames, Calvé, Melba, Nordica, Lehmann—Maurel in a half-dozen inimitable characterizations, Tamagno with his trumpet tones, Schumann-Heink in the full-voiced glory of maturity, Sembrich, Plançon, Lassalle, Alvarez, Van Dyck, Scotti. . . .

And of the men, the greatest by acclamation was Jean de Reszke. For a brief but unforgettable period he dominated the operatic realm.

Now that Patti was following Lind and Nilsson into the realm of legend, grand opera devotees restlessly sought a new object for their affections.

They found it in the "parfit" Knight of the Grail, the "ideal" Raoul (in *Huguenots*), the "greatest Faust of all," and at the height of his achievement, a Tristan and a Siegfried who proved that Wagner's formidable "declamations" could be sung.

A "pleasant, slightly balding gentleman, whose portrait is the pride and peril of Parisian boudoirs," Jean won America by the same qualities that had enslaved Europe. He wrought havoc on American womanhood; the term "matinee idol" might have been coined for him. He sustained his reputation as the most romantic lover on the operatic stage, particularly as the "handsome, stalwart Roméo, gentle in love, fierce in fight." Victor Capoul had blithely worn this mantle twenty years before; one of the ironies of operatic fate placed him as the Tybalt to Jean's Roméo in the Polish singer's first American season. Capoul-Tybalt in truth lay "here slain."

Not only the romantic gentleman and the polished singer who mastered all vocal shortcomings, Jean was the finest artist of the generation, a genuine friend to his colleagues and a man of principle and character—"the only one of his kind," Lilli Lehmann believed.

As Lohengrin's "lieber Schwan" had borne the new hero to Chicago's stage on November 9, 1891, so the Monsalvat dove drew Jean de Reszke off the same stage in the same opera on April 27, 1901. The audience raised a storm; they would hardly let Jean and Nordica, his Elsa, out of sight between curtain calls. Thus Jean said farewell to America, except for a gala at the Metropolitan on April 29, in which he sang an act from *Tristan*. He had come full circle as America's most beloved knight-errant.

Between those two swan-boat excursions lay splendid, songful years for the Metropolitan. Now, despite all disclaimers, the "star system" rose to its zenith. The management might protest that "ensemble" constituted their goal, but Abbey's idea of ensemble still was to cram all the first-rank singers he could obtain into his casts. Constellations rather than single stars made the operatic firmament glorious.

Abbey's "powerful coterie of principals selected from the flower of foreign vocal celebrities" amazed Chicago and ten other cities that were exposed to the galaxy. During the eight seasons that the Metropolitan company functioned in Jean's epoch (one of them without him), the public interest and personal and artistic satisfaction kept the nucleus together: Eames, Calvé, Melba, Nordica, Lehmann.

In his reign on tour, Jean most often acknowledged as his queens three of the five—Eames, Melba and Nordica. A single Radames to Lehmann's Aida in 1891 in Chicago and one Tristan to her Isolde in Boston in 1899 formed the extent of his partnership with the dramatic Lilli; he sang Calvé's Don José only twice, her Faust three times in the spring of 1897.

Chicago also took to its bosom a hero of another stamp: Jean's younger brother Edouard.

"He stepped down from the bus [that had met the train], a full head and shoulders above the men and women who followed. His little brown hat sat on his bushy hair like a chimneypot and around his giant's throat a rare seal collar was tucked against the raw Chicago wind. His right arm, with the elbow at his valet's crown, held a folded comforter with silk lining and tied with satin knots.

"His stride was so wide that two steps took him into the hotel vestibule; and, bending his frame over the book, he wrote in the big generous hand of a man who never orders pints—'Edouard de Reszke.'"

Jean's younger brother suited Chicago's bold, expansive nature down to the last ounce of his gargantuan bulk, which was attached to his six-foot-two frame by many years of joyous feeding. His generosity, his roaring geniality, his jokes, his sheer strength (he could lift with his head the 250-pound Jean

Lassalle who clasped hands around that "giant throat")—all fitted Chicago's idea of a personality. On the stage, other qualities emerged.

From King Henry's first note, the audience sat up in wonder and delight at his impressive and impersonal dignity. His triumph as Count Rudolph in *Sonnambula* was enhanced by Friar Laurence in *Roméo* and St. Bris in *Huguenots;* his Mephisto seemed the apotheosis of deviltry, if outwardly "a gentleman and a jolly good fellow." This role, given Edouard by "God and Gounod," remained a favorite for years, growing mellower rather than more evil, until it became difficult to tell villain from hero.

Jean's first queen, Emma Eames, made her American debut with the brothers at the same Chicago performance of *Lohengrin.* Her beauty struck the eye of the beholder with a lasting impact. "Slender but not thin," as one account described her, "her small throat as round as the Venus of Milo's, her perfect oval face, with high, proud-spirited features, eyes large and somewhat hard, nose with delicate broad nostrils."

"Every patriotic and art-loving subject has reason to be proud of this young uncrowned Queen of Song," the *Chicago Inter-Ocean* chauvinistically proclaimed. "She is a handsome and dignified type of genuine American womanhood, winsomely appealing to the imagination through higher faculties than mere lyric brilliance, domineering sentiment or childlike simplicity."

The friendly relationship between the prima donna and the De Reszkes showed plainly in an interview in Louisville, where the company played three performances in the midst of their first Chicago season. "The brothers always occupy the same room and continually sing to each other . . . and they have a French valet [a lifelong servitor and secretary, Louis Vachet] whose only charge is to assist them. . . . They praise each other but never hesitate to speak of faults." Jean took the *Courier-Journal* reporter to see Eames, "humming the drinking song from *Lucrezia Borgia* along the way.

"It was at once apparent that the tenor is a great favorite of the prima donna's. She said: 'I persuaded him to come to America. They will go wild over you, I told him, and they have. The De Reszkes call me their goddaughter because I made my debut with them. We always sing together and I like Jean's acting.'"

Julian Story, the singer's artist husband, was present during the interview but contributed nothing, although her beauty inspired his most subtle talents as a painter and as designer of her costumes.

A *Brooklyn Eagle* writer quoted Balzac as saying that "God knows his angels on earth by the inflections of their voices. If ever a woman with a Yankee voice succeeds in passing for an angel, Eames can do it." And Jean himself remarked, according to his biographer, Clara Leiser, that he "always liked to sing with Emma Eames; there was always the odor of violets about her."

De Reszke joined Melba only a few times in their first season together, singing Roméo to her Juliette in New York and Faust to her Marguerite in Boston, Chicago and St. Louis.

The Australian arrived in Chicago in 1894 clad in "a tan and brown serge traveling costume trimmed with cream lace and a shade of brown velvet that exactly matched her eyes. She wore a broad-brimmed hat covered with black ostrich tips curled down over masses of jet black hair. Like all prima donnas, Melba has a pet—a ferocious looking Mexican beetle which lay snugly cuddled up under the lace at Madame's $10,000 throat.

" 'Oh, my!' she exclaimed, 'he's going down my back!' She pulled at the chain which held the beetle. 'The gentleman said he wouldn't bite.' The creature looked like a circus elephant, all dressed up in a suit of red, white and blue. Evidently Melba was in terror of the little monster."

The prima donna was never seen hatless off stage. Even on stage, singers invariably appeared in full street costume at rehearsals. An *Inter-Ocean* reporter expressed his astonishment at the Chicago rehearsal for *Lohengrin* in 1891, when "Eames wore gloves and a great fur boa even though the stage setting showed full summertime, and the De Reszkes worked earnestly in tall silk hats."

Melba's triumph in Chicago was as complete and instantaneous as Sembrich's in 1884. "Gifted by nature," the *Inter-Ocean* rhapsodized, "with a graceful personality, queenly figure, arms perfect in proportion, head well poised on dimpled shoulders, expressive eyes, well chiseled features, strong but sensitive mouth . . . her histrionic powers are limited, not much beyond the conventional, but the mesmerism is magic in her voice . . . simply phenomenal in its purity. . . . We have here a new goddess of song!"

When the diva at last began to show histrionic ambitions, in a *Faust* performance of 1896, Hale pounced on her with acerbity:

"Her Marguerite is a more sharply defined creature than before. Yet I prefer the staid and drab coloring of the earlier performance to false vivacity and deliberate acting. Her withdrawal after meeting Faust reminded one of Galatea, frolicsome Galatea, who hid herself that she might be found. Her recollection of the 'noble gentlemen' was almost flippantly amorous; her joy at the casket of jewels not so much girlish glee of surprise as the experienced recognition and acknowledgment of a valuable gift. . . . Now it is artificiality instead of the not indispensable atmosphere of virginal innocence. At the beginning she was ready to fall into Faust's arms [with] no need of demoniac aid."

The breezy Australian entered fully into Jean de Reszke's orbit and acknowledged the tenor to be one of the strongest influences in her development. "He was a god," she wrote in *Melodies and Memories,* "not only in his voice . . . but in his appearance, his acting, his every movement. So utterly wonderful was he that . . . when I found myself singing *Lohengrin* with him without a rehearsal, I burst into tears in the last act and thanked my stars that my singing role for the evening was practically finished. . . . Never has there been an artist like him."

A playful conversation between the two artists during an intermission in *Faust* was recorded by the *Chicago News* in 1896. Melba gravely demanded:

"Jean, do you think we are in love?"

The big, handsome Pole laughed gallantly and, according to the reporter, said in delightful English:

"I do not think it at all; it is my life sentence." Turning to the interviewer he continued: "Melba is my pet Marguerite—we have become so satisfied one with the other that there is a sort of *Faust* bond uniting us at least once a week, don't you see?"

Nordica's progress toward greatness achieved acknowledgment everywhere except from Boston's Hale. Chicago expressed astonished delight at seeing "the majestic Nordica carrying Susanna [in *Figaro*] with piquancy and grace, demureness and daintiness—a trifle too dignified, perhaps, but thoroughly consistent with high art"; compared her singing in *L'Africaine* to "jewels of song that outshone the rich barbaric accompaniment" and complimented her on "total forgetfulness of husbanding her resources"; found her "artistically nonchalant" in the assignment, wildly improbable at that advanced stage of her development, of Philine, and gave her Wagnerian roles full marks, particularly after her initiation at Bayreuth in 1894.

Chicago always cherished a soft spot for *Lohengrin,* and accounted the performance of March 20, 1895, one of the triumphs of the season. Nordica revealed "fullness of meaning, with new gestures properly conceived and placed. The growing of the girl's character to womanhood was evenly and sincerely done."

"She kneeled often," marveled the *Elite,* "and made a graceful recovery of her upright position without use of either hand."

Philip Hale, however, remained captious. "She is self-conscious and her Valentine does not touch the heart," he said of a performance of *Huguenots* in 1894. "Although nature gave her an advantageous face and figure, she has not made the most of her gifts. Her make-up was bad and she moves in lines, not curves." Her Philine "was a promise rather than a well-defined, wholly satisfactory result."

Another *Huguenots* brought Hale's admission that Nordica perhaps improved in action, "not so much in what she now does as in the abandonment of what she formerly did. She evidently has been coached," he judged.

In 1899 she finally won from Hale the admission that her Elsa showed genuine merit. But her Donna Elvira seemed "a cardboard figure." Nordica must have thought despairingly that she would have to start all over again to win a crumb from Hale. He paid scant attention to her first Isolde, being absorbed in the perplexing discovery that he did not much care for *Tristan* well sung after all.

As her substantial figure became more matronly, Nordica determined to exercise. She and several other prima donnas turned to cycling, whose vogue had mounted to the proportions of a rage.

"There is nothing like a bike for enjoyment," Nordica is quoted as saying. "I first tried to ride ten days ago."

For the new sport Nordica wore a brown, rather short skirt, with an Eton jacket, blue shirt with white collar, a red turban with black ostrich plumes. Scalchi's costume was black serge, noted the *Post-Dispatch.*

Nordica's poodle, Turk, accompanied her on the ride, as on other occasions. The previous year, St. Louis had been made aware of opera singers' penchant for pets. William G. B. Carson, in his entertaining history, *St. Louis Goes to the Opera,* admitted that local hotels "were not enthusiastic when it came to canine guests. The Southern and the Planter's remained coldly adamant, but the smaller St. Nicholas relented, and thither went those stars who would not part with their pets.

"To put foot within the recessed portals [of the St. Nicholas] is to be reminded of a New York bench show, with an Italian opera accompaniment."

In Chicago one year prima donna and pet checked in at the Auditorium Annex (the hotel, now the Congress, that was connected by underground passage with the Auditorium itself) in a whirlwind of temperament.

Nordica's poodle, observed a *Herald* reporter, led the procession, a "lank, close-shorn dog with plenty of hair over its eyes and tail and none where most was needed. . . . It dashed past the startled porter and his law against dogs and babies. Three men with pointed whiskers went in pursuit. A motherly woman gasped 'Pierrot!' This was Nordica, the tragic Valentine of *Huguenots*.

"Nordica started by complaining. This is a diva's right. . . . She flounced down in a big chair and vowed that she would sleep there before going to the ninth floor.

"Jean de Reszke, with the graciousness of a knight, offered to surrender his rooms . . . she refused. . . . Edouard de Reszke appeared. His beer had not come and the gas log—he hated it at best—was not consuming half the gas. Couldn't it be taken away?

" 'Turn it out,' mildly suggested the little man who was trying to book three stars at once.

"Nordica had her way and was settled on the parlor floor with the Polish brothers. A new watch of clerks came on duty. About eight, the queenly Melba and *her* court appeared. *She* liked a high place.

"No man or woman on earth demands so much richness as opera stars. They want the best, as soon as they feel sure they know what the best is."

Few shadows of the discord that was to part Jean and Nordica two years later hung over the friends as they received the press. Nordica displayed a fan embroidered with the name "Elsa" in diamonds, the gift of Cosima Wagner. Jean, not his usual tactful self, castigated the theatres in Philadelphia, Baltimore and Washington and vowed, according to the *Tribune,* that he never would sing in them again. (He repented the next season.)

"There are only a few theatres fit to sing in," he cried. "The dirt and filth are an absolute disgrace. Little, cramped dressing rooms are hardly more than cupboards. There is no place to wash one's hands. And the dust! If one moved on stage, a cloud arose and one swallowed a throatful of microbes."

Nordica chimed in: "Yes, and my white gown you ruined! He had to 'wipe up the stage with me' in Washington," she told the reporter. "It is beyond belief that such things exist in the nation's capital."

Baltimore's offending stage was Harris' Academy of Music, which the company would abandon after another season for Music Hall, a remodeled concert hall. Washington's was the Grand Opera House, which Grau continued to patronize until 1900. Philadelphia's, of course, was the famous Academy of Music.

Jean was a chief victim in this spring of 1895 that incapacitated a half-dozen stars. Boston suffered most from the germ that swept through the ranks, operas being changed five times in the course of three weeks and many substitutions marring the perfection of the casts. Patrons were said to be up in arms. The *Chicago Tribune* championed the Boston cause with fervor and urged an organization against the "exactions and small but exasperating tyrannies of opera impresarios."

Abbey and Grau could not be held to blame for their singers' delicate throats. Jean was always terrified of illness; this season set his worst record on the road. For most of his cancellations, substitutions of other tenors could be made, but Boston lost a *Lohengrin* and Chicago a *Meistersinger* because of the tenor's indisposition.

The *Chicago Herald* resumed: "The De Reszkes are the most popular in the company because fame and genius and homage have not turned their heads. Each knew a dozen men in the lobby and each was as demonstrative as foreigners always are until they become Americanized. Edouard puts his arms about men callers, then looks down upon their heads. Jean is full of words and bustles around where Edouard stamps and strides."

Willy Schütz, whose sister was married to Edouard, joined the group. He acted as secretary, general buffer and liaison with the press for the brothers. "Not very strong above the eyes," as James Huneker described him, Willy bulked large in physique, not ashamed to stand beside the six-foot-two Edouard, the six-foot Jean and the equally mountainous Lassalle.

It was undoubtedly Willy who carried the tidings to Jean that his fiancée had been insulted in a Chicago paper, arousing the chivalrous Jean almost to the point of challenging the reporter. Willy had exaggerated. Jean calmed down when he read the report, for it contained nothing more than the gossip which had surrounded Jean for six years. "He has been engaged for seven years," the *Tribune* wrote, and quoted Jean as saying that his long-time sweetheart was finally to obtain her divorce. This was 1896; when Jean returned to America in the fall, he was a married man.

Jean Lassalle, the third member of the trio, towering over six feet, weighing over two hundred pounds, with a chest measurement of fifty and one-half inches, joined the brothers in America for only three seasons, touring Boston, Philadelphia and Brooklyn in 1891-92 and adding five other cities in 1893-94 and 1896-97.

His remarkable Valentin, his exciting Don Giovanni and his artistic but necessarily un-German Sachs and Telramund pleased the cognoscenti, and the impressionable element in Chicago's audience gasped at the sight of his tawny-tinted physique clad in the comparatively scanty costume of Nelusko.

Like the brothers, Lassalle cherished a fondness for sports and for horses; he was also proficient in the murderous French version of boxing and wrestling known as *la savate*. One Chicago admirer of the De Reszkes thought Lassalle grouchy by comparison in 1897.

The trio could always find amusement in its own company on the road, and from its suite would issue gargantuan roars of laughter. A picture of the three lounging at ease was drawn in the *Musical Courier* in the 'nineties:

"Bandying jests . . . someone hums, and instantly the room is flooded with tone, the Great Trio from *William Tell*, perhaps. Jean sings C sharp without effort. Then that rapturous breakdown known as the can-can is indulged in by one of the partners and suddenly a fierce description about the psychic possibilities of *Hamlet* arises and is ended only by a call for fresh beverages.

"These big fellows are men, men. They play billiards, run, wrestle, swim, smoke [Jean gave up cigars, but enjoyed a mild cigarette which the manufacturer named after him] and possibly swear, too."

When they tried their voices in their rooms, the walls shook. Once, coming from Boston where Jean had been ill, "he hummed tunes from *Manon* in the wholesome Chicago atmosphere, and by the time he had reached *Faust* and *Otello* was using notes that had their origin deep in his chest. Edouard put his foot on the loud pedal and hit the keys with sledge hammer blows, yet above all the noise rang Jean's voice, as distinct as a tug whistle on a rainy night."

That Jean reverted to *Otello* for practice throws an interesting light on his preferences, for he considered the Verdi role his most difficult, according to an unusually informative interview in the *Chicago Tribune* in 1895, and sang it only once on tour.

"Both Otello and Don José are contrary to my nature," he was quoted as saying. "Naturalism is disagreeable to me. To die spluttering and spitting—oh, no! It is the stage, not the hospital, where I work."

He liked any role he could act *and* sing. For this reason he rarely appeared in concert and never with pleasure.

"To stand still in dress suit and sing—never!"

After his intensive study of Tristan, and on the eve of singing the exigent role in Chicago, he offered this advice:

"Always learn the words of the libretto fully. Afterward learn the music—absolutely as the composer has written it, without a single change except when it is impossible for your voice, for that is the honesty of art."

He gave as much consideration to the details of character building as to its elemental structure. His most trying moment came during the preparation for the young Siegfried. Should he shave his beloved mustache?

The great controversy, "to beard or not to beard," had raged for years. As early as 1887 the *Boston Globe* had asked: "Should singers and speakers wear smoothly shaven faces? Hair around the mouth tends to impair the utterance in song and speech as projected from the mouth. Most lawyers, ministers and orators are clean shaven; actors, too, as a rule. But foreign singers to a man are hairy about the mouth."

"Singers' hirsute excrescences" continued to annoy the newspaper writers; the *Chicago Sun-Herald* took both men and women to task in 1892. "While Jean de Reszke assumes the same wig and beard as Lohengrin, Faust and Roméo, Eames makes a mistake in the opposite direction by wearing her own natural hair as Elsa."

The writer chided little Martapoura for wearing "a beard half as long as himself, making him look like a Rip Van Winkle dwarf instead of Mercutio." Brooklyn approved the mustache worn by the tenor Mauguiere in the second act of *Carmen*. "José had time to grow it in jail."

Jean had spent hours in fasting and prayer before shaving off the hair that had served to mask his "large, sensuous mouth." Not until an hour before the New York performance was the decision made, and then only after his valet had snipped off the adornment bit by bit until the point of no return was reached. In 1900-01 Jean's single performance of each Siegfried in New York hardly justified the sacrifice, and so both appeared hirsute.

Chicago complained bitterly that the tenor refused to sing there in 1898-99, when he ventured no farther afield than Boston, Philadelphia, Washington and Pittsburgh.

In the following year, his total absence from these shores brought a realization of how much he might be missed. Then, when he returned in 1900-01, five cities shared a scant ten performances among them.

Only New York was treated to the amazing spectacle of the fifty-two-year-old tenor ranging masterfully through the best of his repertory, piling one triumph atop another. There was no Roméo, no Siegfried, and more important, no *Götterdämmerung* Siegfried for the road.

Melba, "the pet Marguerite," and Nordica, Jean's first Isolde and faithful Valentine and Elsa, matched their heroines to his heroes as before. This final season also saw Jean in partnership with three new prima donnas.

Seemingly the most incongruous was the pert Fritzi Scheff, who in her first season at the Metropolitan filled the part of Eva in the two *Meistersinger* performances on tour (Gadski had sung it in the House). Pittsburgh took particular pleasure in the gay, pretty singer, hailing her Musetta as the season's sensation. A hint of her future appeared in the *Dispatch:*

"If Scheff ever becomes a light opera star, this country will enjoy an artist who will revive the favor of Aimée."

Lucienne Bréval played opposite Jean in his only two Philadelphia appearances, *L'Africaine* and *Le Cid*. This stately soprano, handsome in mien and rich in voice, sang little outside of New York in her two seasons with the Metropolitan.

A new Wagnerian heroine arose on the horizon the season before Jean's return, singing Isolde (to Van Dyck's Tristan), the first two Brünnhildes, Elsa and Elisabeth, as well as Valentine and Beethoven's Leonore. Milka Ternina seemed headed for the highest peaks of achievement, but after only four seasons contracted a facial paralysis, said to have been brought on by a cold caught while mountain-climbing.

Tall and majestic in appearance, the Croatian singer gave the impression of beauty though her features were heavy and plain. She was America's first Tosca, introducing Puccini's masterpiece in Jean's last season. Only Boston and Pittsburgh heard the two in *Tristan*.

The still unregenerate Hale spent most of his column in a diatribe against *Tristan's* "illogical and silly libretto," scoffing at the potion scene, which to him suggested that a "sharp attack of colic" had overtaken the lovers. He remarked sarcastically that Jean was evidently indisposed: "he chopped phrases into little bits . . . and saved himself to the extent of often being inaudible." Ternina had already proved herself as "a great artist, an actress to her finger tips."

Pittsburgh was better pleased. De Reszke sang "easily and without strenuous effort . . . and was all we expected. A deadly quietus was given any reports that he is failing."

Jean thus ended his career in America with a succession of richly varied experiences and companions. As the *Chicago Inter-Ocean* repeated: "Blessings brighten as they take their flight."

During the seven brief seasons he graced the American scene he sang only 116 performances in ten cities outside of New York. He never journeyed farther west than St. Louis, and never appeared in Brooklyn.

When it came to replacing him, his roles were divided among four or five tenors. The words "perfection" and "ideal" remained with him to the last: Chicago said his Lohengrin had never been equaled. Thus Jean de Reszke became the Metropolitan's first "indispensable man"—unrivaled until a certain chubby Neapolitan disembarked in 1903.

2. SECOND POKER HAND: STRAIGHT, ACE HIGH

"He touches nothing he does not adorn . . . distinctly original, full of genuine comedy, dashing and dextrous. . . ." "The singer may inspire the fancy or captivate the senses; the actor carries one away upon a flood tide of conviction. . . ." "He is exceedingly handsome, with much of the mobile richness of expression and dark intellectuality so appealing in Otis Skinner."

These Chicago encomiums described Victor Maurel, the one male opera personage who had nothing to fear from "the French trio." Indeed this baritone commanded Philip Hale's attention almost to the exclusion of the De Reszkes and Lassalle during his Indian Summer in America. After the *Otello* of February 26, 1895, Hale wrote:

"Maurel represents Iago as the Demon of Perversity. To describe fully . . . would be to give at length every detail of his business, every mocking and sinister inflection; to dissect his marvelous mastery of the musical phrase; to attempt to portray in words the changes of his extraordinarily mobile face, to paint in words a wealth of gestures, none without meaning. . . . Yet he convinces you that all this is spontaneous."

The Boston premiere of Verdi's *Falstaff* on February 28, 1895, caught Maurel with a sore throat which prohibited him from singing the great soliloquy on honor as well as several pages of cantabile and the soliloquy that opens Act II. Nevertheless Hale compared the work to *Figaro* and *The Barber*. It will lead them, he decided, "because Verdi is a man of our own day . . . and can build on the foundations of others. If Mozart were alive, he might have written *Falstaff*." The critic considered this a "risky judgment," but then he had been forced to eat his prediction that *The Flying Dutchman* would outlive the later music dramas.

Maurel's Amonasro was a triumph in make-up, "his face, walk, pose . . . the savage King, with no trace of the gallant Don Giovanni, the devilish Iago, the toss-pot Falstaff, the shrewd Figaro."

Don Giovanni provided the singing actor with perhaps his greatest opportunity.

"The moment the light fell on his face, the libertine was revealed," Hale wrote, "not to be misunderstood by even the most unsuspicious virgin . . . sensuous, wicked, yet splendid in a fashion; brilliant, alluring, seductive. Such was his authority that even when he lowers himself (to beat Masetto) nine women out of ten in the audience admire him. The tenth looks at him earnestly and wishes she had known him."

The *St. Louis Globe-Democrat* oracle saw in a clouded crystal ball that the music of *Falstaff* "was not rich in invention, but will be successful as long as Maurel is around." The *Post-Dispatch* devoted eight column inches to the description of his elaborate make-up, and the *Republic* recounted a meeting between the famous singer and James J. Corbett. Maurel mistook the boxer's profession and said proudly:

"I too haff kill my man."

Brooklyn, in homespun style, compared a criticism of the baritone's "quarrel with the pitch" to "seeing a fly on the barn without seeing the barn."

Chicago bowed deeply to the veteran singing actor and paid him many compliments. He soon became an object of idolatry to the debutantes, who did not seem to know that he had charmed their mothers twenty years before. Amy Leslie, as usual, "scored a beat" with a personal interview on the subject of concert singing, similar in content to an earlier expression by Jean de Reszke, but different in language, at least as filtered through Miss Leslie's lively pen:

"To *chant* correctly always in the same voice, in the same toilet [te], with the hands full of music and the soul fixed upon the gate money is not lyric art.

"The lyric artist must have security and the balance of a trapeze performer, the dramatic intensity of a tragedian and the . . . adaptability of an archcomedian. Proper clothes are the least of an artist's necessities."

It is certain that this artist explored every resource of his mind and heart toward creating his powerful delineation of Iago before the time arrived to costume the deceiver, yet even that final detail lacked nothing.

His hands were studies in graceful ease and physical perfection, the writer added, "white and shapely . . . of constant interest."

Maurel possessed a sharp tongue always on call. Geraldine Farrar tells the story that her teacher and mentor, Lilli Lehmann, once felt its cutting edge. After a superb performance of *Don Giovanni* the baritone complimented his stately, rather shapeless Donna Anna for her acting and singing in gracious stanzas until she was blushing with pleasure. Then, *sotto voce,* he added: "But for God's sake, burn those costumes!"

Another towering figure, Tamagno, the barrel-chested stentorian, returned to "throw out ringing B flats and C's with the same ease as Sandow

juggles fifty-pound dumbbells" in 1894-95, prompting the *Brooklyn Eagle* to
suggest: "as well criticize a cyclone for its ragged edges."

But the good-natured, buoyant, curly-haired young giant who had endeared himself to Patti and the Arditis five years before had disappeared, at
least in Chicago, where the tenor "seemed large and silent and somber." Perhaps he felt a trifle lost in the rush of praise for the subtlety and distinction of Jean de Reszke—or even for his own closest associate, Maurel.

In opera, when the gods come in, the half-gods do not go, as in Emerson's
poem, but stay on and sing. Abbey's company in the 'nineties enjoyed the
presence of a dozen stellar bodies whose brilliance would have registered first
magnitude in any other skies.

"Room at the top" was the rule on the Metropolitan's roster from 1891 to
1900. At least six sopranos with aspirations in alt left their names for posterity.

Easily the most picturesque of these was the expatriate Californian, Sybil
Sanderson, petted by Paris, showered with jewels by Czar Alexander III, the
cause of a Belgian prince's suicide and the inspiration of three Massenet
operas and one by Saint-Saëns.

When Abbey and Grau succumbed to her European reputation and engaged her for 1894-95, it was for the display of her beauty, her "Eiffel
Tower notes" and her fortune of jewels in *Manon,* which had its first French
productions in New York, Philadelphia, Brooklyn, Baltimore, Washington
and Boston.

The voice that had enchanted Paris and St. Petersburg failed to touch many
of her compatriots, although Philadelphia declared that the singer was "the
incarnation of daintiness, both in voice and person," and Boston's Philip
Hale mentioned many tones "haunting in their sweetness" and praised her
"elegance, rare in these days of boisterous sopranos."

"Any more chic coquette would be difficult to imagine," the *Washington
Post* declared, while Baltimore gasped at her costumes, particularly a "marvelous creation of spangled pink mirror velvet, shaded into rich yellow in
motion."

If any provincial audience shared New York's distaste at Manon's insistence
on wearing her jewels to the convent, no hint of displeasure appeared in the
press. Her severest critics resided in Chicago, where the papers gossiped of
her forthcoming marriage to Antonio Terry, a wealthy Cuban.

One of Sanderson's wedding gifts was the Château of Chenonceaux,
haunted by the ghosts of Diane de Poitiers and Catherine de Médicis. Terry's
generosity even ran to the engagement of the entire Opéra Comique to sing
in his wife's bedroom when she was convalescing from an illness. The opera
was *Esclarmonde,* like the equally forgotten *Le Mage* and the more enduring
Thais, composed by Massenet for his little American friend. Sanderson was
to take one more fling at America, barnstorming with Grau in 1901-02, but
meanwhile she reveled in her luxurious, pampered life in Paris.

Another American soprano, Marie van Zandt, also paid one visit to her
homeland and returned to more congenial surroundings abroad. The daughter of Jennie van Zandt, a popular concert and opera singer, and the grand-
daughter of the famous magician, Signor Blitz, Marie became "the spoiled

child of the Paris Opéra Comique," according to Herman Klein. Delibes wrote *Lakmé* for her.

The scandal that forced her from the Paris stage in 1885 had blown over by the time she came to America. She had been completely vindicated in the charge that she had appeared on the stage intoxicated.

Van Zandt made her debut in Chicago in 1891, one of twelve newcomers including the De Reszkes, Eames and the Ravogli sisters. As Amina in *La Sonnambula,* "this dainty, delicate, captivating dreamer stepped at once into the domain of high art," said the *Inter-Ocean.*

Her deepest failure lay in the characterization, as well as vocalization, of Mignon. The Chicago and Brooklyn performances of Thomas' opera offered one of the strangest contrasts in operatic history: the slender, girlish Van Zandt as Mignon, and the heroic, almost corpulent Lehmann as the giddy Philine. It was hardly fair to the American, in spite of her physical advantages. Lehmann was the "life of the performance" in Chicago and in Brooklyn, although "she seemed as little fitting as a steam locomotive drawing a horse car."

Boston heard *Lakmé* with the original singer (as did Philadelphia) after its February introduction in New York. Hale could find "not one drop of human blood, not one throb of a racked heart in the book and music," but considered Van Zandt's a performance of "singular fascination, savage innocence, and with its touch of maidenly awkwardness."

Marie van Zandt ended her days as a Russian countess in the south of France, after having recaptured the Parisian public in 1896.

Abbey's companies of the 'nineties were further enriched by American lyric sopranos, at least three of whom gleaned critical honors. Sophie Traubmann, a diminutive, dark-haired beauty of the German years, made the transition to Micaelas and Leonoras in the 'nineties. She still climbed the tree to flute the Forest Bird's warning to Siegfried in 1897, her last touring year.

Frances Saville, born in California of a Danish father named Simonsen and a Parisian mother, lived a great deal in Australia (she was the aunt of Frances Alda) and sang a great deal more in Europe. The comely soprano toured only one season of her two with the Metropolitan, but left a lasting impression in several cities as Marguerite, Mistress Ford and Micaela. Her triumph in *Traviata* was complete, according to Chicago's critics. One called her "petite, graceful, with features as clear-cut as a cameo."

It was to be expected that Marie Engle, a Chicagoan, would win her warmest ovations in her home town, where she was called "the poetical, physical and spiritual embodiment of Micaela," and also allowed to sing Juliette and Cherubino. But Boston found her "pleasing" even after Sembrich as Marguerite in *Les Huguenots.*

Abbey tried to keep a plentiful supply of Micaelas on hand, for Calvé seemed to wear them out faster than Josés. In addition to the Americans, the Swedish Sigrid Arnoldson, the French Clementine de Vere (wife of the conductor Sapio who had toured with Patti), the Italian Maria Pettigiani and the Polish Lola Beeth were pressed into service.

Chicago admired De Vere's brilliant upper notes and mass of red curls. Of Beeth's voice many things were said, but only one opinion was held on her beauty, which Chicago described as "a physical and mental caste rare lent the earth."

Arnoldson conquered hearts everywhere, although Chicago and Boston disagreed over her adaptability to Cherubino's doublet and hose. Throughout the tour of 1893-94, she earned the soubriquets "Pocket Venus," "Miniature Nilsson" and even "Swedish Nightingale."

Dramatic heroines were more difficult to come by: Litvinne is remembered for bulk rather than beauty (Hale commented that her Brünnhilde, after "long fire-encircled sleep, shows the perilous consequences of abstaining from exercise"); Libia Drog's voice "scatters as thin as a jet water-blown by the wind"; Mira Heller's Carmen "for once was a dull logy woman"; Mme. Basta-Tavary entered the roster in 1891-92, replacing Lehmann as Donna Anna in Philadelphia, Boston and Brooklyn and singing Carmen for Giulia Ravogli in New York.

Among lower voices, the field was open for Eugenia Mantelli to develop as Ortrud, Amneris and Azucena; for Rosa Olitzka to score as Erda (although she missed the mark as Carmen), and for Marie Brema to display her powerful Ortrud and Brangaene.

Giulia Ravogli, of whose Orfeo great things had been expected, gave America less intense pleasure than Europe had experienced in this and other roles, although one Chicago critic compared her to Viardot, "her soul like a star." She did not return after 1892.

Her sister Sophie, imported to sing Euridice to her Orfeo, proved attractive enough to warrant Orfeo's pursuit.

Zélie de Lussan, whom Brooklyn claimed as its own, sang almost 800 Carmens, but very few of them in American cities. Her most popular role at Covent Garden, the cigarette girl seemed merely coquettish and attractive in 1895 after the searing impression of Calvé.

The carefree Zélie tossed her blue-black, curly hair and remained unruffled, displaying her svelte figure in the comedy roles that better suited her: a dainty Zerlina, a bewitching Cherubino.

Meanwhile, the popular Scalchi marched on undefeated, one of those for whom all excuses are made, all justifications advanced. With what Philip Hale called her "peculiar assortment of voices" she earned a "Pax tecum, Madame, and late may you return to heaven" in 1895, a year before she retired.

"In [Urbain's] imperishable maroon velvet and white satin rig worn for twenty-five years without change of anything except waist measure, she still rolls out those garrison notes from her stalwart chest, breaks systematically when changing register, works as hard as a war horse and smiles at her untiring labors," Amy Leslie noted.

Scalchi sang her last performance on a Metropolitan tour in St. Louis on April 8, 1896, wearing the familiar tights of the *Huguenots* page.

"So grand a performance was never given under more auspicious circumstances," the *Post-Dispatch* exclaimed.

"There is no danger the troupe can go to pieces," remarked the *Chicago Tribune* in the critical season of 1896-97. "Bauermeister is back."

The indestructible Mathilde had come to America with Mapleson, had joined Abbey in 1891 and was to act as the Metropolitan's mainstay until 1905, rising from secondary to major roles in any emergency.

"She has a cast-iron throat and no knowledge of nerves. She sings her own repertory and the repertory of all other women; sings when it storms and when it is pleasant. . . . No jealousies torment her, no ambitions vex her serene spirit. No escorts wait at the stage door, no ardent admirers persecute her, no Chollies throw her roses. She is the sheet anchor of the Italian troupe. . . . Grau's salvation lies in clinging to Bauermeister."

She sat up to study Alice in *Falstaff* because Eames was ill. "Catching Mancinelli's eye, she dropped a curtsey, sang 'Rev-er-en-za!' and the orchestra laughed."

Bauermeister took some of Calvé's high notes in St. Louis, when the famous Carmen faltered; she replaced Lucille Hill as Susanna in Boston, "again showing her versatility, memory, courage and good nature," Hale said warmly. She even took over Zerlina and the *Huguenots* Marguerite in a Boston crisis.

Marie van Cauteren, Bauermeister's closest companion on stage from 1894 to 1903 (except for one season when Maude Roudez sang the Mercedeses, the Poussettes, the Countesses), never aspired to Mathilde's position. Although a Chicago paper called her "popular and lovable . . . she is a woman of mystery. Nobody knows where she lives or goes."

In the 'nineties, tenors found themselves in even fiercer competition than high sopranos. Of a dozen, all but Tamagno perforce gave gracious place to De Reszke.

Fernando de Lucia, the bright eyed, dapper little man with a spiked mustache and a vibrato that was better liked in Europe than America, basked in his brief day in Boston in 1894. His voice "thrilled" Philip Hale, and his passionate interpretation of José and Canio (he had created the *Pagliacci* role for New York earlier in the season) stirred the *Journal* critic for its "remarkable exhibition of natural temperament and dramatic skill. He is a master of his resources . . . sang a marvelous *Vesti la giubba* . . . and in his frenzy in the last act . . . did not lose control."

Hale credited his only disappointment in De Lucia to the role of Wilhelm Meister, in *Mignon*. (The writer always anathematized this and other anemic roles or singers as "walking gentlemen.") The tenor's pictures were selling like wildfire, the critic remarked in a chatty aside. "He has the hearts of girls as well as the hands and voices of Boston's public."

But Boston and Philadelphia did not make a season for the proud tenor; and he never returned.

Giuseppe Russitano gamely came back for more even after being placed as "a general average Italian" on the road. He bore his cross as stand-in for Jean with resignation, though he must have seethed at the *Baltimore Sun's* remark that "he looked like Little Lord Fauntleroy beside the giant frame of his Satanic friend" (Edouard "Méphistophélès" de Reszke).

Brooklyn developed a tolerance to Russitano that amounted almost to fondness. A *Trovatore* of 1894-95 "will go down in history," wrote the *Eagle* critic, "as the night Russitano got two encores. How is not clear, but the little man chirked up . . . like a henpecked husband who finds he can run his own house."

In a Brooklyn *Cavalleria* the following season, the tenor "padded his legs into presentable shape and screwed his courage to the sticking point."

Thomas Salignac, a spry little Frenchman, aroused the dislike of the *San Francisco Examiner* in 1901 for his "reedy voice" and "nauseating nanny of a tremolo." Other cities were kinder, if never effusive, and Salignac remained as long as Grau.

Giuseppe Cremonini promised more in 1895 than he realized in his three seasons with the Metropolitan. Cremonini seemed "an Apollo" to Chicago, while Washington called him "shapely, graceful, handsome, with the sweetest and most satisfactory tenor in many years."

Other tenors proved brief candles indeed. Antonio Ceppi, tall, manly and prepossessing, lacked the voice to match his pulchritude. Albert Lubert, though he sustained his European reputation in a Boston *Carmen* and a Chicago *Navarraise* by the intensity of his acting, stayed for only one season. Georges Mauguiere remained for three, acceptable only in amiable roles. Hale amended his favorite expression to "standing gentleman" in describing Mauguiere.

Among darker male voices the powerful and pervasive Edouard de Reszke practically monopolized the bass repertory in all languages, from kings to clowns. In his first seven seasons on tour, Edouard averaged eight roles and once sang twelve.

His nearest rival, the handsome Pol Plançon, who entered the lists one year after Edouard, immediately shared the roles of King Henry, Méphistophélès and Friar Laurence. Ramfis was also divided by the two giants; then Edouard went on into the buffo's arena, with Leporello and Don Basilio, and into the realm of the Teutonic gods, kings and plain men with Marke, the Wanderer, Hagen and Daland.

Plançon remained in the 'nineties with the dignified elders of French and Italian lineage. His only German role (sung in Italian when he first assumed it) was the Landgraf in *Tannhäuser;* his only god the Jupiter of Gounod's *Philemon et Baucis,* in which he was introduced both to New York and the road.

Plançon's noble art impressed the tour cities from the first; Philadelphia thought him "every inch the lyric artist"; Chicago admired his commanding presence, fine physique and the voice that "rang sonorous and true."

Hale went further to praise "the noble organ used in masterly manner. His singing is full of *nuancirung,* the lower tones without a suspicion of gargarism. No such singing has been heard from any bass in many a year."

By 1897, Chicago believed Edouard outranked in a favorite role. Plançon's Méphistophélès won new distinction for "grace, dash, subtlety . . . impressive make-up, sable costume and rich . . . tonal value."

Other basses subsisted on crumbs dropped from the kingly feast. Occasionally Novara would fall heir to a Plunkett, Arimondi to a Marcel, Pringle to a King Henry, Vinche to a Friar, Abramoff to a Ramfis, Devries to a Méphistophélès. Jean Martapoura, a Belgian nobleman, "bluff and hearty, a wee bit of a man," succeeded to a Nilakantha. Eugène Dufriche, who remained active with the company as a singer until 1908 and then became a stage director, once stepped into Count Almaviva's shoes, vacated by Edouard.

Agostino Carbone, a well-loved buffo, took over Leporello for Edouard on a single occasion but usually busied himself with Masetto and the Bartolos of Mozart and Rossini.

David Bispham's experience in the 'nineties hardly heralded his later tours. The Quaker lad who owed his operatic career to the advice of a Ouija board made his out-of-town Metropolitan debut in Chicago, in the dismal season following Abbey's death.

Lifting the veil of depression for a moment, the *Chicago Tribune* awarded a wreath to Bispham's excellent Kurvenal, noticed several welcome departures from tradition in his Telramund and found his Alberich impressive.

Hale was of the opinion that the bass-baritone overacted and oversang in the Boston *Martha* of April 9. It was the first time Bispham had tried the part; and his most distinguished predecessor in it had dropped dead on the Metropolitan stage two months before.

Armand Castelmary, an old-time favorite, "admirable, venerated, his force and fire preserved, not unkindly treated by the years," gave the road much nostalgic pleasure before his dramatic death in 1897. His only out-of-town appearance that year had been in Brooklyn on January 9, singing the Duke of Verona. Chicago, expecting him with the company in February, was shocked to hear that he had collapsed on the New York stage after Tristan's roughhouse in *Martha*.

Baritones held their own in the 'nineties although Lassalle and Maurel cut into their fattest repertory. Two veterans made brief reappearances. Giuseppe del Puente, the "one and only Escamillo" for many fans of earlier days, supported Patti in her 1892 *Traviatas* in Boston and Philadelphia. Giuseppe Kaschmann, who had shared baritone roles with Del Puente in the Metropolitan's opening season, was pressed into service again in 1895-96.

The merry Ancona, plump, round-faced, the upturned ends of his luxurious mustache quivering, gave the most value for Abbey's money between 1893 and 1897. To Chicago he seemed "well-dressed, radiant, full of extravagant gestures and honeyed phrases." The baritone made a hit with Tonio, commanded respect for his Valentin and repeated the Alfio he had created.

"So fond of society that his face is about as well known off stage as on," according to Detroit, the little man pursued his amiable way as Rigoletto, Escamillo, Telramund.

In his second year Ancona began to notice that with Lassalle gone Maurel wanted a Rigoletto here, a Valentin there. Younger men were pressing hard for other "Ancona roles." Maurizio Bensaude competed only one season, but Giuseppe Campanari settled firmly and outstayed Ancona by many years.

One of the most genuinely admired baritones of the early years, Campa-

nari began his out-of-town duties as the Count di Luna, thought by Philadelphia to be merely picturesque, although Chicago noted the "beautiful
quality of tone, his clarity and finish, his sympathetic quality and his taste."
Campanari had begun his career as a cellist in the Boston Symphony, and
carried his disciplined training over into the world of grease paint and
gestures.

His second major assignment was one that thirty years later brought
fame to Lawrence Tibbett—Ford in *Falstaff*. His "powerfully passionate"
aria compelled a volley of applause in Chicago. In the first year of Ancona's
absence Campanari sang ten roles on tour. Spanning four managerial re-
gimes, he found, in his last year with the Metropolitan, only Scotti, Pini-
Corsi, Gadski and Schumann-Heink who had seen service in the 'nineties—
and none of them within four years of his initiation.

The names of other singers of the 'nineties grow fainter with the years.
Perhaps only Louisville will remember a Signor Gianini (or Giannini), said
to be the brother of the tenor who sang with Mapleson, for Louisville considered in 1891 that he had a "throat of velvet" while other cities found him
commonplace. Albany and Troy have reason to recall Sebastian Montariol,
who sang Roméo to Eames' Juliette in the one city and Elvino to Pettigiani's
Adina in the other, through a brief 1892 series in the midst of the New York
season. Albany may also recall Jane de Vigne, who sang Rosina in its original
mezzo key with Gianini as her Almaviva and Magini-Coletti as Figaro; and
Fernando Valero, the Raoul to the city's own prima donna, Emma Albani.

The excitement engendered by grand opera in the 'nineties heightened as
the new century drew near. Grau carried on with shrewd business acumen,
spreading the glory ever wider—and much thinner. More than a dozen cities
from New England to Nashville, from Canada to Texas, awaited their first
taste of grand opera, Metropolitan style.

3. THE QUEEN OF HEARTS TAKES ALL TRICKS

"She received women callers in bed. Her black hair . . . curled about her
warm white neck and crisped over sheer ruffles of crepe on her *robe de
chambre*—a dusky background for her round, pale face. The single vivid
color was the scarlet thread of her lips, bright as though carmine were
freshly laid on. Her black eyes glittered with traces of recent tears. A great
fur robe of white Persian lamb lay across her bed. In one plump hand she
held a scarlet-bound Flammarion novel, *Urania,* inscribed by the author on
the flyleaf. She was a study in black and white and scarlet."

This *levée à la Bourbon,* as carefully studied as a stage set, gave Chicago
its first intimate glimpse of one of the most fascinating prima donnas of the

Metropolitan's cross-country races. The *Evening Post's* girl columnist scooped her male colleagues: they could report only from the auditorium or hotel parlor the captivating personality of Emma Calvé.

In her first year of travel with the company, Calvé's progress resembled a rising mercury. The warmth crept up through Philadelphia and Brooklyn and rose several degrees in Boston, where Philip Hale found the new singer's Carmen irresistible, even though she did not hesitate to twist a phrase and change a rhythm to gain an effect.

Abbey and Grau wisely chose *Carmen* to launch the new season in Boston and Chicago instead of *Cavalleria* in which Calvé had made her debut in New York and Philadelphia. Her first Chicago audience lacked numbers and vitality—until her witchery took hold. Then patrons and critics were caught up in a frenzy that renewed itself every time she sang. Five Carmens and three Santuzzas hardly assuaged the Chicago desire for Calvé and more Calvé—although the Spanish gypsy invariably commanded more attention than the Sicilian peasant.

Calvé seemed to *be* Carmen.

Perhaps Hale had not launched the famous saying that was to float after Calvé like a shadow, but he gave it the weight of his reputation:

"If she had not sung the role at all, she would have held the audience by her dramatic art," he affirmed.

As the frantic heroine in Massenet's *La Navarraise,* she also showed herself to be a great lyric tragedienne. Comparisons to Olga Nethersole, a fiery actress of the time, and even to Duse, were not considered out of place.

"Before she went to Italy," Hale noted further, "her acting was strictly conventional. Now she is known chiefly as an instrument blown by the lips of passion."

The *Chicago Inter-Ocean* set before its non-opera-going readers a description that should have propelled them toward the Auditorium box office:

"The winds over the Pyrenees must have given her something of a Spanish sense. In personal appearance she fills the eye: tall, dignified, svelte, sumptuous in figure . . . with a picturesque, graceful carriage, a trace of Orientalism in her lithe movements. Her chin is as well defined as a Hebe's, her features clean-cut and remarkably mobile, her mouth is small, with a Cupid's bow in its curve. Her wonderful eyes, dark as night, fill with fine fire, dilating with passionate intensity of emotion, furnishing a remarkable range of expression to a beautiful and characteristic face. . . ."

"This is a true Carmen!" cried the *Times* writer. "The fire of genius blazing in her soul electrified and enthralled. She goes straight to nature . . . the only creature, with hot-blooded, strong animal passion and no soul, that Bizet could have meant."

Carmen's possible impact upon the morals of the community provided fresh discussion among the literalists who viewed Violetta and Manon as fallen women rather than singing actresses and who cringed at the dubious Wagnerian relationships. Buffalo advanced a liberal point of view:

"A woman may be fond of admiration from the male sex and yet be entirely correct morally."

Philadelphia left judgment to a higher—or lower—power. "One almost expected to see Mephisto come up a trap door and politely escort Carmen below, to the accompaniment of red fire and a chorus of imps."

After several years, the *Philadelphia North American* believed her dance to be "more chaste than formerly, yet with a curious touch that is hardly agreeable . . . she danced with her hands, a lithe, creepy sort of thing that suggested snakes and subtlety."

The singer's kittenish ways amused her fans. She refused to learn English, deeming three sentences sufficient: "Come in" . . . "How do you do?" . . . "I love you." Later she took English lessons from Ellen Terry, but could not rid herself of her French accent.

In especially seductive humor one year, she cajoled Sir Henry Irving into giving up his suite in the Chicago Auditorium Annex. The great man not only vacated his rooms with courtesy but later paid a gallant call on her.

Even in plain dress, she fascinated a *Chicago Evening Post* reporter of a later date. "She talks 1,000 words a minute, gives no one else a chance. She talks with her hands, shoulders, fingers and the top of her head."

Further peeps into the diva's private life titillated the nation as much as her magnetism on stage. She told a Cincinnati reporter that Benjamin Constant was painting her portrait on the ceiling of the Paris Opéra Comique.

"Calvé Has a Lover," the *Chicago Mail* proclaimed. "At seven dollars per note, she talks and sings him love letters on recording cylinders. She literally whispers soft nothings . . . 5-6,000 miles away. He is an artist. She objects to writing letters. So, her kisses are preserved."

The end of this idyll was signalized in 1900 by a typical Sunday magazine story in the *San Francisco Examiner,* concluding:

"Duse took to morphine, Calvé took to flight."

During the six seasons in which she sang Carmen with the Metropolitan on tour, Calvé seldom received what critics believed adequate "support." This referred entirely to tenors, for Escamillos were plentiful and often stole scenes from the accepted cynosure, to her irritation. She was once seen to throw her fan petulantly on the table after Lassalle had responded twice to the audience's demand for another chorus of the Toreador Song.

She could handle the undersized tenors often allotted her—De Lucia, Salignac, Saléza—but critics could not understand "why a man of small stature was always chosen for Calvé to spend all evening trying to win." In St. Louis, where *Trilby* headed the current bestseller list, Salignac was compared to Little Billie. "How she loves that little shrimp!" one writer quoted. The dissatisfaction mounted highest one evening in Chicago, "when the greatest Don José of all [Jean de Reszke] sat in a box, while a pygmy [Lubert] occupied the stage."

Chicago won the good fortune of seeing the only two performances on the road of Jean and Emma as José and Carmen. The result was spectacular, although Jean's fans claimed that he prompted her to higher flights than ever before and Calvé's champions, among them the *Herald,* vowed that Jean "was fired by a new inspiration, and superb as he always is, never achieved a greater climax."

Any José had to keep his wits about him or he soon became outplayed, for Calvé thought up new business for each performance. Even Jean found her a "little trying," according to Leiser. She would run about, looking for pursuit, or scatter one prop after another, hoping for a knightly retriever. Jean refused the bait, in one case giving as a reason:

"Well, if she thought I was going to bend down and split my elegant brand-new tights she had better think again."

Her most mischievous trick was to pop a rose into his mouth just as he was about to sing. This flower did not receive the same tender treatment as Carmen's first-act offering.

Probably apocryphal is the tale circulated in California that Calvé got up and left the stage immediately after José stabbed her, whereupon the enraged Jean rushed after her, broke down her dressing room door and dragged her to the stage in a recumbent position. To have her ultimate revenge, she sang his last measures with him.

Because of the limitations of her repertory to such humbly born damsels as Carmen, Marguerite and Santuzza, Calvé rarely had the excuse to dress up on stage as a lady of fashion. This deprivation was more than the singer could bear. One season she dressed for the party at Lillas Pastia's as if it were Sherry's, in a contemporary Worth gown of conch-shell pink chiffon velvet with huge festoons of French knots, a train and a Japanese shawl.

Her extravagant taste for ravishing haberdashery turned perforce to her life off stage. In Boston she displayed her new wardrobe for a few friends, among them a *Globe* reporter. One dinner gown of white moiré had for trimming a two-inch band of ermine around the skirt, a chiffon pleated bodice and a bertha of *duchesse* lace, with acacia blossoms clustered on the shoulder.

The imagination boggles at the vision of Calvé on one of her free nights sweeping through the theatres in Boston or Buffalo, St. Louis or Detroit, trailing ermine under an opera cloak of white broadcloth lined with canary satin, bordered with sable, and a shoulder cape of yellow velvet embroidered in pearls. Nordica's cherry silk or Melba's collar of floor-length sable tails could not compete with her.

Calvé, the healthiest of mortals by her own account, suffered from one disease after another according to the enterprising journals that always found her good copy. Rheumatism in 1897, heart trouble in 1900, the dread cancer in 1901. Grau denied all the rumors and Calvé kept on singing—except when she fell a prey to some minor ailment.

San Francisco surprisingly judged her Carmen as "not roses but violets."

New Haven's *Journal Courier* insisted that "her walk and manner, despite perfect grace always, are those of a low bred woman. When she runs up steps she goes heavily on the flat part of her feet . . . in the last act her fear is that of a dumb animal at bay, never an intellectual fear."

Dismissing the remainder of the cast as "accessories," Hartford's *Times* compared Calvé to "a sunbeam," "the cresting of a wave," "a heart-throb!" . . . and noted that catlike bearing of infinite grace and seductiveness . . .

that sinuous movement of muscle and limb—in short, this figure which in-
carnates all the graces Eve bequeathed to her daughters . . . the quintessence
of the sex as such."

Over the years, the role took on the gradual accretion of Calvé's caprices.
In 1896 Philip Hale found her Boston impersonation "not so deliberately
boisterous or so aggressively athletic as it was two years ago. When she was
last here her singing in certain respects was disappointing . . . a willful
maltreatment of music . . . but now she enchants and thrills as much by
her voice as by her rare dramatic art. She is discreet in the liberties she takes."

In 1897 she showed "remarkable strength and subtlety, though not as
diabolically powerful as when she first startled, amazed and triumphed."

In 1900: "In many respects [Carmen] is diametrically opposed to the
former embodiment. . . . Now a subtle creation of refined cunning, the
physical appeal not dominating. . . . She indulges herself in mental ex-
periments . . . we rub our eyes—is it Calvé?"

In 1902: "How far from the first revelation as a lyric tragedienne of singular charm, power and originality; nevertheless it is still interesting in many
ways, though pitched in a much lower key . . . more colloquial and . . .
suggesting a soubrette. . . . Spontaneity is now capriciousness; the original
plastic art now stiff."

By 1904, Calvé's variations exasperated the critics.

"Calvé dominated everything," remarked the *Chicago Inter-Ocean*, "Conried has not curbed her characteristic independence, even if he cut her salary.
Her asides were numerous and rather plain, her rompings noticeable for
their vigor. . . . She laughed gleefully in the face of Mottl when she attempted
the high note at the end of the quintet and missed. . . . It was quite a frolic.
Reiss, one of those devilish opera comedians, and Dufriche, like a boy out
of school . . . were evidently bent upon 'breaking up' Calvé. She was
laughing before the number was finished and in the encore had a plain case
of . . . giggles.

"Then Navál sang the Flower Song considerably off key, Zuniga tripped
over the doorsill and Calvé giggled some more . . . in the last act [the tenor]
succeeded in so disarranging her black jet gown at the shoulder that for a
moment those within range breathed irregularly. . . . We are sorry not to
be able to record Madame's exact words."

From the "firm, true and artistic touch" that the *Chicago Herald* attributed to the diva in 1894 to the *Chronicle's* review of 1904 marks the passing of more than time:

"The star has risen above the work. She is the picture, the opera, the
frame. . . . She magnifies her own part to the eclipse of the other principals,
chorus and even ballet. She has coarsened, to use no stronger term, an impersonation once superbly artistic."

Grau's long tour of 1901-02 appeared to be a one-woman affair, although
several other equally distinguished ladies were aboard. A year later Calvé's
irresistible force met the immovable body of Heinrich Conried's will to
absolute power. After one stormy season she freed herself from the Metropolitan to pursue her own devices. In that final clash of 1904, the *Chicago*

Tribune found her "clearly tired of the part. . . . She is abusing her voice; has robbed most tones of richness . . . and now resorts to tricks. . . . Mme. Calvé's Carmen is a thing of the past."

4. CHICAGO TAKES A CHANCE

"Chicago, Chicago, That Toddling Town."
(Song by Fred Fischer, 1922)

In 1892 Chicago came into its majority in a new incarnation, full-grown at twenty-one. The "toddle" in the song title of 1922 named a waddling dance step and not the uncertain groping of a youngster's feet. Chicago had passed the toddling stage even before the fire, which in 1871 had drastically changed the city's composition. The sprawling entity of stone and steel that soon relentlessly began to force its boundaries mile after mile along the shore and eventually encroached even into Lake Michigan itself bore little resemblance to its rickety wooden ancestor.

It is conceivable to personify other cities, like ships, by the feminine pronoun—but never Chicago. Chicago is sinew and lust, tough fiber and daring intellect. Even Chicago's beauty is all brawn.

At the end of two decades the city still ached with growing pains. Its restless citizens sampled every newfangled invention. A horseless buggy terrified strollers on Michigan Avenue. With direct telephone service to New York a Chicagoan did business the way he liked—fast. Steam-powered elevated trains roared overhead on a web of trestles in "The Loop," dooming Chicago's downtown streets to darkness and confusion.

Several tentacles of the city's expanding organism reached out for ornaments to cover and adorn the aggressively muscular body. These aesthetic attributes attained their apotheosis in the new Auditorium, which opened in 1889.

For 187 feet on Michigan Avenue, 161 on Wabash Street and 362 on Congress Street, the huge ten-story Romanesque pile, designed by Louis Sullivan and Dankmar Adler, bore witness to Chicago's ambition; its 240-foot, seven-story tower, topped by a smaller rectangle two stories high, signaled to the sky that Chicago's boundless daring had triumphed.

The marbled, stained-glass magnificence of the entrance, the vast lobby with its mosaic floor, the bronze-balustered stairway—all brought gasps of admiration from the beholders. The rectangular ivory and gold audience chamber, with its paintings by Charles Holloway, would seat 5,000, divided among the main floor and boxes (1,800), the main balcony (1,700) and the two upper galleries (750 each). Using the stage, at least 1,000 more could be packed in.

Best of all, in Chicago's fiercely democratic mind, the new theatre had been built for "people," and not only box-holders. Patrons on all floors could enjoy foyers and promenades (narrowing with each higher level, to be sure), "finely furnished, each possessing all conveniences of cloak and retiring rooms."

The stage itself kindled wonder and pride. Mechanical miracles behind the curtain were made possible by a new scientific principle.

"It's all done by hydraulics," Chicago boasted.

Did an opera call for a mountain? a valley? a balcony? terraces rising to a castle? a bridge? a sea undulating gently or stormily? a ship before a gale utterly submerged and its crew with it? The Auditorium stage could produce them all.

Invited to a preview, aldermen and commissioners clustered on the stage platforms, apprehensive but game, and were raised and lowered in vertiginous succession. No cases of seasickness were reported, however, until later in the season, when a soprano succumbed to the rocking of a small boat in *L'Africaine.*

Now Ferd W. Peck's skyscraper was a reality, one of the first of a genre Chicago had recently developed. It had cost $2,700,000, with carrying charges of about $200,000.

Until after the turn of the century a migrant lyric troupe took its chances together with other road companies, vaudeville acts and minstrel shows. The astronomical guarantees that the Metropolitan requires today before moving a wig or a stick of greasepaint from the House had their nearest nineteenth century counterpart in well organized auctions conducted in advance of the company's arrival.

Chicago's most famous auction preceded the opening of the Auditorium. The Windy City's wealthiest men and their wives filled the lower floor of Central Music Hall, reported the *Times.* Only evening dress was lacking to make it a social event of prime order. On the stage sat Ferd Peck and Marcus Mayer, Abbey's representative, with the experienced auctioneers, Franklin H. Head and S. J. Reynolds.

"What am I offered for the first box?" the chant arose; and the bidding was on. Otto Young mentioned $200 and was immediately silenced by George M. Pullman's raise to $500.

"Why, that wouldn't pay for gilding the box," Head chided the sleeping-car magnate.

Columbus R. Cummings entered the fray; railroads and railroad cars went at it hammer and tongs until Pullman quashed his opponent at $1,600.

All thirty-two boxes were snapped up. Adding $6,500 for premiums on seats, the auction yielded $19,990, a figure approximating the cost of one Metropolitan performance today.

The affair was dignified by the presence of many of "the old people"—Beechers, Otises, Drakes, Pullmans, Blackstones, Adams'—all names that strike echoes from Chicago's present economy.

Hobart Chatfield Chatfield-Taylor, "a rich young man who writes newspaper articles and draws horses equally well," according to the *Evening*

News, selected Box 36. Everyone was there—"but where was Potter Palmer?"

The *News* reporter must have missed Palmer in the crowd, because on Dedication Night the occupant of Box 37 shone radiantly in "Eiffel-red crepe, with a round-cut corsage of velvet, a diamond necklace and hair-cluster, a point-lace fan and a *sortie-du-bal* [opera cloak] of palest mauve with ostrich boa—Mrs. Potter Palmer."

By the middle of the decade, Chicago joined the Metropolitan adventure as an active partner rather than merely a compliant host. For a share of the receipts (basically twenty-five percent) the Auditorium supplied scenery, costumes (except those of the stars) and an orchestra—no pick-up mélange of stray musicians but the finely trained ensemble formed in 1891 by Theodore Thomas. That peripatetic conductor had at last settled down to one principal job with the classic remark:

"I would go to hell if they offered me a permanent orchestra."

The Chicago Orchestra played for the Metropolitan visitors until 1900 (except in 1895 when a tour of its own took it out of town), even accompanying the troupe to St. Louis, Louisville and Cincinnati. Its supremacy was questioned only once. At the first rehearsal in 1897, Luigi Mancinelli furiously denounced the men for sloppy discipline and threatened to send for the Metropolitan orchestra. He did not make good his threat and peace was soon restored.

Abbey and Grau did not win every season. Oddly enough their receipts were highest in the two years when Chicagoans were feeling the aftermath of the panic of 1893 and the crippling Pullman strike of 1894. The spring series of 1894 topped the decade's record for the Italian Grand Opera, and in 1895, with all favorite singers safely on the roster except Emma Calvé, speculators still believed it worth while to wait in line to buy tickets for resale at 100 percent profit.

"There must be money in spite of hard times," a reporter concluded.

Chicago society fancied that it had invented a new formula. Ward McAllister coined his famous appellation for New York's exclusive circle in 1892; Chicago was soon remarking that "New York's 400 would have to give way to Chicago's 40,000."

Even in 1894 the season sale amounted only to $13,200 and the average box office for twenty-seven performances came to about $6,800. This represented the maximum Abbey could expect with his ticket price of $3 for the best seat. A fifty-cent increase in 1895—over local protests—brought no additional revenue, for attendance dropped while costs rose.

The most expensive shows, *Aida, Huguenots* and *Faust,* each required $8,500 to mount; the cheapest, *Lucia,* came to $4,500. A glance at the salaries Abbey paid his songbirds reveals the consequential item in his budget.

When Jean de Reszke first came to America he received $10,000 per month for eight performances, plus twenty-five percent of receipts over $5,000. This average of $1,250 per performance was later raised to $1,500 and in 1901 was said to be $2,500. His brother Edouard received $500 or $600 plus ten percent over $5,000. Nellie Melba, beginning at $1,000, rose to a par with Jean, but without the percentage. Emma Eames was paid less at the beginning, but soon commanded a $1,000 fee. Emma Calvé also came reasonably at first, but her popularity ensured a higher cachet almost immediately. By 1896 each performance earned $1,500 for her.

In all Chicago Auditorium programs from 1889 until 1895 (when the reform presumably had been accomplished), appeared an adjuration to enjoy the facilities for a social occasion:

"The audience, especially the ladies, are requested to leave their seats during the intermission."

This innovation, which signalized a crack in the veneer of gentility favored by the Victorian age, was the inspiration of Milward Adams, the tall, energetic manager of the Auditorium. Physically a stalwart specimen, he nevertheless showed the strain of successive opera seasons.

"Adams allowed his whiskers to grow, and they came out gray," the *Evening Post* sympathized.

Each season seemed more notable, more exciting than the one before, like Sheherazade's tales, introducing "some glory that leaves its predecessors in the shadow."

Exponent of "the biggest and the best," Chicago fittingly produced everything to size: the largest and most modern opera house, the highest receipts, the fullest newspaper coverage (with eleven dailies and innumerable specialized journals)—and the juiciest scandals.

Amy Leslie, the one exception to anonymity among music critics in the 'nineties, believed in a press as free as a rotating lawn spray. After the turn of the century Miss Leslie is said to have furnished an item for the other gossip columns by eloping with a bellboy. Until the hunter became the hunted, she filled a column in the *Evening News* with her highly personal views. She displayed a surprising streak of primness in a stubborn crusade against décolletage and took no part in a scandal that swept three prima donnas into a vortex of dismay and indignation in 1894.

Eames and Calvé under the same roof always posed a problem for the temperament-regulators; danger lay inherent in the juxtaposition of the New Englander's flinty reserve and the Frenchwoman's "smoldering volcano." Grau juggled their mutual roles so that one would sing Santuzza and Marguerite in the season the other was absent, but brought them together in *Carmen* in 1893-94—each true to character: Eames the chaste, shy Micaela; Calvé the tempestuous, lawless, full-blooded Carmen.

Perhaps the tension had been building through Calvé's first New York season when Eames sang six times as Micaela. On tour Arnoldson and Pettigiani shared Micaelas, three and three alike, and each companioned Calvé once in Chicago. The third *Carmen* on March 26 and the fourth on March 31 threw ice and fire together once more.

The lid blew off on April 1, with a headline screaming from the *Sunday Times*:

"LYRIC QUEENS WON'T DO! The fight between Eames and Calvé has barred at least Calvé from society's drawing rooms [the story ran]. Eames calls Calvé a 'creature—how could society take her up?' Calvé says she'll slap Eames at their next meeting."

If the date aroused any suspicion that this was meant for an April Fool hoax, the next few paragraphs dispelled it.

"Why look with benign not to say enthusiastic approbation on this turbulent, vociferous, gum-chewing, highly painted Calvé? This tiger lily, too exotic to thrive in gardens of conventionality? Crested notes by discreet footmen, great baskets of gorgeous roses and fragrant violets, suppers, breakfasts, lunches, dinners, always with either French or Italian food. . . . Society whispers that Calvé eats with her knife. . . . She snubs other prima donnas except Melba, who is the friend of her bosom . . . she talks and laughs through others' solos. . . .

"With Melba, Calvé leads the fast set. Two factions exist in the company— the De Reszkes, Arnoldson and her husband and Eames make up the 'decent' set."

The exuberant Australian, who had confessed that Chicago air made her "boisterous," now realized how she might be misinterpreted. She was accused in indelicate terms of choosing between two suitors with the result that her singing in *Rigoletto* fell below par (the performance had approached the nearest to failure of the season, it was true, and Melba's evident indisposition at the beginning gave the scandal-monger a peg on which to hang his scurrilities). "But she forgave her rude lover, for he was in her box Thursday." The attack concluded with the dark prophecy that "some divorces are brewing."

The three outraged prima donnas sprang to the defense of their honor in dignified letters of protest, which the *Times* printed in facsimile.

Calvé called the account "calumnious and injurious"; Nordica complained that the paper "used my name more freely than courtesy permits or truth justifies; an insinuation so strong as to be an attack upon my moral qualities which have never been questioned."

Melba wrote: "You have coupled my name with a man I do not even know. . . . I have been credited with an offense to my womanhood and art, both of which I prize as any honest woman should. I ask full retraction."

The offending *Times* expressed "sincerest regrets that the article referred to should have occasioned distress to the authors of these letters," and disavowed the "slightest intention to inflict pain or do injustice. If unwarrantable inferences have been drawn from the publication there is further occasion for regret which the *Times* greatly deplores."

The tone of this "apology" and the use of the words "unwarrantable inferences" must have infuriated Melba, but she wisely dropped the matter and it was soon forgotten except by the *Dispatch,* which reprinted the entire *Times* article.

The friction between Calvé and Eames continued. Grau threw them together once more as Carmen and Micaela in the New York Spring season. The aftermath was reported in Chicago under the heading, "Calvé Resigns."

"She snatched her hand from Eames in the curtain call . . . 'moulting' combs, scarves, etcetera. . . . De Lucia [the Don José] picked up her scarf and came back with it, but received such a fierce glance that he dropped it and ran as if pursued by the bull."

Melba, asked by the *Evening Post* columnist, The Matinee Girl, if the trouble were over between her colleagues, "looked with straight, serene gaze, and said in even tones: 'I have no idea. I do not know Madame Eames.'"

Calvé did not come to Chicago again until 1896 when Eames was absent, although the two prima donnas "made up" in New York when Eames sang a token Micaela in the winter of 1896 and Calvé insisted on giving her all the flowers.

Calvé and Eames did not sing in the same Metropolitan company in Chicago until 1899. By then Eames was safe from any meeting with the more limited Calvé, being largely preoccupied with Wagner and Mozart operas.

Every season was spiced with at least one episode to set tongues wagging and pens scribbling. Luigi Mancinelli, who enjoyed visiting "dime museums" in his free hours, was arrested by two detectives who insisted that he was a clever thief with a trick coat. The case of mistaken identity was straightened out barely in time for the wrathy Italian conductor to assume his dress clothes and hurry to the pit to conduct *Faust*.

During a performance of *Roméo et Juliette* in 1896 the lovers were interrupted in the balcony scene by a "lunatic," who climbed over the footlights onto the stage. Before he could be ejected, women had fainted, Melba was conveyed in a near-hysterical state to her dressing room and the opera house was in an uproar. Only Jean de Reszke kept his presence of mind, drawing his sword and shouting for the curtain to be lowered.

The *Herald* turned the episode off neatly with the remark that "love has turned many a man's head, but Romeo was never before played with a crazy man in the balcony scene."

Abbey's tragic death in the autumn of 1896 closed an era, although Grau pursued an "all-star" policy of his own into the early century. The dissolution of the firm of Abbey, Schoeffel and Grau, following the season of 1895-96, was brought on by the ill luck of such theatrical figures as Lillian Russell, Réjane, the French comedian Mounet-Sully ("a frost seldom equaled") and even Bernhardt, as much as any operatic loss. Grau, who had grown increasingly responsible for Abbey's affairs, agreed to take over the business by himself and refinanced his projects.

Grau's first independent year was shadowed from the start by the loss of his partner and by prima donna vexations, chiefly Nordica's desertion in a huff at the loss of the *Siegfried* Brünnhilde to Melba, an unlikely and unsuccessful protagonist. The feckless Australian's "appetite exceeded capacity," as she was the first to admit, after her one and only experience of the dramatic role. The strain proved too much for her, and she begged to be relieved of her contract in January, after only one out-of-town appearance in Brooklyn in the more congenial role of Juliette. Since Eames, too, refused to tour, Calvé, the De Reszkes, Plançon and Lassalle upheld the star-spangled reputation of the troupe on the road.

To secure a partner for Jean de Reszke's Siegfried, Grau looked no farther than Edouard's sister-in-law, Félia Litvinne, an enormously fat lady whose voice impressed Chicago by its size and power but who "found it impossible to appear maidenly." This choice further provoked Nordica's ire and precipitated a quarrel with Jean that ruptured a long friendship.

Nordica first claimed that Jean had inspired Melba to the ill-advised step of joining the Valkyrie maidens. Now she accused him of conspiring with Grau to replace her with his relative. Jean denied this with dignity if with some heat. The rift between the two singers was not closed until 1897. Meanwhile Chicago missed Nordica as well as Melba and Eames.

With twenty-five performances, only three fewer than the total of other out-of-town appearances in Brooklyn, Hartford, St. Louis, Louisville, Cincinnati and Boston, Chicago's 1896 vote proved decisive. It was a general "Nay."

Calvé's Carmen still commanded slavish worship—it was thrown into the breach five times—and Marguerite, a new role for her, astonished and delighted Chicagoans by its "gentle girlishness."

Still, the prevailing situation seemed desperate enough to warrant a drastic departure from precedent—lowering prices to a "popular" level. Six operas were subjected to this ignominy during the last week, even *Les Huguenots* going at the bargain rates of $2 in the orchestra, seventy-five cents in the balcony. But all to no avail.

Chicago newspapers might loyally fan the blaze of favor for a local girl, Marie Engle, and might show how deeply they were impressed by a new singer, David Bispham—might even continue to sing the praises of the "famous five." Chicago readers remained indifferent.

From New York came the ultimatum: No opera next year unless a guarantee is forthcoming!

In his distress, Grau found help from his business associates and, more surprisingly, from his singers. To make up deficits, Jean de Reszke gave $4,000, his brother $2,000, Calvé $3,000, Lassalle $2,000. Other contributions came from Grau's firm (he himself wrote a personal check for $2,500), and from Milward Adams for the Auditorium. The company limped on to other commitments, which did not materially improve its condition.

When Nordica turned her back on Grau, rumors spread widely and were eventually confirmed that she, as well as Melba, would join Damrosch's wandering singers. Seeking a foothold since 1891 and denied a place at the Metropolitan, Walter had given sporadic performances here and there, notably three Wagnerian operas as a benefit in Philadelphia in 1894 with Materna, Schott and Fischer, remembered from the previous decade.

In 1895 he had formed his own company and for two seasons had barnstormed through cities large and small. When Grau decided that his troubles did not permit a season in 1897-98, he leased the Metropolitan to Damrosch, who had acquired Charles Ellis as a partner, chiefly to secure Melba.

Chicago as usual provided the touring anchor. Damrosch effected such inroads into Chicago's affections that one newspaper hopefully suggested in 1897 that he take over the entire operatic business. Probably nothing would have pleased Walter better, but the next year Grau bounced back as cheerful and competent as ever, and "all his sins were forgiven him" by Chicago.

Among these sins, the lack of freshness in the repertory disturbed Chicago

very little. Although not premieres, *Orfeo, Otello* and *Cavalleria* had sufficed as novelties in 1891; the American premiere of Massenet's *Werther*
had dignified 1894; *Falstaff* gave Chicago's musicologists their chance to
pontificate in 1895; *La Navarraise* scored a hit with Calvé in 1896; another
Massenet work, *Le Cid,* like *Werther* a starring vehicle for Jean de Reszke,
"excited the most pronounced and spirited ovation" of the bleak 1897. Then
Grau waited until 1902 to produce other novelties from his trunk—*Magic
Flute* and *Manru.* Chicago hardly grumbled; this was, after all, the age of
song and only singers counted.

The heart of the country's railroad system, Chicago had been a way-stop
for every migrant troupe. The city's first opera house, Rice's Theatre, "could
not stand the innovation" and burst into flame during the second performance of *Sonnambula* on July 30, 1850. After the theatre was rebuilt, the
city, like an eligible bachelor, entertained all the visiting ladies but saw no
reason to give its heart to any one.

But in 1907 Henry Russell brought his San Carlo company with Nordica,
Alice Nielsen and Florencio Constantino, and planted a portentous seed.
Unrest at Heinrich Conried's methods had already sprung up.

The decisive step awaited more auspicious circumstances, however, and
was taken under Metropolitan auspices. Three years later, when the New
York company under Giulio Gatti-Casazza had successfully completed the
expensive and harrowing business of suppressing Oscar Hammerstein, and
desired to plant its own roots in strategic grounds, Chicago was offered
Hammerstein's singers and scenery. At last Chicago raised the curtain on its
own opera company, November 3, 1910.

Cleofonte Campanini received the appointment as musical director, and
Andreas Dippel, the first tenor to accede—though not the first to aspire—to
management level, accepted the post of general director for Chicago, thereby
relieving an embarrassing situation in New York. His dissonant duet with
Gatti-Casazza as co-director had grated on too many ears.

Through additional arrangements with Boston and Philadelphia, New
York interchanged repertory and casts in a four-city scheme that promulgated
grand opera on a scale never before—and never since—attempted in
America.

Chicago played its role vigorously at home and on the road as well. Known
as the Chicago-Philadelphia company on the local scene and in New York,
Boston and other cities, the organization reversed its title for annual visits to
the Quaker City.

Subsequent shifts in the balance of operatic ballast brought Chicago's complete autonomy a few years later under different titles.

The local Maecenas, Harold McCormick, with his socially prominent wife,
the former Edith Rockefeller, poured their resources into opera for two
decades.

This period represented "partly the history of Mary Garden's fabulous
career, as she presented one by one her vivid characterizations of a long line
of heroines, mostly scarlet ones," wrote Cecil Smith in *Musical America.*
"McCormick withdrew his support after the season of 1921-22 in which Miss

Garden, in her sole year as director, doubly scandalized her patrons by her performance in *Salome* and by the ease with which she let a deficit of $1,110,-000 accumulate in twelve weeks."

Samuel Insull took over in the sweeping reorganization that followed, and Chicago's prestige continued with the Chicago Civic Opera until the collapse of the financier's utilities empire in 1932. After the debacle Chicago's opera became a "hand-to-mouth" affair, according to Smith, until 1942, when the Metropolitan returned as an old friend after thirty-two years' absence.

The Auditorium is no longer the scene of Chicago's opera gaiety. In 1928 Insull's $30,000,000 Opera House on Wacker Drive usurped the glory. It is still Chicago's home for the Metropolitan, as well as for the new Lyric Opera that has given the city its own company once again.

The Auditorium never recovered. The grand theatre suffered humiliating vicissitudes: it was invaded by vaudeville; converted to a baseball diamond for the annual newsboys' and bootblacks' benefit game and to a cathedral for Reinhardt's *Miracle;* disguised as a bowling alley and a service center during World War II; and once even reduced to servitude as a warehouse.

In 1946 Roosevelt College (now Roosevelt University) bought Sullivan's monument and converted hotel and offices to academic uses, including the Chicago College of Music. But darkness fell on the famous Auditorium.

Part V

GRAU'S BARNSTORMERS

1. OUTPOST ON THE MISSOURI RIVER

The opera train chugged through New England's ruddy autumn hills, bisected New York beside the placid Erie Canal, angled to cross the friendly frontier to the north then returned to pause in the tangled knots of our industrial centers.

In 1899 the tour set its western mark at Kansas City. But in the ensuing two years, it did not stop until Maurice Grau had at last stretched the Metropolitan's perimeter almost to the boundary of the United States. In three touring years, the troupe visited thirty-seven cities, twenty-three for the first time. From Portland, Maine, to San Francisco, from Minneapolis to New Orleans, the special trains wove their complicated patterns.

Along the way, local folk gathered to watch and marvel. There could be no mistaking this for an ordinary band of travelers. An inscription in letters a foot high exulted to the world that this splendid caravan belonged to "The Metropolitan Opera House." To protests that the company resembled a traveling circus, Grau answered that he believed in advertising his product as loudly as possible; the blatant stencil remained.

A holiday spirit, partly thwarted when the wayfarers were confined to a few larger cities, lightened these longer trips. Singers who had spent most of their waking hours between theatre and hotel now felt new freedom and found new friends.

In a small town en route, they all disembarked to stretch their legs, to admire the faraway mountains and to pose for Librarian Mapleson's camera. Suzanne Adams, the new American Juliette, climbed tomboyishly into the engineer's cab; Walter Damrosch (who, not able to "lick 'em," had "j'ined 'em" in 1900) aspired to a different kind of conductor's job and donned a placard identifying himself with Car B. Thomas Salignac, the tiny tenor, and Antonio Pini-Corsi, the corpulent buffo, paired off inevitably for a snapshot.

Edouard de Reszke, still the popular favorite of colleagues and public alike, conquered a superstition that stirred uneasily in his Slavic soul even after years of facing professional lenses and allowed Mapleson to picture him with the bewitching new Viennese soprano, Fritzi Scheff. Ernestine Schumann-Heink boomed her good-natured laugh, then twinkled almost coyly at

79

Plançon, a notable gallant though an implacable bachelor. The huge, hand-somely-bearded bass joyously executed an arabesque *à la* Mercury.

Creature comforts may or may not have been plentiful, depending on whose account one believes. Andrés de Segurola, the dashing Spanish bass-baritone, who made a transcontinental tour before singing a note at the Metropolitan, pictures the company thus in his unpublished memoirs, *Through My Monocle:*

"A milky way of stars, rolling along in nine or ten Pullmans . . . with good food, good drinks, good laughs . . . and a table of poker at which I sat from six to eight hours daily with Dippel, Reiss, Journet, Campanari and Franko."

The monocled *bon vivant* preferred to remain incognito during his early journey with the Metropolitan, for he used a pseudonym, Perello, in his first few appearances, adding his surname later and changing the Perello for Andrés only in New York. He reacted unfavorably to Grau's businesslike, rather brusque manner and did not return to the Metropolitan until 1909.

Comparison with the private car in which she later circled the concert route may have prompted Calvé's confession:

"We were not luxurious in Grau's day . . . small quarters, not always the best arrangements. On some of the long runs we had to carry our own food supplies, for buffets at stations were so poor that we could not eat there. We had merry times at our improvised suppers."

Could the troupe possibly have traveled without a diner? It seems hardly likely, and yet an account in Louisville mentions a stop in Cincinnati for "supper and rest." Smaller cities lacked many of the refinements the opera stars demanded. After learning that the "hummingbirds" she noticed in a southern hotel dining room were in reality flying cockroaches, Emma Eames took to dining in her bedroom.

This expedient was favored by most of the Italian troupers, who, un-daunted by regulations, continued to smuggle skillets into their hotels and cook savory messes in their rooms. Giuseppe Campanari was said to go so far as to make his own spaghetti, taking along a special machine.

Lodovico Viviani, an Italian bass who was entitled to the prefix of "Count," solved the problem with his usual thoroughness and elegance. But his very fastidiousness betrayed him, as Aimé Gerber, long-time paymaster, relates in *Backstage at the Opera.*

Max Hirsch, the box-office treasurer, never lost an opportunity to deflate Viviani's pretensions. As the bass was signing his noble name in a Chicago register, Hirsch playfully tipped over the shiny silk hatbox Viviani never let out of sight. Even Hirsch was surprised as a clattering assortment of pots and pans rolled out on the stone floor. The clerk, who had been slightly cowed by Viviani's impressiveness, now took pleasure in informing him, "No cooking in the rooms, *Count!*"

Melba fell victim to the unkindest practical joke of all. In the midst of her Chicago tribulations in 1894, some wag sent out fifty invitations to a supper party in her name—an extreme seldom resorted to by pranksters. Mischief usually took a less expensive, more professional turn. During the tour of

Louise and Sidney Homer
set sail for Paris, 1910

Scotti, Caruso and Alda
share a joke in Atlanta

anta Journal; Courtesy Musical America

Courtesy Mrs. James B. Riley

"La Geraldir
—Farrar in
radiant mo

Col. W. L. Peel of Atlanta

ourtesy Dr. William H. Kiser, Jr.

bove: Atlanta hospitality. From the left, Rosa Ponselle, Henry M. Atkinson, estival president in Mephisphelean dress, Julia Claussen and John Grant

eft: Lucrezia Bori—"I became a golf fan." Champion Bobby Jones at her left

Giuseppe De Luca entertains Marion Talley and Giovanni Martinelli

Recognizable: Lawrence Tibbett, Louise Hunter, Otto Kahn, Mary Lewis, Ellen Dalossy, Giuseppe Bamboschek and William Gustafson

News Events; Courtesy Musical America

race Moore, in a 1928 hat, with Jackson P.
ick at one of the famous Atlanta barbecues

Above: Reunion—Arturo Toscanini
and Giulio Gatti-Casazza in 1932

Left: An Atlanta party. Rothier,
De Segurola, Caruso (behind Mrs.
Peel), Martin, Scotti and Amato

Stage Manager Désiré Defrère (left) ?
Assistant Manager Max Rudolf explore
Midway in Memphis

"Welcome to Dallas!" The Arthur
L. Kramers greet Edward Johnson

Pote

In Denver the Arthur Oberfelders meet Patrice Munsel, Jan Peerce
(front), Mrs. Peerce, Herbert Graf, Frank St. Leger, Ramon Vinay

Cleveland's Public Square takes note of a famous visitor in a spring snow

Troupers Alessio De Paolis, Frank Guarera, Lorenzo Alvary, form a typical trio

Above: Lauritz and Kleinchen Melchior (right) make sure of their destination

"All aboard!" Risë Stevens urges her colleagues,
Zinka Milanov, Leonard Warren and Ezio Pinza

Thelma Votipka, "fabulous Tip
moves in aura of accomplishme

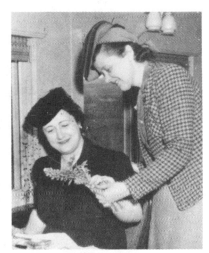

Hayes; Dallas Times-Herald

Above: Breakfast posy for Bruna Castagna from Mary Ellis Peltz

Left: "We're off!" cry Brownlee, Novotna, Ziegler, Jobin, Lewis

N. Y. Times Studio

eft: Chief clown "Nicky" Moscona
rplexes at least one conductor

ight: Heavy duty for a "heavy":
accaloni wheels Inge Manski and
ucker; Paula Lenchner kibitzes

Melançon

"Needs a stitch?" Dresser Angelo inspects an elaborate *Boris* robe

Jennie Cervini settles a chaplet on Lily Pons for a Chicago Gilda

Melançon

Harry G. Schumer,
librarian at work

"Props O. K.?" Ralph Edson,
gaudily capped, says "Yes"

A crucial moment: Henry A.
Fischer has pay checks ready

rchie Cohen, Thomas Hillary, John
lood, magicians of transportation

eft: "Gangway!" A tour begins

"Easy does it!" Louis Edson (right) directs
manoeuvres on the difficult Baltimore stage

Rothschild; Courtesy Musical America

Left: Amelita Galli Curci greets Edward Johnson, Jussi Bjoerling

Below: Not since 1905! The Met arrives in Los Angeles in 1948

Left: New Orleans hardly recognized Cleva, Pelletier, Papi, Leinsdorf

Right: Earle Lewis' hand is quicker than, for one, Eleanor Steber's eye

Schumer

N. Y. Times Studio

Left: War effort. Mona Paulee & Company

Below: Rudolf Bing (seated) waits while Florence Guarino, Francis Robinson worry

Schumer

Everyone asleep but Jerome Hines

Right: In Atlanta Cesare Siepi leads Mrs. Harold N. Cooledge

Below: Oklahoma City idyll for Giuseppe Campora and his bride

Ettore Bastianini waits while Frank
Paola gives Herva Nelli her tickets

Roberta Peters and bridegroom, Bert Fields

Redcap for Blanche Thebom!

"Bon voyage!" Rudolf
Bing cheerily speeds
his troupe departing
without him in 1956

The Northrop Auditorium   The Fair Park Auditor

Left: Brooklyn Academy
of Music, built in 1908

Montreal's Forum becomes an opera house   An opera night at Indiana Univer

The largest Metropolitan audience: 11,352 for *Carmen* in Toronto Maple Leaf Gardens

1901 Montreal's Arena, a skating rink with a decrepit roof, dripped copiously on a *Tannhäuser* cast.

In *Memories and Reflections* Eames, the Elisabeth, describes how "Dippel, egged on by Walter Damrosch, began the series of Weber and Fields jokes that followed us to the Pacific Coast by appearing in the wings holding a huge cotton umbrella, which in conjunction with his Tannhäuser costume put us in a hilarious mood from which we found it difficult to recover."

Grau indulged this friskiness, as natural to opera stars as children's spit-balls and paper airplanes, but he seldom joined in the fun. Even the poker game, his only relaxation, rarely welcomed the manager on tour. Too many hazards occupied his mind.

Yet, according to David Bispham, Grau regarded his profession "in the light of a complicated and highly interesting game." The baritone had watched Grau in intricate discussions of changing casts, while at the same time "hearing a complicated report from the managers of the company, discussing terms of a written agreement with an artist without referring to the document except to prove the artist wrong; speaking three foreign languages in rotation with men of as many nationalities, calling up his Wall Street broker to give orders and evidently calculating the possibility of gains and losses mentally as he spoke."

Grau considered himself to be a cold, shrewd man of business, although most of his colleagues also granted him amiability. His artists even liked him in their grudging way, said Walter Damrosch. They loved to repeat the characterization attributed to Jean de Reszke:

"Grau would give a man a fine cigar but would not offer him a match to light it unless such generosity had been nominated in the bond."

Few credited this manager with any depth of feeling or subtlety of appreciation for music, although he told a Louisville reporter that his taste for grand opera had "grown remarkably."

In a San Francisco interview he insisted that he was not a musician, "had never discovered as much as a single voice and had yet to give his first original production of a new work."

The record of Grau's five seasons as complete master of the Metropolitan's destinies bears him out in the letter if not entirely in the spirit. He introduced several novelties, and although none of them possessed staying power, he did his honest best for Paderewski's *Manru* and Mancinelli's *Ero e Leandro* on the road.

He did not "discover" Puccini's *La Bohème* and *Tosca,* but hustled them into the Metropolitan repertory with commendable alacrity. These were the years when, as he declared in *Musical America,* "a fine ensemble will not attract people; some star must shine out above all the rest, and people will not go to new operas."

He could command any singers he wanted, discoveries or old favorites, for Jean de Reszke's intercession had obtained for him the directorship of Covent Garden after the death of Sir Augustus Harris, and he managed the pair of great opera houses simultaneously for two years. At his behest Ternina, Homer, Schumann-Heink, Adams, Saléza, Van Dyck, Alvarez, Scotti and

Van Rooy came to the Metropolitan; the singing fabric remained strong and golden throughout his stewardship.

"His casts were his form of personal expression," said Gerber.

As he manipulated the hundreds of pieces in his operatic jigsaw puzzle at the turn of the century, he looked almost the same Maurice Grau who had shared bad news with Abbey in Cincinnati on the morning of February 10, 1884. A shade stouter, his skin swarthy, his keen eyes sparsely lashed and lightly hooded, he reminded some observers of a heavily charged electric battery as he paced about nervously, hands in pockets.

Others found him placid and imperturbable, tactful as a woman, just the man to tame the wild prima donna. Chicago reported an exchange between Grau and William Parry, the small, neat stage manager who had been snatched back by Mapleson in Abbey's first raid, but later rejoined the Metropolitan's technical force.

"How is Madame X. today?" Grau asked.

"Oh, Madame is alive," answered Parry.

"Then I'll bet she's kicking."

Touring farther afield than Chicago in the Autumn was unheard of until 1899. Grau decided to use his knowledge of every theatre in the country to build a prosperous network for opera. He even succeeded in selling the performances outright in Kansas City—the beginning of the guarantee system. Wherever a hall could be adapted to his purpose, Grau booked a date.

Kansas City offered the Metropolitan its first experience in one of those immense, barnlike rectangles known as "convention halls." This new auditorium was dedicated on Washington's Birthday, 1899, with two concerts by Sousa's Band.

An injudicious bit of booking turned the opera's opening into a nightmare. Frank Rigo, the Metropolitan's stage technician, and his expert crew arrived in town to convert the hall to the semblance of an opera house. They found a cattle show in progress, the auditorium floor deep in tanbark, the atmosphere reeking of manure. Not until Saturday, October 28, would the last prize Hereford lumber from the premises. On Monday evening, *Carmen* was due to "dedicate Convention Hall in the cause of art."

Rigo's plan called for an apron extension to the 45-foot stage, a proscenium arch and a huge projecting sounding board. Most of the construction was ready; finishing it and installing it became a matter of intensive, driving labor. Painters worked while the cattle were cheered in the hall; hardly had the last customer departed when one crew began shoveling out the tanbark and another repaired the floor.

Dressing rooms with canvas partitions, a row of boxes on the arena floor (provided with hooks "so that persons need not check wraps and hats") and a thousand other conveniences and appurtenances flew into place as if by magic. Checkrooms would be open and attendants on duty as at a Priests of Pallas Ball, the *Journal* informed patrons.

"Tomorrow, grand opera!" exclaimed the paper. "Three words never meant more in the way of artistic and intelligent entertainment to Kansas City."

More capacious even than Mechanics Hall in Boston, Convention Hall accommodated the biggest audience for a Metropolitan performance to that date, possibly invalidating Atlanta's claim some years later. Atlanta's audience of 6,000 for Caruso's local debut in 1910 was said to be the largest ever to hear him in opera but the tenor's first Kansas City appearance in 1905 was estimated to have attracted an even greater number.

Acoustical problems were not easily solved, and the view from far away of the "little stage and bits of little men and women in brilliant lights and colors seemed like an opera in miniature" to the *Star* reporter. "The faces were indistinguishable, but voices floated up sweet and plain, clarified and glorified."

Whatever souvenirs remained from the performance, memory of Calvé was not among them. The prima donna had had "an attack" in St. Louis, not the first of the spells of illness that were to harass Grau's schedules. She arrived in Kansas City with the troupe, and "the swish of her skirts stirred a lively breeze as she walked rapidly toward the gate."

Healthy enough to give the *Journal* representative a long interview, she told him plaintively that she had just designed her own tomb, to be ornamented with statues of herself as Carmen and Ophelia.

Bonnard, the tenor who had traveled with Damrosch the previous year and whom Grau had engaged for the Autumn tour to replace Alvarez, left himself open to the wrath of the goddess by stating publicly that De Lussan was every bit as good as Calvé—he had sung with both and he ought to know. Kansas City liked him and agreed with him about the American. De Lussan remained the standard; Calvé never appeared in opera in Kansas City.

In April, 1900, Convention Hall was destroyed by a fire, but public-spirited citizens now sprang into action with typical Midwest "get-up-and-go." A. E. Stillwell and William Rockhill Nelson led the drive for funds, and a new, fireproof interior was ready in ninety days for the Democratic National Convention on July 4.

Learning from previous opera experience, S. Kronberg, the local impresario, induced Louis W. Shouse, the new hall manager, to block off about one-third of the hall in 1900-01, hoping to create an atmosphere of comparative intimacy. If the series had opened with *Huguenots* or *Lohengrin,* the effect would have been notable, but Grau chose his novelty, *La Bohème,* with the Mad Scene from *Lucia* as its customary pendant for Melba.

"*Bohème* is a gem," remarked the *Journal,* "but Convention Hall is not the place to exhibit gems. There is just a little less interest this season . . . only 5,000 in the audience."

Puccini's "new" opera provided an ideal opportunity for the oracles. Philip Hale thought *Bohème* a triumph, though "the music may shock the purist or confuse the careless." Trenchant Chicago pens were not given a chance at a Metropolitan *Bohème* until 1907. Many prophets solemnly agreed that the soprano part offered "very slim pickings" indeed. The *Kansas City Journal* advanced a typical view:

"Neither the character nor the music of Mimi is showy. . . . This work ranges from light and trifling music and playful recitative to beautiful, sustained concerted numbers. . . . It seems as if Puccini had endeavored to make an ideal compromise between the florid embellishment of Donizetti and the rigid motif service of Wagner. In his orchestration he displays his genius most."

In a gloomy prognostication the *Star's* critic averred that: *"Bohème* is altogether too scholarly to ever rival *Faust*. It does not stream with melody; there is nothing to whistle unless it is the theme of the duet in the third act. . . . Maybe the masses will grow to love it, however, though it is doubtful."

For several years customers did not get their money's worth unless after this "curtain raiser," as in Kansas City, the figure of Melba appeared "with streaming hair and flowing draperies, a wild light in her eyes, a playful, challenging smile on her lips."

The smiling lips of this apparition parted, and "there stole into the darkness a rippling note that danced from head to head until it reached the farthest crevice of the building . . . then the soft-tuned flute spoke out and the mad girl's voice chased it as a woman would have tripped gaily after a butterfly. Now voice, now flute . . . the race grew faster, the woman's eyes wilder, until in one last burst of purest sound Lucia reached the climax of the struggle and, throwing her hands on high, ran from the stage."

Delirium from the *Star's* critic inspired all too few customers for the remainder of the series. Even the solid core of out-of-town patronage weakened. S. Kronberg was heard once more to grumble his annual threat to cease and desist. This time he meant it. After paying Grau $12,500 for three operas the first year and $13,000 in 1900-01, Kronberg told the New York manager that from now on he was on his own. The third year, Kronberg again took charge, but at Grau's risk. The season grossed only $9,159.

Kronberg, who had accepted a job with Grau to set up the local machinery in Lincoln and Minneapolis in 1900-01, performed the same services in 1901-02 for Buffalo, Cleveland and several southeastern cities.

This was the winter of Grau's discontent, his profits and peace of mind nibbled away by the antics of his two wayward prima donnas, Calvé and Sybil Sanderson, and an occasional tantrum by Emma Eames. All three were promised to Kansas City in 1901-02; none was delivered.

The suggestion of Austin Latchaw, the *Journal's* critic, that guarantees from the wealthy men in town be solicited and a subscription basis adopted, fell on barren ground. In spite of a "masterful" *Tannhäuser* and an *Aida* that enrolled a peerless cast—Gadski, Homer, De Marchi, Scotti, Journet and Edouard de Reszke—disillusion had set in.

2. THROUGH THE GOLDEN GATE

It was with the greatest misgivings that Grau signed a contract to appear in "the smallest city in the United States," noted a western newspaper in 1900. Though his path lay in the right direction, it took the zeal of a go-getting citizen to allay his apprehensions. Finally the manager of the Metropolitan

Opera committed himself to three performances in this little community, for which he was to be paid $13,500. The dates agreed upon were November 9 and 10.

The party of the second part signed his name to the contract: Lynden Ellsworth Behymer. The contract was executed in the City of Los Angeles, Los Angeles County, State of California. Although not the smallest among hosts to the Metropolitan, its population of 102,489 ranked it thirty-third in size among cities of the United States, and Los Angeles displayed a seemly modesty.

The "Busy Bee," as Behymer became known to an ever widening circle, electrified the community with his exploit, the first of a lifelong series that was to make him musical czar of the West. He had arrived in Los Angeles in 1886 and it was rumored that he had begun his career as a "scalper." Usher, book reviewer, press agent, playbill publisher and theatre treasurer marked some of the steps that brought him to the position of the nation's most respected regional impresario.

More than any showman of his day Bee realized the advantages of publicity. He was the first manager to quote press reviews in advertisements, according to Howard Swan, author of *Music in the Southwest*. Anyone who could read the *Los Angeles Times* knew that Bee had renovated old Hazard's Pavilion at Olive and Fifth Street, "laying canvas over dirty floors so that the most exquisite toilette need fear nothing." He saw to it, with the glad assistance of the manager, that a page from the Van Nuys Hotel register, burdened with famous names, was reproduced in the papers. He set aside 700 matinee seats at reduced prices for music students and teachers.

On opening night a contingent from Pasadena "swept up before the very door in a special trolley car all blazing with light and gorgeousness." Fifty came from as far away as San Diego, added the *Times*.

Lohengrin won favor over *Bohème* and *Roméo* that first year, perhaps due to the popularity of Nordica, whom the *Express* critic represented lying "prone upon the stage as the last notes were dying out. The great audience heaved a pent-up sigh," continued the reporter. "The curtain fell and the grandest season of opera ever held in Los Angeles was at an end."

The opening of the season had brought a number of outstanding Metropolitan debuts, especially Fritzi Scheff as Musetta, Marcel Journet as Colline, Suzanne Adams as Juliette and Georges Imbart de la Tour as Roméo. Evidently his first appearance as Parpignol so unnerved a tenor named Aristide Masiero that his services as Benvolio faltered the following night. The official program contains the note: "Masiero's music sung by Miss Bridewell." Los Angeles, however, heard nothing amiss; in fact, the *Express* complimented Masiero for his "excellent pronunciation."

Grau heeded the suggestion of the *Times* and repeated *Lohengrin* a second year, bracketing it with *Carmen* and *Huguenots* for a $500 raise in the guarantee, which Behymer cheerfuly met.

San Francisco was Grau's main objective in these two Autumn tours with Los Angeles acting as prologue.

The Golden Gate had seasoned itself to grand opera performances early in its vigorous life. The "Forty-niners" wanted opera, a history compiled for the

WPA Music Project states unequivocally. "They loved opera. They loved gold, good food, adventure and their own great land. . . . The circus gave way; clowns yielded to prima donnas."

The rough miners had to be told to mind their manners, however. A notice in 1851 "respectfully advised gentlemen that if they must eject tobacco juice in church or in the theatre, they be particular to eject it on their own boots and pantaloons instead of the boots and pantaloons of others."

Sonnambula launched San Francisco on its operatic way in 1851, one year after it had performed the same service for Chicago. *Norma* and *Ernani* followed in a Pellegrini Company season at the Adelphi Theatre.

More opera troupes flourished in the 'fifties and 'sixties than in any other period of the same length. A company might give as many as three seasons in one year.

Empty pockets in the early 'seventies deflated the excitement, but in 1879 flagging interest revived under the stimulus of a new form of entertainment. San Francisco's famous Tivoli, launched as a beer garden with the Viennese Ladies' Orchestra playing sweet waltzes and even operatic medleys, became the rage. The ambitious management broke the operatic ice with *H. M. S. Pinafore* and subsequently offered opera of every type, from comic to grand, until 1913. The theatre remained dark only forty nights: twenty-five for renovation, thirteen for deaths and two for dress rehearsals.

Colonel Mapleson paid the first of several visits in 1879, bringing Marie Rôze, Minnie Hauk and Etelka Gerster. Emma Nevada's return to her native state in 1885 fanned enthusiasm to fever heat. (The singer had adopted her stage name from a town near her birthplace, Alpha, Calif., and not from the State of Nevada.) Her triumph rivaled that of Patti.

San Francisco had been clamoring for grand opera since Mapleson's day, happy at anything that came its way but asking for more. The National Opera under Theodore Thomas gave an impressive season before its spectacular collapse; Emma Abbott's troupe paid regular calls until 1891; the Bostonians visited the Baldwin Theatre twice; Emma Juch and Tavary headed companies in 1891-92 and the Hess and Duff troupes were frequent visitors.

Even a fifth-rate troupe drew eager patrons until it became obvious to the public as well as to the critics that a difference always exists "between the lithograph you see outside of the show and the performance that goes on inside the canvas."

Near the end of the century, the Del Conte Company had made history by producing the first *Bohème* in America, straggling up from Mexico to perform in Los Angeles and San Francisco successively. Giuseppe Agostino, the Rodolfo, still lingered as a model in San Francisco's opinion (he would appear once in the opera as a substitute for Caruso in New York in 1903). Damrosch and Ellis brought Melba, Gadski and De Lussan in 1898.

Grau had looked with favor upon San Francisco's opera public since 1890, when he and Abbey had presented Patti and Tamagno during a prosperous February fortnight. The blandishments of the West persuaded him to a step unique in Metropolitan history: he opened a tour on the Pacific Coast.

For two subsequent seasons it seemed as if the balance of power had shifted

1,500 miles from Chicago. Only four cities east of the Mississippi aside from Brooklyn and Philadelphia benefited from the Metropolitan's largesse in 1901 and 1902, in spring tours of from four to five weeks.

Grau promised San Francisco twenty-four performances, more than a Metropolitan manager had ever granted any city except Chicago. As a climax, the entire *Ring* Cycle was expected to excite far-western ears, which had never heard any of the Tetralogy but *Die Walküre.*

"Wagner is no longer a fad; it is a fact," admitted a daily newspaper.

Grau began to wonder on opening night if he had been right to put so many eggs in this western basket. Although the box office showed that satisfactory numbers of San Franciscans occupied the seats of the old Mission Street Opera House, "a cold, gray audience . . . took the singers for granted." Ashton Stevens of the *Examiner* felt sorry for the performers, although he found Melba "as cold as the audience."

Half as many heard *Tannhäuser,* a "fabulous production with great singing," the second night; and even fewer enjoyed a sumptuous *Aida* wherein Nordica shone supreme, Homer's debut with the company brought her instant recognition, Scotti played a fiery, virile Amonasro, Imbart de la Tour's top notes "were enough to bring the gallery downstairs" and Plançon sang superbly.

The next night was Melba's, but in spite of San Francisco's "Melba madness" not enough of the town turned out "to cover all that Mission Street plush," even though *Faust* enjoyed the best production San Francisco had ever witnessed.

Bispham as the Holländer overwhelmed the critic by his superior gifts, but the audience remained undersized; Melba's matinee Lucia brought hardly any improvement.

Stevens pondered gloomily on his city's delinquency. Chicago a few years ago had been offered big shows at bargain counter prices; they went a-begging. That settled Chicago. He concluded:

"This settles San Francisco."

But he despaired too soon. A performance of *Lohengrin* turned the tide; the season sailed full speed out of the doldrums. The town shook off its apathy. Schumann-Heink galvanized the audience as Ortrud; there seemed no limit to Bispham's skill; Nordica was a sensation; Edouard de Reszke added stature to a "big broad night." Only Van Dyck was "in painful voice."

The season which was to be marked with a big red letter in West Coast calendars proceeded smoothly to its apogee: the *Ring* Cycle. These stupendous music-dramas dwarfed all else in the public's anticipation. Significantly San Franciscans showed up in the greatest numbers for the relatively familiar *Die Walküre.* When all four productions had been entered in the record book, San Francisco, still game, picked itself up and turned to *Traviata, Lohengrin* and *Rigoletto* as the season ended.

San Francisco was made of the right metal, Eustace Cullman wrote in the *Bulletin* of the *Ring* experience. "Grau applied the acid and we stood the test."

Others sustained doubts. For all its initial willingness to experiment, San

Francisco's digestive system could not assimilate large doses of the later Wagner. Next year *Walküre* drew the comment from the *Call* that the boxing ring captured more ardent attention.

Siegfried affected one writer as "puerile, tedious and exasperatingly dull," while *Götterdämmerung* held value chiefly for Edouard de Reszke's Hagen. *Meistersinger* and *Tristan* met with the same lack of appreciation except from Stevens, who studied the score for a week and heard Damrosch's lecture.

His paper's news reporter frankly confessed, however, that, aside from the Quintet, "it would require a raise of salary and a span of mules to draw me within four long city blocks of *Meistersinger* again."

Two American girls, similar in their origin, Christian names and eventual destinies, pleased San Francisco in Grau's first season, although Suzanne Adams invariably won a larger slice of approbation than Susan Strong by virtue of a more brilliant talent and showier roles.

Suzanne made her San Francisco debut as Marguerite in a breathtaking production of *Les Huguenots* that paraded "real grand opera" before the dazzled audience. A *Chronicle* reporter singled out Adams from the rest:

"It is doubtful if any prima donna here shows the same intense brilliancy. Her voice is not large, but sound and sympathetic."

"Successful" was the word for Susan as Elisabeth. Otherwise, Miss Strong remained only a name in the *Ring* casts in San Francisco—Gutrune and the *Rheingold* Fricka. When the market for her Brünnhilde, Venus and Sieglinde dwindled, this gently-born young lady (her father was a New York state senator and one-time mayor of Brooklyn) opened an elegant laundry in London, catering to the peers—and royalty—of several realms. Suzanne Adams emulated her sister prima donna when times turned harder and her distinguished husband, the cellist Leo Stern, had died.

San Francisco had never heard of blue laws and saw nothing strange in opera performances on Sunday nights. So Grau allowed no holidays, but played straight through from November 12 to December 2, with matinees on Saturdays. Sundays were "Pop" nights, with admission prices lowered appreciably from the $7 top that prevailed all week. No Sunday night, that season or next, paid for itself except a *Barbiere* that provoked the demonstration of the season for "the greatest Rosina since Patti," Marcella Sembrich. There had been nothing like it, Stevens averred, since Melba sang *The Star-Spangled Banner* in the lesson scene during the Spanish-American War. "People stood in the aisles and whooped and thundered."

While tenors sulked at San Francisco's treatment (Van Dyck, De Marchi, Salignac and Dippel bent their efforts and also strained their vocal cords to no avail), at least four females lived a pampered life.

Sembrich's conquering march appeared the more remarkable for her failure in her own company the previous spring. After two years with Grau, the petite Polishwoman had succumbed to the desire for independence. Her illness in San Francisco revealed the fatal flaw in a one-woman company. Paying off 130 people at the rate of two weeks' salary each and transportation home, the disillusioned prima donna returned to Dresden. The following season, Marcella once more nestled happily in her niche with the Metropolitan company.

Calvé became directly responsible for San Francisco's good fortune in extracting an extra week from Grau's schedule. Her first Carmen produced the desired effect, but she was unable to sing two days later. Grau announced that the ailing diva would seek rest and solace in the green fields of Pasadena and that he would extend the season in order to allow patrons to hear her famous role twice more, canceling plans to revisit Los Angeles and to accept Dallas' rumored offer of $20,000 for a single night.

Three audiences eventually paid $27,836.50 to hear *Carmen* and few thought their money wasted. In interviews with "the man on the street," the *Examiner* quoted a fire commissioner as calling Calvé's Carmen "the greatest thing in the world of opera." An insurance man, however, preferred Collamarini, while an iron magnate was loyal to De Lussan's Carmen.

The more controversy in this case, the merrier for Grau. A teapot tempest that raged around the handsome head of another of his prize songbirds, however, left a faintly bitter aftertaste. Sybil Sanderson, whose wealthy husband had died in Europe, came home once again to try her Manon and Juliette. "Home" to the dainty prima donna meant Sacramento, and most of northern California rallied to welcome the return of a famous daughter.

Sanderson approached her first San Francisco audience with timidity and relied heavily on the prompter. Her own sex meted out the harshest treatment. Blanche Partington wrote in the *Call* that Sanderson could not sing now, whatever she had done in the past, and that she had no place in grand opera.

The exotic prodigal had postponed all social activities until after *Manon* should be behind her. Now she was in no mood for gaiety. She cried herself to sleep, Edward H. Hamilton reported in the *Examiner*, and even wrote indignant letters to the critics. Only one-third of an audience watched her redeem herself as Juliette, when her high, light soprano showed at its best. Sanderson did not appear again on tour, canceling a San Francisco assignment for Marguerite in *Les Huguenots* and a special Los Angeles gala. She was said to be undergoing a throat operation, although this seems doubtful, for she contrived to sing a single performance in New York as Juliette on December 28 and in Philadelphia on New Year's Eve—her farewell to opera and to America. She died in France two years later.

Two earlier Wagner operas, *Lohengrin* and *Tannhäuser,* staunchly held their own in San Francisco, and provided vehicles for several of the Coast's most favored singers. *Lohengrin,* opening the 1901-02 season, gave the city its first glimpse of Emma Eames, who immediately succeeded Johanna Gadski as the Golden Gate's most beloved Elsa since Gadski had replaced Nordica late in the previous season.

Unfortunately for the establishment of a real bond between city and singer, Eames fell ill and had to cancel a *Lohengrin* and a *Faust,* later singing an *Aida* when hardly equal to the task. Her acting, however, proved "a memorable reproach to those who have called this most human and unaffected of prima donnas cold and glacial."

Stevens was inconsolable when Luise Reuss-Belce, a soprano "who looks more like a Greek goddess than others," according to Miss Partington, took Eames's place as Elsa, "attacking the part with a savagery which distorted it out of all poetic meaning."

Gadski made herself immensely popular off stage as well as on, particularly with the press: "After the gossip and backbiting of the ordinary prima donnas, it is good to see this one, so comfortable, generous and German."

At its highest point and twice again, the season owed its happiest moments to Mozart. *Le Nozze di Figaro* filled the opera house as never before.

"Eames may have been greater as Elsa, Sembrich as Violetta, Campanari as Marcello, De Reszke as Méphistophélès, but put them all together and add Scheff at her best in an opera with tunes to tickle the ear and you have a sensation," crowed the *Examiner*. "Walter Damrosch shouted 'Bravo, Seppilli!' from the dress circle and went down and played the drums under Seppilli's baton. The Zephyr duet called out a demonstration like those of twenty years ago. The musicians were all but delirious."

Only one accident marred the perfection. "Eames missed her cue for the 'Dove Song' [sic—'Dove Sono'] and left the stage in an empty wait. After a half-minute of tense silence, Seppilli gave the signal for the next scene. De Reszke and Dufriche [the Count and Antonio] made a hasty entrance, but Eames was in the wings before their short episode ended, and the hands of time turned back for her aria."

Informality in transposing and repeating scenes bothered no one. The encore habit died hard on the road. Three "Toreador Songs" were common in *Carmen,* only one in context. If conductors grew weary of the tasteless business, the singers took over: the tenor Russitano once conducted the orchestra himself for his third rendering of *Di Quella Pira*. When the orchestra left the pit after a performance of *Faust,* the tenor De Lucia, nothing daunted, sang the serenade from *Cavalleria* unaccompanied.

In Boston "Azucena recovered sufficiently from her fainting to bow before she had another attack, and Manrico came out of the locked tower as though he knew the combination . . . or a friendly jailer." In Brooklyn "the delighted Leonora broke into prison, caught the beaming Manrico by the hand and brought him down to the footlights to receive the plaudits of the audience. Then the prisoner trotted dutifully back to jail and they sang the whole scene over again."

In 1896 Hale was ashamed of his fellow Bostonians: "Tell it not in New York, publish it not in Philadelphia! The Soldiers' Chorus [in *Faust*] was redemanded." By the next year he recorded the encore as a simple matter of historical fact. Even the harp solo in *Lucia* was encored in Philadelphia.

Scenes of equal tumult took place at the repeats of *Le Nozze di Figaro* which closed the San Francisco season. Grau could not quarrel with the success of his Pacific stand. Both seasons had proved worth while.

In 1901-02, San Francisco marked the halfway point of the Autumn tour. In 1900-01, Grau had only two weeks on the road before the New York season.

He revisited Kansas City and added Denver, Lincoln and Minneapolis to the roll of Metropolitan cities. "Mr. Grau's priceless singers, bearing aloft the branches of genius," made their Denver bow under circumstances not wholly favorable. An extra performance of *Tannhäuser* had been prefixed to the announced season too late to promote properly. The Broadway Theatre left much to be desired; chorus and ballet crowded the stage—the company evidently "was scaled to larger spaces" as the *Times* admitted.

The opera itself proved "too heavy" for many—the *Republican* confessed that *Tannhäuser* was impossible to understand without a half-dozen hearings, and "not knowing German or the story made it doubly hard." No fault could be found with the remainder of the series.

The Nebraska capital regarded the opera visit as almost as exciting an event as the election, when its most illustrious citizen, William Jennings Bryan, had met his second defeat as candidate for the presidency. Smallest city on the route, Lincoln was required to post a guarantee before Grau consented to stop.

Willard Kimball, who risked $7,500 to bring "the most expensive form of entertainment so that Nebraskans could enjoy the highest form of art without paying more than at the Metropolitan," had founded the University School of Music in 1894 and directed music at the Omaha Exhibition in 1898. He strained every resource to promote this undertaking, a gigantic task for the little city.

Lincoln's new opera house, the Lansing, would not hold the crowds expected for the "largest and strongest opera company in the world." Another reconstruction job for a big auditorium, similar to Kansas City's, was indicated. Work proceeded frantically until after the opera train arrived. Confusion seemed likely to persist; indeed, the performance of the matinee *Faust* had to be delayed an hour. When at last the curtain went up, all the troubles and "the dismal auditorium, half-filled, were forgotten in the magic of the performance." Only one trace of disappointment lingered.

Advance programs had listed alternates in the role of Méphistophélès—Journet and Edouard de Reszke. Lincoln heard Journet. A story printed simultaneously in Lincoln and Kansas City papers explained that the hearty Polish trencherman could not be dissuaded from finishing a "family sized steak" and a huge stein of beer and had consequently missed his train.

Journet was replaced by Viviani at the evening performance of *Lucia,* which John Randolph of the *Nebraska State Journal* deemed "jaded and thin today, but wonderfully tuneful. It is music our grandmothers heard with enthusiasm. . . . Today we prefer the ecstasy of *Tristan und Isolde.*"

The majority of Lincolnians did not agree. The "one-day season" which began in gloom, ended in a storm of enthusiasm.

Minneapolis received the troupe warmly, although a *Journal* writer vouchsafed the opinion that "none of the Grau people are in danger of being drafted for beauty shows."

Exposition Hall, although heated for the duration, put the troupe in a disadvantageous position, Frances H. Robertson of the *Tribune* apologized. Many Minneapolis citizens agreed with her. Pride in being chosen as a

Metropolitan city and shame at the surroundings in which it received the visitors inspired a campaign for a new hall. It was completed by the time Conried came that way in 1905.

3. MARATHON

On October 7, 1901, the opera train steamed out of New York once again, not to return until December 22. During the intervening weeks, the company from the Metropolitan Opera made touring history. In what was to be the last Autumn foray by any troupe from the House, Grau and his songbirds called at twenty-one cities from coast to coast. During the New York season, which measured only slightly more than half the number of performances on the road, they visited Philadelphia fifteen times. In March, Grau set forth again to keep important engagements in Boston, Chicago, Pittsburgh and Baltimore, completing the extraordinary record by a single appearance in Brooklyn.

Total statistics on the season thus read: 145 performances of thirty operas (four in double bills) in twenty-seven cities in fifteen states and Canada.

Grau opened his marathon in Albany. In the effort to pave the way to Canada in two directions, he continued to try various combinations of New York way stops, but opera never became a fixture along the Erie Canal, although the circuit was an old-time favorite for stage troupes. Albany, with its Harmanus Bleecker Hall, well built and commodious with 1,800 seats, commanded occasional visits in after years, but the other towns could not match Albany's box-office yield of $3-4,000 in Grau's time, $7,000 in Gatti-Casazza's.

"Not more than 1,000 Utica people were enthused" when Grau first experimented with the Canal route in 1899. If they wanted opera, they could go to New York and, furthermore, hear Calvé in *Carmen* instead of De Lussan, who, after all, had been popular years before with the Boston Ideals and even before that as a concert singer at Richfield Springs. At a $4 top, not even 1,000 showed up at the Utica Opera House on October 13 for what was to be the city's only Metropolitan performance.

Syracuse, as Utica complained, did receive more consideration. In 1899 Sembrich sang Rosina and Calvé, Carmen in the New Wieting Opera House.

The University town responded with genuine appreciation, which was reflected in many columns of newspaper reviews and interviews. A *Post-Standard* reporter, graciously received by Sembrich, quoted her as expressing the usual nostalgia of the trouper for "a little place to rest," sighing that singers' homes are only perches for birds of passage!

Grau shuttled from Albany to the two Canadian cities, Rochester, Syracuse and Buffalo in 1901. *Lohengrin* was the choice of Albany and Syracuse, with the same cast except that Homer sang "Ostend" (sic) in Syracuse instead of Schumann-Heink.

Buffalo, its 352,000 population comparing favorably with most of the tour cities and even surpassing San Francisco and Cincinnati, still remained unsophisticated in operatic matters. No opera could be too hackneyed in 1896, when the company played in Abbey's own Music Hall with considerable success. Now in the bare, bat-infested Convention Hall, audiences fell off sharply. The opening-night *Faust* contended for the auditors' attention with the chilly temperature of the hall, the leakage of gas and the squeaking seats of latecomers.

Rochester, in spite of its all-time low box-office record for a Metropolitan performance—$332 for *Manon* at the matinee of October 14, 1901—is the only New York town to have reentered the Metropolitan's present-day route books.

Toronto, stubbornly English, and Montreal, as stubbornly French, encountered language difficulties with their early Metropolitan experiences. The *Toronto Globe,* in 1899, attributed the relatively small audience for *Barbiere* to the fact that the opera was not very well known and noted a further drawback in that it was sung in Italian. The *Montreal Gazette* shuddered at the German text for *Tannhäuser,* in 1901, saying that "its strong guttural sounds at first grated on the ear a little, following three operas written in the most polished language of Europe."

Grau consented to his singers' participation in a State Concert in Toronto on October 10, 1901, to honor Their Royal Highnesses, The Duke and Duchess of Cornwall and York, later George V and Queen Mary, whose triumphal progress from coast to coast elicited the best Canada had to give. Even if the receipts of $7,877 exceeded almost any other of the year, the strain on the singers was considerable. Calvé, forced to wait until the Royal party entered, competed through her songs with a brass band, a chorus of fish horns (noisy instruments that irritated even patriotic Canadians), a cavalcade of fire engines and finally a band of pipers.

Massey Hall was not built for a theatre, the *Mail and Empire* reluctantly concluded. When the Metropolitan company next crossed the border in 1952, quarters of an unexpectedly different nature had been prepared for it in Toronto's Maple Leaf Gardens.

Still less appropriate than the comparative refinement of Massey Hall was Montreal's Arena, the skating rink with the leaky roof. Montreal welcomed the troupe once more, in 1911, at the popular theatre known then and now as Her Majesty's, before following Toronto's example by transforming a sports arena into an opera house.

The train headed southward on October 19, as Grau's master plan unfolded. For two weeks a half-dozen southwestern cities buzzed wildly about the glamorous visitors. In all but Louisville the Metropolitan company was breaking new ground. Nashville, Memphis, Atlanta and Birmingham had entertained no troupe of comparable grandeur. New Orleans, however, proud Queen of Opera in the South, proclaimed that its illustrious French Opera House had been occupied by an opera company every season since its opening in 1859 "except in national or local calamity, such as the four years of war and a few dates following disasters."

Louisville, itself a theatre town of no mean pretensions, laid down the red carpet for the fourth time since first it was unrolled for Patti's delicate steps in 1890. Abbey and Grau had always liked to do business with Daniel Quilp, the manager of the Auditorium. He had paid them $25,000 outright for four performances by the Patti-Tamagno troupe and $10,000 for three in 1891.

Daniel Quilp was a pseudonym for Captain William F. Norton, scion of a pious Baptist family, who chose one of Dickens' less attractive characters to mask his theatrical activities from his mother. Mrs. Norton must have led a sheltered life indeed not to have received some inkling of "Willie's" doings. As Melville O. Briney, columnist for the *Louisville Times,* records in her *Fond Recollections,* Norton found himself the possessor of 3,065 chairs, waved his hand toward a vacant corner lot and said: "We'll set 'em out on the lawn, by God! and build an auditorium around 'em."

Norton's Auditorium dominated an entire city block. The Amphitheatre, a huge wooden structure seating more than 3,000, an artificial lake, on which floated a great ship used for performances of *H. M. S. Pinafore,* bicycle tracks through glades and an esplanade offered the town entertainment summer and winter from its dedication on September 23, 1889, by Edwin Booth and Lawrence Barrett.

Before the marathon tour was over two weeks old, Grau's serenity disappeared. Calvé, who had sung three times during the fortnight, refused to continue after Louisville. She had caught cold.

Grau at last persuaded her to board the opera train to Nashville, although she insisted that there was no use in stopping anywhere short of New Orleans, where lived a French doctor who "understood" her. Consternation swept along the telegraph wires between Louisville and three cities that had built their operatic hopes on *Carmen.* Nashville, one day away, presented the direst emergency; a breathing space existed to pacify Memphis and Atlanta.

Before the damaging news could reach the *Nashville Morning Banner,* the Tabernacle Committee and the Philharmonic Society, jointly responsible for the engagement, worked feverishly behind scenes.

Strangely unbeknownst to the contemporary newspaper reporters, who were occupied interviewing Sembrich or chasing "big, florid Germans with blond beards and deep voices or bright and vivacious French and Italians" through hotel corridors, a delegation of three Nashville ladies called on Calvé. They wished to offer felicitations or commiserations or whatever courtesy seemed to be in order—and incidentally to determine for themselves if the singer was *really* ill. But Mrs. T. Graham Hall, Mrs. Brandan and Mrs. Chapman never got past the prima donna's door in the Maxwell House. They were given to understand that not only Madame was ill, but her dog as well (the chef had sent up a beefsteak too well done, the report got around).

Calvé, however, offered to submit to examination by Nashville doctors, and the committee agreed. Doctors W. D. Haggard, Jr., Hillard Wood and George Hunter Price duly peered down the diva's throat and produced what Dr. Price's sister Elizabeth termed fifty-five years later a masterpiece of adroitness in their published report:

"We find her complaining of a bronchial irritation which she insists will incapacitate her to sing tonight. She also states that she will be unable to sing in Memphis and Atlanta, but hopes to sing in New Orleans."

The committee reluctantly settled for Camille Seygard in place of Calvé. The people were satisfied, the *Banner* announced next morning, that the Citizens' Committee did the correct thing in a trying emergency. In spite of cash refunds of $1,018, the house was nearly full, representing "all of the social and musical culture, beauty and wealth in Nashville and nearly all over the state."

Seygard, "with a flaming geranium between her pearly teeth and an impudent swagger," showed the audience to perfection "that she was even more beautiful than Calvé." Destined to become the "pinch-hitter" of the troupe, the Frenchwoman fared better in Nashville than in most of her fourteen substitutions for Calvé, Sanderson, Eames and Scheff.

After all, as Frederick Farrar pointed out philosophically in the *American,* "one singer does not make an opera company by any means," although Grau might have felt like disagreeing at the moment. Still, Sembrich redeemed the engagement by her matchless performance as Rosina the second night.

Ryman Tabernacle was the city's best auditorium, although the chant and holler of the revival meeting had echoed through its walls more often than the opera aria. Captain T. G. Ryman, a retired steamboat owner, had built it "at the behest of the Lord" for the evangelist Sam Paul Jones (who never saw it until he preached at Ryman's funeral). Grand opera encroached on the hallowed premises at last. Captain Ryman could not refuse the Grau engagement but he tried to ensure against any contamination of his sacred premises. During the entire length of both performances the devout man stood beneath the quivering stage, praying at the top of his voice.

Ryman's monument lived on in Nashville, acquiring a chatelaine in Mrs. L. C. Naff, who brought musical visitors to the Tabernacle for fifty years until her retirement in 1956. Her eyes shoot bright blue sparks at any criticism of her beloved auditorium. "It still has the best acoustics anywhere," she maintains, "and those who complain about the hard benches [the original pews installed in 1892] sit longer in church!"

Memphis hungered for grand opera with a passion that overflowed into the surrounding countryside and prompted special trains from many outlying towns; a zest that called for renovation and backstage reconstruction of its Auditorium and that inspired an unprecedented advance sale. Grau's promise of Sembrich in *Faust* compensated for Calvé's defection.

As the curtain rose on *Lohengrin,* the *Commercial Appeal* took note of an audience of 2,800, capacity for the house. "Lovely women of the South and men of many occupations blended with one accord into an enthusiastic multitude which cheered the artists to the echo."

Memphis stood exonerated from an occasional charge of "inartisticness."

The future of grand opera in the city seemed assured. *Faust* was sold out, so that the afternoon *Manon* remained the one unknown element. Memphis knew nothing of the opera and little more of the prima donna scheduled for the title role. When the performance had ended, knowledge of Massenet's music had increased somewhat, but all Memphis gleaned from Sybil Sanderson's performance was that Manon seemed more *souffrante* than any courtesan, except Violetta Valéry, had any right to be.

Sanderson's illness became apparent after the first few moments. She seemed to pause as if lost, reported the *Commercial Appeal* reviewer, and then whispered distinctly enough to be heard in the front rows, "I cannot sing." At the end of the act, Seygard took over.

A legend has grown up in the South that Sanderson partly recovered and found her way back to the stage in the third act, so that two Manons were imploring Des Grieux to return to their arms. But this is obviously a canard.

Memphis had not "universally honored the occasion with evening dress," for, as the society chronicler explained, "grand opera is democratic . . . to the tyro in fashion's art the discomfort of full dress outweighs the sense of duty fulfilled." But Atlanta announced proudly that "full dress will be worn by all occupying seats on the lower floor in the De Give Grand Opera House and a number of elegant toilet[te]s are being designed for Atlanta belles."

Even after the announcement of Calvé's withdrawal, enthusiasm persisted. *Lohengrin* shared headlines with the execution of President McKinley's assassin: "Czolgosz Dies as Fool Dieth!" topped page one of the *Constitution,* but the grim specter of retribution was soon forgotten, while Eames as Elsa, Sanderson as Juliette, and above all, Sembrich as Rosina, captivated Georgians.

Birmingham's one-night stand proved refreshingly lacking in incident for Grau's troupe. The Alabama steel center of 38,000 professed to be less boastful and self-conscious than Memphis or Nashville or Atlanta, and "so in the most modest and unpretentious ways its members have attended the lectures on *Lohengrin* and given an order here and there for a new gown or wrap."

Some small dissatisfaction about the cast found expression, when Birmingham, which had demanded Sembrich, realized afterward that she shone less brilliantly in Wagner than in coloratura roles. William Ryan of the *Age-Herald* yearned for Schumann-Heink, but conceded that giving the role of Ortrud to Carrie Bridewell, a Mississippi girl who had lived in Birmingham, was a stroke of good politics. Boyle and Edwards of the Auditorium paid Grau $5,000 and were said to have cleared $1,000 at a $4 top.

"When Grau comes this way again, standing room will be demanded," the newspaper prophesied; but Conried, not Grau, reaped the harvest so happily seeded in Birmingham.

Grau had intended his four-day stay in New Orleans as a bonbon after a long October feast. By the time he brought the company safely to rest on the shores of Lake Ponchartrain, the manager was ready for the balm of applause—and high subscription figures—from a really exigent audience.

Society had not been better represented on any first night during the best seasons of opera, the *Picayune* stated firmly after *Lohengrin.* Every seat was taken, the aisles packed, and many ladies "bravely stood." Old habitués jubilantly talked of palmy days. The rather unfamiliar opera carried Eames to triumph; Van Dyck, "the best Wagnerian tenor today," opened his last season with the Metropolitan at this performance, and Edouard de Reszke began his tenth in America, "his glorious voice as flexible as a high soprano." Bispham's brilliant and ringing baritone kept the audience in a fever to applaud.

Calvé, "like a splash of sunshine," brought perfection to *Carmen* before an even larger crowd, while Gibert, a favorite New Orleans tenor whom Grau had recruited for the tour, seemed better than ever. Calvé's Carmen, extolled in the newspapers of the time, left little impression on several opera *aficionados* who remember it even today, among them Edward Alexander Parsons and Harry Brunswick Loëb. The latter unkindly described her as "a harp just taken out of the case and not unwrapped."

This public was the first of any sophistication in America to judge the talents of the tenor who had created Cavaradossi in Rome; Emilio de Marchi had made his debut in Buffalo on October 18, but had not been heard again until he sang Raoul in New Orleans. The *Picayune* deemed his voice glorious.

New Orleans also appreciated Sanderson in *Manon* as the exponent of a unique French style, summoned up a few surprisingly warm words for Salignac and thought Homer a revelation as Urbain in *Huguenots*.

Several Autumn tour cities would have been happy to welcome *Tosca* in their repertories, but Grau did not include Puccini's newest opera, perhaps because Milka Ternina, its superb heroine, was not available. Philadelphia, Boston and Chicago had found the work strikingly effective, if not so easily assimilable as *Bohème*, the previous Spring. William H. Sherwood in the Chicago *American* deemed it a marvel, and Philip Hale in Boston believed it to be a step toward Bernhardt's ideal—a play with continuous and expressive music.

Even with the original Cavaradossi at hand, *Tosca* traveled no farther than Philadelphia and Boston in 1901-02, and reaped a single performance in Philadelphia in 1902-03, with Eames and De Marchi.

Three Texas towns had contended for the open dates on Grau's westward trek. Dallas, smallest of the three with a population of 42,000, lay slightly off the route, so Grau chose Houston and San Antonio for one-night stands, promising *Lohengrin* to each.

The opera vied for Houston's attention with the news of three more oil "spouters," and with a campaign to prohibit the carrying of deadly weapons. A letter to the editor of the *Post* deplored "too many personal conflicts and a consequent tendency to violence and bloodshed." But opera meant more to the *Post*—and to the wayfarers from a dozen outlying towns who assembled in the old city Auditorium—than mere pomp and show:

"Those who presented themselves for music's gracious ministrations were strengthened, comforted and spiritually uplifted by the contemplation and sympathetic reception of the heroic heights of harmonious polyphony and refreshing streams of melody which delighted the ear and heart all through the long score."

Backstage in the crude auditorium, however, all was not "harmonious polyphony." Lying at some distance from the center of town, the building had been harnessed to the Citizens' Electric Light plant, but no similar link to a plumbing system had been thought necessary. Certain facilities were entirely absent in the dressing rooms, and the Ortrud, shaken by pre-performance nerves, was heard to demand a substitute.

"No vessel, no performance!" she shrieked in contralto tones of unequaled power, range and vibrance. While she fumed, a distracted auditorium official made a house-to-house canvass in the sparsely populated neighborhood, asking an embarrassing question at each door. At last his heroic efforts were rewarded. Bearing the desired article under an overcoat he had foresightedly thought to carry, he scurried back to the auditorium stage door. The performance—and Madame's comfort—were assured.

San Antonio lacked none of the amenities, and its picturesqueness caught the fancy of the traveling troupe, who would have liked to explore the quaint city more thoroughly.

In 1901 Grau settled his company for one night in the Opera House, on the west side of Alamo Plaza. The audience gathered at 7 o'clock, "magnificent in point of brilliance as well as numbers," and wildly applauded "the dignity, glory and stateliness of Wagner." The *Express* critic showed some disappointment at first in Sembrich's Elsa, but "she grew on the audience." Jacques Bars, in a rare assignment to a leading role, proved a "sweet-voiced tenor, whose first notes bespoke him a true artist."

Grau's company provided as keen a cultural excitement as any since the San Antonio visit of Oscar Wilde in 1882. The death of the witty esthete in 1900 had renewed Texas memories of an event described by Mrs. Franz Stumpf in a history of San Antonio's famous Hotel Menger. Wilde caused a sensation with his "colorful, light-brown overcoat, yellow silk waistcoat, blue tie, lemon-yellow gloves and green morocco bag" as well as with his lecture on "Decorative Art." Texans failed to appreciate his long hair and "his posing in stained-glass attitudes."

After a month on the West Coast, Grau's company returned through Missouri, Indiana and Ohio. Attendance dropped discouragingly in St. Louis, Kansas City, Cleveland and Cincinnati, and in Indianapolis Grau encountered the most adverse circumstances of the tour. English's Opera House, where he had played in 1899, was not available, and he had been forced into Tomlinson Hall, a large room over City Market, inadequate in every respect.

On the bitter December day, with temperatures predicted at ten degrees below zero, the opera train arrived late from St. Louis. Customers shivering in the freezing hall for two hours were eventually told to get refunds at the box office; the matinee *Roméo et Juliette* had to be canceled.

Scenery for *Lohengrin* was hoisted through the windows, and the audience that evening huddled in coats and wondered how much of Wagner's music they had missed under the victorious "clanks" of the steam radiators.

In a reasonably profitable spring tour to Boston, Chicago, Pittsburgh and Baltimore, Grau's new production of *Magic Flute* drew curious thousands in the two larger cities, and theatres invariably filled for *Carmen* with Calvé and Alvarez, and for *Figaro* with a superlative cast.

Nevertheless, Grau was through. He had intimated as much in San Francisco, when he spoke his mind freely to Ashton Stevens of the *Examiner,* "peeling the opera business of the last coating of romance with a frankness almost ferocious." His usual buoyancy seemed deflated; he may have even stopped his tuneless whistling that drove superstitious singers to the brink of tantrums.

"Grau must assume all the risks," Stevens quoted him as saying. "Well, Grau is tired, and after thirty years of it, Grau will retire . . . I shall quit while the luck is still hot; and the funeral of Maurice Grau will not be paid for by his friends."

This was true prophecy: Grau had multiplied his opera earnings many times by canny stock-market manipulations; he became the first opera impresario to depart with a nest egg.

"Only a fool or a madman will take up where I leave off," he told Stevens.

Heedless of this warning, a half-dozen claimants to his title and perquisites made themselves heard when he announced his abdication in the middle of his 1902-03 season. The American continent, which had known and respected the doughty little manager for three decades, saw him no more. France was to be his home until his death on March 14, 1907.

Part VI

CONRIED: MAN OF THE THEATRE

1. STEEL LOSES TO THE IRON WILL

In an elaborate prospectus entitled "Grand Opera Tour Across the Continent, Season 1905," Heinrich Conried appears as "Rejuvenator of the Opera." The first year of his regime had been not without its mishaps, admitted the brochure's writer, but *"Conried* had had his baptism of *fire,* he had been in the *crucible!"* As new plans were announced, "the *Sneer* and *Curled* lip were again in harness. *But this man Conried had caught his second wind! Artistic Finesse* came to his aid, as did courage and daring, also quiet and unyielding determination."

Conried had not only "caught his second wind" but he had found the ideal bellows to direct a stream of grandiloquent press-agentry in his van. Gustave Schlotterbeck's rich hyperbole, its italics and exclamation points as thick as paste diamonds in stage jewelry, had hitherto been confined within the columns of the Pittsburgh *Post.* The effusive critic had managed the Metropolitan's Pittsburgh season in 1903-04 and at Conried's behest had represented the company in Cincinnati and Chicago. In 1904-05 he was entrusted with the exploitation of Conried's first transcontinental tour.

Schlotterbeck's efforts, described by himself in the prospectus as "vigorous, intelligent and absolutely truthful publicity," admirably suited Conried's flamboyant nature.

The emphasis placed on the personality of management in America had touched Grau's sense of irony. He told Ashton Stevens in San Francisco that singers, seeing the manager's name prominently displayed in the programs, would ask with unconcealed amusement, "What part do you sing, Mr. Grau?"

Conried was never one to shun the spotlight. A three-quarter length portrait, showing a cluster of decorations on his evening coat lapel, occupied the first inside page of the 1905 prospectus, surrounded by a laurel wreath and topped by a lyre.

His first taste of power had made an indelible impression. Taking over the Bremen Stadttheater when a mere boy, he soon came to "recognize no one as above him," according to his biographer, Montrose J. Moses. "From then on he adopted an imperious manner which instilled confidence into those under him, but which gained for him many enemies."

Adolf Neuendorff, who in 1886 was to conduct the Metropolitan Company on its "rebel" tour, brought Conried to America in 1877 to take charge of the Germania Theatre. The next year the immigrant became artistic director of the Thalia Theatre. For several years he was associated with Rudolph Aronson in producing operas at the New York Casino, then returned to the German stage to direct the Irving Place Theatre, where his phenomenal success recommended him most strongly to the Metropolitan's directors, in spite of his conspicuous lack of actual operatic experience.

Conried did not win the nation's supreme operatic post without opposition. When Grau's failing health made it imperative that he be replaced before the end of the 1902-03 season in order to insure the continuity of the company, bids for the lease of the House poured in upon the directors. Newspapers in many cities picked their own candidates and frequently changed them from week to week, so that one day it was possible to read that Charles A. Ellis of Boston stood the best chance; next day John Duss, a band leader, had threatened through his manager R. E. Johnson to withdraw the Metropolitan orchestra and many singers under his control if he were not selected.

John B. Schoeffel, Abbey's and Grau's former partner, saw his name in the lists; others suggested were Frederick Charles of the New Orleans French Opera, Daniel Frohman, Charles Frohman and Henry Russell. Even the singer David Bispham "had the temerity" to covet the position, as he confessed in his autobiography.

As February began the competition had narrowed down to three in addition to Conried. According to which paper one read in which city, Walter Damrosch or Henry W. Savage (who had headed the only English-speaking troupe ever to inhabit the Metropolitan, in a pre-season series in 1901) or even George W. Wilson of Pittsburgh was the favorite. By Lincoln's Birthday, Savage had dropped out. The other two strove mightily behind scenes to impress the board with their good intentions and splendid backing.

Damrosch had raised the required $150,000 backing for the Metropolitan post, but had not been able to coax a letter of recommendation from Grau, who acted as a sort of elder statesman through all the campaigning.

Wilson seemed to many observers (even outside of Pittsburgh, which quite naturally embraced his candidacy as a matter of *amour propre*) to be the leading contender. His long career as a practical manager was cited: he had been transplanted in 1891 by Theodore Thomas to Chicago, as secretary of the Bureau of Music of the World's Fair. In his native Boston, he had written criticism for the *Daily Traveler,* annotated the program notes for the Boston Symphony and for ten years had published the *Musical Year Book of the United States.* After managing the Chicago Symphony for one year, he was summoned to Pittsburgh in 1895.

Andrew Carnegie's representatives believed Wilson the right man to run the "great new artistic movement" that was afoot in the steel capital. He took charge of Carnegie Music Hall and the Pittsburgh Art Society and helped organize the Pittsburgh Symphony.

Grau had accepted Wilson's first invitation in 1899 and had returned to Pittsburgh every year thereafter, pleased at the mounting receipts and the attentive audiences. In 1901 Duquesne Garden, a huge, car-barn that had been turned into a skating rink, was remodeled for opera. Wilson, who had crowded the 2,000-seat Grand Opera House at a $6.25 top for four perform- ances, now coped successfully with 4,000 seats at a $6 top for five. When Wilson sought Grau's post, he believed that Grau himself approved.

Wilson was summoned from a sickbed to New York on Lincoln's Birthday and learned that the deadline for the $150,000 guarantee had been advanced from March 1 to February 13, the next day, when the Metropolitan board meeting was scheduled. By frantic cabling and long-distance phoning he raised $200,000 within twenty-four hours on a legal holiday. Among his guarantors were Charles M. Schwab, president of United States Steel, who was enjoying a Riviera holiday at Cannes at the moment, and other steel magnates chosen from the seventy-six rich men who had backed his projects in Pittsburgh.

The "Battle of the Millionaires" was opened: standing for Damrosch was Samuel Untermeyer, the famous lawyer; behind Wilson ranged most of the "Steel Trust"; supporting Conried was Jacob Schiff, a member of Kuhn, Loeb and Company and director of nineteen corporations, who had pledged himself to Damrosch if Conried failed.

Only thirteen members of the board were present in George G. Haven's office that Friday the thirteenth; it was an unlucky number for Damrosch and Wilson. Seven voted for Conried; six are said to have voted for Dam- rosch. When the chips were down, the Metropolitan preferred New York's millionaires to Pittsburgh's. The decision was made unanimous at a full board meeting the next day.

Though chagrined, Wilson settled back into his orchestra routine, handing over the Metropolitan's visits to Schlotterbeck. When Conried came to Pitts- burgh in 1903-04 it was to the Nixon Theatre (seating 2,160), which would be the Metropolitan's home until its last visit in 1910. Wilson died on March 18, 1908, just seventeen days after Conried's resignation from the Metro- politan.

The rumor that Damrosch, on the strength of his big minority vote, would be taken into almost equal partnership with Conried or at least given a high post quickly proved false. Conried let it be known that he and he alone would rule his new kingdom.

With a will stiffened to iron by years of absolute command in the theatre, he immediately laid down the law upon his succession to the highest operatic post in America. In an interview the very day of the formal announcement that he had won the negotiations, he charted a plain course for the opera:

He would have the best singers that money could buy—and many new singers . . . but he would subordinate stars to ensemble. He would show novelty in production of new and entertaining works. There would be no rushing over to Philadelphia and Brooklyn for one-night stands: "The time spent in catching cold on the cars and in extra work in public in the neigh- boring cities will be given to rehearsal." Discipline, discipline—that was to be the watchword: "I am afraid the artists don't realize what downright re-hearsals mean."

As for the star system, "I warrant I can put a star on one night and an ensemble opera the next and draw as great a crowd. . . ."

And, finally: "No one is absolutely necessary to success. . . . If I felt dependent on any one person I should seek another as alternate or close up my theatre."

Brave promises these, which he was forced to eat almost to a word. Hardly one of them was realized.

Perhaps a Napoleonic complex underlay the actions of this small, corpulent man who tried to appear taller by affecting a crest of thick, black hair at one end and high-heeled suede boots at the other. "Formerly it was the star who managed the opera house; now it is I," he told Chicago. But unfortunately for Conried's claims to absolute authority, his wagon had become hitched willy-nilly to the most refulgent star of all times: Enrico Caruso.

His complete dependence upon this single voice not only belied one of his early promises but made another impossible to fulfill: he neglected to secure the great French and some Italian talent that played into Oscar Hammerstein's hands and further increased that pugnacious impresario's power.

In his five-year term Conried offered nine "novelties," including the sensational and short-lived *Salome* and the pirated *Parsifal* which with *Madama Butterfly, Hänsel und Gretel* and *Manon Lescaut* became staples of the repertory. Others that reached any part of the road more remote than Philadelphia included *Iris* and *Fledermaus*. Of several revivals, only *L'Elisir d'Amore* has lived.

Needless to say, the threat to excommunicate Philadelphia never materialized. Brooklyn automatically disqualified itself by the loss of the Academy of Music, which was destroyed by fire on November 30, 1903.

When Conried's term was finished and the record could be seen in retrospect, the two milestones of his five years were admitted to be his production of *Parsifal* and the exploitation of Caruso. At first the road enjoyed neither. The tenor sang five times in Philadelphia in his—and Conried's—initial season, but journeyed no farther afield because Conried had contracted for too little of his time. Neither did the bruited *Parsifal* reach the circuits until 1904-05.

The first tour of the Conried Metropolitan Opera Company pushed no farther west than Cincinnati. When the German wing occupied itself in New York and Philadelphia in early March, the Italians and French split a week between Buffalo and Washington; then the entire company traveled to Chicago for a fortnight. Two performances in Cincinnati, five in Pittsburgh, sixteen in Boston and single stands in Providence, Hartford, Springfield and New Haven completed the round.

Nor did Conried leave the bounds of the conventional in his repertory and principals, but drew heavily on his inheritance from Grau. Calvé's Carmen led the parade numerically with eight performances; *Faust,* starring a new and not overpopular soprano, Aino Ackté, ranked second with seven. Ternina's Tosca, Isolde and three Brünnhildes, Sembrich's Violetta and

Rosina, Gadski's *Walküre* Brünnhilde, Pamina and Countess Almaviva remained favorite ladies in the provinces, while Plançon continued to enchant auditors with his sauve Méphistophélès, and Van Rooy still seemed the ideal Wotan and Kurvenal (except to the *Pittsburgh Commercial-Gazette* reviewer, who remembered Fischer too clearly).

Sembrich no longer had to reckon with "that pestiferous little Scheff" in *Zauberflöte,* the *Chicago Inter-Ocean* pointed out, referring to an incident the previous year. Papageno (Campanari) and his Papagena (Scheff) had so charmed the audience that applause for them persisted even after Sembrich made her entrance for the Queen of the Night's second solo. Hisses to quiet the applause increased the bedlam. Sembrich, believing the hisses to be for her, ran furiously from the stage and refused to sing again. Newspapers waxed hot in partisanship over the affair, several taking the prima donna's part, others the soubrette's.

Sembrich accomplished both arias with éclat this time. The Papagena was the long-suffering Camille Seygard, who seldom earned enough applause to hold up any performance. On this occasion she was preoccupied with costume changes, for she sang the First Lady as well.

Several beloved prima donnas absented themselves from Conried's first season—Nordica and Eames chief among them. Melba had been off the roster since 1901. Both Schumann-Heink and Scheff were trying their wings in comic opera; the soprano's held steady, but the contralto's let her down with a thump. All but Scheff returned for a season or two before Conried's banner fell.

At the end of his initial year, further to unbalance the seesawing roster, Calvé and Gadski departed, airing their grievances widely. Calvé by now considered herself beyond discipline, and Gadski stated plainly in Philadelphia that "vocal artists cannot be bullied, driven or whipped into getting around for 8 a.m. rehearsal like the little German actors of Conried's little German theatre."

Gadski would return after two seasons; the Frenchwoman never. Meanwhile Conried added three personages who took root in America's affections from the first.

The advent of the statuesque Olive Fremstad ranked only just below that of Caruso and *Parsifal* in a New York critic's eyes; the road soon agreed. As Lilli Lehmann had been introduced to the American public in the incongruous role of Carmen, so her pupil, a later embodiment of the towering Wagnerian heroines, first appeared before an out-of-town audience as Santuzza. Philadelphia remained cool to her charms, justifiably after *Cavalleria,* but less understandably when she had shown what Chicago called an "ideal" Venus, and a Sieglinde that both Boston and Chicago were to reverence.

The Quaker City reviewers woke up to the new sensation in their midst only after Fremstad's Carmen in 1905, another role that she quickly cast aside in America, although it had been uniquely her own in Germany. The *Ledger* accounted the Swedish-American's gypsy portrayal "startling, vivid, dominating."

In the midst of a "very bad" performance of *Tannhäuser*—largely the fault of Alfred Hertz, the *Boston Transcript* insisted, "the frightful din being in no way due to exuberance of temperament but solely to coarseness and rudeness of concept"—Fremstad's Venus stood out as "graceful and agreeable to look at." Above all, continued the critic, "she sang with exquisite skill, intelligence and a lovely tone."

Edyth Walker, a young American, sang Amneris, Ortrud, Brangaene and Erda to the deep satisfaction of Conried's first tour cities, and settled down to a three-year occupation of her own special niche.

Otto Goritz, who fulfilled the promise of a long stay (until the German repertory was cast out in World War I) surprised Chicago by his "truly exquisite voice" as Wolfram. Boston thought he lacked "purity of vocal style" as Papageno and presented "an even more disagreeable Alberich than most, though less vocally tiresome." The baritone at last came into his own in Pittsburgh, where an encore was demanded for his Papageno aria.

Pittsburghers did not seem unduly swayed by the exhortations of the Metropolitan's new "public relations" expert; they had lived with him for several years and had become accustomed to "Schlotterbeckia."

After apostrophizing Grau's 1902 production of *Aida* as "shades of the bejeweled orchid, the golden jasmine and the fabulous asphodel," the *Post* critic asked himself rhetorically if he had not been too enthusiastic. His answer: "Not so, not one whit. The materialistic is no longer everything with us . . . an ideal or two are not amiss . . . so welcome thrice, Lord Enthusiasm; hail, hail chief Optimist! *bas, bas* Mephisto Pessimist!"

After one of Alfred Hertz' typically energetic performances, Schlotterbeck headed his review: *"Donnerwetter! Donnerwetter! zerplatzen, meine Herren.* . . . Hertz' ebullient temperament never intended him for a two-armed man!"

It was Schlotterbeck, of course, who found "the very air drunken" at *La Fille du Régiment.* "It staggered, heaved, reeled and rolled. Sembrich, that seven-mooned coloratura, was stung by the intoxicating currents and from her throat issued such tones as put the flush of deep-seated envy upon the rich *limpidezza* of the mellow-voiced flute."

The *Post* critic had been quoted in 1902 at some length in the *New York Sun*:

"Nervously, even violently intent all day yesterday were the heartstrings of nearly 10,000 opera patrons who attended two presentations. . . . Quickened was the flow of blood by the thrill of heaven-scaling ensembles and of solo performances that were spangled with the diamond light of pristine brilliance. High were the beating of the waves of enthusiasm which washed from the auditorium across the footlights and immersed soloists, orchestra and chorus with results most infectious . . ." and so on and so on.

The *Sun* commented, in the fashion of today's *New Yorker*:

". . . in the waves, what happened to the footlights?"

Schlotterbeck once described Calvé's Carmen as a "lovely, seductive, devilish octopus, supple as leather, cold as night, terrible in its very softness," and then confessed that "superlatives falter." Fortunately for the *Post's* readers, and later for the recipients of 100,000 Metropolitan prospectuses, neither superlatives nor involved, inverted, infinitely ornamental sentences ever ceased to flow from this eager pen until its work was done.

2. THE GUILELESS FOOL WHO MADE A FORTUNE

Heinrich Conried had thrown the main burden of his first season on the pirated Wagnerian Festival Play, *Parsifal*, surviving the storm of remonstrance from Bayreuth and the concerted attack of a number of clergymen who condemned the work as sacrilegious. This double-barreled opposition, far from throwing a damper on Conried's daring project, only fanned the fires of curiosity to ravening proportions. *Parsifal* became the thing to see, regardless of the doubled prices Conried charged at the Metropolitan, having cannily withheld his *coup* from the regular subscription lists.

The manager fed the excitement on the road by examining local stages in 1904 with the view to the necessary conversion for the spectacle and by allowing the controversy to rage on over his leonine head. By the time the Guileless Fool was ready to travel in 1905, the chosen sixteen cities had been raised to a state of exaltation—or, as some put it, reduced to a state of drivel.

The amount of newsprint pressed into *Parsifal's* service, the lectures, the "readings," the analyses, the debates—"Is *Parsifal* a religious expression or only a fable?"—exceeded any manifestations ever before summoned up for a cultural event. The countrywide, quasi-devotional *brouhaha* attending *Parsifal's* introduction in nineteen performances has never since been equaled, even in this day of streamlined public relations and network communications.

A prospectus devised by Gustave Schlotterbeck set the tone, a nice blend of the lurid and the reverent, the material and the artistic. Thirty-five of its sixty-four pages told the story of Conried, his Opera School and the tour. Twenty-nine exhorted readers to buy choice merchandise, chiefly pianos, although corsets ("Kabo's have no brass eyelets"), Mumm's "Extra Dry" and "Selected Brut," bathroom fixtures and the "Wonderful White—ideal car for shopping and for evening use—" begged genteelly for attention.

Parsifal had been reserved exclusively for performance at Bayreuth, Cosima Wagner had protested at the first inkling of Conried's proposal, which she condemned as illegal and irreverent. The manager persisted; Wagner's widow resorted to court action. Conried argued that no copyright protected the work outside of the continent: that he had found *Parsifal* scores on the open market in London. As for irreverence, "it is morally inadmissible that a handful of people, even though they should be Wagner's heirs, can decide whether a great, immortal work shall be revealed or denied to an admiring

world. All humanity has an ideal right to the creations of its greatest minds."
Bayreuth had made no protest, he added, when the work had been given in
concert form in Brooklyn under Anton Seidl in 1890.

To the stricture of the clergy Conried countered that there had been nothing wrong with accepting money for tickets to witness *Parsifal* at Bayreuth
—therefore it had been a theatrical performance and not a church service.

The Metropolitan manager stood on secure legal grounds, though his position may have been ethically indefensible, as many continued to believe even
after the New York court found in his favor. Cosima never relented; her
wrath spilled over on the singers as well. Any who participated in the rapine
would never be allowed to darken the shrine of the master again or sing in
the Festspielhaus.

This interdiction chiefly affected Alois Burgstaller, a notable exponent of
the title role. Others, too, among them Olive Fremstad, who soon made the
role of Kundry almost exclusively her own, feared the "Bayreuth curse" and
anticipated some manifestation at every performance.

The odd hour at which the curtain was set to rise threw Americans into a
dither of excitement and speculation. How to dress for an event that began
at 5:30 (when the tired business man was usually just leaving his office), ad-
journed for an hour and a half and then resumed at 8:30?

Not only was *Parsifal* the most esoteric entertainment ever offered the
American public, it was also the most expensive since Patti's ill-fated tour of
1881. The top price of $10 for a seat added a fillip of exclusivity that appealed
to snobbish society.

The *"Parsifal* tour" extended to the West Coast, embracing Boston, Pittsburgh, Cincinnati, Chicago, Minneapolis, Omaha, Kansas City and Salt Lake
City on the way. Boston and Chicago witnessed the "novelty" twice each
during a week's span; San Francisco asked for and received three performances; the other towns were content with one each. After Los Angeles, the
fourteen additional productions that Conried carried thus far were shipped
home and *Parsifal* journeyed on alone, returning east through most of the
towns Grau had visited in 1901.

As anticipation rose to fever heat, Conried learned with dismay that his
piracy had borne strange fruit—an imitator. Henry W. Savage, a defeated
candidate for the director's Metropolitan post, had paid him the highest
compliment. Retooling his American opera company for a big job, he had
produced an English version of the disputed Wagner work and was blithely
touring the country, preceding Conried into most of his towns by a slim
margin, sometimes only days. The inevitable comparisons did not always
favor the Metropolitan's production. Taking Boston to task for preferring
Savage's "chromo" to his genuine production, Conried sounded not like
a "petulant person," Philip Hale thought, but "expressed the deep-rooted
grief of a philanthropist who finds those whom he would benefit indifferent
and ungrateful."

Conried maintained this lofty sense of injured dignity until the company
reached Chicago. There, to add salt to the Metropolitan manager's wound,
Savage cheerily issued a challenge to a *"Parsifal* duel," setting the stakes at

a fair box-office intake, $8,000. Conried "Ignored the Defi," as a *Chicago Chronicle* headline put it, but could not resist launching a few sizzling verbal rockets at his adversary, "shaking his lion's mane" the while:

"Savage's challenge is so ridiculous, so silly, I don't care to discuss it. . . . He only wants to advertise his production. I have no desire to help. . . . He has copied my production in every detail. Why? Good business, of course. I could have made a million last year if I had sent *Parsifal* on the road. But artistic aims prohibited me."

The larger stages he occupied gave Conried an advantage but Savage commanded greater mobility. Even with Eugène Castel-Bert's advance visits, many stages resisted transformation. Surprisingly the Chicago Auditorium with its hydraulically controlled platforms could not furnish the illusion of Kundry rising out of the depths at Klingsor's call. Burns Mantle, the *Inter-Ocean's* theatre "newsman" of the day, considered this lack a good excuse for not asking Nordica (who divided the role with Fremstad in Boston, Chicago and San Francisco) to ride up on a trap door.

While the Metropolitan's second act showed an improvement on Bayreuth's, in Chicago's opinion, the transformation barely equaled Savage's. Awkwardness of stage management made illusion difficult to preserve: Kundry's couch was pushed on stage while a piece of flower scenery was pulled off; the line for the spear remained plainly visible throughout, and the final transformation from the enchanted garden to withered desert was accomplished by merely raising the flower scenery in full light.

Both productions boasted a winding panorama similar to Bayreuth's. As Gurnemanz and Parsifal strolled toward the Temple of the Grail, the scene passed rapidly behind them—when it worked properly. In Kansas City, the Metropolitan's drop curtain caught on the panorama at an embarrassing moment, whereas Savage's transformation in the Willis Wood Theatre had been "a triumph of stagecraft."

One mishap after another plagued Conried's troupe in Kansas City. The train arrived an hour late and could not be accommodated in the depot proper but stopped at a tower near the south end. In the eyes of the *Journal* reporter, the scene resembled a nightmare. Baggage was piled up anyhow; no porters showed up. The singers were forced to walk seventy-five yards through a confusing tangle of tracks, trains and baggage, dodging trucks and fighting thick black smoke that came down from the engine "in ominous clouds."

A truck barely missed Fremstad's maid; the prima donna screamed and jumped against a train coach. She would not move until the reporter promised to escort her up the dark and narrow passage to the station.

Abuse in three languages spouted from the tired, hungry, frantic singers. After another tangle of confusion on the carriage platform, the crowd finally dispersed. The *Star* representative followed Fremstad, Burgstaller and Robert Blass to the Midland Hotel. The two men were assigned a room together.

"Not for us!" expostulated Blass.

"Sing together we will; room together we won't!" echoed Burgstaller.

The Midland's orchestra was playing "Back, Back to Baltimore" at the moment. The singers did not recognize the tune but found significance in the words, and forthwith departed to the Baltimore Hotel.

The gremlins had only just begun their mischief. Because of "faulty stage construction" the performance was delayed a half hour. Three times the trumpets sounded (a Bayreuth touch that deeply impressed American cities); three times disappointment followed. At the fourth summons, the curtain rose. But the damage had been done. At 6:45, when intermission was scheduled, Kansas City rose in a block and left the hall. Patrons had made dinner reservations in swanky restaurants, the *Journal* explained, and "no *Parsifal* neophyte was going to permit his 'ham and' to grow cold, even though the bass viols droned and the bugles blew and grand opera stars sang their heads off!"

Castel-Bert had discovered that Parsifal's spear could not be made to stand upright in the Kansas City Convention Hall stage floor, so he ordered a hole to be bored and a bracing inserted below stage; then he warned Burgstaller, the Parsifal.

The tenor accordingly sought the prepared spot and carefully plunged the spear into the hole. To his horror, the shaft sank out of sight up to its head. Someone had removed the bracing. Poor Parsifal reached down and drew out the weapon, but he could not make it stand. Finally he tipped it like Pisa's tower and finished the scene. But the audience laughed; some of the devotional atmosphere was dissipated.

Nevertheless, *Parsifal* was accounted a great experience, and one which Kansas City treasured in memory side by side with Caruso's first appearance in *Pagliacci*. Barrett and Oakford, who had assumed responsibility for the engagement, established something of a record for Kansas City, with box-office figures that compared favorably to those in most of the tour cities. Because Convention Hall was so commodious, the top price was reduced to $4, the lowest for *Parsifal* on the tour; still the gross amounted to $12,622, $122 more than Kronberg had paid for three performances in 1899.

The controversy over *Parsifal's* religious content still raged. In spite of the humorous *contretemps* in Kansas City, the *Journal* critic vouchsafed for the atmosphere of "some great religious festival in a cathedral" that prevailed.

In the *Chicago Examiner* Harriet Monroe described the performance as a "delicious spectacle," but averred that *Parsifal,* "instead of being a simple act of faith (Wagner never was completely contrite) is a statuesque, medieval pose like Tolstoy's *Resurrection*. It lacks high sincerity, profound conviction. . . . Wagner does not in his deepest heart believe in his hero. . . . *Parsifal* is always a pageant, never in the least a rite."

The *Los Angeles Express* critic, one of the few who adopted a frivolous tone, declared that "Males find it hard to understand why Parsifal should resist . . . that Kundry Kiss! It made Parsifal clutch his stomach with a gesture that expressed intense enjoyment or intense pain—one did not know which."

The *San Francisco Examiner* produced a gem that Schlotterbeck, recognizing a fellow embroiderer, culled to use in subsequent advertisements:

"*Parsifal* transcends hysteria. The English language, full as it is and

founded on great conceptions, has but one word which covers such a performance—'gigantic.' *Parsifal* takes possession of you and holds you as a
great horror or a great beauty would. You cannot think of anything else, you
cannot smile and whisper to your neighbor, you cannot frame your thoughts.
As the wonderful symphony beats in on you, sex and individuality disappear
in the maelstrom of the allegory, for you are Amfortas, you are Kundry, you
are Parsifal, you are Klingsor."

Birmingham, where this example of the "great conceptions" of the English
language was most prominently displayed, reacted timidly. In spite of advance fanfare, $7 and $10 tickets moved sluggishly. On April 25, two days
before the performance, Conried reduced all orchestra seats to $5. This stimu-
lated sales in Birmingham, the penultimate city on tour, but stirred resent-
ment in Nashville, where the final performance was scheduled in the Ven-
dome Theatre on April 29.

Whatever he may have yielded to his rival in stagecraft, Conried bested
Savage in the musical elements of his *Parsifal* production. Walter Henry
Rothwell proved no match for the exuberant Hertz, who commanded a peerless orchestra of sixty. Florence Wickham, Louise Kirkby-Lunn and Hanna
Mara, Savage's alternates as Kundry, and Alois Pennarini and Francis Mac-
lennan, who sang Parsifal, lacked the full artistic stature of Conried's protagonists for those roles—Fremstad and Nordica, Burgstaller and Dippel.

In other parts, Van Rooy and Goritz (Amfortas), Journet and Mühlmann
(Titurel), Blass and Journet (Gurnemanz) and Mühlmann and Goritz
(Klingsor) overweighted their opposite numbers: Johannes Bischoff and
Franz Egenieff, Robert Kent Parker, Putnam Griswold and Ottley Cran-
ston, and Homer Lind and J. Parker Coombs.

William Foster Apthorp, in his last year with the *Boston Transcript*, had
said of Burgstaller in *Meistersinger* that he "convinced one before five minutes that he *was* Walther. As with Irving's Hamlet, one instinctively transfers
the actor's peculiarities to the character and so takes them for granted." Burgstaller similarly accomplished identification with Parsifal; he seemed the
character to the life.

One performance in San Francisco subjected the tenor to a severe strain,
as the headlines in the *Chronicle* revealed:

"Sings Role with a Breaking Heart—Burgstaller, Bowed with Grief at
Mother's Death, Lives His Part."

"Few of the thousands who listened . . . entranced, enraptured . . . knew
that his heart was breaking for the love and the loss of his dear little peasant
mother far away," the sentimental account rambled on. "She lay dead in the
simple mountain home in Upper Bavaria, the home from which her boy was
lured to the bigger world because he, as none other, could sing the greatest
role the master of the world of song created."

Those who did know watched the tenor with particular sympathy in the
passage where Kundry tells Parsifal of his mother's anguish and death. Several viewers claimed that both Kundry (Nordica) and Parsifal wept, the
tears of the temptress and the "reine Thor" mingling throughout the ordeal.

Fremstad's triumph as Kundry was complete everywhere except in her home town. Although she had not been born in Minnesota, Minneapolis had fallen into the habit of claiming the Scandinavian diva because of her youthful days there, and professed to be hurt at what it termed her later superciliousness. This opinion grieved Fremstad, who tried very hard to counteract it, but lacked ease in a situation that called for tact and unbending.

The queenly soprano demonstrated "the full fruition of her vocal gifts" in the opinion of W. B. Chamberlain of the *Journal*, "but she was not as alluring in face, attitude and voice as her predecessor (Kirkby-Lunn), who surpassed her in vitalizing the contradictory character of Kundry. In the defiant and morose aspects of the character Fremstad seemed more nearly ideal."

On this occasion the town's interest was divided between the performances and the new building that sheltered them. "There is no fellow to the Minneapolis Auditorium," the *Journal* exulted, "either in ancient temple or modern theatre. It is not a copy of any building, though of classic style, rather a consistent adaptation of Grecian Doric to modern requirements." Its 2,507 "conventional folding opera-type green plush seats" were satisfactorily occupied during the Metropolitan season.

Amid the columns devoted to symbolism, staging, local behavior and virtues of the individual singers, comparatively little space was allotted to *Parsifal's* music itself. Few critics ventured out into such dangerous depths. Philip Hale's successor on the *Boston Journal* found that "after the thin, small voice of played-out Italian opera, the majestic fullness of the colossal German" was welcome. But Hale himself, though he thought the performance one of uncommon merit, stood fast on his anti-Wagner promontory. "Some may wax hysterical over *Parsifal* and with uprolled eyes declare it to be a divine message. Others, and we of them, believe the work as a whole to be the last effort of the tired brain of an old man."

A few who, like Glenn Dillard Gunn of the *Chicago Inter-Ocean*, had worshiped at the Bayreuth shrine, contented themselves with comparisons: "Hertz' tempos were much slower than Bayreuth, but he was justified." Those to whom *Parsifal* came as a new and overwhelming experience, even Miss Eugenie Wehrmann, "the South's great musical genius" who wrote a special column for the *Houston Chronicle*, were inclined to hedge or gush. Miss Wehrmann hedged.

Marie Alice Phillips in the *Atlanta Journal* chose the flowery path, describing the music as "a marvelous deep rumbling of wonderful harmonies, which fairly makes one gasp for breath and struggle to keep down a creeping fear of falling under the magic of Klingsor's black art."

The perplexing question of applause arose in each city. Omaha found it difficult to restrain enthusiasm at the entrance of Parsifal in spite of requests that any demonstration be confined to the second act. Chicago hissed down the few extroverts who were determined to respond at forbidden junctures; Kansas City thought that Wagner would have been heartbroken at the noisy citizens who expressed themselves too freely. Los Angeles refused to follow the "Wagner cult" to absolute silence, while Houston proclaimed its rugged individualism by justifying applause as "the American way," and upholding those "whom the worshipers would class among the *hoi polloi*."

Equally vexing was the problem of what the *Los Angeles Express* termed "pre-digestion."

"I hope to get something out of it," a woman in white was quoted by the *Minneapolis Journal.* "I've been to all the lectures and the English version and played the motives—haven't thought to read anything else for weeks."

"Aren't you afraid you're overtrained?" asked her companion.

Many business men—and some of their wives—solved the puzzle of what to wear by going home at the intermission, snatching a bite of food and changing into evening clothes for the final session. L. E. Behymer, the Los Angeles impresario, published a request that evening dress be the rule for the entire performance, but "Bee's advice was not taken," said the *Express,* and "many business suits appeared in the evening." Handsome, light dresses, "but high-necked," formed the prevailing Minneapolis style; a minister remarked that "no one wants the consciousness of his own or neighbors' clothes thrust in between him and such high ideas." Omaha indulged in "gilded luxury, but somewhat modified."

Despite its high prices, *Parsifal* commanded such crowds as had rarely been drawn together in the tour cities. Conried had gambled successfully: when his books were closed on the 1905 tour, the Guileless Fool had earned $167,000, probably an all-time record for any single opera production.

3. LOGE BRINGS DOWN THE HOUSE

No black-winged shadow brushed across the sky to warn the Metropolitan Opera voyagers that the spring of 1906 would be different from any other. No omen darkened the spirits of the superstitious opera stars.

The annual hegira began sunnily enough in Baltimore, where an opera-hungry crowd, eager to emerge from the gloom cast by the previous year's calamitous fire, paid $19,666 to cheer Caruso in two appearances. For the first time in what was to be an enduring custom, the opera played in the Lyric Theatre, which normally held 2,300. More than 3,000 tested the elasticity of its walls when Caruso sang Faust. The tramp of feet drowned out the tenor's first silvery notes; a dozen women fainted.

Washington greeted the new tenor with more decorum if no less enthusiasm. A distinguished visitor backstage sought out the singing hero of the evening, but Caruso thought it a joke that the President of the United States should be asking to see him, and ignored the summons. His embarrassment when he came face to face with President Roosevelt, who was waiting patiently, mounted to the point of anguish. "T. R." heaped further coals of fire on the penitent singer by asking him to sing at the White House and presenting him with a large, autographed photograph, which Caruso cherished thenceforth.

Pittsburgh, attempting a full week instead of the usual four or five performances, had to admit that it had ordered more opera than it could digest; only $43,000 of an expected $70,000 materialized.

Chicago's week had sold out, three Caruso appearances bringing $12,600 each, but the total lacked $5,000 of the previous year's, when *Parsifal* was an additional drawing card.

Conried told Chicago bluntly that he could not afford to experiment with further performances in that city. Then he returned to New York, allowing Ernest Goerlitz, his second-in-command, and Charles W. Strine, his new touring manager, to carry on.

St. Louis ran a lower temperature than anticipated. Goerlitz, echoing Abbey and Grau, pronounced a malediction with threats of boycott, adding sarcastically that perhaps the town would prefer *Buster Brown* to the opera. St. Louis retorted that bringing the opera during Holy Week was an insult.

When Kansas City turned in only $8,585 for two performances, Goerlitz' temper had worn off and his scolding took on an almost perfunctory tone. His thoughts already anticipated a California triumph.

In the early hours of April 13, the caravan turned its face to the West. Only three principals were not on the special train: Lillian Nordica, who had gone no farther than Chicago; Heinrich Knote, the German tenor, and Lina Abarbanell, the ingénue from the Irving Place Theatre who had been the company's first Hänsel. Philip Crispano, a property man who later headed this complicated department, also missed the trip, fidgeting restlessly through convalescence from an emergency appendectomy.

Conried had known what he was doing when he sent the company to San Francisco again. The Golden Gate had rewarded him richly, its citizens subscribing $120,000 in advance of the two weeks' opera season. Goerlitz expressed his gratification to the local management and to Frank Garlichs, the company treasurer, and passed through the iron door onto the stage.

In the unshaded rays of a single work-lamp, the magnificent pillars and golden lions of Solomon's throne room glimmered faintly; all lay in readiness for the arrival of the Queen of Sheba.

Historians were to write of the Mission Street Opera House that its curtain had risen on only 255 nights of grand opera in thirty years. Tonight's *Queen of Sheba* would mark its 254th.

Goerlitz, unaware of the imminence of destiny, stepped to the footlights and gazed up through the dusky audience chamber to where a proud crystal chandelier shivered through the deep shadows. Then he decided to make a final check of the storage rooms.

In any other city only one or two productions would be trucked into the opera house at one time, but in San Francisco the long, daily barge haul from the Southern Pacific depot in Oakland was deemed impractical. Conried's settings for the nineteen tour operas consequently reposed under one roof.

Disappointingly *The Queen of Sheba* possessed no allure for San Francisco that night. "Opera Crowd Cold," ran Ashton Stevens' headline.

The second night told a happier story. Caruso broke the ice; his sultry, passionate Don José swept away all the reserve of the San Francisco audience,

Fremstad's Carmen seemed pale and overshadowed. Later she claimed that she had sung with effort, fighting a strange lethargy that amounted almost to a premonition on that April 17.

Caruso felt no such foreboding. With customary expansiveness he held court in his dressing room, then went to bed late at the Palace Hotel contented with the evening's éclat. Shaken out of a light slumber by an unusual noise, which he described as if someone had thrown himself on the bed in the next room and then hit the wall with a "biff, boof br-r-am!" he dashed across the heaving floor and pulled up the window shade.

What he saw and heard made him tremble with fear—buildings toppling against the pearly dawn sky like toys knocked over by a petulant child; screams and shouts of terror. He remained spellbound for a long, suspended moment, in which he thought of "40,000 different things" and he seemed to sing the whole of *Carmen* all over again. At last he gathered his faculties and called for his valet. Martino came immediately and solicitously helped his master into a few clothes.

In the corridor Caruso encountered Antonio Scotti. The baritone had awakened with a feeling of seasickness. He reached for the light button, but no electricity responded. When he tried to unlock the door, the key was gone; he finally found it on the floor amid scraps of fallen plaster.

On the sixth floor Bessie Abott, the new protégée of Jean de Reszke, who as Micaela had vowed in song only a few hours before not to fear anything, was nearly thrown out of bed. Everything rocked more violently than a ship at sea. She heard a noise that she could not understand—"indescribable rumblings and grinding sounds, as if bones of earth were cracking and being crushed in the jaws of some giant monster."

As Miss Abott tumbled out of bed great strips of plaster peeled off from the ceiling in grotesque coils, writhing through the room. The crystal chandelier hurtled past her and broke into shards on the floor. She cut her feet cruelly in gaining the door. Her maid joined her in the stumbling, panicky crowd on the staircases.

No one seemed to know what had happened. Miss Abott was ashamed to hear herself ask idiotic questions, joining the babbling chorus that echoed through the Palace. Across the street a fire had broken out; its heat penetrated scorchingly even into the lobby. Miss Abott decided to return to her room to dress.

Cursing his lame leg, Alfred Hertz pulled on a pair of trousers and a coat, ducked the falling chandelier, clutched his room key, numbered 615, and hobbled painfully down five flights.

Down the hall, Edyth Walker's trunk landed in the middle of her bed a moment after she had vacated it. Her piano danced awkwardly into the middle of the tipsy room. She hurriedly dressed and snatched up a sealskin jacket and a small sofa pillow. Several interminable moments passed before she could wrench open her door, which had bent and jammed.

Marion Weed, also from the sixth floor, reached the ground in time to see the Call Building a few doors away buckle and fall. She dashed back upstairs, packed a trunk, and lugged it down, only to abandon it because falling timber barred the exits.

Josephine Jacoby, another American singer, disregarded the hubbub in the Palace lobby and hastened back to her room to dress fully. She packed a bag with her jewels, got into a brown tailored suit, but slipped her feet into Frasquita's flimsy golden slippers.

Farther uptown in fashionable Union Square the thirteen-story St. Francis Hotel sheltered three Metropolitan singers. From a room on the top floor Andreas Dippel, the company's old reliable, looked at his heavy gold pocket watch. Its hour hand stood at 5; its minute hand moved jerkily from 12 to 13. He hurried down twelve flights, stopping at the sixth floor to see if Marcella Sembrich was safe.

The little Polish prima donna thought the world had come to an end. Shocked and crying she ran out of her suite in her night clothes and bare feet; only coming to her senses when a gentleman gallantly placed an overcoat around her quivering shoulders. Between temblors her maid helped her into underclothes and a light blue suit.

Pol Plançon, awake in the dawn, suddenly experienced the sensation of a bird in a swinging cage. For once neglecting his usual finicky elegance, he appeared in Union Square in underwear and overcoat.

Preferring private luxury to a hotel, Emma Eames had taken up residence with friends on Taylor Street atop Nob Hill. Her coolness and sense of superiority to fate persisted through the hours that followed. Her first thought after she had extricated herself from the peril of a heavily canopied bedstead was of the matinee performance of *Le Nozze di Figaro*, in which she was billed as the Countess. She tried vainly to telephone Goerlitz and decided there would be no matinee.

Individual as always, Olive Fremstad had leased a suite at St. Dunstan's Hotel in Van Ness Avenue, some distance from her colleagues. The tremor that shook the façade from her hotel loosened hardly a petal from her crimson roses of the night before. As she picked her way down stairs made rickety and railless, the flowers obsessed her. She sent a porter up to fetch them. For several hours she hugged the long-stemmed blossoms to her heart as she sat in the little park across the street and breathed the sulphurous air. Then she gave the flowers one by one to the swarming refugees.

In a less pretentious hostelry called The Oaks, orchestra players and comprimario singers fled for their lives amid showers of masonry. Taurino Parvis, a young baritone with two years' experience under Conried, managed to don his underwear and tuck a precious violin under his arm. The baritone Eugene Dufriche and his wife, a member of the orchestra, had thoughts only for the expensive Érard harp, which reposed in the Opera House. They set off toward Third and Mission Streets, but they were too late.

Goerlitz, like Eames, was concerned primarily with his schedule. He found Strine, assigned him to look after the women and round up the company in Union Square, then hastened to the Opera House.

In this first hour of the death struggle of a glamorous and bewitching city, no one spared a thought to the bundles of morning newspapers already dumped beside newsstands. Their front pages told that a great fund had been raised for sufferers from the recent eruption of Mt. Vesuvius.

Caruso would not learn for many days that Blanche Partington of the *Call* wanted to rechristen the night's opera *Don José* in his honor. Fremstad would not know that Ashton Stevens of the *Examiner* had called her "dutchy." Bessie Abott remained happily ignorant of Stevens' appellation of "phantom soprano."

Caruso and Fremstad and Abott and all of their *confrères* had assumed unrehearsed roles in a more exigent drama. Few, however, thought in dramatic terms; only Hertz is credited with comparing the holocaust to *Götterdämmerung*. The 300 members of the opera company were preoccupied with reality.

Along the 270-mile trail of the San Andreas Fault, the earth cracked open from northwest to southeast that morning, shaking and grinding and tearing at everything in its path. San Franciscans knew it instantly for what it was; they had experienced the lesser stirrings of this giant before. The visitors learned fast.

In that brief and terrible April morning, water mains, gas mains, sewers, telephone connections, street car lines and telegraph cables snapped. Live wires were exposed; stoves overturned; flues cracked. As Jack London, a devoted San Franciscan, wrote for *Collier's Weekly* a few days later:

"All the cunning adjustments of a twentieth century city had been smashed by the earthquake. . . . All the shrewd contrivances and safeguards of men had been thrown out of gear by thirty seconds' twitching of the earth-crust."

Tongues of flame leaped into the air from a score of tindery frame shacks south of Market Street. Within minutes Loge assumed supreme command. Hoses were limp and empty from the beginning. Dynamite remained the only weapon against the fierce, consuming element.

The straggling file of refugees to the north and west became a torrent: toiling up hills, choking streets, spilling into small green oases of squares and parks, settling down to watch in dazed disbelief as destruction came ever closer, moving on at last when the rain of ash grew thicker and the suffocating smoke heralded the hungry flames.

A second vicious shock lasted half as long but the earth continued to shudder for twenty-four hours.

Around the experiences of the opera visitors legends grew like weeds, nourished by inflamed imaginations and the fallibility of the human memory. Each informant added a new "fact."

Legends clustered thickest around the chubby person of the chief tenor. Caruso was seen in many strange circumstances. In a fur coat, with a towel around his neck, he sobbed on Hertz' shoulder. Scantily clad, he sat on a valise in the street, begging for a pair of trousers. Antonio Scotti saw him come out of his room fully dressed. Caruso himself remembered that his valet helped him don socks, shoes, trousers and a coat.

Campanari saw the valet "with absolutely nothing on," capering about, crying in Italian for a towel. Caruso remembered him as cool and self-possessed, decently clothed.

When the tenor first realized what had happened, he was heard trying out his high C through the corridors in the Palace Hotel. His voice had failed him.

Alexander Krasoff, a Russian tenor who had renewed his acquaintance of 1905 with Caruso after the *Carmen* performance, crossed the Bay from Berkeley to keep a breakfast engagement with the tenor. Caruso had promised him an autographed picture as a souvenir. Krasoff could not find his friend at the Palace, and sadly returned home.

In the lobby of the St. Francis Hotel Caruso was overheard (by the photographer Arnold Genthe) to mutter: " 'Ell of a place! 'Ell of a place! I never come back here." At the time he was dressed in pajamas and a fur coat and was smoking the inevitable cigarette. He compared Vesuvius favorably with San Francisco.

Caruso had reached the St. Francis after many painful incidents. While the faithful Martino ran up and down stairs, fetching the last of three small trunks, Caruso stood on Market Street guarding the other two. A rough man (Chinese by some accounts) tried to steal one. Caruso yelled for help, and a soldier, recognizing him as the opera singer, made the thief "skidoo."

The tenor wandered aimlessly all day. His and Scotti's luggage, according to the baritone, was conveyed on a wagon to the house of a Dr. Bachman, outside the danger zone, where Caruso lay under a tree in the Bachman yard all night.

Caruso remembered sleeping on the hard ground, but in Lafayette Square or Golden Gate Park. Wherever he walked, the precious photograph of Teddy Roosevelt went with him. The talisman served as a passport into Lafayette Square. A soldier halted Caruso at the point of a bayonet, but when he glimpsed the huge picture said, "Any friend of T. R.'s is a friend of mine," and showed the tenor to a place on the grass.

Martino kept track of his master and the luggage as well, and when Thursday dawned, produced a frail cart with a horse and a man to drive it. Perched on top of his three perilously rescued trunks, the world's greatest tenor moved slowly through the ruins of a city he would never see again.

Once in Oakland, Caruso opened his trunks and shared with any who needed—and could wear—his raiment. Hertz arrived in New York wearing Caruso's shirt.

Another legend pictured Fremstad as a kind of a Viking Florence Nightingale. She saved an invalid woman from the third floor of her hotel, then like a ministering angel she tended the wounded in the park nearby, spending money recklessly for food, wine and bandages and working from daylight till night without food. She neither confirmed nor denied the pretty story.

With her trunks safely in the street, the prima donna served coffee and bread over them. The improvised tables were carted away to the Oakland ferry on Thursday with the help of St. Dunstan's manager, a Mr. Wheedon.

The name of Bessie Abott was also inscribed in San Francisco's book of heroines. Miss Abott and her maid, lucky to find a carriage, soon drove to a friend's home on Telegraph Hill and left their trunks. Then the singer made the long pilgrimage to an improvised hospital at Mechanics Pavilion, opposite the shattered City Hall. The lack of water proved an almost insuperable hindrance to the care for the wounded.

Everywhere she saw deeds of heroism. Everyone, she thought, forgot himself; the city was transformed into a place of heroes.

Miss Abott's friends had chosen the wrong side of Telegraph Hill. The Neapolitan fishermen saved their cottages at the top by soaking blankets in Chianti, but the singer's friends possessed no wine cellar. Their house and $25,000 worth of Miss Abott's possessions were lost.

Edyth Walker found her way to Golden Gate Park after a harrowing day. She reassured the frightened chorus women who clustered in Union Square like lost sheep. The contralto lent her sofa pillow to an exhausted woman.

Alfred Hertz found a German saloon and nourished himself on cheese and sausage and beer on Wednesday. But before he could make a second meal Mayor Schmitz' martial law had closed the haven; Hertz was obliged to subsist on sardines and cocoa. He wandered to the zoo in Golden Gate Park and slept uneasily in an abandoned street car, frightened by the roars of the disturbed lions. The self-control and discipline of the San Franciscans deeply impressed this German drill master.

Marion Weed, with a fine disregard for distances and geography, set off to walk around the Bay to Oakland. She wound up in Golden Gate Park and, like Hertz, found an old street car to sleep in. Thursday morning she and Josephine Jacoby accepted a ride toward the ferry. Their companions drove drunkenly into an area where house after house was being dynamited in a vain effort to stem the flames.

The two women got out and walked through the nightmare of Chinatown past bodies lying in heaps, through rubble and over hillocks where sidewalks had been, skirting huge cracks in the streets and dodging falling bricks. Men cooked their meals at fires in the middle of the streets until soldiers ordered the fires extinguished.

Emma Eames dressed herself with her usual fastidiousness. Then she and her host, Dr. Harry Tevis, descended the few blocks to the St. Francis and persuaded Sembrich, Dippel and Plançon to join them on the hill. Sembrich brought her diamond and pearl necklace and some money but in her nervous state came away without a coat. Eames supplied her with one. The story still persists that all through their ordeal the two prima donnas carried on a current feud and never spoke directly to each other.

The afternoon passed in a state of suspended animation. Dr. Tevis had a habit of saying after each tremor: "Go on, go on! Shake a little faster!" Eames played patience, much to the indignation of Plançon, who called her a "rock."

Warned that the house might be surrounded by fire, they packed coats, blankets and a few valuables in a carriage retained by Dr. Tevis. Eames' companion, Miss Fetridge, and Sembrich's maid, Frieda, were not allowed to walk, though the others went on foot to North Beach.

The expanse of vacant lots to the north was jammed with refugees. The singers slept fitfully under the strange mixture of dew and soot, surrounded by strange companions, menaced by strange animals. Plançon roused to find a cow sniffing wetly at him and yelled for help. Eames drove the beast away with a flick of her handkerchief. At dawn they moved up the hill to allow a procession of prisoners to shuffle past them toward the new jail at Fort Mason.

They saw a man in his underwear holding a phonograph under one arm. A woman passed by, carrying a cage of birds. A man who had saved only a large and elaborate clock suddenly threw it on the street where it broke into a thousand pieces. The sun rose blood red.

The little party separated, Eames and her entourage to travel with Dr. Tevis to his home near San José, where the prima donna wrote for the *Associated Press* the clearest personal account to emerge from the opera folk.

Sembrich reached the opera's special train in time, leaving $40,000 worth of personal effects and costumes behind her.

Plançon's loss was equally sizable. At first he railed at fate, calling the catastrophe a visitation upon him for not having gone home to Paris for his niece's marriage. Sembrich told him tartly that it was a pity so many had suffered for his small sin. Later Plançon admitted that he had been amazed by the Americans' calmness and coolness. The Latin races—ah, they might well go to pieces under such conditions.

Plançon's personal grooming provided a target for comment from his colleagues. Scotti alone noted that the French bass had been caught by the first shock before he had time to dye his beard, now greenish in the morning light. No one else mentioned this lapse. Sembrich described his first impromptu costume euphemistically as "shirtsleeves." Jacoby later saw him "faultlessly dressed even to a boutonniere." He arrived in New York in a light suit and overcoat.

Dippel, who minimized his own good deeds, saw wealthy women carrying clothes and provisions to ragged unfortunates and commented on the essential goodness of human nature. The tenor claimed that he slept on the bank of a reservoir, contradicting Eames' story. He smiled at the wax dummies in store windows, melted into grotesque shapes.

Archangelo Rossi was alleged to have stood on a corner near the Palace Hotel, singing *Vecchia zimarra* at the top of his voice—presumably to prove that he still could. The basso's frenzy subsided as the hours dragged by. For a whole day and night he had to be satisfied with three crackers and a glass of milk.

Giuseppe Campanari, on the other hand, endured the hazardous hours with a surprisingly light heart and considerable humor. After the first shock he dressed, even to garters and stickpin. Then he waited for death. When it did not oblige he went downstairs.

Meeting Arturo Vigna in the street, he borrowed $10 from the conductor, who had tucked some money in a pajama pocket. Campanari hastened to a telegraph office and paid $5 to expedite his wire. It was one of the first to arrive in New York, informing his family that all was well. He signed it "Papa."

The baritone then walked to the house of his brother-in-law and was dumfounded to find the family on the veranda munching cakes and drinking tea. "Heavens! A picnic," he thought.

Next day he took his niece and went down into chaos to find either food or the opera company. He bought a bottle of whiskey and a corkscrew and talked a Chinese merchant into giving him a box of biscuits for $1.50.

After a whole side of a street was blown up almost in their faces, he sent his niece home. Now scores of dogs began to follow him, slavering, as he believed, for the biscuits. "Not a bit of it," he told them. He collected a batch of newspapers; they would be interesting twenty years hence.

Campanari studied the people. They laughed when a house caught fire. He felt no fear and walked around like an imbecile. He lost count of time. Noticing some men drinking in a bar (the mayor's proclamation had out lawed the sale or possession of liquor; this resort must have been extremely well hidden), he decided to get drunk himself. One man flashed a huge roll of money. A thug demanded it. The man shot him dead.

The wanderer moved on. That night he slept on the grass. He wondered vaguely if a man could exist on grass. He seemed to be trying. He appeared at the Oakland railroad station unshaven and unshorn, borrowed a collar from Dippel, bought a shirt for thirty-five cents and a tie for ten cents. When he reached New York he looked like an immigrant, his kit still tied in a gay blanket over his shoulder.

"Such a change," is all he said before he embraced his son Christopher.

Louise Homer, the comely American contralto, reached the Oakland rendezvous in a state of shock, wearing what was called a "wrapper" over a pair of her husband's trousers. Sidney and Louise had both fled from the Palace with masculine garb. A Mr. Pope on Pacific Avenue gave the Homers shelter, allowing them to sleep in his car. His cook gave Mme. Homer a pair of shoes five or six sizes too big, the only shoes she possessed until she reached Chicago.

Hers was the most serious plight among the singers. At Des Moines Dr. W. D. McFaul boarded the train and advised her removal to a hospital in Chicago, where she slowly recovered.

Adelaide Thomas, one of the young girls in Conried's Opera School, had been allowed by her Pittsburgh parents to go on the tour because Mme. Homer would be near to keep an eye on her. The contralto's father had been the preacher at the church where Adelaide's mother sang. Adelaide worshiped the older girl. Even in her distress Homer "was always a lady."

Adelaide, with the buoyancy of youth, fended nicely for herself in the emergency. With other junior members, Lucille Lawrence, Lucy Call and Jeanne Jomelli among them, she boarded the train without mishap. This was only the first of three earthquakes in her eventful career.

Marie Rappold arrived in a truck loaded with thirty other members of the company, collected by the diligent Strine. At last all of the singers came out of jeopardy. One by one their stories emerged. Jacques Bars had run out of his hotel to be confronted with an automobile filled with corpses. Marcel Journet and Robert Blass had hired a cab, but the driver decamped with the horse. The two men drew the vehicle out of the danger zone and made it their bedroom for the night.

Albert Reiss and Bernard Bégué lost everything. The librarian Mapleson, the repetiteurs Morgenstern and Schindler and the chorus master Pietro Napoli arrived destitute. Max Hirsch saved his mother's picture and one business suit.

Alois Burgstaller rescued a hen from a burning house and roared happily (he found it difficult to speak softly) that he was going to teach it the "Voodbird song" from *Siegfried*. Adolf Mühlmann boasted two crocodiles as trophies. Charles Henry Meltzer, the acting press representative, fondled an armadillo, given to him by a soldier at the zoo. Bianca Froelich, the *première danseuse,* carried two Mexican hats as her only baggage.

Only Frederick Rullman, a former Grau partner, a ticket broker and founder of the Metropolitan's libretto concession, had no tale of shock to tell. Under the effects of a hilarious celebration after the opera, he had slept through the first hours of terror.

Goerlitz had done a superhuman job. By Thursday night everyone had been accounted for and all except Eames were in Oakland ready to board the Chicago and Northwestern's "Overland" or a later train that was to be routed through New Orleans. Strine had made many trips back and forth to convey the choristers and the ballet, who had been lodged in the foreign quarter under Telegraph Hill and who miraculously clung in groups throughout the agonizing thirty-six hours. Goerlitz refused to take credit.

"They all just got together," he said.

Goerlitz' own Wednesday and Thursday had been not without unhappy incident. He paid a man $25 to take his luggage and the opera's subscription books to the St. Francis Hotel. When that hostelry fell vulnerable, Goerlitz joined the multitude of the "have-nots."

Almost immediately it became apparent that the Opera House would be an early victim to the fire that crawled from roof to roof behind it. No wind blew, but the searing heat created its own wings.

Goerlitz watched helplessly as the first red tongue licked at the plain three-story building. The successive shocks of the earth's convulsions had shaken down the wooden balconies and sent the famous chandelier crashing into the orchestra well. Few dared enter the doomed structure. Ten out of fifty-five precious instruments were retrieved by reckless musicians before the walls collapsed. Only thirty trunks could be extricated. Nine carloads of scenery, properties, costumes, music and personal clothing were destroyed.

As the roof plummeted onto the stage where Carmen had met her death barely twelve hours before, the Metropolitan administrator turned away with a shudder.

Wearily he hopped a ride on an old cart to friends on Clay Street, where fourteen sleepers shared a few mattresses. All night long the manager sat on the steps. A woman asked him to help revive her child; the infant's skull had been crushed. The dull grinding noise of thousands of trunks scraping over the pavement came to his ears—the sound that had obsessed Arnold Genthe and other writers. Thursday he got to Oakland and by heroic efforts arranged for the two trains.

While San Francisco still writhed on its funeral pyre the opera troupe started home. The stricken city blazed on until Saturday morning. While the opera stars, destitute but thankful to be alive, sped over mountains and desert, San Francisco's fabled phoenix rose out of her ashes and summoned her citizens to return and build again.

In Los Angeles the trains were allowed a brief stop so that the passengers could buy toothbrushes or whatever they thought vital. Sembrich purchased a bright red kimono. Otto Goritz bargained for a gaudy shirt and socks "at which the East will marvel."

In New York, meanwhile, two days of uncertainty had frayed the nerves of the opera personnel and relatives of the travelers. After a long vigil, Conried heard that Nathan Franko's wife had received a reassuring message about the musicians. Wednesday night a stagehand called in wild excitement to say that he had heard from a carpenter that all were safe.

Rumors began to spread that Franko's message had reported Caruso, Sembrich and Eames as missing. Sembrich's husband, Professor Stengel, was distraught. When at last he learned through the eastern agent of the Southern Pacific that the entire company was on its way home, Stengel wired his wife: "Leave for New York at once."

Her overwrought friends could not help laughing.

On Monday at 12:50 P.M. the "Overland" arrived in Chicago. In the crowd that met the train were Milward Adams, the Auditorium manager; F. Wright Neumann, local impresario, and Charles E. Nixon, *Musical America's* correspondent. The three posed for a photograph with the refugees. Everyone wore hats—the women, surprisingly elaborate affairs, the men, derbies or fedoras. Three of the women Sembrich, still in her light-blue suit, among them—boasted fur boas. Caruso kept firm hold of Roosevelt's photograph.

Adams told the singers that the Actors' Fund Benefit had been diverted to the earthquake victims and would bring in $6,600.10.

As soon as Conried learned that his flock had suffered no fatality, he turned his mind to figures. He would lose $210,000 on his properties, for which insurance would recompense him only $50,000. He would be obliged to refund $118,000 to San Francisco ticket buyers—if they could be found. The artists must be paid to the end of their contracts. Conried determined further to give each male chorister a new suit and $5, each woman a $15 bonus.

When a reporter pestered him about replacement of the demolished scenery he snapped:

"I have already given orders to reserve time and workmen. But I am not Oscar Hammerstein and cannot have these things done without time!"

As the Twentieth Century Limited approached, bringing a part of his company, Conried sent Aimé Gerber, his paymaster, to buy $200 worth of roses and himself conveyed them to Albany, where he boarded the homecoming train. The manager had little chance to deliver the blossoms at first because of what the *Times* described as a friendly assault by tenors, sopranos, contraltos and baritones "falling on his stout neck, kissing him and crying affectionate greetings." The same moving scene was reenacted when the silk-hatted impresario met the remainder of his troupe in Philadelphia two days later.

Most of the singers jumped nervously at any sudden jolt or unusual noise. Fremstad screamed at a flashlight photograph. But these symptoms soon wore off. The majority of the company boarded ships for Europe within a few days. Caruso and Journet made a detour to Paris to order new costumes for the Covent Garden season. Hertz still kept his hotel key as a memento.

Sembrich, touched by the plight of the chorus and orchestra, gave one of her famous benefits, playing both the violin and piano as well as singing. Of the total receipts $7,691 went to replace the musicians' instruments, $2,435 to the chorus and technicians.

Goerlitz, who seemed to one reporter "in surprisingly good health" and to another "a veritable wreck with cheeks hollowed, beard ragged and eyes dimmed," barely caught his breath before he was dispatched back to San Francisco to supervise one of the most monumental refunding operations in history. At first the Metropolitan representative demanded proof of ticket purchase but soon waived any such formality and paid on demand. The infinitesimal amount of overpayment spoke well for San Franciscans' honor.

The summer slipped by; another season impended. The House opened its doors as usual, with new singers, new costumes, new scenery—and the old spirit.

The Metropolitan, too, rejoiced in the sign of the phoenix.

4. THE STARS REMAIN

Heinrich Conried's penultimate season (actually the last in which he was actively concerned with the tours) promised to be his brightest. Nerves shattered by the San Francisco ordeal had mended by November. Although the budget tipped woefully out of balance, the Metropolitan benefited artistically from the scenic replacements. The shocking experience, however, proved only the first in a series of trials that led to Conried's collapse.

The manager's health began to be a subject of public comment during the summer. What was diagnosed as "locomotor ataxia" and later sciatic neuritis made walking and standing difficult. He was called on to do both under circumstances that caused both physical and mental torture.

A week before the season was to open, Caruso was arrested for having allegedly accosted a woman in the Central Park Zoo monkey house. The episode not only brought painful notoriety to both tenor and manager, but caused Conried to stand long hours in the crowded courtroom. Technically the case went against Caruso in spite of his protestations of innocence, but cast no shadow on the faith of his friends. And his audiences in New York, Philadelphia and Boston were wildly acclamatory at his first appearances. The *Philadelphia Ledger* complained indeed that the interest in the tenor's return and curiosity about the new soprano, Lina Cavalieri, obscured the significance of their novel vehicle, Giordano's *Fedora*.

Never again would Caruso's hold on the public be questioned. The American newspapers might make capital of his common-law wife and their two children; of the divorce suit instituted by her husband after the lady had eloped with her chauffeur; of breach-of-promise suits and skirmishes with assorted blackmailers and Black Hand villains. But the American public's sympathy never wavered.

The tenor encountered stage mishaps in unusually large numbers on tours, perhaps attracting them by his superstitious fears—accidental stabbings, falls, tumbling scenery. His millions of admirers were vitally concerned. When he suffered an attack of parotitis in Boston, his audiences worried. He appeared in *Gioconda,* but to Philip Hale "his suffering visibly chastened his ardor." Mumps could be dangerous at the age of thirty-two.

Once assured in 1906 that his stellar songbird would continue to lay only golden eggs, Conried, though frequently an absentee general, planned his next campaign—for *Salome*. He intended that the feverish eroticism of Herod's court should become as familiar to American operagoers as the consecrated temple of Monsalvat. The seven-veiled dancer was to reap as much cash and *réclame* as the Guileless Fool. But a squeamish element among the boxholders demanded that the management take the "operatic offal" (W. J. Henderson's redolent phrase) off the boards. Thus Conried lost what surely would have been a *succès de Grand Guignol* on the road.

Tour cities were not to see a Metropolitan production of *Salome* for twenty-seven years; meanwhile Oscar Hammerstein picked up the work as a strong card in the operatic hand he was playing—with traditional beginner's luck—against the Metropolitan.

Hammerstein, opening the Manhattan Opera House in New York in 1906, was just emerging as an opera director to be reckoned with. The stimulus of his competition could be held directly responsible for the feverish expansion undertaken by the Metropolitan in 1909.

At first the older institution underrated this adversary. But Hammerstein was out for blood—the Metropolitan's and Conried's. His antipathy to the established house was no secret; Hammerstein liked nothing better than talking for publication.

Hammerstein and Conried, singularly alike in their drive for power, had fallen out long ago, when the German refugee backed a play in which the Austrian actor appeared. Vincent Sheean, in his recent Hammerstein biography, emphasizes that the mighty Oscar ordinarily did not cherish grudges, but that Conried aroused in him a unique loathing. Sheean believes that Hammerstein was "inclined to see the hairy hand of Conried" in any of his tribulations as long as the latter lived.

A large measure of audacity backed by a first-class opera director in the person of Cleofonte Campanini and a few top-ranking singers—Maurice Renaud, Alessandro Bonci, Charles Dalmorès and Mario Sammarco—carried Hammerstein through his first Manhattan season. He produced no novelty but filled his new opera house almost every night. An alarm bell sounded in the Metropolitan's inner counsels.

Conried reacted to this new nettle in his operatic meadow by attempting raids on his challenger's flock. He was successful only in inducing Alessandro Bonci to change sides. Bonci's very name sent tremors through Caruso, as that of Van Dyck had affected Jean de Reszke. For three seasons thereafter, as a Boston observer put it, the tiny tenor "kept Caruso on his mettle." Bonci's "miraculously clear, sweet, resonant voice, used with consummate art," graced the roles Conried occasionally filched from Caruso's repertory on the road as well as the few Bonci could keep for his own. Many tour cities regarded him as Caruso's equal. In fact, the *Pittsburgh Post* critic, Schlotterbeck's successor, Jennie Irene Mix, contended that no other tenor should be "mentioned in the same sentence."

The operatic war that was soon to rage through a half-dozen cities would not concern Conried, however. Hammerstein did not cast a covetous eye at Philadelphia, the object of his first infiltration, until the spring of 1908; his two performances there on March 19 and 26 (*Lucia* to show off his dazzling coloratura soprano, Tetrazzini, and *Louise* to introduce his magnetic "singing actress," Mary Garden) occurred after the announcement of Conried's resignation.

All of Conried's troubles notwithstanding—and a financial panic broke in 1907 to add to them—the last tour under his supervision bore every mark of success. The majority of his twelve cities delivered gate receipts that exceeded the previous year's average by as much as $1,200.

No city was allowed more than a week, but the route extended as far west as Omaha (including stopovers in Cincinnati, St. Louis and Kansas City) and as far north as Minneapolis and St. Paul.

Goerlitz and all the opera personnel complimented St. Paul on its new "wonder building" in 1907 and expressed gratification at the respectable average of $7,797 per performance. The *Pioneer-Press* marveled that "scenery wagons could be driven right on stage and unloaded." Audiences of 3,000 were neatly contained in the smaller of the two chambers that were separated by removable wings.

Across the river in Minneapolis the final performance was *Tosca* with Emma Eames in the title role. Shortly after the first act a messenger brought the news that the singer was a "free woman," divorced from Julian Story. She rushed into the arms of a dear friend and was quoted by the *Journal* as exclaiming, "Now you will hear me sing!"

"And how she sang!" the *Journal* summed up. "Never so well in her life!"

Chicago had been grumbling in a steady crescendo for three seasons. Glenn Dillard Gunn fumed in the *Inter-Ocean* that "Conried's standard grows lower every year," and W. L. Hubbard proclaimed with equal heat in the *Tribune* that "the desire for the almighty dollar is more in evidence in the present 'artistic' rule than when commercialism was the acknowledged purpose."

Although Hubbard railed at Conried for using *Salome* "as bait" long after the Judean princess had been shelved, 1907 was judged Conried's most laudable season. Felix Borowski pointed out in the *Post* that the demand for tickets was unprecedented. "Lines of music students, country cousins and others" extended far into Congress Street.

Conried offered attractions that Chicago—and the other cities—could not afford to miss. Two feminine headliners had aroused special curiosity: Geraldine Farrar and Lina Cavalieri. The little American had conquered the discriminating Berlin public and, it was hinted, the heart of the young crown prince as well. A ravishing charmer, she fitted into the courts and opera houses of Europe with extraordinary compatibility in spite of a New England upbringing. New York, although unfavorably preconditioned by the wave of European adulation that heralded the girlish prima donna, had quickly capitulated. Now the road followed suit.

The day after her Philadelphia debut, the *Ledger* printed one of its rare interviews, using as an excuse that Philadelphia looked on Farrar as one of its own by virtue of her father's stardom at first base in its National League baseball team. The interviewer discovered that the singer possessed a will of her own and a "bland indifference to those who opposed her." Her originality in costuming her heroines came to early notice: "Beauty is essential," she claimed, and for beauty "she would sacrifice even appropriateness," assuming a high, modern coiffure for Marguerite in *Faust* instead of the conventional blonde swinging plaits, and appearing as "a Mignon who glitters with spangles."

The year's craze for Puccini, signaled by the presence of the composer to witness first Metropolitan performances of his *Manon Lescaut* and *Madama Butterfly,* spread to the road, where his works led even Wagner's in number of performances—twenty to thirteen. Only one flaw sullied Conried's pleasure in the success of *Butterfly:* Savage scooped him here as in *Parsifal* with an English production on the circuit as well as in New York.

Puccini's own favorite heroine soon became the darling of American opera houses as well, and Farrar's most popular role as long as she remained with the Metropolitan. Philadelphia found her "radiant" as the frail, passionate Cio-Cio-San. Chicago discovered that she possessed the "rarest and most precious of guiding powers: brains," in addition to a lovely and responsive voice, capable of a "wide variety of gradations and colorings."

When she sang Elisabeth, her favorite at the time, Cincinnati responded with an ovation such as "seldom was accorded a newcomer." Boston's current high priest, the formidable H. T. Parker of the *Transcript,* paid tribute freely to a home-town talent, noting that she changed "fully and illusively" in each of four roles, "not merely in external disguise and cast of features, but in the very quality of her tones."

Farrar's appeal as a personality stemmed from the piquant contrast of American independence and candor with European sophistication. Lina

Cavalieri was wholly an exotic. Either would have supplied enough excitement for any one opera company. Conried engaged both.

Cavalieri came from the gutters of Rome. She sold flowers on street corners and sang in cafes. Her beauty still stirs the senses even from aging photographs. As a living presence she dominated the early century, trailing Russian princes in her wake. America offered no royalty to conquer; Cavalieri consoled herself with merchant princes.

Philadelphia alone had the opportunity to succumb to her charms when she sang in *Fedora, Bohème, Pagliacci* and *Manon Lescaut.* The next year she created the title role in *Adriana Lecouvreur* and repeated *Bohème* for Philadelphia, also singing *Manon Lescaut* in Baltimore and Boston. Olin Downes judiciously paid tribute to her talent in the *Boston Post,* recognizing her cleverness and pronouncing her "an instant success."

The Tosca that later stunned Boston was under Hammerstein's wing. Andrés de Segurola describes it temptingly as an affair of "white Caucasian ermine, glowing white satin and luscious flesh, topped by the deep green emeralds of tiara, necklace and brooch."

In Conried's final year one of the most memorable figures of operatic history flashed across American skies, vanishing almost immediately in a cloud of misunderstanding. America was not ready for the peculiar greatness of Feodor Chaliapin, said many—among them the bass himself. Others suspected that the reverse might be true. The Russian artist sang four roles during his brief passage, repeating three of them exclusively in Philadelphia.

His success as Mefistofele in Boito's opera was unquestioned in the eyes of the Quaker City *Press,* "not only in the naked audacities of the reading of the role but also the vocal treatment." "Naked" audacities extended to the huge frame of the bass, stripped to a loincloth and painted gray, reminding John Curtis of a dead body. Philadelphia politely ignored what New York deemed disgusting in his Don Basilio, merely noting that the performance of *Barbiere* "struck a low water mark." His Leporello was dismissed as "low comedy." Not until 1921 would the offended singer make his peace with America.

One of Conried's last gestures was to restore the German wing to some semblance of strength. The addition of Gustav Mahler to the conducting staff kindled the Wagner and Mozart singers to new efforts. "A past master of appraising comparative values," in the *Philadelphia Enquirer's* opinion, the great conductor permitted "no languishing sentimentality," said the *Ledger. Tristan* was reduced to a reasonable length, thereby ministering to the comfort of that tyrant of the American stage, the "tired business man."

Mahler's triumph in Boston was termed "epoch-making" by the *Journal,* while the *Globe* described him as "no apostle of noise." Hertz took over the few remaining German performances on the road, so that Chicago and Pittsburgh were deprived of the renaissance. Mahler did not go beyond Brooklyn and Philadelphia in his second season and in his third and last did not tour at all.

Miraculously there was no shortage of heldentenors. Alois Burgstaller, inherited from Grau, appeared in *Meistersinger* as well as giving consistent service in *Parsifal* on the 1905 tour. His tall frame and boyish face became familiar to Boston, Philadelphia and Chicago in four other Wagnerian roles during the last three Conried seasons.

Heinrich Knote, who amused Baltimore by his habit of addressing all his colleagues by full titles ("Herr Geheimrat Goerlitz," "Herr Intendant Hertz"), traveled as far west as Kansas City in 1906, but in his final year, 1908, sang only in Philadelphia. He gave the Quaker City its most satisfactory Lohengrin in years "from the point of pure singing."

Carl Burrian remained the Tannhäuser assigned to Philadelphia and Brooklyn, singing other roles intermittently until he retired in 1913. Each year one or more tenors (sometimes as many as four) parceled out Wagnerian roles among themselves—Schmedes, Jörn, Anthes, Hyde, Jadlowker, Hensel and even Slezak, although the big Czech never dipped into the deeper waters of the Ring. And always Dippel, ever reliable, sang his own and everybody's roles—twenty-six in three languages during eight touring seasons.

Fremstad's incandescent Isolde was revealed to Philadelphia, Boston and Chicago in 1907-08, repeated in Philadelphia next season and in Philadelphia and Boston in 1909-10. Thereafter the road was denied this most illustrious creation, although her Elsa, a role she enjoyed least of all, was widely circulated.

One of the last truly to deserve the title of "Diva," Fremstad traveled in great style, scorning the economies of her adored teacher, Lilli Lehmann. Mary Watkins Cushing, her faithful "buffer," relates in her perceptive *Rainbow Bridge* the hilarious circumstances attending every journey. Sheets soaked in hot water and sprayed with pine oil were draped in train compartments; bathtubs in hotel suites filled with steaming water and pine oil to condition the air for her sensitive throat.

"Madame liked to go to the dining car . . . she detested lukewarm food. . . . She always wore a veil over her mouth like an houri, and I, no matter what the weather, would carry a large muff."

This ornament was in reality a camouflage for the dog, Mimi. Miss Watkins hardly ever enjoyed her meals, "for the muff kept showing too lively an interest in the contents of my plate."

Conried's purposeful bolstering of the German wing, an area into which Hammerstein could not follow, led him to engage Berta Morena, whose "bewitching grace" as Elisabeth awoke echoes of Ternina in Philadelphia; Martha Leffler-Burkhard, whose *Walküre* Brünnhilde impressed Paul Rosenfeld of the *Chicago Examiner* as "beautiful and exuberant"; and Louise Kirkby-Lunn, the serviceable contralto from Savage's company. Johanna Gadski aspired to higher Wagnerian realms each season; and Ernestine Schumann-Heink returned for a few performances in 1907, contrasting Wagner's heavy roles with a cackling witch in *Hänsel und Gretel*.

An era ended with the retirement of Pol Plançon. The debonair French bachelor had commanded critical respect and enchained feminine hearts for fifteen years. Appropriately his last role on the road was his most popular: Méphistophélès, sung in Pittsburgh on April 26, 1908. Without seeming aware that she was delivering a valedictory, Jennie Irene Mix, in her *Post* summary, paid him the finest compliment a veteran could have wished for: "Plançon was the one star supreme."

Among other singers who wrote *finis* to their Metropolitan careers, none had been more useful than Marcel Journet. After his first season in 1900 the stylish French bass had plunged into major competition with Plançon and Edouard de Reszke. In eight years he sang thirty roles on the road, nine more than Plançon. Valuable as he was to Grau and Conried (and to the Chicago Opera in the years to come), Journet nevertheless could not rival Plançon in the public's favor.

At some juncture in the ill-fated tour of 1905-06, the little Bauermeister slipped out of sight. A great to-do had been made for several seasons over the threatened retirement of the "indispensable" seconda, but she, to a lesser degree like Patti, lingered on. In 1906 she may have traveled no farther than Washington. Bauermeister was listed in San Francisco's advance programs, but her name does not occur in the accounts of the earthquake.

Conried's time was fast running out. Long before his formal resignation, Metropolitan directors had signed a contract with Giulio Gatti-Casazza. At a cost of $90,000, the board bought the "president's" interest in the company. Conried outlived his "Conried Metropolitan Opera" by scarcely a year. On April 27, 1909, he died in Meran, Italy. The Metropolitan, having insured his life, was richer by $150,000.

Conried was not present when the last company that bore his name played his tour finale on April 29, 1908, in Pittsburgh, to the accompaniment of the flames of *Die Walküre*. Appropriately he ended his tenure in the House with *Götterdämmerung*.

Part VII

GATTI'S QUARTER CENTURY

1. THE MERRY WAR: A TALE OF SEVEN CITIES

The second year of Gatti-Casazza's regime as general manager of the Metropolitan Opera has gone down in history as the most stimulating for the patron of opera and the most disastrous for opera management ever known in America. Never before and never since has so much grand opera been available to the populations of seven United States cities. Three opera houses were regularly open in New York: the Metropolitan itself; the New Theatre (the Metropolitan's Opéra Comique venture) and Oscar Hammerstein's Manhattan Opera House. More than 300 performances of opera were crowded between November 8 and April 2 in the metropolis.

Across the Brooklyn Bridge, the Metropolitan performed on twenty Mondays and one Tuesday in the creamy-yellow brick Academy of Music on Lafayette Avenue which Brooklyn had proudly dedicated the previous year. Not to be outdone, Philadelphia undertook to support twenty-five Metropolitan representations. Baltimore's quota jumped from the customary three or four in the spring to a startling twenty during the season. One week in January and another in March were allotted to Boston.

To carry out this grandiose scheme, the Metropolitan engaged a double orchestra, Italian and German choruses and a list of 101 principals. Ten solo singers did not leave New York, but more than that number were hired for the out-of-town engagements, several from the separate roster of the New Theatre, which endured only one season.

The intricate schedule called for simultaneous performances in two cities on fifty-six occasions. Even as *Gioconda* opened the House, the German wing was performing *Tannhäuser* in Brooklyn. It is apparent what resources a company must command to be able to show *Falstaff* in New York while *Rigoletto* is being played in Boston; *Aida* in Baltimore while *Lohengrin* is given in New York; *Pagliacci* and the ballet *Coppélia* in New York while Boston enjoys *Die Meistersinger*.

At the end of this remarkable operatic shuttling, only half the travel story had been told. One company set off in April for thirty-three performances in

131

Chicago; another headed for Pittsburgh to begin a tour of ten cities that would end in Atlanta on May 7.

No wonder that the international madhouse, as one journal dubbed the Metropolitan colossus, should need guideposts on the road. The complications were so obvious and the trail so arduous that the management issued booklets showing maps of the cities visited and tabulating dates and hotels.

The grand total of these peregrinations lagged only one behind Grau's record of 145 in 1901-02; but 1910 stands unique in Metropolitan history for the season's European pendant. Leading artists of the company and its chorus and ballet took ship in May for France and performed seventeen times before the books could be closed on the achievements of 1909-10.

The Metropolitan's sudden mania for expansion had not originated in the mind of its new general manager; on the contrary, Giulio Gatti-Casazza went on record as being firmly opposed to such dizzy flights. Gatti stepped into an ambiguous situation without warning. Although he had weathered ten seasons as *generalissimo* at La Scala, the new general manager was unknown to many Americans. Some members of the board evinced disquiet over the possibility that the Italian might pass over the German repertory, a staple since the late De Reszke days.

Arturo Toscanini, who had agreed to come to America if Gatti were in command, was thought like him to be a fervent nationalist. Why take chances when a man whom everybody knew and respected could be counted on to champion the German works? Dippel was ripe for retirement as an artist; the wider sphere of management appealed to him as to other tenors past and future. He was well liked by the public and had powerful friends in high places. Dippel was told somewhat ambiguously that he could "work by the side" of the director. Gatti-Casazza remained in ignorance of this appointment until his arrival on the New York pier.

Confronted by the *fait accompli*, Gatti, by his own account "a man who never talks a great deal," bided his time. Because he was a professional, his chances of survival mounted with each rash move of his colleague. If he could not hold all the reins, he tried at least to snaffle some of Dippel's more venturesome sallies. But Dippel was bent on "fighting fire with fire," as he described the master plan for defeating Oscar Hammerstein at his own game of aggrandizement. Gatti had to acknowledge that this challenge must be met.

If the rivalry had been contained within the New York-Philadelphia axis, desperate measures might not have seemed imperative. But in every one of the four other old strongholds that constituted the Metropolitan's modest tour of 1908-09, Gatti encountered Hammerstein's outreaching tentacles. Chicago was treated to Mary Garden in *Salome* and *Jongleur de Notre Dame* among other gems in the Manhattan's provocative bill of fare; Brooklyn, Baltimore and Pittsburgh were similarly drawn into the irrepressible Oscar's budding empire. The Metropolitan could not even get into Boston: Hammerstein had secured a lease on the city's only operatic shrine, the fifty-five-year-old Boston Theatre.

In 1909-10, Hammerstein added Washington, which, while not currently involved, still belonged in the Metropolitan's orbit.

Of the seven outlying citadels stormed by Hammerstein, Brooklyn was least affected. Oscar, whose passion for acquiring real estate amounted to mania, bought a possible opera-house site in the borough, as well as another in Cleveland; but this threat died before birth. Brooklyn continued to open the Academy doors to the Metropolitan until two seasons after Gatti's departure. By the end of 1937, even the five performances to which the season had shrunk (from ten or twelve in the 'twenties), were thought to keep too many Brooklynites from buying New York subscriptions. The time-honored association fizzled out.

Ever since the Brooklyn Institute of Arts and Sciences had erected a new Academy of Music in 1908 it had been a "subway series." In the years that had passed since Brooklyn's decision to become a borough of Greater New York, the huge, fiercely independent community had begun to smart under an inferiority complex. The uneasy partnership with Manhattan, which Brooklynites unequivocally call "New York," created an ambivalence which has carried over into cultural life. Brooklyn resents the superiority of Manhattan's entertainment resources while patronizing them to the detriment of its own. The Brooklynite professes to desire yet only halfheartedly supports local musical institutions.

The Metropolitan's first season in the new Academy brought out box-office receipts which were never again achieved. Fourteen performances averaged $9,872 (the fifteenth, a matinee of *Hänsel und Gretel*, earned only $2,165). Subscribers paid $5 apiece but single tickets for opening night cost $10.

The 1908 inaugural night on November 14 gave the borough an evening the more glorious for its anticipation by two days of the Manhattan opening. The New York dailies covered the event with their usual (and to Brooklyn infuriating) note of condescension. Geraldine Farrar sang "The Star-Spangled Banner" amid unfurling flags; the *Times* believed that "the heart of every Brooklynite must have been particularly joyous." In the side boxes "the cream of Brooklyn society was separated from the milk of kith and kin"; the *Telegram* expressed mild surprise that "the same etiquette was displayed as in New York."

The *American* delivered the final pat on the head:

"Caruso's celebrated high C (in *Faust*) made Brooklyn sit up and feel 'as if it belonged.' "

In spite of many happy evenings in its acoustically excellent and comfortable theatre (the old Academy had been cramped and usually kept at a freezing temperature), Brooklyn came to be suspected of a jinx by many members of the company. Today's saying, "Anything can happen in Brooklyn," which arises from the antics of its baseball team, might have applied also to the Metropolitan's hegiras across the bridge.

Blizzards had a way of waiting until Brooklyn days to strike: once a *Lohengrin* truck broke down in the storm and the chorus had to improvise a concert; again—and on a Christmas afternoon—a stalled taxi made Anna Meitschik fifty minutes late for her appearance as the Witch in *Hänsel und*

Gretel. A ballet entitled *Czar and Carpenter,* scheduled for an afterpiece, was hastily moved up between the acts of the fairy opera, creating a weird sequence. The *Eagle* chided the *"Hexe"* for abandoning her characteristic mode of travel, adding that "taxicabs are not so reliable as broomsticks."

Perhaps Brooklyn was too close to home. Louise Homer allowed only a normal time to cross the river for an *Aida* in 1916-17, but the elevator in her Manhattan apartment perversely stuck between floors. A very nervous Amneris barely reached the transpontine Temple of Phtha in time.

Illnesses can occur anywhere, but those that struck in Brooklyn were always specially remembered. Fremstad sang too soon after an illness; it was a Brooklyn *Tannhäuser.* Her chauffeur refused to entrust the car to the inevitable snowstorm, so Madame and her entourage traveled by subway, to the astonishment of all the passengers, including herself.

Martha had to be cut short in 1909 because of Elvira de Hidalgo's fainting spells. Frances Alda's appendix burst during an *Otello* the same year—Slezak handled his Desdemona with unnecessary roughness, many observers thought. The soprano underwent an emergency operation at 3 A.M. in her hotel.

But the blackest day in Brooklyn history was the Saturday in 1920 when a horrified audience saw Caruso struggle bravely to finish the first act of *L'Elisir d'Amore* although every note brought a new gush of blood from his mouth. The hemorrhage that cut short the Brooklyn performance presaged the end; Caruso never sang on the road again and appeared only three times afterward in the House.

Because Brooklyn occupied an early place in the Metropolitan's calendar, even opening the season three times, several artists made their debuts there: the tenors Orville Harrold and Umberto Macnez, the baritone Clarence Whitehill, and the bass Adamo Didur among them.

An unscheduled "debut" of which Brooklyn was proud brought Arturo Toscanini in his first out-of-town appearance (on November 23, 1908) replacing Francesco Spetrino, who had effected his debut with the company in Brooklyn's opening. Spetrino hurt his foot and was out of action for several days. Toscanini conducted *Tosca* for him in the House and *Rigoletto* in Brooklyn, both without rehearsal—the first of the miraculous accomplishments that were to found a new legend.

This *Rigoletto* marked Sembrich's final appearance in Brooklyn. The 1908-09 season also signalized the farewell of Emma Eames. Each of the prima donnas sang four times out of town, dividing their favors between Brooklyn and Philadelphia. Sembrich received her final dazzle of tributes, tears and applause on the road at a Philadelphia *Rigoletto* on January 5. Eames sang her last Countess Almaviva in Brooklyn on February 4 with no fanfare whatever. Philadelphia had remarked her coolness in snuffing out a fire caused by candle drippings in her first—and last—local *Tosca* on December 15. The *Bulletin* admired her for "never stepping out of character," an epitaph to be treasured by the lady who was seldom credited with entering fully into any role.

Baltimore sustained the harshest consequences of the new opera war. A small and fairly consistent customer for three or four spring performances since the days of Abbey, Schoeffel and Grau, the elegant, mannerly city suddenly found itself at the center of an operatic whirlpool.

In 1908 the Metropolitan's contract with Baltimore for four performances during the season omitted the usual clause stipulating that no previous opera must be given within a certain period. Hammerstein advanced his first performance, *Lucia,* to January 4, hoping to take the cream off the Metropolitan's January 20 *Butterfly,* for it seemed a foregone conclusion that the first in the field would carry off the most profits. The ticket sale for both companies was held the same day; and to confound the pessimists, both series moved briskly. Baltimore began to believe in its oft-repeated contention that it could support as many operas as Philadelphia. The chance was immediately offered.

Hammerstein had erected an opera house in Philadelphia to combat the Metropolitan; very well, the Metropolitan would counter by establishing its own fortification just to the south. Otto H. Kahn, acting for the directors, bought the Baltimore Lyric Theatre and announced sweeping renovations.

Furthermore, Dippel promised twenty evenings of opera, contingent on a guarantee of $7,500 for each. Henry Walters was the first to sign his name for $10,000; Frank A. Munsey, proprietor of the *News,* made up the final $1,800 of a $100,000 fund. Baltimore flung itself into the enticing new project with unwonted abandon. The opening *Tannhäuser* fulfilled all dreams of glory. Society, diplomats from Washington, jewels, perfumes, expensive corsages and excited talk filled the theatre; 400 were turned away. The box office rang to the tune of $7,855. Dippel promised "to give Baltimore the very best." Manager Bernard Ulrich rubbed his hands together in glee and announced that any surplus would be placed in a fund to Baltimore's credit next year.

With seven performances crossed off, it became apparent that Baltimore's "eyes were bigger than its stomach" for opera. The city watched the dream fade before the inexorable figures. Cautiously at first and then despairingly the newspapers reported each performance in terms of deficit under the guarantee. The $100,000 fund lacked half of being enough. The total intake was $99,683, leaving a deficit of more than $50,000.

Still, Baltimoreans who took little account of fiscal problems cherished shining memories: President and Mrs. Taft's visit to hear John Forsell's "gorgeous" Figaro in *Barbiere; Gioconda;* Alma Gluck's first Marguerite anywhere ("a joy to the eye"); the debuts of Glenn Hall, Walter Hyde and Jane Noria; and the farewell of Lillian Nordica in *Trovatore,* actually her final performance with the Metropolitan.

Ulrich joined the Chicago Opera and, from the vantage point of his new affiliation, persuaded Baltimore to try another operatic visitor. Except for a single performance of *Königskinder* in 1912, the Metropolitan bypassed Baltimore until 1927, when a new group, spearheaded by the energetic and tactful Frederick R. Huber, initiated a fresh chapter in cordial relations.

Meanwhile the Lyric Theatre had to get along without the drastic improvements that Kahn had envisioned. Out of all his and Ulrich's grandiose plans, only new murals around the proscenium arch, a smoking room to replace the bar and a refurbished lounge for ladies materialized. Improvements have been instituted piecemeal in the intervening years, but the Lyric still lacks a façade and many backstage facilities. Its charm and atmosphere are confined to the auditorium.

Hammerstein's inroads on the Metropolitan's territory had far-reaching if indirect consequences in Pittsburgh. Here the vein of opera enthusiasm might have petered out in any case. In 1909 Charles Wakefield Cadman complained in the *Dispatch* that "New York is conferring no special favor upon a city of Pittsburgh's size, culture and means in giving us a brand of opera like last night's." He referred to a *Faust* in which only Farrar shone. Giovanni Zenatello, whom Hammerstein had lent to Gatti when Caruso became too ill to tour, appeared ill at ease "in a strange garret"; Didur was "atrocious"; Fornia, "commonplace"; Amato, "insignificant." The other papers took a less virulent tone throughout the short season, but everyone was disturbed by the screaming child Trouble who had to be put off the stage by an exasperated Farrar in the third act of *Madama Butterfly*.

Next season Pittsburgh was the chief complainant in the case against the split tour. Although it enjoyed a *Lohengrin* with Fremstad, Jadlowker and Soomer, and a *Tosca* with Farrar, Jadlowker and Scotti, Pittsburgh felt cheated. John Forsell performed his "striking" Tonio and Rosina van Dyck her "delightful" Gretel; Riccardo Martin "justified expectations" as Canio; Jane Osborn-Hannah was a "vision of loveliness" as Elisabeth and Jane Noria seemed "perfectly adapted for Wagner"—still Pittsburgh was unhappy. Caruso was absent. So were Bonci, Slezak, Gadski, Destinn and Alda.

"The Left Wing of the Metropolitan Opera closed a rather disastrous engagement . . . [while the] Right Wing is now in Chicago," the *Post* concluded indignantly.

Pittsburgh never entered the Metropolitan orbit again. The overexpansion of 1910 led to a retrenchment; and when the Metropolitan began once more to spread its influence widely, Cleveland became so strong a contender that all cities within a radius of 500 miles bowed to its superior claims.

If the Metropolitan had not won in Pittsburgh or Baltimore, neither had Hammerstein. The battle moved to other arenas. Hammerstein gave Boston two seasons of diverting performances. His *Elektra* with Mariette Mazarin successfully challenged Gatti's *Aida* on the opening night of 1909 with a jammed house, while two rows of boxes "showed wide gaps where there might have been handsomely dressed people" to applaud the Verdi.

Chicago and Boston reacted almost identically to the "merry opera war" and its aftermath. Both cities had been feeling artistic growing pains and the chauvinistic desire to foster opera houses of their own. Henry Russell had recently supplied an incentive with his San Carlo Company; in 1909 he settled in Boston in a new opera house built largely through the efforts of Eben D. Jordan, Boston's most influential patron of music. The Metropolitan, with an eye to schemes almost as comprehensive as Hammerstein's, invited Jordan to their board; and Otto H. Kahn became a Boston director. Cooperation in exchange of artists between the two units lasted through the hectic opera merry-go-round of 1909-10, and for several seasons a few of Boston's leading singers—notably Alice Nielsen, Maria Claessens, Antonio Pini-Corsi and Florencio Constantino—remained on the New York roster.

The Metropolitan left Boston exclusively to its home-grown product in 1910-11, 1912-13, 1913-14. After the demise of Russell's troupe the New York company returned for visits in 1915-16 and 1916-17. Thereafter the Massachusetts field was abandoned to other touring groups until 1934, when a firm, new basis for friendship with the Metropolitan was secured.

Chicago already had an opera house; all it wanted was a company to call its own. Sooner than anyone could have expected, just such a company dropped into Chicago's lap. The decision was fought out in Philadelphia, where the trouble had begun.

2. OLD FAITHFUL FLIRTS WITH A RIVAL

Philadelphia, dowager among hostesses, has inscribed only four "not-at-homes" to the Metropolitan in an engagement book covering more than seventy years of friendly association. In 1884-85 and 1889-90 Damrosch regretfully bypassed the city; but in 1896-97, having left the Metropolitan to head his own company, he negotiated successfully with Abbey and Grau for a division of spheres of interest for one season. He chose Philadelphia; the Metropolitan went to Chicago (a disastrous alternative as it happened). After the Metropolitan's suspension during 1897-98 Grau brought the reorganized company back to the Quaker City. Since then only the depression year of 1934-35, when the Philadelphia Orchestra undertook an opera season of its own and lost upward of $300,000, has spoiled the perfect record.

It is ironic to reflect that the guarantees Philadelphia has raised for the Metropolitan since 1899 were continuations of the efforts originally made by zealous admirers in Damrosch's behalf.

Though indubitably most faithful among all Metropolitan cities, Philadelphia did not bar a decorous flirtation or two with beguiling strangers. Hospitality to opera from other cities may have deepened her sympathy for indigenous opera growths as well.

Her consciousness of the delights of "the stage" has been heightened, perhaps, since she overcame her Quaker preoccupation with original sin. Whatever atavistic pangs of conscience may nag her dreams, Philadelphia has been addicted to opera for a century—the life span of her illustrious opera house.

On January 26, 1957, the Academy of Music marked its centenary, exactly 100 years since the new center of culture for the little red brick city of 500,-000 was inaugurated with a great ball. The first opera, *Il Trovatore,* came a month later on February 25, 1857.

It had been a bold decision to place the hall so far from Fourth and Market

Streets, the center of town. Largely determinate was the quiet of the residential neighborhood, since become the teeming vortex of the city's roar. A nationwide competition had selected Napoleon Le Brun and Gustavus Punge as architects.

With commendable honesty they offered a choice between beauty within or without, claiming that both could not be accomplished for the $250,000 available. With equally commendable wisdom John B. Budd and his directors chose to concentrate on a beautiful interior. Although the façade was planned so that a marble facing could be attached, none ever was. Today the building is still "as plain as a market house" and 100 years dirtier.

But its audience chamber is the envy of every concert and opera society in America. The unexampled excellence of acoustics is due to Le Brun's passion for the subject. He modeled the Academy after La Scala, securing good results from a large, dry well under the parquet and a corresponding dome in the ceiling. Sounding boards in the orchestra pit and around the back walls of the auditorium, a hollow chamber in the form of a semicircular promenade, thick walls around the entrance lobby and the addition of tons of cow-hair mixed with the cement may account for the glorious sounds in the Academy's auditorium.

The handsome chandelier, which was brought from New York's Crystal Palace in Bryant Square, still twinkles high above, seeming very close to the cramped devotees in the top reaches of the Amphitheatre, Philadelphia's euphemism for "peanut heaven." It is obvious to these occupants of "plain" seats that the architect never sat through *Die Meistersinger* on one of them.

In 1950, while making such necessary alterations as a new fire curtain, stacks of decaying scenery, defying identification, were thrown out—all that remained of the "largest and most varied stock of any place of amusement in the country" in the 1870's. In the same year the Philadelphia Orchestra bought the controlling interest in the American Academy of Music (still the official name), and together with an Academy association headed by Stuart Lochheim keeps the centenarian in a reasonably healthy state.

Plans for the Academy's 100th birthday took into account the imperative need for a few renovations, so that patrons of the jubilee concert followed by a grand ball were asked to pay as much as $1,500 for a lower box. That the building has hitherto needed so little repair is undoubtedly due to the fact that the shell was allowed to stand through the weather of two years without a roof.

The Philadelphia Academy of Music is the only auditorium the Metropolitan still visits after seventy-three years of almost continuous use. As we have seen, Abbey had recourse to the Chestnut Street Opera House for a part of his first tour, later transferring to the Academy. The only other break was the ten-year hiatus after Philadelphia's flirtation with Oscar Hammerstein.

In the fall of 1908 Hammerstein's Philadelphia Opera House was the talk of the town. He had not waited for the walls to weather; indeed he gave his son Arthur, who always implemented Oscar's wild plans, only a few months to build the house, deliberately setting his opening night for November 17 to clash with the Metropolitan's. Arthur got the roof on seven days ahead of schedule; whereupon Oscar gave a huge *al fresco* supper to the critics and "men about town." John Curtis remembered that the stairs were improvised and the railings temporary, but "an up-to-date phonograph played grand opera records, and white-aproned cooks served steaks and champagne."

On opening night long kid gloves and broadcloth shoulders rubbed against paint that was not quite dry; nevertheless "the whole city was at Oscar Hammerstein's feet," according to Curtis and other insurgents. He was the only one since Gustav Hinrichs had launched the first of many summer seasons in 1888 to "look at Philadelphia as something better than one-night stands." Mayor John E. Reyburn bestowed his patronage on the new house and a segment of Philadelphia society, headed by G. Heide Norris, counsel for the Philadelphia Orchestra, endeavored to make a civic project out of Hammerstein.

The twin operatic attraction tried Philadelphia loyalties sorely. Nevertheless the Academy glittered as brightly as its new rival. The performance of *La Bohème* was unusually brilliant, with Caruso and Sembrich and new scenery. A smoking room for men only, the first in the Academy, had been installed. Fifty applications were received for one of the Drexel boxes, offered for sublet because the family was in mourning.

Numerous boxholders attended both affairs, leaving relatives or friends as stand-ins. Never had such an operatic night been vouchsafed Philadelphia. Many of almost equal splendor were to follow. The Metropolitan stepped up its schedule to two performances a week; Hammerstein was essaying five!

Something had to give. On New Year's Eve the proprietor of the new theatre castigated Philadelphia and its financiers for not giving him a guarantee similar to the Metropolitan's. Dippel countered by offering to waive the guarantee. No guarantor had been called on for five years anyway. But luckily the committee voted to maintain it. At the end of the season only seven of twenty-four performances had topped $7,000 guarantee level.

Hammerstein was feeling the pinch even more severely. He tried to borrow $400,000 from Norris, but the latter refused without mortgages on both the Philadelphia and Manhattan houses. Edward T. Stotesbury then stepped into the picture, advancing $67,000 to meet Hammerstein's current deficits and taking a $400,000 mortgage on the Philadelphia house.

Another season went by before the reckless Hammerstein finally overreached himself. Sentiment swung away from him, particularly when he branded the Metropolitan personnel as a "bunch of antediluvian lemons."

Otto H. Kahn announced in April that Hammerstein was to be paid a million and a quarter to give up. Title to the Philadelphia Opera House, promptly renamed the "Metropolitan," was included in the transaction, but not the Manhattan; however, Oscar was enjoined not to produce grand opera there or in other strategic cities for ten years. The Metropolitan took over the American rights to operas, scores and properties of the Manhattan and contracts with its leading artists.

Stotesbury immediately formed the Metropolitan Opera Company of Philadelphia with himself as president. All the while he had been a Metro-

politan director and a partner in the house of Morgan; Hammerstein's
biographer advances the theory that his motives were "more complex" than
Kahn's, indeed the latter may have acted solely from altruism.

With the beginning of 1910-11, its twentieth season in Philadelphia, the
Metropolitan deserted the Academy for the new house, where 1,000 additional
subscribers could be accommodated. Considerable delicate maneuvering had
reassigned the boxes; and society presented an unbroken rank again for the
first time on December 13, when Morena, Fremstad and Slezak starred in
Tannhäuser.

A week later the "second performance in the world" of Puccini's *Fanciulla
del West* delighted H. T. Craven of the *Inquirer,* achieving "an accent of
the picturesque to a degree never before associated with the lyric stage." Puccini volunteered the compliment that "Philadelphia is a real American city,
more American even than New York."

The war was over. Dippel had won in principle; but his inflation had cost
the Metropolitan $300,000 in addition to the Hammerstein "cease and desist"
money, which came out of private pockets. It also cost Dippel his job. He was
politely asked if he would care to manage the new Chicago-Philadelphia
Opera, created with Hammerstein stars as a nucleus. He solved many problems by accepting.

Gatti was now in full command. Not since Abbey had a Metropolitan impresario looked the part. His tall, imposing figure, his full beard and soft,
dark eyes, his inscrutable expression all indicated the man of importance. He
best lived up to George P. Upton's earlier definition: "Rarely if ever gregarious. Dwells apart; as unapproachable as the Grand Lama. Usually a very
exalted person with a handsome brilliant in his cravat and wrinkled brow
above it."

Gatti thus explained his own wrinkled brow: "The theatre is nothing but
difficulty. A manager walks on a razor edge. He should have a hand of the
best-tempered steel in a glove of the richest and most attractive velvet."

Gatti's "steel hand" revealed itself in his first edict: "No more touring."

The inevitable deflation hit the swollen roster first, especially the oversized
orchestra and chorus. Max Hirsch, veteran road man, announced his retirement. Dippel's severance brought other changes: John Brown was advanced
to be business comptroller; into Brown's place stepped young Earle R. Lewis,
destined to become box-office treasurer and in 1937 Edward Johnson's assistant general manager.

Fortunately for the sake of the national status of the Metropolitan Gatti
changed his mind before the end of the season. The spring tours continued,
at least in token form, until the 'twenties, when the route burgeoned once
more.

From 1911 to 1915 the Metropolitan's visits to Philadelphia were bracketed
in one subscription plan with the Philadelphia-Chicago company. When the
latter failed, its successor also competed during its lifetime for Quaker City
interest. But Philadelphia's most dangerous flirtation was happily past.

In the ten years the Metropolitan occupied its own house, the names of
Stotesbury, Biddle, De Witt Cuyler, Drexel, Yarnall and Van Rensselaer in-

sured that all was well "out front," while on stage the parade of stars never diminished. On April 18, 1912, several boxes remained empty because many Philadelphians were mourning their kin, lost in the sinking of the Titanic. The next night all boxes except Stotesbury's were filled to hear Caruso and Gadski in *Aida*. The tenor was greater than ever, claimed the *Ledger*.

Three years later the same paper found Caruso a sober, matured artist, "to whom several seasons of prudence have restored much of the power of a perilously strained and overused voice. The annoying cough that had become almost an affliction was little in evidence."

Comparative austerity in the first year of the war did not lessen the brilliance on the opening night except that the Stotesburys omitted their annual supper dance for 200, taking only thirty friends to the Ritz-Carlton for supper. Philadelphians of the period insisted they would never forget Geraldine Farrar's "strongly individual Carmen, to which, perhaps, she imparted too much of the street Arab"; yet when Margarete Matzenauer stepped into the part unexpectedly, it was as if "heat-lightning" flashed across the stage, even though the contralto's heroic build "made a considerable lapful for José" [Martinelli].

Gatti was scolded by the *Ledger* in 1915 for not allowing Frances Alda, whom he married in 1910, to appear more often, saying that the manager was *too* impartial—an opinion which many New York critics did not share. Alda made an "ideal" Manon for Philadelphia. Supreme, too, was Maria Barrientos as Lucia, now that Sembrich had departed. Philadelphia admired Adamo Didur extravagantly as Boris, the *Ledger* opining that it was the most vivid characterization of 1916-17.

Artur Bodanzky proved his "right to inherit the mantle of the able and faithful Hertz," when he made his debut with *Lohengrin* in 1915, "reining in the orchestra as he would a full-blooded horse." Jacques Urlus was the Wagnerian tenor of the moment, "untrammeled by the leading strings of the prompter's box." Frieda Hempel's delicious voice "threaded in intricate coloratura measures with surpassing skill, comeliness and authority."

Before Hertz' retirement he had denounced Philadelphia in a New York paper for not knowing when *Lohengrin* "begins and ends." In the middle of the bridal procession the curtain dropped "like a pall." He stopped the orchestra and shouted for the curtain to be raised but was drowned out "by that terrible audience which supposed the act was over." When the curtain finally did go up, a "vulgar stagehand in shirtsleeves was hanging to it . . . like grim death." As the unfortunate man reached a height of about ten feet, he let go, and scampered off among the bridal party into the wings. The *Ledger* blamed "execrable" stage management, but it is highly probable that Hertz pushed the wrong button when he gave a cue to the organ.

Perhaps the most famous incident in the Philadelphia Metropolitan Opera House was Caruso's assumption of a bass role for the first and only time in his career, singing the "Coat Song" in *La Bohème*. The story has been recounted in many versions but the most circumstantial account appears in the autobiography of Andrés de Segurola. The bass was hoarse even during a luncheon with Caruso at Del Pezzo's in New York. On the train he tried his voice; it was worse. Caruso mocked him to perfection, and promised jokingly to sing in his place. When the time came, the bass held the tenor to his promise, in spite of Caruso's *sotto voce* protests. "I pulled him toward the left corner of the stage . . . seated myself on a chair, held Caruso next to me and whispered, 'Enrico, save me, save me.'

"Polacco signaled and Caruso began singing—glorious, grand, generous fellow that he was. . . . At the end he was trembling . . . said he had never been so nervous on the stage."

Segurola places this celebrated occurrence in 1916; the Caruso biography says 1915; but an eyewitness, Max de Schauensee, today's critic for the *Bulletin,* vouches for December 23, 1913, and suggests that Caruso took the initiative in the kindly substitution.

The incident passed unnoticed by the Philadelphia audience and critics. Caruso made a special Victor record of *Vecchia zimarra* in bass register as a souvenir for the three principals, and according to Segurola gave the bass his complete Rodolfo costume as an extra favor, "from your understudy."

Stotesbury grew tired of his burden in 1920 and put the Metropolitan Opera House up for sale in April. A syndicate of motion picture interests bought it for $650,000; Hammerstein's Pride became a dance floor and variety house. The Metropolitan turned back to the Academy.

But that ancient house was on the auction block too. Quick thinking and united action, urged by Edward W. Bok and Charlton Yarnall, effected a four-party agreement among the Philadelphia Orchestra, Metropolitan Opera, Academy Association and a citizens' group stipulating the lease of the Academy for five years. President George Fales Baker reduced the rental substantially. A committee headed by Mrs. George Horace Lorimer and including Mrs. Alexander Biddle and Dr. Herbert J. Tily worked valiantly. Alfred Hoegerle, whose management activities reached back into the 'eighties with Hinrichs at the Grand Opera House and included the recent decade at the Philadelphia Metropolitan, was put in charge at the Academy, replacing Siegfried Behrens, a former Philadelphian conductor.

The Metropolitan seasons went on without a break, in spite of the strenuous reshuffling necessary to fit nearly 4,000 subscribers in a 2,910 capacity house. *Eugen Onegin* closed the Metropolitan with a box office of $10,896 on April 20; *La Juive* opened the Academy on November 30 with the incredible return of $21,677, a record due to increased prices for the event, but still unbroken until 1926. The only sad note of the evening was sounded in retrospect: it was Caruso's final appearance in Philadelphia.

Philadelphia has been justly proud of its record as a "premiere city," boasting the first American performances of a score of celebrated operas, from *Der Freischütz* in 1825 and *Faust* in 1863 to *Cavalleria Rusticana* in 1891 and *Manon Lescaut* in 1894. Metropolitan novelties have been almost without exception shared immediately with Old Faithful, so that Philadelphia's calendar has resembled New York's through the years.

Cancellations have been rare—in fact, nonexistent since 1918, when the wartime fuel law closed the Academy and Philadelphia lost a *Traviata.* In 1909 Toscanini's production of *La Wally* was withdrawn at the last moment because of Destinn's illness; but the *Bulletin* showed where consolation might be found: "Of course everyone will flock to hear the first *Pelléas et Mélisande* with Garden and Dalmorès at Hammerstein's." A similar last-minute cancellation occurred in 1895, when Maurel is said to have refused to sing in *Rigoletto* with Marie van Cauteren, who was to replace the ailing Melba. Manager Behrens told the enraged customers who had been standing outside in the bitter cold for two hours that Maurel's costumes had not arrived.

The Metropolitan has shown a penchant for introducing important singers through the medium of Philadelphia performances, Risë Stevens, Blanche Thebom, Gladys Swarthout, Salvatore Baccaloni and Herbert Janssen among them. Seven singers, almost the entire cast of *Die Verkaufte Braut,* made their Metropolitan debuts in Philadelphia in 1936, including Norman Cordon and George Rasely.

Philadelphia's current problems fall generally under two headings: space and money. Mrs. George Haly, the Metropolitan's Philadelphia representative since 1949, keeps track of old subscribers and tries to find room for new ones. The opera's ballooning budget in 1957 precipitated a rise in seat prices of $1 each, which brings a parquet subscription to $60 for six performances. Henry P. McIlhenny, chairman of the Philadelphia committee, conducted a drive for $15,000, in which subscribers were asked for extra donations from $25 down to $5 for each ticket.

Tradition is even more important than money to Philadelphia, however. And the Metropolitan means tradition, as well as enjoyment of the kind the city particularly relishes. Philadelphia hopes never to lose its status as the Metropolitan's Good Neighbor.

3. SOUTHERN COMFORT

Like her Metropolitan Opera guests of many Aprils, Atlanta is a prima donna herself, one of her analytical sons admitted recently. This accounts for the striking affinity between Atlanta and Geraldine Farrar—and also for their quarrel. "It was the dramatic temperament of both of them," elaborated the *Journal's* Frank Daniel. "Scarlet O'Hara did not accidentally emanate from this city."

"Atlanta wants to be a lady and have fun on the side, too," says Ernest Rogers, author of *Peachtree Parade,* after thirty-five years on the *Journal.* Her dual nature helps Atlanta to show "more friendly warmth" than most northern cities and more "get-up-and-go" than most southern ones.

This happy blend has wrought a perfect atmosphere for grand opera. Atlanta has played host to the Metropolitan Opera for thirty-three seasons with a grace and largesse that can be only termed regal.

Everything about opera week comes in large sizes and must be described in superlatives. In a "week" of four days is crowded a lifetime of enjoyment. The houses are sold out long in advance (the new Fox Theatre inheriting this euphoric condition in 1947 from the older, larger Auditorium). In elegance the audience bows only to the Metropolitan itself on opening night—and shows more homogeneity from box to balcony.

Two newspapers (formerly three) devote so much space to opera that when the news and feature stories, society columns, advance analyses, reviews, photographs, editorials, interviews, cartoons and versified satires are clipped, only lacy shreds remain.

As for the parties—Atlanta's famous parties. . . . Other cities may compete in the gaiety or elaborateness of a single function, but Atlanta's parties begin when the first opera curtain falls and (almost literally) end each day barely in time to change from evening to daytime apparel—or vice versa. Francis Robinson, favorite ambassador from the Metropolitan to Atlanta's court, quoted Rudolf Bing as moaning, on his visit as general manager: "Work has stopped; sleep has stopped."

The lavishness of yesterday established the tradition for Atlanta's unparalleled hospitality. Still, no hostess today attempts to rival Mrs. John W. Grant, who frequently entertained Bori, or Mrs. John Edgar Murphy, who practically adopted Geraldine Farrar, according to the Murphys' daughter, Mrs. James B. Riley. A lunch table in the Murphy house at Peachtree and Fourteenth Streets might glisten with silver baskets filled with little cakes whose pink icing showed songbirds and the initials "G. F."; or twinkle with a huge bunch of electrically lighted green grapes. On one occasion a hundred canary birds sang throughout the house in sweet competition with an orchestra on the porch.

The Atlanta Opera Guild, founded in 1949 through the inspiration of Lucrezia Bori and the efforts of Mrs. Harold N. Cooledge, has become the official luncheon hostess to more than 450 guests in the Biltmore nowadays, with ceremonies including music by young singers of the company. Mrs. Edward Van Winkle, Mrs. Green Warren and Mrs. Erroll Hay have served the Guild successively as president.

An elder generation regrets the abandonment of the old-fashioned barbecue at the Druid Hills Golf Club, where Atlanta remembers Edward Ziegler, assistant general manager, drinking *Brüderschaft* with the beloved baritone Giuseppe de Luca in Seidels of foaming brew . . . Jackson P. Dick, son-in-law of a former president and himself now president of the Festival Association, politely sharing a plate of spareribs with Grace Moore . . . Chaliapin leading an impromptu band of clowning confrères while Louise Hunter, named "Atlanta's Sweetheart" when she sang later in light opera, danced an expert Charleston.

The fine careless rapture that inspired Lucrezia Bori to sing "Clavelitos" while stamping her tiny feet in delicate precision on the supper table and throwing carnations at the gentlemen has not evaporated. Revelers of recent days have been known to escort Eleanor Steber to the train clinking their champagne glasses in perpetual motion as they toasted her glowing beauty.

BOSTON THEATRE

MPKINS & HILL . . . . Proprietors
GENE TOMPKINS . . . . Manager

MR. HENRY E. ABBEY'S

rand Italian Opera Company

FROM THE

METROPOLITAN OPERA HOUSE, NEW YORK.

ING MANAGER . . . . MR. MAURICE GRAU

THIS EVENING

GOUNOD'S OPERA,

FAUST

ST . . . . Sig. ITALO CAMPANINI
PHISTOPHELES . . . . Sig. FRANCO NOVARA
ENTINO . . . . Sig. GIUSEPPE DEL PUENTE
GNER . . . . Sig. CONTINI
BEL . . . . Mme. SOFIA SCALCHI
RTA . . . . Mme. E. LABLACHE
——AND——
RGHERITA . . . . Mme. CHRISTINE NILSSON

ical Director and Conductor . . . . Sig. VIANESI

The Costumes are entirely new, and were manufactured at Venice by D.
OLI, under the supervision of Mr. HENRY DAZIAN.

e Managers . . . . MM. CORANI and .
asurer . . . . Mr. CHARLES H. MA
ness Manager . . . . MR. MARCUS R

URSDAY . . . . LUCIA DI LAMME
DAY . . . . IL TROV
TURDAY MATINEE . . . .
TURDAY EVENING . . . . LA SONNA
NDAY NIGHT . . . GRAND CONCERT --- POPULAR
NUARY 3 . . . . ELKS' ANNUAL B

The WEBER Pianos are used by Mr. Abbey's Opera Company.

Pianos used at this Theatre are from the celebrated manufactory of CHICKERIN
The Cabinet Organs are from the manufacturers, MASON & HAMLIN.

ERA GLASSES TO LET AT THE STAND IN THE FRONT

ORS OPEN AT 1.30 and 7.15. . . . . BEGINS AT 2

Rare Book Division, Boston Public Library

Opera Caravan's first port of call

Henry Eugene Abbey,
"a gambler in stars"

Walery, London

Christine Nilsson, Abbey's touring
queen. ". . . *lèse majesté* in Boston"

Italo Campanini, tenor.
". . . the couch tipped"

Mora

Music Division N. Y. Public Library

Giuseppe del Puente, "curly-haired and handsome Spaniard, a true Escamillo"

Courtesy Musical Courier

Left: Sofia Scalchi, "idol in tights."
". . . a peculiar assortment of voices"

CHICAGO OPERA HOUSE

FIRE PROOF

...RTON & CO.   DAVID HENDERSON,

≻PROGRAMME≺

...S—Commencing Monday Evening, A...

...d German O...

WITH THE FULL STRENGTH OF THE

...METROPOLITAN OPERA...

TUESDAY EVENING, APRIL 23,

...E WALKU...

Music Drama, in 3 Acts, by Richard Wagner.

...nhilde...Frau Lehmann.
...ricka...Louise Meisling.
Sieglinde...Frl. Kaschoska

Falk   *Falk*
Walter Damrosch   Edmund C. Stanton

Schaarwächter, Berlin

Max Alvary, "tall, handsome, gallant" a fine Tannhäuser

Victor Maurel as Don Giovanni—"so the libertine is revealed—wicked, alluring"

Lilli Lehmann as The Queen of Sheba; "womanlike, she had nothing to say"

Right: Edouard de Reszke ". . . never orders pints." Fritzi Scheff at right

Jean de Reszke, "pleasant, slightly balding gentleman, gentle in love, fierce in fight"

Maurice Grau (left)—"a fool or a madman will take up after me"

Emma Calvé—"instrument blown by passion's lips"

Falk

Emma Eames as Marguerite— "always an odor of violets"

Dupont, Courtesy Musical America

Nellie Melba, "a new goddess, never seen hatless offstage"

Benque, Paris

Höffert, Berlin

Lillian Nordica and Turk, both welcome at the hotel

Francesco Tamagno, clarion-voiced tenor,
"turns a good-natured face to the world"

Adelina Patti and entourage in the Diva's private car—"provincial eyes opened"

Marceau, L. A.

Andreas Dippel, "old standby." Right, Ernestine Schumann-Heink

Marcella Sembrich (right) and Suzanne Adams

Debonair Pol Plançon —"an era ended"

...u's barnstormers stop for a breath of desert air during the first
... to the Pacific Coast ever made by a Metropolitan Opera company

Frueh; St. Louis Post-Dispatch

Above: Conried and Savage meet in St. Louis for one of their road skirmishes

Left: Mathilde Bauermeister, peerless comprimaria—"no ambitions, no escorts"

Below: George W. Wilson of Pittsburgh —his millionaires lost to Conried's

ght: Among the opera gypsies
David Bispham (front, center)

ow: Alois Burgstaller with
ert Reiss, Eugène Dufriche

Mapleson Collection

Mapleson Collection

Courtesy, Moses' "Heinrich Conried"

Brown; Courtesy Musical America

ove: Heinrich Conried, "imperious
nner . . . a will stiffened to iron"

ht: Olive Fremstad—"she played
senkavalier to earthquake victims"

San Francisco welcomes Caruso's debut
and "the world's greatest coloratura"

Sketches by Caruso. Left: Alfred Hertz.
Below: the tenor fleeing the earthquake

San Francisco Examiner

London Sketch; Courtesy Musical America

San Francisco refugees arrive in Chicago. Present: Nahan Franko, Edyth Walker, Robert Blass, Marcella Sembrich, Bella Alten, Ernest Goerlitz, Enrico Caruso

Courtesy Tompkins' "History of the Boston Theatre"
It all began here—the famous Boston Theatre

Briol; Courtesy Musical America
Cincinnati's Music Hall today

Title Insurance & Trust Co., L. A.
The old Hazards Pavilion, Los Angeles

Courtesy Chicago Historical Society
The Chicago Auditorium on opening night

Philadelphia Academy of Music

McClure; Denver Public Library Western Collect
Denver's ornate Broadway Theatre

Where Beniamino Gigli once offered "Home on the Range" at the Piedmont Driving Club, Jerome Hines rises to his handsome six-foot-four and booms out "Ol' Man River" to the satisfaction of Atlantans of 1955. Once Gadski sang "Coon Songs" with a band; now Mildred Miller holds the Capital Club crowd spellbound with nostalgic Viennese melodies.

In the late 'twenties the new bass sensation, Ezio Pinza, shocked a society audience by singing naughty verses to "The Parade of the Wooden Soldiers," written by sports writer O. B. Keeler, an opera fan in spite of himself.

A glory of the past are the masquerade balls at the Atlanta Biltmore Hotel where Georgians loved to meet their operatic heroes and heroines on equal ground, with the assistance of the Metropolitan's make-up and costume departments. Henry M. Atkinson, president of the Atlanta Festival Association at the time, especially fancied his disguise one season as Méphistophélès. Even Otto H. Kahn, who enjoyed his visits to Atlanta, advising everybody to "Buy South—best tip on the market," once donned powdered wig, doublet and hose.

The same flair for organization that prompted Gatti-Casazza to compliment Atlanta on "the only method by which grand opera can ever be made a success outside of New York" has always been applied to extra-curricular affairs as well. Today it is even decided who is to ride in whose car to the climactic supper party at the Piedmont Driving Club. Experts of the present are the indefatigable Junior League women, who spent 8,957 hours of volunteer work in the typical season of 1955 on ticket sales, promotion, publicity and the sale of advertising for the elaborate programs. Their annual reward is several thousand dollars for charity, plus the satisfaction of making work out of play. Nancy McLarty, their public relations wizard, remains a lodestone in the shifting patterns of new committees each year.

Even the weather man produces his best samples for opera week—"he would be lynched if he didn't help the beauty, wealth and chivalry of the South to a week of Caruso and Culture," a New York newspaper predicted in advance of Atlanta's first opera festival. The brilliance of the sun and the sudden release from New York makes the singers "play outdoors like happy children," reports the *Atlanta Journal*. Only a few cold snaps, the latest in 1955, have leadened skies "as lovely as the dreams of Cavaradossi," in the words of Mabelle Wall, one of a long line of Georgian newspaperwomen. To see Atlanta without its mantle of dogwood and azalea is to miss the usual radiance of opera week.

Atlanta reckons "opera" (its unadorned term for the Metropolitan panoply, equated with Boston's "symphony") from 1910, preferring to ignore Grau's three-day visit in 1901 and Conried's 1905 *Parsifal*. One is tempted to concede the point except for purposes of historical record. The Atlanta Festival Association of 1910 brought a new concept into being. Guarantees had occasionally been obtained by the traveling company in years past; but the idea of supplanting local management by a citizens' committee did not take firm hold until Atlanta showed the way.

Many observers give Farrar credit for the entire sequence of events. As one of several soloists for the May Festival that dedicated Atlanta's new Auditorium in 1909, La Geraldine knew that the committee had yearned for Caruso as well, resigning themselves to Zenatello when the greater tenor fell ill.

"Why don't you bring the opera—with Caruso—next year?" the soprano is supposed to have suggested graciously. Victor Lamar Smith, a prepossessing lawyer who was chairman of the festival committee, consulted a director of the Auditorium building committee, "Colonel" William Lawson Peel, spruce president of the American National Bank.

Smith made an exploratory trip to New York. Fortunately for the new aspirant to Metropolitan favors, Kahn was in Europe—he declared later that he would have dismissed the project as "crazy"—and Smith's chief transactions were with the travel-minded Dippel.

The Metropolitan demanded $50,000 for five performances. Atlanta topped the sum by $1,000 in little more than twenty-four hours with the help of the three newspapers.

Directors of the Music Festival Association, of which Colonel Peel was made president and Smith secretary, not only bought their own seats and boxes, but "toiled like beavers," said Smith. C. B. Bidwell, the young and eager treasurer, wore out his eyes behind their rimless glasses with night work.

The committee spent $20,000 to raise the Auditorium stage roof. The Metropolitan donated the red velvet curtain recently replaced by gold damask.

Until the once-disappointed town assured itself that Caruso was really coming, ticket sales lagged. One director left town in order not to face the debacle. But after the tenor appeared in the flesh, $20,000 worth of tickets were sold in one day; the festival went over the top. Caruso's debut audience of 7,042 was claimed as a record even for him. Hirsch flatteringly declared that the Metropolitan had never sung to so many people (27,042) or such an amount of money ($71,030.50) in one week.

The jubilant Association cleared about $10,000, which was applied to the purchase of a new $50,000 organ for the Auditorium. Atlanta thrilled to the presence of Caruso, Farrar, Gadski, Homer, Scotti and Amato. The *Journal* had secured a scoop by sending W. B. Seabrook to Chicago so that he could ride back on the opera train. The writer reported that Caruso had been the victim of a practical joke through a newspaper story claiming he wanted to adopt a son. Thousands of ragamuffins showed up and pestered the unfortunate tenor, who was having enough trouble already with a Black Hand threat.

Farrar and Caruso both sang for the inmates of the Federal Penitentiary, inspiring columns of "sob stories"; Caruso clapped Farrar's picture hat on his head at the automobile race track while the soprano swathed herself in twelve yards of veiling to take a scorching ride with Ralph de Palma (who later won a race in his Fiat 60).

Thus Atlanta placed itself in thrall to opera almost overnight. Never was she to become wholly immune to the alluring siren, for although the song faded twice from her ears, it always returned, more compelling than before.

Farrar reigned as undisputed queen in the early days. "Atlanta adored her —and deplored her," Frank Daniel remembers. "All Southern girls are supposed to be beautiful; all Yankee girls homely. Yet this gorgeous creature came from Massachusetts—a *spinster* to boot!—glittering, incomparable, a symbol of shining achievement. . . . Was it any wonder that Atlanta alternately wooed Miss Farrar and warred against her?"

Her peek-a-boo blouse, with its tantalizing glimpses of coy bows on her camisole caused a minor scandal at Mrs. Murphy's luncheon and a raid on ribbon counters next day.

Farrar's first day in Atlanta typified the dichotomy of the city's earlier make-up: part Dixie hoyden, part *grande dame*. With her mother she had taken a suite in the Piedmont Hotel. Next year she stayed at the celebrated Georgian Terrace, and in subsequent visits lived in her private railroad car. She recently recalled her initiation into Atlanta society:

"Rather early in the morning came a rat-a-tat at the door. It was Mrs. Peel, the colonel's wife and head of the local D.A.R., with five other ladies. They had come to look me over."

Mrs. Peel, who carried a heavy cane and bore a remarkable resemblance to Queen Victoria, finally spoke:

"You're the nawth'n singah."

For the moment Farrar passed off the encounter with her ready charm and wit, and went on to an eleven o'clock luncheon that brought the lighter side of Atlanta into focus.

"Mrs. Riccardo Martin and I thought the delicious beverage in the tall, frosted, silver glasses was iced tea," she confessed. "Luckily it wasn't a matinee day."

For five seasons thereafter Farrar played enchantress to Atlanta's willing slave. Each of her roles was judged more captivating than the last, although the audience chastised her unconventional Carmen by making a great fuss over Alda's Micaela. Then when she withdrew from *Faust* the rumor circulated busily that she had imbibed too freely.

"That singers drank too much was a superstition here," Daniel commented. "Matter of fact, all the drinking was in the audience."

Farrar remained absent from Atlanta for five seasons after 1915. When she returned it was to mingled triumph and defeat. The Zaza that all men, most writers and some women thought fascinating seemed to the dowagers the ultimate outrage. In Atlanta one can choose between a dozen conflicting versions of what Farrar actually did on the stage that afternoon of April 27, 1920. Perpetrated at a matinee, her actions seemed the more censurable.

In the light of the difference of opinion between her defenders and detractors, Farrar's own account may be enlightening. Even then she looked on the affair as a prank. "And everything I did contributed to the character of Zaza, the demimondaine," she said recently.

"The idea of raising the skirt and perfuming the panties with an atomizer originated with Belasco, the playwright. As for the 'strip tease' they accused me of, I changed clothes down to a chemise. [So quickly and expertly was this accomplished that many could not believe they had witnessed it at all.]

My second-act dress was designed to be tantalizing—black lace over pink chiffon." The rumor spread rapidly, later confirmed by Farrar, that the saucy prima donna, having been told to "go the limit" by several Festival directors, sent notes to her friends suggesting that they sit on one side of the stage in order not to miss the undress show. The rush to left side, front row seats was noticeable.

Farrar was not invited to return by the Festival Association, but after her retirement from opera in 1922, she was engaged to give a concert in Wesley Memorial Church. Atlanta had not forgotten; the church was closed to her. Farrar gave the concert in the Auditorium, which was jammed.

The prima donna returned Atlanta's love but shrugged off its denunciation. Atlanta still suspects ruefully that it got the worst of the argument.

Other prima donnas took their turns in Atlanta's hierarchy, none more cherished than Lucrezia Bori. After twenty-two curtain calls at her debut as Antonia in *Les Contes d'Hoffmann* in 1912, Bori occupied her special place in Atlanta's heart and scrapbooks. The photographs still look chic, even in the awkward fashions of a bygone period. Cloche hats could not dim her beauty; nor knee-length waistlines conceal her supple figure.

It tickled Atlanta's pride to bring together two of its idols, Bori and Bobby Jones. The golf champion, at the height of his fame, found numerous admirers among the opera folk, particularly Otto Kahn and Earle R. Lewis, whose partiality for the Atlanta links was one factor in his moving there to live after he retired as assistant general manager.

One day, by Bori's account, she watched Kahn and Jones drive, fascinated at her first sight of the game. Jones handed her a club and teed up a ball for her.

"I evidently understood everything he told me to do," she said, "because when I swung at the ball, off it went into the air, to my great delight, without chopping the green. From that moment I became a golf fan and great admirer of Bobby Jones—and I think he admired me, too!"

When Bori returned to assist in the foundation of the Opera Guild, O. B. Keeler expressed Atlanta's sentiments: "That darling Lucrezia—the perennial *jeune fille* of opera!"

The last year of the First World War brought an unhappy hiatus in the Metropolitan's southern journeys, but in 1919 the break was mended. Atlanta's appetite for great singing, whetted by the deprivation, found satisfaction in the new prima donna, Rosa Ponselle. Two years previously she had appeared with her sister, Carmela, billed as the Ponzillo Sisters, in Atlanta's Forsyth Theatre and "not a bit ashamed of it," as she declared in an interview. The tall, vivacious soprano immediately won her way into Atlanta's graces by her performance in *Forza del Destino* and went on to become "dangerously near the greatest of all." Atlanta was desolated when she arrived in 1925 too ill (from a vaccination in Canada) to sing; but cheered her valiant spirit when she roused herself to add a *Cavalleria* to the scheduled *Tosca* on Saturday night. The Auditorium capacity had been reduced to 5,439 seats, and every one was occupied.

Atlanta, in common with the rest of the opera world, has succumbed regularly to "coloratura fever," shouting its approval of Barrientos, Galli-Curci, Talley, Munsel, Pons and Peters. But even with a predilection for "glamor girls" Atlanta slights no one.

No singer ever left Atlanta without experiencing her distinctive brand of allegiance and esteem.

No tenor has ever quite erased Caruso as memory or legend. Periodically some newspaper will recall that he rewarded a young clarinet player with an expensive watch for doubling the voice part softly in *Celeste Aida* so that he could keep on pitch at his debut; that he broke into song on the street one day in an attempt to soothe a screaming child, collecting a crowd while the child screamed louder than ever.

His multi-colored haberdashery and long cigarette holder are not forgotten; the sight of him waving in purple pajamas to friends in the street from a window in his top-story suite (he always reserved the entire floor); his wide grin as he drove through the town in an open car; his capers and jokes and infinite good nature; his companion with the unpronounceable name of Scognamillo.

Dozens of Caruso cartoons occupy places of honor in Atlanta shrines, among them a charming series in the Peels' guest book, now in the possession of Dr. William H. Kiser, Jr., a grand-nephew.

The "fullest moment" that Atlanta knew was when Caruso's voice rang out over a thunderous accompaniment in the National Anthem's closing line —"the land of the free"—signalizing America's entry into the war.

Dapper Antonio Scotti eclipsed Douglas Fairbanks and John Drew in feminine Atlanta's affections from the start. A tailor rushed to the door as the baritone walked by, gazed at the tight coat, the square shoulders, the ultra-correct trousers. Then he went back and changed a few entries on his customer's order blank.

O. B. Keeler admired the baritone extravagantly for his strong constitution, which withstood early morning setting-up exercises "with a tall bottle, siphon, glasses and ice."

Annual rumors of Scotti's impending marriage to Farrar delighted the sentimental; annual denials raised others' hopes. But Scotti "was not made for marriage," concluded Miss Farrar herself. Scotti left Atlanta, as he left his life, a bachelor.

"Big Charlie" Chaliapin, as reporters dubbed the convivial bass, roared through four seasons, with a single role each year. "Who is this giant, this colossus? . . . who is the man with such divine powers? Who is this actor?" demanded Pierre van Paassen, the Unitarian minister who later became a best-selling author, and meanwhile turned out music criticism with more warmth than accuracy. Of Marion Telva's "heavenly tenor" (sic) in the Polish scene of *Boris* he wrote that it climbed "with passionate fervor as the embrace takes place."

Chaliapin attended all the formal parties but he preferred to forswear Society with a capital letter in favor of an intimate evening with a few cronies, sampling "the wine of the country," according to Dudley Glass, who added liveliness to each of Atlanta's three newspapers during a long career.

"Georgia's prohibition-era moonshine was strong enough to take the enamel off your teeth," Glass remembered, "but Chaliapin thought it resembled his native vodka. Of course, when Billy Guard was around we had to drink his *grappa*."

William J. Guard, the press representative who fitted the popular conception of an artist, with long, thin locks, straggling string tie to match and a broad-brimmed black hat, had been Gatti's prize legacy from Hammerstein. Until his death in 1932 he carried out his duties with the urbane charm of an Irishman, the doggedness of a prospector for gold and the resourcefulness of an ace newspaper man—all of which he had been.

Giovanni Martinelli, Beniamino Gigli and Giacomo Lauri-Volpi in turn nobly lived up to Atlanta's requirements for the "ideal" tenor; Edward Johnson's fine art and winning personality made an early impression. The town showed its warm interest in the rising young baritone, Lawrence Tibbett, who sang his first Telramund there.

The distaff members of the daily press took an important place: Nana Tucker wrote long descriptions of opera plots. Louise Dooly, Louise Barili (a grand-niece of Patti), Helen Knox Spain, Mabelle Wall and Marguerite Bartholomew added moonlight, roses and commonsense.

Keeler was not the only sports expert drafted to referee in the opera arena. The great Fuzzy Woodruff of the *Constitution* complained that an opera jag had demoralized his entire staff. His headline, "Bohème K. O.'s Fans" made opera—and boxing—history.

Glass added to the merriment with his versified *Operas in Jazz* in the *Georgian*. Ernest Rogers adopted the formula for a series in the *Journal*. In a survey for the W. P. A. Writers' Project, Eldin Burton complained that "there was never any serious attempt at discriminating criticism . . . in this (1910) or any other season." But Atlantans and their visitors loved it.

Financial skies remained clear until 1922, when the guarantors were called on for the first time. The deficit amounted to $24,000 only, according to C. Howard Candler, who became treasurer in 1923, and the assessment only twenty-five percent, but the warning sign was patent. Candler watched anxiously through the next few seasons. Among the five children of Asa Candler, founder of the Coca-Cola fortune, he had always showed the deepest interest in the Festival.

The greatest ticket sale in Atlanta history occurred in 1926, Candler stated, with receipts of $130,000 for seven operas. Colonel Peel died in 1927; his last act: signing the current Metropolitan contract. Atkinson took over for two gay but unprofitable seasons. Then, in 1930, with a reluctance that only half masked her relief, Atlanta relinquished part of her week to Richmond. Cotton had slumped; the guarantors thought it the better part of prudence to do without opera for a while.

The "while" stretched into a decade. Then Atlanta's mixture of shrewdness and charm revealed itself in an individual. One of the city's most beautiful women signed a Metropolitan contract alone. Both she and Atlanta deserve credit for the outcome of her daring.

Mrs. Harold N. Cooledge, as president of the Atlanta Music Club, believed the restoration of the Metropolitan season would be a fitting climax to the club's Silver Jubilee season. The business men shied away at first, but this determined lady approached them without asking for money. One by one agreed on a broad and general basis that, yes, it might be fine to have the Metropolitan. Yes, they would help. . . .

For professional aid Mrs. Cooledge enlisted Marvin McDonald, originator of several famous concert series in the South. McDonald went to New York, to be received with "keen pleasure" by Edward Johnson, who had been the Metropolitan general manager since 1935.

When the contract arrived in Atlanta, Harold Cooledge was in a hospital, too ill to be consulted. His intrepid wife put her signature to a $40,500 obligation without knowing how she was to meet it. When Cooledge recovered, he sighed philosophically: "There goes my paint factory."

He need not have worried. Three performances brought in approximately $52,000. For two years subsequently the beautiful lady, by now staunchly backed by many former directors of the old Association, won complete vindication.

Another lapse, marking four war years, did not cool the newly awakened comradeship between the Metropolitan and its southern hostess. In 1947 the Association was resumed with Jackson P. Dick as president and an affiliation with the Junior League accomplished by its president, Mrs. James Frazier.

Atlanta's latest smiling decade has twice been ruffled. In 1948 "one of the best-dressed audiences came within a hook-and-eye of witnessing one of the worst-dressed *Carmens* ever seen on any stage," Celestine Sibley reported in the *Constitution*. "A flood, several railroad washouts and a pair of bushy eye brows were to blame," according to her colleague, Howell Jones.

The eyebrows belonged to John L. Lewis, whose union had called a coal strike reducing travel to a trickle. The Metropolitan's cars had to be hitched to regular trains, The Peach Queen and the Piedmont. Both ran into trouble, delaying the company's arrival. Risë Stevens and Kurt Baum improvised costumes with scarves, and the experienced Licia Albanese, substituting for Claudia Pinza, sang in a black street dress.

The other disturbance was serious. In 1949 John Garris, a gifted German character tenor, was found murdered in an alley after the company had departed for Memphis. The stunning shock to the personnel was intensified by the presence of an Atlanta police lieutenant who followed the company to Memphis, Dallas and Los Angeles. Under the extreme nervous tension, the singers earned the right to be called good troupers, performing without a hitch.

From recent guarded statements by another member of the Atlanta police, one can infer a belief in the guilt of an early suspect, a vagrant. But the trail grew cold long ago. The case remains on the books as "unsolved."

The sense of sorrow and strain lessened with time. By the next season, tragedy had returned where it belongs in an opera company: on the stage.

Atlanta continues to combine business and beauty in true southern style; and her men and women alike treasure opera week as pure enchantment. The city today could not duplicate the experience of Mayor Robert Maddox, a Festival supporter who inadvertently arrived late one night at the Auditorium. The doorman refused him admittance with this explanation:

"Mistah Mayah, suh, if I was to open them big doors right now, 4,000 husbands would come a-runnin' out!"

4. *ITALIANI IN PARIGI*

The Parisian public was agog; gossip darted like a swallow and twittered like a starling along the boulevards. *"L'Opéra Italien"* was arriving for a season at the Théâtre du Châtelet. As the chief delight one could hear M. Caruso in three new roles while the exquisite Cavalieri would appear with him in M. Puccini's version of *Manon Lescaut,* never before given in the French capital because of a delicate deference to M. Massenet.

"Audacieux!" cried the conservative inhabitants of *le monde théâtral* when informed by the sanguine M. Gabriel Astruc, Parisian representative of the New York Metropolitan Opera, that M. Gatti-Casazza would attempt full-scale grand opera in the outmoded Châtelet in May, 1910.

"Épatant!" exclaimed the arbiters of fashion, to whom the exotic had become almost a passion—Shakespeare and the fine arts of English domestic life, Russian ballet, American devices for comfort and convenience—and even German music. Just figure to yourself: had not the three Puccini works in the repertory of the Opéra-Comique necessitated the engagement of an Italian conductor?

From other quarters came less admiring expressions. Resentful whispers began to be heard from certain local *ateliers* and editorial rooms: disgruntled singers muttered about *"le snobisme";* while a few chauvinistic composers (who also happened to be critics) sharpened their vocabularies and waited for the chance to prove that Italian opera and "Italian" singers fell woefully short of French standards!

Otto Kahn had decided in favor of the Paris expedition without much urging from Gatti. Both were convinced by Astruc that the venture was feasible, might be profitable, and certainly would add to the prestige of the Metropolitan. Putting behind him all thoughts of the disastrous double tour, which, after all, had ended on a crescendo in Atlanta, and dismissing the money paid to Hammerstein as well spent, the godfather of the Metropolitan sent a chosen flock of songbirds off on the S. S. George Washington and the Kaiser Wilhelm II to Cherbourg.

The grand opera stars "burst upon Paris in a constellation of such magnitude and brilliance that Parisians forgot all about Halley's comet," a reporter cabled the *New York World*. With so much beauty at hand, customs officials "lost their heads and nearly forgot to make the visitors go through the usual formalities." A ballet corps and the Metropolitan's chorus swelled the invading troupe to more than 200.

Gatti's original plan encompassed fifteen performances: three each of *Aida, Cavalleria Rusticana* and *Pagliacci, Otello, Falstaff* and *Manon Lescaut.* An overwhelming demand for Caruso nights soon threatened to leave *Otello* and *Falstaff* without audiences; Astruc kept the balance by a "tie-in" requirement that stated in effect: "No elder Verdi, no Caruso." At last it became apparent that the *haut monde* could not be contained in one first night. Astruc persuaded Gatti to anticipate his official opening on May 21 by a public "dress rehearsal" on May 19.

Only two days remained between the departure from the Châtelet of a company playing a melodrama entitled *The Man with Two Heads* and the first *Aida* curtain.

This put it squarely up to the backstage experts: Edward Seidle, technical director, and Frederick Hosli, chief machinist. At their first glimpse of the Châtelet, "homely without as well as within," they agreed with other uncharitable Americans that it reminded them of nothing so much as a dilapidated old barn. "Why, it dates from one of the Napoleons!" Seidle told a New York interviewer.

Heroically they set to work. Local stage hands had to be persuaded verbally and financially to stir themselves out of a firmly-rooted lethargy; masses of antiquated scenery were pushed into corners to make room somehow for the heavily-built New York mountings; ground cloths, too long for French railroad cars and consequently towed to Paris from Le Hâvre on special canal barges, covered the wide, splintery boards that showed cracks big enough to catch a prima donna's heel.

Thanks to the depth of the stage and the miracles performed by a combined American-French-Italian staff, Parisians saw *Aida* much as it had been shown in New York. A hundred small hitches plagued the dress rehearsal, but nobody seemed to care except the technicians.

Impressive as were the lavish settings, rich costumes, remarkable chorus effects (which Paris did not expect), and fine individual singing (which it did), the glory of the preview lay elsewhere. In the pit the imperious Arturo Toscanini revealed to Paris what magic could be wrought even with a strange orchestra. And in the theatre, an audience such as Paris had not seen for two generations preened itself in an *"éblouissement de toilettes et de diamants."*

Even the famous audiences in the Ventadour, elegant theatre of the Second Empire, could not compare, admitted Raoul Brévannes in *Figaro.* Nor could those boasted by Stendhal at La Scala.

"What a hall! What a public! What cascades of precious stones! What beauties! What charms! What names, *enfin!"*

The deeply impressed reporter proceeded to list a hundred or so of these names "at random," beginning with nobility in the persons of *la duchesse* d'Uzès nee Montemart and S. A. (Her Highness) *la princesse* Lucien Murat, proceeding to M. Lepine, *préfet de police,* M. and Mme. Jean de Reszke,

M. Gabriel d'Annunzio, and ending with a score of singers, among them Farrar, who was singing at the Opéra-Comique.

Minister Briand represented the French government; diplomats attended in force, with Ambassador Bacon heading the American corps. Mrs. William K. Vanderbilt presided in her box (she would attend every performance); E. T. Stotesbury came from Philadelphia; Mrs. Potter Palmer (who scorned diamonds in favor of giant turquoises), came from Chicago.

Two nights later the official opening scintillated no less brightly, boasting an equal number of exalted personages and a smoother performance. The famous "flower basket," as the two tiers of boxes in the first balcony were called, coruscated with an array of feminine pulchritude and adornment. Cartier was said to have estimated the jewels to be worth $3,000,000; the Countess Colloredo-Mansfeld took honors for the finest collection of pearls, and Doña Catalina Lassa de Baró of Havana displayed the most resplendent diamonds.

Underlying the festive atmosphere, tension plucked at the nerves of performers and observers alike. For several days a cabal against "The Italians" had been building. (The Metropolitan's own name was never used by the French papers.) French opera singers pointedly stayed away from a champagne party given by Astruc, although the composers Dukas, De Lara, Hahn, Charpentier and Saint-Saëns attended. For several days certain journals voiced a local spite at the brilliant Metropolitan invasion.

Gil Blas had led the way with an attack on Toscanini and Gatti, evidently inspired by a French singer, Marie Delna. This contralto had lost a bitter argument with the conductor in New York, and had not been asked to return.

The journal had made fun of Toscanini's conducting from memory; quoted Delna to the effect that the conductor had only one friend, the prompter; and reached its lowest level of malice on May 21, the day of the opening, by accusing Toscanini and Gatti of angling for a Legion of Honor decoration.

That evening a boisterous, unruly crowd pushed into the gallery, obviously bent on mischief. As Toscanini came out for the second act, the hostile element unleashed a tumult of boos and hisses, screamed epithets and curses. Toscanini continued calmly to conduct; his masterful arm could be seen to sweep down in its long curved beat, but not a note could be heard over the uproar, to which was added applause from the stalls and boxes as a counter-measure.

On the stage, Louise Homer, the only American singer in the cast, began her scene as Amneris. Her mouth moved; but no voice was audible. Suddenly a moment of quiet fell. Homer's lovely tones floated out, miraculously quelling the disturbance. Even the gallery fell silent after a few of their ringleaders had been ejected. The coolness and gallantry of Homer and Toscanini were acknowledged in what one newspaper termed "almost an apotheosis."

"Honorable" journals gave the extraordinary season its due, although a tinge of pique continued to color the reports of several malcontents, among them Pierre Lalo. *Gil Blas,* however, repented to the extent of pronouncing

Alda's Desdemona a triumph, and softened its opinion of her impresario-husband.

This *volte-face* caused considerable amusement in knowledgeable circles. Conclusive evidence that the shift was due to something other than conscience is revealed in a note signed "W. J. Guard" on a Metropolitan scrapbook page directly beneath the offending and the "reconstructed" paragraphs. The cost of the change of heart was "exactly 2,000 francs, my own price," wrote Guard.

Caruso had been a hero to the Parisian public since his earlier appearances in *Rigoletto* and *Fedora;* now Toscanini and Amato joined the tenor on his pedestal. The baritone sang in five of the six operas; he was idolized as Amonasro, Tonio, Iago, Alfio and Lescaut. The conductor's transformation of the hundred rather lukewarm gentlemen who constituted Paris' celebrated Colonne Orchestra electrified the city.

Andrés de Segurola, who watched the first rehearsal, was amused at the men's facial expressions: sneers, diffidence or professional nonchalance (*je m'en fichisme*). As the "little great Maestro" took hold with his customary thoroughness, inspiration and discipline, the "gentlemen" straightened up in their chairs and began to play better than they knew they could. At the end they broke into a vociferous ovation.

From then on "they obeyed every crook of Toscanini's finger and shade of facial expression," as one Paris music lover put it; in *Falstaff,* he was "the soul, the very terrible and moving soul, of this perfectly harmonious spectacle," in the eyes of *Figaro's* critic.

While the public cheered Destinn and Rappold as Aida, Fremstad and Jadlowker in *Cavalleria*, Slezak in *Otello*—a triumph second only to Caruso's in many opinions—and Scotti in *Falstaff*, the composer-critics busily wrote columns of analysis and opinion about the works themselves. Verdi's late masterpieces provided their meat; the public preferred the *verismo* operas.

Both audiences and writers discovered unforeseen delights in *Manon Lescaut.* Not alone for its own charms, but also for the unexpected heroine, Puccini's opera won first place in the series. Shortly after the company arrived, Cavalieri became ill—it was rumored that all was not well with her appendix but that she preferred to avoid an operation rather than scar her beautiful skin. Gatti needed a Manon desperately.

"Where can I find what Toscanini wants now?" De Segurola quotes the manager as asking. "He demands a talented singer, young and dainty enough to impersonate the role so well known to Parisian audiences—an artist with an Italian voice and French looks. Where is that four-leafed clover?"

Exactly fitting Toscanini's description was a Spanish singer whom De Segurola had heard as Mimi in Milan the year before. The Spanish bass claims credit for suggesting Lucrezia Bori to Gatti, and he may well deserve it. In any case Bori made an immediate impression.

"*Une toute jeune fille,*" Gabriel Fauré said of her, using the phrase that was to follow the enchanting Bori through her career and beyond it. "Her voice is facile, fresh and charming in timbre; her acting showed no affectation."

Gatti immediately invited the new prima donna to the Metropolitan, but she was not free until 1912, when Puccini's *Manon* again served as her debut role.

The Paris introduction of Puccini's early opera coincided with news of his latest work. Behind the scenes, Gatti signed a contract for the world premiere of *La Fanciulla del West*.

The success of the first three performances of *Manon Lescaut* encouraged the impresario to add two extras to his schedule. The impressionable public still came in flocks. Never, agreed the scribes, had there been such a brilliant season.

The "Italians" had asked and received more money for their performances than any other theatre including the Opéra; their prices—an $8 top—had been cheerfully paid. Gatti took in $172,892, an average of $10,500 a night, which surprised everyone, including the Metropolitan financiers.

In addition to its artistic influence, the Metropolitan season produced two unforeseen by-products: M. Carré of the Opéra-Comique defensively raised prices twenty-five per cent; and M. Begusseau, secretary of the Châtelet, faced three duels from outraged *citoyens* who were jostled by *gendarmes* in the crowds outside the theatre.

In the week before they departed, artists of the Metropolitan company joined others in a gala benefit at the Opéra that set the town talking and raised 200,000 francs for the survivors of the submarine Pluviôse, which had recently sunk in an accident. The audience contained an even greater number of distinguished persons than graced the Châtelet's opening night. For the first time in forty years a work was sung in German at the Paris Opéra—the second act of *Tristan und Isolde* with Fremstad, Burrian, Homer, Hinckley, Reiss and Ananian. Toscanini conducted. Farrar, Caruso, Scotti and Alten sang the third act from *Bohème;* the *Otello* cast repeated an act; and the final scene from *Faust* made a stirring conclusion.

As the company said *"adieu,"* great plans were bruited for further international jaunts. Proposals involving an exchange with Sir Thomas Beecham in London received serious consideration. The company hoped to storm the seven hills of Rome and conquer another discriminating public. Such international projects were never realized. The roster might include envoys from practically every civilized country on earth, but the Metropolitan remained on the North American continent in the forty-six years to come.

5. NEW DIMENSIONS AND OLD FRIENDS

When Maurice Grau retired as an impresario in 1903, he advocated some reforms for grand opera astonishing from the old "star-system" magnate. Above all, he urged that "everything should be done to make opera attractive to the multitude."

Of all the Metropolitan's tour cities, Cleveland may justly claim to have filled Grau's prescription most satisfactorily. A city with a big auditorium and big ideas, Cleveland determined to acquire a grand opera season tailored to its own measurements.

Metropolitan performances in the Ohio metropolis have broken so many records that a "box score" of attendance and receipts is no longer published in the local dailies—it has ceased to be news. Nor are later figures available to challenge the $30,291 for *Rigoletto* with Talley in 1926, and, more remarkable for a new work, $30,700 for *Peter Ibbetson* in 1931.

The task of filling Public Auditorium's 9,000 seats for a week of opera raised Cleveland's sights even beyond the committee of guarantors that was rapidly becoming the norm for Metropolitan hospitality. Guarantors were indispensable, of course, but Cleveland went beyond them into its own city government, and, moving dramatically outside of its borders, extended its influence in a circle with a diameter of 500 miles.

In a moment of crisis in 1926, brought on by the collapse of a group that had sponsored the Metropolitan for three seasons, William R. Hopkins, city manager, intervened. Finding that direct municipal sponsorship would be illegal under the city charter, Hopkins seized on the idea of using an existing Public Auditorium Advisory Committee as a nucleus for an opera committee. The Northern Ohio Opera Association was formed under this guise.

Hopkins, a "glorious name in this story," according to Senator Robert J. Bulkley (whose meed is no less) persisted until Otto Kahn's confidence had been restored in Cleveland's good will and responsibility. The Metropolitan signed a contract for five years. Then the city manager called a meeting, at which Bulkley "talked too much and too enthusiastically" and was promptly drafted as chairman. With Lincoln G. Dickey, manager of the Auditorium, and Harold J. (better known as "Johnny") Miskell, a public relations and promotion expert since become general manager, the new committee set out to broaden the base of operations.

The intent from the very outset was to democratize the system of opera management. Hopkins published an official appeal to the citizens of northern Ohio for 500 additional guarantors. Experience showed, he explained, that not more than ten per cent would be called the first year; five per cent the second year. By the third, the enterprise should be self-sustaining.

On this basis, more than $200,000 was raised among 400 guarantors. Enthusiasm and gate receipts remained high throughout the five-year span. "We had a surplus in 1932, but our guarantee had expired, and depression made us cautious," said Bulkley. "We asked the Met if they would play for what we had in the bank. They chewed it over and finally agreed to four performances. But it cost just as much to promote four as twice the number."

In 1931 Detroit had made a strong bid for the opera. To show its sense of active partnership, the Cleveland City Council had authorized the use of Public Auditorium without rent from 1932-36 unless any performance made $900 profit. The newspapers looked jubilantly into the future, seeing another five-year contract and rosy prospects. "Operatic industry is leading us out of our well-known depression," crowed James H. Rogers in the *Plain Dealer*. But, as Archie Bell ruefully admitted in the *News,* "Cleveland bragged just before it fell." Reluctant to broach the subject to guarantors, the committee decided to suspend after the 1932 season.

For the next four years the Metropolitan swung in a modest orbit that extended no farther than Rochester to the west, Boston to the north, and Washington to the south, adding a few performances in White Plains and Newark, and continuing what was to be a twelve-year association with Hartford. The company had inaugurated the luxurious Bushnell Memorial Hall with *Tosca* on November 25, 1930 in a festive atmosphere compounded of ermine, silk hats, curious bystanders and Jeritza's temperament.

The prima donna arrived with three maids and four trunks, prepared to hang her own curtains at the dressing room windows. But Bushnell Hall had provided pleasing draperies as well as a grand piano, a divan and vases of snapdragons. Except for the tobacco smoke—which Martinelli also deplored—the tempestuous Tosca was happy. Smoke did not bother Scotti, who bought his own delicately scented Russian filter cigarettes and reminisced about his previous visit to the Parsons Theatre for *Faust* in 1904.

In 1937 the Metropolitan returned to Cleveland, where it has been very much at home ever since. Bulkley had no compunctions about asking for money, this time on a perpetual basis. Guarantors signed self-renewing agreements. The Northern Ohio Opera Association notifies a guarantor by November 1 of each year; if he has not canceled by the deadline of January 1, his pledge is automatically reinstated. Cancellations have been negligible, due chiefly to deaths. When a guarantor dies, the committee waits a decent interval, then invites survivors to join.

The billing, "Northern Ohio Opera Association in cooperation with the City of Cleveland" is not an idle one, the partnership not a marriage in name only. The city-owned Auditorium, not allowed to operate commercially, makes its reasonable rentals on annual contracts.

Civic groups, schools (which benefit by low-priced midweek matinees), industry and other cultural enterprises take a vital interest in Cleveland's Metropolitan Week. For several years the Sherwin-Williams Paint Company, which sponsored the Auditions of the Air, were hosts at a pre-season concert by current and past winners. Wilfred Pelletier would conduct the Cleveland Orchestra, and the program would be based on the year's repertory.

The absence of jealousy between the orchestra and the visiting opera is refreshing in a competitive musical world. Thomas L. Sidlo, the opera chairman from 1938 until his death in 1955, was also president of the Cleveland Orchestra Association for seventeen years.

Cleveland's "democracy" extends into a realm where it carries extra meaning—ticket prices. What Archie Bell called the "high-hats" still pay the toll—but "the derbies, fedoras and whoopee-caps get a bargain." Top prices rose gradually through the years to $10, but the low has remained at $1.20. High school students pay $1.25 no matter where they sit at the special matinees. As many as 1,000 seats outside of the good sight lines are given to the blind during the week.

Until Toronto entered the Metropolitan lists in 1952 with its 12,000-seat sports arena, Cleveland had the most gigantic operatic machinery in existence. Ohio still operates on a lavish scale second to none. Basically helpless without the populous area surrounding it, Cleveland depends for fifty per cent of the Auditorium's audiences on out-of-town patronage.

Cities within its sphere of influence may clamor for the return of the Metropolitan, but as long as Cleveland gives its inimitable service, the opera company is content. Such former Metropolitan customers as Pittsburgh, Cincinnati, Buffalo, Toledo and Detroit have never succeeded in applying the reentering wedge.

"They have not been able to build a tradition," Senator Bulkley gives as a reason for the eclipse of these cities. "Cleveland is now an 'opera town.'"

With its customary efficiency and grasp of large projects, the association set up box offices in outlying communities: forty in 1955. The oddest agency is in Canton, Ohio, where an automobile club passes out opera tickets along with road information. Special trains, planes and buses bring the devotees from far and near. Mrs. Flora Ward Hineline charters a plane in Toledo; her party dresses at home and returns the same evening.

Quizzes and contests based on the opera are a Cleveland specialty in the newspaper linage annually surrendered to opera. Hotels and restaurants and transportation agencies, not to mention retailers, become very busy and happy each April.

With an amplification system that ranks with the best and the recent installation of air-conditioning, Public Auditorium shelters its huge audiences in comfort.

Understandably Cleveland is too absorbed in Opera Present to take even a fleeting look at Opera Past. After Grau's *Lohengrin, Faust* and *Meistersinger* in 1901 at Gray's Armory, Gatti brought the company to Keith's Hippodrome in 1910 and 1911. The live geese trained for Farrar's *Königskinder* in 1911 showed unusual vivacity before the performance because of the presence of mice under the stage. (At least they made less disturbance than the elephants once left behind by a circus.) Full dress in the audience was a rarity. The *Leader* commented loftily: "We do not wish to encourage that sort of thing."

At the beginning of the 'twenties a Cleveland real estate broker who had once sung in the Metropolitan chorus ardently desired to bring the opera to his home town. Philip Miner met only denial from Kahn and Ziegler until Public Auditorium became a reality in 1923. Then the Metropolitan signed for seven performances the first year, ten each the second and third. Kahn made a dedicatory speech at the opening in 1923, complimenting cities "with clean operatic slates and unsophisticated audiences for taking the leadership."

By the end of 1926 it was apparent that Miner, the short redhead with the tall ambitions, had built on shaky foundations, which fell away from under others' feet as well as his own. It required frantic effort to shore up the structure.

The machinery runs smoothly now, but no one is inclined to take the Metropolitan for granted. Emergencies may lie just around the corner. Sidlo's death threw the committee into a quandary until Vernon Stouffer, head of the chain of restaurants and a member of the Metropolitan's National

Council, was elected to fill the post. The 1955 season, unaccountably shy at the box office, used up much of the reserve fund. Fortunately, 1956 proved a good vintage year for Cleveland's opera wine.

Top stars—one to an opera, preferably two—and favorite operas spell bliss for Cleveland, Senator Bulkley still maintains. Departure from either absolute threatens the box office. When 8,000 people agreed with the *Plain Dealer*'s Herbert Elwell that "nothing short of an iron will could resist Jepson's radiance of personal charm as Thais" and that "Flagstad is a miracle," all was well. Arthur Shepherd continued the joyous paean in the *Press* when Pons sang with the "God-given, blithesome ease of a bird in the first flush of spring," and when a "non-Wagnerian star like Stevens came along, with a 38" bust, a 27" waist and 38" hips, a gay smile and mischief in her eyes."

Cleveland takes a chance now and then on a "novelty," perhaps remembering the pleasant fate of *Peter Ibbetson*. To date ("knock on wood," adjures Johnny Miskell) no scheduled opera has been changed, although the normal number of replacements among singers occur. The psychology of substitutions works well, particularly for an unknown, Senator Bulkley believes. The public is usually sympathetic; the newcomer gives his best. Swarthout's last-minute assumption of the role of Adalgisa in *Norma* in 1931 without rehearsal is still cited as a Cleveland highlight.

The substitution of one well-known star for another creates problems among their respective fans. John Brownlee, called on to sing Germont for Baritone X in a matinee *Traviata*, found cabs scarce and gladly accepted a ride to the Auditorium with two girls. The two had come from Buffalo to hear X, they informed him. They raved about X. Finally Brownlee informed them that he was sorry they wouldn't hear X. They were desolated to learn that a substitute would take their idol's place. "Who would dare try?" one wailed as they drew up to the Auditorium stage door.

"I would," said Brownlee, politely assisting them from the cab.

The story goes that the two startled girls sent a new favorite a bunch of flowers after the performance.

No official parties command the presence of staff and stars nowadays—the Opera Balls of the past have been abandoned in favor of intimate luncheons and suppers. Senator Bulkley gave an announcement party for Marion Telva when the contralto became engaged to Elmer R. Jones in 1928. The warm friendliness, the red carpets, the flowers, the large gestures and small attentions Cleveland bestows on the visiting opera troupe make it one of the most pleasant stopovers.

On the way home from Cleveland in 1923 the Metropolitan paused to renew acquaintance with a city it had not seen for more than twenty years. A personal invitation had been extended by Rochester's leading philanthropist, George Eastman, who had made "Kodak" a word accepted by Webster, and had heightened his own and Rochester's fame by building a music school and theatre.

Eastman wanted the Metropolitan in his handsome theatre, and he was willing to pay the bills. This strange, shy man made friends cautiously and never married. He hired a string quartet for Sunday evenings and a full-time organist to play to him at breakfast every morning at 7:30 on the pipe organ installed in his residence. Employing the Metropolitan was much the same kind of gesture except that 3,000 people could enjoy it with him, instead of the select few at his Sunday evenings, over which presided as hostesses a succession of society leaders.

The cost of the Metropolitan's two-day visits in 1923 stunned the populace —although there were no deficits to pay. "The expense of one performance would maintain the average high class attraction for more than a week," marveled the *Democrat-Chronicle*. A. J. Warner, arbiter of musical taste for many years from the columns of this paper as well as the *Times-Union*, honored his city for assuming "a cosmopolitan and metropolitan aspect that must have caused many a citizen to wonder if he were really awake."

Eastman died in 1932, but his personal touch had been withdrawn from certain of his beneficiaries a few years before; and the Metropolitan continued its Rochester visits under the sponsorship of the Civic Music Association, an administrative group formed to channel Rochester's musical activities in many directions.

A single opera now sufficed for Rochester. Quite naturally, when Howard Hanson's *Merry Mount* experienced its year of glory at the Metropolitan, Rochester loyally demanded the opus of its chief musical citizen. Hanson, as director of the Eastman School and conductor of many orchestral events, was the hero of 1934.

Goddard Lieberson, a Columbia recording executive of today, wrote in the *Journal* that the Metropolitan "might have been kinder to the authors in the scenery they supplied," and that "Leonora Corona brought a good deal visually to her role."

Jack F. Dailey has succeeded the late Arthur M. See as manager of the Civic Music Association, and desires to keep the Metropolitan as a regular visitor to Rochester, deploring the one or two recent lacunae in its annual record.

In the same year that Cleveland established the firm Metropolitan base on which it rests today, a "charter member" returned to the fold. Baltimore had welcomed Abbey in 1884 and Grau and Conried after him, but after its plethora of opera in 1910 the city lost interest for a decade. Its opera house languished for an equal period under Kahn's absentee ownership. One day Kahn's representative told A. R. Doehme over a Baltimore luncheon table that the Lyric was to be sold for a garage. Doehme sprang into action, enlisted a group of citizens to sell $25 shares in a Lyric Company, headed by Dr. Hugh R. Young, whose father-in-law had performed a parallel service for the original theatre, then named Music Hall. By dint of strenuous campaigning, the new champions won a battle that was touch-and-go up to the last minute before a November 1 deadline.

Baltimore, the first and until recently the only city to offer music official support, can also boast the only municipal director of music, the celebrated Frederick R. Huber. When "Freddie" was appointed director of the Lyric in 1920 he had already been publicity director for Peabody Conservatory, had helped organize the Baltimore Symphony and assisted "Baltimur," as its loving natives know the city, to be the first to adopt a flag and anthem.

The Metropolitan had wanted to include Baltimore on its 1923 tour, but local guarantors had moved too sluggishly. By 1927 the omens were propitious. Within four days fifty-five guarantors gave $1,000 each toward four performances.

The Chicago Opera had become a frequent caller of late, and was to end its current season on February 18. Huber tried to hold back the Metropolitan news until the Chicago engagement was secure, but it leaked out—and without mention of Kahn's name. One of Kahn's close friends, A. Davies Warfield, president of Seaboard Air Line (he was fond of attaching his private car to the opera train for the trip to Atlanta) immediately withdrew his support. Huber coaxed Warfield back to the guarantors' committee. The Baltimore season would have missed the sparkle of the lavish entertainments at his home, Manor Glen, where opera stars indulged in milking contests among other diversions.

When the Lyric curtain opened on the Metropolitan for the first time in fifteen years, revealing a resplendent production of *Turandot,* a new page appeared in the tour books—a page discreetly embossed in formal lettering and illuminated with heraldic crests. Baltimore brought courtliness back to opera-going in a generation that had learned to live without refinements.

To make patrons dress-conscious, Huber ordered gray and maroon costumes for the entire Lyric staff of doormen, ushers and maids. Wilson B. Pearson, chief usher (a bank teller by day), bears the broad, crimson stripe of diplomacy across his bosom; all ushers wear white gloves. Souvenir program vendors must bark their wares in full dress.

"White tie" was *de rigueur* in the house for many years; depression and war persuaded Huber to relax his rule to the extent of "black tie."

Backstage a kind of "aristocratic democracy" prevailed, according to one reporter's highly colored account. Each dressing room was furnished exactly like the next; all bore stars on their doors. Two call boys were dressed as lackeys in French gray with gold braid.

In 1929 a small hall at the rear of the balcony, known as the Little Lyric, was eliminated to add balcony space. The gain: 694 seats.

Juggling dates in the spring to avoid Holy Week is problem enough with Easter a movable holiday, but Baltimore adds to Metropolitan complications with a racing season that brooks no competition. Maryland opera dates fall nowadays in late March; before 1933 the opera was the high spot of a "little season that blossomed after Easter, complementing the three April steeplechases." Even society reporting sometimes took on a tinge of the track, with Madison Calvert listing the occupants of the Lyric's "official paddock."

Tickets for the box Huber retains for himself have not borne numbers since the year President Taft arrived without warning, causing an embarrassing wait while seats were found for his party. "If I had had blank tickets, I could have shuffled people around more easily," said Huber.

No president has visited Baltimore since, although all are traditionally invited. Mrs. Woodrow Wilson and Mrs. Herbert Hoover were distinguished guests in 1932. Diplomats are frequent patrons.

Baltimore remembers as high spots in its opera-going Bori's farewell to the stage in 1936, when Mayor Jackson presented her with a silver jewel case and mispronounced her name three different ways; Ponselle's engagement to Carle Jackson, the Mayor's son (and her subsequent marriage and divorce); and John Charles Thomas' opera debut in his home town as Athanael in *Thais* in 1939.

Encores persisted as late as 1942, when Beecham allowed Leonard Warren to repeat the "Toreador Song," which had taken the house by storm.

In his sixteen consecutive years and the eleven since a two-year break in 1942-43 and 1943-44, Huber set a good many records of which he is proud. He never called on a guarantor; never departed from a "high-society" basis; never allowed an organization to be a sponsor (refusing Hutzler's department store although Hutzlers as individuals were loyal guarantors); never split a box; and never made a cent for himself. Opera prices rose to $5 for the cheapest seat; $10 for orchestra; $12.50 for boxes. Standing room cost $3.

The Lyric's 2,620 seats were invariably bought in advance; but prices cannot go above a certain point, while opera costs continue to soar. In 1954 the Opera Club, which took over the sponsoring duties as a non-profit-making corporation in 1928, decided to withdraw.

A new group with Dr. Harry R. Slack as president set about a rejuvenation. It includes Miss Ponselle, whose palatial establishment in Green Spring Valley, Villa Pace, is open to a constant stream of friends, students and poodles.

Huber, as managing director of his beloved Lyric, continues to advise the committee and to schedule dates. Through the years he has managed to add improvements—new seats, a set for the symphony, a new marquee, fresh curtains in the boxes, a new orchestra pit even if the façade can never be completed because a stubborn owner refuses to sell part of the frontage. Baltimore hopes that the prediction of a magazine article will never come true: "If Huber ever resigns, a crash of thunder and cymbals would dissolve the Lyric instantaneously into dust."

Washington rejoined the opera caravan beside Baltimore in 1927, but remained only five years. Mrs. Katie Wilson Greene hired the big Auditorium, which was filled to its 6,000 capacity for three operas at an $8.80 top.

Gatti-Casazza expressed amazement in a *Herald* interview that the nation's capital possessed no opera house. The *Times* showed interest in the impresario's ability to smooth the ruffled feathers of high-strung singers, and in Chaliapin's extra-large bed.

Next season the impresario moved to Poli's Theatre and raised prices to $10; four performances fell $10,000 under the guarantee of $60,000, although all boxes were filled, to the credit of Mrs. Robert Low Bacon, local chairman. President and Mrs. Coolidge attended the opening *Norma,* but departed after the first act "in accordance with the president's custom at grand opera," the *Post* explained. Mrs. Hoover was seen at two performances.

The opera arrived on the front pages of Washington's newspapers for the first time in 1930. Mrs. Hoover was ill, therefore Vice-President Curtis, the guest of Mrs. Thomas F. Walsh, represented the White House. The *Post* considered the Fox Theatre, seating 3,500, the most adequate in Washington.

Although in 1931 the current chairman claimed a surplus of $3,000 even after paying deficits of other seasons, Mrs. Greene was forced by illness to give up this taxing project. The opera did not return for eleven years.

In 1952 and 1953 Washington engagements were accomplished by the joint forces of a New York impresario, S. Hurok, and a Washington bureau headed by Mrs. Constance Snow. Three performances the first year met with success; four in the second year lost money for the backers. In 1954-55 Patrick Hayes, a Washington concert manager, made another attempt in Loew's Capitol Theatre (formerly the Fox), presenting *Traviata* and *Faust*. The Gounod opera failed to please the public, with the result that fifty guarantors were called on for four-fifths of their pledge. A single performance of *Figaro* in 1955-56 promised good fortune for everyone. Washington trusted to retain its foothold in the Metropolitan's scheme.

Another long-time friend to celebrate reunion with the New York company after a long absence was Boston, which for sixteen years had looked elsewhere for operatic enlightenment. In Gatti's penultimate season, Anita Davis Chase, a native New Yorker who had learned some secrets of management from the revered Charles A. Ellis, brought the Metropolitan back to Boston.

"Honest opera returned last evening," the *Transcript* candidly proclaimed after the opening *Aida* on April 2, 1934. But the familiar initials H. T. P. did not appear at the end of the story. Henry T. Parker had died of pneumonia four days before, after working valiantly to promote the opera season he would not live to enjoy.

This "small, fierce-eyed individual . . . as indigenous to Boston as G. B. S. to London . . . the man who broke the back of English prose" inspired many other tributes in addition to this one by David McCord in *Theatre Arts Monthly*. His place in Boston was never filled, even though many vigorous and individual pens carried on. Philip Hale, his archenemy, outlived him by only eight months.

With the exception of 1942-43, when gasoline rationing posed difficulties for too many of the Hub's elderly guarantors, Mrs. Chase remained at the helm until 1954, when she was succeeded by Harriet O'Brien. Her unhappiest moments in twenty years came in the annual refusal of checks amounting to more than $20,000. Among her most joyous memories she counts the promotion of interest among schools which she saw grow to rewarding proportions. As an example she cited "one man who bought fourteen seats for a *Carmen* a few years ago, and came back in 1954 with an order for 1,000— from the same school."

The Metropolitan moved from the Boston Opera House to a theatre bearing its own name—although no relation—in 1941. Every seat of its 4,000 was a good seat, Mrs. Chase declared. "And the Metropolitan Theatre was so clean! They shampooed every carpet; every dressing room was painted like a china plate. We loved working there. The only difficulty was the shallow stage."

When the theatre became too deeply involved in film commitments, the opera returned to the Boston Opera House, to continue in a close bond with its oldest partner.

Part VIII

EDWARD JOHNSON:
AMBASSADOR-AT-LARGE

1. FROM PAMPAS TO CAMPUS

"When you saw those three stride arm in arm across the lobby, their silk hats and patent leather pumps glistening, their white ties crisp and immaculate, their tail coats dancing behind them, you knew the Met had come to town," a Dallas resident nostalgically recalled just the other day.

This well groomed trio—Edward Johnson, Frank St. Leger and Earle R. Lewis, wearing what for them were "work clothes"—symbolized for Dallas the tingling excitement of grand opera from the inception of the modern era. Although technically considered a reunion, since Conried had brought *Parsifal* to the Dallas Opera House in 1905, the Metropolitan's arrival in 1939 virtually constituted a new start.

In the intervening generation Dallas had grown to eight times its former size and had absorbed culture as a dry arroyo takes into itself the flash flood of the desert. For a city that already boasted America's most publicized fashion shop, biggest book store and least necessary skyscrapers, grand opera was an ever recurrent dream. Other companies had paid fleeting visits, but Dallas continued to yearn for the Metropolitan.

When at last the mutual rediscovery was accomplished, "both parties were simply charmed, and the meeting showed many of the signs of a love affair," wrote John Rosenfield, the only music critic in America who presides over an entire "Amusements" section in a daily and Sunday newspaper. Rosenfield's reputation is nationwide through several brilliant appearances on the Metropolitan Opera Quiz during the Saturday afternoon broadcasts, while his advice and approval in the columns of the *Morning News* remain the *sine qua non* for Dallas in all musical and theatrical matters.

The tour of 1939 marked the first in a period of gradual expansion. As wanderlust reawakened, the Metropolitan found an ingratiating ambassador-at-large in its new general manager.

Gatti had retired in 1935 and Herbert Witherspoon was appointed, only to die at his desk of a heart attack in May. Edward Johnson, who had been named as an associate, stepped into the top position. Already a favorite with tour audiences as a polished lyric tenor, as impresario Johnson showed tact and an infectious enthusiasm that delighted guarantors and average citizens alike, while his gift for repartee endeared him to the newspaper fraternity. When the most gregarious "boss" the Metropolitan had ever known left his post in 1949, his collection of trophies included keys to a dozen cities, a Confederate bond and flag (from Atlanta) and innumerable scrolls testifying to his popularity.

The emissary from Dallas was Arthur L. Kramer, a lawyer and department store owner who had never forgotten his early musical training. He brought the news from Johnson's office that his city might be allowed to share a week with New Orleans. Dallas, with what Frank Goodwyn described in *Lone-Star Land* as a penchant for "continuous materialization of seemingly extravagant air castles," promptly raised $136,800, more than twice the amount of underwriting for the final Chicago Opera season a decade before.

Since that first bold gesture, Dallas has never found out what an unsuccessful opera season might cost. Devotedly Kramer served the Grand Opera Association as president until his death in 1951. His son, Arthur, Jr., has taken over the direction of the opera as well as A. H. Harris & Co.

From top stars to engineers and hairdressers, the Metropolitan loves this Texas city, for it is the only one to invite every member of the company— more than 300 strong—to a supper dance after opening night. This unique gambol, each year following a different motif in decoration, is held alternately in the two hotels, the Adolphus and the Baker.

Every season brings some new lyric joy and some piquant comment from Rosenfield. "Grace Moore's bedroom key was not the only key lost in the first act of *La Bohème*," he wrote in 1939. After "an operatic strip tease" by Lakmé in 1940, the company "got down to music" with *Walküre,* deeply satisfying the Wagner-hungry Texans. *Rosenkavalier* in 1946 proved "a triumph of music over matter," for the condition of the sets was deplorable. Welitch's sensational Tosca gave Dallas a "high-voltage esthetic shock" in 1950; when the movie version of *Samson and Delilah* played at the same time as the opera, Rosenfield headed an omnibus review: "The dame is the same."

The Metropolitan's rendezvous with New Orleans was suspended between 1941 and 1947; Dallas took on a fifth performance in 1942 with some reluctance. New Orleans had supported only three in 1941, and had barely made its guarantee, although both Louisianans and the opera folk had relished the short stay. The *Times-Picayune* critic, however, finding himself "buried in a thicket of bass fiddles" which had overflowed the pit in the inadequate Municipal Auditorium, could only report that "the bass fiddles were excellent."

When the opera resumed wider tours after two war years, a zig-zag trail in 1947—Chicago-Atlanta-Dallas-New Orleans—caused severe headaches in the booking office. Dallas was asked to relinquish her sovereignty in Texas to allow stopovers in San Antonio and Houston.

"Dallas Is Tolerant," a newspaper reported, but open grumbling persisted until Kramer threw his whole weight behind the change, emphasizing that the situation was desperate. Johnson had appealed to him in his friendly way and Kramer had agreed to take sole responsibility, providing only that Dallas should come first on the calendar and that no repertory be duplicated. The gesture was called "gracious" in Houston.

In the same season occurred the disastrous explosion at Texas City. Metropolitan artists gave their services for a concert, raising $10,000 to help the sufferers, the company's first benefit of the kind on tour since the Cincinnati flood in 1884. A heat wave put the orchestra men in shirt sleeves but did not militate against "the Metropolitan's most artistic season thus far," in Rosenfield's opinion.

Dallas entertains its distinguished visitors in the Fair Park Auditorium, seating 4,500, one of the colorful buildings annually occupied by the State Fair. The city has resolved the difficulty of opera competition within its state borders by keeping its own patronage up to a healthy level.

San Antonio remained in the Metropolitan parade only one season, 1946-47. San Antonians were already busy with an opera festival founded in association with their orchestra, and featuring Metropolitan stars for top roles each season.

"For Houston, art is a social obligation . . . to be tolerated only as a prize fighter tolerates tails at a banquet," believes author Goodwyn. Customers all over the world will pay for cotton, oil and chemicals whether or not the Metropolitan gives its annual pair of performances. The Southwest's doyenne of concert managers, Mrs. Edna W. Saunders is a soft-spoken and tough-minded lady with snow-white hair who has been seasoned by years of promoting the Chicago Opera and booking every great artist in the concert world for Houston audiences. The Metropolitan appears as the climax to her blue-ribbon list, but is additionally dignified by a separate association, set up as a tax-exempt body.

Sir Thomas Beecham's remark about the Queen of Texas boom towns has become a classic: "Houston would be a beautiful city if they ever finished it." In a metropolis Mrs. Saunders describes as "a bed of ants, running all over the place and doing a lot of things all at once," the manager sometimes wonders how many among her audiences are real music lovers, but adds that she doesn't care "as long as they come."

No Metropolitan guarantor has ever been assessed, but Mrs. Saunders remains adamant about revealing figures—whether gains or losses. In this respect she claims to be a rock against which even the persistent trade paper *Variety* "stubs its toe."

Aida was given "at Egyptian temperature" in Houston's first Metropolitan season at the old City Auditorium, according to Hubert Roussel, who writes about music and many other things at great length in the Houston *Post*. The orchestra had stripped off its coats, according to good old Texas custom, but many patrons, "attempting to live up to Metropolitan fashions, sat sweltering in formal dress." Orchids wilted and pearl lorgnette handles slithered from white-gloved fingers.

The Metropolitan, in company with Mrs. Saunders' other attractions, recently moved to Music Hall, a model of modern design and equipment, seating 3,010. In spite of the boon of its air conditioning, Mrs. Saunders entertains the idea of returning to the larger hall. No complaint from the artists reached the manager in the eight years of the steam-bath atmosphere of City Auditorium, although one wonders at the fortitude of Blanche Thebom, who winds her long hair around her neck as Ortrud, regardless of the latitude in which *Lohengrin* is performed.

"The Met Goes to College!" This favorite headline has appeared almost annually in one newspaper or another since April 13, 1942, when the opera troupe first set foot officially on a university campus. Ward G. Biddle, vice-president and treasurer of Indiana University, in his additional capacity as director of programs, had wished for the Metropolitan so passionately that he insisted I. U.'s new auditorium be built with the opera's requirements in mind. He consulted Johnson, and commissioned Lee Simonson to design the stage.

The result is a hall second to none on the Metropolitan's tour. Technicians sigh with relief when the company reaches Bloomington; the stage is well-nigh perfect, and only the scenery, costumes and props need to be unpacked. Donald H. Horton, auditorium manager, and his staff purr at the annual compliments.

Aida proved a good choice for the opening show. In the handsome audience chamber students, faculty, townspeople, Hoosiers from all over the state, and Kentuckians long deprived of the Metropolitan filled the 3,788 comfortable seats and applauded Bampton, Carron, Castagna, Warren and Cordon.

In the vast lobby known as the Hall of Murals because of Thomas Hart Benton's magnificent Indiana scenes (a gift from the state legislature) and in the foyers where Hoosier paintings hang proudly, the talk concerned Bloomington's undisputed claim to a place on the Metropolitan's schedule thenceforth. The governing committee gaped in amazement when they saw a profit of $243. They had expected none; and none ever again materialized. One reason is that the student ticket sales—at $1 each—have increased from twenty to fifty per cent of the house.

The Metropolitan did indeed return to Bloomington in 1946, this time for two performances, a quota since maintained. Biddle died the same year; he did not long enjoy the fulfillment of his dream. He was succeeded by Harold W. Jordan, who had assisted with the original opera negotiations and who remains program director for the University's full music schedule.

From the moment the train pulls in, the company knows that life is going to be different in Bloomington from any other roadstop. No shortage of porters here; boys in turtle-neck sweaters vie for the privilege of toting the stars' luggage. Metropolitan artists joyously greet former colleagues, now faculty members: Frank St. Leger, Charles Kullman, Dorothee Manski, Anna Kaskas and Agnes Davis.

Then the company scatters to the four corners of the campus. Housing is still a problem. When a projected addition to the Union Building is completed, everyone can bide under one roof; meanwhile, the ballet girls still batter their precious toes against rocks on the dark path from the dormitory to the hall.

A pattern of social events was set long ago. Monday night the students give a party for 2,000 in the Men's Quadrangle. This is the outcome of an early year's impromptu serenade of the ballet girls by the college boys, gradually joined by barefoot co-eds and opera choristers until the scene resembled the *Meistersinger* riot.

On Tuesday afternoon patrons and University and Metropolitan officials form a receiving line for more than 1,000 guests in the Union Alumni Hall. Two cicerones for each artist make sure that everybody meets everybody else. The University president entertains the artists at supper the second night.

What pleases the company most is the chance to witness an opera performance with which it has had absolutely nothing to do. Every year Wilfred C. Bain, dean of the Music School, is pleased to show one of the opera department's productions, which, especially the impressive *Parsifal,* have won national acclaim.

Ernst Hoffman's tragic death in an automobile accident in 1955 deprived the department of its mainstay, but Hans Busch, the gifted stage designer, and St. Leger among others have carried on.

Meanwhile another Indiana campus beckoned. Purdue University at Lafayette, only a few miles away, had antedated Bloomington by two years in building an opulent auditorium to house its convocations, lectures and special events. Dr. R. B. Stewart, vice-president and treasurer, coveted the Metropolitan for this sleek Hall of Music, whose fine lines and proportions disguised its true vastness—6,146 seats.

As a technical school Purdue embraces no fine arts departments, but its concert course is comprehensive, and many big shows have played in the Hall of Music. The Metropolitan, biggest of all, came to Lafayette in 1945, with some thought of alternating between the two branches of Indiana University.

The Bloomington dovecotes fluttered; this was too close to home. The Metropolitan bypassed Lafayette for two years, then in 1948 returned, limiting the Purdue promotion to the local community, with no public ticket sale and no advertising. Selling the big house under such conditions was impossible. Even after the restriction was raised, sellouts have not been common, *Carmen* in 1952 coming closest, according to Ross Smith, head of convocations and lectures (and director of Purdue's active theatre group).

Acoustics present no problem even without amplification, avers John Ditamore, a Purdue graduate in electrical engineering who has managed the Hall of Music from its inception.

Lafayette's Metropolitan evening, following Bloomington's two, creates a little Indiana festival. Walter Whitworth of the *Indianapolis News,* Henry Butler of the *Times* and Corbin Patrick of the *Star* cover both impartially, being careful to set their watches back—or is it forward?—as they go from the "fast time" of Bloomington to the Standard Time of Lafayette.

Minneapolis sealed a bargain twelve years ago that brought the Metropolitan to its third campus. The annual season in Northrop Auditorium is such big business and managed so professionally that one could easily overlook the fact that the University of Minnesota is the prime factor in this felicitous arrangement—that is, unless one happens to be a Minnesotan. In that northern state everyone knows that the University is part of a triumvirate opera sponsorship that includes the Minneapolis Symphony Orchestra Association and a citizens' committee.

The University's stately white-pillared hall was standing dark too many nights a week to suit the chief of the Civic and Commerce Association, a bustling man named Perry Williams. Arthur Gaines, the bluff, jovial manager of the symphony, agreed. Together they approached James S. Lombard, director of the University's Department of Concerts and Lectures, who possessed an entrée to University councils and who had won a reputation for hard-headedness when dealing with New York managers for his artists' courses in Northrop Memorial and the 200 concerts annually given in the state as a service of his department.

Once the necessary University sanction had been received, the plan moved swiftly to completion. Stanley Hawks, who had seen a number of years of diplomatic service, was deemed the ideal chairman for the state-wide sponsors' group (later extending through the Northwest and into Canada). His committee easily raised the $50,000 guarantee fund the University Board of Regents had stipulated before authorizing a contract. The great adventure had begun.

In 1955 as in 1945 the four operas that have become standard for Minneapolis acted like a magnet for pilgrims from eleven states and Canada. Winnipeg has set up its own box office. Fans think nothing of driving 200 miles to and from the short festival.

The profits, always divided between the orchestra and the University, grow slimmer, for local expenses have almost doubled. With its half the University has made up the deficits of the local Metropolitan Auditions of the Air for three years, and has underwritten such special projects as Herbert Graf's book, *Opera for the People,* and John K. Sherman's history of the Minneapolis Symphony, *Music and Maestros.*

Perhaps the most festive of all seasons was 1947, when three out of the four operas—*Figaro, Butterfly* and *Lohengrin*—featured weddings, one critic pointed out. *Faust,* the fourth, "skipped the ceremony."

Minneapolis was enthralled to discover through a newspaper interview that you do not wish good luck to a singer but you invite him instead, if he is a German, to break his neck (*"Hals und bein bruch"*), while if he is an Italian, you hope that he may be eaten by a wolf (*"In bocca al lupo"*).

"Tops in Tights" ran the banner line over a rotogravure feature in the *Tribune,* which graphically compared George London's charms to those of Pinza, Brownlee, Siepi, Caruso, Tibbett, Peerce, Jean and Edouard de Reszke, Bjoerling and Hackett.

When Eugene Ormandy flew to conduct *Fledermaus* in the city where he had directed the orchestra some years before, John Sherman in the *Star* called him a "cherubic and dynamic maestro," and remarked "how odd and refreshing it was to hear the audience break out in laughter . . . instead of remaining mum . . . as all good little opera audiences do."

Twin City critics remain staunchly independent although mergers have overtaken a pair of journals in each city. Of the Metropolitan's new mounting for *Faust* in 1954, "debatable" was John H. Harvey's word in the *St. Paul Dispatch-Pioneer-Press.* "Partly effective; a major gain over the previous corny one," opined Norman Houk in the *Minneapolis Tribune,* while from his desk opposite Houk's—the new regime has retained both critics—Sherman told his *Star* readers that *Faust* was "a pleasant surprise—bold and striking in at least three scenes."

Minneapolis treasures its personal meetings with the stars at parties in the homes of Stanley Hawks, Leonard Lampert, Jr., Samuel Maslon and other Twin Cities social leaders. The Opera Association held a reception for many years at a smart club, and Mr. and Mrs. Frederick L. Weyerhaeuser and the Lombards have entertained jointly. Leo Pflaum's Friday "brunch" is an established custom.

The three-pronged sponsorship continues with amiability and efficiency. Boris Sokoloff has taken Gaines' place as symphony manager, but Hawks still heads the citizens' committee (as well as the symphony), and Lombard continues to manage the series with a firm hand and a shrewd sense of values.

2. ONCE AGAIN, COAST-TO-COAST

For the Metropolitan Opera the two middle years of the Second World War reduced travel to the vestige of a memory. Cleveland was the only survivor among tour cities in 1943. The courage of its subscribers in voting not to break the cherished affiliation stimulated Edward Johnson to undertake a token tour. He gambled on two weeks in Chicago and picked up a Rochester date on the way home. The following year he added a Boston week and a single *Tannhäuser* in Milwaukee.

Then in 1945 the general manager took a step which rapidly accelerated the recovery of the road: he turned for assistance in booking to two professionals, Marks Levine and Sol Hurok. It was the first time since Herman Grau's foray in 1886 that outsiders had assumed tour direction. Levine, as head of the concert department of the NBC Artists Service (later National Concert and Artists Corporation), had been close to the Metropolitan for many years, representing Flagstad, Melchior and a dozen others. Hurok, a bold operator who handled unwieldy touring aggregations and princely sums of money with equal aplomb, agreed after a single conversation to participate fifty-fifty in raising guarantees and in profits—if any. Francis Robinson, already working for Hurok and dividing his spare time between road work for Katherine Cornell and publicity for the Berkshire Festival, began his experience as Metropolitan "contact man."

Their contract, known as the "Levine-Hurok Folly," guaranteed to the company $78,000 a week the first year, $80,000 thereafter, plus railroad fares. Only after two years of losses did they begin to collect a ten per cent commission—"but with an average of $100,000 a week, we did not complain," said Levine. "And besides, the five years of work and travel with the Met were the most pleasant I ever spent."

Atlanta, Boston, Baltimore, Cleveland and Rochester kept exclusive control within their self-sufficient local associations, but other cities, which grew in number from four in 1945 to eleven in 1949, gladly accepted the Levine-Hurok services. The majority have remained loyal Metropolitan hosts to this day.

The Southeast proved an unexpectedly fertile field for expansion. Levine's old friend, Michaud Moody, who had been called in by Richmond's Civic Music Association to take charge of the half week "graciously relinquished by Atlanta" in 1930, had happily received two performances in 1941 and again in 1942, placing one in his regular Celebrity Series each year. In 1948 he found himself on Levine's route for a *Traviata* and has since twice bid successfully for Bing's attention. The artists always hope for an overnight stay in order to visit the flowering gardens of Virginia's capital or to make a pilgrimage to nearby Williamsburg.

Chattanooga's first experience with the Metropolitan occurred in the middle of a railroad strike in 1946. On May 19, with the nation's traffic snarled, a five-day truce was announced. The company left Dallas, due for *Carmen* and *Butterfly* in Memphis before Chattanooga's *Rigoletto* on May 22. The truce was up at 4 o'clock the next afternoon, but the Metropolitan train slid through Washington and home without intervention.

For the second and latest time, Johnson brought the troupe to Chattanooga in 1948, again at the behest of Clint McDade, a local publisher and orchid grower. For several years it was the endearing custom of this ardent opera lover to airmail his fragile, lovely blossoms to favorite singers on birthdays or important openings.

Memphis has afforded the Metropolitan a rare example of a "one-man show" in I. L. Myers, known almost universally as "Ike." His nearest counterpart, the late George Eastman, left little personal imprint on Metropolitan history, whereas "Ike's" individuality lies at the core of the opera's transactions with Memphis. Behind an impassive, almost sardonic façade, Myers approaches his objectives with a passion that burns away obstacles. His chief goal: every cultural advantage that he can bring to his home town. For all his decorations by foreign governments, his friendships among artists everywhere, this citizen of the world turns to Tennessee for deepest satisfaction.

"Ike" admits that he is a "lone wolf" and fidgets when confronted with multiple opinions. Anecdotes that hide the facts in an aura of legend reveal his *modus operandi*. The first concerns his introduction to the Metropolitan.

On one of his annual trips to New York to buy artists for his Appreciation Arts course (founded in 1931), Myers met Marks Levine in the elevator at 711

Fifth Avenue, the old NBC building. It was 1945 and Levine had the Metropolitan very much in mind. "How about it?" he asked. "Fine!" said "Ike." The deal was closed before the elevator reached Levine's floor. "Considering that 'Ike' had committed himself to $35,000 of his own money, and Levine's office was on the third floor," a Metropolitan official commented, "that's more than $10,000 a floor."

The second story involves another Metropolitan official who waited for his money after the Memphis engagement until the last possible moment before leaving the Peabody Hotel for the train. A hint brought immediate action. "Ike" walked over to the hotel cashier's desk and made out a counter check— "five figures, no stub, no receipt, nothing—and off we went to the station."

After poor attendance at *Rosenkavalier* in 1948 (his third season), Myers brought only one opera for each of three years, "to create a shortage and increase the demand." Two have been the rule since, except in 1954. "I could make money with one," stated this unusual manager, "but I'd rather lose money and have fun." His risks are assumed, a close friend insists, against a modest income from a paper business.

Opera balls, inaugurated in 1953, raise money for the Mid-South Opera Guild. Mrs. Herbert Darnell, Hugo Dixon and William R. Kent made of the 1955 edition at the King Cotton Hotel one of the gayest and most beautifully appointed. Lobster flown from Maxim's in Paris provided both entrée and "conversation piece."

In 1947 *Le Nozze di Figaro* contended with the street fair that celebrated the annual debarkation of the King and Queen of Cotton from their barge on the Mississippi River. It was an abnormally hot evening, so several Ellis Auditorium windows were kept open. Many loyal opera patrons were forced to tune one ear to Mozart and the other to a calliope that joined Bidu Sayao in several high notes.

"Never again, if I can help it, will the opera conflict with Cotton Carnival," vowed "Ike." So far, it never has.

From Johnson's earliest days as general manager fanciful visions of "regional" opera had flitted through his mind, he confided recently. He saw New York, Chicago and San Francisco as partners in the exchange of scenery and top artists, though otherwise maintaining autonomous forces. Believing the Midwest to be a natural hub, he had broached the project to Robert Hall McCormick, Chicago Opera Association president in the early 'forties. But the dream receded as emergencies at home and the rebuilding of the tours occupied his attention.

"Witherspoon, in a desire to give opportunities to American artists, had let a million dollars' worth of contracts expire," Johnson recalled. "The concert agencies at once picked them up, so that we could no longer command the artists' time at home, much less on tour. We started then with no money —and no company."

In the gradual development of both personnel and finances, the tours played a steady role in the 'thirties. Three new factors generated interest at home and abroad. The founding of The Metropolitan Opera Guild in 1935 by Mrs. August Belmont, assisted by Mrs. Herbert Witherspoon, soon strengthened the Metropolitan's position throughout the country while the lively *Opera News,* edited by Mary Ellis Peltz, gave knowledge and pleasure to a growing Guild membership, many of whom knew opera chiefly through the Saturday afternoon broadcasts sponsored since 1940 by the Texas Company. Further public excitement on a national scale was aroused by the Auditions of the Air, which from 1935 provided young American talent for the Metropolitan and also gave many communities a feeling of intimacy through their candidates.

In 1948 the road quivered in apprehension at the news that the Metropolitan would shut its doors because of what were said to be "insuperable" difficulties with the unions. After an uneasy summer, the word went out that all was well; the tour would proceed as scheduled.

Johnson had a particular reason for keeping this migration intact: a siren song from 3,600 miles away had brought back the regional vision, but with a different western anchor. For three years an organization known as Greater Los Angeles Plans (inevitably shortened to GLAP) had been sponsoring ambitious projects, including the annual visits of the San Francisco Opera, while quietly gathering large real estate holdings.

Whether the idea originated with Ray W. Smith, GLAP's master mind, or with Dr. Charles H. Strub, a colorful Angelino who combined dentistry with promotion of baseball and race tracks, it came full-blown to Johnson's desk: a new opera house for Los Angeles; a western home for the Metropolitan. Meanwhile the Met was urged to make a trial trip, playing in the old Shrine Auditorium. A tempting guarantee of $275,000 waited.

Johnson often explained the intention of the Metropolitan, as a national company, to avoid discrimination between cities and to accept all that could be worked into the schedule. He was fond of illustrating this impartiality with a story, told with a naughty twinkle that luncheon and banquet audiences found irresistible.

A small boy ran to a policeman and asked his help to separate his father and another man, who were fighting.

"Which is your father?" asked the officer.

"I dunno. That's what they're fighting about."

George A. Sloan, president of the Metropolitan Opera Association, shared Johnson's ardent desire to expand westward. The 1948 tour could be stretched to include Los Angeles by reactivating Denver and one other way station on the homeward trip. Levine, although he opposed the project on two grounds, financial (obvious) and political (San Francisco's opera considered Los Angeles exclusive territory), enlisted the dynamic Arthur Oberfelder of Denver for three performances and found a courageous lady in Lincoln, Mrs. Richard W. Smith, who agreed to shoulder the burden of a single show.

The Los Angeles trek started badly. In El Paso, the train hit a car that crossed the tracks just before the barrier went down. Several Mexicans were killed. A two-hour police investigation threw the schedule out of kilter. Still, the curtain went up on *Carmen* on time before a record audience in Shrine Auditorium.

To Levine's surprise and Johnson's gratification the fortnight brought a stunning success. GLAP officials uttered philanthropic sentiments; Dr. Strub, who had been made vice-president of a special opera committee, gave a costly party at the California Club; Albert Goldberg of the *Times* sensed a "deeper undercurrent of satisfaction that East and West had joined hands." Mildred Norton in the *News* evoked the past: "since the Met's last visit in 1905 women's skirts have gone from above the ankles to above the knees and back again." It seemed a pity that L. E. Behymer, "the perennial old caliph of culture," had died the previous autumn.

Johnson was vindicated in daring to produce *Peter Grimes;* Britten's opera caused a sensation. To Patterson Greene of the *Examiner* the work was "the most exciting since *Der Rosenkavalier.*"

A second season was immediately entered in the route books. History threatened to repeat itself by a railroad delay in El Paso (fortunately minus fatalities). Ramon Vinay, Nicola Moscona and Herbert Graf made a sortie across the Mexican border in search of souvenirs. Because all three were foreign-born, border officials resisted their re-entry until someone from the company came to rescue them.

Even though the mayor proclaimed a special Opera Week, the 1949 season deflated hopes of any lasting East-West entente. Los Angeles turned captious. It was a mistake to repeat *Peter Grimes;* the impact had worn off. Some jitters were attributed to the aftermath of the Garris tragedy. Only *Carmen* and *Traviata* (each given twice), *Rigoletto* and *Aida* lived up to both financial and critical standards.

The dream was over. New York woke up to the impracticality of a lengthy trip with only lukewarm hosts at the end of it; Los Angeles expiated her feeling of guilt by turning her full loyalty to San Francisco.

Denver, where Oberfelder had joined Myers in the category of lone guarantor for his city, let the Met go with reluctance. The impresario had paid a deficit in 1949, but was still game.

"Denver's bluebloods almost got to pulling hair over who would entertain," *Time* reported. "Hazel Oberfelder, wife of the local promotor, cleared all invitations. Guests were taken from one party and deposited at another; persons not in favor got no stars . . . by the time the opera left town half of Denver's society was not speaking to the other half."

The pretty Pat Smith's heroic effort in Lincoln brought the town in force to the University of Nebraska's Coliseum to hear *Tosca.* Even though guarantors had to make up a loss of about $8,000, Lincoln would have tried again, but the engagement echoed Grau's single shot of 1900.

In 1949 the company accepted an invitation of several years' standing from the *Des Moines Register* and *Tribune* to play KRNT Theatre in Des Moines, returning each year to the well-equipped stage of the "largest legitimate theatre in the United States" (it seats 4,139). Duane C. Peterson, manager until 1953, and R. C. Fraser, who succeeded him, have found the Metropolitan an expensive but entirely worthwhile attraction. Drake University students rush to fill the 298 minimum-priced seats—if they haven't already signed up backstage as supers. Eddie Scott, his six feet four inches and 230 pounds encased in smart green livery, has greeted patrons at the center door since the beginning.

Des Moines boasts one of the country's largest organized concert audiences but confessed to a relatively unsophisticated opera public until recently, except for a sturdy devotion to the Met's Saturday broadcasts. Clifford Bloom, the leading critic, keeps his readers well informed in the *Register*. It is nevertheless possible to hear a resident of some nearby town insist on an opera "with melody, because that's what we country kids like."

When the Metropolitan's booking team made overtures to St. Louis in 1945, the city had not seen the troupe since Guy Golterman (later active in many local operatic enterprises) had transformed the enormous Coliseum into a "palm bower" for *Bohème, Trovatore, Faust* and *Madama Butterfly* in 1910.

William Zalken, manager of the St. Louis Symphony, agreed that the orchestra's society would make a good sponsor and signed a contract for three performances in May 1946 in Kiel Auditorium's Opera House. The company's intermittent visits to the familiar city since then have not all been so felicitous as the first, which sold out from the initial announcement, but St. Louis still wants the Metropolitan whenever it will say "yes."

The western tours had eliminated Chicago, where the company had played since 1943 "on its own," always with a loss, and Milwaukee, where Margaret Rice had sponsored three brief seasons in the Auditorium. The *Milwaukee Journal* thought *Tannhäuser* with Marjorie Lawrence as Venus "approached perfection," but grumbled at a double dose of Wagner (*Tristan* and *Walküre*) the next year, and showed very little warmth for *Madama Butterfly* in the third.

Chicago offered a period of security to the Metropolitan only in 1950, when the experienced Harry Zelzer fitted its engagement into the efficient operation of his Allied Arts Corporation, which is responsible for most of the Windy City's visiting musical attractions.

The metropolis lived up to its nickname in providing one of the most dramatic incidents of Johnson's regime. The coal strike of 1946 brought an emergency curfew in Chicago just as the opera season was due to open. Public buildings could be lighted only from 2 to 6 P.M. Levine and Hurok in Minneapolis and Robinson in Chicago (all men with "high foreheads") felt sure that their remaining hairs were graying overnight.

After many hectic hours, the brilliant idea occurred to someone that one of the new maritime ships anchored at the Twelfth Street docks might be brought up the river to the Opera House and used as a generator. Cutting through red tape as only opera generals can, the manager of the Metropolitan found himself the lessee of the good ship "Mainsheet Eye," on payment of a $25,000 deposit against damages to the Maritime Commission.

Tied up—but only by one line—against the Wacker Drive Opera House, the ship prepared to do her duty by grand opera. But a careless crew left her virtually unmanned at the coffee break, and the famous Chicago wind snapped the single line with a gusty flip. Wallowing clumsily in the narrow

Chicago River, the 325-foot vessel was bound to collide with something. It chose the *News* building, with consequent publicity.

By the time the errant "Mainsheet Eye" had been retrieved $10,000 damages were incurred. But the day—or rather, the nights—were saved, and the opera stage and lobby (not enough current could be generated for the house itself) showed the only rays of light in Chicago's black week. The performances were crowded—"Chicago had no other place to go," said Levine—but partnership with the "Mainsheet Eye" wiped out all the profits.

Part IX

RUDOLF BING: OLD BORDERS, NEW FRIENDS

During the Metropolitan's most comprehensive tour since Grau's marathon in 1901-02, Rudolf Bing dramatically crossed the Canadian border to play in a city that had not seen a Metropolitan production since Grau's visit fifty years before.

The august company, which had mounted its elaborate shows in practically every type of four-walled building, had never before invaded a sports arena until it banished ice hockey temporarily from Toronto's Maple Leaf Gardens. (Only a spoilsport historian would recall the Montreal skating rink-cum-opera house that Grau had inhabited in that same 1901 hegira.)

Furthermore Toronto's audiences in the reconstituted Gardens were of indisputably record size—43,344 for four performances. Since this averaged well over 10,000 for each opera, even Cleveland had to bow. A $10 top ensured equally exalted totals in another important department.

The management of Maple Leaf Gardens had wooed the Metropolitan for twelve years with mortifying results. The Met refused, as June Callwood put it in *Maclean's,* the popular Canadian magazine, "because (a) playing on a hockey rink represented a return to savagery besides being an acoustical sacrilege, and (b) Canada didn't know opera from first base."

Then Toronto's Rotary Club took over, an irrepressible body with a flair for successful promotion in the Gardens. Spectacles ranging from softball to an ice revue with Canada's Olympic winner Barbara Ann Scott had brought large sums into the club's coffers for its extensive philanthropies. In 1950 Stanley Reid, special events chairman, went after the Met in typical "do-or-die" fashion. Of his other two choices, the Uruguay soccer team had been disbanded by a governmental ukase and David Webster of the Sadler's Wells Ballet, after a horrified glance at the bleak expanse of the Gardens, politely regretted.

Reid and Conn Smythe, the millionaire owner of Maple Leaf Gardens, met Edward Johnson, whom Canada claimed as her own, over a cup of tea at the Royal York. Later Reid and Douglas Morris, the Garden's technical director, flew to Cleveland to witness opera in the auditorium nearest in size to Toronto's. All to no avail.

Not until midway in Bing's first season did Reid wear down the Metropolitan's resistance to the extent of sending Horace Armistead to view the premises with an expert eye. Armistead hurried back with what Miss Call-

179

wood listed as "seating capacity, cleanliness, a solution to the acoustical problems, seating capacity, an exact scale model of a stage and seating capacity.
. . ." He also reported that an open stage was feasible. The contract was
signed in June.

Still the Metropolitan could not quite credit Toronto's "optimism" in de-
manding an entire week. Three days would surely suffice. When large seg-
ments of the Gardens were sold out in advance, the amazed New Yorkers
added a fourth performance.

Meanwhile, Montreal had caught the fever. The adventuresome impresario
Nicholas Koudriavtzeff believed that the Forum, most profitable sports arena
of its kind in America, could also be transformed into an opera house. Three
performances were accorded Montreal.

Before Toronto's first operatic mass scene took place, miracles had been
wrought in the monster auditorium. An original misunderstanding of the
term "open stage" faced Reid and Morris after 40,000 tickets had already
been sold. Existing steel trusses were not strong enough to hold the iron
grid that Armistead specified and could not be reinforced in time. Many
ideas were tried and rejected.

At last six wooden columns of Douglas fir were ordered at a cost of $20,000.
Each was two feet in diameter and eighty-seven feet long—about the height
of a seven-story building. Maneuvering these giants through the city, even
in dawn hours when traffic was lightest, required a special police permit and
practiced navigation. Once erected, with two 100-foot wooden trusses on top,
a grid could be mounted from which to hang the heavy scenic drops and
curtains.

The Rotary Club assumed all expenses, to the tune of $65,000—a massive
curtain and side "legs," arm chairs with leather seats for the "boxes" and
blue canvas seats for other floor positions, thirteen miles of rope, a floor
ramp, lights, amplification. Twenty-five thousand dollars remained for their
charity. The Gardens, which took a quarter of the gross receipts the first
year, subsequently put up an iron grid at their own expense and shared fifty-
fifty from then on. By 1954 a pleasant margin of profit appeared for both.

Aida christened the new opera arena on May 26, 1952. Toronto's 10,000
hardly recognized their Maple Leaf Gardens except for the moon-faced
timing clocks, visible on three sides (the fourth was hidden by the heavily
curtained stage), and the familiar orangeade and hot dog vendors in the
lobby. On the floor where the Maple Leafs were wont to clash sticks over a
square block of ice, 1,000 red and white chairs were arranged in squares of
eight, separated by white velvet ropes. The distinctive patterns of blue, green
and gray that mark seat locations of various prices—the Gardens' original
device—soon were obliterated as the eager crowd settled down.

By the end of the engagement Toronto and the Metropolitan had adjusted
to each other in complete amity. The unprecedented audience for *Carmen*
the third evening—quoted in round figures as 12,000, actually 11,352 by count
—taught a new lesson: success does not always succeed. To remedy the poor
sight lines, black curtains were stretched from the stage to the walls in 1953.
This cut off more than 2,000 seats but ensured good visibility for the remain-

ing 9,000. Refinements in the amplification system have had a soothing effect on Toronto's ears as well. Since Coronation year a great portrait of Elizabeth Regina on the wall opposite the stage commands all eyes as it is brilliantly spotlighted during the singing of the national anthem.

The Gardens' pride in the unusual visitor shows at every turn. Spencer Gaylord Evans, the friendly and personable public relations man whom everybody knows as "Spiff," points to a mural photograph of that mammoth first-night audience which occupies a place of honor with Toronto's heroes of the puck.

In addition to Hugh Thompson and Jack Karr of the *Star*, George Kidd of the *Telegram* and John Kraglund of the *Globe and Mail,* who cover Toronto's musical life, sports writers inevitably take a hand in their erstwhile kingdom, signing up as supers and reporting their sensations.

The official party tendered by the mayor on the Royal York roof has sparkled with merriment except on the occasion when someone forgot to deliver the invitations and all the artists trooped to the birthday fete of a colleague.

To the traditional red carpet and floral greetings attendant on a Metropolitan arrival, Toronto adds the final civilized touch. Every member of the company has been registered in advance at the Royal York and needs only pick up a key. This is regal welcome indeed to tired singers who often must join the line of traveling salesmen at several hotel desks along the route.

Montreal's transition from ice hockey to lyric drama brought the comment from the *Gazette's* sage, Thomas Archer, that "with present-day electrical equipment and the right engineer you can make any indoor hall into a good theatre." "The Forum comes closer to reproducing the elegant atmosphere of the Met," wrote June Callwood in *Maclean's,* "with crimson rugs . . . portraits of forgotten patrons and wide, curving staircases. . . . Cracks in the elderly cement walls are stuffed with hair felt. This gives a cozy effect. The audience snuggles down between burgundy drapes, parted into sections with strips of rugs and potted palms."

In this cosmopolitan city, with its extremes of wealth and dual French and English population, sports magnates sponsor opera without any profit to themselves. After the first two years Canadian Arena, the company that owns the Forum, decided to back up Koudriavtzeff and spent about $200,000 on improvements, including a new grid. If women attend in fancy clothes the seats must be adequate, the Forum contended, so $30,000 went for upholstered chairs.

In spite of the critics' tolerance—Eric McLean of the *Star* had found the first year's *Aida* "reasonably distinct"—a new sound system was installed by a CBC television expert.

Frank Selke came to manage the Forum in 1946 after twenty-five years as assistant manager of Maple Leaf Gardens. When Conn Smythe, his former boss, said to him, "You run your business with your heart; I run mine with my head," no compliment could have pleased Selke more. His pride in the Forum is not lessened by the fact that Toronto outdraws Montreal in opera attendance. The Montreal building does not hold so many opera customers at a time, Selke pointed out. With the stage almost exactly in the center of the huge enclosure, only 6,500 seats can be offered.

Forum personnel show a lively, if somewhat diffident interest in the exotic visitor. Superintendent Hunter is distressed because the new microphones can be seen, "but then you have to dream a little about opera anyway, so you can dream away the mikes." Camille des Roches, publicity representative, speaks for the French Canadians when he wonders how the average family with six children can afford opera.

The season that brought Canada back into the Metropolitan family was Bing's own marathon, for although he added a few performances in the tours to come the eighteen cities (plus Philadelphia) of 1951-52 stand as his record. Furthermore the Metropolitan sponsored an ill-fated tour of a separate company in the Kanin-Gérard production of *Fledermaus,* which had created a sensation in regular road performances. The young singers included Brenda Lewis, Jon Crain, Virginia MacWatters, William Horne, Laura Castellano, John Tyers and Kenneth Schon. Tibor Kozma was the conductor.

Opening in Philadelphia on September 24, *Fledermaus,* Jr., played in thirty-three cities. Overly ambitious booking, the competition of a Hurok troupe simultaneously playing the Strauss work as *Rosalinda* and the tragic death of the tenor Donald Dame in Lincoln combined to shadow the venture.

In the days when Dallas worried lest Houston usurp her opera rights in Texas, another contender's name had been mentioned, but Oklahoma City did not enter the active lists until Johnson's last season. The city "with an oil well in every back yard" accepted opera gratefully from the Oklahoma Publishing Company, which controls both newspapers, the *Daily Oklahoman* and *Times,* as well as radio and television outlets. Needless to say, the annual advent of "Glamor and Glitter" is adequately publicized, but because of direct mailing, each performance is two-thirds sold out before any public announcement appears.

"We don't dare advertise," declared James Burge, manager of the publishing company's special events: "we would get too much mail."

The only year that this prosperous operation failed to make its profit coincided with the removal of the federal sales tax and Oklahoma City's lowering of its top price from $9 to $8. Even so, everything would have been all right, Burge thought, "but the English *Bohème* was our downfall."

Conventional Oklahoma City, which cannot be persuaded that any fashionable business location exists except two city blocks hallowed by tradition, did not warm to Howard Dietz' literary revelation of Bohemian life. Critics Tracy Silvester and Alan Jenkins, however, thought it "superb," "a priceless jewel." Everyone rallied for *Rigoletto* the following year and *Cavalleria* and *Pagliacci* in 1955—"There's a Loud Week Coming!" wrote Aline Jean Trainor in the *Oklahoman* to herald the *verismo* twins.

Although Birmingham received the Johnson company jubilantly in 1942, ten years were to elapse before operatic stars again "fell on Alabama." Since 1952 the steel city marks its calendar every May for the Metropolitan. Marvin McDonald, who had performed a similar service for one Atlanta regime, provides the business management for the sponsor, the Birmingham Music

Club. A club member, Mrs. E. T. Bozenhard, acts as box-office treasurer. "Bozey" occasionally demonstrates what seems to be clairvoyance by calling off a subscriber's seat number before being told. As the Auditorium seats 5,500, this is no mean feat.

"All keyed up like a concertmaster's fiddle," wrote Lily May Caldwell, affectionately regarded in the Southeast as a leading cultural oracle through the columns of the News, and no less a music lover than the thousands of Alabamans she was describing.

Appropriately, the Metropolitan assisted in the Music Club's Golden Jubilee in 1955, as it had been present when the club was founded. Few of the members—certainly not the vivacious young president, Mrs. William I. Grubb—remember Conried's Parsifal in 1905. A thriving Opera Guild and Junior League, as well as an opera committee within the club, work hard behind the scenes and then join in the merriment crammed into two dizzying days—luncheons at "The Club" atop one of the city's suburban mountains, merry parties, perhaps at the home of Mr. and Mrs. Preston H. Haskell, Jr., or another of Birmingham's warmhearted hostesses. The view from Mrs. Morris W. Bush's lofty home is breathtaking, the hospitality exquisite at every level of its three landscaped terraces.

Birmingham can add to its opera lore the spectacle of Rudolf Bing, in impish mood, wearing top hat ("too large") and sideburns ("they tickle"), earnestly conducting the stage orchestra in the Kermesse scene in Faust. Because a spotlight dazzled him, the general manager almost missed a cue to stop, but critical opinion, shared by Kurt Adler in the pit, granted Bing "a clean, firm beat."

The new general manager inherited a tour machine that could not have failed to meet his criteria of order, teamwork and discipline. The pattern had been set by Levine and Hunck and kept intact in the single year between their retirement and the new regime. Two of Bing's right bowers were already wise in the ways of the road, for in addition to Francis Robinson, Max Rudolf had assisted St. Leger in his administrative capacity and was thoroughly familiar with railroad complexities. The efficient Frank Paola also remained.

Among a million other facts, Rudolf also knew that in Atlanta and Cleveland certain artists each year were "musts," while Bloomington and Des Moines would not ask for special singers; that Jewish singers are popular in Canada and Chicago, and that Boston likes Scandinavians and Germans—and Irish, whenever they come along.

Today's team is more methodical and concentrated than yesterday's, but today's tours require the utmost in method and concentration—as well as the dash of genius and sheer despotism that has always been a requisite.

Bing took to the road heralded by more publicity than any Metropolitan chief had ever received, a good deal of it of the type to create apprehension that "things would change"—of course, for the worse.

Philadelphia's first taste of the new order, the stunning production of Don Carlo, clearly revealed change in the improved visual aspect of the stage. The new Armistead settings for Cavalleria and Pagliacci showed the extremes to which a radical departure could go. No two opinions existed about *Don Carlo* in its subsequent four showings on the road; twenty arose over the controversial "Twins."

When *Faust* performed its function of opening a season for the *nth* time, Baltimore saw no reason to believe that the Metropolitan would be so very different. De Los Angeles, Di Stefano and Siepi lent the charm of old-fashioned *bel canto,* and the scenery barely held together for its perilous trip through the Lyric's basement. But *Fledermaus* showed the fresh, clean side of the coin.

So it went throughout this tour and subsequent ones. "Something old and something new" but always something to talk about.

As for Bing himself, "thin, angular, reticent and a bit forbidding," as John Rosenfield found him in Dallas in 1951, the general manager remained as great a puzzle to the public and press as Gatti had been. By 1955 he had accustomed himself to the onslaught of the American music-lover who wants to come as close as possible to his (or her) heroes—opera impresarios have fallen in that category since Grau's day.

The Metropolitan's general management has alternated regularly between the professional and the performer—Abbey, Stanton and Grau, Gatti and Bing representing the former, Damrosch, Conried, Dippel and Johnson the latter.

When Bing suavely compares a roomful of southern women to flowers, his gallantry seems a trifle studied; but when he paces back and forth in the wings, listening to a soprano, who has substituted for an indisposed Mimi, and suddenly exclaims: "She is singing like an angel! an angel!" one feels the words spoken from the heart. This is the professional at home in his world.

After nearly three-quarters of a century, many things seem much the same on the Metropolitan road.

There is the same story about Mrs. Malaprop and the coloratura: "Isn't it a shame she has to have that little instrument play along with her to keep on pitch?"

The same quality of improvisation comes to the fore now and then, when in spite of nearly faultless planning, a singer will be allowed to step into a role when he has not meshed with the ensemble. If it is an experienced trouper like Lily Pons, no harm comes from Bob Herman's coaching her every step and position in the new *Barbiere* production from the wings, like a towerman "talking a plane to land." And Memphis, which asked specially for its beloved Lily, is charmed.

The traditions and superstitions of day before yesterday remain in today's pattern. Kirsten Flagstad followed her own ritual: a glass of champagne after each performance that satisfied her. Set Svanholm, the third Metropolitan tenor to become an opera manager—he took over direction of the Royal Swedish Opera in 1955—liked to munch an apple immediately after singing. His friends along the route honored the tradition.

Illnesses still strike unexpectedly in dramatic circumstances. Astrid Varnay, noted for her emergency flights to help stricken sopranos, herself became the victim of acute appendicitis in the midst of a Boston performance and had to give way to Maxine Stellman.

Yesterday it was Bauermeister; today it is Votipka—the fabulous "Tippy," who moves in an aura of recognized accomplishment. She keeps very much to herself on tour, friendly but reserved; however, unlike Marie van Cauteren, Bauermeister's sister comprimaria, not as "a woman of mystery." The trusted De Paolis and Cehanovsky today walk in the footsteps of the Bada and Ananian of yesterday and the Vanni and Viviani of the day before.

The Italians still cluster to themselves and have little to say to anyone who cannot speak their language. *Bohème* is still the most difficult of all standard operas to put on, with its dozens of props and complicated chorus entrances and exits. William Parry nominated it for the honor in Grau's time; Ralph and Louis Edson echo him today. It also remains one of the most popular, and hence is always taken as a "buffer," or spare, in case of emergency.

One great difference between Abbey and Bing would cause some heart burning among the married folk of opera, if they knew of it. "Traveling expenses for several voiceless wives and husbands are paid out by Abbey," the St. Louis paper noted long ago. Still, this is probably not enough incentive for the Kurt Baums or the young Norman Scotts to want to turn back the clock. Sandra Warfield and James McCracken, the only married couple in the company of today, do not share the problem—both their fares are paid as singers.

The curtain closes as Rigoletto's despairing cry rings through Toronto's Maple Leaf Gardens. Leonard Warren and Roberta Peters, Richard Tucker, Rosalind Elias and Georgio Tozzi come out for a half-dozen curtain calls (no solo bows these days—Bing's order!). The train is waiting. On June 3 the 1956 tour ends as the special train pulls into Grand Central Station.

At the Metropolitan forty-six weeks later, Concertmaster Felix Eyle puts his violin into its case, turns to shake hands with friends that crowd down to the rail, and goes home to pack. John Mundy, orchestra manager, calls a good-night in British tones; Henry Wrong, secretary of the planning committee for the projected new Metropolitan Opera House, waves blithely. David Pardoll spends ten minutes in his little office just at the head of the steps leading from the stage, the nexus of the production departments.

On the huge stage, the crew hurries to strike the *Tosca* set in record time. The trucks are waiting. The 1957 opera caravan departs tomorrow.

METROPOLITAN OPERA TOUR CASTS

1883–84—1955–56

Listed Chronologically

Many casts before 1917 have been based on advance listings, company advertisements, programs and newspaper reviews. Where a complete cast could not be ascertained or verified, a question mark has been placed after the doubtful cast or performer. Since 1917, casts have been based on official Metropolitan Opera tour programs.

When one opera was substituted for another the names of both operas appear. The verified substitution of one performer for another is similarly shown.

Key: (c) conductor. (d) debut with company. (l) local singer; not member of company. (t) tour only: specially engaged or member of company not listed in Seltsam's *Metropolitan Opera Annals*.

1889-90A indicates Abbey's tour with Patti.

1 8 8 3 – 8 4

BOSTON

ABBEY GRAND OPERA COMPANY
Henry E. Abbey, *Manager*
All operas sung in Italian

December 26
FAUST/Vianesi (c)
Faust : Campanini
Marguerite : Nilsson
Méphistophélès : Novara
Valentin : Del Puente
Siébel : Scalchi
Marthe : E.Lablache
Wagner : Contini

December 27
LUCIA DI LAMMERMOOR
Vianesi (c)
Lucia : Sembrich
Ashton : Del Puente
Edgardo : Campanini
Alisa : Forti
Raimondo : Augier
Arturo : Fornaris
Normanno : Grazzi

December 28
IL TROVATORE/Vianesi (c)
Leonora : Valleria
Manrico : Stagno
Count di Luna : Kaschmann
Azucena : Scalchi
Inez : Forti
Ferrando : Augier
Ruiz : Grazzi

December 29 (mat.)
MIGNON/Vianesi (c)
Mignon : Nilsson
Philine : Valleria
Wilhelm : Capoul
Lothario : Del Puente
Laerte : Corsini
Jarno : Contini
Frederic : Scalchi

December 29
LA SONNAMBULA
Campanini (c)
Adina : Sembrich
Elvino : Campanini
Rodolfo : Novara
Alessio : Corsini
Notary : Grazzi
Lisa : Corani
Teresa : E.Lablache (?)

December 30
CONCERT/Vianesi (c)
STABAT MATER (Rossini)
Fursch-Madi (?), Campanini
(?), Trebelli, Novara, Louise

188

Lablache, Kaschmann,
Mirabella

December 31
LA TRAVIATA/Vianesi (c)
Violetta : Sembrich
Alfredo : Capoul
Germont : Augier
(for Del Puente)
Flora : E.Lablache
Annina : Forti
Gastone : Fornaris
Baron Douphol : Grazzi
Marquis d'Obigny : Corsini
Dr. Grenvil : Contini

January 1
LA GIOCONDA/Vianesi (c)
La Gioconda : Nilsson
Laura : Fursch-Madi
Alvise : Novara
La Cieca : Scalchi
Enzo : Stagno
Barnaba : Del Puente
Zuane : Augier
Singer : Contini
Isepo : Grazzi
Steersman : Barberis

January 2
IL BARBIERE DI SIVIGLIA
Vianesi (c)
Almaviva : Stagno
Dr. Bartolo : Corsini
Rosina : Sembrich
Figaro : Del Puente
Don Basilio : Mirabella
Berta : E.Lablache
Fiorello : Contini
Sergeant : Grazzi

January 3
LOHENGRIN/Vianesi (c)
King Henry : Novara
Lohengrin : Campanini
Elsa : Nilsson
Telramund : Kaschmann
Ortrud : Fursch-Madi
Herald : Contini

January 4
MARTHA/Vianesi (c)
Harriet : Valleria
Nancy : Scalchi
Lionel : Stagno
Plunkett : Del Puente
Tristan : Corsini

January 5 (mat.)
FAUST
Same as Dec. 26 except:
Faust : Capoul
Valentin : Kaschmann

January 5
CARMEN *(first by Abbey Co.)*
Campanini (c)
Carmen : Trebelli

Don José : Campanini
Micaela : Valleria
Escamillo : Del Puente
Zuniga : Augier
Morales : Contini
Frasquita : Corani
Mercedes : L.Lablache
Dancaire : Corsini
Remendado : Grazzi

BROOKLYN

January 7
CARMEN
Same (?) as Jan. 5

January 8
FAUST
Same as Dec. 26 except:
Faust : Capoul
Valentin : Kaschmann

January 10
DON GIOVANNI (for *Lucia*)
Vianesi (c)
Don Giovanni : Kaschmann
Donna Anna : Fursch-Madi
Donna Elvira : Valleria
Zerlina : Trebelli
Commendatore : Augier
Don Ottavio : Stagno
Leporello : Mirabella (?)
Masetto : Corsini (?)

PHILADELPHIA

January 14
FAUST
Same (?) as Dec. 26 except:
Valentin : Kaschmann

January 15
LUCIA DI LAMMERMOOR
Same as Dec. 27 except:
Edgardo : Capoul
(for Campanini)

January 16
IL TROVATORE
Same as Dec. 28 except:
Azucena : Trebelli

January 17
DON GIOVANNI (for *Barbiere*)
Same as Jan. 10

January 18
LA GIOCONDA
Same as Jan. 1 except:
Enzo : Capoul (for Stagno)

January 19 (mat.)
MARTHA (for *Traviata*)
Campanini (c)
Same (?) as Jan. 4 except:
Nancy : Lablache
Plunkett : Kaschmann

Tristan : Augier
Sheriff : Corsini

January 19
CARMEN
Same as Jan. 5 except:
Micaela : Corani (for
    Valleria)
Frasquita : L.Lablache
Mercedes : E.Lablache

CHICAGO
January 21
FAUST
Same (?) as Dec. 26 except:
Faust : Capoul
    (for Campanini)
Valentin : Kaschmann

January 22
LUCIA DI LAMMERMOOR
Same as Dec. 27 except:
Edgardo : Stagno

January 23
LOHENGRIN
Same as Jan. 3
(*Last scene omitted, Campa-
nini ill.*)

January 24
DON GIOVANNI
Same as Jan. 10 except:
Zerlina : Scalchi

January 25
IL BARBIERE DI SIVIGLIA
Same as Jan. 2 except:
Almaviva : Capoul

January 26 (mat.)
FAUST
Same as Dec. 26 except:
Faust : Capoul
Valentin : Kaschmann

January 26
CARMEN
Same (?) as Jan. 5

January 27
CONCERT/Vianesi (c)
STABAT MATER (Rossini)
Trebelli, Louise Lablache,
Fursch-Madi, Stagi, Capoul,
Kaschmann, Mirabella, Augier

January 28
LA GIOCONDA
Same as Jan. 1

January 29
LA SONNAMBULA
Same as Dec. 29

January 30
MIGNON
Same as Dec. 29 except:

Lothario : Novara

January 31
LA TRAVIATA
Same as Dec. 31 except:
Germont : Del Puente

February 1
ROBERT LE DIABLE
Vianesi (c)
Alice : Fursch-Madi
Isabella : Valleria
Abbess : Cavalazzi (dancer)
Raimbaut : Stagi (?)
Bertram : Mirabella
Herald : Fornaris
Robert : Stagno
Cavaliers : Corsini, Contini,
    Grazzi

February 2 (mat.)
MARTHA
Same as Jan. 4 except:
Harriet : Sembrich
Nancy : Trebelli
Lionel : Campanini

February 2
LA GIOCONDA
Same as Jan. 1 except:
Enzo : Capoul

ST. LOUIS
February 4
IL TROVATORE
Same as Dec. 28 except:
Azucena : Trebelli

February 5
FAUST
Same as Dec. 26

February 6
LUCIA DI LAMMERMOOR
    Campanini (c)
Same as Dec. 27 except:
Ashton : Kaschmann
Edgardo : Stagno

February 7
CARMEN
Same as Jan. 5

February 8
LA GIOCONDA/Campanini (c)
Same as Jan. 1 except:
Laura : L.Lablache
    (for Fursch-Madi)

February 9 (mat.)
IL BARBIERE DI SIVIGLIA
    Campanini (c)
Same (?) as Jan. 2 except:
Almaviva : Stagi
Dr. Bartolo : Mirabella

Don Basilio : Corsini

February 9
DON GIOVANNI/Campanini (c)
Same as Jan. 10 except:
Donna Anna : E.Lablache (?)
Zerlina : Scalchi
Don Ottavio : Campanini

CINCINNATI
February 11
FAUST
Same (?) as Dec. 26

February 12
LE PROPHÈTE/Vianesi (c)
John of Leyden : Stagno
Fidès : Scalchi
Bertha : Valleria
Jonas : Stagi
Mathisen : Contini
Zacharias : Mirabella
Oberthal : Guadagnini
Soldier : Grazzi
Peasant : Risdelli

February 13 (mat.)
LUCIA DI LAMMERMOOR
Same (?) as Dec. 27 except:
Ashton : Kaschmann

February 14
LA GIOCONDA
Same (?) as Jan. 1 except:
Enzo : Campanini

February 15
IL TROVATORE
Same (?) as Dec. 28 except:
Azucena : Trebelli

February 16 (mat.)
DON GIOVANNI
Same as Jan. 10 except:
Donna Elvira : Nilsson
Zerlina : Sembrich
Don Ottavio : Campanini

February 17 (mat.)
CONCERT/Vianesi (c)
(For benefit of flood relief)

February 18
LA SONNAMBULA
Same (?) as Dec. 29 except:
Lisa : Barabino (t)
Alessio : Contini

February 19
MIGNON
Same (?) as Dec. 29 except:
Giuseppe : Grazzi

February 20 (mat.)
ROBERT LE DIABLE
Same as Feb. 1

189

February 21
HAMLET (*first by Abbey Co.*)
Vianesi (c)
Ophelia : Sembrich
Hamlet : Kaschmann
Ghost : Augier
Claudius : Mirabella
Queen : Scalchi
Laertes : Stagi
Horatio : Contini
Polonius : Corsini

February 22
MEFISTOFELE/Campanini (c)
Marguerite : Nilsson
Helen of Troy : Nilsson
Martha : Trebelli
Pantalis : Trebelli
Mefistofele : Mirabella
Faust : Campanini
Wagner : Grazzi
Nereus : Grazzi

February 23
MARTHA
Same as Jan. 4 except:
Harriet : Sembrich
Sheriff : Contini

WASHINGTON
February 25
FAUST
Same as Dec. 26

February 26
LUCIA DI LAMMERMOOR
Same as Dec. 27 except:
Ashton : Kaschmann
Edgardo : Stagno

February 27
LA GIOCONDA
Same (?) as Jan. 1 except:
Enzo : Campanini

February 28
DON GIOVANNI
Vianesi (c?)
Same as Jan. 10 except:
Zerlina : Scalchi

BALTIMORE
February 29
IL BARBIERE DI SIVIGLIA
Same as Jan. 2 except:
Almaviva : Capoul
(for Stagno)

March 1 (mat.)
CARMEN
Same as Jan. 5

March 1
FAUST
Same as Dec. 26 except:

Faust : Capoul
(for Campanini)
Valentin : Kaschmann
Siébel : L.Lablache
(for Scalchi)

BOSTON
March 3
HAMLET
Same as Feb. 21 except:
Marcello : Grazzi

March 4
MEFISTOFELE
Same as Feb. 22

March 5
ROBERT LE DIABLE
Same as Feb. 1

March 6
DON GIOVANNI
Same as Jan. 10 except:
Donna Elvira : Nilsson
Zerlina : Sembrich
Don Ottavio : Campanini

March 7
LE PROPHÈTE
Same (?) as Feb. 12 except:
Peasant : Mascotti

March 8 (mat.)
IL BARBIERE DI SIVIGLIA
Same as Jan. 2 except:
Almaviva : Capoul

March 8
LA GIOCONDA
Same as Jan. 1 except:
Enzo : Campanini

March 29 (mat.)
CONCERT/Campanini (c)
Sembrich, Trebelli, Campanini,
Kaschmann

PHILADELPHIA
April 14
LES HUGUENOTS/Vianesi (c)
Marguerite : Sembrich
St. Bris : Kaschmann
Valentine : Nilsson
Nevers : Del Puente
Tavannes : Grazzi
Meru : Corsini
Raoul : Campanini
Marcel : Mirabella
Urbain : Scalchi
Bois Rosé : Stagi
Lady of Honor : Alberti (t)

April 15
ROBERT LE DIABLE
Same as Feb. 1 except:
Isabella : Corani

April 16
ROMÉO ET JULIETTE
Vianesi (c)
(Not given in New York)
Juliette : Sembrich
Stephano : L.Lablache
Gertrude : E.Lablache
Roméo : Campanini
Tybalt : Stagi
Benvolio : Grazzi
Mercutio : Del Puente
Gregorio : Corsini
Paris : Contini
Capulet : Augier
Friar Laurence : Mirabella
Duke of Verona : Mascotti

April 17
MIGNON
Same as Dec. 29 except:
Philine : Corani
Lothario : Novara

April 18
LE PROPHÈTE
Same as Feb. 12 except:
Bertha : Corani
Peasant : Mascotti

April 19 (mat.)
LOHENGRIN
Same as Jan. 3 except:
Herald : Augier

April 19
IL BARBIERE DI SIVIGLIA
Same as Jan. 2 except:
Almaviva : Stagi

1 8 8 4 – 8 5

DAMROSCH GRAND OPERA
COMPANY
Walter Damrosch, *Manager*
All operas sung in German

CHICAGO
February 23
TANNHÄUSER/Damrosch (c)
Hermann : Kögel
Tannhäuser : Schott
Wolfram : Robinson
Walther : Junck (t)
Biterolf : Miller
Heinrich : Kemlitz
Reinmar : Wolf
Elisabeth : Materna
Venus : Slach
Shepherd : Frau Kemlitz

February 24
LE PROPHÈTE/Damrosch (c)
John of Leyden : Schott
Fidès : Brandt

Bertha : Martinez
Oberthal : Staudigl
Jonas : Kemlitz
Mathisen : Miller
Zacharias : Kögel

February 25
LA JUIVE/Lund (c)
Rachel : Materna
Princess : Slach
Eleazar : Udvardy
Brogni : Kögel
Leopold : Kemlitz
Ruggiero : Miller
Albert : Paché

February 26
GUILLAUME TELL
Damrosch (c)
Tell : Robinson
Walter Furst : Kögel
Melchthal : Miller
Arnold : Udvardy
Leutold : Wolf
Fisherman : Paché
Gessler : Staudigl
Rudolf : Kemlitz
Matilde : Martinez
Hedwig : Brandt
Jemmy : Slach

February 27
MASANIELLO/Damrosch (c)
Alphonso : Kemlitz
Elvira : Martinez
Masaniello : Schott
Fenella : Torri (dancer)
Pietro : Kögel

February 28 (mat.)
TANNHÄUSER
Same as Feb. 23

February 28
FIDELIO (for *Orfeo*)
Damrosch (c)
Don Fernando : Staudigl (?)
Pizarro : Robinson
Florestan : Udvardy
Leonore : Brandt
Rocco : Miller
Marzelline : Slach
Jaquino : Kemlitz (?)

March 2
LOHENGRIN/Damrosch (c)
King Henry : Staudigl (?)
Lohengrin : Schott (?)
Elsa : Slach (?)
Telramund : Robinson (?)
Ortrud : Brandt (?)
Herald : Abramoff (t) (?)

March 3
LA JUIVE
Same as Feb. 25

March 4
LE PROPHÈTE
Same as Feb. 24

March 5
TANNHÄUSER
Same as Feb. 23 except:
Wolfram : Staudigl

March 6
FIDELIO (for *Huguenots*)
Same as Feb. 28 except:
Pizarro : Staudigl
(for Robinson)
Marzelline : Frau Kemlitz

March 7 (mat.)
LOHENGRIN
Same (?) as Mar. 2

March 7
DER FREISCHÜTZ/Lund (c)
Ottokar : Robinson
Agathe : Frau Robinson
Aennchen : Poppenberg (l)
Max : Udvardy
Caspar : Kögel
Bridesmaid : Stern
Hermit : Staudigl

March 8
LE PROPHÈTE
Same as Feb. 24 except:
Bertha : Frau Robinson

March 10
DIE WALKÜRE/Damrosch (c)
Wotan : Staudigl
Fricka : Brandt
Brünnhilde : Materna
Siegmund : Schott
Sieglinde : Slach
Hunding : Kögel
Helmwige : Frau Robinson
Gerhilde : Brandt
Ortlinde : Stern
Rossweisse : Brandl
Grimgerde : Kemlitz
Waltraute : Stahlke
Siegrune : Hock
Schwertleite : Morse

March 11
DIE WALKÜRE
Same as Mar. 10

March 12
LA DAME BLANCHE
Damrosch (c)
(First time by the company.
Not given in New York)
Anna : Slach
Jenny : Frau Kemlitz
Margarethe : Brandt
George Brown : Udvardy

MacIrton : Wolf
Dickson : Kemlitz
Gaveston : Miller

March 13
LOHENGRIN
Same (?) as Mar. 2

March 14 (mat.)
DIE WALKÜRE
Same as Mar. 10

March 14
DON GIOVANNI/Damrosch (c)
Don Giovanni : Robinson (?)
Donna Anna : Frau
Robinson (?)
Donna Elvira : Brandt (?)
Zerlina : Martinez (?)
Commendatore :
Abramoff (?)
Don Ottavio : Udvardy (?)
Leporello : Staudigl (?)
Masetto : Miller (?)

CINCINNATI

March 16
LOHENGRIN
Same as Mar. 2

March 17
LA JUIVE
Same as Feb. 25

March 18
LE PROPHÈTE
Same as Feb. 24

March 19
TANNHÄUSER
Same (?) as Feb. 23 except:
Wolfram : Staudigl

March 20
FIDELIO
Same (?) as Feb. 28 except:
Don Fernando : Wolf

March 21 (mat.)
LOHENGRIN
Same as Mar. 2

March 21
DER FREISCHÜTZ
Same (?) as March 7 except:
Aennchen : Frau
Kemlitz (?)

BOSTON

April 6
LE PROPHÈTE
Same as Feb. 24

April 7
TANNHÄUSER
Same as Feb. 23 except:
Walther : Kemlitz

191

Heinrich : Paché
Shepherd : Stern

April 8
FIDELIO
Same as Feb. 28 except:
Don Fernando : Wolf
Don Pizarro : Staudigl

April 9
LOHENGRIN
Same as Mar. 2 except:
Herald : Miller

April 10
LA JUIVE/Damrosch (c)
Same as Feb. 25

April 11 (mat.)
TANNHÄUSER
Same as Feb. 23 except:
Walther : Kemlitz
Heinrich : Paché
Shepherd : Stern

April 11
ORFEO ED EURIDICE
Damrosch (c)
(Not given in New York)
Orfeo : Brandt
Euridice : Slach
Amor : Hock

April 13
DIE WALKÜRE
Same as Mar. 10 except:
Schwertleite : Schanz

April 14
LOHENGRIN
Same as Mar. 2 except:
Herald : Miller

April 15
TANNHÄUSER
Same as Feb. 23 except:
Tannhäuser :
    Charles R. Adams
    (l—special engagement)
Wolfram : Staudigl
Walther : Kemlitz
Heinrich : Paché
Venus : Martinez
Shepherd : Stern

April 16
DIE WALKÜRE/Lund (c)
Same as Mar. 10 except:
Schwertleite : Schanz

April 17
FIDELIO
Same as Feb. 28 except:
Don Fernando : Wolf
Pizarro : Staudigl
Rocco : Kögel
Marzelline : Martinez

April 18 (mat.)
DIE WALKÜRE
Same (?) as Mar. 10 except:
Schwertleite : Schanz

April 18
LA DAME BLANCHE
Same as Mar. 12 except:
Anna : Martinez
Margarethe : Schanz

1 8 8 5 – 8 6

GERMAN GRAND OPERA
COMPANY
Herman Grau, *Manager*
All operas sung in German

PHILADELPHIA

December 21
TANNHÄUSER/Seidl (c)
Hermann : Fischer
Tannhäuser : Sylva
Wolfram : Robinson
Walther : Alvary
Biterolf : Lehmler
Heinrich : Kemlitz
Reinmar : Sänger
Elisabeth : Seidl-Kraus
Venus : Slach
Shepherd : Klein

December 22
LE PROPHÈTE/Damrosch (c)
John of Leyden : Stritt
Bertha : Lehmann
Fidès : Brandt
Oberthal : Staudigl
Jonas : Dworsky
Mathisen : Kaufmann
Zacharias : Lehmler

December 23
CARMEN/Seidl (c)
Carmen : Lehmann
Don José : Alvary
Micaela : Seidl-Kraus
Escamillo : Robinson
Zuniga : Lehmler
Morales : Alexy
Frasquita : Slach
Mercedes : Goldsticker
Dancaire : Kemlitz
Remendado : Kaufmann

December 24
LOHENGRIN/Seidl (c)
King Henry : Fischer
Lohengrin : Stritt
Elsa : Seidl-Kraus
Telramund : Robinson
Ortrud : Brandt
Herald : Alexy

December 25
DIE WALKÜRE
Damrosch (c)
Wotan : Fischer
Fricka : Brandt
Brünnhilde : Lehmann
Siegmund : Stritt
Sieglinde : Slach
Hunding : Lehmler
Helmwige : Brandl
Gerhilde : Brandt
Ortlinde : Klein
Rossweisse : Escott
Grimgerde : Frau Kemlitz
Waltraute : Henniges
Siegrune : Eschenbach
Schwertleite : Goldsticker

December 26 (mat.)
TANNHÄUSER
Same as Dec. 21

December 28
LOHENGRIN
Same as Dec. 24

December 29
CARMEN
Same as Dec. 23 except:
Don José : Stritt (for Sylva)

December 30
LE PROPHÈTE
Same as Dec. 22 except:
John of Leyden : Sylva

December 31
TANNHÄUSER
Same as Dec. 21 except:
Elisabeth : Krämer-Wiedl

January 1
DIE WALKÜRE
Same as Dec. 25 except:
Sieglinde : Seidl-Kraus

January 2 (mat.)
DIE WALKÜRE
Same as Dec. 25 except:
Wotan : Staudigl

CHICAGO

March 15
RIENZI/Neuendorff (c—t)
Cola Rienzi : Sylva
Irene : Krämer-Wiedl
Steffano : Staudigl
Adriano : Frau Staudigl (t)
Paolo Orsini : Robinson
Raimondo : Lehmler
Baroncelli : Kemlitz
Cecco del Vecchio : Sänger
Messenger :
    Januschowsky (t)

March 16
LOHENGRIN/Neuendorff (c)
Same as Dec. 24 except:
King Henry : Staudigl
Lohengrin : Alvary
Ortrud : Goldsticker
Herald : Kaufmann

March 17
RIENZI
Same as Mar. 15

March 18
FAUST/Neuendorff (c)
Faust : Alvary
Marguerite : Seidl-Kraus
Méphistophélès : Fischer
Valentin : Robinson
Siébel : Januschowsky (t)
Martha : Frau Kemlitz
Wagner : Sänger

March 19
LOHENGRIN/Neuendorff (c)
Same as Dec. 24 except:
King Henry : Staudigl
Lohengrin : Alvary
Ortrud : Goldsticker
Herald : Lehmler

March 20 (mat.)
RIENZI
Same (?) as Mar. 15

March 20
FIDELIO/Neuendorff (c)
(Not given in New York)
Don Fernando : Lehmler
Pizarro : Staudigl
Florestan : Alvary
Leonore : Krämer-Wiedl
Rocco : Fischer
Marzelline :
   Januschowsky (t)
Jacquino : Krämer

March 22
DIE KÖNIGIN VON SABA
   Neuendorff (c)
King Solomon : Robinson
Queen of Sheba :
   Frau Staudigl (t)
Sulamith : Seidl-Kraus
Astaroth : Januschowsky (t)
Assad : Alvary
High Priest : Fischer
Baal Hanan : Sänger

March 23
TANNHÄUSER/Neuendorff (c)
Same as Dec. 21 except:
Hermann : Lehmler
Wolfram : Staudigl
Walther : Krämer
Biterolf : Kaufmann

Elisabeth : Krämer-Wiedl
Venus : Januschowsky (t)
Shepherd : Frau Kemlitz

March 24
DIE KÖNIGIN VON SABA
Same as Mar. 22 except:
Queen of Sheba :
   Krämer-Wiedl

March 25
TANNHÄUSER/Neuendorff (c)
   (for *Prophète*)
Same as Dec. 21 except:
Hermann : Lehmler
Wolfram : Staudigl
Walther : Krämer
Biterolf : Kaufmann
Elisabeth : Krämer-Wiedl
Venus : Januschowsky (t)
Shepherd : Frau Kemlitz

March 26
DIE KÖNIGIN VON SABA
Same as Mar. 22 except:
Queen of Sheba :
   Krämer-Wiedl

March 27 (mat.)
DIE KÖNIGIN VON SABA
Same (?) as Mar. 22

March 27
RIENZI
Same (?) as Mar. 15

ST. LOUIS
March 29
DIE KÖNIGIN VON SABA
Same as Mar. 22

March 30
TANNHÄUSER/Neuendorff (c)
Same as Dec. 21 except:
Hermann : Lehmler
Wolfram : Staudigl
Walther : Krämer
Biterolf : Kaufmann
Venus : Januschowsky (t)
Shepherd : Frau Kemlitz

March 31
DIE KÖNIGIN VON SABA
Same (?) as Mar. 22 except:
Sulamith :
   Krämer-Wiedl (?)
Astaroth : Goldsticker (?)

April 1
RIENZI
Same (?) as Mar. 15 except:
Steffano : Fischer

April 2
LOHENGRIN/Neuendorff (c)
Same as Dec. 24 except:

Lohengrin : Alvary
Elsa : Krämer-Wiedl
Telramund : Staudigl
Ortrud : Goldsticker
Herald : Kemlitz

April 3 (mat.)
DIE KÖNIGIN VON SABA
Same (?) as Mar. 22

April 3
RIENZI
Same (?) as Mar. 15

April 4
FIDELIO
*Extra performance. Benefit
for Grau.*
Same (?) as Mar. 20

CINCINNATI
April 5
DIE KÖNIGIN VON SABA
Same as Mar. 22

April 6
RIENZI
Same as Mar. 15 except:
Steffano : Fischer

April 7
DIE KÖNIGIN VON SABA
Same (?) as Mar. 22

CLEVELAND
April 8
RIENZI
Same as Mar. 15 except:
Steffano : Fischer

April 9
DIE KÖNIGIN VON SABA
Same as Mar. 22 except:
Astaroth : Goldsticker

April 10 (mat.)
LOHENGRIN/Neuendorff (c)
King Henry : Lehmler
Lohengrin : Alvary
Elsa : Krämer-Wiedl
Telramund : Staudigl
Ortrud : Goldsticker
Herald : Kemlitz

April 10
TANNHÄUSER/Neuendorff (c)
Same as Dec. 21 except:
Hermann : Lehmler
Wolfram : Staudigl
Walther : Krämer
Biterolf : Kaufmann
Venus : Januschowsky (t)
Shepherd : Frau Kemlitz

1 8 8 8 - 8 9

GERMAN GRAND OPERA
COMPANY
Edmund C. Stanton, *Manager*
All operas sung in German

PHILADELPHIA

March 25
DIE MEISTERSINGER
Seidl (c)
Hans Sachs : Fischer
Pogner : Beck
Eva : Kaschowska
Magdalene : Reil
Walther : Alvary
Beckmesser : Mödlinger
Kothner : Grienauer
Vogelgesang : Mittelhauser
Nachtigall : Doré
Zorn : Bartels (t)
Eisslinger : Göttich
Moser : Hoppe
Ortel : Doerfler
Schwarz : Eiserbeck
Foltz : Witt
David : Sedlmayer
Night Watchman : Doré

March 26
DAS RHEINGOLD/Seidl (c)
Wotan : Fischer
Donner : Doré (?)
Froh : Mittelhauser
Loge : Alvary
Alberich : Beck
Mime : Sedlmayer
Fasolt : Mödlinger
Fafner : Weiss
Fricka : Meisslinger
Freia : Klein
Erda : Reil
Woglinde : Traubmann
Wellgunde : Kaschowska
Flosshilde : Reil

March 27
DIE WALKÜRE/Seidl (c)
Wotan : Fischer
Fricka : Meisslinger
Brünnhilde : Triloff (t)
Siegmund : Kalisch
Sieglinde : Lehmann
Hunding : Weiss
Helmwige : Traubmann
Gerhilde : Seidlmayer
Ortlinde : Klein
Rossweisse : Miron
Grimgerde : Hartmann
Waltraute : Reil
Siegrune : Egenor
Schwertleite : Göttich

March 28
SIEGFRIED/Seidl (c)
Siegfried : Alvary

194

Mime : Sedlmayer
Wanderer : Fischer
Alberich : Mödlinger
Fafner : Weiss
Erda : Reil
Brünnhilde : Lehmann
Forest Bird : Traubmann

March 29
GÖTTERDÄMMERUNG
Seidl (c)
Siegfried : Kalisch
Gunther : Beck
Hagen : Fischer
Brünnhilde : Lehmann
Gutrune : Meisslinger
Woglinde : Traubmann
Wellgunde : Kaschowska
Flosshilde : Reil
(Norn, Alberich, Waltraute
scenes omitted)

March 30 (mat.)
DIE MEISTERSINGER
Same as Mar. 25 except:
Walther : Jäger (t)

BOSTON

April 1
DAS RHEINGOLD
Same as Mar. 26 except:
Donner : Grienauer

April 2
DIE WALKÜRE
Same as Mar. 27 except:
Wotan : Grienauer (for
Fischer)

April 3
SIEGFRIED
Same as Mar. 28 except:
Alberich : Beck
Erda scene omitted

April 5
GÖTTERDÄMMERUNG
Same as Mar. 29

April 6 (mat.)
DAS RHEINGOLD
Same as Mar. 26 except:
Donner : Grienauer

April 6
TANNHÄUSER/Seidl (c)
Hermann : Muehe
Tannhäuser : Jäger (t)
Wolfram : Grienauer
Walther : Mittelhauser
Biterolf : Mödlinger
Heinrich : Sedlmayer
Reinmar : Doré
Elisabeth : Traubmann
Venus : Lehmann
Shepherd : Kaschowska

April 8
DIE MEISTERSINGER
Same as Mar. 25

April 9
DAS RHEINGOLD
Same (?) as Mar. 26

April 10
DIE WALKÜRE
Same as Mar. 27 except:
Brünnhilde : Lehmann
Sieglinde : Kaschowska

April 11
SIEGFRIED
Same as Mar. 28 except:
Erda scene omitted

April 12
GÖTTERDÄMMERUNG
Same as Mar. 29

April 13 (mat.)
DIE MEISTERSINGER
Same as Mar. 25

MILWAUKEE

April 16
DAS RHEINGOLD
Same as Mar. 26 except:
Donner : Grienauer

April 17
DIE WALKÜRE
Same as Mar. 27 except:
Brünnhilde : Lehmann
Sieglinde : Kaschowska

April 18
SIEGFRIED
Same as Mar. 28 except:
Erda scene omitted

April 20
GÖTTERDÄMMERUNG
Same as Mar. 29

CHICAGO

April 22
DAS RHEINGOLD
Same as Mar. 26 except:
Donner : Grienauer

April 23
DIE WALKÜRE
Same as Mar. 27 except:
Brünnhilde : Lehmann
Sieglinde : Kaschowska

April 24
SIEGFRIED
Same as Mar. 28 except:
Erda scene omitted

April 25
GÖTTERDÄMMERUNG
Same (?) as Mar. 29

April 26
DIE MEISTERSINGER
Same (?) as Mar. 25

April 27 (mat.)
TANNHÄUSER
Same as Apr. 6 except:
Tannhäuser : Kalisch
Venus : Meisslinger

April 27
FIDELIO/Seidl (c)
Don Fernando : Mödlinger
Don Pizarro : Beck
Florestan : Alvary
Leonore : Lehmann
Rocco : Fischer
Marzelline : Traubmann
Jaquino : Sedlmayer
Prisoners : Göttich, Doré

April 29
SIEGFRIED
Same as Mar. 28 except:
Erda scene omitted

April 30
GÖTTERDÄMMERUNG
Same as Mar. 29

May 1
DIE MEISTERSINGER
Same as Mar. 25 except:
Walther : Jäger (t)

May 2
TANNHÄUSER
Same as April 6 except:
Tannhäuser : Kalisch
Venus : Meisslinger

May 3
LOHENGRIN/Seidl (c)
King Henry : Fischer
Lohengrin : Alvary
Elsa : Kaschowska
Telramund : Grienauer
Ortrud : Meisslinger
Herald : Mödlinger

May 4 (mat.)
DIE MEISTERSINGER
Same as Mar. 25

May 4
LOHENGRIN
Same as May 3

ST. LOUIS

May 6
DAS RHEINGOLD
Same as Mar. 26 except:
Donner : Grienauer

May 7
DIE WALKÜRE
Same as Mar. 27 except:
Brünnhilde : Lehmann
Sieglinde : Kaschowska

May 8
SIEGFRIED
Same as Mar. 28 except:
Erda scene omitted

May 9
GÖTTERDÄMMERUNG
Same as Mar. 29

May 10
DIE MEISTERSINGER
Same as Mar. 25

May 11 (mat.)
TANNHÄUSER
Same (?) as Apr. 6 except:
Tannhäuser : Kalisch
Venus : Meisslinger

1889-90A

ITALIAN GRAND OPERA
Henry E. Abbey, *Manager*

CHICAGO

December 9
DEDICATION OF THE
AUDITORIUM
Patti soloist; chorus and
orchestra

December 10
ROMÉO ET JULIETTE
Sapio (c)
Juliette : Patti
Stephano : Fabbri
Gertrude : Bauermeister
Roméo : Ravelli
Tybalt : Perugini
Benvolio : Bieletto
Mercutio : Del Puente
Paris : Lucini
Gregorio : Cernusco
Capulet : De Vaschetti
Friar Laurence : Marcassa

December 11
GUILLAUME TELL/Arditi (c)
William Tell : Zardo
Arnold : Tamagno (Am.d)
Walter Furst : Marcassa
Melchthal : Novara
Matilde : Valda
Jemmy : Bauermeister
Hedwig : Claire
Fisherman : Vanni
Leutold : De Vaschetti
Gessler : Migliara
Rudolf : Bieletto

December 12
FAUST/Arditi (c)
Faust : Ravelli
Marguerite : Albani
Méphistophélès : Novara
Valentin : Mareschalchi
Siébel : Synnerberg
Marthe : Bauermeister
Wagner : De Vaschetti

December 13
IL TROVATORE/Arditi (c)
Leonora : Valda (for
Nordica)
Manrico : Tamagno
Count di Luna : Del Puente
Azucena : Fabbri
Inez : Bauermeister
Ferrando : De Vaschetti
Ruiz : Bieletto
Gypsy : Lucini

December 14 (mat.)
LUCIA DI LAMMERMOOR
Sapio (c)
Lucia : Patti
Ashton : Mareschalchi
Edgardo : Ravelli
Alisa : Bauermeister
Raimondo : Carbone
Arturo : Vanni
Normanno : Bieletto

December 16
AIDA/Arditi (c)
King : De Vaschetti
Amneris : Synnerberg
Aida : Nordica
Radames : Tamagno
Amonasro : Zardo
Ramfis : Novara
Messenger : Bieletto

December 17
SEMIRAMIDE/Sapio (c)
Semiramide : Patti
Arsace : Fabbri
Idreno : Vicini
Oroe : Castelmary
Ghost of Ninus : De
Vaschetti
Assur : Marcassa

December 19
GUILLAUME TELL
Same as Dec. 11

December 20
IL TROVATORE
Same as Dec. 13 except:
Leonora : Nordica

December 21
MARTHA/Sapio (c)
Harriet : Patti

Nancy : Fabbri
Lionel : Ravelli
Plunkett : Marcassa
Tristan : Carbone
Sheriff : De Vaschetti

December 23
LES HUGUENOTS/Arditi (c)
Marguerite : Pettigiani
St. Bris : Carbone
Valentine : Albani
Nevers : Del Puente
Cossé : Lucini
Tavannes : Bieletto
Meru : Parini
Retz : De Vaschetti
Raoul : Ravelli
  (for Tamagno)
Marcel : Castelmary
Urbain : Fabbri
Maurevert : Migliara
Bois Rosé : Vanni
Lady of Honor :
  Bauermeister

December 24
LA TRAVIATA/Sapio (c)
Violetta : Patti
Alfredo : Ravelli
Germont : Mareschalchi
Flora : Claire
Annina : Bauermeister
Gastone : Vanni
Baron Douphol : Migliara
Marquis D'Obigny : Bieletto
Dr. Grenvil : De Vaschetti

December 26
AIDA
Same as Dec. 16

December 27
LA SONNAMBULA/Sapio (c)
Amina : Patti
Elvino : Ravelli
Rodolfo : Marcassa
Lisa : Bauermeister
Teresa : Claire
Alessio : Migliara
Notary : Bieletto

December 28 (mat.)
FAUST (for *Huguenots*)
Same as Dec. 12 except:
Faust : Vicini

December 30
LUCIA DI LAMMERMOOR
Same as Dec. 14

December 31
LES HUGUENOTS (for *Otello*)
Same as Dec. 23 except:
Marguerite : Bauermeister
Lady of Honor : Filomena

January 1
SEMIRAMIDE
Same as Dec. 17

January 2
OTELLO/Arditi (c)
Otello : Tamagno
Desdemona : Albani
Iago : Del Puente
Emilia : Synnerberg
Cassio : Perugini
Roderigo : Bieletto
Lodovico : Castelmary
Montano : De Vaschetti

January 3
OTELLO
Same as Jan. 2

January 4 (mat.)
IL BARBIERE DI SIVIGLIA
Sapio (c)
Almaviva : Vicini
Dr. Bartolo : Carbone
Rosina : Patti
Figaro : Mareschalchi
Don Basilio : Marcassa
Berta : Bauermeister
Fiorello : Bieletto

MEXICO

January 11
SEMIRAMIDE
Same (?) as Dec. 17

January 12
GUILLAUME TELL
Same (?) as Dec. 11

January 14
AIDA
Same (?) as Dec. 16

January 15
LUCIA DI LAMMERMOOR
Same (?) as Dec. 14

January 16
IL TROVATORE
Same (?) as Dec. 13 except:
Leonora : Nordica (?)

January 18
OTELLO
Same (?) as Jan. 2

Jan. 19 (mat.)
OTELLO
Same (?) as Jan. 2

January 19
SEMIRAMIDE
No data

January 21
LES HUGUENOTS
Same (?) as Dec. 23 except:
Raoul : Tamagno (?)

January 22
IL BARBIERE DI SIVIGLIA
Same (?) as Jan. 4

January 23
L'AFRICAINE
Selika : Nordica (?)
Vasco da Gama :
  Tamagno (?)
(Others not listed)

January 25
LINDA DI CHAMOUNIX
Linda : Patti
(Others not listed)

January 26 (mat.)
IL TROVATORE
Same (?) as Dec. 13 except:
Leonora : Nordica (?)

January 26
FAUST
Same (?) as Dec. 12

January 28
L'AFRICAINE (for *Aida*)
No data

January 29
LA TRAVIATA (Benefit for
  Patti)
Same (?) as Dec. 24

January 30
AIDA
Same (?) as Dec. 16

January 31
OTELLO (Benefit for
  Tamagno)
Same (?) as Jan. 2

February 1
SEMIRAMIDE
Same (?) as Dec. 17

February 2 (mat.)
CARMEN (Benefit for
  Nordica)

February 2
GUILLAUME TELL
Same (?) as Dec. 11

SAN FRANCISCO

February 10
GUILLAUME TELL
Same as Dec. 11

February 11
SEMIRAMIDE
Same as Dec. 17

February 12
OTELLO
Same as Jan. 2

February 13
IL TROVATORE
Same as Dec. 13

February 14
FAUST
Same as Dec. 12 except:
Méphistophélès : Castelmary
Valentin : Zardo

February 15 (mat.)
LA SONNAMBULA
Same as Dec. 27

February 15
AIDA
Same as Dec. 16

February 17
LES HUGUENOTS
Same as Dec. 23 except:
Raoul : Tamagno

February 18
LUCIA DI LAMMERMOOR
Same as Dec. 14

February 19
L'AFRICAINE/Sapio (c)
Don Pedro : Novara
Don Diego : Migliara
Inez : Pettigiani
Vasco da Gama : Tamagno
Don Alvaro : Vanni
Nelusko : Zardo
Selika : Nordica
Grand Inquisitor :
   Castelmary
Grand Brahmin :
   De Vaschetti
Anna : Bauermeister
Usher : Bieletto

February 20
MARTHA
Same as Dec. 21

February 21
MEFISTOFELE/Arditi (c)
Marguerite : Albani
Helen of Troy : Albani
Martha : Synnerberg
Pantalis : Synnerberg
Mefistofele : Castelmary
   (Part I); Novara (Part II)
Faust : Tamagno
Wagner : Bieletto
Nereus : Bieletto

February 22 (mat.)
LA TRAVIATA
Same as Dec. 24

February 22
OTELLO
Same as (?) as Jan. 2

DENVER
February 27
FAUST (for *Semiramide*)
Same as Dec. 12 except:
Valentin : Zardo

February 28
OTELLO
Same as Jan. 2

March 1 (mat.)
MARTHA
Same as Dec. 21

March 1
IL TROVATORE
Same as Dec. 13 except:
Leonora : Nordica
Azucena : Synnerberg

OMAHA
March 3
IL TROVATORE
Same (?) as Dec. 13 except:
Leonora : Nordica
Manrico : Vicini (for
   Tamagno)
Azucena : Synnerberg

March 4 (mat.)
IL BARBIERE DI SIVIGLIA
Same as Jan. 4 except:
Almaviva : Ravelli

LOUISVILLE
March 6
OTELLO
Same as Jan. 2

March 7
SEMIRAMIDE
Same (?) as Dec. 17

March 8 (mat.)
FAUST
Same (?) as Dec. 12

March 8
LES HUGUENOTS
Same (?) as Dec. 23 except:
Valentine : Nordica
St. Bris : Zardo
Raoul : Tamagno

CHICAGO
March 10
L'AFRICAINE
Same as Feb. 19 except:
Nelusko : Mareschalchi

March 11
LINDA DI CHAMOUNIX
Linda : Patti
Pierotto : Fabbri
Arditi (c)

Maddelena : Bauermeister
Charles : Ravelli
Antonio : Mareschalchi
Prefect : Marcassa
Marquis : Carbone

March 12
OTELLO
Same as Jan. 2

March 13
LAKMÉ/Sapio (c)
Lakmé : Patti
Mallika : Fabbri
Gerald : Ravelli
Frederic : Mareschalchi
Nilakantha : Marcassa
Hadji : Vanni

March 14
OTELLO
Same as Jan. 2

March 15
SEMIRAMIDE
Same as Dec. 17

BOSTON
March 17
OTELLO
Same as Jan. 2

March 18
SEMIRAMIDE
Same as Dec. 17

March 19
IL TROVATORE
Same as Dec. 13 except:
Leonora : Nordica
Azucena : Synnerberg

March 20 (mat.)
MARTHA
Same as Dec. 21

March 20
GUILLAUME TELL
Same as Dec. 11 except:
Walter Furst : Castelmary
Matilde : Pettigiani

March 21
FAUST
Same as Dec. 12 except:
Faust : Vicini
Marguerite : Nordica
Méphistophélès : Castelmary
Valentin : Zardo

March 22 (mat.)
OTELLO
Same (?) as Jan. 2

March 22
LAKMÉ
Same (?) as Mar. 13

197

PHILADELPHIA

April 3
OTELLO
Same as Jan. 2 except:
Desdemona : Nordica

April 10
FAUST
Same as Dec. 12 except:
Méphistophélès : Castelmary
Valentin : Zardo
(for Del Puente)

April 21 (mat.)
LAKMÉ
Same as Mar. 13 except:
Frederic : Migliara

1 8 8 9 – 9 0

GERMAN GRAND OPERA
Edmund C. Stanton, *Manager*
All operas sung in German

BOSTON
April 7
TANNHÄUSER/Damrosch (c)
Hermann : Behrens
Tannhäuser : Kalisch
Wolfram : Reichmann
Walther : Mittelhauser
Biterolf : Arden
Heinrich : Paché
Reinmar : Doré
Elisabeth : Lehmann
Venus : Traubmann
Shepherd : Miron

April 8
GUILLAUME TELL
Damrosch (c)
William Tell : Reichmann
Arnold : Perotti
Walter Furst : Fischer
Melchthal : Beck
Matilde : Traubmann
Jemmy : Kaschowska
Hedwig : Huhn
Fisherman : Gorski
Leutold : Doré
Gessler : Behrens
Rudolf : Mittelhauser

April 9
NORMA/Damrosch (c)
Oroveso : Fischer
Norma : Lehmann
Pollione : Kalisch
Adalgisa : Kaschowska
Clotilde : Miron
Flavio : Mittelhauser

April 10
LOHENGRIN/Damrosch (c)
King Henry : Behrens
Lohengrin : Perotti
Elsa : Wiesner
Telramund : Reichmann
Ortrud : Huhn
Herald : Arden

April 11
DIE MEISTERSINGER
Damrosch (c)
Hans Sachs : Fischer
Pogner : Beck
Eva : Kaschowska
Magdalene : Huhn
Walther : Kalisch
Beckmesser : Arden
Kothner : Doré
Vogelgesang : Mittelhauser
Nachtigall : Schuster (t)
Zorn : Paché
Eisslinger : Göttich
Moser : Bartels
Ortel : Doerfler
Schwarz : Eisenbeck
Foltz : Hoffman (t)
David : Gorski
Night Watchman : Doré

April 12
TANNHÄUSER
Same as Apr. 7 except:
Tannhäuser : Perotti
Wolfram : Beck

April 14
LES HUGUENOTS
Damrosch (c)
(Not given in New York)
Marguerite : Traubmann
St. Bris : Behrens
Valentine : Lehmann
Nevers : Beck
Cossé : Gorski
Tavannes : Mittelhauser
Meru : Doré
Raoul : Perotti
Marcel : Fischer
Urbain : Kaschowska
Maurevert : Arden
Bois Rosé : Mittelhauser
Lady of Honor : Miron
Night Watchman : Doré

April 15
DER FLIEGENDE HOLLÄNDER
Damrosch (c)
Senta : Wiesner
Mary : Huhn
Dutchman : Reichmann
Erik : Kalisch
Daland : Behrens
Steersman : Mittelhauser

April 16
FIDELIO/Damrosch (c)
(Not given in New York)
Don Fernando : Arden
Don Pizarro : Beck
Florestan : Kalisch
Leonore : Lehmann
Rocco : Fischer
Marzelline : Traubmann
Jaquino : Gorski
Prisoners : Paché, Doré

April 17
DIE MEISTERSINGER
Same (?) as Apr. 11

April 18
DON GIOVANNI
Damrosch (c)
Don Giovanni : Reichmann
Donna Anna : Lehmann
Donna Elvira : Kaschowska
Zerlina : Traubmann
Commendatore : Behrens
Don Ottavio : Kalisch
Leporello : Fischer
Masetto : Arden

April 19 (mat.)
LOHENGRIN
Same (?) as Apr. 10

CHICAGO
April 21
TANNHÄUSER
Same as Apr. 7 except:
Hermann : Fischer

April 22
GUILLAUME TELL
Same as Apr. 8 except:
Walter Furst : Behrens

April 23
DIE MEISTERSINGER
Same as Apr. 11 except:
Moser : Hoppe (t)

April 24
LA JUIVE/Damrosch (c)
Rachel : Lehmann
Eudora : Traubmann
Eleazar : Perotti
Cardinal : Fischer
Prince Leopold : Gorski
Ruggiero : Arden
Alberto : Doré

April 25
LOHENGRIN
Same as Apr. 10 except:
Elsa : Kaschowska
Herald : Mittelhauser

April 26 (mat.)
TANNHÄUSER
Same as Apr. 7 except:
Hermann : Fischer

April 28
UN BALLO IN MASCHERA
Damrosch (c)

Riccardo : Perotti
Renato : Reichmann
Amelia : Lehmann
Ulrica : Huhn
Oscar : Kaschowska
Silvano : Mittelhauser
Sam : Arden
Tom : Behrens

April 29
DER FLIEGENDE HOLLÄNDER
Same as Apr. 15 except:
Mary : Von Doenhoff (t)
Daland : Fischer

April 30
FIDELIO
Same as Apr. 16 except:
Don Fernando : Doré

May 1
DIE KÖNIGIN VON SABA
Damrosch (c)

Solomon : Beck
Queen of Sheba : Wiesner
Astaroth : Huhn
Sulamith : Traubmann
Assad : Perotti
High Priest : Behrens
Baal Hanan : Arden

May 2
NORMA
Same as Apr. 9

May 3 (mat.)
DIE KÖNIGIN VON SABA
Same as May 1 except:
Solomon : Reichmann

May 5
DER BARBIER VON BAGDAD
Damrosch (c)

Caliph : Beck
Cadi Mustapha : Mittelhauser
Margiana : Traubmann
Bostana : Huhn
Nureddin : Kalisch
Barber (Abu Hassan) : Fischer

DIE PUPPENFEE (Ballet)

CHICAGO
May 6
DON GIOVANNI
Same as Apr. 18 except:
Commendatore : Doré
Don Ottavio : Perotti
Leporello : Behrens

May 7
LOHENGRIN
Same as Apr. 10 except:
Herald : Mittelhauser

May 8
DER BARBIER VON BAGDAD
DIE PUPPENFEE (Ballet)
Same as May 5

May 9
DIE WALKÜRE
Damrosch (c)

Wotan : Fischer
Fricka : Huhn
Brünnhilde : Lehmann
Siegmund : Perotti
Sieglinde : Kaschowska
Hunding : Behrens
Helmwige : Traubmann
Gerhilde :
Von Doenhoff (t)
Ortlinde : Krügermann (t)
Rossweisse : Miron
Grimgerde : Hartmann
Waltraute : Huhn
Siegrune : Egenor
Schwertleite : Göttich (t)

May 10 (mat.)
DER BARBIER VON BAGDAD
DIE PUPPENFEE (Ballet)
Same as May 5

1891 – 92

ITALIAN GRAND OPERA
Abbey, Schoeffel and Grau,
Managers
For 1891-92 only, (d) signifies
debut in America

CHICAGO
November 9
LOHENGRIN/Vianesi (c)
King Henry :
E. de Reszke (d)
Lohengrin :
J. de Reszke (d)
Elsa : Eames (d)
Telramund :
Magini-Coletti (d)
Ortrud : G. Ravogli (d)
Herald : Serbolini

November 11
ORFEO ED EURIDICE
Vianesi (c)
Orfeo : G. Ravogli
Euridice : S. Ravogli (d)
Amor : Bauermeister

November 13
LA SONNAMBULA/Vianesi (c)
Adina : Van Zandt (d)

Elvino : Gianini (d)
Rodolfo : E. de Reszke
Lisa : Klein
Teresa : Cernusco (t)
Alessio : Rinaldini
Notary : Grossi

November 14 (mat.)
LOHENGRIN
Same as Nov. 9

November 16
ROMÉO ET JULIETTE
Vianesi (c)
Juliette : Eames
Stephano : De Vigne (d)
Gertrude : Bauermeister
Roméo : J. de Reszke
Tybalt : Capoul
Benvolio : Rinaldini
Mercutio : Martapoura (d)
Gregorio : De Vaschetti
Capulet : Vinche (d)
Friar Laurence : E. de Reszke
Duke of Verona : Viviani

November 18
DINORAH/Vianesi (c)
Dinorah : Van Zandt
Goatherds : G. Ravogli, Klein
Corentino : Gianini
Harvester : Grossi
Huntsman : Viviani
Hoel : Magini-Coletti

November 20
LES HUGUENOTS/Vianesi (c)
Marguerite : Pettigiani
St Bris : E. de Reszke
Valentine : Albani
Nevers : Magini-Coletti
Cossé : Rinaldini
Tavannes : Cernusco
Retz : Viviani
Raoul : J. de Reszke
Marcel : Vinche
Urbain : Scalchi
Maurevert : De Vaschetti
Bois Rosé : Grossi
Lady of Honor : Bauermeister

November 21 (mat.)
LA SONNAMBULA
Same as Nov. 13

November 23
OTELLO/Saar (c)
Otello : J. de Reszke
Desdemona : Albani
Iago : Camera (d)
Emilia : Scalchi
Cassio : Capoul
Roderigo : Rinaldini
Lodovico : Serbolini
Montano : Viviani

November 25
RIGOLETTO/Vianesi (c)
Duke : Valero (d)
Rigoletto : Camera
Gilda : Albani
Sparafucile : Vinche
Maddalena : Scalchi
Giovanna : Bauermeister
Monterone : Viviani
Marullo : De Vaschetti
Borsa : Rinaldini
Ceprano : Cernusco
Countess : Klein

November 26 (mat.)
FAUST/Vianesi (c)
Faust : J. de Reszke
Marguerite : Eames
Méphistophélès : E. de Reszke
Valentin : Martapoura
Siébel : Scalchi
Marthe : Bauermeister
Wagner : De Vaschetti

November 27
NORMA/Saar (c)
Oroveso : Serbolini
Norma : Lehmann
Pollione : Kalisch
Adalgisa : Pettigiani
Clotilde : Bauermeister
Flavio : Rinaldini

November 28 (mat.)
MARTHA/Saar (c ?)
Harriet : Van Zandt
Nancy : Scalchi
Lionel : Valero
Plunkett : E. de Reszke
Tristan : Carbone

November 30
MIGNON/Saar (c ?)
Mignon : Van Zandt
Philine : Lehmann
Wilhelm : Valero
Lothario : Vinche
Laerte : Carbone
Jarno : De Vaschetti
Frederic : Scalchi
Antonio : Cernusco

December 2
FAUST
Same as Nov. 26

December 4
LA TRAVIATA—*Act I*
Vianesi (c)
(Not given in New York)
Violetta : Albani
Alfredo : Gianini
Flora : Klein
Gastone : Rinaldini
Baron Douphol : De Vaschetti
Marquis d'Obigny : Grossi
Dr. Grenvil : Viviani

CAVALLERIA RUSTICANA
Vianesi (c)
Santuzza : Eames
Turiddu : Valero
Lola : Scalchi
Alfio : Camera
Lucia : Bauermeister

December 5 (mat.)
LES HUGUENOTS
Same as Nov. 20 except:
St. Bris : Serbolini
Nevers : Martapoura

December 5
DON GIOVANNI/Vianesi (c)
Don Giovanni :
Magini-Coletti
Donna Anna : Lehmann
Donna Elvira : S. Ravogli
Zerlina : Van Zandt
Commendatore : Serbolini
Don Ottavio : Kalisch
Leporello : E. de Reszke
Masetto : Rinaldini

LOUISVILLE
December 7
LOHENGRIN
Same as Nov. 9

December 8 (mat.)
LA SONNAMBULA
Same (?) as Nov. 13

December 8
LES HUGUENOTS
Same (?) as Nov. 20 except:
St. Bris : Serbolini
Raoul : Valero

CHICAGO
December 9
CONCERT/Vianesi, Saar (c)
First anniversary of Auditorium. Acts from *Trovatore,
Otello, Barbiere, Carmen.
Majority of company
participating*

December 10
AIDA/Saar (c)
King : Viviani
Amneris : G. Ravogli
Aida : Lehmann
Radames : J. de Reszke
Amonasro : Magini-Coletti
Ramfis : Serbolini
Messenger : Grossi

December 11
MARTHA
Same as Nov. 28

December 12 (mat.)
LOHENGRIN/Saar (c)
Same as Nov. 9 except:

King Henry : Vinche
Lohengrin : Valero
Elsa : Albani
Telramund : Camera

BROOKLYN
January 5
MIGNON
Same as Nov. 30

ALBANY
January 25
ROMÉO ET JULIETTE/Saar (c)
Same (?) as Nov. 16 except:
Roméo : Montariol
Capulet : Magini-Coletti
Friar Laurence : Vinche

TROY
January 29
LA SONNAMBULA
Same (?) as Nov. 13 except:
Adina : Pettigiani
Elvino : Montariol
Rodolfo : Serbolini

ALBANY
January 30 (mat.)
IL BARBIERE DI SIVIGLIA
(c—?)
Almaviva : Gianini (?)
Dr. Bartolo : Carbone
Rosina : De Vigne
Figaro : Magini-Coletti
Don Basilio : Serbolini
Berta : Bauermeister (?)
Fiorello : Rinaldini

January 30
LES HUGUENOTS
Same (?) as Nov. 20 except:
St. Bris : Serbolini
Raoul : Valero

BROOKLYN
February 2
LES HUGUENOTS
Same (?) as Nov. 20 except:
St. Bris : Lassalle
Raoul : Valero
Marcel : E. de Reszke

PHILADELPHIA
February 4
FAUST
Same as Nov. 26

February 11
ROMÉO ET JULIETTE
Same as Nov. 16 except:
Capulet : Magini-Coletti
Friar Laurence : Vinche

February 16
ORFEO ED EURIDICE
Same as Nov. 11

CAVALLERIA RUSTICANA
Same as Dec. 4 except:
Lola : G. Ravogli

February 18
MIGNON
Same as Nov. 30 except:
Philine : Pettigiani (for
Lehmann)
Wilhelm : Montariol

BROOKLYN
March 1
DON GIOVANNI
Same as Dec. 5 except:
Don Giovanni : Lassalle
Donna Anna : Tavary (d)
Masetto : Carbone

PHILADELPHIA
March 3 (mat.)
DON GIOVANNI/Saar (c?)
Same as Dec. 5 except:
Don Giovanni : Lassalle
Donna Anna : Tavary (for
Lehmann)
Masetto : Carbone

BROOKLYN
March 8
ORFEO ED EURIDICE
Same (?) as Nov. 11

CAVALLERIA RUSTICANA
Same (?) as Dec. 4 except:
Santuzza : Tavary (for
Eames)
Lola : G. Ravogli

PHILADELPHIA
March 10
LES HUGUENOTS
Same as Nov. 20 except:
St. Bris : Lassalle
Raoul : Montariol
Marcel : E. de Reszke

BOSTON
March 14
LES HUGUENOTS
Same as Nov. 20 except:
St. Bris : Lassalle
Marcel : E. de Reszke
Urbain : G. Ravogli

March 15
LAKMÉ/Vianesi (c)
Lakmé : Van Zandt
Mallika : De Vigne
Ellen : Klein
Rose : Bauermeister
Nilakantha : E. de Reszke
Frederic : Martapoura

Hadji : Rinaldini
Gerald : Montariol

March 16
ROMÉO ET JULIETTE
Same as Nov. 16 except:
Tybalt : Montariol
Capulet : Magini-Coletti

March 18
ORFEO ED EURIDICE
Same (?) as Nov. 11

CAVALLERIA RUSTICANA
Same (?) as Dec. 4 except:
Lola : G. Ravogli
Alfio : Magini-Coletti

March 19 (mat.)
MARTHA/Arditi (c)
Same as Nov. 28 except:
Harriet : Patti
Nancy : Fabbri
Plunkett : Novara

March 19
FAUST
Same as Nov. 26 except:
Valentin : Lassalle
Siébel : De Vigne

March 21
DIE MEISTERSINGER/Seidl (c)
Hans Sachs : Lassalle
Pogner : Serbolini
Eva : Albani
Magdalene : Bauermeister
Walther : J. de Reszke
Beckmesser : Carbone
Kothner : Delasco
Vogelgesang : Grossi
Nachtigall : Cernusco
Zorn : Rinaldini
Eisslinger : Claus
Moser : Furst
Ortel : De Vaschetti
Schwarz : Viviani
Foltz : Mira
David : Montariol
Night Watchman : Delasco

March 22
SEMIRAMIDE/Arditi (c)
(Not given in New York)
Semiramide : Patti
Arsace : Fabbri
Idreno : Rinaldini
Oroe : Viviani
Ghost of Ninus : De Vaschetti
Assur : Novara

March 23
LOHENGRIN
Same as Nov. 9

March 25
DON GIOVANNI
Same as Dec. 5 except:

Don Giovanni : Lassalle
Donna Anna : Tavary
Donna Elvira : Albani
Don Ottavio : Campanini
Masetto : Carbone

March 26 (mat.)
FAUST
Same as Nov. 26 except:
Valentin : Lassalle
Siébel : De Vigne

March 26
LA TRAVIATA/Arditi (c)
Same as Dec. 4 except:
Violetta : Patti
Alfredo : Valero
Germont : Del Puente
Annina : Bauermeister
Gastone : Viviani
Marquis d'Obigny : Rinaldini

PHILADELPHIA
March 29
LAKMÉ
Same as Mar. 15 except:
Nilakantha : Martapoura
(for E. de Reszke)
Frederic : Carbone

April 26
MARTHA/Arditi (c)
Same as Nov. 28 except:
Harriet : Patti
Nancy : Fabbri
Lionel : Guille
Plunkett : Novara
Sheriff : Proverba (t)

1893–94

PHILADELPHIA
December 5
FAUST/Mancinelli (c)
Faust : J. de Reszke
Marguerite : Eames
Méphistophélès : E. de Reszke
Valentin : Martapoura
Siébel : Guercia
Marthe : Bauermeister
Wagner : De Vaschetti

December 7
PHILEMON ET BAUCIS
Bevignani (c)
Baucis : Arnoldson
Jupiter : Plançon
Philemon : Mauguiere
Vulcan : Castelmary

CAVALLERIA RUSTICANA
Bevignani (c)
Santuzza : Calvé
Turiddu : Vignas

Lola : Ibles (d—for Guercia)
Alfio : Dufriche
Lucia : Bauermeister

December 12
LOHENGRIN/Mancinelli (c)
King Henry : Plançon
Lohengrin : Vignas
Elsa : Nordica
Telramund : Ancona
Ortrud : Guercia
Herald : De Vaschetti

December 14
LUCIA DI LAMMERMOOR
  Mancinelli (c)
Lucia : Melba
Ashton : Dufriche
Edgardo : Vignas
Alisa : Bauermeister
Raimondo : Carbone
Arturo : Mastrobuono
Normanno : Rinaldini

December 19
ORFEO ED EURIDICE
  Bevignani (c)
Orfeo : Scalchi
Euridice : Colombati
Amor : Bauermeister

PAGLIACCI/Mancinelli (c)
Nedda : Tavary (t—for
  Melba)
Canio : De Lucia
Tonio : Ancona
Beppe : Guetary
Silvio : De Gromzeski

BROOKLYN
December 21
LUCIA DI LAMMERMOOR
Same as Dec. 14

December 30
FAUST/Bevignani (c)
Same as Dec. 5 except:
Faust : De Lucia
Méphistophélès : Plançon
Siébel : Scalchi

PHILADELPHIA
January 2
CARMEN/Bevignani (c)
Carmen : Calvé
Don José : De Lucia
Micaela : Arnoldson (for
  Eames)
Escamillo : Ancona
Zuniga : Viviani
Morales : De Gromzeski
Frasquita : Bauermeister
Mercedes : Ibles
Dancaire : Carbone
Remendado : Rinaldini

January 9
RIGOLETTO/Bevignani (c)
Duke : De Lucia
Rigoletto : Ancona
Gilda : Melba
Sparafucile : Castelmary
Maddalena : Scalchi
Giovanna : Bauermeister
Monterone : De Vaschetti
Marullo : Viviani
Borsa : Rinaldini
Ceprano : Cernusco
Countess : Ibles

January 11
FAUST (for *Roméo*)
Same as Dec. 5 except:
Faust : Mauguiere
Méphistophélès : Plançon
Valentin : Lassalle
Wagner : Viviani

January 16
SEMIRAMIDE/Mancinelli (c)
Semiramide : Melba
Arsace : Scalchi
Idreno : Guetary
Oroe : Castelmary
Ghost of Ninus : De Vaschetti
Assur : Colonnesi (t—for
  E. de Reszke)

BROOKLYN
January 16
CARMEN
Same as Jan. 2

PHILADELPHIA
January 18
CARMEN
Same as Jan. 2

BROOKLYN
January 23
LOHENGRIN
Same (?) as Dec. 12 except:
King Henry : E. de Reszke
Telramund : Dufriche
Ortrud : Domenech

January 30
PAGLIACCI
Same as Dec. 19 except:
Nedda : Elandi (t—for
  Arnoldson)
Tonio : Dufriche
Silvio : De Gromzeski

CAVALLERIA RUSTICANA
Same (?) as Dec. 7 except:
Lola : Guercia
Alfio : Martapoura

PHILADELPHIA
February 1
TANNHÄUSER/Mancinelli (c)
Hermann : Plançon
Tannhäuser : Vignas
Wolfram : Vignas
Walther : Mastrobuono
Biterolf : Viviani
Heinrich : Rinaldini
Reinmar : De Vaschetti
Elisabeth : Melba
Venus : Nordica
Shepherd : Guercia

February 8
LE NOZZE DI FIGARO
  Bevignani (c)
Almaviva : E. de Reszke
Countess : Eames
Susanna : Nordica
Figaro : Ancona
Cherubino : Arnoldson
Marcellina : Bauermeister
Bartolo : Carbone
Basilio : Rinaldini
Don Curzio : Mastrobuono
Antonio : De Vaschetti

BROOKLYN
February 17
CARMEN
Same (?) as Jan. 2 except:
Micaela : Pettigiani

BOSTON
February 26
FAUST
Same as Dec. 5 except:
Faust : Mauguiere (for
  J. de Reszke)
Valentin : Lassalle
Siébel : Scalchi

February 27
CARMEN
Same as Jan. 2 except:
Micaela : Pettigiani

February 28
LE NOZZE DI FIGARO
Same as Feb. 8

March 1
ROMÉO ET JULIETTE
  Mancinelli (c)
Juliette : Melba
Stephano : Guercia
Gertrude : Bauermeister
Roméo : J. de Reszke
Tybalt : Mauguiere
Benvolio : Rinaldini
Mercutio : Martapoura
Gregorio : De Vaschetti

Capulet : Dufriche
Friar Laurence : Plançon
Duke of Verona : Castelmary

March 2
PAGLIACCI
Same as Dec. 19 except:
Nedda : Arnoldson

CAVALLERIA RUSTICANA
Same as Dec. 7 except:
Lola : Guercia
Alfio : Martapoura

March 3 (mat.)
LUCIA DI LAMMERMOOR
Same as Dec. 14

March 3
FAUST
Same as Dec. 5 except:
Valentin : Lassalle
Siébel : Scalchi

March 4
CONCERT/Mancinelli,
    Bevignani (c)
Mauguiere, Plançon,
    Arnoldson, Melba, Guercia

March 5
LES HUGUENOTS/Bevignani (c)
Marguerite : Pettigiani
St. Bris : Lassalle
Valentine : Nordica
Nevers : Ancona
Cossé : Rinaldini
Tavannes : Cernusco
Retz : Viviani
Raoul : J. de Reszke
Marcel : E. de Reszke
Urbain : Scalchi
Maurevert : De Vaschetti
Bois Rosé : Mastrobuono
Lady of Honor : Bauermeister

March 6
MIGNON/Bevignani (c)
(Not given in New York)
Mignon : Calvé
Philine : Nordica
Wilhelm : De Lucia
Lothario : Plançon
Laerte : Carbone
Jarno : De Vaschetti
Frederic : Scalchi
Antonio : Cernusco

March 7
ROMÉO ET JULIETTE
Same as Mar. 1 except:
Juliette : Eames

March 8 (mat.)
CARMEN
Same as Jan. 2 except:

Carmen : Arnoldson (for
    Calvé)
Micaela : Pettigiani

March 8
SEMIRAMIDE
Same as Jan. 16 except:
Assur : E. de Reszke

March 9
LOHENGRIN
Same as Dec. 12 except:
Lohengrin : J. de Reszke
Telramund : Lassalle
Ortrud : Domenech

March 10 (mat.)
FAUST/Bevignani (c)
Same as Dec. 5 except:
Faust : Mauguiere
Marguerite : Melba
Méphistophélès : Plançon

March 10
CARMEN
Same (?) as Jan. 2 except:
Escamillo : Lassalle

CHICAGO

March 12
FAUST
Same as Dec. 5 except:
Valentin : Ancona
Siébel : Scalchi

March 13
CARMEN
Same as Jan. 2 except:
Micaela : Pettigiani

March 14
LE NOZZE DI FIGARO
Same as Feb. 8

March 15
L'AFRICAINE/Mancinelli (c)
Don Pedro : E. de Reszke
Don Diego : Viviani
Inez : Pettigiani
Vasco da Gama : J. de Reszke
Don Alvaro : Mastrobuono
Nelusko : Lassalle
Selika : Nordica
Grand Inquisitor : Castelmary
Grand Brahmin :
    De Vaschetti
Anna : Bauermeister

March 16
LUCIA DI LAMMERMOOR
Same as Dec. 14

March 17 (mat.)
CARMEN
Same as Jan. 2

March 17
FAUST
Same as Dec. 5 except:
Valentin : Lassalle
Siébel : Scalchi

March 19
LOHENGRIN
Same as Dec. 12 except:
Lohengrin : J. de Reszke
Elsa : Eames
Telramund : Lassalle
Ortrud : Domenech

March 20
SEMIRAMIDE
Same as Jan. 16

March 21
PHILEMON ET BAUCIS
Same as Dec. 7

CAVALLERIA RUSTICANA
Same as Dec. 7 except:
Lola : Guercia
Alfio : Ancona

March 22
ROMÉO ET JULIETTE
Same (?) as Mar. 1 except:
Friar Laurence : E. de Reszke

March 23
MIGNON
Same as Mar. 6 except:
Mignon : Arnoldson (for
    Calvé)

March 24 (mat.)
FAUST
Same as Dec. 5 except:
Valentin : Lassalle
Siébel : Scalchi

March 26
CARMEN
Same as Jan. 2 except:
Don José : J. de Reszke
Micaela : Eames
Escamillo : Lassalle

March 27
RIGOLETTO
Same as Jan. 9 except:
Rigoletto : Dufriche

HAMLET—*Act 4* : Melba

March 28
PAGLIACCI
Same as Dec. 19 except:
Nedda : Arnoldson

CAVALLERIA RUSTICANA
Same as Dec. 7 except:

Lola : Guercia
Alfio : Martapoura

March 29
WERTHER/Mancinelli (c)
(American premiere)
Werther : J. de Reszke
Albert : Martapoura
Bailiff : Carbone
Schmidt : Guetary
Johann : De Vaschetti
Charlotte : Eames
Sophie : Arnoldson

March 30
AIDA/Bevignani (c)
King : Castelmary
Amneris : Scalchi
Aida : Nordica
Radames : Vignas
Amonasro : Lassalle
Ramfis : E. de Reszke
Messenger : Rinaldini

March 31 (mat.)
LUCIA DI LAMMERMOOR
Same as Dec. 14

March 31
CARMEN
Same as Jan. 2 except:
Don José : J. de Reszke
Micaela : Eames
Escamillo : Lassalle

April 2
LES HUGUENOTS
Same as Mar. 5 except:
Nevers : De Gromzeski

April 3
CAVALLERIA RUSTICANA
Same as Dec. 7 except:
Lola : Guercia
Alfio : Martapoura

PAGLIACCI
Same as Dec. 19 except:
Nedda : Arnoldson

April 4
TANNHÄUSER
Same as Feb. 1 except:
Venus : Pevny (for Nordica)
Shepherd : Bauermeister
(Ended with "Evening Star"
due to illness of Vignas)

LUCIA—*Mad Scene* : Melba

April 5
LOHENGRIN
Same as Dec. 12 except:
Lohengrin : J. de Reszke
Elsa : Eames

204

Telramund : Lassalle
Ortrud : Domenech

April 6
FAUST
Same as Dec. 5 except:
Faust : Mauguiere
Marguerite : Melba
Valentin : Lassalle
Siébel : Scalchi

April 7 (mat.)
ROMÉO ET JULIETTE
Same as Mar. 1 except:
Juliette : Eames
Friar Laurence : E. de Reszke

April 7
CARMEN
Same as Jan. 2

ST. LOUIS
April 9
FAUST
Same as Dec. 5 except:
Marguerite : Melba (for
Eames)
Valentin : Lassalle
Siébel : Scalchi

April 10
CARMEN
Same as Jan. 2 except:
Micaela : Pettigiani (for
Arnoldson)

April 11 (mat.)
LOHENGRIN
Same as Dec. 12 except:
Lohengrin : J. de Reszke
Telramund : Lassalle
Ortrud : Domenech

April 11
LUCIA DI LAMMERMOOR
Same as Dec. 14

April 12
PAGLIACCI
Same as Dec. 19 except:
Nedda : Arnoldson

CAVALLERIA RUSTICANA
Same as Dec. 7 except:
Lola : Guercia
Alfio : Martapoura

April 13
ROMÉO ET JULIETTE
Same (?) as Mar. 1 except:
Friar Laurence : E. de Reszke

April 14 (mat.)
CARMEN
Same as Jan. 2 except:

Micaela : Pettigiani
Escamillo : Martapoura

April 14
LE NOZZE DI FIGARO
Same as Feb. 8 except:
Almaviva : Dufriche

1 8 9 4 – 9 5

PHILADELPHIA
December 4
CARMEN/Bevignani (c)
Carmen : De Lussan
Don José : Russitano (d)
Micaela : Hill (d)
Escamillo : Ancona
Zuniga : Viviani
Morales : De Vaschetti
(for De Gromzeski)
Frasquita : Bauermeister
Mercedes : Van Cauteren
Dancaire : Carbone
Remendado : Rinaldini

December 11
OTELLO/Mancinelli (c)
Otello : Tamagno
Desdemona : Eames
Iago : Maurel
Emilia : Mantelli
Cassio : Mauguiere
Roderigo : Rinaldini
Lodovico : Mariani
Montano : De Vaschetti
Herald : Viviani

BROOKLYN
December 13
OTELLO
Same as Dec. 11 except:
Desdemona : Nordica

PHILADELPHIA
December 18
AIDA/Bevignani (c)
King : Mariani
Amneris : De Vigne (for
Mantelli)
Aida : Drog
Radames : Tamagno
Amonasro : Bensaude
Ramfis : Plançon
Messenger : Rinaldini
Priestess : Bauermeister

BROOKLYN
December 20
FAUST/Bevignani (c)
Faust : Russitano
Marguerite : Melba
Méphistophélès : Plançon
Valentin : Ancona

Siébel : Scalchi
Marthe : Bauermeister
Wagner : Viviani

PHILADELPHIA
January 8
Il Trovatore/Bevignani (c)
Leonora : Drog
Manrico : Tamagno
Count di Luna : Campanari
Azucena : Mantelli
Inez : Van Cauteren
Ferrando : Mariani
Ruiz : Vanni
Gypsy : Rinaldini

January 10
Faust/Mancinelli (c)
Same as Dec. 20 except:
Faust : Mauguiere
Valentin : Bensaude

BROOKLYN
January 10
Il Trovatore
Same as Jan. 8 except:
Manrico : Russitano (for Tamagno)
Azucena : De Vigne (for Mantelli)

PHILADELPHIA
January 15
Don Giovanni/Mancinelli (c)
Don Giovanni : Maurel
Donna Anna : Nordica
Donna Elvira : Eames
Zerlina : De Lussan
Commendatore : Abramoff
Don Ottavio : Russitano
Leporello : E. de Reszke
Masetto : Carbone

BROOKLYN
January 17
Carmen/Saar (c)
Same as Dec. 4 except:
Don José : Mauguiere
Micaela : Eames
Escamillo : Campanari
Zuniga : De Vaschetti
Morales : De Gromzeski

PHILADELPHIA
January 22
Manon/Bevignani (c)
Manon : Sanderson
Lescaut : Ancona
Des Grieux : Mauguiere
Count Des Grieux : Plançon
Poussette : Bauermeister
Javotte : Van Cauteren
Rosette : De Vigne
Guillot : Carbone
De Brétigny : De Gromzeski

January 24
Pagliacci/Bevignani (c)
(for *Huguenots*)
Nedda : De Lussan
Canio : Russitano
Tonio : Campanari
Beppe : Vanni
Silvio : De Gromzeski

Cavalleria Rusticana
Bevignani (c)
Santuzza : Heller
Turiddu : Tamagno
Lola : Mantelli
Alfio : Bensaude
Lucia : Bauermeister

January 29
La Traviata/Saar (c)
Violetta : Nordica
Alfredo : Russitano
Germont : Bensaude (for Campanari)
Flora : Bertinetti (t)
Annina : Bauermeister
Gastone : Vanni
Baron Douphol : Viviani
Marquis d'Obigny : Rinaldini
Dr. Grenvil : De Vaschetti

BROOKLYN
January 29
Manon
Same as Jan. 22 except:
Poussette : Miramar
Guillot : Castelmary

PHILADELPHIA
January 31
Aida (for *Guillaume Tell*)
Same as Dec. 18 except:
Amneris : Mantelli
Ramfis : E. de Reszke
(for Plançon)

February 7 (mat.)
Falstaff/Mancinelli (c)
Falstaff : Maurel
Ford : Campanari
Fenton : Russitano
Dr. Caius : Vanni
Bardolph : Rinaldini
Pistol : Nicolini
Mistress Ford : Eames
Anne : De Lussan
Dame Quickly : Scalchi
Mistress Page : De Vigne

February 7
Les Huguenots/Bevignani (c)
Marguerite : Melba
St. Bris : Plançon
Valentine : Nordica
Nevers : Ancona
Cossé : Vanni

Tavannes : Rinaldini
Retz : Viviani
Raoul : J. de Reszke
Marcel : E. de Reszke
Urbain : De Vigne
Maurevert : De Vaschetti
Bois Rosé : Vanni
Lady of Honor : Bauermeister

BROOKLYN
February 14
Falstaff
Same as Feb. 7

BALTIMORE
February 18
Lohengrin/Mancinelli (c)
King Henry : Plançon
Lohengrin : J. de Reszke
Elsa : Nordica
Telramund : Ancona
Ortrud : Mantelli
Herald : Abramoff

February 19
Otello
Same as Dec. 11

February 20 (mat.)
Faust/Mancinelli (c)
Same as Dec. 20 except:
Méphistophélès : E. de Reszke
Valentin : Campanari

February 20
Manon
Same as Jan. 22 except:
Lescaut : Bensaude

WASHINGTON
February 21
Lohengrin
Same as Feb. 18

February 22
Otello
Same as Dec. 11

February 23 (mat.)
Faust/Mancinelli (c?)
Same as Dec. 20 except:
Méphistophélès : E. de Reszke

February 23
Manon
Same as Jan. 22 except:
Lescaut : Bensaude

BOSTON
February 25
Les Huguenots
Same as Feb. 7 except:
Urbain : Scalchi

February 26
Otello
Same as Dec. 11

February 27
CARMEN (for *Manon*)
Same as Dec. 4 except:
Don José : Mauguiere
Escamillo : Campanari
Morales : De Gromzeski

February 28 (mat.)
LES HUGUENOTS
Same as Feb. 7 except:
Raoul : Russitano (for
J. de Reszke)
Urbain : Mantelli

February 28
FALSTAFF
Same as Feb. 7 except:
Pistol : Mariani

March 1
IL TROVATORE
Same as Jan. 8

March 2 (mat.)
RIGOLETTO/Bevignani (c)
Duke : Russitano
Rigoletto : Ancona (for
Maurel)
Gilda : Melba
Sparafucile : Mariani
Maddalena : Scalchi
Giovanna : Bauermeister
Monterone : Viviani
Marullo : De Vaschetti
Borsa : Rinaldini
Ceprano : Cernusco
Countess : Van Cauteren
Page : Michaelena (t)

March 2
FAUST/Mancinelli (c)
Same as Dec. 20 except:
Faust : Mauguiere
Marguerite : Eames
Méphistophélès : E. de Reszke
Valentin : Bensaude
Siébel : De Vigne

March 3
CONCERT/Bevignani (c)
STABAT MATER (Rossini)
Nordica, Scalchi, Mauguiere,
Plançon

SAMSON ET DALILA
Mancinelli (c)
Dalila : Mantelli
Samson : Tamagno
High Priest : Meyn (l—for
Campanari)
Abimelech : Plançon
Old Hebrew : Plançon
Messenger : Vanni
Philistines : Rinaldini,
De Vaschetti

206

March 4
LES HUGUENOTS (for
Lohengrin)
Same as Feb. 7 except:
Marguerite : Bauermeister
Raoul : Russitano
Urbain : Van Cauteren

March 5
DON GIOVANNI
Same as Jan. 15

March 6 (mat.)
FAUST/Mancinelli (c?)
Same as Dec. 20 except:
Faust : D'Aubigné (for
Mauguiere)
Valentin : Campanari
Wagner : De Vaschetti

March 6
CARMEN (for *Guillaume Tell*)
Same as Dec. 4 except:
Carmen : Heller
Don José : Mauguiere
Morales : De Gromzeski

March 7
FALSTAFF (for *Figaro*)
Same as Feb. 7 except:
Pistol : Mariani

March 8
ROMÉO ET JULIETTE
Mancinelli (c)
Juliette : Melba
Stephano : De Vigne
Gertrude : Bauermeister
Roméo : J. de Reszke
Tybalt : Mauguiere
Benvolio : Rinaldini
Mercutio : De Gromzeski
Gregorio : De Vaschetti
Capulet : Plançon
Friar Laurence : E. de Reszke
Duke of Verona : Viviani

March 9 (mat.)
MANON
Same as Jan. 22 except:
Lescaut : Bensaude
Poussette : Miramar

March 10
OTELLO
Same as Dec. 11 except:
Desdemona : Drog (for
Eames)

CHICAGO

March 11
LES HUGUENOTS
Same as Feb. 7 except:
Urbain : Scalchi

March 12
OTELLO
Same as Dec. 11 except:
Desdemona : Nordica (for
Drog)
Cassio : Vanni

March 13
ROMÉO ET JULIETTE
(for *Manon*)
Same as Mar. 8 except:
Duke of Verona : Castelmary

March 14
FALSTAFF
Same as Feb. 7 except:
Pistol : Mariani

March 15
AIDA
Same as Dec. 18 except:
Amneris : Mantelli
Amonasro : Ancona

March 16 (mat.)
OTELLO
Same as Dec. 11

March 16
LES HUGUENOTS
Same as Feb. 7 except:
Urbain : Scalchi

March 18
FAUST/Mancinelli (c)
Same as Dec. 20 except:
Faust : J.de Reszke
Marguerite : Eames
Méphistophélès : E.de Reszke

March 19
RIGOLETTO
Same as Mar. 2 except:
Rigoletto : Maurel
Sparafucile : Castelmary

March 20
LOHENGRIN
Same as Feb. 18

March 21
DON GIOVANNI
Same as Jan. 15 except:
Donna Anna : Drog (for
Nordica)

March 22
IL TROVATORE
Same as Jan. 8

March 23 (mat.)
LES HUGUENOTS
Same as Feb. 7 except:
Raoul : Russitano (for
J. de Reszke)
Urbain : Mantelli

March 23
FALSTAFF
Same as Feb. 7 except:
Fenton : Mauguiere
Pistol : Mariani

March 25
CARMEN (for *Meistersinger*)
Same as Dec. 4 except:
Don José : Mauguiere
Micaela : Eames
Escamillo : E. de Reszke
Morales : De Gromzeski

March 26
LUCIA DI LAMMERMOOR
Bevignani (c)
Lucia : Melba
Ashton : Bensaude
Edgardo : Russitano
Alisa : Bauermeister
Raimondo : Abramoff
Arturo : Vanni
Normanno : Rinaldini

CAVALLERIA RUSTICANA
Bevignani (c)
Santuzza : Heller
Turiddu : Tamagno
Lola : De Vigne
Alfio : Campanari (for
Ancona)
Lucia : Bauermeister

March 27 (mat.)
LOHENGRIN
Same as Feb. 18

March 27
LE NOZZE DI FIGARO
Bevignani (c)
Almaviva : E. de Reszke
Countess : Eames
Susanna : Hill
Figaro : Maurel
Cherubino : De Lussan
Marcellina : Bauermeister
Bartolo : Carbone
Basilio : Rinaldini
Don Curzio : Vanni
Antonio : De Vaschetti

March 28
AIDA
Same as Dec. 18 except:
Amneris : Mantelli
Aida : Nordica
Amonasro : Ancona
Ramfis : Abramoff

March 29
ROMÉO ET JULIETTE
Same as Mar. 8 except:
Juliette : Eames
Mercutio : Campanari

Capulet : De Gromzeski
(for Plançon)
Duke of Verona : Castelmary

March 30 (mat.)
FAUST/Mancinelli (c)
Same as Dec. 20 except:
Faust : Mauguiere
Méphistophélès : E. de Reszke
(for Plançon)

March 30
IL TROVATORE
Same as Jan. 8 except:
Leonora : Nordica

ST. LOUIS

April 1
LES HUGUENOTS
Same (?) as Feb. 7 except:
St. Bris : Mariani
Urbain : Scalchi

April 2
OTELLO
Same as Dec. 11 except:
Emilia : De Vigne
Cassio : Vanni

April 3 (mat.)
FAUST/Mancinelli (c)
Same as Dec. 20 except:
Faust : Mauguiere
Méphistophélès : E. de Reszke
(for Plançon)
Valentin : Bensaude (for
Ancona)

April 3
DON GIOVANNI
Same as Jan. 15 except:
Donna Elvira : Van Cauteren
(for Hill)
Leporello : Carbone (for
E. de Reszke)
Masetto : Rinaldini

April 4
DIE MEISTERSINGER
Mancinelli (c)
Hans Sachs : E. de Reszke
Pogner : Abramoff
Eva : Eames
Magdalene : Bauermeister
Walther : J. de Reszke
Beckmesser : Carbone
Kothner : Campanari
Vogelgesang : Vanni
Nachtigall : Borin(?)
Zorn : Rinaldini
Eisslinger : Paris (?)
Moser : Maestri (?)
Ortel : De Vaschetti (?)
Schwarz : Viviani
Foltz : Cernusco (?)

David : D'Aubigné
Night Watchman : Viviani

April 5
IL TROVATORE
Same as Jan. 8

April 6 (mat.)
LUCIA DI LAMMERMOOR
Same (?) as Mar. 26

April 6
FALSTAFF
Same (?) as Feb. 7

BOSTON

April 9
LOHENGRIN
Same as Feb. 18 except:
King Henry : E. de Reszke

April 10
LE NOZZE DI FIGARO
Same as Mar. 27 except:
Susanna : Bauermeister
(for Hill)
Marcellina : Van Cauteren
(for Bauermeister)

April 11 (mat.)
ROMÉO ET JULIETTE
Same as Mar. 8 except:
Mercutio : Campanari
Capulet : De Gromzeski
(for Plançon)
Duke of Verona : Castelmary

April 11
AIDA
Same as Dec. 18 except:
Amneris : Mantelli
Aida : Nordica
Amonasro : Maurel
Ramfis : Abramoff (for
Plançon)
Messenger : Vanni

April 12
PAGLIACCI
Same as Jan. 24 except:
Tonio : Ancona

CAVALLERIA RUSTICANA
Same as Jan. 24 except:
Santuzza : Drog
Turiddu : Del Papa (1—for
Tamagno)
Lola : De Vigne

April 13 (mat.)
LUCIA DI LAMMERMOOR
Same as Mar. 26

April 13
FAUST/Mancinelli (c)
Same as Dec. 20 except:

Faust : Mauguiere
(for J. de Reszke)
Marguerite : Eames
Méphistophélès : E. de Reszke
Valentin : Campanari
Wagner : De Vaschetti

April 14
CONCERT/Bevignani (c)
STABAT MATER (Rossini)
Nordica, De Vigne, Tamagno,
Plançon. Also Ancona, Heller

1 8 9 5 - 9 6

BROOKLYN
December 17
CARMEN/Bevignani (c)
Carmen : Calvé
Don José : Lubert
Micaela : Traubmann
(for Saville)
Escamillo : Ancona
Zuniga : De Vries (?)
Morales : De Longprez (?)
Frasquita : Bauermeister
Mercedes : Van Cauteren
Dancaire : Carbone
Remendado : Rinaldini

December 24
TANNHÄUSER/Seidl (c)
Hermann : Bucha
Tannhäuser : Wallnöfer
Wolfram : Kaschmann
Walther : Mirsalis (?)
Biterolf : Livermann (?)
Heinrich : Riedel (?)
Reinmar : Viviani (?)
Elisabeth : Beeth
Venus : Traubmann
Shepherd : Kitzu (?)

December 31
LOHENGRIN/Seidl (c)
King Henry : Plançon
Lohengrin : Cremonini (?)
Elsa : Nordica
Telramund : Ancona
Ortrud : Brema
Herald : De Vaschetti

January 7
FAUST/Bevignani (c)
Faust : Lubert
Marguerite : Saville
Méphistophélès : E. de Reszke
Valentin : Ancona
Siébel : Scalchi
Marthe : Bauermeister
Wagner : Viviani (?)

208

January 14
RIGOLETTO/Bevignani (c)
Duke : Cremonini (for
Russitano)
Rigoletto : Kaschmann
Gilda : Melba
Sparafucile : Castelmary
Maddalena : Scalchi
Giovanna : Bauermeister
Monterone : Viviani (?)
Marullo : De Vaschetti (?)
Borsa : Rinaldini (?)
Ceprano : Cernusco (?)
Countess : Van Cauteren
LUCIA—*Mad Scene* : Melba

January 21
PHILEMON ET BAUCIS
Bevignani (c)
Baucis : Engle
Philemon : Mauguiere
Vulcan : Castelmary
Jupiter : Plançon

CAVALLERIA RUSTICANA
Bevignani (c)
Santuzza : Calvé
Lola : Olitzka (?)
Turiddu : Russitano (for
Lubert)
Alfio : Ancona
Lucia : Bauermeister

January 28
FALSTAFF/Seppilli (c)
Falstaff : Maurel
Ford : Campanari
Fenton : Cremonini
Dr. Caius : Vanni
Bardolph : Rinaldini
Pistol : Arimondi
Mistress Ford : Saville
Anne : Beeth
Dame Quickly : Scalchi
Mistress Page : Kitzu (?)

February 4
LES HUGUENOTS/Bevignani (c)
Marguerite : Engle
St. Bris : Plançon
Valentine : Nordica
Nevers : Ancona
Cossé : Vanni (?)
Tavannes : Rinaldini (?)
Retz : Viviani (?)
Raoul : Russitano
Marcel : Arimondi
Urbain : Scalchi
Maurevert : De Vaschetti (?)
Bois Rosé : De Longprez (?)
Lady of Honor :
Bauermeister (?)

February 13
CARMEN
Same (?) as Dec. 17 except:
Micaela : Saville

BOSTON

February 17
FAUST
Same (?) as Jan. 7 except:
Faust : J. de Reszke
Marguerite : Melba
Valentin : Maurel

February 18
CARMEN
Same (?) as Dec. 17 except:
Micaela : Saville

February 19
LES HUGUENOTS
Same (?) as Feb. 4 except:
Marguerite : Melba
Nevers : Maurel
Raoul : J. de Reszke
Marcel : E. de Reszke

February 20
LUCIA DI LAMMERMOOR *(Acts
I, II, III)* Bevignani (c)
Lucia : Melba
Ashton : Campanari
Edgardo : Russitano
Alisa : Bauermeister
Raimondo : Arimondi
Arturo : Vanni
Normanno : Rinaldini

CAVALLERIA RUSTICANA
Same as Jan. 21 except:
Turiddu : Cremonini
Lola : Engle

February 21
TRISTAN UND ISOLDE/Seidl (c)
Tristan : J. de Reszke
Isolde : Nordica
King Marke : E. de Reszke
Kurvenal : Kaschmann
Brangaene : Olitzka (for
Brema)
Melot : Riedel
Shepherd : Mirsalis

February 22 (mat.)
CARMEN/(c?)
Same (?) as Dec. 17 except:
Micaela : Engle

February 22
FALSTAFF
Same (?) as Jan. 28

February 23
CONCERT—LA DAMNATION
DE FAUST/Seidl (c)
Marguerite : Nordica
Faust : Lubert
Brander : Castelmary
Méphistophélès : Plançon

February 24
ROMÉO ET JULIETTE
Bevignani (c)

Juliette : Melba
Stephano : Hunt
Gertrude : Bauermeister
Roméo : J. de Reszke
Tybalt : Mauguiere
Benvolio : Rinaldini
Mercutio : De Vries
Gregorio : De Vaschetti
Capulet : Plançon
Friar Laurence : E. de Reszke
Duke of Verona : Castelmary

February 25
AIDA *(Acts I, II, III)*
Bevignani (c)

King : Arimondi
Amneris : Mantelli
Aida : Nordica
Radames : Russitano
Amonasro : Kaschmann
Ramfis : Plançon
Messenger : Vanni
Priestess : Bauermeister

LA NAVARRAISE/Bevignani (c)

Anita : Calvé
Garrido : Plançon
Araguil : Lubert
Ramon : Mauguiere
Bustamente : De Vries

February 26
MANON/Bevignani (c)

Manon : Melba
Lescaut : Maurel
Des Grieux : J. de Reszke
Count des Grieux : Plançon
Poussette : Bauermeister
Javotte : Van Cauteren
Rosette : Hunt
Guillot : Castelmary
De Brétigny : De Vries

February 27
IL TROVATORE (for *Mefistofele*)
Seppilli (c)

Leonora : Nordica
Manrico : Russitano
Count di Luna : Campanari
Azucena : Mantelli
Inez : Bauermeister
Ferrando : Arimondi
Ruiz : Vanni
Gypsy : Rinaldini

February 28
LOHENGRIN

Same as Dec. 31 except:
King Henry : E.de Reszke
Lohengrin : J. de Reszke
Telramund : Kaschmann
Herald : Livermann

February 29 (mat.)
FAUST

Same (?) as Jan. 7 except:
Faust : Cremonini
Marguerite : Melba
Méphistophélès : Plançon
Valentin : Campanari

February 29
CARMEN

Same as Dec. 17 except:
Carmen : Olitzka (for Calvé)
Micaela : Beeth

BALTIMORE
March 2
FAUST (for *Roméo*)

Same (?) as Jan. 7 except:
Faust : Cremonini
Méphistophélès : Plançon
Siébel : Mantelli

March 3
ROMÉO ET JULIETTE

Same as Feb. 24

March 4 (mat.)
AIDA

Same as Feb. 25 except:
King : Castelmary
Amneris : Brema
Radames : Wallnöfer

March 4
FALSTAFF

Same (?) as Jan. 28

WASHINGTON
March 5
CARMEN

Same (?) as Dec. 17

March 6
ROMÉO ET JULIETTE

Same as Feb. 24

BALTIMORE
March 7 (mat.)
CARMEN/Saar (c)

Same (?) as Dec. 17 except:
Micaela : Engle
Escamillo : De Vries
Zuniga : Viviani

WASHINGTON
March 7 (mat.)
AIDA

Same (?) as Feb. 25 except:
King : Plançon
Ramfis : Castelmary

March 7
FALSTAFF

Same (?) as Jan. 28

PHILADELPHIA
March 9
FAUST

Same (?) as Jan. 7 except:
Faust : J. de Reszke
Marguerite : Melba
Valentin : Maurel

March 10
CARMEN

Same (?) as Dec. 17 except:
Micaela : Saville

March 11 (mat.)
LES HUGUENOTS

Same (?) as Feb. 4 except:
Marguerite : Melba
St. Bris : Arimondi
Nevers : Maurel
Raoul : J. de Reszke
Marcel : E. de Reszke

March 11
LOHENGRIN

Same (?) as Dec. 31 except:
Elsa : Beeth
Telramund : Kaschmann
Ortrud : Mantelli

March 12
RIGOLETTO

Same (?) as Jan. 14 except:
Duke : Russitano
Rigoletto : Maurel

LA NAVARRAISE

Same (?) as Feb. 25

March 13
TRISTAN UND ISOLDE

Same (?) as Feb. 21 except:
Brangaene : Brema

March 14 (mat.)
LUCIA DI LAMMERMOOR

Same as Feb. 20 except:
Edgardo : Cremonini
Raimondo : Carbone

CAVALLERIA RUSTICANA

Same as Jan. 21 except:
Turiddu : Lubert
Lola : Engle

March 14
FALSTAFF

Same (?) as Jan. 28

BUFFALO
March 16
LES HUGUENOTS

Same (?) as Feb. 4 except:
Marguerite : Melba
Nevers : Maurel
Raoul : J. de Reszke
Marcel : E. de Reszke

March 17

CARMEN
Same (?) as Dec. 17 except:
Micaela : Saville

March 18 (mat.)
FAUST
Same (?) as Jan. 7 except:
Faust : Cremonini
Marguerite : Melba
Méphistophélès : Plançon
Valentin : Maurel

March 18
AIDA
Same as Feb. 25 except:
King : De Vaschetti
Amneris : Brema
Ramfis : Arimondi

DETROIT

March 19
CARMEN
Same (?) as Dec. 17 except:
Micaela : Saville

March 20
FAUST
Same (?) as Jan. 7 except:
Faust : Cremonini
Marguerite : Melba
Méphistophélès : Plançon
Valentin : Campanari

March 21 (mat.)
AIDA
Same as Feb. 25

March 21
FALSTAFF
Same (?) as Jan. 28 except:
Fenton : Mauguiere

CHICAGO

March 23
FAUST
Same (?) as Jan. 7 except:
Faust : J. de Reszke
Marguerite : Melba
Valentin : Kaschmann

March 24
CARMEN
Same (?) as Dec. 17 except:
Micaela : Engle

March 25
LES HUGUENOTS
Same (?) as Feb. 4 except:
Marguerite : Melba
Raoul : J. de Reszke
Marcel : E. de Reszke
Urbain : Mantelli (for
    Scalchi)

March 26
LA TRAVIATA *(Acts I, II, III)*
    Bevignani (c)
Violetta : Saville
Alfredo : Russitano
Germont : Ancona
Flora : Van Cauteren
Annina : Bauermeister
Gastone : Vanni
Baron Douphol : Viviani
Marquis d'Obigny :
    Rinaldini
Dr. Grenvil : De Vaschetti

CAVALLERIA RUSTICANA
Same as Jan. 21 except:
Turiddu : Cremonini
Lola : Engle
Alfio : Campanari

March 27
TRISTAN UND ISOLDE
Same (?) as Feb. 21 except:
Brangaene : Brema

March 28 (mat.)
CARMEN
Same (?) as Dec. 17 except:
Micaela : Saville (for
    Beeth)

March 28
RIGOLETTO
Same (?) as Jan. 14 except:
Rigoletto : Maurel
LUCIA—*Mad Scene* : Melba

March 30
ROMÉO ET JULIETTE
Same as Feb. 24
*(Performance interrupted by
    lunatic who climbed on
    stage. He was arrested and
    jailed)*

March 31
IL TROVATORE
Same as Feb. 27 except:
Inez : Van Cauteren

LA NAVARRAISE
Same (?) as Feb. 25

April 1
FAUST
Same (?) as Jan. 7 except:
Faust : J. de Reszke
Marguerite : Melba
Valentin : Maurel

April 2
LOHENGRIN
Same (?) as Dec. 31 except:
Telramund : Kaschmann

April 3
LUCIA DI LAMMERMOOR
Same as Feb. 20 except:
Edgardo : Cremonini

CAVALLERIA RUSTICANA
Same as Jan. 21 except:
Lola : Engle

April 4 (mat.)
LES HUGUENOTS
Same as Feb. 4 except:
Marguerite : Melba
Nevers : Maurel
Raoul : J. de Reszke
Marcel : E de Reszke
Urbain : Olitzka (for
    Scalchi)

April 4
CARMEN
Same (?) as Dec. 17 except:
Micaela : Saville

ST. LOUIS

April 6
ROMÉO ET JULIETTE
Same as Feb. 24

April 7
CARMEN
Same (?) as Dec. 17 except:
Micaela : Beeth

April 8 (mat.)
LA TRAVIATA
Same (?) as Mar. 26

CAVALLERIA RUSTICANA
Same as Jan. 21 except:
Turiddu : Cremonini
Lola : Engle
Alfio : Campanari

April 8
LES HUGUENOTS
Same (?) as Feb. 4 except:
Marguerite : Melba
Nevers : Maurel
Raoul : J. de Reszke
Marcel : E. de Reszke

April 9
FAUST (for *Rigoletto*)
Same (?) as Jan. 7 except:
Faust : Cremonini
Marguerite : Beeth
Méphistophélès : Plançon
Valentin : Maurel

April 10
LOHENGRIN/Saar (c)
Same as Dec. 31 except:
King Henry : E. de Reszke
Lohengrin : J. de Reszke
Telramund : Kaschmann

April 11 (mat.)
CARMEN
Same (?) as Dec. 17 except:
Micaela : Saville
Escamillo : De Vries
Zuniga : Viviani

April 11
AIDA/Seppilli (c?)
Same (?) as Feb. 25 except:
Amonasro : Ancona

1 8 9 6 – 9 7

BROOKLYN
January 7
ROMÉO ET JULIETTE
Mancinelli (c)
Juliette : Melba
Stephano : Belina
Gertrude : Bauermeister
Roméo : Salignac
Tybalt : Bars
Benvolio : Corsi (?)
Mercutio : Campanari
Gregorio : De Vaschetti (?)
Capulet : De Vries
Friar Laurence : Plançon
Duke of Verona : Castelmary

NEW HAVEN
January 11
CARMEN/Bevignani (c)
Carmen : Calvé
Don José : Salignac
Micaela : Traubmann
Escamillo : Ancona
Zuniga : De Vries
Morales : Bars
Frasquita : Bauermeister
Mercedes : Van Cauteren
Dancaire : Viviani
Remendado : Corsi

BROOKLYN
January 19
LOHENGRIN/Seidl (c)
King Henry : Plançon
Lohengrin : Cremonini
Elsa : Eames
Telramund : Ancona
Ortrud : Mantelli
Herald : De Vaschetti

HARTFORD
January 26
CARMEN
Same (?) as Jan. 11 except:
Micaela : Engle

BROOKLYN
January 28
LES HUGUENOTS/Saar (c)
Marguerite : De Vere
St. Bris : Lassalle

Valentine : Litvinne
Nevers : Ancona
Cossé : Vanni (?)
Tavannes : Corsi (?)
Retz : Viviani (?)
Raoul : Ceppi
Marcel : E. de Reszke
Urbain : Mantelli
Maurevert : De Vaschetti (?)
Bois Rosé : Bars (?)
Lady of Honor :
  Bauermeister (?)

February 11
FAUST/Mancinelli (c?)
Faust : Cremonini (for
  Salignac)
Marguerite : Calvé
Méphistophélès : Plançon
Valentin : Ancona
Siébel : Mantelli
Marthe : Bauermeister
Wagner : Viviani (?)

CHICAGO
February 22
CARMEN/Mancinelli (c)
Same as Jan. 11 except:
Micaela : De Vere
Escamillo : Lassalle

February 23
LES HUGUENOTS/Bevignani (c)
Same (?) as Jan. 28 except:
St. Bris : Plançon
Raoul : J. de Reszke

February 24
MARTHA/Bevignani (c)
Harriet : Engle
Nancy : Mantelli
Lionel : Cremonini
Plunkett : E. de Reszke
Tristan : Viviani
Sheriff : De Vaschetti
Servant : Cernusco

February 25
FAUST
Same (?) as Feb. 11 except:
Valentin : Campanari

February 26
TRISTAN UND ISOLDE/Seidl (c)
Tristan : J. de Reszke
Isolde : Litvinne
King Marke : E. de Reszke
Kurvenal : Bispham
Brangaene : Olitzka
Melot : Von Hübbenet
Shepherd : Riedel
Steersman : D'Aubigné

February 27 (mat.)
CARMEN
Same as Jan. 11 except:

Micaela : Engle
Escamillo : Lassalle

March 1
L'AFRICAINE/Mancinelli (c)
Don Pedro : E. de Reszke
Don Diego : Viviani
Inez : Engle
Vasco da Gama :
  J. de Reszke
Don Alvar : Bars
Nelusko : Lassalle
Selika : Litvinne
Grand Inquisitor : Plançon
Grand Brahmin : Plançon
Anna : Bauermeister
Usher : Corsi

March 2
MEFISTOFELE/Mancinelli (c)
Marguerite : Calvé
Helen of Troy : Calvé
Martha : Mantelli
Pantalis : Mantelli
Mefistofele : Plançon
Faust : Cremonini
Wagner : Corsi
Nereus : Corsi

March 3
AIDA/Bevignani (c)
King : De Vaschetti
Amneris : Mantelli
Aida : Litvinne
Radames : Ceppi
Amonasro : Campanari
Ramfis : E. de Reszke
Messenger : Vanni
Priestess : Bauermeister

March 4
CARMEN
Same as Jan. 11 except:
Don José : J. de Reszke
Micaela : De Vere
Escamillo : Lassalle

March 5
IL TROVATORE/Bevignani (c)
Leonora : Traubmann
Manrico : Ceppi
Count di Luna : Campanari
Azucena : Olitzka
Inez : Van Cauteren
Ferrando : De Vaschetti
Ruiz : Vanni
Gypsy : Corsi

March 6 (mat.)
FAUST
Same (?) as Feb. 11 except:
Faust : J. de Reszke
Méphistophélès : E. de Reszke

March 8
LE CID/Mancinelli (c)
Roderigo : J. de Reszke

211

Don Diego : E. de Reszke
King : Lassalle
Count de Gormas : Plançon
St. James : Bars
Moorish Envoy : Bars
Don Arias : Corsi
Don Alonzo : De Vaschetti
Infanta : De Vere
Chimène : Litvinne

March 9
CARMEN
Same as Jan. 11 except:
Micaela : Engle
Escamillo : Lassalle

March 10
LOHENGRIN/Seidl (c)
King Henry : E. de Reszke
Lohengrin : J. de Reszke
Elsa : Litvinne
Telramund : Bispham
Ortrud : Olitzka
Herald : De Vries

March 11
FAUST
Same (?) as Feb. 11

March 12
SIEGFRIED/Seidl (c)
Siegfried : J. de Reszke
Mime : Von Hübbenet
Wanderer : E. de Reszke
Alberich : Bispham
Fafner : Viviani
Erda : Olitzka
Brünnhilde : Litvinne
Forest Bird : Traubmann

March 13 (mat.)
MARTHA
Same as Feb. 24

March 15
PHILEMON ET BAUCIS
Bevignani (c)
(Not given in New York)
Baucis : Engle
Philemon : Salignac
Vulcan : Bispham
Jupiter : Plançon

CAVALLERIA RUSTICANA
Bevignani (c)
Santuzza : Calvé
Turiddu : Cremonini
Lola : Belina
Alfio : Campanari
Lucia : Bauermeister

March 16
LES HUGUENOTS/Bevignani (c)
Same (?) as Jan. 28 except:
St. Bris : Plançon

March 17
FAUST
Same (?) as Feb. 11 except:
Faust : J. de Reszke
Méphistophélès : E. de Reszke

March 18
DON GIOVANNI/Mancinelli (c)
Don Giovanni : Lassalle
Donna Anna : Litvinne
Donna Elvira : Traubmann
Zerlina : Engle
Commendatore :
De Vaschetti
Don Ottavio : Cremonini
Leporello : E. de Reszke
Masetto : Bispham

March 19
CARMEN
Same as Jan. 11 except:
Escamillo : Lassalle

March 20 (mat.)
SIEGFRIED
Same as Mar. 12

March 20
ROMÉO ET JULIETTE
Same as Jan. 7 except:
Juliette : Engle
Duke of Verona : Viviani

ST. LOUIS
March 22
FAUST
Same (?) as Feb. 11 except:
Faust : J. de Reszke
Méphistophélès : E. de Reszke
Valentin : Campanari

March 23
LES HUGUENOTS/Bevignani (c)
Same (?) as Jan. 28 except:
St. Bris : Plançon

March 24 (mat.)
CARMEN/Mancinelli (c)
Same (?) as Jan. 11 except:
Micaela : Engle
Escamillo : Lassalle

March 24
IL TROVATORE
Same (?) as Mar. 5

March 25
SIEGFRIED
Same (?) as Mar. 12

LOUISVILLE
March 26
CARMEN/Mancinelli (c)
Same as Jan. 11 except:

Micaela : Engle
Escamillo : Lassalle

March 27 (mat.)
FAUST/Bevignani (c)
Same (?) as Feb. 11 except:
Marguerite : De Vere

March 27
LOHENGRIN
Same (?) as Mar. 10

CINCINNATI
March 29
CARMEN/Mancinelli (c)
Same (?) as Jan. 11 except:
Micaela : De Vere
Escamillo : Lassalle

March 30
SIEGFRIED
Same as Mar. 12

March 31 (mat.)
MARTHA
Same (?) as Feb. 24

March 31
FAUST
Same (?) as Feb. 11 except:
Faust : Salignac
Siébel : Olitzka

April 1
AIDA
Same (?) as Mar. 3 except:
Ramfis : Plançon

April 2
LOHENGRIN/Saar (c)
Same as Mar. 10

April 3 (mat.)
CARMEN
Same (?) as Jan. 11 except:
Micaela : Engle

April 3
IL TROVATORE
Same (?) as Mar. 5 except:
Azucena : Mantelli

BOSTON
April 5
SIEGFRIED
Same (?) as Mar. 12

April 6
FAUST
Same (?) as Feb. 11

April 7
LOHENGRIN
Same as Mar. 10

April 8
CARMEN
Same as Jan. 11 except:
Micaela : De Vere
Escamillo : Lassalle

April 9
MARTHA
Same as Feb. 24 except:
Tristan : Bispham

April 10
FAUST
Same (?) as Feb. 11 except:
Faust : J. de Reszke
Méphistophélès : E. de Reszke
Valentin : Campanari

1 8 9 8 – 9 9

GRAU GRAND OPERA COMPANY
Maurice Grau, *Manager*

CHICAGO
November 7
LOHENGRIN/Mancinelli (c)
King Henry : Pringle (for
  E. de Reszke)
Lohengrin : Dippel
Elsa : Eames
Telramund : Bispham
Ortrud :
  Schumann-Heink (d)
Herald : Mühlmann (for
  Pringle)

November 8
ROMÉO ET JULIETTE
Mancinelli (c)
Juliette : Adams (d)
Stephano : Djella (d)
Gertrude : Bauermeister
Roméo : Saléza (d)
Tybalt : Bars
Benvolio : Vanni
Mercutio : Albers (d)
Gregorio : Meux (d)
Capulet : Devries (d)
Friar Laurence : Plançon
Duke of Verona : Dufriche

November 9
TANNHÄUSER/Schalk (c—d)
Hermann : Plançon
Tannhäuser : Van Dyck (d)
Wolfram : Bispham
Walther : Bars
Biterolf : Mühlmann
Heinrich : Meffert (d)
Reinmar : Meux
Elisabeth : Eames
Venus : Pevny (for
  Schumann-Heink)
Shepherd : Meisslinger

November 10
IL BARBIERE DI SIVIGLIA
  Mancinelli (c)
Almaviva : Salignac
Dr. Bartolo : Carbone
Rosina : Sembrich
Figaro : Campanari
Don Basilio : Devries
Berta : Bauermeister
Fiorello : Meux
Sergeant : Vanni

November 11
FAUST/Mancinelli (c)
Faust : Saléza
Marguerite : Adams
Méphistophélès : Plançon
Valentin : Albers
Siébel : Mantelli
Marthe : Bauermeister
Wagner : Meux

November 12 (mat.)
LOHENGRIN
Same as Nov. 7

November 12
LA TRAVIATA/Bevignani (c)
Violetta : Sembrich
Alfredo : Salignac
Germont : Campanari
Flora : Roudez (d)
Annina : Bauermeister
Gastone : Vanni
Baron Douphol : Bars
Marquis d'Obigny : Pringle
  (for Piroia)
Dr. Grenvil : Dufriche

November 14
TANNHÄUSER
Same as Nov. 9 except:
Wolfram : Albers

November 15
LUCIA DI LAMMERMOOR
  Mancinelli (c)
Lucia : Sembrich
Alisa : Bauermeister
Edgardo : Saléza
Ashton : Campanari
Raimondo : Pringle
Arturo : Vanni
Normanno : Piroia (d)

November 16
AIDA/Mancinelli (c)
King : Pringle
Amneris : Mantelli
Aida : Nordica
Radames : Dippel
Amonasro : Campanari
Ramfis : Plançon
Messenger : Vanni
Priestess : Bauermeister

November 17
ROMÉO ET JULIETTE
Same as Nov. 8 except:
Capulet : Plançon
Friar Laurence : E. de Reszke

November 18
DIE WALKÜRE/Schalk (c)
Wotan : Mühlmann (for
  Bispham)
Fricka : Schumann-Heink
Brünnhilde : Nordica
Siegmund : Van Dyck
Sieglinde : Eames
Hunding : Pringle
Helmwige : Pevny
Gerhilde : Roudez
Ortlinde : Bauermeister
Rossweisse : Bach
Grimgerde : Djella
Waltraute :
  Schumann-Heink
Siegrune : Mantelli
Schwertleite : Meisslinger

November 19 (mat.)
IL BARBIERE DI SIVIGLIA
Same as Nov. 10

November 19
FAUST/Bevignani (c)
Same as Nov. 11 except:
Méphistophélès : Devries

November 21
LE NOZZE DI FIGARO
  Bevignani (c)
Almaviva : E. de Reszke
Countess : Eames
Susanna : Sembrich
Figaro : Campanari
Cherubino : Engle
Marcellina : Bauermeister
Bartolo : Carbone
Basilio : Vanni
Don Curzio : Maestri
Antonio : Dufriche

November 22
MARTHA/Bevignani (c)
Harriet : Engle
Nancy : Mantelli
Lionel : Salignac
Tristan : Carbone
Plunkett : E. de Reszke
Sheriff : Dufriche
Servant : Cernusco

November 23
DIE WALKÜRE
Same as Nov. 18

November 24
IL BARBIERE DI SIVIGLIA
  Bevignani (c)
Same as Nov. 10 except:

Don Basilio : E. de Reszke
(for Devries)

November 25
LES HUGUENOTS/Bevignani (c)
Marguerite : Engle
St. Bris : Devries
Valentine : Nordica
Nevers : Albers
Cossé : Vanni
Tavannes : Piroia
Retz : Meux
Raoul : Saléza
Marcel : E. de Reszke
Urbain : Mantelli
Maurevert : Dufriche
Bois Rosé : Bars
Ladies of Honor : Roudez,
Bauermeister

November 26 (mat.)
LUCIA DI LAMMERMOOR
Bevignani (c)
Same as Nov. 15 except:
Edgardo : Ceppi

BROOKLYN
January 3
IL BARBIERE DI SIVIGLIA
Same (?) as Nov. 10 except:
Don Basilio : E. de Reszke

January 10
LOHENGRIN/Schalk (c)
Same as Nov. 7

January 26
FAUST/Bevignani (c)
Same (?) as Nov. 11 except:
Méphistophélès : E. de Reszke

PHILADELPHIA
January 31
TANNHÄUSER
Same (?) as Nov. 9 except:
Venus : Nordica

February 2
IL BARBIERE DI SIVIGLIA
Same (?) as Nov. 10 except:
Don Basilio : E. de Reszke

BROOKLYN
February 3
IL TROVATORE/Bevignani (c)
Leonora : Nordica
Manrico : Ceppi
Count di Luna : Campanari
Azucena : Mantelli
Inez : Bauermeister (?)
Ferrando : Pringle (?)
Ruiz : Vanni (?)

February 9
ROMÉO ET JULIETTE
Same (?) as Nov. 8

PHILADELPHIA
February 21
LOHENGRIN/Schalk (c)
Same as Nov. 7 except:
King Henry : E. de Reszke
Lohengrin : Van Dyck

February 23
LES HUGUENOTS
Mancinelli (c)
Same as Nov. 25 except:
St. Bris : Plançon
Raoul : J. de Reszke

February 28
DIE WALKÜRE
Same (?) as Nov. 18 except:
Wotan : Van Rooy
Brünnhilde : Brema
Rossweisse : Djella (?)
Grimgerde :
Molka-Kellog (?)

March 2
ROMÉO ET JULIETTE
Bevignani (c)
Same as Nov. 8 except:
Friar Laurence : E. de Reszke

March 7
DON GIOVANNI/Bevignani (c)
Don Giovanni : Maurel
Donna Anna : Nordica
Donna Elvira : Adams
(for Schumann-Heink)
Zerlina : Engle(?)
Commendatore : Devries (?)
Don Ottavio : Salignac
Leporello : E. de Reszke
Masetto : Carbone (?)

March 9
RIGOLETTO/Bevignani (c)
Duke : Salignac
Rigoletto : Campanari
Gilda : Sembrich
Sparafucile : Devries (?)
Maddalena : Mantelli (?)
Giovanna :
Bauermeister (?)
Monterone : Dufriche (?)
Marullo : Meux (?)
Borsa : Vanni (?)
Ceprano : Cernusco (?)
Countess : Roudez (?)

BOSTON
March 27
LOHENGRIN/Schalk (c)
Same as Nov. 7 except:
King Henry : E. de Reszke
Lohengrin : J. de Reszke
Elsa : Nordica

March 28
TANNHÄUSER
Same as Nov. 9 except:
Wolfram : Albers
Venus : Engle

March 29 (mat.)
ROMÉO ET JULIETTE
Bevignani (c)
Same as Nov. 8

March 29
LES HUGUENOTS
Mancinelli (c)
Same (?) as Nov. 25 except:
Marguerite : Sembrich
St. Bris : Plançon
Nevers : Maurel
Raoul : J. de Reszke

March 30
DIE WALKÜRE
Same as Nov. 18 except:
Wotan : Van Rooy
Brünnhilde : Brema
Rossweisse : Djella
Grimgerde : Molka-Kellog

March 31
IL BARBIERE DI SIVIGLIA
Same as Nov. 10 except:
Don Basilio : E. de Reszke

April 1 (mat.)
FAUST/Bevignani (c)
Same as Nov. 11 except:
Faust : J. de Reszke
Marguerite : Eames

April 1
DON GIOVANNI/Mancinelli (c)
Same (?) as Mar. 7 except:
Donna Anna : Lehmann
Donna Elvira : Nordica
Zerlina : Sembrich

April 2
CONCERT/Mancinelli (c)
Plançon, Van Rooy, Van
Dyck, Adams, Brema, Stern
(cellist)

April 3
TRISTAN UND ISOLDE
Schalk (c)
Tristan : J. de Reszke
Isolde : Lehmann
King Marke : E. de Reszke
Kurvenal : Van Rooy
Brangaene : Brema
Melot : Pringle
Steersman : Meux
Shepherd : Meffert

April 4
LE NOZZE DI FIGARO
Same as Nov. 21 except:
Cherubino : Adams

April 5 (mat.)
LOHENGRIN/Schalk (c)
Same as Nov. 7 except:
King Henry : E. de Reszke
Lohengrin : Van Dyck
Elsa : Nordica

April 5
FAUST/Bevignani (c)
Same as Nov. 11 except:
Faust : J. de Reszke
Méphistophélès : E. de Reszke

April 6
ERO E LEANDRO
Mancinelli (c)
Prologo : Mantelli
Ero : Eames
Leandro : Saléza
Ariofarne : Plançon
Una Voce dal Mare : Pringle

April 7
LES HUGUENOTS
Same as Nov. 25 except:
St. Bris : Plançon
Nevers : Campanari
Raoul : J. de Reszke

April 8 (mat.)
DON GIOVANNI
Same as Mar. 9 except:
Donna Anna : Lehmann
Donna Elvira : Nordica
Zerlina : Sembrich

April 8
ROMÉO ET JULIETTE
Same as Nov. 8 except:
Mercutio : Dufriche (?)
Duke of Verona :
  Pringle (?)

BALTIMORE
April 10
LOHENGRIN/Schalk (c)
Same as Nov. 7 except:
King Henry : E. de Reszke
Lohengrin : J. de Reszke
Elsa : Nordica
Herald : Pringle

April 11
LA TRAVIATA/Mancinelli (c)
Same as Nov. 12 except:
Baron Douphol : Meux
Marquis d'Obigny :
  Cernusco
Dr. Grenvil : Pringle

April 12 (mat.)
FAUST
Same as Nov. 11 except:
Marguerite : Eames
Valentin : Campanari
Siébel : Meisslinger

April 12
DIE WALKÜRE
Same as Nov. 18 except:
Wotan : Van Rooy
Brünnhilde : Brema
Sieglinde : Lehmann
Hunding : Bispham
Rossweisse : Djella
Grimgerde : Bach

WASHINGTON
April 13
LOHENGRIN/Schalk (c)
Same as Nov. 7 except:
King Henry : E. de Reszke
Lohengrin : J. de Reszke
Elsa : Nordica
Herald : Pringle

April 14
LA TRAVIATA/Mancinelli (c)
Same as Nov. 12 except:
Violetta : Nordica (for
  Sembrich)
Baron Douphol : Meux
Marquis d'Obigny :
  Cernusco
Dr. Grenvil : Pringle

April 15 (mat.)
FAUST
Same as Nov. 11 except:
Marguerite : Eames
Valentin : Campanari
Siébel : Meisslinger

April 15
DIE WALKÜRE
Same as Nov. 18 except:
Wotan : Van Rooy
Brünnhilde : Brema
Sieglinde : Lehmann
Hunding : Bispham
Rossweisse : Djella
Grimgerde : Bach

PITTSBURGH
April 17
LOHENGRIN/Schalk (c)
Same as Nov. 7 except:
King Henry : E. de Reszke
Lohengrin : J. de Reszke
Elsa : Nordica
Herald : Pringle

April 18
ROMÉO ET JULIETTE
Same as Nov. 8 except:

Roméo : Salignac
Tybalt : Vanni
Benvolio : Maestri
Mercutio : Campanari
Capulet : Plançon
Friar Laurence : E. de Reszke
Duke of Verona : Pringle

April 19 (mat.)
FAUST
Same as Nov. 11 except:
Marguerite : Eames
Valentin : Campanari
Siébel : Meisslinger

April 19
DIE WALKÜRE
Same as Nov. 18 except:
Wotan : Van Rooy
Brünnhilde : Brema
Siegmund : Dippel (for
  Van Dyck)
Sieglinde : Lehmann
Gerhilde : Bauermeister
Ortlinde : Roudez
Rossweisse : Djella
Grimgerde : Bach

PHILADELPHIA
April 20
TRISTAN UND ISOLDE
Same as Apr. 3 except:
Isolde : Nordica
Kurvenal : Bispham
Brangaene :
  Schumann-Heink

1 8 9 9 – 0 0

NEW HAVEN
October 10
FAUST/Mancinelli (c)
Faust : Bonnard (t)
Marguerite : Calvé
Méphistophélès : E. de Reszke
Valentin : Illy (d)
Siébel : Olitzka
Marthe : Bauermeister
Wagner : Meux

SPRINGFIELD
October 11
IL BARBIERE DI SIVIGLIA
Mancinelli (c)
Almaviva : Salignac
Dr. Bartolo : Pini-Corsi (d)
Rosina : Sembrich
Figaro : Campanari
Don Basilio : Devries
Berta : Bauermeister
Fiorello : Meux
Sergeant : Vanni

1899–00

ALBANY
October 12
FAUST
Same as Oct. 10 except:
Faust : Dippel
Valentin : Campanari

UTICA
October 13
CARMEN/Mancinelli (c)
Carmen : De Lussan
Don José : Bonnard
Micaela : Adams
Escamillo : Illy
Zuniga : Devries
Morales : Bars
Frasquita : Bauermeister
Mercedes : Van Cauteren
Dancaire : Dufriche
Remendado : Queyla (d)

SYRACUSE
October 14 (mat.)
IL BARBIERE DI SIVIGLIA
Hinrichs (c—t)
Same as Oct. 11

October 14
CARMEN
Same as Oct. 13 except:
Carmen : Calvé
Zuniga : Meux

MONTREAL
October 16
LA TRAVIATA/Mancinelli (c)
Violetta : Sembrich
Alfredo : Dippel
Germont : Campanari
Flora : Van Cauteren
Annina : Bauermeister
Gastone : Vanni
Baron Douphol : Bars
Marquis d'Obigny : Pringle
Dr. Grenvil : Dufriche

October 17
CARMEN
Same as Oct. 13 except:
Carmen : Calvé
Don José : Salignac
Escamillo : Campanari

October 18
ROMÉO ET JULIETTE
Juliette : Adams
Stephano : Olitzka
Gertrude : Bauermeister
Roméo : Bonnard
Tybalt : Bars
Benvolio : Vanni
Mercutio : Illy
Gregorio : Meux
Capulet : Plançon

Friar Laurence : E. de Reszke
Duke of Verona : Dufriche

October 19
FAUST/Hinrichs (c)
Same as Oct. 10 except:
Faust : Dippel
Méphistophélès : Plançon

TORONTO
October 20
IL BARBIERE DI SIVIGLIA
Same as Oct. 11 except:
Don Basilio : E. de Reszke

October 21 (mat.)
FAUST/Hinrichs (c)
Same as Oct. 10 except:
Faust : Dippel
Marguerite : Adams
Méphistophélès : Plançon
Marthe : Van Cauteren

October 21
CARMEN
Same as Oct. 13 except:
Carmen : Calvé
Micaela : De Vere
Escamillo : Campanari

DETROIT
October 23
CARMEN
Same as Oct. 13

October 24
IL BARBIERE DI SIVIGLIA
Same as Oct. 11 except:
Don Basilio : E. de Reszke

October 25 (mat.)
MIGNON/Hinrichs (c)
Mignon : De Lussan
Philine : Adams
Wilhelm : Bonnard
Lothario : Plançon
Laerte : Queyla
Jarno : Dufriche
Frederic : Olitzka
Antonio : Meux

October 25
FAUST
Same as Oct. 10 except:
Faust : Dippel
Valentin : Dufriche

CLEVELAND
October 26
IL BARBIERE DI SIVIGLIA
Same as Oct. 11 except:
Dr. Bartolo : Sonnino (t—for
Pini-Corsi)
Don Basilio : E. de Reszke

October 27
ROMÉO ET JULIETTE
(for *Carmen*)
Same as Oct. 18 except:
Capulet : Devries
Friar Laurence : Plançon

October 28 (mat.)
LA TRAVIATA
Same as Oct. 16 except:
Alfredo : Salignac

October 28
FAUST/Hinrichs (c?)
Same as Oct. 10 except:
Faust : Dippel
Marguerite : Adams
Méphistophélès : Plançon

KANSAS CITY
October 30
CARMEN/Hinrichs (c)
Micaela : De Vere
Escamillo : Campanari

October 31 (mat.)
MIGNON
Same as Oct. 25 except:
Mignon : De Vere (for
De Lussan)
Wilhelm : Salignac

October 31
FAUST
Same as Oct. 10 except:
Faust : Dippel
Marguerite : Sembrich
Valentin : Campanari

ST. LOUIS
November 1
CARMEN/Hinrichs (c)
Same as Oct. 13 except:
Carmen : Calvé
(*Calvé's voice failed in last
act and Bauermeister sang
some high notes*)

November 2
IL BARBIERE DI SIVIGLIA
Hinrichs (c)
Same as Oct. 11 except:
Don Basilio : E. de Reszke

November 3
FAUST/Hinrichs (c)
Same as Oct. 10 except:
Faust : Dippel
Marguerite : Adams (for
Calvé)
Méphistophélès : Plançon

November 4 (mat.)
LA TRAVIATA/Hinrichs (c)
Same as Oct. 16 except:
Alfredo : Salignac (for
Dippel)

November 4
LOHENGRIN/Hinrichs (c)
King Henry : E. de Reszke
Lohengrin : Van Dyck
Elsa : Strong
Telramund : Mühlmann
Ortrud : Olitzka
Herald : Pringle

INDIANAPOLIS
November 6
IL BARBIERE DI SIVIGLIA
Same as Oct. 11 except:
Don Basilio : E. de Reszke

LOUISVILLE
November 7
FAUST
Same as Oct. 10 except:
Faust : Dippel
Marguerite : Adams

November 8 (mat.)
MIGNON
Same as Oct. 25 except:
Philine : De Vere

November 8
IL BARBIERE DI SIVIGLIA
Same as Oct. 11 except:
Dr. Bartolo : Dufriche
(for Pini-Corsi)

CINCINNATI
November 9
IL BARBIERE DI SIVIGLIA
Same as Oct. 11 except:
Dr. Bartolo : Dufriche
(for Pini-Corsi)
Don Basilio : E. de Reszke

November 10
LOHENGRIN/Mancinelli (c)
Same as Nov. 4 except:
Elsa : Ternina (d)
Ortrud : Schumann-Heink

November 11 (mat.)
MIGNON
Same as Oct. 25 except:
Wilhelm : Salignac

November 11
FAUST
Same as Oct. 10 except:
Faust : Saléza
Marguerite : Sembrich
Valentin : Campanari

CHICAGO
November 13
TANNHÄUSER/Paur (c—d)
Hermann : Plançon
Tannhäuser : Dippel
(for Van Dyck)

Wolfram : Bispham
Walther : Bars
Biterolf : Mühlmann
Heinrich : Queyla
Reinmar : Meux
Elisabeth : Strong (for Ternina)
Venus : Nordica (for Ternina)
Shepherd : Olitzka

November 14
LE NOZZE DI FIGARO
Mancinelli (c)
Almaviva : E. de Reszke
Countess : Eames
Susanna : Sembrich
Figaro : Campanari
Cherubino : De Lussan
Marcellina : Bauermeister
Bartolo : Pini-Corsi
Basilio : Vanni
Don Curzio : Maestri
Antonio : Dufriche

November 15
LES HUGUENOTS
Mancinelli (c)
Marguerite : Adams
St. Bris : Plançon
Valentine : Nordica
Nevers : Scotti (d)
Cossé : Vanni
Tavannes : Queyla
Retz : Meux
Raoul : Dippel
Marcel : E. de Reszke
Urbain : Mantelli
Maurevert : Dufriche
Bois Rosé : Bars
Ladies of Honor : Bauermeister, Van Cauteren
Watchman : Pringle

November 16
CARMEN
Same as Oct. 13 except:
Carmen : Calvé
Don José : Saléza
Escamillo : Campanari

November 17
LOHENGRIN/Mancinelli (c)
Same as Nov. 4 except:
Lohengrin : Dippel (for Van Dyck)
Elsa : Eames
Ortrud : Schumann-Heink

November 18 (mat.)
FAUST
Same as Oct. 10 except:
Faust : Saléza

Méphistophélès : Plançon
Valentin : Campanari
Siébel : Mantelli

November 18
MIGNON/Saar (c)
Same as Oct. 25 except:
Wilhelm : Salignac
Lothario : Devries

November 20
IL BARBIERE DI SIVIGLIA
(Acts II and III)
Same as Oct. 11 except:
Don Basilio : E. de Reszke
Berta : Van Cauteren

CAVALLERIA RUSTICANA
Mancinelli (c)
Santuzza : Calvé
Lola : Mantelli
Turiddu : Dippel
Alfio : Dufriche
Lucia : Bauermeister

November 21
TANNHÄUSER
Same as Nov. 13 except:
Elisabeth : Eames
Venus : Strong

November 22
CARMEN
Same as Oct. 13 except:
Carmen : Calvé
Don José : Saléza
Escamillo : Campanari

November 23
DON GIOVANNI/Mancinelli (c)
Don Giovanni : Scotti
Donna Anna : Nordica
Donna Elvira : De Vere
Zerlina : Sembrich
Commendatore : Devries
Don Ottavio : Salignac
Leporello : E. de Reszke
Masetto : Pini-Corsi

MILWAUKEE
November 24
IL BARBIERE DI SIVIGLIA
Saar (c)
Same as Oct. 11 except:
Don Basilio : E. de Reszke
Berta : Pratti (t)
Fiorello : Sonnino (t—for Meux)

CHICAGO
November 24
DIE WALKÜRE/Paur (c)
Wotan : Mühlmann
Fricka : Schumann-Heink
Brünnhilde : Ternina

Siegmund : Dippel (for
  Van Dyck)
Sieglinde : Eames
Hunding : Pringle
Helmwige : De Vere
Gerhilde : Van Cauteren
Ortlinde : Bauermeister
Rossweisse : Broadfoot (d)
Grimgerde : Bach
Waltraute : Schumann-Heink
Siegrune : Mantelli
Schwertleite : Olitzka

November 25 (mat.)
DON GIOVANNI

Same as Nov. 23 except:
Zerlina : De Lussan
Leporello : Pini-Corsi
Masetto : Dufriche

November 25
AIDA/Paur (c)

King : Pringle
Amneris : Mantelli
Aida : Strong
Radames : Saléza
Amonasro : Plançon
Messenger : Vanni
Priestess : Bauermeister

November 27
FAUST

Same as Oct. 10 except:
Faust : Saléza
Méphistophélès : Plançon
Valentin : Scotti

November 28
LOHENGRIN/Mancinelli (c)

Same as Nov. 4 except:
Lohengrin : Dippel
Elsa : Ternina
Ortrud : Schumann-Heink

November 29
LE NOZZE DI FIGARO
  Bevignani (c)

Same as Nov. 14

November 30 (mat.)
CARMEN/Bevignani (c)

Same as Oct. 13 except:
Carmen : Calvé
Don José : Salignac
Escamillo : Scotti
Frasquita : Van Cauteren
  (for Bauermeister)
Mercedes : Bertinetti
  (t—for Van Cauteren)

November 30
IL TROVATORE/Bevignani (c)

Leonora : Nordica
Manrico : Dippel
Count di Luna : Campanari

Azucena : Mantelli
Inez : Van Cauteren
  (for Bauermeister)
Ferrando : Pringle
Ruiz : Vanni

December 1
ROMÉO ET JULIETTE
  Bevignani (c)

Same as Oct. 18 except:
Juliette : Eames
Roméo : Saléza
Capulet : Devries

December 2 (mat.)
DIE WALKÜRE

Same as Nov. 24 except:
Wotan : Bertram (d)
Brünnhilde : Nordica
Sieglinde : Strong

December 2
RIGOLETTO/Bevignani (c)

Duke : Salignac
Rigoletto : Scotti
Gilda : Sembrich
Sparafucile : Devries
Maddalena : Olitzka
Giovanna : Bauermeister
Monterone : Dufriche
Marullo : Meux
Borsa : Vanni
Ceprano : Cernusco
Countess : Van Cauteren

BOSTON

December 4
CARMEN

Same as Oct. 13 except:
Carmen : Calvé
Don José : Salignac
Escamillo : Campanari

December 5
LE NOZZE DI FIGARO

Same as Nov. 14

December 6 (mat.)
LOHENGRIN (for *Tannhäuser*)
  Paur (c)

Same as Nov. 4 except:
King Henry : Pringle
Lohengrin : Dippel
Telramund : Bertram
Ortrud : Schumann-Heink
Herald : Mühlmann

December 6
CARMEN (for *Cavalleria* and
  Pagliacci) Bevignani (c)

Same as Oct. 13 except:
Carmen : Calvé
Don José : Salignac
Escamillo : Scotti

December 7
AIDA/Mancinelli (c)

Same as Nov. 25 except:
Aida : Nordica
Amonasro : Scotti

December 8
LOHENGRIN/Mancinelli (c)

Same as Nov. 4 except:
Lohengrin : Dippel
Elsa : Eames
Telramund : Bertram
Ortrud : Schumann-Heink
Herald : Mühlmann

December 9 (mat.)
FAUST/Bevignani (c)

Same as Oct. 10 except:
Faust : Saléza
Méphistophélès : Plançon
Valentin : Campanari
Siébel : Mantelli

December 9
DON GIOVANNI

Same as Nov. 23 except:
Don Giovanni : Bertram
Zerlina : De Lussan

December 10
CONCERT/Paur (c)

Bars, Olitzka, Mühlmann,
  Adams, Scotti, Pringle (for
  Strong)

December 11
LES HUGUENOTS/Bevignani (c)

Same as Nov. 15 except:
Marguerite : Sembrich
Valentine : Ternina
Nevers : Illy

December 12
ROMÉO ET JULIETTE

Same as Oct. 18 except:
Juliette : Eames
Stephano : Mantelli
Roméo : Alvarez (d)

December 13 (mat.)
CARMEN

Same as Oct. 13 except:
Carmen : Calvé
Don José : Salignac
Escamillo : Scotti (for
  Campanari)

December 13
DER FLIEGENDE HOLLÄNDER
  Paur (c)

Senta : Ternina
Mary : Schumann-Heink
Dutchman : Bertram
Erik : Dippel
Daland : Pringle
Steersman : Bars

December 14
LE NOZZE DI FIGARO
Same as Nov. 14 except:
Susanna : De Vere
Bartolo : Pringle

PORTLAND, ME.
December 14
IL BARBIERE DI SIVIGLIA
Bevignani (c)
Same as Oct. 11 except:
Dr. Bartolo : Dufriche
Figaro : Pini-Corsi
Berta : Van Cauteren
Sergeant : Meux (for
Bauda—t)

BOSTON
December 15
FAUST
Same as Oct. 10 except:
Faust : Alvarez
Méphistophélès : Plançon
Valentin : Scotti

December 16 (mat.)
DIE WALKÜRE
Same as Nov. 24 except:
Wotan : Bertram
Brünnhilde : Nordica
Sieglinde : Ternina

December 16
IL BARBIERE DI SIVIGLIA
Bevignani (c)
Same as Oct. 11 except:
Dr. Bartolo : Dufriche (for
Pini Corsi)
Don Basilio : E. de Reszke

December 17
CONCERT/Bevignani (c)
Broadfoot, Scotti, Adams,
Stern (cellist)

PHILADELPHIA
December 26
FAUST/Bevignani (c)
Same as Oct. 10 except:
Faust : Alvarez
Marguerite : Adams (for
Eames)
Méphistophélès : Plançon
Valentin : Campanari
Siébel : Mantelli

December 28
TANNHÄUSER
Same as Nov. 13 except:
Tannhäuser : Van Dyck
Wolfram : Bertram
Elisabeth : Gadski (for
Ternina)
Venus : Strong

January 2
LOHENGRIN/Paur (c)
Same as Nov. 4 except:
Elsa : Nordica
Telramund : Bertram
Ortrud : Schumann-Heink
Herald : Mühlmann

January 4 (mat.)
CARMEN/Bevignani (c)
Same as Oct. 13 except:
Carmen : Calvé
Don José : Saléza
Escamillo : Campanari

January 9
DER FLIEGENDE HOLLÄNDER
Same as Dec. 13 except:
Senta : Gadski
Daland : E. de Reszke
Steersman : Breuer (t)

January 11
LE NOZZE DI FIGARO
Same as Nov. 14

January 16
LE PROPHÈTE/Mancinelli (c)
John of Leyden : Alvarez
Fidès : Schumann-Heink
Bertha : Adams
Jonas : Bars
Mathisen : Devries
Zacharias : E. de Reszke
Oberthal : Plançon

January 18 (mat.)
IL BARBIERE DI SIVIGLIA
Bevignani (c)
Same as Oct. 11 except:
Don Basilio : E. de Reszke
Sergeant : Meux

January 23
DON PASQUALE/Bevignani (c)
Norina : Sembrich
Ernesto : Salignac
Dr. Malatesta : Scotti
Don Pasquale : Pini-Corsi
Notary : Queyla

CAVALLERIA RUSTICANA
Bevignani (c)
Same as Nov. 20 except:
Turiddu : Saléza
Alfio : Campanari

January 25
DON GIOVANNI
Same as Nov. 23

January 30
DIE MEISTERSINGER/Paur (c)
Hans Sachs : Van Rooy
Pogner : Bertram

Eva : Gadski
Magdalene :
   Schumann-Heink
Walther : Dippel
Beckmesser : Friedrichs
Kothner : Mühlmann
Vogelgesang : Vanni
Nachtigal : Borin
Zorn : Queyla
Eisslinger : Bertinetti
Moser : Maestri
Ortel : Meux
Schwarz : Weber
Foltz : Cernusco
David : Breuer
Night Watchman : Pringle

February 1 (mat.)
FAUST/Bevignani (c)
Same as Oct. 10 except:
Faust : Saléza
Valentin : Scotti

February 6
DAS RHEINGOLD/Paur (c)
Wotan : Van Rooy
Donner : Devries
Froh : Dippel
Loge : Van Dyck
Alberich : Friedrichs
Mime : Breuer
Fasolt : Mühlmann
Fafner : Pringle
Fricka : Brema
Freia : Strong
Erda : Schumann-Heink
Woglinde : Pevny
Wellgunde : Olitzka
Flosshilde : Schumann-Heink

BROOKLYN
February 6
CARMEN/Bevignani (c)
Same as Oct. 13 except:
Carmen : Calvé
Don José : Saléza
Escamillo : Campanari

PHILADELPHIA
February 8
DIE WALKÜRE
Same as Nov. 24 except:
Wotan : Van Rooy
Brünnhilde : Brema
Siegmund : Van Dyck
Sieglinde : Strong
Helmwige : Pevny
Grimgerde : Molka-Kellog
Siegrune : Bouton

February 13
SIEGFRIED/Paur (c?)
Siegfried : Dippel
Mime : Breuer
Wanderer : Van Rooy

Alberich : Friedrichs (?)
Fafner : Pringle (?)
Erda : Schumann-Heink
Brünnhilde : Ternina
Forest Bird : Pevny

February 15
GÖTTERDÄMMERUNG/Paur (c)
Siegfried : Dippel
Gunther : Mühlmann
Hagen : E. de Reszke
Alberich : Friedrichs
Brünnhilde : Nordica
Gutrune : Strong (?)
Waltraute : Schumann-Heink
Woglinde : Pevny (?)
Wellgunde :
    Molka-Kellog (?)
Flosshilde : Olitzka (?)
First Norn : Schumann-Heink
Second Norn : Olitzka
Third Norn : Pevny (?)

February 22
AIDA/Bevignani (c)
Same as Nov. 25 except:
King : Devries
Amneris : Broadfoot (for
    Mantelli)
Aida : Eames
Radames : Perotti
Amonasro : Scotti
Ramfis : E. de Reszke (for
    Plançon)

March 6
TRISTAN UND ISOLDE/Paur (c)
Tristan : Van Dyck
Isolde : Ternina
King Marke : E. de Reszke
Kurvenal : Van Rooy
Brangaene : Schumann-Heink
Melot : Pringle (?)
Steersman : Meux (?)
Shepherd : Breuer (?)
Sailor's Voice : Bars (?)

March 8 (mat.)
LES HUGUENOTS/Bevignani (c)
Same (?) as Nov. 15 except:
St. Bris : Dufriche (for
    Devries)
Valentine : De Vere (for
    Nordica)
Raoul : Cornubert

BROOKLYN
March 12
FAUST/Bevignani (c)
Same as Oct. 10 except:
Faust : Salignac
Méphistophélès : Plançon
Valentin : Scotti
Siébel : Mantelli
Wagner : Occillier

220

PHILADELPHIA
March 13
IL TROVATORE
Same as Nov. 30 except:
Manrico : Perotti

PAGLIACCI/Bevignani (c—?)
Nedda : Adams (for De
    Lussan)
Canio : Cornubert (?)
Tonio : Scotti
Beppe : Bars
Silvio : Mühlmann (?)

March 15
CARMEN/Bevignani (c)
Same (?) as Oct. 13 except:
Carmen : Calvé
Don José : Salignac
Escamillo : Plançon
Zuniga : Meux
Morales : Vanni

PITTSBURGH
April 16
IL BARBIERE DI SIVIGLIA
    Bevignani (c)
Same as Oct. 11 except:
Don Basilio : E. de Reszke
Berta : Van Cauteren
Sergeant : Queyla

CAVALLERIA RUSTICANA
Same as Jan. 23 except:
Turiddu : Bars
Alfio : Mühlmann

April 17
TANNHÄUSER
Same as Nov. 13 except:
Tannhäuser : Van Dyck
Wolfram : Bertram
Elisabeth : Ternina
Venus : Strong
Shepherd : Schumann-Heink

April 18 (mat.)
CARMEN/Bevignani (c)
Same as Oct. 13 except:
Carmen : Calvé
Don José : Salignac
Escamillo : Plançon
Zuniga : Meux

April 18
DON GIOVANNI/Bevignani (c)
Same as Nov. 23 except:
Commendatore : Pringle
Don Ottavio : Dippel

WASHINGTON
April 19
AIDA/Bevignani (c)
Same (?) as Nov. 25 except:

Radames : Perotti
Ramfis : E. de Reszke
Messenger : Queyla

April 20
DON GIOVANNI/Bevignani (c)
Same as Nov. 23 except:
Zerlina : De Lussan
Commendatore : Pringle
Don Ottavio : Dippel

April 21 (mat.)
CARMEN/Bevignani (c)
Same (?) as Oct. 13 except:
Carmen : Calvé
Don José : Salignac
Escamillo : Scotti
Zuniga : Meux

April 21
FAUST/Bevignani (c)
Same as Oct. 10 except:
Faust : Van Dyck
Marguerite : Sembrich
Méphistophélès : Plançon
Valentin : Campanari
Siébel : Mantelli

BALTIMORE
April 23
CARMEN/Bevignani (c)
Same as Oct. 13 except:
Carmen : Calvé
Don José : Salignac
Micaela : De Vere
Escamillo : Scotti
Zuniga : Meux

April 24
TANNHÄUSER
Same as Nov. 13 except:
Wolfram : Bertram

1 9 0 0 – 0 1

LOS ANGELES
November 9
LA BOHÈME/Mancinelli (c)
Rodolfo : Cremonini
Marcello : Campanari
Schaunard : Gilibert (d)
Colline : Journet (d)
Mimi : Melba
Musetta : Scheff (d)
Benoit : Dufriche
Parpignol : Masiero (d)
Alcindoro : Dufriche

LUCIA—*Mad Scene* : Melba

November 10 (mat.)
ROMÉO ET JULIETTE
    Mancinelli (c)
Juliette : Adams

Stephano : Bridewell
Gertrude : Bauermeister
Roméo :
    Imbart de la Tour (d)
Tybalt : Bars
Benvolio : Masiero (?)
Mercutio : Sizes (d)
Gregorio : Viviani
Capulet : Journet
Friar Laurence : Plançon
Duke of Verona : Dufriche

(*Official program states that
Carrie Bridewell sang for
Masiero, but no verification
of this odd substitution was
possible*)

November 10
LOHENGRIN/Damrosch (c)
King Henry : E. de Reszke
Lohengrin : Dippel
Elsa : Nordica
Telramund : Mühlmann
Ortrud : Olitzka
Herald : Dufriche

SAN FRANCISCO
November 12
ROMÉO ET JULIETTE

Same as Nov. 10 except:
Juliette : Melba
Roméo : Saléza
Gregorio : Dufriche
Capulet : Plançon
Friar Laurence : E. de Reszke

November 13
TANNHÄUSER/Damrosch (c)

Hermann : Blass (d)
Tannhäuser : Van Dyck
Wolfram : Bispham
Walther : Bars
Biterolf : Mühlmann
Heinrich : Von Hübbenet
Reinmar : Viviani
Elisabeth : Gadski
Venus : Strong
Shepherd : Olitzka

November 14
AIDA/Mancinelli (c)

King : Journet
Amneris : Homer (d)
Aida : Nordica
Radames : Imbart de la Tour
Amonasro : Scotti
Ramfis : Plançon
Messenger : Masiero
Priestess : Bauermeister

November 15
FAUST/Mancinelli (c)

Faust : Saléza
Marguerite : Melba
Méphistophélès : Plançon

Valentin : Campanari
Siébel : Homer
Marthe : Bauermeister
Wagner : Dufriche

November 16
DER FLIEGENDE HOLLÄNDER
    Damrosch (c)

Senta : Gadski
Mary : Olitzka
Dutchman : Bispham
Erik : Dippel
Daland : Blass
Steersman : Bars

November 17 (mat.)
LUCIA DI LAMMERMOOR
    Mancinelli (c)

Lucia : Melba
Alisa : Bauermeister
Edgardo : Cremonini
Ashton : Campanari
Raimondo : Journet
Arturo : Bars
Normanno : Masiero

November 17
LOHENGRIN

Same as Nov. 10 except:
Lohengrin : Van Dyck
Telramund : Bispham
Ortrud : Schumann-Heink
Herald : Mühlmann

November 18
IL TROVATORE/Mancinelli (c)

Leonora : Nordica
Manrico : Dippel
Count di Luna : Dufriche
Azucena : Olitzka
Inez : Van Cauteren
Ferrando : Journet
Ruiz : Masiero

November 19
LA BOHÈME

Same as Nov. 9

November 20
DON GIOVANNI/Mancinelli (c)

Don Giovanni : Scotti
Donna Anna : Nordica
Donna Elvira : Gadski
Zerlina : Scheff
Commendatore : Journet
Don Ottavio : Salignac
Leporello : E. de Reszke
Masetto : Pini-Corsi

November 21
TANNHÄUSER

Same as Nov. 13

November 22
ROMÉO ET JULIETTE

Same as Nov. 10 except:

Juliette : Melba
Roméo : Saléza
Gregorio : Dufriche
Capulet : Plançon
Friar Laurence : E. de Reszke
Duke of Verona : Gilibert

November 23
LES HUGUENOTS/Flon (c—d)

Marguerite : Adams
St. Bris : Plançon
Valentine : Nordica
Nevers : Scotti
Cossé : Masiero
Tavannes : Von Hübbenet
Retz : Viviani
Raoul : Dippel
Marcel : E. de Reszke
Urbain : Olitzka
Maurevert : Dufriche
Bois Rosé : Bars
Ladies of Honor :
    Bauermeister, Van Cauteren

November 24 (mat.)
LOHENGRIN

Same as Nov. 10 except:
King Henry : Blass
Lohengrin : Van Dyck
Elsa : Gadski
Telramund : Bispham
Ortrud : Schumann-Heink

November 24
FAUST

Same as Nov. 15 except:
Méphistophélès : E. de Reszke

November 25
TANNHÄUSER

Same as Nov. 13 except:
Hermann : Plançon
Tannhäuser : Dippel
Wolfram : Mühlmann
Biterolf : Gilibert
Elisabeth : Strong
Venus : Marilly (d)

November 26
DAS RHEINGOLD/Damrosch (c)

Wotan : Mühlmann
Donner : Dufriche
Froh : Bars
Loge : Van Dyck
Alberich : Bispham
Mime : Von Hübbenet
Fasolt : Blass
Fafner : Journet
Fricka : Strong
Freia : Marilly
Erda : Schumann-Heink
Woglinde : Scheff
Wellgunde : Olitzka
Flosshilde : Schumann-Heink

1900–01

November 27
DIE WALKÜRE/Damrosch (c)
Wotan : Bispham
Fricka : Schumann-Heink
Brünnhilde : Nordica
Siegmund : Van Dyck
Sieglinde : Gadski
Hunding : Blass
Helmwige : Scheff
Gerhilde : Van Cauteren
Ortlinde : Bauermeister
Rossweisse : Bridewell
Grimgerde : Olitzka
Waltraute : Schumann-Heink
Siegrune : Marilly
Schwertleite : Homer

November 28
SIEGFRIED/Damrosch (c)
Siegfried : Dippel
Mime : Von Hübbenet
Wanderer : E. de Reszke
Alberich : Bispham
Fafner : Blass
Erda : Schumann-Heink
Brünnhilde : Nordica
Forest Bird : Scheff

November 29
LA BOHÈME
Same as Nov. 9 except:
Rodolfo : Saléza

November 30
GÖTTERDÄMMERUNG
Damrosch (c)
Siegfried : Dippel
Gunther : Mühlmann
Hagen : E. de Reszke
Brünnhilde : Nordica
Gutrune : Strong
Waltraute : Schumann-Heink
Woglinde : Scheff
Wellgunde : Bridewell
Flosshilde : Schumann-Heink
(Norn, Alberich scenes
omitted)

December 1 (mat.)
LA TRAVIATA/Mancinelli (c)
Violetta : Melba
Alfredo : Cremonini
Germont : Campanari
Flora : Van Cauteren
Annina : Bauermeister
Gastone : Masiero
Baron Douphol : Bars
Marquis d'Obigny : Dufriche
Doctor Grenvil : Gilibert

December 1
LOHENGRIN
Same as Nov. 10 except:
King Henry : Blass
Lohengrin : Van Dyck

Elsa : Gadski
Ortrud : Schumann-Heink

December 2
RIGOLETTO/Flon (c)
Duke : Saléza
Rigoletto : Scotti
Gilda : Adams
Sparafucile : Journet
Maddalena : Homer
Giovanna : Bauermeister
Monterone : Gilibert
Marullo : Viviani
Borsa : Masiero
Ceprano : Fanelli (t)
Countess : Van Cauteren

DENVER
December 5
TANNHÄUSER
Same as Nov. 13 except:
Hermann : Plançon
Tannhäuser : Dippel
Wolfram : Bertram
Elisabeth : Strong
Venus : Nordica

December 6
LA BOHÈME
Same as Nov. 9 (followed by
LUCIA—Mad Scene : Melba)

December 7
LES HUGUENOTS
Same as Nov. 23 except:
Valentine : Gadski
Nevers : Sizes

December 8 (mat.)
ROMÉO ET JULIETTE
Same as Nov. 10 except:
Roméo : Salignac
Capulet : Gilibert

December 8
LOHENGRIN
Same as Nov. 10 except:
Telramund : Bertram
Ortrud : Schumann-Heink
Herald : Mühlmann

KANSAS CITY
December 10
LA BOHÈME
Same as Nov. 9 (followed by
LUCIA—Mad Scene : Melba)

December 11 (mat.)
LES HUGUENOTS
Same as Nov. 23 except:
Nevers : Sizes
Raoul : Imbart de la Tour
Marcel : Journet

December 11
LOHENGRIN
Same as Nov. 10 except:
Elsa : Gadski
Telramund : Bertram
Ortrud : Schumann-Heink
Herald : Mühlmann

LINCOLN
December 12 (mat.)
FAUST (for Roméo)/Flon (c)
Same as Nov. 15 except:
Faust : Salignac
Marguerite : Adams
Méphistophélès : Journet
Valentin : Scotti
Siébel : Olitzka

December 12
LUCIA DI LAMMERMOOR
Same as Nov. 17 except:
Raimondo : Viviani

MINNEAPOLIS
December 13
LES HUGUENOTS
Same as Nov. 23 except:
Urbain : Homer

December 14
LA BOHÈME
Same as Nov. 9 (followed by
LUCIA—Mad Scene : Melba)

December 15 (mat.)
TANNHÄUSER
Same as Nov. 13 except:
Hermann : Plançon
Tannhäuser :
Imbart de la Tour
Wolfram : Mühlmann
Biterolf : Gilibert

December 15
LOHENGRIN
Same as Nov. 10 except:
Telramund : Bertram
Ortrud : Schumann-Heink
Herald : Mühlmann

PHILADELPHIA
December 20
FAUST
Same as Nov. 15 except:
Faust : Cremonini
Méphistophélès : E. de Reszke

December 25
LOHENGRIN
Same as Nov. 10 except:
Telramund : Bispham
Ortrud : Schumann-Heink
Herald : Mühlmann

December 27 (mat.)
TANNHÄUSER
Same as Nov. 13 except:
Hermann : Plançon
Wolfram : Bertram

January 1
LA BOHÈME
Same as Nov. 9 except:
Rodolfo : Saléza

January 3
FIDELIO/Damrosch (c)
Don Fernando : Mühlmann
Don Pizarro : Bertram
Florestan : Dippel
Leonore : Ternina
Rocco : Blass
Marzelline : Scheff
Jaquino : Von Hübbenet

January 8
LES HUGUENOTS
Same as Nov. 23 except:
Valentine : Gadski
Nevers : Sizes
Raoul : Saléza
Urbain : Homer

January 10
DIE WALKÜRE
Same as Nov. 27 except:
Wotan : Bertram
Fricka : Olitzka
Brünnhilde : Ternina
Grimgerde : Molka-Kellog
Waltraute : Olitzka
Schwertleite : Remi

January 15
AIDA/Flon (c)
Same as Nov. 14 except:
King : Mühlmann
Radames : Saléza
Ramfis : Journet

January 17 (mat.)
MEFISTOFELE/Mancinelli (c)
Marguerite : MacIntyre
Helen of Troy : MacIntyre
Pantalis : Homer
Martha : Homer
Mefistofele : Plançon
Faust : Cremonini
Wagner : Masiero
Nereus : Masiero

January 22
LE CID/Mancinelli (c)
Chimène : Bréval
Infanta : Adams
Roderigo : J. de Reszke
Count de Gormas : Plançon
King : Sizes
St. James : Bars

Moorish Envoy : Dufriche
Don Arias : Masiero
Don Alonzo : Viviani
Don Diego : E. de Reszke

January 24
DAS RHEINGOLD
Same as Nov. 26 except:
Wotan : Bertram
Froh : Dippel
Fasolt : Mühlmann
Freia : Scheff

January 29
DIE WALKÜRE
Same as Nov. 27 except:
Wotan : Bertram
Sieglinde : Ternina
Schwertleite : Remi

January 31
SIEGFRIED
Same as Nov. 28

February 5
GÖTTERDÄMMERUNG
Same as Nov. 30 except:
Flosshilde : Olitzka

February 7 (mat.)
LA BOHÈME
Same as Nov. 9 except:
Rodolfo : Saléza
LUCIA—*Mad Scene* : Melba

February 14
TANNHÄUSER (for *Tosca*)
Same as Nov. 13 except:
Wolfram : Bertram

February 21
DON GIOVANNI/Flon (c)
Same as Nov. 20 except:
Donna Elvira : MacIntyre

February 28 (mat.)
RIGOLETTO
Same as Dec. 2 except:
Rigoletto : Campanari
Gilda : Melba
Ceprano : Cernusco

CAVALLERIA RUSTICANA
Flon (c)
Santuzza : Gadski
Lola : Homer
Turiddu : Salignac (for Cremonini)
Alfio : Pini-Corsi (for Scotti)
Lucia : Bauermeister

February 28
TOSCA/Mancinelli (c)
Tosca : Ternina
Cavaradossi : Cremonini

Scarpia : Scotti
Angelotti : Dufriche
Sacristan : Gilibert
Spoletta : Bars
Sciarrone : Viviani
Jailer : Cernusco

March 5
L'AFRICAINE/Flon (c)
Don Pedro : Journet (for E. de Reszke)
Don Diego : Dufriche (for Journet)
Inez : Adams
Vasco da Gama : J. de Reszke
Don Alvar : Bars
Nelusko : Campanari
Selika : Bréval
Grand Inquisitor : Plançon
Grand Brahmin : Plançon
Anna : Bauermeister
Usher : Masiero

BROOKLYN

March 21
LOHENGRIN
Same as Nov. 10 except:
King Henry : Blass
Telramund : Bispham
Ortrud : Schumann-Heink
Herald : Mühlmann

BOSTON

April 1
FAUST
Same as Nov. 15 except:
Marguerite : Adams
Valentin : Scotti

April 2
LES HUGUENOTS
Same as Nov. 23 except:
Valentine : Bréval

April 3 (mat.)
AIDA/Flon (c)
Same as Nov. 14 except:
Radames : Saléza
Amonasro : Campanari

April 3
PAGLIACCI (for *Trovatore*)
Flon (c)
Nedda : Scheff
Canio : Salignac
Tonio : Scotti
Beppe : Masiero
Silvio : Mühlmann

CAVALLERIA RUSTICANA
Same as Feb. 28 except:
Lola : Bridewell

April 4
TOSCA
Same as Feb. 28

223

April 5

LOHENGRIN
Same as Nov. 10 except:
Telramund : Bertram
Ortrud : Schumann-Heink
Herald : Mühlmann

April 6 (mat.)

LA BOHÈME
Same as Nov. 9 (followed by
LUCIA—*Mad Scene* : Melba)

April 6

TANNHÄUSER
Same as Nov. 13 except:
Tannhäuser : Dippel
Wolfram : Bertram
Elisabeth : Ternina

April 7

CONCERT/Mancinelli (c)
REQUIEM (Verdi) : Nordica,
Schumann-Heink, Salignac,
Plançon

April 8

ROMÉO ET JULIETTE
Same as Nov. 10 except:
Juliette : Melba
Roméo : Saléza
(for J. de Reszke)
Gregorio : Dufriche
Capulet : Plançon
Friar Laurence : E. de Reszke
Duke of Verona : Gilibert

April 9

DIE WALKÜRE
Same as Nov. 27 except:
Wotan : Bertram
Fricka : Olitzka
Brünnhilde : Bréval
Siegmund : Dippel
Sieglinde : Ternina
Grimgerde : Bach (t)
Waltraute : Olitzka
Schwertleite : Remi

April 10 (mat.)

FAUST
Same as Nov. 15 except:
Faust : J. de Reszke

April 10

DON GIOVANNI/Flon (c)
Same as Nov. 20 except:
Donna Elvira : MacIntyre
Zerlina : Bauermeister
(for Scheff)

April 11

TOSCA (for *Siegfried*)
Same as Feb. 28

224

April 12

TRISTAN UND ISOLDE
Damrosch (c)
Tristan : J. de Reszke
Isolde : Nordica
King Marke : E. de Reszke
Kurvenal : Bertram
Brangaene : Schumann-Heink
Melot : Mühlmann
Steersman : Von Hübbenet
Shepherd : Von Hübbenet
Sailor's Voice : Bars

April 13 (mat.)

LES HUGUENOTS
Same as Nov. 23 except:
Marguerite : Melba
Valentine : Bréval
Raoul : Saléza
Urbain : Homer

April 13

DIE MEISTERSINGER
Damrosch (c)
Hans Sachs : Bertram
Pogner : Blass
Eva : Scheff
Magdalene : Schumann-Heink
Walther : Dippel
Beckmesser : Bispham
Kothner : Mühlmann
Vogelgesang : Masiero
Nachtigall : Viviani
Zorn : Quesnel
Eisslinger : Bertinetti
Moser : Maestri
Ortel : Froelich
Schwarz : Weber
Foltz : Cernusco
David : Von Hübbenet
Night Watchman : Dufriche

PITTSBURGH

April 15

TRISTAN UND ISOLDE
Same as Apr. 12 except:
Isolde : Ternina

April 16

LA BOHÈME
Same as Nov. 9 (followed by
LUCIA—*Mad Scene* : Melba)

April 17

LES HUGUENOTS
Same as Nov. 23 except:
Urbain : Homer

April 18 (mat.)

FAUST/Flon (c)
Same as Nov. 15 except:
Faust : Cremonini
Siébel : Bridewell

April 18

DIE MEISTERSINGER
Same as Apr. 13 except:
Hans Sachs : E. de Reszke
Walther : J. de Reszke
Night Watchman : Viviani

CINCINNATI

April 19

DIE WALKÜRE
Same as Nov. 27 except:
Wotan : Bertram
Brünnhilde : Ternina
Siegmund : Dippel
Sieglinde : Strong
Schwertleite : Remi

April 20 (mat.)

TRISTAN UND ISOLDE
Same as Apr. 12 except:
Kurvenal : Bispham

April 20

LUCIA DI LAMMERMOOR
Flon (c)
Same as Nov. 17

CAVALLERIA RUSTICANA
Same as Feb. 28 except:
Santuzza : MacIntyre
Alfio : Scotti

CHICAGO

April 22

FAUST/Flon (c)
Same as Nov. 15 except:
Faust : J. de Reszke
Méphistophélès : E. de Reszke

April 23

DON GIOVANNI/Flon (c)
Same as Nov. 20 except:
Donna Elvira : Adams
Don Ottavio : Cremonini

April 24 (mat.)

LUCIA DI LAMMERMOOR
Same as Nov. 17 except:
Edgardo : Salignac

CAVALLERIA RUSTICANA
Same as Feb. 28 except:
Santuzza : MacIntyre
Turiddu : Dippel
Alfio : Campanari

April 24

TOSCA/Flon (c)
Same as Feb. 28 except:
Sacristan : Pini-Corsi

April 25

LES HUGUENOTS
Same as Nov. 23 except:

Marguerite : Melba
Raoul : J. de Reszke
Urbain : Homer

April 26

TANNHÄUSER

Same as Nov. 13 except:
Hermann : Plançon
Tannhäuser : Dippel
Wolfram : Bertram
Elisabeth : Ternina

April 27 (mat.)

LOHENGRIN

Same as Nov. 10 except:
Lohengrin : J. de Reszke
Telramund : Bertram
Ortrud : Schumann-Heink
Herald : Mühlmann

April 27

IL TROVATORE/Flon (c)

Same as Nov. 18 except:
Manrico : Gauthier (d)

RIGOLETTO—Act 4 (for *Pagliacci*)

Same as Dec. 2 except:
Duke : Salignac

1 9 0 1 – 0 2

ALBANY

October 7

LOHENGRIN/Damrosch (c)

King Henry : Blass
Lohengrin : Dippel
Elsa : Eames
Telramund : Mühlmann
Ortrud : Schumann-Heink
Herald : Dufriche

MONTREAL

October 8

CARMEN/Flon (c)

Carmen : Calvé
Don José : Salignac
Micaela : Scheff
Escamillo : Declery
Zuniga : Dufriche
Morales : Bars
Frasquita : Bauermeister
Mercedes : Van Cauteren
Dancaire : Gilibert
Remendado : Vanni

October 9

FAUST/Seppilli (c)

Faust : Gibert (t)
Marguerite : Sembrich
Méphistophélès : Journet
Valentin : Declery
Siébel : Bridewell
Marthe : Bauermeister
Wagner : Dufriche

October 10 (mat.)

MANON/Flon (c)

(Not given in New York)
Manon : Sanderson
Lescaut : Dufriche
Des Grieux : Salignac
Count des Grieux : Declery
Poussette : Marilly
Javotte : Bridewell
Rosette : Van Cauteren
Guillot : Gilibert
De Brétigny : Bars

October 10

TANNHÄUSER/Damrosch (c)

Hermann : Blass
Tannhäuser : Dippel
Wolfram : Mühlmann
Walther : Bars (for Reiss)
Biterolf : Vanni
Heinrich : Gilibert
Reinmar : Viviani
Elisabeth : Eames
Venus : Reuss-Belce (d)
Shepherd : Bridewell

TORONTO

October 10

STATE CONCERT/Seppilli (c)

Journet, Scheff, Homer,
Gilbert, Calvé, Perello (the
name used by Andrés de
Segurola, both as a first and
surname)

October 11

LOHENGRIN

Same as Oct. 7 except:
Elsa : Sembrich
Ortrud : Homer

October 12 (mat.)

ROMÉO ET JULIETTE/Flon (c)

Juliette : Seygard (d—for
Sanderson)
Stephano : Bridewell
Gertrude : Bauermeister
Roméo : Gibert
Tybalt : Bars
Mercutio : Declery
Gregorio : Viviani
Capulet : Gilibert
Friar Laurence : Perello
Duke of Verona : Dufriche

October 12

CARMEN/Seppilli (c)

Same as Oct. 8 except:
Escamillo : Journet
Morales : Vanni
Remendado : Reiss (d)

ROCHESTER

October 14 (mat.)

MANON

Same as Oct. 10

October 14

CARMEN/Seppilli (c)

Same as Oct. 8 except:
Don José : Gibert
Escamillo : Journet
Morales : Vanni
Remendado : Reiss

SYRACUSE

October 15

LOHENGRIN

Same as Oct. 7 except:
Ortrud : Homer

BUFFALO

October 16

FAUST/Seppilli (c)

Same as Oct. 9 except:
Faust : Salignac
Valentin : Campanari

October 17

CARMEN

Same as Oct. 8 except:
Don José : Gibert
Escamillo : Journet
Remendado : Reiss

October 18

AIDA/Seppilli (c—for Flon)

King : Mühlmann
Amneris : Homer
Aida : Eames
Radames : De Marchi (d)
Amonasro : Campanari
Ramfis : Perello
Messenger : Vanni
Priestess : Bauermeister

October 19 (mat.)

LOHENGRIN

Same as Oct. 7 except:
Elsa : Sembrich

October 19

MANON

Same as Oct. 10 except:
Lescaut : Declery
Count des Grieux : Journet

LOUISVILLE

October 21

CARMEN

Same as Oct. 8 except:
Don José : Gibert
Escamillo : Journet
Remendado : Reiss

October 22 (mat.)

LA TRAVIATA/Seppilli (c)

Violetta : Sembrich
Alfredo : Salignac
Germont : Campanari
Flora : Van Cauteren

1901–02

Annina : Bauermeister
Gastone : Vanni
Baron Douphol : Bars
Marquis d'Obigny : Dufriche
Dr. Grenvil : Gilibert

October 22
LOHENGRIN
Same as Oct. 7 except:
Telramund : Bispham
Herald : Mühlmann

NASHVILLE

October 23
CARMEN
Same as Oct. 8 except:
Carmen : Seygard (for
  Calvé)
Don José : Gibert
Escamillo : Journet
Remendado : Reiss

October 24
IL BARBIERE DI SIVIGLIA
  Seppilli (c)
(Not given in New York)
Almaviva : Salignac
Dr. Bartolo : Tavecchia (d)
Rosina : Sembrich
Figaro : Campanari
Don Basilio : Perello
Berta : Bauermeister
Fiorello : Viviani
Sergeant : Vanni

MEMPHIS

October 25
LOHENGRIN
Same as Oct. 7 except:
Telramund : Bispham
Herald : Mühlmann

October 26 (mat.)
MANON
Same as Oct. 10 except:
Manon : Seygard (for
  Sanderson in middle of
  opera)

October 26
FAUST (for *Carmen*)
Same as Oct. 9 except:
Valentin : Campanari
Siébel : Homer

ATLANTA

October 28
LOHENGRIN
Same as Oct. 7 except:
Telramund : Bispham
Herald : Mühlmann

October 29 (mat.)
ROMÉO ET JULIETTE
Same as Oct. 12 except:
Juliette : Sanderson

226

Friar Laurence : Journet

October 29
IL BARBIERE DI SIVIGLIA
Same as Oct. 24

BIRMINGHAM

October 30
LOHENGRIN
Same as Oct. 7 except:
Elsa : Sembrich
Ortrud : Bridewell

NEW ORLEANS

October 31
LOHENGRIN
Same as Oct. 7 except:
King Henry : E. de Reszke
Lohengrin : Van Dyck
Telramund : Bispham
Herald : Mühlmann

November 1
CARMEN
Same as Oct. 8 except:
Don José : Gibert
Escamillo : Journet
Remendado : Reiss

November 2 (mat.)
MANON
Same as Oct. 10 except:
Lescaut : Declery
Count des Grieux : Journet

November 2
LES HUGUENOTS/Flon (c)
Marguerite : Sembrich
St. Bris : Journet
Valentine : Gadski
Nevers : Scotti
Cossé : Vanni
Tavannes : Reiss
Retz : Viviani
Raoul : De Marchi
Marcel : E. de Reszke
Urbain : Homer
Maurevert : Dufriche
Bois Rosé : Bars
Ladies of Honor :
  Bauermeister, Van Cauteren

November 3
FAUST
Same as Oct. 9 except:
Marguerite : Adams (for
  Calvé)

HOUSTON

November 4
LOHENGRIN/Franko (c)
Same as Oct. 7 except:
Telramund : Bispham
Herald : Mühlmann

SAN ANTONIO

November 5
LOHENGRIN/Franko (c)
Same as Oct. 7 except:
Lohengrin : Bars
Elsa : Sembrich
Telramund : Bispham

LOS ANGELES

November 8
CARMEN
Same as Oct. 8 except:
Micaela : Marilly (for
  Scheff)
Escamillo : Campanari
Remendado : Reiss

November 9 (mat.)
LOHENGRIN
Same as Oct. 2 except:
Elsa : Sembrich
Telramund : Bispham
Herald : Mühlmann

November 9
LES HUGUENOTS
Same as Nov. 8 except:
Marguerite : Adams

SAN FRANCISCO

November 11
LOHENGRIN
Same as Oct. 7 except:
King Henry : E. de Reszke
Lohengrin : Van Dyck
Telramund : Bispham
Herald : Mühlmann

November 12
LES HUGUENOTS
Same as Nov. 2 except:
Marguerite : Adams

November 13
LA TRAVIATA
Same as Oct. 22

November 14
TANNHÄUSER
Same as Oct. 10 except:
Tannhäuser : Van Dyck
Wolfram : Bispham
Biterolf : Mühlmann
Heinrich : Reiss
Shepherd : Scheff

November 15
DIE WALKÜRE/Damrosch (c)
Wotan : Bispham
Fricka : Schumann-Heink
Brünnhilde : Reuss-Belce
Siegmund : Dippel
Sieglinde : Gadski
Hunding : Blass

Helmwige : Scheff
Gerhilde : Van Cauteren
Ortlinde : Bauermeister
Rossweisse : Bridewell
Grimgerde : Seygard
Waltraute : Schumann-Heink
Siegrune : Marilly
Schwertleite : Homer

November 16 (mat.)
FAUST
Same as Oct. 9 except:
Faust : Dippel
Méphistophélès : E. de Reszke
Valentin : Campanari
Siébel : Homer

November 16
MANON
Same as Oct. 10 except:
Count des Grieux : Journet

November 17
LA BOHÈME/Seppilli (c)
(Not given in New York)
Rodolfo : De Marchi
Marcello : Campanari
Schaunard : Gilibert
Colline : Perello de Segurola
Mimi : Adams
Musetta : Repetto (1—for
  Scheff)
Benoit : Dufriche
Parpignol : Vanni
Alcindoro : Dufriche

November 18
ROMÉO ET JULIETTE
Same as Oct. 12 except:
Juliette : Sanderson
Roméo : Salignac
Gregorio : Dufriche
Capulet : Journet
Friar Laurence : E. de Reszke
Duke of Verona : Gilibert

November 19
LE NOZZE DI FIGARO
  Seppilli (c)
Almaviva : E. de Reszke
Countess : Eames
Susanna : Sembrich
Figaro : Campanari
Cherubino : Scheff
Marcellina : Bauermeister
Bartolo : Tavecchia
Basilio : Reiss
Don Curzio : Maestri
Antonio : Dufriche

November 20
CARMEN
Same as Oct. 8 except:
Micaela : Adams
Escamillo : Scotti

Zuniga : Declery
Remendado : Reiss

November 21
DIE MEISTERSINGER
  Damrosch (c)
Hans Sachs : E. de Reszke
Pogner : Blass
Eva : Gadski
Magdalene :
  Schumann-Heink
Walther : Dippel
Beckmesser : Bispham
Kothner : Mühlmann
Vogelgesang : Vanni
Nachtigall : Viviani
Zorn : Engel (t)
Eisslinger : Bighinelli
Moser : Maestri
Ortel : Dufriche
Schwarz : Cernusco
Foltz : Fanelli
David : Reiss
Night Watchman : Dufriche

November 22
CARMEN
Same as Oct. 8 except:
Carmen : Seygard (for
  Calvé)
Don José : De Marchi
Micaela : Adams
Escamillo : Scotti
Zuniga : Declery
Morales : Dufriche
Remendado : Reiss

November 23 (mat.)
LOHENGRIN
Same as Oct. 7 except:
Lohengrin : Van Dyck
Elsa : Reuss-Belce (for
  Eames)
Telramund : Bispham
Herald : Mühlmann

November 23
IL BARBIERE DI SIVIGLIA
  Seppilli (c)
Same as Oct. 24 except:
Don Basilio : E. de Reszke

November 24
LES HUGUENOTS
Same as Nov. 2 except:
Marguerite : Adams (for
  Sanderson)
St. Bris : Mühlmann
Raoul : Dippel
Marcel : Journet

November 25
FAUST
Same as Oct. 9 except:
Faust : Salignac

Marguerite : Seygard (for
  Eames)
Méphistophélès : E. de Reszke
Valentin : Campanari

November 26
DIE WALKÜRE
Same as Nov. 15 except:
Siegmund : Van Dyck

November 27
DON PASQUALE/Flon (c)
Norina : Sembrich
Dr. Malatesta : Scotti
Don Pasquale : Tavecchia
Ernesto : Salignac
Notary : Vanni

PAGLIACCI/Flon (c)
Nedda : Scheff
Canio : De Marchi
Tonio : Campanari
Beppe : Reiss
Silvio : Declery

November 28
DIE MEISTERSINGER
Same as Nov. 21

November 29
AIDA/Flon (c)
Same as Oct. 18 except:
Amonasro : Scotti
Ramfis : Journet

November 30 (mat.)
IL BARBIERE DI SIVIGLIA
Same as Oct. 24 except:
Don Basilio : E. de Reszke

November 30
CARMEN
Same as Oct. 8 except:
Don José : De Marchi
Escamillo : Journet
Zuniga : Declery
Morales : Dufriche

December 1
LOHENGRIN
Same as Oct. 7 except:
Elsa : Gadski
Telramund : Bispham
Ortrud : Homer
Herald : Mühlmann

December 2 (mat.)
LE NOZZE DI FIGARO
Same as Nov. 19

December 2
LA BOHÈME
Same as Nov. 17 except:
Marcello : Scotti
Musetta : Scheff

Cavalleria Rusticana
Flon (c)
Santuzza : Calvé
Lola : Bridewell
Turiddu : Salignac
Alfio : Declery
Lucia : Bauermeister

December 3
Tristan und Isolde
Damrosch (c)
Tristan : Van Dyck
Isolde : Reuss-Belce
King Marke : E. de Reszke
Kurvenal : Bispham
Brangaene : Homer
Melot : Mühlmann
Steersman : Reiss
Shepherd : Reiss
Sailor's Voice : Bars

December 4
Carmen
Same as Oct. 8 except:
Micaela : Adams
Escamillo : Scotti
Zuniga : Declery
Morales : Dufriche
Remendado : Reiss

December 5 (mat.)
Tannhäuser
Same as Oct. 10 except:
Wolfram : Bispham
Biterolf : Mühlmann
Heinrich : Reiss
Elisabeth : Gadski

December 5
Le Nozze di Figaro
Same as Nov. 19

KANSAS CITY
December 9
Roméo et Juliette
Same as Oct. 12 except:
Stephano : Marilly
Roméo : Salignac
Friar Laurence : E. de Reszke

December 10 (mat.)
Tannhäuser
Same as Oct. 10 except:
Wolfram : Bispham
Biterolf : Mühlmann
Heinrich : Reiss
Elisabeth : Reuss-Belce
Venus : Marilly

December 10
Aida
Same as Oct. 18 except:
King : Journet
Aida : Gadski
Amonasro : Scotti
Ramfis : E. de Reszke

ST. LOUIS
December 11
Roméo et Juliette
Same as Oct. 12 except:
Roméo : Salignac
Gregorio : Dufriche
Capulet : Journet
Friar Laurence : E. de Reszke
Duke of Verona : Gilibert

December 12 (mat.)
Tannhäuser
Same as Oct. 10 except:
Heinrich : Reiss
Elisabeth : Gadski
Venus : Homer

December 12
Faust
Same as Oct. 9 except:
Faust : Salignac
Méphistophélès : E. de Reszke
Valentin : Scotti

December 13
Aida
Same as Oct. 18 except:
King : Journet
Radames : Dippel (for
De Marchi)

INDIANAPOLIS
December 14
Lohengrin
Same as Oct. 7 except:
King Henry : E. de Reszke
Lohengrin : Bars (for
Dippel)
Elsa : Gadski
Telramund : Bispham
Herald : Mühlmann

CINCINNATI
December 16
Tannhäuser
Same as Oct. 10 except:
Wolfram : Bispham
Biterolf : Mühlmann
Heinrich : Reiss

December 17
Roméo et Juliette
(for *Huguenots*)
Same as Oct. 12 except:
Juliette : Adams
Roméo : Salignac
Gregorio : Dufriche
Capulet : Journet
Friar Laurence : E. de Reszke
Duke of Verona : Gilibert

December 18 (mat.)
Die Meistersinger
Same as Nov. 21

December 18
Manon
Same as Oct. 10 except:
Manon : Seygard (for
Sanderson)
Lescaut : Declery
Count des Grieux : Journet

December 19
Aida
Same as Oct. 18 except:
Radames : Dippel (for
De Marchi)
Amonasro : Scotti
Ramfis : E. de Reszke

CLEVELAND
December 20
Lohengrin (for *Roméo*)
Same as Oct. 7 except:
Lohengrin : Bars
Elsa : Gadski
Telramund : Bispham
Herald : Mühlmann

December 21 (mat.)
Faust (for *Lucia*)
Same as Oct. 9 except:
Faust : Salignac
Marguerite : Adams
Valentin : Scotti
Siébel : Homer

December 21
Die Meistersinger
Same as Nov. 21 except:
Eva : Reuss-Belce (for
Gadski, who sang Elsa
unexpectedly the day
before)

PHILADELPHIA
December 26
Tristan und Isolde
Same as Dec. 3 except:
Isolde : Ternina
King Marke : Blass
Brangaene :
Schumann-Heink

December 31
Roméo et Juliette
Same as Oct. 12 except:
Juliette : Sanderson
Gertrude : Van Cauteren
Roméo : Salignac
Gregorio : Dufriche
Capulet : Journet
Friar Laurence : E. de Reszke
Duke of Verona : Gilibert

January 2
Carmen
Same as Oct. 8 except:
Don José : Alvarez

Micaela : Adams
Escamillo : Journet
Zuniga : Declery
Remendado : Reiss

January 7

TOSCA/Flon (c)

Tosca : Ternina
Cavaradossi : De Marchi
Scarpia : Scotti
Angelotti : Dufriche
Sacristan : Gilibert
Spoletta : Bars
Sciarrone : Viviani
Jailer : Cernusco
Shepherd : Bridewell

January 9

DIE MEISTERSINGER

Same as Nov. 21 except:
Zorn : Lawson

January 14

LE NOZZE DI FIGARO

Same as Nov. 19 except:
Basilio : Vanni

January 16

LOHENGRIN

Same as Oct. 7 except:
Elsa : Gadski
Telramund : Van Rooy
Herald : Mühlmann

January 21

PAGLIACCI

Same as Nov. 27 except:
Nedda : Seygard

LA FILLE DU RÉGIMENT
Flon (c)

Marie : Scheff
La Marquise : Van Cauteren
Tonio : Salignac
Sulpice : Gilibert
Hortensius : Dufriche
Corporal : Viviani

January 23 (mat.)

AIDA

Same as Oct. 18 except:
Aida : Chalia (t—for Eames)
Ramfis : Journet
Priestess : Marilly

January 28

FAUST

Same as Oct. 9 except:
Faust : Van Dyck
Marguerite : Calvé
Valentin : Campanari
Wagner : Viviani (for
  Dufriche)

January 30

IL BARBIERE DI SIVIGLIA

Same as Oct. 24 except:
Don Basilio : E. de Reszke
Berta : Van Cauteren

February 4

MESSALINE/Flon (c)

Messaline : Calvé
Tyndaris : Marilly
La Citharède : Van Cauteren
Tsilla : Roslyn
Leuconoe : Mapleson
Helion : Alvarez
Myrtille : Journet
Olympias : Journet
Myrrhon : Gilibert
Gallas : Declery
Rameur de Galère :
  Dufriche
Mime Alexandrin : Viviani
Poète d'Atellanes : Giaccone
Le Leono : Vanni
Marchand d'Eau : Maestri
L'Edile : Judels
Harés : Scotti

February 6

DIE ZAUBERFLÖTE
Damrosch (c)

Sarastro : E. de Reszke
Tamino : Dippel
High Priest : Dufriche
Priests : Mühlmann, Vanni
Queen of the Night :
  Sembrich
Pamina : Eames
Ladies : Ternina, Van
  Cauteren, Bridewell
Papageno : Campanari
Papagena : Scheff
Monostatos : Reiss
Genii : Marilly, Randall,
  Bouton
Guards : Dufriche, Maestri

February 13 (mat.)

DIE WALKÜRE/Flon (c)

Same as Nov. 15 except:
Wotan : Van Rooy
Siegmund : Van Dyck
Helmwige : Seygard
Grimgerde : Bouton
Waltraute : Maurer

February 18

MANRU/Damrosch (c)

Ulana : Sembrich
Hedwig : Homer
Asa : Scheff
Manru : Van Bandrowski
Oros : Mühlmann
Jagu : Blass
Urok : Bispham

BOSTON

March 10

AIDA

Same as Oct. 18 except:
Amonasro : Scotti
Ramfis : Journet
Priestess : Marilly

March 11

TOSCA

Same as Jan. 7

March 12 (mat.)

LOHENGRIN

Same as Oct. 7 except:
King Henry : E. de Reszke
Lohengrin : Van Dyck
Elsa : Gadski
Telramund : Van Rooy
Herald : Mühlmann

March 12

CARMEN

Same as Oct. 8 except:
Don José : Alvarez
Micaela : Adams
Escamillo : Journet
Zuniga : Declery
Frasquita : Marilly
Mercedes : Bridewell
Remendado : Reiss

March 13

DIE ZAUBERFLÖTE

Same as Feb. 6 except:
Second Lady : Homer
Second Genie : Van Cauteren
Third Genie : Randall

March 14

LE CID/Flon (c)

Chimène : Du Cial
Infanta : Adams
Roderigo : Alvarez
Count de Gormas : Journet
King : Gilibert
St. James : Bars
Moorish Envoy : Dufriche
Don Arias : Vanni
Don Alonzo : Viviani
Don Diego : E. de Reszke

March 15 (mat.)

FAUST

Same as Oct. 9 except:
Faust : Van Dyck
Marguerite : Seygard
  (for Calvé)
Valentin : Campanari

March 15

MANRU

Same as Feb. 18

March 16

CONCERT/Damrosch (c)

REQUIEM MASS (Verdi)

229

1901–02

Gadski, Schumann-Heink,
Salignac, Bispham

March 17
TANNHÄUSER

Same as Oct. 10 except:
Tannhäuser : Van Dyck
Wolfram : Van Rooy
Biterolf : Mühlmann
Heinrich : Reiss
Elisabeth : Ternina
Venus : Homer

March 18
LE NOZZE DI FIGARO

Same as Nov. 19 except:
Bartolo : Gilibert

March 19 (mat.)
CARMEN

Same as Oct. 8 except:
Escamillo : Scotti
Frasquita : Marilly
Mercedes : Bridewell
Remendado : Reiss

March 19
LES HUGUENOTS

Same as Nov. 2 except:
Marguerite : Adams
Valentine : Bréval
Nevers : Declery
Raoul : Alvarez

March 20
LOHENGRIN (for *Tristan*)

Same as Oct. 7 except:
King Henry : E. de Reszke
Lohengrin :
Van Bandrowski
Elsa : Ternina

March 21
OTELLO/Seppilli (c)

Otello : Alvarez
Desdemona : Eames
Iago : Scotti
Emilia : Homer
Cassio : Bars
Roderigo : Vanni
Lodovico : Journet
Montano : Dufriche
Herald : Viviani

March 22 (mat.)
DIE ZAUBERFLÖTE

Same as Feb. 6 except:
Sarastro : Blass
Pamina : Gadski
Second Lady : Homer
Second Genie :
Van Cauteren
Third Genie : Randall

230

March 22
CAVALLERIA RUSTICANA

Same as Dec. 2 except:
Turiddu : De Marchi

PAGLIACCI

Same as Nov. 27 except:
Canio : Salignac
Tonio : Scotti
Silvio : Mühlmann

March 23
CONCERT/Flon (c)

Campanari, Adams

STABAT MATER (Rossini)

Gadski, Bridewell (for
Schumann-Heink), Dippel,
Journet

CHICAGO

March 31
AIDA

Same as Oct. 18 except:
Amonasro : Scotti
Ramfis : Journet
Priestess : Marilly

April 1
TANNHÄUSER (for *Tosca*)

Same as Oct. 10 except:
Hermann : Mühlmann
Wolfram : Van Rooy
Heinrich : Reiss
Elisabeth : Ternina

April 2 (mat.)
LOHENGRIN

Same as Oct. 7 except:
King Henry : E. de Reszke
Lohengrin : Van Dyck
Elsa : Gadski
Telramund : Bispham

April 2
CARMEN

Same as Oct. 8 except:
Don José : Alvarez
Escamillo : Journet
Zuniga : Declery
Frasquita : Van Cauteren
(for Marilly)
Mercedes : Bridewell
Remendado : Reiss

April 3
DIE ZAUBERFLÖTE

Same as Feb. 6 except:
Pamina : Gadski (for
Eames)
Second Lady : Homer
Second Genie : Bauermeister
Third Genie : Van Cauteren

April 4
LE CID

Same as Mar. 14 except:
Infanta : Marilly

April 5 (mat.)
FAUST

Same as Oct. 9 except:
Faust : Dippel
Marguerite : Calvé
Valentin : Campanari

April 5
MANRU

Same as Feb. 18 except:
Country Girl : Van Cauteren

April 6
CONCERT/Damrosch (c)

REQUIEM MASS (Verdi)

Gadski, Schumann-Heink,
Salignac, Bispham

April 7
DAS RHEINGOLD/Damrosch (c)

Wotan : Van Rooy
Donner : Dufriche
Froh : Bars
Loge : Van Dyck
Alberich : Bispham
Mime : Reiss
Fasolt : Mühlmann
Fafner : Blass
Fricka : Reuss-Belce
Freia : Marilly
Erda : Schumann-Heink
Woglinde : Scheff
Wellgunde : Bridewell
Flosshilde : Schumann-Heink

April 8
DIE WALKÜRE

Same as Nov. 15 except:
Wotan : Van Rooy
Brünnhilde : Ternina
Siegmund : Van Dyck
Sieglinde : Reuss-Belce
(for Eames)
Schwertleite : Virgil (t)

April 9 (mat.)
CARMEN

Same as Oct. 8 except:
Micaela : Marilly
Escamillo : Campanari
Remendado : Reiss

April 9
LES HUGUENOTS

Same as Nov. 2 except:
Valentine : Bréval
Meru : Dufriche
Raoul : Alvarez
Urbain : Seygard (for
Homer)

April 10
SIEGFRIED/Damrosch (c)
Siegfried : Dippel
Mime : Reiss
Wanderer : Van Rooy
Alberich : Bispham
Fafner : Blass
Erda : Schumann-Heink
Brünnhilde : Ternina
Forest Bird : Seygard
  (for Scheff)

April 11
DIE ZAUBERFLÖTE

Same as Feb. 6 except:
First Lady : Seygard
Second Lady : Homer
Papagena : Seygard (for
  Scheff)
Second Genie : Bauermeister
Third Genie : Van Cauteren

April 12 (mat.)
PAGLIACCI

Same as Nov. 27 except:
Nedda : Seygard
Canio : Salignac (for
  De Marchi)
Tonio : Scotti

CAVALLERIA RUSTICANA

Same as Dec. 2 except:
Turiddu : Bars (for
  Salignac)
Alfio : Dufriche

April 12
GÖTTERDÄMMERUNG
  Damrosch (c)

Siegfried : Van Bandrowski
Gunther : Mühlmann
Hagen : E. de Reszke
Brünnhilde : Ternina
Gutrune : Reuss-Belce
Waltraute : Schumann-Heink
Woglinde : Scheff
Wellgunde : Bridewell
Flosshilde : Schumann-Heink
(Norn, Alberich scenes
  omitted)

April 13
CONCERT/Flon (c)
Campanari, Marilly

STABAT MATER (Rossini)
Gadski, Schumann-Heink,
  Salignac (for Dippel),
  Bispham

PITTSBURGH
April 14
AIDA

Same as Oct. 18 except:
Radames : Dippel (for

De Marchi)
Amonasro : Scotti
Ramfis : E. de Reszke
Priestess : Marilly

April 15
MANRU

Same as Feb. 18 except:
Asa : Seygard (for Scheff)

April 16 (mat.)
CARMEN

Same as Oct. 8 except:
Don José : Alvarez
Micaela : Marilly
Escamillo : Scotti
Zuniga : Declery
Morales : Dufriche
Remendado : Reiss

April 16
LOHENGRIN

Same as Oct. 7 except:
King Henry : E. de Reszke
Lohengrin : Van Dyck
Elsa : Ternina
Telramund : Van Rooy

April 17
LE NOZZE DI FIGARO

Same as Nov. 19 except:
Cherubino : Seygard (for
  Scheff)
Bartolo : Gilibert

BALTIMORE
April 18
CARMEN

Same as Oct. 8 except:
Don José : Alvarez
Micaela : Marilly
Escamillo : Journet
Zuniga : Declery
Morales : Dufriche
Frasquita : Van Cauteren
Mercedes : Bauermeister
Remendado : Reiss

April 19 (mat.)
TRISTAN UND ISOLDE

Same as Dec. 3 except:
Isolde : Ternina
Kurvenal : Van Rooy
Brangaene : Schumann-Heink

April 19
MANRU

Same as Feb. 18 except:
Asa : Seygard (for Scheff)

BROOKLYN
April 22
CARMEN

Same as Oct. 8 except:
Micaela : Marilly

Escamillo : Scotti
Zuniga : Declery
Morales : Dufriche

1902–03

PHILADELPHIA
December 2
OTELLO/Mancinelli (c)

Otello : Alvarez
Desdemona : Eames
Iago : Scotti
Emilia : Marilly
Cassio : Bars
Roderigo : Vanni
Lodovico : Journet
Montano : Dufriche
Herald : Bégué

December 9
LA TRAVIATA/Mancinelli (c)

Violetta : Sembrich
Alfredo : Dani
Germont : Scotti
Flora : Van Cauteren
Annina : Bauermeister
Gastone : Vanni
Baron Douphol : Bars
Marquis d'Obigny : ? (for
  Bégué)
Dr. Grenvil : Dufriche

December 11 (mat.)
LOHENGRIN/Hertz (c)

King Henry : Blass
Lohengrin : Anthes
Elsa : Gadski
Telramund : Bispham
Ortrud : Schumann-Heink
Herald : Mühlmann

December 16
LE PROPHÈTE/Flon (c)

John of Leyden : Alvarez
Fidès : Schumann-Heink
Bertha : Marilly
Jonas : Bars
Mathisen : Declery
Zacharias : E. de Reszke
Oberthal : Journet
Anabaptist : Cernusco
Officer : Bégué
Citizen, Peasant : Vanni

December 23
TANNHÄUSER/Hertz (c)

Hermann : Blass
Tannhäuser : Anthes
Wolfram : Bispham
Walther : Bars
Heinrich : Reiss
Reinmar : Dufriche
Elisabeth : Gadski

231

Venus : Homer
Shepherd : Bridewell

December 30
LES HUGUENOTS/Flon (c)
Marguerite : Gifford (d)
St. Bris : Journet
Valentine : Gadski
Nevers : Scotti
Cossé : Vanni
Tavannes : Reiss
Retz : Bégué
Raoul : Alvarez
Marcel : E. de Reszke
Urbain : Scheff
Maurevert : Dufriche
Bois Rosé : Bars
Ladies of Honor :
  Bauermeister, Van Cauteren

January 6
TOSCA/Mancinelli (c)
Tosca : Eames
Cavaradossi : De Marchi
Scarpia : Scotti
Angelotti : Dufriche
Sacristan : Gilibert
Spoletta : Bars
Sciarrone : Bégué
Jailer : Cernusco
Shepherd : Bridewell

January 8 (mat.)
LA BOHÈME/Mancinelli (c)
Rodolfo : De Marchi
Marcello : Campanari
Schaunard : Gilibert
Colline : Journet
Mimi : Sembrich
Musetta : Seygard
Benoit : Dufriche
Parpignol : Vanni
Alcindoro : Dufriche

January 13
IL BARBIERE DI SIVIGLIA
  Mancinelli (c)
Almaviva : Salignac
Dr. Bartolo : Gilibert
Rosina : Sembrich
Figaro : Campanari
Don Basilio : E. de Reszke
Berta : Bauermeister
Fiorello : Bégué
Sergeant : Vanni

WASHINGTON
January 20
PHILEMON ET BAUCIS/Flon (c)
(Not given in New York)
Jupiter : Journet
Philemon : Salignac
Vulcan : Gregory (t)
Baucis : Seygard

PHILADELPHIA
January 20
FAUST/Mancinelli (c)
Faust : Alvarez
Marguerite : Marilly (for
  Eames)
Méphistophélès : E. de Reszke
Valentin : Scotti
Siébel : Bridewell
Marthe : Bauermeister
Wagner : Dufriche

January 27
DAS RHEINGOLD/Hertz (c)
Wotan : Van Rooy
Donner : Mühlmann
Froh : Bars
Loge : Anthes
Alberich : Bispham
Mime : Reiss
Fasolt : Blass
Fafner : Elmblad
Fricka : Reuss-Belce
Freia : Marilly
Erda : Schumann-Heink
Woglinde : Scheff
Wellgunde : Bridewell
Flosshilde : Schumann-Heink

January 29
DIE WALKÜRE/Hertz (c)
Wotan : Van Rooy
Fricka : Reuss-Belce
Brünnhilde : Nordica
Siegmund : Burgstaller (d)
Sieglinde : Gadski
Hunding : Elmblad
Helmwige : Seygard
Gerhilde : Van Cauteren
Ortlinde : Bauermeister
Rossweisse : Bridewell
Grimgerde : Egener
Waltraute : Maurer
Siegrune : Marilly
Schwertleite : Homer

February 3
SIEGFRIED/Hertz (c)
Siegfried : Burgstaller
Mime : Reiss
Wanderer : Van Rooy
Alberich : Bispham
Fafner : Elmblad
Erda : Kirkby-Lunn
Brünnhilde : Nordica
Forest Bird : Scheff

February 5 (mat.)
GÖTTERDÄMMERUNG/Hertz (c)
Siegfried : Burgstaller
Gunther : Mühlmann
Hagen : Blass
Alberich : Bispham
Brünnhilde : Nordica

Gutrune : Reuss-Belce
Waltraute : Homer
Woglinde : Scheff
Wellgunde : Bridewell
Flosshilde : Homer

February 10
ERNANI/Flon (c)
Elvira : Sembrich
Giovanna : Bauermeister
Ernani : De Marchi
Don Carlo : Scotti
Don Ruy Gomez : E. de
  Reszke
Iago : Bégué
Don Riccardo : Vanni

February 17
LA FILLE DU RÉGIMENT
  Flon (c)
Marie : Sembrich
Marquise : Van Cauteren
Tonio : Salignac
Sulpice : Gilibert
Hortensius : Dufriche
Corporal : Bégué

PAGLIACCI/Flon (c)
Nedda : Seygard
Canio : Dani
Tonio : Scotti
Beppe : Reiss
Silvio : Declery

February 26
AIDA/Flon (c)
King : Mühlmann
Amneris : Homer
Aida : Gadski
Radames : Alvarez
Amonasro : Scotti
Ramfis : Journet
Messenger : Vanni
Priestess : Marilly

March 3
TRISTAN UND ISOLDE/Hertz (c)
Tristan : Anthes
Isolde : Nordica
King Marke : Blass
Kurvenal : Van Rooy
Brangaene : Homer
  (for Schumann-Heink)
Melot : Mühlmann
Shepherd : Reiss
Steersman : Walther
Sailor's Voice : Bars

March 10
DON PASQUALE/Flon (c)
Norina : Sembrich
Ernesto : Dani
Malatesta : Scotti
Don Pasquale : Gilibert
Notary : Vanni

March 12

DIE ZAUBERFLÖTE
Mancinelli (c)
Sarastro : E. de Reszke
Tamino : Salignac
High Priest : Dufriche
Priests : Mühlmann, Vanni
Queen of the Night :
   Sembrich
Pamina : Gadski
Ladies : Seygard, Homer,
   Bridewell
Papageno : Campanari
Papagena : Scheff
Monostatos : Reiss
Genii : Marilly, Bouton,
   Mapleson
Guards : Dufriche, Maestri

March 17

DIE MEISTERSINGER/Hertz (c)
Hans Sachs : Van Rooy
Pogner : Blass
Eva : Gadski
Magdalene : Maurer
Walther : Burgstaller
Beckmesser : Bispham
Kothner : Mühlmann
Vogelgesang : Vanni
Nachtigall : Dufriche
Zorn : Conde
Eisslinger : Bighinelli
Moser : Maestri
Ortel : Rodeschi
Schwarz : Fanelli
Foltz : Cernusco
David : Reiss
Night Watchman : Dufriche

BOSTON

March 23

LA FILLE DU RÉGIMENT
Same as Feb. 17

PAGLIACCI/Mancinelli (c)
Same as Feb. 17 except:
Nedda : Scheff
Canio : Alvarez

March 24

LOHENGRIN
Same as Dec. 11 except:
King Henry : E. de Reszke
Elsa : Nordica

March 25 (mat.)

DIE MEISTERSINGER
Same as Mar. 17 except:
Pogner : Mühlmann (for
   Blass—also sang Kothner)
Magdalene : Schumann-
   Heink

March 25

LA TRAVIATA
Same as Dec. 9 except:
Marquis d'Obigny : Dufriche
Doctor Grenvil : Bégué

March 26

IL TROVATORE/Mancinelli (c)
Leonora : Vicini (t—for
   Nordica)
Manrico : De Marchi
Count di Luna : Campanari
Azucena : Homer
Inez : Bauermeister
Ferrando : Journet
Ruiz : Vanni

March 27

LE PROPHÈTE
Same as Dec. 16

March 28 (mat.)

LA BOHÈME
Same as Jan. 8 except:
Musetta : Scheff

March 28

DIE WALKÜRE
Same as Jan. 29 except:
Fricka : Schumann-Heink
Grimgerde : Maurer
Waltraute : Schumann-Heink

March 29

CONCERT/Mancinelli (c)
ERO E LEANDRO (Excerpts)
Schumann-Heink, Gadski
STABAT MATER (Rossini)
Gadski, Schumann-Heink,
   Salignac, Journet

March 30

DON GIOVANNI/Mancinelli (c)
Don Giovanni : Scotti
Donna Anna : Nordica
Donna Elvira : Gadski
Zerlina : Scheff
Commendatore : Journet
Don Ottavio : Salignac
Leporello : E. de Reszke
Masetto : Gilibert

March 31

DON PASQUALE
Same as Mar. 10

CAVALLERIA RUSTICANA
Flon (c)
Santuzza : Seygard
Lola : Bridewell
Turiddu : De Marchi
Alfio : Campanari
Lucia : Bauermeister

April 1 (mat.)

AIDA/Mancinelli (c)
Same as Feb. 26 except:
Amonasro : Campanari

April 1

SIEGFRIED
Same as Feb. 3 except:

Fafner : Blass
Erda : Schumann-Heink
Forest Bird : Seygard

April 2

DIE ZAUBERFLÖTE
Same as Mar. 12 except:
Second Genie : Van Cauteren

April 3

FAUST/Flon (c)
Same as Jan. 20 except:
Marguerite : Scheff

April 4 (mat.)

CARMEN/Mancinelli (c)
Carmen : Seygard
Don José : De Marchi
Micaela : Gadski
Escamillo : Journet
Zuniga : Declery
Morales : Bégué
Frasquita : Padroni (t—for
   Bauermeister)
Mercedes : Van Cauteren
Dancaire : Gilibert
Remendado : Reiss

April 4

GÖTTERDÄMMERUNG
Same as Feb. 5 except:
Siegfried : Anthes (for
   Burgstaller)
(Alberich, Rhine maidens
   omitted because Bispham
   and Schumann-Heink were
   ill)

CHICAGO

April 7

LA FILLE DU RÉGIMENT
Same as Feb. 17

PAGLIACCI/Mancinelli (c)
Same as Feb. 17 except:
Nedda : Scheff
Canio : Alvarez

April 8

DIE WALKÜRE
Same as Jan. 29 except:
Wotan : Bispham
Fricka : Schumann-Heink
Hunding : Blass
Helmwige : Scheff
Grimgerde : Seygard
Waltraute : Schumann-Heink

April 9

DIE MEISTERSINGER
Same as Mar. 17 except:
Magdalene : Schumann-
   Heink
Walther : Anthes

April 10
FAUST
Same as Jan. 20 except:
Marguerite : Scheff
Valentin : Campanari

April 11 (mat.)
TRISTAN UND ISOLDE
Same (?) as Mar. 3 except:
King Marke : E. de Reszke
Brangaene : Schumann-Heink

April 11
AIDA
Same as Feb. 26 except:
Radames : De Marchi

April 13
DON GIOVANNI
Same as Mar. 30 except:
Zerlina : Sembrich

April 14
UN BALLO IN MASCHERA
Mancinelli (c)
Amelia : Gadski
Ulrica : Homer
Oscar : Scheff
Riccardo : De Marchi
Renato : Campanari
Samuel : E. de Reszke
Tom : Journet
Silvano : Dufriche
Justice : Bégué
Servant : Vanni

April 15
SIEGFRIED
Same as Feb. 3 except:
Fafner : Blass
Erda : Schumann-Heink

April 16
DON PASQUALE
Same as Mar. 10

CAVALLERIA RUSTICANA
Same as Mar. 31

April 17
LE PROPHÈTE
Same as Dec. 16

April 18 (mat.)
DIE ZAUBERFLÖTE/Flon (c)
Same as Mar. 12 except:
Second Genie : Van Cauteren
(Sembrich omitted aria in Act II, ostensibly because applause for Scheff and Campanari in preceding duet overlapped her entrance.)

April 18
GÖTTERDÄMMERUNG/Hertz (c)
Same as Feb. 5 except:
Waltraute : Schumann-Heink
Flosshilde : Schumann-Heink

CINCINNATI
April 20
FAUST (for *Prophète*) Flon (c)
Same as Jan. 20 except:
Marguerite : Seygard
Valentin : Campanari

April 21 (mat.)
DIE ZAUBERFLÖTE/Flon (c)
Same as Mar. 12 except:
First Genie : Bauermeister
Second Genie : Van Cauteren

April 21
SIEGFRIED
Same as Feb. 3 except:
Erda : Schumann-Heink
(for Maurer)
Fafner : Blass
Forest Bird : Seygard

PITTSBURGH
April 22
LE PROPHÈTE
Same as Dec. 16

April 23
SIEGFRIED
Same as Feb. 3 except:
Fafner : Blass
Erda : Schumann-Heink
Forest Bird : Seygard

April 24
LA FILLE DU RÉGIMENT
Same as Feb. 17

PAGLIACCI
Same as Feb. 17 except:
Nedda : Scheff
Canio : De Marchi
Tonio : Campanari

April 25 (mat.)
DON GIOVANNI/Flon (c)
Same as Mar. 30 except:
Donna Elvira : Van Cauteren
(for Marilly)
Zerlina : Sembrich
Commendatore : Blass (for Journet)

April 25
DIE MEISTERSINGER
Same as Mar. 17 except:
Magdalene : Schumann-Heink
Walther : Anthes

1 9 0 3 – 0 4

CONRIED METROPOLITAN
OPERA COMPANY
Heinrich Conried, *Manager*

PHILADELPHIA
December 29
RIGOLETTO/Vigna (c)
Duke : Caruso
Rigoletto : Scotti
Gilda : Sembrich
Sparafucile : Journet
Maddalena : Homer
Giovanna : Bauermeister
Monterone : Dufriche
Marullo : Bégué (?)
Borsa : Masiero (?)
Ceprano : Cernusco (?)
Countess : Mapleson
Page : Förnsen

January 5
LOHENGRIN/Mottl (c)
King Henry : Blass
Lohengrin : Kraus
Elsa : Gadski
Telramund : Van Rooy
Ortrud : Walker
Herald : Mühlmann

January 12
CAVALLERIA RUSTICANA
Vigna (c)
Santuzza : Fremstad
Lola : Homer
Turiddu : Dippel
Alfio : Campanari
Lucia : Bauermeister

PAGLIACCI/Vigna (c)
Nedda : Seygard
Canio : Caruso
Tonio : Scotti
Beppe : Reiss
Silvio : Guardabassi

January 19
TOSCA/Vigna (c)
Tosca : Ternina
Cavaradossi : Caruso
Scarpia : Scotti
Angelotti : Dufriche
Sacristan : Rossi
Spoletta : Bars
Sciarrone : Bégué
Jailer : Cernusco
Shepherd : Bouton

January 26
TANNHÄUSER/Hertz (c)
Hermann : Plançon
Tannhäuser : Dippel (for Kraus)
Wolfram : Goritz

Walther : Reiss
Biterolf : Mühlmann
Heinrich : Bayer
Reinmar : Dufriche
Elisabeth : Gadski
Venus : Fremstad
Shepherd : Delsarta

February 2
AIDA/Vigna (c)
King : Mühlmann
Amneris : Walker
Aida : Gadski
Radames : Caruso
Amonasro : Scotti
Ramfis : Plançon
Messenger : Masiero
Priestess : Schaeffer

February 9
CARMEN/Mottl (c)
Carmen : Calvé
Don José : Dippel
Micaela : Lemon
Escamillo : Journet
Zuniga : Bégué
Morales : Guardabassi
Frasquita : Ralph
Mercedes : Jacoby
Dancaire : Dufriche
Remendado : Reiss

February 18 (mat.)
FAUST/Hinrichs (c)
Faust : Navál
Marguerite : Ackté (d)
Méphistophélès : Plançon
Valentin : Scotti
Siébel : Walker
Marthe : Bauermeister
Wagner : Dufriche

February 23
L'ELISIR D'AMORE/Franko (c)
Adina : Sembrich
Gianetta : Bouton
Nemorino : Navál
Belcore : Scotti
Dulcamara : Rossi

COPPELIA (Ballet—2 Acts)
Franko (c)
Swanhilda : Varesi
Franz : Braun
Poupee : Gellford
Coppelius : Francioli
Le Bourgmestre : Romeo

March 1
TRISTAN UND ISOLDE
Mottl (c)
Tristan : Kraus
Isolde : Weed (for Ternina)
King Marke : Kloepfer
Kurvenal : Van Rooy

Brangaene : Walker
Steersman : Walther
Shepherd : Reiss
Sailor's Voice : Bars
(Last act cut because Kraus broke down)

March 7
DAS RHEINGOLD/Hertz (c)
Wotan : Van Rooy
Donner : Mühlmann
Froh : Bars
Loge : Burgstaller
Alberich : Goritz
Mime : Reiss
Fasolt : Kloepfer
Fafner : Blass
Fricka : Fremstad
Freia : Seygard
Erda : Poehlmann (for Walker)
Woglinde : Weed
Wellgunde : Ralph
Flosshilde : Poehlmann

WASHINGTON
March 7
FAUST
Same as Feb. 18 except:
Siébel : Jacoby

PHILADELPHIA
March 8
DIE WALKÜRE/Mottl (c)
Wotan : Mühlmann (for Goritz)
Fricka : Homer
Brunnhilde : Gadski
Siegmund : Kraus
Sieglinde : Fremstad
Hunding : Kloepfer
Helmwige : Kronold
Gerhilde : Heidelbach
Ortlinde : Ralph
Rossweisse : Schueler
Grimgerde : Poehlmann
Waltraute : Bouton
Siegrune : Van Dresser
Schwertleite : Homer

WASHINGTON
March 8
IL BARBIERE DI SIVIGLIA
Hinrichs (c)
Almaviva : Dippel
Dr. Bartolo : Rossi
Rosina : Sembrich
Figaro : Campanari
Don Basilio : Journet
Berta : Bauermeister
Fiorello : Masiero
Sergeant : Bégué

March 9
CARMEN/Hinrichs (c)
Same as Feb. 9 except:
Don José : Navál
Micaela : Norelli
Escamillo : Campanari
Frasquita : Bauermeister
Remendado : Masiero

PHILADELPHIA
March 11
SIEGFRIED/Mottl (c)
Siegfried : Burgstaller
Mime : Reiss
Wanderer : Van Rooy
Alberich : Goritz
Fafner : Kloepfer
Erda : Walker
Brünnhilde : Weed (for Ternina)
Forest Bird : Lemon

BUFFALO
March 11
FAUST
Same as Feb. 18 except:
Valentin : Campanari
Siébel : Jacoby

PHILADELPHIA
March 12 (mat.)
GÖTTERDÄMMERUNG/Hertz (c)
Siegfried : Dippel (for Kraus)
Gunther : Mühlmann
Hagen : Blass
Alberich : Goritz
Brünnhilde : Januschowsky (for Gadski)
Gutrune : Weed
Waltraute : Homer
Woglinde : Seygard
Wellgunde : Ralph
Flosshilde : Homer
(Norn Scene omitted)

BUFFALO
March 12
LA TRAVIATA/Hinrichs (c)
Violetta : Sembrich
Alfredo : Navál
Germont : Scotti
Flora : Jacoby
Annina : Bauermeister
Gastone : Masiero
Baron Douphol : Bars
Marquis d'Obigny : Bégué
Doctor Grenvil : Dufriche

CHICAGO
March 14
DIE WALKÜRE
Same as Mar. 8 except:
Wotan : Van Rooy

1903–04

Brünnhilde : Ternina
Siegmund : Burgstaller
Hunding : Blass
Helmwige : Seygard
Gerhilde : Schueler
Rosswiesse : Bauermeister
Siegrune : Lemon

March 15
FAUST
Same as Feb. 18 except:
Faust : Dippel
Siébel : Jacoby

March 16
CARMEN
Same as Feb. 9 except:
Don José : Navál

March 17
DIE ZAUBERFLÖTE/Mottl (c)
Sarastro : Plançon
Tamino : Dippel
High Priest : Mühlmann
Priests : Masiero, Dufriche
Queen of the Night :
    Sembrich
Pamina : Gadski
Three Ladies : Seygard,
    Homer, Poehlmann
Papageno : Campanari
Papagena : Seygard
Monostatos : Reiss
Three Genii : Lemon,
    Bouton, Mapleson
Guards : Masiero, Dufriche

March 18
TRISTAN UND ISOLDE
Same as Mar. 1 except:
Isolde : Ternina
King Marke : Blass
Steersman : Dufriche (for
    Walther)

March 19 (mat.)
IL BARBIERE DI SIVIGLIA
Same as Mar. 8 except:
Almaviva : Bars

CAVALLERIA RUSTICANA
    Hinrichs (c)
Same as Jan. 12 except:
Santuzza : Calvé
Lola : Jacoby
Turiddu : Navál
Alfio : Mühlmann

March 19
TANNHÄUSER
Same as Jan. 26 except:
Elisabeth : Ackté

March 21
SIEGFRIED
Same as Mar. 11 except:

236

Fafner : Blass
Brünnhilde : Ternina

March 22
L'ELISIR D'AMORE
Same as Feb. 23

March 23
LOHENGRIN/Hertz (c)
Same as Jan. 5 except:
Elsa : Ackté
Telramund : Goritz

March 24
LE NOZZE DI FIGARO/Mottl (c)
Almaviva : Journet
Countess : Gadski
Susanna : Sembrich
Figaro : Campanari
Cherubino : Seygard
Marcellina : Bauermeister
Bartolo : Rossi
Basilio : Reiss
Antonio : Dufriche

March 25
TOSCA/Franko (c)
Same as Jan. 19 except:
Cavaradossi : Dippel

March 26 (mat.)
CARMEN
Same as Feb. 9 except:
Don José : Navál
Escamillo : Campanari

March 26
GÖTTERDÄMMERUNG
Same as Mar. 12 except:
Siegfried : Kraus
Brünnhilde : Gadski
(Alberich, Norn scenes
    omitted)

CINCINNATI
March 28 (mat.)
DIE WALKÜRE
Same as Mar. 8 except:
Wotan : Van Rooy
Siegmund : Burgstaller
Hunding : Blass
Helmwige : Seygard
Gerhilde : Lemon
Rosswiesse : Jacoby
Siegrune : Bauermeister

March 28
LA TRAVIATA
Same as Mar. 12 except:
Germont : Campanari
Annina : Poehlmann (for
    Bauermeister)

PITTSBURGH
March 29
TRISTAN UND ISOLDE
Same as Mar. 1 except:

Isolde : Ternina
King Marke : Blass
Steersman : Dufriche (for
    Walther)

March 30
DIE ZAUBERFLÖTE
Same as Mar. 17 except:
Sarastro : Blass
Priests : Harden, Stellmach
    (t)
First Lady : Weed
Second Lady : Ralph
Papageno : Goritz
First Guard : Bayer

March 31
CARMEN
Same as Feb. 9 except:
Don José : Navál
Escamillo : Campanari

April 2 (mat.)
GÖTTERDÄMMERUNG
Same as Mar. 12 except:
Siegfried : Burgstaller
Brünnhilde : Ternina
(Alberich, Norn scenes
    omitted)

April 2
FAUST
Same as Feb. 18

BOSTON
April 4
LOHENGRIN
Same as Jan. 5 except:
Elsa : Ackté
Telramund : Goritz

April 5
CARMEN
Same as Feb. 9 except:
Don José : Navál

April 6 (mat.)
DIE ZAUBERFLÖTE
Same as Mar. 17 except:
Sarastro : Blass
Tamino : Kraus
Priests : Harden, Stellmach
First Lady : Weed
Second Lady : Ralph
Papageno : Goritz
First Guard : Bayer

April 6
TOSCA/Franko (c)
Same as Jan. 19 except:
Cavaradossi : Dippel

April 7
DIE WALKÜRE/Hertz (c)
Wotan : Van Rooy
Hunding : Blass

Helmwige : Seygard (?)
Gerhilde : Jacoby (?)
Rossweisse : Weed (for
Bauermeister) (?)
Siegrune : Lemon (?)

April 8
IL BARBIERE DI SIVIGLIA
Same as Mar. 8

CAVALLERIA RUSTICANA
Hinrichs (c)
Same as Jan. 12 except:
Santuzza : Calvé
Turiddu : Navál
Alfio : Mühlmann

April 9 (mat.)
ROMÉO ET JULIETTE/Mottl (c)
Juliette : Ackté
Stephano : Bouton
Gertrude . Bauermeister
Roméo : Navál
Tybalt : Bars
Mercutio : Bégué
Gregorio : Dufriche
Capulet : Journet
Friar Laurence : Plançon
Duke of Verona : Mühlmann

April 9
TRISTAN UND ISOLDE/Hertz (c)
Same as Mar. 1 except:
Isolde : Ternina
King Marke : Blass
Steersman : Dufriche (for
Walther)

April 11
AIDA/Hinrichs (c)
Same as Feb. a except:
Amneris : Homer
Radames : Dippel
Amonasro : Campanari
Priestess : Poehlmann

April 12
SIEGFRIED
Same as Mar. 11 except:
Fafner : Blass
Brünnhilde : Ternina

April 13 (mat.)
FAUST
Same as Feb. 18 except:
Faust : Dippel
Valentin : Campanari
Siébel : Jacoby

April 13
L'ELISIR D'AMORE
Same as Feb. 23

COPPELIA (Ballet) Franko (c)
Same as Feb. 23 except:
Franz : Hesch
Le Bourgmestre : Muzio

April 14
TANNHÄUSER
Same as Jan. 26 except:
Tannhäuser : Kraus
Elisabeth : Ackté
Shepherd : Seygard

April 15
LE NOZZE DI FIGARO
Same as Mar. 24 except:
Almaviva : Scotti

April 16 (mat.)
CARMEN
Same as Feb. 9

April 16
GÖTTERDÄMMERUNG
Same as Mar. 12 except:
Siegfried : Kraus
Brünnhilde : Gadski (for
Ternina)
(Alberich, Norn scenes
omitted)

PROVIDENCE

April 19
LA TRAVIATA
Same as Mar. 12 except:
Alfredo : Dippel
Germont : Campanari

HARTFORD

April 20
FAUST
Same as Feb. 18 except.
Siébel : Jacoby

SPRINGFIELD

April 21
LA TRAVIATA
Same as Mar. 12 except:
Alfredo : Dippel
Germont : Campanari

NEW HAVEN

April 22
CARMEN/Hinrichs (c)
Same as Feb. 9 except:
Don José : Navál
Micaela : Norelli
Escamillo : Campanari
Frasquita : Bauermeister
Remendado : Masiero

1904–05

PHILADELPHIA

December 6
ROMÉO ET JULIETTE
Franko (c)
Juliette : Eames
Stephano : Lemon (?)

Gertrude : Bauermeister (?)
Roméo : Saléza
Tybalt : Bars (?)
Mercutio : Parvis
Gregorio : Bégué (?)
Capulet : Journet
Friar Laurence : Plançon
Duke of Verona :
Mühlmann (?)

December 13
AIDA/Vigna (c)
King : Mühlmann
Amneris : Walker
Aida : Eames
Radames : Caruso
Amonasro : Scotti
Ramfis : Plançon
Messenger : Giordani
Priestess : Schaeffer

December 27
CAVALLERIA RUSTICANA (for
Bohème) Vigna (c)
Santuzza : De Macchi
Lola : Jacoby
Turiddu : Saléza
Alfio : Giraldoni
Lucia : Bauermeister

PAGLIACCI/Vigna (c)
Nedda : Alten
Canio : Caruso
Tonio : Scotti
Beppe : Reiss
Silvio : Parvis

January 3 (mat.)
LOHENGRIN/Franko (c)
King Henry : Blass
Lohengrin : Knote
Elsa : Nordica
Telramund : Goritz
Ortrud : Homer
Herald : Mühlmann

January 10
LUCIA DI LAMMERMOOR
Vigna (c)
Lucia : Sembrich
Ashton : Parvis
Edgardo : Caruso
Alisa : Bauermeister
Raimondo : Journet
Arturo : Bars
Normanno : Giordani

January 17
TRISTAN UND ISOLDE/Hertz (c)
Tristan : Knote
Isolde : Nordica
King Marke : Blass
Kurvenal : Van Rooy
Brangaene : Homer (for
Fremstad)

Melot : Mühlmann
Steersman : Walther
Shepherd : Reiss
Sailor's Voice : Bars

January 24
LA BOHÈME/Vigna (c)
Rodolfo : Caruso
Marcello : Scotti
Schaunard : Parvis
Colline : Journet
Mimi : Sembrich
Musetta : Alten
Benoit : Rossi
Parpignol : Zecchi
Alcindoro : Rossi
Sergeant : Gili
Customs Officer : Fanelli

January 31
DIE MEISTERSINGER/Hertz (c)
Hans Sachs : Van Rooy
Pogner : Blass
Eva : Acké (for Alten)
Magdalene : Homer
Walther : Burgstaller
Beckmesser : Greder (for
   Goritz)
Kothner : Mühlmann
Vogelgesang : Rand
Nachtigall : Dufriche
Zorn : Bayer
Eisslinger : Lapini
Moser : Rudolfi
Ortel : Baillard
Schwarz : Lötzsch
Foltz : Werner
David : Reiss
Night Watchman : Dufriche

February 7
CARMEN/Vigna (c)
Carmen : Fremstad
Don José : Saléza
Micaela : Acké
Escamillo : Journet
Zuniga : Bégué
Morales : Parvis
Frasquita : Ralph
Mercedes : Jacoby
Dancaire : Dufriche
Remendado : Reiss

February 14
FAUST/Vigna (c)
Faust : Saléza
Marguerite : Eames
Méphistophélès : Journet
Valentin : Scotti
Siébel : Jacoby
Marthe : Bauermeister
Wagner : Bégué

February 21
FLEDERMAUS/Franko (c)
Eisenstein : Dippel

Rosalinda : Sembrich
Adele : Alten
Ida : Elliott
Alfred : Reiss
Orlofsky : Walker
Dr. Falke : Greder
Frank : Goritz
Dr. Blind : Mühlmann
Frosch : Hänseler

DIE PUPPENFEE (ballet)

February 28
LA GIOCONDA/Vigna (c)
La Gioconda : Nordica
Laura : Homer
Alvise : Plançon
La Cieca : Walker
Enzo : Caruso
Barnaba : Giraldoni
Zuane : Bégué
Singer : Dufriche
Isepo : Giaccone
Monk : Bégué

BOSTON
March 6
LUCIA DI LAMMERMOOR
Same as Jan. 10 except:
Normanno : Giaccone

March 7
PARSIFAL/Hertz (c)
Amfortas : Van Rooy
Titurel : Journet
Gurnemanz : Blass
Parsifal : Burgstaller
Klingsor : Goritz
Kundry : Nordica
A Voice : Jacoby
Knights of the Grail : Bayer,
   Greder
Esquires : Moran, Braendle,
   Reiss, Alberti
Flower Maidens : Lemon,
   Talma (for Rockwell), Law-
   rence, Call (for Alten),
   Heidelbach, Mulford

March 8
CAVALLERIA RUSTICANA
   Franko (c)
Same as Dec. 27 except:
Lola : Homer
Turiddu : Bars (for Dippel)

PAGLIACCI
Same as Dec. 27

March 9 (mat.)
PARSIFAL
Same as Mar. 7 except:
Titurel : Mühlmann
Kundry : Fremstad
Third Esquire : Rudolfi

Flower Maidens : Poehlmann
   (t), Alten, Ralph, Jacoby
   (3rd, 4th, 5th, 6th)

March 9
FLEDERMAUS
Same as Feb. 21 except:
Orlofsky : Weed
Frosch : Bayer
Ivan : Rudolfi (for Franke)

March 10
LA GIOCONDA
Same as Feb. 28 except:
Singer : Rossi

March 11 (mat.)
LES HUGUENOTS/Vigna (c)
Marguerite : Sembrich
St. Bris : Plançon
Valentine : De Macchi
Nevers : Scotti
Cossé : Zecchi
Tavannes : Giaccone
Meru : Greder
Retz : Bégué
Raoul : Saléza
Marcel : Journet
Urbain : Walker
Maurevert : Dufriche
Bois Rosé : Bars
Ladies of Honor :
   Bauermeister, Mulford
Night Watchman : Parvis

March 11
DIE MEISTERSINGER
Same as Jan. 31 except:
Eva : Alten
Beckmesser : Goritz
Eisslinger : Eisler (for
   Franke)
Ortel : Greder

PITTSBURGH
March 13
LUCIA DI LAMMERMOOR
Same as Jan. 10 except:
Normanno : Giaccone

March 14
PARSIFAL
Same as Mar. 7 except:
Titurel : Mühlmann
Kundry : Fremstad
Flower Maidens : Poehlmann,
   Jacoby, Ralph (2nd, 5th,
   6th)

March 15 (mat.)
LES HUGUENOTS
Same as Mar. 11 except:
Valentine : Nordica
Cossé : Rand
Urbain : Jacoby
Maurevert : Rossi

March 15

DIE MEISTERSINGER
Same as Jan. 31 except:
Eva : Alten
Walther : Dippel
Beckmesser : Goritz
Eisslinger : Eisler
Ortel : Greder

March 16

LA GIOCONDA
Same as Feb. 28 except:
La Gioconda : De Macchi
Singer : Rossi (for Dufriche)

CINCINNATI

March 17

PARSIFAL
Same as Mar. 7 except:
Kundry : Fremstad
Flower Maidens : Poehlmann,
Ralph, Jacoby (3rd, 5th,
6th)

March 18 (mat.)

LES HUGUENOTS
Same as Mar. 11 except:
St. Bris : Mühlmann (for
Plançon)
Valentine : Nordica
Cossé : Rand
Raoul : Dippel
Urbain : Alten
Maurevert : Rossi (for
Dufriche)

March 18

LA GIOCONDA
Same as Feb. 28 except:
La Gioconda : De Macchi

CHICAGO

March 20

LUCIA DI LAMMERMOOR
Same as Jan. 10 except:
Normanno : Giaccone

March 21

PARSIFAL
Same as Mar. 7 except:
Flower Maidens : Poehlmann,
Jacoby, Ralph (2nd, 5th,
6th)

March 22

CAVALLERIA RUSTICANA
Franko (c)
Same as Dec. 27 except:
Lola : Homer
Turiddu : Dippel

PAGLIACCI
Same as Dec. 27

March 23 (11:30 A.M.)

PARSIFAL
Same as Mar. 7 except:
Titurel : Mühlmann
Kundry : Fremstad
Third Esquire : Rudolfi
Flower Maidens : Poehlmann,
Jacoby, Ralph (2nd, 5th,
6th)

March 23

FLEDERMAUS
Same as Feb. 21 except:
Orlofsky : Weed
Frosch : Bayer
Ivan : Franke

March 24

LA GIOCONDA
Same as Feb. 28 except:
Singer : Rossi (for Dufriche)

March 25 (mat.)

LES HUGUENOTS
Same as Mar. 11 except:
Cossé : Rand
Maurevert : Rossi

March 25

DIE MEISTERSINGER
Same as Jan. 31 except:
Eva : Alten
Beckmesser : Goritz
Eisslinger : Franke
Ortel : Greder

MINNEAPOLIS

March 27

PARSIFAL
Same as Mar. 7 except:
Titurel : Mühlmann
Kundry : Fremstad
Flower Maidens : Poehlmann,
Jacoby, Ralph (3rd, 6th,
5th)

March 28 (mat.)

LES HUGUENOTS
Same as Mar. 11 except:
St. Bris : Mühlmann
Valentine : Nordica
Cossé : Rand
Raoul : Dippel
Urbain : Homer
Maurevert : Rossi

March 28

CAVALLERIA RUSTICANA
Franko (c)
Same as Dec. 27 except:
Turiddu : Bars
Alfio : Bégué

PAGLIACCI
Same as Dec. 27 except:
Tonio : Goritz

OMAHA

March 29

PARSIFAL
Same as Mar. 7 except:
Titurel : Mühlmann
Kundry : Fremstad
Third Esquire : Rudolfi
Flower Maidens : Poehlmann,
Ralph, Jacoby (3rd, 5th,
6th)

March 30

LUCIA DI LAMMERMOOR
Same as Jan. 10 except:
Normanno : Giaccone

KANSAS CITY

March 31

PARSIFAL
Same as Mar. 7 except:
Titurel : Mühlmann
Kundry : Fremstad
Third Esquire : Rudolfi
Flower Maidens : Poehlmann,
Ralph, Jacoby (3rd, 5th,
6th)

April 1 (mat.)

LES HUGUENOTS
Same as Mar. 11 except:
St. Bris : Mühlmann
Valentine : Nordica
Cossé : Rand
Raoul : Dippel
Urbain : Homer
Maurevert : Rossi
Bois Rosé : Giaccone (for
Bars)

April 1

CAVALLERIA RUSTICANA
Franko (c)
Same as Dec. 27 except:
Turiddu : Bars
Alfio : Bégué

PAGLIACCI
Same as Dec. 27 except:
Tonio : Goritz

SALT LAKE CITY

April 4

CONCERT/Vigna (c)
Alten, De Macchi, chorus

STABAT MATER (Rossini)
Nordica, Jacoby (for Homer),
Dippel, Journet

SAN FRANCISCO

April 6

RIGOLETTO/Vigna (c)
Duke : Caruso
Rigoletto : Parvis (for
Scotti after Act II)

239

Gilda : Sembrich
Sparafucile : Journet
Maddalena : Homer
Giovanna : Bauermeister
Monterone : Mühlmann
Marullo : Bégué
Borsa : Giaccone
Ceprano : Greder
Countess : Mapleson
Page : Elliott
Guard : Fanelli

April 7
PARSIFAL
Same as Mar. 7 except:
Titurel : Mühlmann
Flower Maidens : Poehlmann,
Jacoby, Ralph (2nd, 5th,
6th)

April 8 (mat.)
CAVALLERIA RUSTICANA
Franko (c)
Same as Dec. 27 except:
Turiddu : Dippel
Alfio : Bégué

PAGLIACCI
Same as Dec. 27 except:
Nedda : Lemon (for Alten)

April 8
LES HUGUENOTS
Same as Mar. 11 except:
St. Bris : Mühlmann
Valentine : Nordica
Cossé : Rand
Raoul : Dippel
Urbain : Homer
Maurevert : Rossi

April 9
CONCERT/Vigna (c)
Alten, Franko (violinist),
De Macchi

STABAT MATER (Rossini)
Nordica, Homer, Dippel,
Journet

April 10
LUCIA DI LAMMERMOOR
Same as Jan. 10 except:
Arturo : Giaccone
Normanno : Reiss

April 11
PARSIFAL
Same as Mar. 7 except:
Titurel : Mühlmann
Kundry : Fremstad
Third Esquire : Rudolfi
(for Reiss)
Flower Maidens : Poehlmann,
Jacoby, Ralph (2nd, 5th,
6th)

April 12
LA GIOCONDA
Same as Feb. 28 except:
Alvise : Journet
La Cieca : Jacoby
Barnaba : Scotti

April 13 (11:30 A.M.)
PARSIFAL
Same as Mar. 7 except:
Titurel : Mühlmann
Kundry : Fremstad
Third Esquire : Rudolfi
Flower Maidens : Poehlmann,
Jacoby, Ralph (2nd, 5th,
6th)

April 13
FLEDERMAUS
Same as Mar. 9 except:
Orlofsky : Weed
Frosch : Bayer

April 14
CAVALLERIA RUSTICANA
Same as Dec. 27 except:
Turiddu : Bars (for Dippel)
Alfio : Bégué

PAGLIACCI
Same as Dec. 27 except:
Tonio : Goritz

April 15 (mat.)
DIE MEISTERSINGER
Same as Jan. 31 except:
Eva : Alten
Magdalene : Jacoby
Beckmesser : Goritz
Eisslinger : Eisler (for
Franke)
Ortel : Greder

April 15
LA GIOCONDA
Same as Feb. 28 except:
Alvise : Journet
La Cieca : Jacoby
Barnaba : Scotti

LOS ANGELES

April 17
PARSIFAL
Same as Mar. 7 except:
Titurel : Mühlmann
Kundry : Fremstad
Third Esquire : Rudolfi
Flower Maidens : Poehlmann,
Jacoby, Ralph (2nd, 5th,
6th)

April 18
LUCIA DI LAMMERMOOR
Same as Jan. 10 except:
Alisa : Poehlmann
Normanno : Giaccone

DALLAS

April 21
PARSIFAL
Same as Mar. 7 except:
Titurel : Mühlmann
Gurnemanz : Journet
Parsifal : Dippel
Kundry : Fremstad
Third Esquire : Rudolfi
Flower Maidens : Poehlmann,
Jacoby, Ralph (2nd, 5th,
6th)

HOUSTON

April 22
PARSIFAL
Same as Mar. 7 except:
Amfortas : Goritz
Titurel : Mühlmann
Klingsor : Mühlmann (for
Greder)
Kundry : Weed
Third Esquire : Rudolfi
(for Reiss)
Flower Maidens : Poehl-
mann, Talma, Jacoby, Ralph
(2nd, 3rd, 5th, 6th)

NEW ORLEANS

April 24
PARSIFAL
Same as Mar. 7 except:
Amfortas : Goritz
Titurel : Mühlmann
Klingsor : Mühlmann
Kundry : Fremstad
Third Esquire : Rudolfi
Flower Maidens : Poehlmann,
Jacoby, Ralph (2nd, 5th,
6th)

ATLANTA

April 26
PARSIFAL
Same as Mar. 7 except:
Amfortas : Goritz
Titurel : Mühlmann
Gurnemanz : Journet
Parsifal : Dippel
Klingsor : Mühlmann
Kundry : Fremstad
Third Esquire : Rudolfi
Flower Maidens : Poehlmann,
Mulford, Jacoby, Ralph
(2nd, 3rd, 5th, 6th)

BIRMINGHAM

April 27
PARSIFAL
Same as Mar. 7 except:
Amfortas : Goritz
Titurel : Mühlmann
Klingsor : Mühlmann
Kundry : Weed

Third Esquire : Rudolfi
Flower Maidens : Poehlmann,
Mulford, Jacoby, Ralph
(2nd, 3rd, 5th, 6th)

NASHVILLE
April 29
PARSIFAL
Same as Mar. 7 except:
Amfortas : Goritz
Titurel : Mühlmann
Klingsor : Mühlmann
Kundry : Fremstad
Third Esquire : Rudolfi
Flower Maidens : Poehlmann,
Mulford, Jacoby, Ralph
(2nd, 3rd, 5th, 6th)

1 9 0 5 – 0 6

PHILADELPHIA
December 5
LA FAVORITA/Vigna (c)
Leonora : Walker
Inez : Jomelli
Fernando : Caruso
Alfonso : Scotti
Balthazar : Plançon
Don Gasparo : Bars

December 12
FLEDERMAUS/Franko (c)
Eisenstein : Dippel
Rosalinda : Sembrich
Adele : Alten
Ida : Elliott
Alfred : Reiss
Orlofsky : Weed
Dr. Falke : Crogor
Frank : Goritz
Dr. Blind : Mühlmann
Frosch : Hänseler (t)

December 19
DIE WALKÜRE/Hertz (c)
Wotan : Van Rooy
Fricka : Homer
Brünnhilde : Walker
Siegmund : Burgstaller
Sieglinde : Fremstad
Hunding : Blass
Helmwige : Jomelli
Gerhilde : Call (for Alten)
Ortlinde : Bauermeister
Rossweisse : Jacoby
Grimgerde : Mulford
Waltraute : Weed
Siegrune : Ralph
Schwertleite : Homer

December 26
RIGOLETTO/Vigna (c)
Duke : Caruso
Rigoletto : Scotti

Gilda : Sembrich
Sparafucile : Journet (?)
Maddalena : Jacoby
Giovanna : Bauermeister (?)
Monterone : Mühlmann (?)
Marullo : Bégué (?)
Borsa : Paroli (?)
Ceprano : Dufriche (?)
Countess : Lawrence (?)
Page : Vail (?)

January 2
DIE KÖNIGIN VON SABA
Hertz (c)
Queen of Sheba : Walker
Sulamith : Rappold
Astaroth : Alten
Assad : Knote
King Solomon : Van Rooy
High Priest : Blass
Baal Hanan : Mühlmann
Voice : Bayer

January 4 (mat.)
HÄNSEL UND GRETEL
Franko (c)
Hänsel : Arbarbanell
Gretel : Alten
Witch : Homer
Gertrude : Weed
Sandman : Mulford (?)
Dewman : Glanville (?)
Peter : Goritz

January 9
SIEGFRIED (for *Tosca* due
to chorus strike) Hertz (c)
Siegfried : Knote
Mime : Reiss
Wanderer : Van Rooy
Alberich : Goritz
Fafner : Blass
Brünnhilde : Nordica
Erda : Jacoby
Forest Bird : Alten

January 16
TOSCA/Vigna (c)
Tosca : Eames
Cavaradossi : Dippel
Scarpia : Scotti
Angelotti : Dufriche
Sacristan : Rossi
Spoletta : Paroli
Sciarrone : Bégué
Jailer : Foglia
Shepherd : Mulford

January 23
LA BOHÈME/Vigna (c)
Rodolfo : Caruso
Marcello : Campanari
Schaunard : Parvis
Colline : Journet
Mimi : Sembrich

Musetta : Alten
Benoit : Dufriche
Parpignol : Paroli
Alcindoro : Rossi
Sergeant : Foglia
Customs Officer : Fanelli

January 30
DON GIOVANNI/Franko (c)
Don Giovanni : Scotti
Donna Anna : Nordica
Donna Elvira : Jomelli
Zerlina : Sembrich
Commendatore : Mühlmann
Don Ottavio : Dippel
Leporello : Journet
Masetto : Rossi

February 6
AIDA/Vigna (c)
King : Muhlmann
Amneris : Walker
Aida : Eames
Radames : Caruso
Amonasro : Campanari
Ramfis : Plançon
Messenger : Paroli
Priestess : Lawrence

February 13
GÖTTERDÄMMERUNG/Hertz (c)
Siegfried : Knote
Gunther : Mühlmann
Hagen : Blass
Brünnhilde : Nordica
Gutrune : Weed
Waltraute : Walker
Woglinde : Alten
Wellgunde : Ralph
Flosshilde : Mulford

February 20
CARMEN/Vigna (c)
Carmen : Fremstad
Don José : Caruso
Micaela : Abott
Escamillo : Scotti
Zuniga : Bégué
Morales : Parvis
Frasquita : Ralph
Mercedes : Jacoby
Dancaire : Dufriche
Remendado : Reiss

March 1 (mat.)
FAUST/Franko (c)
Faust : Caruso
Marguerite : Abott
Méphistophélès : Plançon
Valentin : Campanari
Siébel : Jacoby
Marthe : Bauermeister
Wagner : Bégué

241

1905–06

BALTIMORE

March 19
MARTHA/Vigna (c)
Harriet : Sembrich
Nancy : Walker
Lionel : Caruso
Plunkett : Plançon
Tristan : Rossi
Sheriff : Dufriche

March 20
LOHENGRIN/Hertz (c)
King Henry : Journet
Lohengrin : Knote
Elsa : Rappold
Telramund : Goritz
Ortrud : Homer
Herald : Mühlmann

March 21 (mat.)
DIE WALKÜRE
Same as Dec. 19 except:
Helmwige : Call
Gerhilde : Alten

March 21
FAUST
Same as Mar. 1 except:
Marguerite : Eames
Valentin : Scotti
Marthe : Poehlmann (for
Bauermeister)

WASHINGTON

March 22
DIE KÖNIGIN VON SABA
Same as Jan. 2

March 23
LUCIA DI LAMMERMOOR
Vigna (c)
Lucia : Sembrich
Ashton : Parvis
Edgar : Caruso
Alisa : Bauermeister
Raimondo : Journet
Arturo : Bars
Normanno : Paroli

March 24 (mat.)
TOSCA
Same as Jan. 16

March 24
HÄNSEL UND GRETEL
Same as Jan. 4

PAGLIACCI/Vigna (c)
Nedda : Alten
Canio : Caruso
Tonio : Campanari
Beppe : Reiss
Silvio : Parvis

PITTSBURGH

March 26
DIE KÖNIGIN VON SABA
Same as Jan. 2

March 27
CARMEN
Same as Feb. 20 except:
Escamillo : Journet

March 28 (mat.)
LE NOZZE DI FIGARO
Franko (c)
(Not given in New York)
Almaviva : Scotti
Countess : Eames
Susanna : Sembrich
Figaro : Campanari
Cherubino : Alten
Marcellina : Poehlmann
Bartolo : Rossi (?)
Basilio : Reiss
Don Curzio : Paroli (?)
Antonio : Dufriche

March 28
LOHENGRIN
Same as Mar. 20 except:
King Henry : Blass

March 29
LA BOHÈME
Same as Jan. 23 except:
Mimi : Abott

March 30
DIE WALKÜRE
Same as Dec. 19 except:
Helmwige : ?
Gerhilde : Alten
Ortlinde : Poehlmann

March 31 (mat.)
DON PASQUALE/Vigna (c)
Norina : Sembrich
Ernesto : Dippel
Malatesta : Scotti
Don Pasquale : Rossi
Notary : Foglia

HÄNSEL UND GRETEL
Same as Jan. 4 except:
Dewman : Shearman (t)

March 31
FAUST
Same as Mar. 1 except:
Marguerite : Eames
Marthe : Poehlmann

CHICAGO

April 2
DIE KÖNIGIN VON SABA
Same as Jan. 2

April 3
FAUST
Same as Mar. 1 except:
Marguerite : Eames
Valentin : Scotti
Marthe : Poehlmann

April 4 (mat.)
DON PASQUALE
Same as Mar. 31

HÄNSEL UND GRETEL
Same as Jan. 4 except:
Dewman : Shearman

April 4
LOHENGRIN
Same as Mar. 20 except:
King Henry : Blass
Telramund : Van Rooy
Ortrud : Walker

April 5
CARMEN
Same as Feb. 20 except:
Escamillo : Journet

April 6
TOSCA
Same as Jan. 16

April 7 (mat.)
MARTHA
Same as Mar. 19 except:
Nancy : Homer
Sheriff : Foglia

April 7
TANNHÄUSER/Hertz (c)
Hermann : Blass (?)
Tannhäuser : Burgstaller
Wolfram : Goritz
Walther : Reiss (?)
Biterolf : Mühlmann
Heinrich : Bayer (?)
Reinmar : Dufriche (?)
Elisabeth : Rappold
Venus : Fremstad
Shepherd : Alten

ST. LOUIS

April 9
MARTHA
Same as Mar. 19 except:
Nancy : Homer
Servant : Foglia

April 10
LOHENGRIN
Same as Mar. 20 except:
King Henry : Blass
Telramund : Van Rooy
Ortrud : Walker

242

April 11 (mat.)
FAUST
Same as Mar. 1 except:
Marguerite : Eames
Marthe : Poehlmann

April 11
PAGLIACCI
Same as Mar. 24 except:
Canio : Bars
Tonio : Scotti

HÄNSEL UND GRETEL
Hertz (c)
Same as Jan. 4 except:
Hänsel : Mattfeld (t—for
Freund)

KANSAS CITY
April 12 (mat.)
LOHENGRIN
Same as Mar. 20 except:
King Henry : Blass
Telramund : Van Rooy
Ortrud : Walker

April 12
MARTHA
Same as Mar. 19 except:
Nancy : Homer
Servant : Foglia

SAN FRANCISCO
April 16
DIE KÖNIGIN VON SABA
Same as Jan. 2 except:
Assad : Dippel

April 17
CARMEN
Same as Feb. 20 except:
Escamillo : Journet
*(Season cut short by
earthquake)*

1 9 0 6 – 0 7

PHILADELPHIA
December 4
ROMÉO ET JULIETTE/Bovy (c)
Juliette : Farrar
Stephano : Jacoby
Gertrude : Neuendorff
Roméo : Rousselière
Tybalt : Bars
Mercutio : Simard
Capulet : Journet
Friar Laurence : Plançon
Duke of Verona : Mühlmann

December 11
TANNHÄUSER/Hertz (c)
Hermann : Blass

Tannhäuser : Burrian
Wolfram : Van Rooy
Walther : Reiss
Biterolf : Mühlmann
Heinrich : Bayer
Reinmar : Gunther
Elisabeth : Fleischer-Edel
Venus : Fremstad
Shepherd : Alten

December 20
LAKMÉ/Bovy (c)
Lakmé : Sembrich
Mallika : Jacoby
Ellen : Simeoli (for
Glanville)
Rose : Mattfeld
Mrs. Benson : Poehlmann
Gerald : Rousselière
Frederick : Simard
Nilakantha : Journet
Hadji : Bars

December 27
FEDORA/Vigna (c)
Fedora : Cavalieri
Olga : Alten
Loris Ipanov : Caruso
De Siriex : Scotti
Dimitri : Mattfeld
Désiré : Paroli
Baron Rouvel : Paroli
Cyril : Bégué
Borov : Mühlmann
Grech : Dufriche
Lorek : Navarini
Savoyard : Jacoby
Lasinski : Voghera

January 3
FAUST/Bovy (c)
Faust : Rousselière
Marguerite : Farrar
Méphistophélès : Plançon
Valentin : Stracciari
Siébel : Jacoby
Marthe : Simeoli
Wagner : Bégué

January 8
LOHENGRIN/Hertz (c)
King Henry : Blass
Lohengrin : Burrian
Elsa : Eames
Telramund : Van Rooy
Ortrud : Kirkby-Lunn
Herald : Mühlmann

January 15
MARTHA/Vigna (c)
Harriet : Sembrich
Nancy : Homer
Lionel : Caruso
Plunkett : Journet
Tristan : Rossi
Sheriff : Dufriche (?)

January 24
SIEGFRIED/Hertz (c)
Siegfried : Burgstaller
Mime : Reiss
Wanderer : Van Rooy
Alberich : Goritz
Fafner : Blass
Erda : Kirkby-Lunn
Brünnhilde : Fleischer-Edel
Forest Bird : Rappold

January 29
CARMEN/Bovy (c)
Carmen : Fremstad
Don José : Rousselière
Micaela : Rappold
Escamillo : Journet
Zuniga : Bégué
Morales : Simard
Frasquita : Mattfeld
Mercedes : Jacoby
Dancaire : Dufriche
Remendado : Reiss

January 31
LA BOHÈME (for *Manon
Lescaut*)/Vigna (c)
Rodolfo : Dippel
Marcello : Scotti
Schaunard : Simard
Colline : Journet
Mimi : Cavalieri
Musetta : Alten
Benoit : Dufriche
Parpignol : Paroli
Alcindoro : Rossi
Sergeant : Dragoni
Customs Officer : Navarini

February 5
CAVALLERIA RUSTICANA
Vigna (c)
Santuzza : Boninsegna
Lola : Jacoby
Turiddu : Dippel
Alfio : Stracciari
Lucia : Simeoli

PAGLIACCI/Vigna (c)
Nedda : Cavalieri
Canio : Rousselière
Tonio : Scotti
Beppe : Reiss
Silvio : Simard

February 7 (mat.)
AIDA/Vigna (c)
King : Mühlmann
Amneris : Homer
Aida : Eames
Radames : Caruso
Amonasro : Stracciari
Ramfis : Plançon
Messenger : Paroli
Priestess : Lawrence

1906–07

February 14
MADAMA BUTTERFLY
Vigna (c)

Cio-Cio-San : Farrar
B. F. Pinkerton : Caruso
Sharpless : Stracciari
Suzuki : Homer
Kate Pinkerton : Mapleson
Goro : Reiss
Yamadori : Paroli
Uncle-Priest : Mühlmann
Imperial Commissioner :
  Bégué
Yakuside : Rossi

February 19
TRISTAN UND ISOLDE/Hertz (c)

Tristan : Burrian
Isolde : Gadski
King Marke : Blass
Kurvenal : Van Rooy
Brangaene : Homer
Melot : Mühlmann
Steersman : Bayer
Shepherd : Reiss
Sailor's Voice : Reiss

February 21
MANON LESCAUT/Vigna (c)

Manon : Cavalieri
Des Grieux : Caruso
Lescaut : Scotti
Geronte : Rossi
Edmondo : Bars
Lamplighter : Reiss
Innkeeper : Bégué
Commandante : Bégué
Singer : Simeoli
Dancing Master : Paroli
Sergeant : Navarini

February 26
DIE WALKÜRE/Hertz (c)

Wotan : Goritz (for
  Van Rooy)
Fricka : Kirkby-Lunn
Brünnhilde : Gadski
Siegmund : Burgstaller
Sieglinde : Fremstad
Hunding : Blass
Helmwige : Call
Gerhilde : Alten
Ortlinde : Ralph
Rossweisse : Jacoby
Grimgerde : Poehlmann
Waltraute : Weed
Siegrune : Mattfeld
Schwertleite : Wöhning

March 5
HÄNSEL UND GRETEL
Hertz (c)

Hänsel : Mattfeld
Gretel : Alten
Witch : Homer

Gertrude : Weed
Sandman : Moran
Dewman : Shearman
Peter : Goritz

PAGLIACCI

Same as Feb. 5 except:
Nedda : Farrar
Canio : Caruso
Tonio : Stracciari

March 7 (mat.)
LA BOHÈME

Same as Jan. 31 except:
Rodolfo : Caruso
Mimi : Sembrich
Parpignol : Raimondi
Alcindoro : Dufriche

BALTIMORE
March 25
LA BOHÈME

Same as Jan. 31 except:
Rodolfo : Caruso
Mimi : Farrar
Parpignol : Raimondi
Alcindoro : Dufriche

March 26
HÄNSEL UND GRETEL

Same as Mar. 5

PAGLIACCI/Bovy (c)

Same as Feb. 5 except:
Nedda : Alten
Canio : Caruso
Tonio : Stracciari
Beppe : Bars

March 27
TOSCA/Vigna (c)

Tosca : Eames
Cavaradossi : Dippel
Scarpia : Scotti
Angelotti : Dufriche
Sacristan : Navarini
Spoletta : Bars
Sciarrone : Bégué
Jailer : Navarini
Shepherd : Lawrence

WASHINGTON
March 28
MADAMA BUTTERFLY

Same as Feb. 14 except:
Kate Pinkerton : Lawrence
Yamadori : Dufriche
Yakuside : Dragoni

March 30 (mat.)
FAUST

Same as Jan. 3 except:
Faust : Dippel
Marguerite : Eames

Valentin : Scotti
Marthe : Poehlmann

March 30
AIDA

Same as Feb. 7 except:
Aida : Rappold
Ramfis : Journet
Messenger : Raimondi

BOSTON
April 1
FAUST

Same as Jan. 3 except:
Faust : Dippel
Méphisthophélès : Journet
  (for Plançon)
Marthe : Poehlmann

April 2
TOSCA

Same as Mar. 27 except:
Cavaradossi : Caruso
Shepherd : Jacoby

April 3 (mat.)
MADAMA BUTTERFLY

Same as Feb. 14 except:
B. F. Pinkerton : Dippel
Sharpless : Scotti
Suzuki : Jacoby (for Homer)
Kate Pinkerton : Lawrence
Yamadori : Dufriche
Yakuside : Dragoni

April 3
TRISTAN UND ISOLDE

Same as Feb. 19 except:
Tristan : Burgstaller
Brangaene : Schumann-Heink

April 4
MARTHA

Same as Jan. 15 except:
Harriet : Mattfeld (for
  Abott)
Nancy : Jacoby (for Homer)
Tristan : Dufriche
Sheriff : Navarini

April 5
TANNHÄUSER

Same as Dec. 11 except:
Tannhäuser : Burgstaller
Wolfram : Goritz
Reinmar : Dufriche
Elisabeth : Farrar

April 6 (mat.)
AIDA

Same as Feb. 7 except:
Amneris : Jacoby (for
  Homer)
Messenger : Raimondi

April 6
HÄNSEL UND GRETEL
Same as Mar. 5 except:
Witch : Jacoby

PAGLIACCI
Same as Feb. 5 except:
Nedda : Farrar
Canio : Bars

CHICAGO
April 8
L'AFRICAINE/Vigna (c)
Don Pedro : Plançon
Don Diego : Mühlmann
Inez : Rappold
Vasco da Gama : Caruso
Don Alvar : Bars
Nelusko : Stracciari
Selika : Fremstad
Grand Inquisitor : Journet
Grand Brahmin : Journet
Anna : Poehlmann (for
 Mattfeld)
Usher : Raimondi

April 9
TRISTAN UND ISOLDE
Same as Feb. 19 except:
Tristan : Burgstaller
Brangaene : Schumann-Heink

April 10 (mat.)
AIDA
Same as Feb. 7 except:
Amneris : Jacoby
Messenger : Raimondi

April 10
MADAMA BUTTERFLY
Same as Feb. 14 except:
B. F. Pinkerton : Dippel
Sharpless : Scotti
Suzuki : Jacoby
Kate Pinkerton : Lawrence
Yamadori : Dufriche
Yakuside : Dragoni

April 11
TANNHÄUSER
Same as Dec. 11 except:
Tannhäuser : Burgstaller
Wolfram : Goritz
Reinmar : Dufriche
Elisabeth : Farrar

April 12
LA BOHÈME
Same as Jan. 31 except:
Rodolfo : Caruso
Mimi : Ciaparelli (t)
Parpignol : Raimondi
Alcindoro : Dufriche

April 13 (mat.)
TOSCA
Same as Mar. 27

April 13
HÄNSEL UND GRETEL
Same as Mar. 5 except:
Witch : Jacoby
Dewman : Vail

PAGLIACCI
Same as Feb. 5 except:
Nedda : Alten
Canio : Caruso
Tonio : Stracciari

CINCINNATI
April 15
AIDA
Same as Feb. 7 except:
Amneris : Jacoby (for
 Homer)
Aida : Rappold
Ramfis : Journet
Messenger : Raimondi

April 16 (mat.)
TANNHÄUSER
Same as Dec. 11 except:
Tannhäuser : Burgstaller
Reinmar : Dufriche
Elisabeth : Farrar

April 16
HÄNSEL UND GRETEL
Same as Mar. 5 except:
Witch : Schumann-Heink
Dewman : Vail

ST. LOUIS
April 17
AIDA
Same as Feb. 7 except:
Amneris : Jacoby (for
 Homer)
Ramfis : Journet
Messenger : Raimondi

April 18 (mat.)
MADAMA BUTTERFLY
Same as Feb. 14 except:
B. F. Pinkerton : Dippel
Sharpless : Scotti
Suzuki : Jacoby
Kate Pinkerton : Lawrence
Yamadori : Dufriche
Yakuside : Dragoni

April 18
TANNHÄUSER
Same as Dec. 11 except:
Tannhäuser : Burgstaller
Wolfram : Goritz
Reinmar : Dufriche
Elisabeth : Rappold

April 19
LA BOHÈME
Same as Jan. 31 except:
Rodolfo : Caruso
Marcello : Stracciari
Mimi : Ciaparelli
Parpignol : Raimondi
Alcindoro : Dufriche

KANSAS CITY
April 20 (mat.)
TOSCA
Same as Mar. 27 except:
Shepherd : Jacoby

April 20
LA BOHÈME
Same as Jan. 31 except:
Rodolfo : Caruso
Marcello : Stracciari
Mimi : Farrar
Parpignol : Raimondi
Alcindoro : Dufriche

OMAHA
April 22 (mat.)
PAGLIACCI
Same as Feb. 5 except:
Nedda : Farrar
Canio : Bars

HÄNSEL UND GRETEL
Same as Mar. 5 except:
Witch : Jacoby (for Homer)
Dewman : Vail

April 22
LA BOHÈME
Same as Jan. 31 except:
Rodolfo : Caruso
Marcello : Stracciari
Mimi : Ciaparelli (for Abott)
Parpignol : Raimondi
Alcindoro : Dufriche

ST. PAUL
April 23
TANNHÄUSER
Same as Dec. 11 except:
Tannhäuser : Dippel (for
 Burgstaller)
Reinmar : Dufriche
Elisabeth : Eames
Shepherd : Mattfeld

April 24 (mat.)
PAGLIACCI
Same as Feb. 5 except:
Nedda : Farrar
Canio : Bars

HÄNSEL UND GRETEL
Same as Mar. 5 except:
Witch : Jacoby
Dewman : Vail

April 24
LA BOHÈME

Same as Jan. 31 except:
Rodolfo : Caruso
Marcello : Stracciari
Mimi : Ciaparelli
Musetta : Mattfeld
Parpignol : Raimondi
Alcindoro : Dufriche

MINNEAPOLIS
April 25
MADAMA BUTTERFLY

Same as Feb. 14 except:
B. F. Pinkerton : Dippel
Sharpless : Scotti
Suzuki : Jacoby
Kate Pinkerton : Lawrence
Yamadori : Dufriche
Yakuside : Dragoni

April 26 (mat.)
AIDA

Same as Feb. 7 except:
Amneris : Jacoby
Aida : Rappold
Ramfis : Journet
Messenger : Raimondi

April 26
TOSCA

Same as Mar. 27

MILWAUKEE
April 27 (mat.)
TANNHÄUSER

Same as Dec. 11 except:
Tannhäuser : Dippel (for
   Burgstaller)
Reinmar : Dufriche
Elisabeth : Farrar

April 27
HÄNSEL UND GRETEL

Same as Mar. 5 except:
Witch : Jacoby
Dewman : Vail

PAGLIACCI

Same as Feb. 5 except:
Nedda : Alten
Canio : Caruso
Tonio : Stracciari

1 9 0 7 – 0 8

PHILADELPHIA
November 26
MEFISTOFELE/Ferrari (c)

Marguerite : Farrar
Helen of Troy : Rappold
Martha : Girerd

Pantalis : Jacoby
Mefistofele : Chaliapin
Faust : Martin
Wagner : Tecchi
Nereus : Tecchi

December 3
RIGOLETTO/Ferrari (c)

Duke : Bonci
Rigoletto : Stracciari
Gilda : Sembrich
Maddalena : Jacoby
Giovanna : Girerd
Sparafucile : Journet
Monterone : Mühlmann
Marullo : Bégué
Borsa : Tecchi
Ceprano : Dufriche
Countess : Lawrence
Page : Vail
Guard : Navarini

December 10
DIE MEISTERSINGER/Hertz (c)

Hans Sachs : Van Rooy
Pogner : Blass
Eva : Gadski
Magdalene : Mattfeld
Walther : Knote
Beckmesser : Goritz
Kothner : Mühlmann
Vogelgesang : Bayer
Nachtigall : Dufriche
Ortel : Friedberg
Moser : Quesnel
Zorn : Hindemeyer
Eisslinger : Ricker
Schwarz : Waterous
Foltz : Gunther
David : Reiss
Night Watchman : Dufriche

December 31
IL BARBIERE DI SIVIGLIA
Ferrari (c)

Almaviva : Bonci
Dr. Bartolo : Baracchi
Rosina : Fornia (for
   Sembrich)
Figaro : Campanari
Berta : Girerd
Don Basilio : Chaliapin
Fiorello : Bégué
Notary : Tecchi

January 7
LOHENGRIN/Hertz (c)

King Henry : Blass
Lohengrin : Knote
Elsa : Eames
Telramund : Goritz
Ortrud : Kirkby-Lunn (for
   Homer)
Herald : Mühlmann

January 14
ADRIANA LECOUVREUR
Ferrari (c)

Adriana : Cavalieri
Princess : Jacoby
Jouvenot : Mattfeld
Dangeville : Girerd
Maurizio : Caruso
Abbé : Lucas
Michonnet : Scotti
Prince de Bouillon : Journet
Quinault : Baracchi
Poisson : Raimondi
Majordomo : Navarini

January 17
MADAMA BUTTERFLY
Ferrari (c)

Cio-Cio-San : Farrar
B. F. Pinkerton : Caruso
Sharpless : Scotti
Suzuki : Jacoby
Kate Pinkerton : Lawrence
Goro : Reiss
Yamadori : Dufriche
Uncle-Priest : Mühlmann
Imperial Commissioner :
   Bégué
Yakuside : Baracchi

January 21
LA TRAVIATA/Ferrari (c)

Violetta : Sembrich
Alfredo : Bonci
Germont : Stracciari
Flora : Mattfeld
Annina : Girerd
Gastone : Tecchi
Baron Douphol : Navarini
Marquis d'Obigny : Bégué
Doctor Grenvil : Dufriche

January 28
TRISTAN UND ISOLDE
Mahler (c)

Tristan : Knote
Isolde : Fremstad
King Marke : Blass
Kurvenal : Van Rooy
Brangaene : Homer
Melot : Mühlmann
Steersman : Bayer
Shepherd : Reiss
Sailor's Voice : Reiss

February 4
IRIS/Ferrari (c)

Iris : Eames
Geisha : Fornia
Beauty : Menconi
Vampire : Hesch
Death : Jirasek
Osaka : Caruso
Kyoto : Scotti
Blindman : Journet

Ragpicker : Tecchi
Peddler : Raimondi

February 11
DIE WALKÜRE/Mahler (c)
Wotan : Van Rooy
Fricka : Kirkby-Lunn
Brünnhilde : Gadski
Siegmund : Burgstaller
Sieglinde : Fremstad
Hunding : Blass
Helmwige : Fornia
Gerhilde : Alten
Ortlinde : Weed
Rossweisse : Jacoby
Grimgerde : Langendorf
Waltraute : Kirkby-Lunn
Siegrune : Mattfeld
Schwertleite : Wöhning

February 18
DON GIOVANNI/Mahler (c)
Don Giovanni : Scotti
Donna Anna : Weed (for
    Eames)
Donna Elvira : Fornia
Zerlina : Farrar
Commendatore : Blass
Don Ottavio : Bonci
Leporello : Chaliapin
Masetto : Baracchi

February 25
LA BOHÈME/Ferrari (c)
Rodolfo : Bonci
Marcello : Scotti
Schaunard : Bégué
Colline : Baracchi
Mimi : Cavalieri
Musetta : Deleyne
Benoit : Fin...che
Parpignol : Tecchi
Alcindoro : Dufriche
Sergeant : Navarini

March 3
IL TROVATORE/Ferrari (c)
Leonora : Eames
Manrico : Caruso
Count di Luna : Stracciari
Azucena : Homer
Inez : Mattfeld
Ferrando : Mühlmann
Ruiz : Raimondi (for Tecchi)
Gypsy : Navarini

March 10
TANNHÄUSER/Hertz (c)
Hermann : Blass
Tannhäuser : Dippel (for
    Burrian after Act I)
Wolfram : Van Rooy
Walther : Reiss
Biterolf : Mühlmann
Heinrich : Bayer

Reinmar : Gunther
Elisabeth : Morena
Venus : Fremstad
Shepherd : Alten

March 17
AIDA/Ferrari (c)
King : Mühlmann
Amneris : Kirkby-Lunn
Aida : Eames
Radames : Caruso
Amonasro : Scotti
Ramfis : Plançon
Messenger : Tecchi
Priestess : Lawrence

March 24 (mat.)
SIEGFRIED/Mahler (c)
Siegfried : Burrian
Mime : Reiss
Wanderer : Van Rooy
Alberich : Goritz
Fafner : Blass
Erda : Kirkby-Lunn
Brünnhilde : Fremstad
Forest Bird : Alten

March 31 (mat.)
TOSCA/Ferrari (c)
Tosca : Eames
Cavaradossi : Caruso
Scarpia : Scotti
Angelotti : Dufriche
Sacristan : Baracchi
Spoletta : Lucas
Sciarrone : Bégué
Jailer : Navarini
Shepherd : Lawrence (for
    Jacoby)

BOSTON

April 6
IRIS
Same (?) as Feb. 4 except:
Blindman : Mühlmann
Ragpicker : Navarini

April 7
LA BOHÈME
Same as Feb. 25 except:
Marcello : Stracciari
Mimi : Farrar

April 8 (mat.)
IL TROVATORE
Same as Mar. 3 except:
Leonora : Fornia
Ruiz : Tecchi

April 8
DIE WALKÜRE
Same as Feb. 11 except:
Brünnhilde : Leffler-
    Burckhard
Siegmund : Burrian
Sieglinde : Morena
Grimgerde : Wakefield

April 9
DON GIOVANNI
Same as Feb. 18 except:
Donna Anna : Eames
Commendatore : Mühlmann
Leporello : Blass
Masetto : Dufriche

April 10
MANON LESCAUT/Ferrari (c)
Manon : Cavalieri
Lescaut : Scotti
Des Grieux : Caruso
Geronte : Baracchi
Edmondo : Lucas
Balletmaster : Delwary
Musician : Mattfeld
Sergeant : Navarini
Lamplighter : Reiss
Captain : Bégué

April 11 (mat.)
TRISTAN UND ISOLDE
Same as Jan. 28 except:
Tristan : Burgstaller

April 11
MIGNON/Bovy (c)
Mignon : Farrar
Philine : Abott
Wilhelm : Bonci
Lothario : Plançon
Laerte : Lucas
Jarno : Mühlmann
Frederic : Jacoby

BALTIMORE

April 13
MANON LESCAUT
Same as Apr. 10 except:
Lescaut : Stracciari
Lamplighter : Tecchi
Innkeeper : Bégué

April 14
LA TRAVIATA
Same as Jan. 21 except:
Violetta : Farrar
Germont : Scotti
Flora : Lawrence

April 15
IL TROVATORE
Same as Mar. 3 except:
Inez : Girerd
Ferrando : Bégué
Ruiz : Tecchi

WASHINGTON

April 16
LA BOHÈME
Same as Feb. 25 except:
Mimi : Abott (for Cavalieri)
Customs Officer : Dragoni

April 18 (mat.)

MIGNON

Same as Apr. 11 except:
Jarno : Bégué

April 18

CAVALLERIA RUSTICANA
Ferrari (c)
(Not given in New York)

Santuzza : Fornia
Lola : Jacoby
Turiddu : Martin
Alfio : Stracciari
Lucia : Girerd

PAGLIACCI/Ferrari (c)

Nedda : Dereyne
Canio : Caruso
Tonio : Scotti
Beppe : Reiss
Silvio : Sarto

CHICAGO

April 20

LA BOHÈME

Same as Feb. 25 except:
Mimi : Farrar
Musetta : Mattfeld
Customs Officer : Dragoni

April 21

IL TROVATORE

Same as Mar. 3 except:
Ruiz : Tecchi

April 22 (mat.)

FAUST/Bovy (c)

Faust : Martin
Marguerite : Farrar
Méphistophélès : Plançon
Valentin : Stracciari
Siébel : Jacoby
Marthe : Mattfeld
Wagner : Bégué

April 22

DIE WALKÜRE/Hertz (c)

Same as Feb. 11 except:
Wotan : Goritz
Fricka : Homer
Brünnhilde : Leffler-
    Burckhard
Siegmund : Burrian
Waltraute : Homer
Schwertleite : Wakefield

April 23

CAVALLERIA RUSTICANA

Same as Apr. 18 except:
Alfio : Bégué
Lucia : Mattfeld

PAGLIACCI

Same as Apr. 18 except:
Nedda : Alten
Silvio : Mühlmann

248

April 24

MIGNON

Same as Apr. 11

April 25 (mat.)

IRIS

Same (?) as Feb. 4 except:
Blindman : Mühlmann

April 25

TRISTAN UND ISOLDE/Hertz (c)

Same (?) as Jan. 28 except:
Tristan : Burgstaller
Kurvenal : Goritz

PITTSBURGH

April 27

FAUST

Same as Apr. 22 except:
Faust : Caruso
Marguerite : Eames
Valentin : Campanari

April 28

LA BOHÈME

Same as Feb. 25 except:
Mimi : Ciaparelli (for
    Abott)
Musetta : Alten
Customs Officer : Dragoni

April 29 (mat.)

IL TROVATORE

Same as Mar. 3 except:
Count di Luna : Campanari
Ruiz : Tecchi

April 29

DIE WALKÜRE/Hertz (c)

Wotan : Goritz
Fricka : Langendorff
Brünnhilde : Weed
Ortlinde : Vail
Waltraute : Wakefield
Schwertleite : Homer (for
    Lawrence)

1 9 0 8 – 0 9

METROPOLITAN OPERA
COMPANY
Giulio Gatti-Casazza, Andreas
Dippel, *Managers*

BROOKLYN

November 14

FAUST/Spetrino (c—d)

Faust : Caruso
Marguerite : Farrar
Méphistophélès : Didur (d)
Valentin : Noté (d)
Siébel : Fornia
Marthe : Mattfeld
Wagner : Ananian

PHILADELPHIA

November 17

LA BOHÈME/Spetrino (c)

Rodolfo : Caruso
Marcello : Scotti
Schaunard : Rossi
Colline : Didur
Mimi : Sembrich
Musetta : L'Huillier (d)
Benoit : Ananian
Parpignol : Bada
Alcindoro : Paterna
Sergeant : Missiano
Customs Officer : Tecchi

BROOKLYN

November 23

RIGOLETTO/Toscanini (c—
    for Spetrino)

Duke : Quarti (for Bonci)
Rigoletto : Amato
Gilda : Sembrich
Sparafucile : Didur
Maddalena : Homer
Monterone : Bozzano
Marullo : Ananian
Borsa : Tecchi
Countess : Mapleson

PHILADELPHIA

November 24

FAUST/Hageman (c—t)

Same as Nov. 14

December 1

AIDA/Toscanini (c)

King : Rossi
Amneris : Homer
Aida : Destinn
Radames : Caruso
Amonasro : Amato
Ramfis : Didur
Messenger : Bada
Priestess : Sparkes

BROOKLYN

December 2

DIE WALKÜRE/Hertz (c)

Wotan : Feinhals
Fricka : Homer
Brünnhilde : Gadski
Siegmund : Schmedes
Sieglinde : Fremstad
Hunding : Hinckley
Helmwige : Fornia
Gerhilde : Sparkes
Ortlinde : Van Dyck
Rossweisse : Randa
Grimgerde : Niessen-Stone
Waltraute : Homer
Siegrune : Mattfeld
Schwertleite : Wöhning

PHILADELPHIA
December 8
TIEFLAND/Hertz (c)
Sebastiano : Feinhals
Tommaso : Hinckley
Moruccio : Mühlmann
Marta : Destinn
Pepa : Fornia
Antonia : Mattfeld
Rosalia : Randa
Nuri : L'Huillier
Pedro : Schmedes
Nando : Reiss

BROOKLYN
December 14
TIEFLAND
Same as Dec. 8

PHILADELPHIA
December 15
TOSCA/Spetrino (c)
Tosca : Eames
Cavaradossi : Bonci
Scarpia : Scotti
Angelotti : Ananian
Sacristan : Paterna
Spoletta : Bada
Sciarrone : Bégué
Jailer : Missiano
Shepherd : Randa

December 22
LUCIA DI LAMMERMOOR
Spetrino (c)
Lucia : Sembrich
Ashton : Campanari
Edgardo : Bonci
Alisa : Mattfeld
Arturo : Bada
Raimondo : Rossi
Normanno : Tecchi

BROOKLYN
December 22
MADAMA BUTTERFLY
Toscanini (c)
Cio-Cio-San : Farrar
B. F. Pinkerton : Martin
Sharpless : Scotti
Suzuki : Fornia
Kate Pinkerton : Mapleson
Goro : Reiss
Yamadori : Tecchi
Uncle Priest : Mühlmann
Imperial Commissioner :
    Bégué

PHILADELPHIA
December 29
MADAMA BUTTERFLY
Same as Dec. 22 except:
Cio-Cio-San : Destinn
B. F. Pinkerton : Caruso

Sharpless : Amato (for
    Scotti)
Goro : Bada
Yakuside : Paterna

BROOKLYN
January 4
IL TROVATORE/Spetrino (c)
Leonora : Eames
Manrico : Caruso
Count di Luna : Amato
Azucena : Gay
Inez : Mattfeld
Ferrando : Rossi
Ruiz : Tecchi
Gypsy : Missiano

PHILADELPHIA
January 5
RIGOLETTO/Spetrino (c)
Same (?) as Nov. 23 except.
Duke : Bonci
Rigoletto : Campanari
Maddalena : Niessen-Stone
Giovanna : Wöhning
Ceprano : Tretti
Page : Borniggia

January 7 (mat.)
TRISTAN UND ISOLDE
    Mahler (c)
Tristan : Schmedes
Isolde : Fremstad
King Marke : Blass
Kurvenal : Feinhals
Brangaene · Homer
Melot : Mühlmann
Steersman : Bayer
Shepherd : Reiss
Sailor's Voice : Reiss

January 12
CARMEN/Toscanini (c)
Carmen : Gay
Don José : Caruso
Micaela : Rappold
Escamillo : Noté
Zuniga : Bégué
Morales : Cibelli
Frasquita : Fornia
Mercedes : Niessen-Stone
Dancaire : Bada
Remendado : Paterna

BROOKLYN
January 14
CARMEN
Same (?) as Jan. 12

PHILADELPHIA
January 19
LE VILLI/Toscanini (c)
Anna : Alda
Roberto : Bonci (for Martin)
Guglielmo : Amato

CAVALLERIA RUSTICANA
    Toscanini (c)
Santuzza : Destinn
Turiddu : Caruso
Lola : Gay
Alfio : Amato
Lucia : Mattfeld

BALTIMORE
January 20
MADAMA BUTTERFLY
Same as Dec. 22 except:
Cio-Cio-San : Destinn
B. F. Pinkerton : Caruso
Goro : Bada
Yakuside : Paterna

BROOKLYN
January 26
CAVALLERIA RUSTICANA
    Spetrino (c)
Same as Jan. 19 except:
Turiddu : Grassi (d)
Lucia : Niessen-Stone

PAGLIACCI/Spetrino (c)
Nedda : Fornia
Canio : Martin
Tonio : Amato
Beppe : Bada
Silvio : Campanari

PHILADELPHIA
January 26
LE NOZZE DI FIGARO
    Muhler (c)
Almaviva : Scotti
Countess · Eames
Susanna : Sembrich
Figaro : Didur
Cherubino : Farrar
Marcellina : Mattfeld
Bartolo : Rossi
Basilio : Reiss
Don Curzio : Maestri
Antonio : Dufriche (t)
Barbarina : L'Huillier

January 28 (mat.)
IL TROVATORE
Same as Jan. 4 except:
Leonora : Rappold
Count di Luna : Campanari
Azucena : Flahaut (for
    Homer)
Ferrando : Bozzano

February 2
DIE MEISTERSINGER/Hertz (c)
Hans Sachs : Feinhals
Pogner : Hinckley
Eva : Destinn
Magdalene : Homer
Walther : Jörn

Kothner : Mühlmann
Beckmesser : Goritz
Vogelgesang : Bayer
Nachtigall : Schubert
Zorn : Delwary
Eisslinger : Koch
Moser : Sundermann
Ortel : Triebner
Schwarz : Waterous
Foltz : Lötzsch
David : Reiss
Night Watchman : Ananian

BROOKLYN
February 4
LE NOZZE DI FIGARO
Mahler (c)
Same as Jan. 26 except:
Bartolo : Paterna
Don Curzio : Tecchi
Antonio : Ananian
Barbarina : Sparkes

February 6 (mat.)
HÄNSEL UND GRETEL
Hertz (c)
(Not given in New York)
Hänsel : Mattfeld
Gretel : Van Dyck
Witch : Homer
Gertrude : Kaschowska
Sandman : Snelling
Dewman : Sparkes
Peter : Goritz

BALTIMORE
February 10
FAUST
Same as Nov. 19 except:
Faust : Martin
Marguerite : Alda (for
Farrar)
Siébel : L'Huillier

PHILADELPHIA
February 16
TANNHÄUSER/Hertz (c)
Hermann : Blass
Tannhäuser : Burrian
Wolfram : Goritz (for
Feinhals)
Walther : Reiss
Biterolf : Mühlmann
Heinrich : Bayer
Reinmar : Gunther
Elisabeth : Morena
Venus : Fremstad
Shepherd : Sparkes

BROOKLYN
February 17
DIE MEISTERSINGER
Same (?) as Feb. 2

PHILADELPHIA
February 18
MANON/Spetrino (c)
Manon : Farrar
Lescaut : Scotti
Des Grieux : Jörn (for
Caruso)
Count des Grieux : Noté
Poussette : Sparkes
Javotte : Van Dyck
Rosette : Mattfeld
Guillot : Bada (for Reiss)
De Brétigny : Bégué
Innkeeper : Bozzano
Guards : Cibelli, Paterna

February 23
MADAMA BUTTERFLY
Same as Dec. 22 except:
B. F. Pinkerton : Grassi
Goro : Bada
Yakuside : Paterna

February 25
DIE VERKAUFTE BRAUT
Mahler (c)
Kruschina : Blass
Kathinka : Mattfeld
Marie : Destinn
Micha : Mühlmann
Agnes : Wakefield
Wenzel : Reiss
Hans : Jörn
Kezal : Didur
Springer : Marlow (t)
Esmeralda : L'Huillier
Muff : Bayer

March 2
DON PASQUALE/Spetrino (c)
Norina : De Pasquali
Ernesto : Grassi
Doctor Malatesta : Scotti
Don Pasquale : Paterna
(for Campanari)
Notary : Cibelli

PAGLIACCI
Same as Jan. 26 except:
Nedda : De Pasquali (for
Destinn)
Canio : Caruso
Silvio : Cibelli

March 4
DAS RHEINGOLD/Hertz (c)
Wotan : Soomer
Donner : Waterous
Froh : Jörn
Loge : Burrian
Alberich : Goritz
Mime : Reiss
Fasolt : Mühlmann
Fafner : Blass
Fricka : Fremstad

Freia : L'Huillier
Erda : Homer
Woglinde : Sparkes
Wellgunde : Mattfeld
Flosshilde : Ranzenberg

BROOKLYN
March 5
LA TRAVIATA (c?)
Violetta : De Pasquali
Alfredo : Bonci
Germont : Amato

BALTIMORE
March 8
HÄNSEL UND GRETEL
Same as Feb. 6

PAGLIACCI
Same (?) as Jan. 26 except:
Nedda : De Pasquali (for
Destinn)
Canio : Caruso
Silvio : LeComte

PHILADELPHIA
March 11
DIE WALKÜRE
Same (?) as Dec. 2 except:
Wotan : Soomer
Siegmund : Anthes
Sieglinde : Morena
Rossweisse : Ranzenberg

BROOKLYN
March 15
DIE VERKAUFTE BRAUT
Same (?) as Feb. 25

PHILADELPHIA
March 16
FALSTAFF/Toscanini (c)
Sir John Falstaff : Scotti
Ford : Campanari
Fenton : Grassi
Dr. Caius : Bada
Bardolph : Reiss
Pistol : Rossi
Mistress Ford : Destinn
Anne : Alda
Dame Quickly : Gay
Mistress Page : Ranzenberg

March 18
SIEGFRIED/Hertz (c)
Siegfried : Burrian
Mime : Reiss
Wanderer : Soomer
Alberich : Goritz
Fafner : Hinckley
Erda : Homer
Brünnhilde : Gadski
Forest Bird : Sparkes

BROOKLYN

March 24

AIDA

Same (?) as Dec. 1 except:
Radames : Martin

PHILADELPHIA

March 25

GÖTTERDÄMMERUNG/Hertz (c)

Siegfried : Burrian
Gunther : Mühlmann
Hagen : Hinckley
Alberich : Goritz
Brünnhilde : Gadski
Gutrune : Fornia
Waltraute : Homer
Woglinde : Sparkes
Wellgunde : Mattfeld
Flosshilde : Homer
(Norn scene omitted)

BALTIMORE

March 29

LA BOHÈME

Same as Nov. 17 except:
Rodolfo : Bonci
Marcello : Amato
Schaunard : Bozzano
Mimi : Farrar
Musetta : Sparkes
Parpignol : Orlandi
Sergeant : Raimondi
Customs Officer : Carreri (t)

BROOKLYN

April 5

LA BOHÈME

Same as Nov. 17 except:
Rodolfo : Bonci
Marcello : Amato
Schaunard : Bozzano
Mimi : Farrar
Musetta : Mattfeld

CHICAGO

April 12

AIDA

Same as Dec. 1 except:
Radames : Zenatello (t)

April 13

DIE MEISTERSINGER

Same as Feb. 2 except:
Hans Sachs : Soomer
Pogner : Blass
Eva : Gadski
Schwarz : Gunther

April 14 (mat.)

LUCIA DI LAMMERMOOR

Same as Dec. 22 except:
Lucia : De Pasquali
Ashton : Amato
Normanno : Bedeschi

CAVALLERIA RUSTICANA
Spetrino (c)

Same as Jan. 19 except:
Santuzza : Morena
Turiddu : Martin
Lola : Ranzenberg

April 14

FALSTAFF/Spetrino (c—for
Toscanini)

Same as Mar. 16 except:
Pistol : Didur

April 15

MADAMA BUTTERFLY

Same as Dec. 22 except:
B. F. Pinkerton : Zenatello
Kate Pinkerton : Sparkes
Goro : Bada
Yakuside : Paterna

April 16

DIE WALKÜRE

Same (?) as Dec. 2 except:
Wotan : Soomer
Siegmund : Anthes
Sieglinde : Morena
Rossweisse : Ranzenberg
Grimgerde : Böhn (t)

April 17 (mat.)

LA BOHÈME

Same as Nov. 17 except:
Rodolfo : Bonci
Marcello : Amato
Schaunard : Didur
Colline : Rossl
Mimi : Farrar
Musetta : Mattfeld (for
Sparkes)
Customs Officer : Raimondi

April 17

DIE VERKAUFTE BRAUT
Hertz (c)

Same as Feb. 25 except:
Kruschina : Witherspoon
Springer : Bayer
Muff : Burgstaller

April 18

PARSIFAL/Hertz (c)

Amfortas : Amato
Titurel : Witherspoon
Gurnemanz : Hinckley
Parsifal : Anthes (for
Burrian)
Klingsor : Goritz
Kundry : Fremstad
A Voice : Homer
Knights of the Grail :
Bayer, Mühlmann
Esquires : Fornia, Wakefield,
Reiss, Harden

Flower Maidens : Sparkes,
Fornia, Van Dyck,
L'Huillier, Wakefield,
Mattfeld

April 19

LE NOZZE DI FIGARO
Hertz (c)

Same as Jan. 26 except:
Countess : Gadski
Susanna : De Pasquali
Bartolo : Paterna
Don Curzio : Bada
Antonio : Ananian
Peasant Girls : Sparkes,
Wakefield

April 20

TANNHÄUSER

Same as Feb. 16 except:
Hermann : Hinckley
Tannhäuser : Jörn

April 21 (mat.)

FAUST

Same (?) as Nov. 19 except:
Faust : Zenatello
Marguerite : Alda
Valentin : Amato (?)

April 21

TRISTAN UND ISOLDE
Hertz (c?)

Same (?) as Jan. 7 except:
Tristan : Anthes
Isolde : Gadski
King Marke : Hinckley
Kurvenal : Goritz

April 22 (mat.)

MADAMA BUTTERFLY

Same as Dec. 29 except:
Kate Pinkerton : Sparkes
Goro : Bada
Yakuside : Paterna

April 22

HÄNSEL UND GRETEL
Hageman (c—for Hertz)

Same as Feb. 6

PAGLIACCI

Same as Jan. 26 except:
Nedda : De Pasquali
Canio : Zenatello
Tonio : Scotti
Silvio : Bégué

April 23

AIDA

Same as Dec. 1 except:
Amneris : Flahaut
Aida : Rappold
Radames : Martin (for
Zenatello)

MANON
April 24 (mat.)

Same (?) as Feb. 18 except:
Count des Grieux : Rossi
Poussette : Fornia
Javotte : L'Huillier
Rosette : Wakefield
Guillot : Reiss

April 24
GÖTTERDÄMMERUNG
Toscanini (c)

Same (?) as Mar. 25 except:
Siegfried : Anthes
Wellgunde : Wakefield (?)

April 25 (mat.)
IL TROVATORE

Same as Jan. 4 except:
Leonora : Adaberto
Manrico : Martin (for
  Zenatello)
Inez : Borniggia
Ferrando : Witherspoon
Ruiz : Bada

April 25
DIE VERKAUFTE BRAUT
Hertz (c)

Same as Feb. 25 except:
Kruschina : Witherspoon
Marie : Gadski
Springer : Bayer
Muff : Burgstaller

PITTSBURGH
April 26
FAUST

Same as Nov. 14 except:
Faust : Zenatello
Valentin : Amato

April 27
TANNHÄUSER

Same as Feb. 16 except:
Hermann : Hinckley
Tannhäuser : Jörn
Elisabeth : Gadski
Venus : Kaschowska

April 28 (mat.)
MADAMA BUTTERFLY

Same as Dec. 22 except:
B. F. Pinkerton : Grassi
Kate Pinkerton : L'Huillier
Goro : Bada
Yakuside : Paterna

April 28
AIDA

Same as Dec. 1 except:
Aida : Rappold
Radames : Zenatello

252

1909 – 10

BROOKLYN
November 8
MANON/Podesti (c—d)

Manon : Farrar
Des Grieux : Jörn
Lescaut : Dutilloy (d)
Count des Grieux : Rossi
Poussette : Sparkes
Javotte : Van Dyck
Rosette : Wakefield
Guillot : Reiss
De Brétigny : Régis (d)
Guards : Missiano,
  Reschiglian (d)

PHILADELPHIA
November 9
AIDA/Toscanini (c)

King : Rossi
Amneris : Homer
Aida : Gadski
Radames : Caruso
Amonasro : Amato
Ramfis : Hinckley
Messenger : Bada
Priestess : Sparkes

November 11 (mat.)
MADAMA BUTTERFLY
Podesti (c)

Cio-Cio-San : Farrar
B. F. Pinkerton : Martin
Sharpless : Scotti
Suzuki : Fornia
Kate Pinkerton : Mapleson
Goro : Reiss
Uncle-Priest : Mühlmann
Yamadori : Gianoli-Galletti
  (d)
Yakuside : Bourgeois (d)
Imperial Commissioner :
  Bégué

BALTIMORE
November 12
TANNHÄUSER/Hertz (c)

Hermann : Hinckley
Tannhäuser : Jörn
Wolfram : Goritz
Walther : Hall (d)
Biterolf : Mühlmann
Heinrich : Bayer
Reinmar : Gunther
Elisabeth : Gadski
Venus : Noria (d)
Shepherd : Sparkes

BROOKLYN
November 15
TANNHÄUSER

Same as Nov. 12 except:
Tannhäuser : Burrian

Wolfram : Whitehill (d)
Walther : Reiss

PHILADELPHIA
November 16
LA BOHÈME/Podesti (c)

Rodolfo : Bonci
Marcello : Amato
Schaunard : Didur
Colline : Rossi
Mimi : Nielsen (d)
Musetta : Alten
Benoit : Gianoli-Galletti
Parpignol : Tecchi
Alcindoro : Gianoli-Galletti
Sergeant : Missiano
Customs Officer : Tecchi

November 18
TANNHÄUSER

Same as Nov. 12 except:
Tannhäuser : Burrian
Wolfram : Whitehill

BROOKLYN
November 22
MADAMA BUTTERFLY

Same as Nov. 11 except:
Cio-Cio-San : Destinn
B. F. Pinkerton : Caruso
Sharpless : De Segurola
Yamadori : Tecchi
Uncle-Priest : Wulman

BALTIMORE
November 23
LA TRAVIATA/Podesti (c)

Violetta : Lipkowska
Alfredo : Bonci
Germont : Campanari
Flora : Niessen-Stone
Annina : Mattfeld
Gastone : Tecchi
Baron Douphol : Missiano
Marquis d'Obigny :
  Mühlmann
Doctor Grenvil : Ananian

PHILADELPHIA
November 23
OTELLO/Toscanini (c)

Otello : Slezak
Desdemona : Alda
Iago : Amato (for Scotti)
Emilia : Wickham
Cassio : Bada
Roderigo : Audisio
Lodovico : Witherspoon (for
  Hinckley)
Montano : Reschiglian
Herald : Bégué

BROOKLYN
November 29
TOSCA/Tango (c)

Tosca : Farrar

Cavaradossi : Martin
Scarpia : Scotti
Angelotti : Ananian
Sacristan : Gianoli-Galletti
Spoletta : Bada
Sciarrone : Reschiglian
Jailer : Missiano
Shepherd : Wickham

PHILADELPHIA
November 30
LA GIOCONDA/Toscanini (c)

La Gioconda : Destinn
Laura : Fabbri (for Homer)
Alvise : De Segurola
La Cieca : Meitschik
Enzo : Caruso
Barnaba : Amato
Zuane : Bégué
Singer : Missiano
Isepo : Tecchi

December 2
DIE VERKAUFTE BRAUT
Hertz (c)

Kruschina : Witherspoon
Kathinka : Mattfeld
Marie : Destinn
Micha : Mühlmann
Agnes : Wakefield
Wenzel : Reiss
Hans : Jörn
Kezal : Didur
Springer : Bayer
Esmeralda : Gluck
Muff : Burgstaller

BALTIMORE
December 3
TOSCA
Same as Nov. 29 except:
Spoletta : Devaux
Shepherd : Snelling

BROOKLYN
December 6
LOHENGRIN/Hertz (c)
King Henry : Hinckley
Lohengrin : Jörn
Elsa : Gadski
Telramund : Goritz
Ortrud : Homer
Herald : Witherspoon

BALTIMORE
December 7
OTELLO/Podesti (c)
Same as Nov. 23 except:
Lodovico : De Segurola
Herald : Rometi (t)

PHILADELPHIA
December 7
TOSCA
Same as Nov. 29 except:

Tosca : Fremstad
Cavaradossi : Bonci (for
Martin)
Spoletta : Devaux (for Bada)
Sciarrone : Bégué
Shepherd : Snelling

BROOKLYN
December 13
MARTHA/Podesti (c)
(Not given in New York)
Harriet : De Pasquali
Nancy : Fabbri
Lionel : Bonci
Plunkett : Didur
Tristan : Gianoli-Galletti

PHILADELPHIA
December 14
LOHENGRIN
Same as Dec. 6 except:
Elsa : Fremstad
Ortrud : Wickham
Herald : Mühlmann

December 16
IL TROVATORE/Tango (c)
Leonora : Nordica
Manrico : Slezak
Count di Luna : Gilly
Azucena : Flahaut (for
Meitschik)
Inez : Borniggia
Ferrando : Rossi
Ruiz : Tecchi
Gypsy : Daracchi

BALTIMORE
December 17
IL MAESTRO DI CAPELLA
Podesti (c)
(From New Theatre)
Barnaba : Pini-Corsi
Bonetto : Bada
Gertrude : Gluck

BALLET DIVERTISSEMENT :
Rita Sacchetto

PAGLIACCI/Bendix (c)
Nedda : Noria
Canio : Caruso
Tonio : Amato
Beppe : Bada
Silvio : Gilly

BROOKLYN
December 20
IL TROVATORE
Same as Dec. 16 except:
Leonora : Gadski
Inez : Mattfeld
Ferrando : Witherspoon
Ruiz : Audisio

PHILADELPHIA
December 21
WERTHER/Tango (c)
Werther : Clément
Albert : Dutilloy
Le Bailli : Pini-Corsi
Schmitt : Devaux
Johann : Bourgeois
Bruhlmann : Koch
Charlotte : Farrar
Sophie : Gluck (for Heliane)
Kathchen : Michaelis

BALTIMORE
December 22
IL TROVATORE/Podesti (c)
Same as Dec. 16 except:
Azucena : Meitschik
Inez : Mattfeld

BROOKLYN
December 25 (mat.)
HÄNSEL UND GRETEL
Hertz (c)
Hänsel : Mattfeld
Gretel : Alten
Witch : Meitschik
Gertrude : Wickham
Peter : Goritz
Sandman : Snelling
Dewman : Sparkes

CZAR AND CARPENTER (Ballet)
Rothmeyer (c—for Bendix)

December 27
FAUST/Podesti (c)
Faust : Jörn
Marguerite : Noria (for
Farrar)
Méphistophélès : Didur
Valentin : Gilly
Siébel : Fornia
Marthe : Niessen-Stone
Wagner : Ananian

PHILADELPHIA
December 28
IL MAESTRO DI CAPELLA
Tanara (c—t)
Same as Dec. 17

BALLET DIVERTISSEMENT
Bendix (c)

PAGLIACCI/Tango (c)
Same as Dec. 17 except:
Silvio : Reschiglian (for
Gilly)

December 30 (mat.)
CAVALLERIA RUSTICANA
Podesti (c)
Santuzza : Destinn
Turiddu : Martin

Lola : Wickham
Alfio : Gilly
Lucia : Mattfeld

HÄNSEL UND GRETEL
Same as Dec. 25

BALTIMORE
December 31
HÄNSEL UND GRETEL
Same as Dec. 25 except:
Gretel : Van Dyck
Sandman : Sparkes
Dewman : Snelling

BALLET DIVERTISSEMENT
Bendix (c)

January 1 (mat.)
PARSIFAL/Hertz (c)
Amfortas : Whitehill
Titurel : Witherspoon
Gurnemanz : Blass
Parsifal : Burrian
Klingsor : Goritz
Kundry : Fremstad
A Voice : Wickham
Knights of the Grail :
  Bayer, Mühlmann
Esquires : Sparkes, Wakefield,
  Reiss, Haupt
Flower Maidens : Sparkes,
  Fornia, Van Dyck, Gluck,
  Mattfeld, Wakefield

BROOKLYN
January 3
IL MAESTRO DI CAPELLA
Tanara (c)
Same as Dec. 17 except:
Gertrude : Fornia

PAGLIACCI/Tango (c)
Same (?) as Dec. 17 except:
Nedda : Farrar (for Destinn)
Canio : Martin

BALLET DIVERTISSEMENT
Bendix (c)

PHILADELPHIA
January 4
TRISTAN UND ISOLDE
Toscanini (c)
Tristan : Burrian
Isolde : Fremstad (for
  Gadski)
King Marke : Blass
Kurvenal : Amato
Brangaene : Homer
Melot : Mühlmann
Steersman : Bayer
Shepherd : Reiss
Sailor's Voice : Hall

254

BALTIMORE
January 5
LA BOHÈME
Same as Nov. 16 except:
Marcello : Gilly
Schaunard : Pini-Corsi
Colline : Didur
Mimi : Alda
Benoit : Ananian
Parpignol : Bada

BOSTON
January 10
TRISTAN UND ISOLDE
Same as Jan. 4 except:
Brangaene : Wickham (for
  Homer)

PHILADELPHIA
January 11
MANON
Same as Nov. 8 except:
Count des Grieux :
  De Segurola
Poussette : Heliane
Javotte : Dubois
Rosette : Mattfeld
Guillot : Bada
De Brétigny : Reschiglian
Guard : Minot (t)
Servant : De Lievin

BOSTON
January 13
LOHENGRIN
Same as Dec. 6 except:
Telramund : Forsell
Ortrud : Wickham

January 14
TOSCA
Same as Nov. 29 except:
Angelotti : Rossi
Sciarrone : Bégué
Shepherd : Snelling

January 15 (mat.)
PARSIFAL
Same as Jan. 1 except:
Gurnemanz : Hinckley

January 15
HÄNSEL UND GRETEL
Same as Dec. 25

PAGLIACCI/Tango (c)
Same as Dec. 17 except:
Beppe : Reiss
Silvio : Reschiglian

BROOKLYN
January 17
AIDA
Same as Nov. 9 except:
Amneris : Flahaut

Aida : Destinn
Ramfis : Didur
Priestess : ? (for Sparkes)

PHILADELPHIA
January 18
CZAR UND ZIMMERMANN
Hertz (c)
(From New Theatre)
Peter the First : Forsell
Peter Ivanov : Reiss
Van Bett : Goritz
Marie : Alten
General Lefort : Mühlmann
Lord Syndham : Blass
Marquis de Chateauneuf :
  Jörn
Widow Browne : Mattfeld

BALTIMORE
January 19
AIDA/Podesti (c)
Same as Nov. 9 except:
Amneris : Flahaut (for
  Homer)
Radames : Slezak
Amonasro : Gilly
Ramfis : De Segurola
Priestess : Borniggia

PHILADELPHIA
January 25
LA FILLE DE MADAME ANGOT
Tango (c)
(From New Theatre)
Ange Pitou : Clément
Pompounet : Dutilloy
Larivaudiere : Pini-Corsi
Trénitz : Devaux
Louchard : Bourgeois
Cadet : Rossi
Guillaume : Bégué
Buteux : Ananian
Officer : Reschiglian
Incroyable : Rouvroy (t)
Clairette : Alda
Mlle. Lange : Maubourg
Amarante : Roma (t)
Javotte : Bernis (t)
Thérèse : Cabanier (t)
Babet : Legrande (t)
Mme. Delaunay : Gellys (t)
Hersilie : De Lievin

BROOKLYN
January 31
FRA DIAVOLO/Hertz (c)
Fra Diavolo : Clément
Milord : Devaux
Pamela : Maubourg
Lorenzo : Régis
Matteo : Ananian
Zerline : Alten
Beppo : Reiss
Giacomo : Bourgeois

PHILADELPHIA
February 1
FAUST
Same (?) as Dec. 27 except:
Faust : Jadlowker
Marguerite : Farrar
Siébel : Heliane

BALTIMORE
February 2
LA GIOCONDA
Same as Nov. 30

BROOKLYN
February 7
ALESSANDRO STRADELLA
Bendix (c)
Stradella : Slezak
Bassi : Mühlmann
Leonore : Gluck
Malvolio : Goritz
Barbarino : Reiss

BALLET DIVERTISSEMENT
Bendix (c)

PHILADELPHIA
February 8
DIE WALKÜRE/Hertz (c)
Wotan : Soomer
Fricka : Homer
Brünnhilde : Gadski
Siegmund : Burrian
Sieglinde : Fremstad
Hunding : Hinckley
Helmwige : Fornia
Gerhilde : Sparkes
Örtlinde : Van Dyck
Rossweisse : Wickham
Grimgerde : Niessen-Stone
Waltraute : Homer
Siegrune : Mattfeld
Schwertleite : Wöhning

February 10
RIGOLETTO/Podesti (c)
Duke : Caruso
Rigoletto : Amato
Gilda : De Pasquali
Sparafucile : De Segurola
Maddalena : Niessen-Stone
Giovanna : Mattfeld
Monterone : Rossi
Marullo : Bégué (?)
Borsa : Audisio
Ceprano : Ananian
Countess : Mapleson
Page : Borniggia

BALTIMORE
February 11
MADAMA BUTTERFLY
Same as Nov. 11 except:
Goro : Bada

Yamadori : Devaux
Uncle-Priest : Wulman

BROOKLYN
February 14
L'ATTAQUE DU MOULIN
Tango (c)
(From New Theatre)
Françoise : Noria
Dominique : Clément
Marcelline : Delna
Miller : Gilly
German Captain :
De Segurola
Sentinel : Régis
Drummer : Ananian
French Captain : Devaux
Geneviève : Heliane
Sergeant : Bégué

PHILADELPHIA
February 15
GERMANIA/Toscanini (c)
Giovanni Palmi : Rossi
Federico Loewe : Caruso
Carlo Worms : Amato
Crisogono : Pini-Corsi
Ricke : Destinn
Jane : Heliane
Lene Armuth : Mattfeld
Jebbel : Sparkes
Stapps : Didur
Luigi : Wulman
Carlo Körner : Nepoti
Hedvige : Mattfeld
Peters : Baracchi
Chief of Police : Missiano
Lady : Wickham
Youth : Barillo

BALTIMORE
February 16
RIGOLETTO/Tango (c)
Same (?) as Feb. 10 except:
Duke : Bonci
Rigoletto : Baklanoff (t)
Gilda : Nielsen
Sparafucile : Rossi
Monterone : Mühlmann

BROOKLYN
February 21
LA BOHÈME
Same as Nov. 16 except:
Marcello : Gilly
Schaunard : Reschiglian
Colline : De Segurola
Mimi : Farrar
Benoit : Ananian
Customs Officer : Maresi

PHILADELPHIA
February 24
L'ATTAQUE DU MOULIN
Same as Feb. 14

BALTIMORE
February 25
ALESSANDRO STRADELLA
Same as Feb. 7

PAGLIACCI/Voghera (c—t)
Same as Dec. 17 except:
Nedda : Fornia
Canio : Martin
Tonio : Forsell
Beppe : Reiss

BROOKLYN
February 28
OTELLO
Same as Nov. 23 except:
Iago : Scotti
Lodovico : De Segurola

PHILADELPHIA
March 1
FRA DIAVOLO
Same as Jan. 31

BALTIMORE
March 2
FAUST
Same as Dec. 27 except:
Faust : Bonci
Marguerite : Gluck
Méphistophélès : De Segurola
Marthe : Mattfeld
Wagner : Bégué

BROOKLYN
March 7
LA GIOCONDA
Same as Nov. 30 except:
Laura : Homer

PHILADELPHIA
March 8
PARSIFAL
Same as Jan. 1 except:
Parsifal : Jörn

March 10
AIDA
Same as Nov. 9

BALTIMORE
March 11
IL BARBIERE DI SIVIGLIA
Podesti (c)
Almaviva : Bonci
Dr. Bartolo :
Gianoli-Galletti
Rosina : De Hidalgo
Figaro : Forsell
Don Basilio : De Segurola
Berta : Mattfeld
Fiorello : Reschiglian
Sergeant : Audisio

255

BALLET DIVERTISSEMENT :
Pavlowa and Mordkin

BROOKLYN
March 14
IL BARBIERE DI SIVIGLIA
Tanara (c)
Same as Mar. 11 except:
Dr. Bartolo : Pini-Corsi
Berta : Borniggia

BALTIMORE
March 16
MANON/Tanara (c)
Same as Nov. 8 except:
Lescaut : Scotti
Poussette : Heliane
Guillot : Devaux
Guard : Minot
Servant : Cabanier

BROOKLYN
March 21
RIGOLETTO/Tango (c)
Same (?) as Feb. 10 except:
Rigoletto : Campanari (for
Amato)
Gilda : De Hidalgo
Maddalena : Maubourg
Giovanna : Borniggia
Borsa : Bada

BALTIMORE
March 22
DIE WALKÜRE
Same as Feb. 8 except:
Wotan : Whitehill
Fricka : Flahaut
Siegmund : Hyde (d)
Hunding : Blass
Grimgerde : Wakefield
Waltraute : Flahaut
Siegrune : Mattfeld

BOSTON
March 28
AIDA
Same as Nov. 9 except:
Aida : Destinn
Ramfis : De Segurola
Priestess : ? (for Sparkes)

March 29
MADAMA BUTTERFLY
Same as Nov. 11 except:
Goro : Bada
Uncle-Priest : Wulman
Imperial Commissioner :
Reschiglian

BROOKLYN
March 29
DER FREISCHÜTZ/Hertz (c)
Ottokar : Goritz

Cuno : Mühlmann
Agathe : Gadski
Aennchen : Alten
Caspar : Blass
Max : Jadlowker
Samiel : Bayer
Hermit : Witherspoon
Kilian : Reiss
Bridesmaids : Sparkes, Case,
Heliane

BOSTON
March 30 (mat.)
MARTHA
Same as Dec. 13 except:
Henrietta : De Hidalgo
Nancy : Homer
Sheriff : Wulman

COPPELIA (Ballet)
Swanhilda : Pavlowa
Frantz : Mordkin
Poupée : De Lievin
Coppelius : Saracco
Bourgmestre : Morandi

March 30
LA BOHÈME
Same as Nov. 16 except:
Rodolfo : Caruso
Marcello : Gilly
Schaunard : Pini-Corsi
Colline : De Segurola
Mimi : Gluck
Musetta : Sparkes
Sergeant : Cottino (t)

April 2 (mat.)
TOSCA
Same as Nov. 29 except:
Spoletta : Devaux
Sciarrone : Bégué
Shepherd : Snelling

April 2
DIE MEISTERSINGER
Toscanini (c)
Hans Sachs : Soomer
Pogner : Blass
Eva : Gadski
Magdalene : Wickham
Walther : Jörn (for Slezak)
Beckmesser : Goritz
Kothner : Mühlmann
Vogelgesang : Hall
Nachtigall : Rehkopf
Zorn : Bayer
Eisslinger : Koch
Moser : Otto
Ortel : Triebner
Schwarz : Gunther
Foltz : Reiner
David : Reiss
Night Watchman : Ananian

BROOKLYN
April 4
MADAMA BUTTERFLY
Tanara (c)
Same as Nov. 11 except:
B. F. Pinkerton : Hyde
Kate Pinkerton : Heliane
Imperial Commissioner :
Reschiglian

BALLET DIVERTISSEMENT :
Pavlowa and Mordkin

SPLIT TOUR—Part 1

CHICAGO
April 4
LA GIOCONDA
Same as Nov. 30 except:
Laura : Homer
La Cieca : Meitschik

April 5
RIGOLETTO
Same as Feb. 10 except:
Duke : Bonci
Rigoletto : Campanari (for
Amato)
Gilda : Nielsen
Sparafucile : Didur
Maddalena : Meitschik
Marullo : Ananian
Borsa : Bada
Ceprano : Missiano
Countess : Maubourg

April 6 (mat.)
LA BOHÈME
Same as Nov. 16 except:
Rodolfo : Caruso
Marcello : Campanari
Musetta : Sparkes
Benoit : Pini-Corsi
Parpignol : Bada
Alcindoro : Pini-Corsi

April 6
OTELLO
Same as Nov. 23 except:
Iago : Scotti
Emilia : Maubourg
Lodovico : De Segurola

April 7
L'ELISIR D'AMORE/Podesti (c)
Adina : De Pasquali
Gianetta : Mattfeld
Nemorino : Bonci
Belcore : Campanari
Dulcamara : Pini-Corsi

CAVALLERIA RUSTICANA
Same as Dec. 30 except:
Lola : Maubourg

AIDA

April 8

Same as Nov. 9 except:
Radames : Slezak
Amonasro : Gilly
Ramfis : De Segurola

April 9 (mat.)
GERMANIA

Same as Feb. 15 except:
Lene Armuth : Maubourg
Hedvige : Maubourg

April 9
MARTHA/Voghera (c)

Same as Dec. 13 except:
Harriet : Nielsen
Nancy : Homer
Tristan : Pini-Corsi
Sheriff : Wulman

April 11
MADAMA BUTTERFLY
Toscanini (c)

Same as Nov. 11 except:
Kate Pinkerton : Sparkes
Goro : Bada
Yamadori : Devaux
Uncle-Priest : Wulman
Yakuside : Cerri (t)

April 12
IL TROVATORE/Podesti (c)

Same as Dec. 16 except:
Leonora : Gadski
Count di Luna : Amato

April 13 (mat.)
IL BARBIERE DI SIVIGLIA

Same as Mar. 11 except:
Dr. Bartolo : Pini-Corsi
Figaro : Campanari
Don Basilio : Didur
Berta : Borniggia
Fiorello : Bégué

April 13
AIDA

Same as Nov. 9 except:
Aida : Destinn
Amonasro : Gilly
Ramfis : De Segurola
Priestess : Borniggia

April 14
OTELLO

Same as Nov. 23 except:
Emilia : Maubourg
Lodovico : De Segurola

April 15
LA GIOCONDA

Same as Nov. 30 except:
Laura : Homer
La Cieca : Fabbri
Enzo : Martin

April 16 (mat.)
IL MAESTRO DI CAPELLA
Podesti (c)

Same as Dec. 17

LA TRAVIATA—*Act I*

Same as Nov. 23 except:
Violetta : De Pasquali
Flora : Maubourg
Gastone : Audisio
Baron Douphol : Marina (t)
Marquis d'Obigny : Bégué

RIGOLETTO—*Act IV*

Same as Feb. 16 except:
Rigoletto : Campanari
Gilda : De Hidalgo
Sparafucile : De Segurola
Maddalena : Maubourg

LUCIA DI LAMMERMOOR—
Act III

Lucia : De Pasquali
Raimondo : Rossi

April 16
CAVALLERIA RUSTICANA

Same as Dec. 30 except:
Santuzza : Gadski
Lola : Maubourg
Lucia : Borniggia

PAGLIACCI/Podesti (c)

Same as Dec. 17 except:
Nedda : Alten

April 18
DIE MEISTERSINGER

Same as Apr. 2 except:
Walther : Slezak

April 19
MADAMA BUTTERFLY

Same as Nov. 11 except:
B. F. Pinkerton : Hyde
Kate Pinkerton : Sparkes
Goro : Bada
Uncle-Priest : Wulman
Imperial Commissioner :
Reschiglian

April 20 (mat.)
FAUST

Same as Dec. 27 except:
Faust : Caruso
Marguerite : Gluck
Méphistophélès : De Segurola
Marthe : Maubourg

April 20
IL MAESTRO DI CAPELLA

Same as Dec. 17 except:
Gertrude : Fornia

DON PASQUALE/Voghera (c)

Norina : Nielsen

Ernesto : Bonci
Doctor Malatesta : Scotti
Don Pasquale : Pini-Corsi
Notary : Tecchi

April 21
LA BOHÈME

Same as Nov. 16 except:
Rodolfo : Jadlowker
Marcello : Campanari
Schaunard : Pini-Corsi
Colline : De Segurola
Benoit : Ananian
Customs Officer : Maresi

April 22
IL BARBIERE DI SIVIGLIA
(for *Rigoletto*—"by
request")

Same as Mar. 11 except:
Dr. Bartolo : Pini-Corsi
Figaro : Campanari
Berta : Borniggia
Fiorello : Bégué

April 23 (mat.)
MARTHA

Same as Dec. 13 except:
Harriet : Nielsen
Nancy : Homer
Plunkett : Rossi
Tristan : Pini-Corsi
Sheriff : Wulman

April 23
FRA DIAVOLO/Bendix (o for
Hertz)

Same as Jan. 31 except:
Beppo : Gianoli-Galletti

April 24
PARSIFAL

Same as Jan. 1 except:
Gurnemanz : Hinckley
Parsifal : Jörn
A Voice : Meitschik

April 25
TOSCA

Same as Nov. 29 except:
Spoletta : Devaux
Sciarrone : Bégué
Shepherd : Koch-Böhm (t)

April 26
LOHENGRIN

Same as Dec. 6 except:
Lohengrin : Jadlowker
Elsa : Fremstad
Telramund : Soomer

April 27 (mat.)
HÄNSEL UND GRETEL
Hageman (c—t)

Same as Dec. 25 except:

257

1909–10

Sandman : Wakefield
Dewman : Heliane

PAGLIACCI/Tango (c)
Same as Dec. 17 except:
Nedda : De Pasquali
Tonio : Forsell
Beppe : Reiss
Silvio : Reschiglian

April 27
TANNHÄUSER
Same as Nov. 12 except:
Hermann : Witherspoon
Wolfram : Soomer
Walther : Reiss
Elisabeth : Destinn
Venus : Fremstad

April 28
DIE WALKÜRE
Same as Feb. 8 except:
Wotan : Whitehill
Siegmund : Hyde
Sieglinde : Osborn-Hannah
Hunding : Blass
Grimgerde : Wakefield
Schwertleite : Koch-Böhm

April 29
LA BOHÈME
Same as Nov. 16 except:
Rodolfo : Caruso
Marcello : Campanari
Schaunard : Pini-Corsi
Colline : De Segurola
Mimi : Ciaparelli
Musetta : Sparkes
Sergeant : Cottino
Customs Officer : Maresi

April 30 (mat.)
MADAMA BUTTERFLY
Tanara (c)
Same as Nov. 11 except:
B. F. Pinkerton : Hyde
Uncle-Priest : Wulman
Imperial Commissioner :
Reschiglian

April 30
DIE VERKAUFTE BRAUT
Morgenstern (c)
Same as Dec. 2 except:
Kezal : Goritz
Esmeralda : Heliane

SPLIT TOUR—Part 2

BALTIMORE
April 5
LOHENGRIN
Same as Dec. 6 except:
Lohengrin : Jadlowker

258

Elsa : Fremstad
Ortrud : Wickham

April 6
CZAR UND ZIMMERMANN
Bendix (c)
Same as Jan. 18 except:
Widow Browne : Hinsen
(t—for Mattfeld)
Officer : Bayer
Cantor : Burgstaller

PITTSBURGH
April 7
LOHENGRIN
Same as Dec. 6 except:
Lohengrin : Jadlowker
Elsa : Fremstad
Telramund : Soomer
Ortrud : Wickham

April 8
TOSCA
Same as Nov. 29 except:
Cavaradossi : Jadlowker
Spoletta : Devaux
Sciarrone : Mühlmann
Jailer : Bourgeois
Shepherd : Koch-Böhm

April 9 (mat.)
HÄNSEL UND GRETEL
Hageman (c)
Same as Dec. 25 except:
Gretel : Van Dyck
Sandman : Wakefield
Dewman : Case

PAGLIACCI/Tango (c)
Nedda : Alten
Canio : Martin
Tonio : Forsell
Beppe : Régis
Silvio : Reschiglian

April 9
TANNHÄUSER
Same as Nov. 12 except:
Hermann : Blass
Wolfram : Whitehill
Elisabeth : Osborn-Hannah
Shepherd : Fornia

CLEVELAND
April 11
MARTHA/Voghera (c)
Same as Dec. 13 except:
Nancy : Homer
Lionel : Caruso
Sheriff : Rossi

April 12
LOHENGRIN
Same as Dec. 6 except:
Elsa : Fremstad

Telramund : Soomer
Ortrud : Wickham

April 13 (mat.)
HÄNSEL UND GRETEL
Same as Dec. 25 except:
Gretel : Van Dyck (for
Alten)

PAGLIACCI/Tango (c)
Nedda : Alten (for Noria)
Canio : Jörn
Tonio : Forsell
Beppe : Régis
Silvio : Reschiglian

April 13
MADAMA BUTTERFLY
Tanara (c)
Same as Nov. 11 except:
B. F. Pinkerton : Hyde
Suzuki : Mattfeld
Goro : Bada
Yamadori : Devaux

TOLEDO
April 14
LOHENGRIN
Same as Dec. 6 except:
King Henry : Blass
Lohengrin : Jadlowker
Elsa : Fremstad
Ortrud : Wickham
Herald : Mühlmann

DETROIT
April 15
TANNHÄUSER
Same as Nov. 12 except:
Hermann : Witherspoon
Wolfram : Whitehill
Walther : Reiss
Elisabeth : Osborn-Hannah
Shepherd : Heliane

April 16 (mat.)
HÄNSEL UND GRETEL
Hageman (c)
Same as Dec. 25 except:
Gretel : Van Dyck
Sandman : Wakefield
Dewman : Heliane

PAGLIACCI/Tanara (c)
Nedda : Courtenay
Canio : Jadlowker
Tonio : Forsell
Beppe : Reiss
Silvio : Reschiglian

April 16
MADAMA BUTTERFLY
Tanara (c)
Same as Nov. 11 except:
B. F. Pinkerton : Hyde

Kate Pinkerton : Sparkes
Yamadori : Devaux

MILWAUKEE
April 18
AIDA/Podesti (c—for
Toscanini)
Same as Nov. 9 except:
Aida : Destinn
Amonasro : Campanari (for
Amato)
Ramfis : Didur
Priestess : Laurier

April 19
LOHENGRIN
Same as Dec. 6 except:
Lohengrin : Jadlowker
Elsa : Fremstad
Telramund : Whitehill
Ortrud : Wickham

April 20 (mat.)
HÄNSEL UND GRETEL
Hageman (c)
Same as Dec. 25 except:
Dewman : Heliane

PAGLIACCI/Tango (c)
Same as Dec. 17 except:
Canio : Martin
Tonio : Forsell
Beppe : Reiss
Silvio : Reschiglian

April 20
TANNHÄUSER
Same as Nov. 12 except:
Hermann : Blass
Wolfram : Soomer
Shepherd : Oerner (t)

ST. PAUL
April 21
LOHENGRIN
Same as Dec. 6 except:
Elsa : Fremstad
Telramund : Whitehill

April 22 (mat.)
HÄNSEL UND GRETEL
Hageman (c)
Same as Dec. 25 except:
Gretel : Van Dyck (for
Alten)
Sandman : Wakefield
Dewman : Heliane

PAGLIACCI/Tango (c)
Same as Dec. 17 except:
Tonio : Forsell
Silvio : Reschiglian

April 22
AIDA/Tanara (c)
Same as Nov. 9 except:

King : Witherspoon
Amneris : Flahaut
Radames : Martin
Priestess : Laurier

April 23 (mat.)
MADAMA BUTTERFLY
Tanara (c)
Same as Nov. 11 except:
B. F. Pinkerton : Hyde
Kate Pinkerton : Heliane
Goro : Bada
Yamadori : Garden (t)
Yakuside : Cerri
Imperial Commissioner :
Reschiglian

April 23
DIE VERKAUFTE BRAUT
Morgenstern (c)
Same as Dec. 2 except:
Hans : Jadlowker
Kezal : Goritz

ST. LOUIS
April 25
LA BOHÈME
Same as Nov. 16 except:
Rodolfo : Caruso
Schaunard : Reschiglian
Colline : De Segurola
Mimi : Gluck (for Alda)
Musetta : Courtenay
Benoit : Ananian
Alcindoro : Pini-Corsi
Sergeant : Cottino

April 26
IL TROVATORE/Podesti (c)
Same as Dec. 16 except:
Leonora : Gadski
Manrico : Martin
Count di Luna : Amato

April 27 (mat.)
FAUST
Same as Dec. 27 except:
Faust : Bonci
Méphistophélès : De Segurola
Marthe : Maubourg

April 27
MADAMA BUTTERFLY
Tanara (c)
Same as Nov. 11 except:
B. F. Pinkerton : Hyde
Kate Pinkerton : Oerner
Goro : Bada
Yakuside : Cerri

INDIANAPOLIS
April 28
CAVALLERIA RUSTICANA
Tango (c)
Same as Dec. 30 except:

Turiddu : Jadlowker
Lola : Maubourg
Lucia : Borniggia

PAGLIACCI/Tango (c)
Same as Dec. 17 except:
Canio : Martin

April 29
IL TROVATORE
Same as Dec. 16 except:
Leonora : Gadski
Manrico : Martin
Azucena : Homer
Ruiz : Audisio

LOUISVILLE
April 30 (mat.)
RIGOLETTO
Same as Feb. 16 except:
Rigoletto : Amato
Gilda : De Hidalgo
Sparafucile : Hinckley
Maddalena : Meitschik
Giovanna : Borniggia
Monterone : Rossi
Marullo : Ananian
Ceprano : Missiano
Countess : Maubourg

April 30
CAVALLERIA RUSTICANA
Tango (c)
Same as Dec. 30 except:
Santuzza : Fremstad
Lola : Maubourg
Turiddu : Jadlowker
Lucia : Borniggia

PAGLIACCI/Tango (c)
Same as Dec. 17 except:
Nedda : Courtenay (for
De Pasquali)
Canio : Jadlowker

ATLANTA
May 2
LOHENGRIN
Same as Dec. 6 except:
King Henry : Blass
Elsa : Fremstad
Herald : Mühlmann

May 4 (mat.)
TOSCA
Same as Nov. 29 except:
Sacristan : Bourgeois
Sciarrone : Bégué

May 4
AIDA/Tanara (c)
Same as Nov. 9 except:
Ramfis : Blass
Priestess : Oerner

May 6
MADAMA BUTTERFLY
Tanara (c)
Same as Nov. 11 except:
Suzuki : Mattfeld
Kate Pinkerton : Oerner
Yamadori : Bada

May 7
HÄNSEL UND GRETEL
Same as Dec. 25 except:
Gretel : Van Dyck
Witch : Reiss
Sandman : Wakefield
Dewman : Case

PAGLIACCI/Tango (c)
Same as Dec. 17 except:
Beppe : Reiss
Silvio : Reschiglian

PARIS
May 19
AIDA (Public dress rehearsal)
Same as Nov. 9 except:
Aida : Destinn
Ramfis : De Segurola
Priestess : Roma (t)

May 21
AIDA
Same as Nov. 9 except:
Aida : Destinn
Ramfis : De Segurola
Priestess : Roma

May 23
CAVALLERIA RUSTICANA
Toscanini (c)
Santuzza : Fremstad
Turiddu : Jadlowker
Lola : Roma
Alfio : Amato
Lucia : Maubourg

PAGLIACCI/Podesti (c)
Same as Dec. 17 except:
Nedda : Alten
Silvio : Costa (t)

May 25
OTELLO
Same as Nov. 23 except:
Emilia : Maubourg
Lodovico : De Segurola
Roderigo : Reiss

May 27
CAVALLERIA RUSTICANA
Same (?) as May 23

PAGLIACCI
Same (?) as Dec. 17 except:
Nedda : Alten (?)
Silvio : Costa (?)

260

May 30
OTELLO
Same as Nov. 23 except:
Emilia : Maubourg
Lodovico : De Segurola
Roderigo : Reiss

June 1
AIDA
Same as Nov. 9 except:
Aida : Rappold (t)
Ramfis : De Segurola
Priestess : Roma

June 3
FALSTAFF/Toscanini (c)
(Not given in New York)
Falstaff : Scotti
Ford : Campanari
Fenton : Jadlowker
Dr. Caius : Bada
Bardolph : Reiss
Pistol : Rossi
Mistress Ford : Alten
Anne : Alda
Dame Quickly : Homer
Mistress Page : Maubourg

June 6
FALSTAFF
Same (?) as June 3

June 9
MANON LESCAUT/Toscanini (c)
(Not given in New York;
first time in Paris)
Manon : Bori (d)
Lescaut : Amato
Des Grieux : Caruso
Geronte : Pini-Corsi
Edmondo : Reiss (?)
Dancing Master : Bada (?)
Singer : Di Kowska (?)

June 10
OTELLO
Same as Nov. 23 except:
Emilia : Maubourg
Lodovico : De Segurola
Roderigo : Reiss

June 13
MANON LESCAUT
Same (?) as June 9

June 15
FALSTAFF
Same (?) as June 3

June 17
MANON LESCAUT
Same (?) as June 9

June 19
GALA CONCERT/Podesti,
Toscanini (c)
Farrar, Alda, Caruso,

Amato, Fremstad, Burrian,
Homer, Hinckley, De
Segurola, Alten, Scotti,
Slezak, Reiss, Ananian,
Maubourg, Bada, Reschiglian

June 20
AIDA
Same as Nov. 9 except:
Aida : Rappold
Ramfis : De Segurola
Priestess : Roma

June 22
CAVALLERIA RUSTICANA
Same (?) as May 23

PAGLIACCI
Same (?) as Dec. 17 except:
Silvio : Costa (?)

June 23
MANON LESCAUT
Same (?) as June 9

June 25
MANON LESCAUT
Same (?) as June 9

1 9 1 0 – 1 1

Giulio Gatti-Casazza, *Manager*

ALBANY
November 15
MADAMA BUTTERFLY
Toscanini (c)
Cio-Cio-San : Farrar
B. F. Pinkerton : Martin
Sharpless : Scotti
Suzuki : Mattfeld
Kate Pinkerton : Mapleson
Goro : Bada
Yamadori : Bourgeois (?)
Uncle-Priest : Bégué (?)
Yakuside : Cerri (?)
Imperial Commissioner :
Reschiglian (?)

BROOKLYN
November 19
IL TROVATORE/Podesti (c)
Leonora : Rappold
Manrico : Slezak
Count di Luna : Amato
Azucena : Homer
Inez : Borniggia
Ferrando : Witherspoon
Ruiz : Audisio

November 26
ORFEO ED EURIDICE
Toscanini (c)
Orfeo : Homer

Euridice : Rappold
Amor : Sparkes
A Happy Shade : Gluck

December 3
TANNHÄUSER/Hertz (c)
Hermann : Hinckley
Tannhäuser : Burrian
Wolfram : Goritz
Walther : Hall
Biterolf : Hinshaw
Heinrich : Bayer
Reinmar : Gunther
Elisabeth : Weidt (d—for
Morena)
Venus : Fremstad
Shepherd : Sparkes

PHILADELPHIA
December 13
TANNHÄUSER
Same as Dec. 3 except:
Tannhäuser : Slezak
Wolfram : Soomer
Elisabeth : Morena

December 20
LA FANCIULLA DEL WEST
Toscanini (c)
Minnie : Destinn
Dick Johnson : Caruso
Jack Rance : Amato
Nick : Reiss
Ashby : Didur
Sonora : Gilly
Trin : Bada
Sid : Rossi
Bello : Reschiglian
Harry : Audisio
Joe : Hall
Happy : Pini-Corsi
Larkens : Bégué
Billy : Bourgeois
Wowkle : Mattfeld
Jake Wallace : De Segurola
Jose Castro · Missiano
Pony Express Rider : Belleri

December 27
ORFEO ED EURIDICE
Same as Nov. 26 except:
Amor : Gluck

BALLET DIVERTISSEMENT:
Pavlowa and Mordkin

BROOKLYN
January 3
CAVALLERIA RUSTICANA
Podesti (c)
Santuzza : Morena
Turiddu : Martin
Lola : Flahaut
Alfio : Frascona (t—for
Gilly)
Lucia : Mattfeld

PAGLIACCI/Podesti (c)
Nedda : Gluck
Canio : Caruso
Tonio : Amato
Beppe : Bada
Silvio : Reschiglian

PHILADELPHIA
January 10
MADAMA BUTTERFLY
Same (?) as Nov. 15 except:
Suzuki : Fornia
Imperial Commissioner :
Romolo

BROOKLYN
January 17
LOHENGRIN/Hertz (c)
King Henry : Hinckley
Lohengrin : Slezak
Elsa : Fremstad
Telramund : Soomer
Ortrud : Homer
Herald : Hinshaw

January 24
KÖNIGSKINDER/Hertz (c)
King's Son : Jörn
Goose Girl : Farrar
Fiddler : Goritz
Witch : Wickham
Woodcutter : Didur
Broommaker : Reiss
Child : Engel
Innkeeper's Daughter :
Wickham
Stable Maid : Mattfeld

January 31
LA BOHÈME/Podesti (c)
Rodolfo : Smirnoff
Marcello : Scotti
Schaunard : Reschiglian
Colline : De Segurola
Mimi : Nielsen
Musetta : Alten
Benoit : Pini-Corsi
Parpignol : Bada
Alcindoro : Pini-Corsi
Sergeant : Missiano

February 7
RIGOLETTO/Podesti (c)
Duke : Smirnoff
Rigoletto : Amato
Gilda : Lipkowska
Sparafucile : De Segurola
Maddalena : Flahaut
Giovanna : Mattfeld
Monterone : Rossi
Marullo : Bégué (?)
Borsa : Bada
Ceprano : Reschiglian (?)
Countess : Mapleson (?)
Page : Borniggia (?)

PHILADELPHIA
February 14
KÖNIGSKINDER
Same as Jan. 24 except:
Witch : Homer
Senior Councillor : Reiner
Innkeeper : Pini-Corsi
Tailor : Bayer
Gatekeepers : Ruysdael,
Hinshaw

BROOKLYN
February 21
MADAMA BUTTERFLY
Same (?) as Nov. 15 except:
B. F. Pinkerton : Jadlowker
Imperial Commissioner :
Romolo

February 28
TOSCA/Podesti (c)
Tosca : Fremstad
Cavaradossi : Jadlowker
Scarpia : Scotti
Angelotti : Rossi
Sacristan : Pini-Corsi
Spoletta : Bada (?)
Sciarrone : Bégué (?)
Jailer : Missiano (?)
Shepherd : Snelling (?)

March 7
AIDA/Podesti (c)
King : Rossi
Amneris : Claessens
Aida : Destinn
Radames : Martin
Amonasro : Amato
Ramfis : Didur
Messenger · Audisio
Priestess : Sparkes

March 14
OTELLO/Toscanini (c)
Otello : Slezak
Desdemona : Rappold
Iago : Scotti
Emilia : Maubourg
Cassio : Bada
Roderigo : Audisio
Lodovico : De Segurola
Montano : Reschiglian (?)
Herald : Bégué

March 18
LA FANCIULLA DEL WEST
Same as Dec. 20 except:
Dick Johnson : Bassi

March 21
PARSIFAL/Hertz (c)
Amfortas : Amato
Titurel : Hinshaw (?)
Gurnemanz : Witherspoon

Parsifal : Jörn
Klingsor : Goritz
Kundry : Fremstad
A Voice : Wickham (?)
Knights of the Grail :
Bayer, Hinshaw (?)
Esquires : Sparkes, Wake-
field, Reiss, Hall (?)
Flower Maidens : Sparkes,
Fornia, Van Dyck, Alten,
Mattfeld, Wakefield

PHILADELPHIA
March 28
LOHENGRIN (for *Meistersinger*)
Same as Jan. 17 except:
King Henry : Witherspoon
Elsa : Gadski
Telramund : Goritz

April 4
LA GIOCONDA/Toscanini (c)
La Gioconda : Destinn
Laura : Homer
Alvise : De Segurola
La Cieca : Claessens
Enzo : Martin
Barnaba : Amato
Zuane : Bégué
Singer : Missiano
Isepo : Audisio

April 11
PARSIFAL
Same (?) as Mar. 21

MONTREAL
April 17
TANNHÄUSER
Same as Dec. 3 except:
Hermann : Witherspoon
Tannhäuser : Slezak
Walther : Reiss
Reinmar : Ruysdael
Elisabeth : Fremstad
Venus : Gluck

April 18
AIDA/Toscanini (c)
Same as Mar. 7 except:
Amneris : Homer
Amonasro : Scotti
Ramfis : De Segurola

April 19 (mat.)
FAUST/Podesti (c)
Faust : Jörn
Marguerite : Alten
Méphistophélès : Didur
Valentin : Gilly
Siébel : Maubourg
Marthe : Mattfeld
Wagner : Bégué

262

April 19
MADAMA BUTTERFLY
Podesti (c)
Same as Nov. 15 except:
Suzuki : Fornia
Kate Pinkerton : Sparkes
Goro : Venturini
Yamadori : Audisio
Uncle-Priest : Bégué
Imperial Commissioner :
Romolo

CLEVELAND
April 20
OTELLO
Same as Mar. 14 except:
Iago : Amato
Cassio : Venturini

April 21
TANNHÄUSER
Same (?) as Dec. 3 except:
Hermann : Witherspoon
Tannhäuser : Jörn
Walther : Reiss
Reinmar : Ruysdael
Elisabeth : Fremstad
Venus : Gluck

April 22 (mat.)
AIDA/Toscanini (c)
Same as Mar. 7 except:
Amneris : Homer
Ramfis : De Segurola

April 22
KÖNIGSKINDER
Same as Jan. 24 except:
Senior Councillor :
Reiner (?)
Innkeeper : Ruysdael (?)
Tailor : Bayer (?)
Gatekeepers : Maran,
Hinshaw (?)

CINCINNATI
April 24
KÖNIGSKINDER
Same (?) as Jan. 24 except:
Witch : Homer

April 25 (mat.)
OTELLO
Same (?) as Mar. 14 except:
Cassio : Venturini

April 25
DIE VERKAUFTE BRAUT
Hertz (c)
Kruschina : Witherspoon
Kathinka : Mattfeld
Marie : Destinn
Micha : Ruysdael
Agnes : Wakefield
Wenzel : Reiss

Hans : Jörn
Kezal : Goritz
Springer : Bayer
Esmeralda : Gluck
Muff : Burgstaller

ATLANTA
April 27
LA GIOCONDA
Same as Apr. 4 except:
Singer : Reschiglian

April 28
KÖNIGSKINDER
Same as Jan. 24 except:
Senior Councillor : Reiner
Innkeeper : Ruysdael
Tailor : Bayer
Gatekeepers : Maran,
Hinshaw

April 29 (mat.)
IL TROVATORE
Same as Nov. 19 except:
Manrico : Martin
Count di Luna : Gilly
Gypsy : Carlo (t)

April 29
OTELLO
Same (?) as Mar. 14 except:
Desdemona : Alda (t)
Iago : Amato
Cassio : Venturini

1 9 1 1 – 1 2

BROOKLYN
November 11
MADAMA BUTTERFLY
Toscanini (c)
Cio-Cio-San : Farrar
B. F. Pinkerton : Martin
Sharpless : Scotti
Suzuki : Fornia
Kate Pinkerton : Mapleson
Goro : Bada
Yamadori : Audisio
Uncle-Priest : Bégué
Imperial Commissioner :
Romolo

PHILADELPHIA
November 21
LA GIOCONDA/Toscanini (c)
La Gioconda : Destinn
Laura : Wickham
Alvise : De Segurola
La Cieca : Orridge (d)
Enzo : Caruso
Barnaba : Amato
Zuane : Bégué
Singer : Missiano
Isepo : Audisio

BROOKLYN
November 25
IL TROVATORE/Sturani (c)
Leonora : Gadski
Manrico : Martin
Count di Luna : Amato
Azucena : Orridge
Inez : Borniggia
Ferrando : Rossi
Ruiz : Audisio
Gypsy : Missiano

PHILADELPHIA
November 28
MADAMA BUTTERFLY
Same as Nov. 11 except:
Yakuside : Cerri

December 5
GÖTTERDÄMMERUNG/Hertz (c)
Siegfried : Burrian
Gunther : Weil
Hagen : Griswold
Alberich : Goritz
Brünnhilde : Gadski
Gutrune : Fornia
Woglinde : Sparkes
Wellgunde : Alten
Flosshilde : Wickham
(Norn, Waltraute scenes
omitted)

BROOKLYN
December 9
HÄNSEL UND GRETEL
Hertz (c)
Hänsel : Mattfeld
Gretel : Alten
Witch : Reiss
Gertrude : Fornia (for
Wickham)
Peter : Goritz
Sandman : Wakefield
Dewman : Case

CAVALLERIA RUSTICANA
Sturani (c)
Santuzza : Gadski
Lola : Maubourg
Turiddu : Jadlowker
Alfio : Gilly
Lucia : Borniggia

PHILADELPHIA
December 12
LOBETANZ/Hertz (c)
Lobetanz : Jadlowker
Princess : Gadski
King : Hinshaw
Girls : Sparkes, Case
Forester : Ruysdael
Hangman : Sannee
Prisoners : Ruysdael, Bayer,
Ananian, Burgstaller

Old Prisoner : Buckreus
Youth : Murphy

BROOKLYN
December 16
LOBETANZ
Same as Dec. 12 except:
Princess : Rappold
Girl : Wakefield
Judge : Witherspoon

PHILADELPHIA
December 19
TOSCA/Toscanini (c)
Tosca : Farrar
Cavaradossi : Martin
Scarpia : Scotti
Angelotti : Rossi
Sacristan : Pini-Corsi
Spoletta : Bada
Sciarrone : Bégué
Jailer : Ananian
Shepherd : Maubourg

BROOKLYN
December 26
LOHENGRIN/Hertz (c)
King Henry : Griswold
Lohengrin : Hensel
Elsa : Gadski (for Fremstad)
Telramund : Weil
Ortrud : Wickham
Herald : Hinshaw

January 2
LA BOHÈME/Sturani (c)
Rodolfo : Caruso
Marcello : Gilly
Schaunard : Didur
Colline : Rossi
Mimi : Gluck
Musetta : Sparkes
Benoit : Ananian
Parpignol : Audisio
Alcindoro : Bourgeois
Sergeant : Reschiglian

PHILADELPHIA
January 9
LA BOHÈME
Same as Jan. 2 except:
Colline : De Segurola

BROOKLYN
January 13
TANNHÄUSER/Hertz (c)
Hermann : Witherspoon
Tannhäuser : Burrian
Wolfram : Weil
Walther : Reiss
Biterolf : Hinshaw
Heinrich : Bayer
Reinmar : Ruysdael
Elisabeth : Fremstad

Venus : Gluck
Shepherd : Sparkes

PHILADELPHIA
January 16
SIEGFRIED/Hertz (c?)
Siegfried : Hensel
Mime : Reiss
Wanderer : Griswold
Alberich : Goritz
Fafner : Ruysdael
Erda : Matzenauer
Brünnhilde : Fremstad
Forest Bird : Sparkes (?)

BROOKLYN
January 20
FAUST/Sturani (c)
Faust : Martin
Marguerite : Farrar
Méphistophélès : Rothier
Valentin : Gilly
Siébel : Oerner
Marthe : Mattfeld
Wagner : Bégué

PHILADELPHIA
January 23
LOHENGRIN/Hertz (c)
King Henry : Witherspoon
Lohengrin : Jadlowker
Elsa : Destinn
Telramund : Goritz
Ortrud : Matzenauer
Herald : Weil

BROOKLYN
January 27
CAVALLERIA RUSTICANA
Same as Dec. 9 except:
Santuzza : Destinn
Lola : Wickham
Turiddu : Martin

PAGLIACCI/Sturani (c)
Nedda : Gluck
Canio : Caruso
Tonio : Amato
Beppe : Bada
Silvio : Reschiglian

PHILADELPHIA
January 30
VERSIEGELT/Hertz (c)
Braun : Weil
Else : Alten
Frau Gertrud : Gadski
Frau Willmers : Mattfeld
Bertel : Jadlowker
Lampe : Goritz
Neighbor Knote : Reiner
Champion Marksman :
Ruysdael

1911–12

PAGLIACCI
Same as Jan. 27 except:
Nedda : Fornia
Tonio : Gilly

BROOKLYN

February 3
SIEGFRIED
Same (?) as Jan. 16 except:
Siegfried : Burrian
Erda : Homer
Brünnhilde : Morena

February 13
DIE VERKAUFTE BRAUT
Hertz (c)
Kruschina : Witherspoon
Kathinka : Mattfeld
Marie : Destinn
Micha : Ruysdael
Agnes : Wakefield
Wenzel : Reiss
Hans : Hensel
Kezal : Didur
Springer : Bayer
Esmeralda : Case
Muff : Burgstaller

February 20
TOSCA
Same as Dec. 19 except:
Tosca : Fremstad
Scarpia : Amato

February 27
OTELLO/Sturani (c)
Otello : Slezak
Desdemona : Alda
Iago : Scotti
Emilia : Maubourg
Cassio : Bada
Roderigo : Audisio
Lodovico : De Segurola
Montano : Reschiglian
Herald : Bégué

March 5
KÖNIGSKINDER/Hertz (c)
King's Son : Jadlowker
Goose Girl : Farrar
Fiddler : Goritz
Witch : Wickham
Woodcutter : Didur
Broommaker : Reiss
Child : Gascoyne
Senior Councillor : Reiner
Innkeeper : Pini-Corsi
Innkeeper's Daughter :
  Wickham
Tailor : Bayer
Stable Maid : Mattfeld
Gatekeepers : Bourgeois,
  Hager

March 12
AIDA/Sturani (c)
King : Rossi
Amneris : Matzenauer
Aida : Gadski
Radames : Caruso
Amonasro : Gilly
Ramfis : De Segurola
Messenger : Bada
Priestess : Sparkes

March 19
DIE WALKÜRE/Hertz (c)
Wotan : Weil
Fricka : Wickham
Brünnhilde : Matzenauer
  (for Morena)
Siegmund : Jörn
Sieglinde : Gadski
Hunding : Ruysdael
Helmwige : Fornia
Gerhilde : Sparkes
Ortlinde : Van Dyck
Rossweisse : Oerner
Grimgerde : Wakefield
Waltraute : Wickham
Siegrune : Mattfeld
Schwertleite : Jungmann

BOSTON

April 15
TANNHÄUSER
Same as Jan. 13 except:
Hermann : Griswold
Tannhäuser : Slezak
Elisabeth : Gadski
Venus : Fremstad

April 16
KÖNIGSKINDER
Same as Mar. 5 except:
King's Son : Jörn
Innkeeper's Daughter : Fornia
Gatekeeper : Ruysdael (for
  Rudell)

April 17 (mat.)
CAVALLERIA RUSTICANA
Same as Dec. 9 except:
Lola : Wickham
Turiddu : Martin
Lucia : Mattfeld

PAGLIACCI
Same as Jan. 27 except:
Nedda : Nielsen
Beppe : Reiss
Silvio : Gilly

April 17
LOHENGRIN
Same as Dec. 26 except:
Lohengrin : Jörn
Elsa : Fremstad
Telramund : Goritz
Ortrud : Homer

PHILADELPHIA

April 18
LA BOHÈME
Same as Jan. 2 except:
Rodolfo : Martin
Marcello : Scotti
Colline : De Segurola
Mimi : Farrar
Musetta : Alten
Parpignol : Bada
Alcindoro : Pini-Corsi

April 19
AIDA
Same (?) as Mar. 12 except:
King : Hinshaw
Amneris : Homer
Amonasro : Amato

BALTIMORE

April 20 (mat.)
KÖNIGSKINDER
Same as Mar. 5 except:
King's Son : Jörn
Innkeeper's Daughter : Fornia
Gatekeeper : Ruysdael (for
  Rudell)

ATLANTA

April 22
AIDA
Same as Mar. 12 except:
King : Hinshaw
Amneris : Homer

April 23 (mat.)
LA BOHÈME
Same as Jan. 2 except:
Rodolfo : Martin
Marcello : Scotti
Schaunard : Reschiglian
Colline : De Segurola
Mimi : Farrar
Musetta : Alten
Alcindoro : Pini-Corsi
Sergeant : Cotterini (t—for
  Reschiglian)

April 24
IL TROVATORE
Same as Nov. 25 except:
Leonora : Rappold
Count di Luna : Gilly
Azucena : Homer
Gypsy : Cotterini (for
  Reschiglian)

April 25 (mat.)
CAVALLERIA RUSTICANA
Same as Dec. 9 except:
Lola : Wickham
Turiddu : Jörn
Alfio : Reschiglian
Lucia : Mattfeld

PAGLIACCI
Same as Jan. 27 except:
Nedda : Alten
Tonio : Scotti

April 26
FAUST/Hageman (c—t)
Same as Jan. 20 except:
Faust : Jörn
Marguerite : Gluck (for
    Farrar)
Méphistophélès : Griswold
Siébel : Fornia
Wagner : Ananian

April 27 (mat.)
TANNHÄUSER
Same as Jan. 13 except:
Hermann : Griswold
Tannhäuser : Slezak
Wolfram : Goritz
Elisabeth : Gadski
Venus : Rappold

April 27
RIGOLETTO/Sturani (c)
Duke : Caruso
Rigoletto : Gilly
Gilda : Gluck
Sparafucile : De Segurola
Maddalena : Wickham
Giovanna : Borniggia
Monterone : Ananian
Marullo : Sampieri (t)
Borsa : Bada
Ceprano : Reschiglian
Countess : Borniggia

1 9 1 2 – 1 3

ALBANY
November 12
LA BOHÈME/Sturani (c)
Rodolfo : Martin
Marcello : Gilly
Schaunard : Didur
Colline : De Segurola
Mimi : Farrar
Musetta : Alten
Benoit : Pini-Corsi
Parpignol : Audisio (?)
Alcindoro : Pini-Corsi
Sergeant : Audisio

BROOKLYN
November 16
RIGOLETTO/Sturani (c)
Duke : Macnez (d)
Rigoletto : Amato
Gilda : Bori
Sparafucile : Rothier
Maddalena : Maubourg
Giovanna : Borniggia (for
    Mattfeld)

Monterone : Ananian (?)
Marullo : Rossi
Borsa : Bada
Ceprano : Reschiglian
Countess : Mapleson
Page : Borniggia

PHILADELPHIA
November 19
TANNHÄUSER/Hertz (c)
Hermann : Witherspoon
Tannhäuser : Burrian
Wolfram : Weil
Walther : Reiss
Biterolf : Hinshaw
Heinrich : Bayer
Reinmar : Ruysdael
Elisabeth : Fremstad
Venus : Rappold
Shepherd : Sparkes

BROOKLYN
November 23
LA BOHÈME
Same (?) as Nov. 12 except:
Marcello : Amato
Musetta : Sparkes
Benoit : Ananian (?)
Sergeant : Reschiglian (?)

PHILADELPHIA
November 26
MADAMA BUTTERFLY
    Sturani (c)
Cio-Cio-San : Farrar
B. F. Pinkerton : Martin
Sharpless : Scotti
Suzuki : Fornia
Kate Pinkerton : Mapleson
Goro : Bada
Yamadori : Audisio
Uncle-Priest : Bégué
Yakuside : Cerri
Imperial Commissioner :
    Romolo

BROOKLYN
November 30
AIDA/Sturani (c)
King : Rossi
Amneris : Homer
Aida : Rappold
Radames : Slezak
Amonasro : Gilly
Ramfis : Rothier
Messenger : Audisio (?)
Priestess : Sparkes (?)

PHILADELPHIA
December 3
LA BOHÈME/Polacco (c)
Same (?) as Nov. 12 except:
Rodolfo : Caruso
Marcello : Amato

Musetta : Sparkes
Benoit : Ananian
Sergeant : Reschiglian

BROOKLYN
December 7
TANNHÄUSER/Morgenstern
    (c—for Hertz)
Same as Nov. 19 except:
Wolfram : Goritz (for Weil)
Venus : Matzenauer

PHILADELPHIA
December 10
DIE MEISTERSINGER/Hertz (c)
Hans Sachs : Weil
Pogner : Witherspoon
Eva : Destinn
Magdalene : Mattfeld
Walther : Slezak
Beckmesser : Goritz
Kothner : Hinshaw
Vogelgesang : Murphy
Nachtigall : Gaston Martin
Zorn : Bayer
Eisslinger : Hughes
Moser : Audisio
Ortel : Ananian
Schwarz : Heidenreich
Foltz : Hager
David : Reiss
Night Watchman : Pini-Corsi

BROOKLYN
December 14
IL TROVATORE/Sturani (c)
Leonora : Rappold
Manrico : Martin
Count di Luna : Amato
Azucena : Homer
Inez : Borniggia
Ferrando : Rossi
Ruiz : Audisio

PHILADELPHIA
December 17
TOSCA/Sturani (c)
Tosca : Farrar
Cavaradossi : Martin
Scarpia : Amato
Angelotti : Rossi
Sacristan : Pini-Corsi
Spoletta : Bada
Sciarrone : Bégué
Jailer : Ananian
Shepherd : De Mette

BROOKLYN
December 24
CAVALLERIA RUSTICANA
    Polacco (c)
Santuzza : Destinn
Lola : Duchène
Turiddu : Martin

1912–13

Alfio : Gilly
Lucia : Maubourg

PAGLIACCI/Polacco (c)
Nedda : Bori
Canio : Caruso
Tonio : Amato
Beppe : Bada
Silvio : Reschiglian

January 4
DIE WALKÜRE/Hertz (c)
Wotan : Griswold
Fricka : Robeson (for
  Matzenauer)
Brünnhilde : Gadski
Siegmund : Burrian
Sieglinde : Fremstad
Hunding : Ruysdael
Helmwige : Sparkes
Gerhilde : Alten
Ortlinde : Curtis
Rossweisse : Fornia
Grimgerde : Mulford
Waltraute : Robeson
Siegrune : Mattfeld
Schwertleite : Duchène

PHILADELPHIA
January 7
LA GIOCONDA/Polacco (c)
La Gioconda : Destinn
Laura : Homer
Alvise : De Segurola
La Cieca : Duchène
Enzo : Caruso
Barnaba : Gilly
Zuane : Bégué
Singer : Reschiglian
Isepo : Audisio

BROOKLYN
January 11
ORFEO ED EURIDICE
Toscanini (c)
Orfeo : Homer
Euridice : Gadski
Amor : Sparkes
A Happy Shade : Case

PHILADELPHIA
January 14
DIE ZAUBERFLÖTE/Hertz (c)
Sarastro : Witherspoon
Tamino : Slezak
High Priest : Weil
Two Priests : Kriedler,
  Althouse (?)
Queen of the Night : Parks
Pamina : Gadski
Three Ladies : Curtis,
  Mulford, Homer
Papageno : Goritz
Papagena : Alten

Monostatos : Reiss
Three Genii : Sparkes, Case,
  Mattfeld
Guards : Althouse (?),
  Ruysdael (?)

January 21
ORFEO ED EURIDICE
Polacco (c)
Same as Jan. 11 except:
Amor : Alten (for Sparkes)
A Happy Shade : Curtis
  (for Case)

BROOKLYN
January 25
MADAMA BUTTERFLY
Toscanini (c)
Same (?) as Nov. 26 except:
Imperial Commissioner :
  Rossi

PHILADELPHIA
January 28
MANON/Toscanini (c)
Manon : Farrar
Lescaut : Gilly
Des Grieux : Caruso
Count des Grieux : Rothier
Poussette : Sparkes
Javotte : Maubourg
Rosette : Duchène
Guillot : Reiss
De Brétigny : De Segurola
Innkeeper : Ananian
Guards : Reschiglian, Bégué
Servant : Savage

BROOKLYN
February 4
DIE MEISTERSINGER
Same as Dec. 10 except:
Hans Sachs : Buers (d)
Eva : Gadski
Walther : Jörn
Foltz : Ruysdael (for
  Hager)

February 11
LES CONTES D'HOFFMANN
Polacco (c)
Olympia : Hempel
Giuletta : Duchène
Antonia : Bori
Hoffmann : Macnez
Nicklausse : Maubourg
Lindorf : Ruysdael
Coppelius : Didur
Dapertutto : Gilly
Miracle : Rothier
Cochenille : Reiss
Franz : Reiss
Pitichinaccio : Bada
Luther : Bégué

Nathaniel : Audisio
Hermann : Ananian
Spalanzani : De Segurola
Schlemil : De Segurola
Crespel : Rossi

February 25
LA TRAVIATA/Sturani (c)
Violetta : Hempel
Alfredo : Macnez
Germont : Gilly
Flora : Maubourg
Annina : Mattfeld
Gastone : Bada
Baron Douphol : Reschiglian
Marquis d'Obigny : Bégué
Doctor Grenvil : Ananian

March 4
TOSCA/Toscanini (c)
Same (?) as Dec. 17 except:
Tosca : Fremstad
Cavaradossi : Caruso
Scarpia : Scotti
Shepherd : Maubourg (?)

March 11
LOHENGRIN/Hertz (c)
King Henry : Griswold
Lohengrin : Urlus
Elsa : Destinn
Telramund : Buers
Ortrud : Robeson (for
  Homer)
Herald : Hinshaw

PHILADELPHIA
March 25
LES HUGUENOTS/Polacco (c)
Marguerite : Hempel
St. Bris : Rothier
Valentine : Destinn
Nevers : Gilly
Cossé : Audisio
Tavannes : Bada
Meru : Ananian
Retz : Bégué
Raoul : Caruso
Marcel : Braun
Urbain : Alten
Maurevert : Rossi
Bois Rosé : Bada
Lady of Honor : Mattfeld
Night Watchman :
  Reschiglian

ALBANY
April 15
HÄNSEL UND GRETEL
Hageman (c)
Hänsel : Mattfeld
Gretel : Alten
Witch : Robeson
Gertrude : Fornia
Peter : Goritz

266

Sandman : De Mette
Dewman : Van Dyck

PAGLIACCI/Sturani (c)
Nedda : Destinn
Canio : Jörn
Tonio : Amato
Beppe : Bada
Silvio : Reschiglian

ATLANTA
April 21
MANON LESCAUT/Sturani (c)
Manon : Bori
Lescaut : Scotti
Des Grieux : Caruso
Geronte : De Segurola
Edmondo : Bada
Ballet Master : Reiss
Innkeeper : Ananian
Musician : Duchène
Sergeant : Reschiglian
Lamplighter : Audisio
Captain : Morandi

April 22 (mat.)
LA TRAVIATA
Same as Feb. 25 except:
Germont : Amato

April 23
CYRANO DE BERGERAC
Hertz (c)
Cyrano : Amato
Roxane : Alda
Duenna : Mattfeld
Lise : Van Dyck
Mother Superior : Robeson
Christian : Martin
Ragueneau : Reiss
De Guiche : Griswold
Le Bret : Hinshaw
Two Musketeers : Ruysdael, Reiner
Montfleury, Cadet : Laurier (t)
Monk : Pini-Corsi

April 24 (mat.)
LA GIOCONDA/Toscanini (c)
Same as Jan. 7

April 25
LES CONTES D'HOFFMANN
Hageman (c)
Same as Feb. 11 except:
Giulietta : Fornia
Hoffmann : Jörn
Coppelius : Rothier
A Voice : Duchène

April 26 (mat.)
LUCIA DI LAMMERMOOR
Sturani (c)
(Not given in New York)
Lucia : Hempel

Alisa : Mattfeld
Edgardo : Macnez
Ashton : Amato
Raimondo : Rossi
Arturo : Bada
Normanno : Audisio

April 26
TOSCA/Toscanini (c)
Same as Dec. 17 except:
Tosca : Destinn
Cavaradossi : Caruso
Scarpia : Scotti
Spoletta : Audisio
Shepherd : Maubourg

1913 – 14

ALBANY
November 18
TOSCA/Polacco (c)
Tosca : Fremstad
Cavaradossi : Martinelli
Scarpia : Scotti
Angelotti : Rossi
Sacristan : Pini-Corsi
Spoletta : Bada
Sciarrone : Bégué
Jailer : Ananian
Shepherd : Borniggia
(t—for Maubourg)

BROOKLYN
November 22
LA BOHÈME/Polacco (c)
Rodolfo : Cristalli (d)
Marcello : Gilly
Schaunard : Didur
Colline : Rossi
Mimi : Bori
Musetta : Alten
Benoit : Ananian
Parpignol : Audisio
Alcindoro : Pini-Corsi
Sergeant : Reschiglian

PHILADELPHIA
November 25
AIDA/Polacco (c)
King : Rossi
Amneris : Matzenauer
Aida : Destinn
Radames : Caruso
Amonasro : Gilly
Ramfis : Rothier
Messenger : Bedeschi
(t—for Audisio)
Priestess : Borniggia
(for Sparkes)

BROOKLYN
November 29
FAUST/Hageman (c)
Faust : Jörn

Marguerite : Farrar
Méphistophélès : Rothier
Valentin : Gilly
Siébel : Fornia
Marthe : Mattfeld
Wagner : Bégué

PHILADELPHIA
December 2
MADAMA BUTTERFLY
Toscanini (c)
Cio-Cio-San : Destinn
B. F. Pinkerton : Martinelli
Sharpless : Scotti
Suzuki : Fornia
Kate Pinkerton : Mapleson
Goro : Bada
Yamadori : Audisio
Uncle-Priest : Bégué
Imperial Commissioner : Romolo

BROOKLYN
December 13
LES CONTES D'HOFFMANN
Polacco (c)
Olympia : Case (for Hempel)
Giulietta : Duchène
Antonia : Bori
Hoffmann : Jörn
Nicklausse : Maubourg
Lindorf : Ruysdael
Coppelius : Didur
Dapertutto : Gilly
Miracle : Rothier
Crespel : Reiss
Pitichinaccio : Bada
Franz : Reiss
Luther : Bégué
Nathanael : Audisio
Hermann : Ananian
Spalanzani : De Segurola
Schlemil : De Segurola
Crespel : Rossi
The Voice : Robeson

PHILADELPHIA
December 16
TANNHÄUSER/Hertz (c)
Hermann : Braun
Tannhäuser : Urlus
Wolfram : Weil
Walther : Reiss
Biterolf : Schlegel
Heinrich : Bayer
Reinmar : Ruysdael
Elisabeth : Gadski
Venus : Fremstad
Shepherd : Curtis

BROOKLYN
December 20
LA TRAVIATA/Polacco (c)
Violetta : Hempel

1913–14

Alfredo : Cristalli
Germont : Amato
Flora : Maubourg
Annina : Mattfeld
Gastone : Bada
Baron Douphol : Reschiglian
Marquis d'Obigny : Bégué
Doctor Grenvil : Ananian

PHILADELPHIA
December 23
LA BOHÈME
Same as Nov. 22 except:
Rodolfo : Caruso
Marcello : Scotti
Schaunard : Pini-Corsi
Colline : De Segurola
Mimi : Alda
Alcindoro : Ananian

BROOKLYN
December 30
TANNHÄUSER
Same as Dec. 16 except:
Walther : Althouse

PHILADELPHIA
January 6
TRISTAN UND ISOLDE
Toscanini (c)
Tristan : Urlus
Isolde : Gadski
King Marke : Braun
Kurvenal : Weil
Brangaene : Ober
Melot : Schlegel
Steersman : Bayer
Shepherd : Murphy
Sailor's Voice : Murphy

BROOKLYN
January 13
KÖNIGSKINDER/Hertz (c)
King's Son : Jörn
Goose Girl : Farrar
Fiddler : Goritz
Witch : Ober
Woodcutter : Ruysdael
Broommaker : Reiss
Child : Foerster
Senior Councillor : Reiner
Innkeeper : Leonhardt
Innkeeper's Daughter : Fornia
Tailor : Bayer
Stable Maid : Mattfeld
Gatekeepers : Schlegel,
  Fuhrmann

PHILADELPHIA
January 20
DIE ZAUBERFLÖTE/Hertz (c)
Sarastro : Braun
Tamino : Jörn
High Priest : Griswold

Two Priests : Murphy,
  Schlegel
Queen of the Night : Hempel
Pamina : Destinn
Three Ladies : Curtis,
  Eubank, Robeson
Papageno : Goritz
Papagena : Alten
Monostatos : Reiss
Three Genii : Van Dyck,
  Cox, Mattfeld

BROOKLYN
January 27
MADELEINE/Polacco (c)
Madeleine Fleury : Alda
Nichette : Sparkes
Chevalier de Mauprat :
  Pini-Corsi
François : Althouse
Didier : De Segurola
Coachman : Reiner
Servants : Laufer, Buckreus,
  Sappio

PAGLIACCI/Polacco (c)
Nedda : Alten
Canio : Caruso
Tonio : Amato
Beppe : Bada
Silvio : Reschiglian

February 3
DER ROSENKAVALIER/Hertz (c)
Princess von Werdenberg :
  Hempel
Baron Ochs : Goritz
Octavian : Ober
Von Faninal : Weil
Sophie : Case
Marianne : Fornia
Valzacchi : Reiss
Annina : Mattfeld
Police Commissioner :
  Schlegel
Majordomo of Princess :
  Audisio
Majordomo of Von Faninal :
  Murphy
Notary : Ruysdael
Innkeeper : Bayer
Singer : Jörn
Orphans : Cox, Van Dyck,
  Braslau
Milliner : Maubourg
Leopold : Burgstaller
Animal Vendor : Sappio
Negro Boy : Weinstein

PHILADELPHIA
February 10
TOSCA/Toscanini (c)
Same as Nov. 18 except:
Cavaradossi : Caruso
Shepherd : Braslau

BROOKLYN
February 17
AIDA
Same as Nov. 25 except:
Amneris : Ober
Aida : Gadski
Radames : Martin
Messenger : Bada
Priestess : Sparkes

February 24
TOSCA
Same as Nov. 18 except:
Cavaradossi : Martin
Shepherd : Braslau

PHILADELPHIA
March 3
MADELEINE
Same as Jan. 27

PAGLIACCI
Same as Jan. 27

March 10
BORIS GODUNOV/Polacco (c—
  for Toscanini)
Boris Godunov : Didur
Fyodor : Braslau
Xenia : Case (for Sparkes)
Nurse : Duchène
Shuiski : Bada
Shchelkalov : Reschiglian
Pimen : Rothier
Grigori : Althouse
Marina : Ober
Varlaam : De Segurola
Missail : Audisio
Innkeeper : Maubourg
Officer : Rossi
Lavitski : Schlegel
Chernikovski : Reschiglian
Boyar : Murphy (for
  Mariani)

BROOKLYN
March 17
LOHENGRIN/Hertz (c)
King Henry : Witherspoon
Lohengrin : Berger
Elsa : Fremstad
Telramund : Goritz
Ortrud : Ober
Herald : Schlegel

March 24
LA GIOCONDA/Polacco (c)
La Gioconda : Destinn
Laura : Homer
Alvise : De Segurola
La Cieca : Duchène
Enzo : Caruso
Barnaba : Amato
Zuane : Bégué

268

Singer : Reschiglian
Isepo : Audisio

April 7
DIE WALKÜRE/Hertz (c)
Wotan : Weil
Fricka : Homer
Brünnhilde : Gadski
Siegmund : Berger
Sieglinde : Fremstad
Hunding : Ruysdael
Helmwige : Sparkes
Gerhilde : Van Dyck
Ortlinde : Curtis
Rossweisse : Fornia
Grimgerde : Eubank
Waltraute : Robeson
Siegrune : Mattfeld
Schwertleite : Duchène

April 21
ORFEO ED EURIDICE
Toscanini (c)
Orfeo : Homer
Euridice : Gadski
Amor : Sparkes
A Happy Shade : Case

ATLANTA
April 27
MANON/Toscanini (c)
Manon : Farrar
Lescaut : Gilly
Des Grieux : Caruso
Count des Grieux : Rothier
Poussette : Sparkes
Javotte : Van Dyck
Rosette : Duchène
Guillot : Reiss
De Brétigny : De Segurola
Innkeeper : Ananian
Guards : Reschiglian,
  Righi (t)
Servant : Duchène (for
  Savage)

April 28 (mat.)
IL TROVATORE/Hageman (c)
(Not given in New York)
Leonora : Gadski
Manrico : Martin
Count di Luna : Amato
Azucena : Ober
Inez : Mattfeld
Ferrando : Rossi
Ruiz : Bada
Gypsy : Reschiglian

April 29
DER ROSENKAVALIER
Same as Feb. 3 except:
Von Faninal : Leonhardt
Majordomo of Von Faninal :
  Bayer

Singer : Cristalli
Orphans : Sparkes, Robeson
  (for Braslau)
Milliner : Martin (for
  Molet)
Negro Boy : Hoyler

April 30
UN BALLO IN MASCHERA
Toscanini (c)
Riccardo : Caruso
Renato : Amato
Amelia : Gadski
Ulrica : Duchène
Oscar : Hempel
Silvano : Reschiglian
Samuel : De Segurola
Tom : Rothier
Judge : Bada
Servant : Audisio

May 1
MADAMA BUTTERFLY
Same as Dec. 2 except:
Cio-Cio-San : Farrar
B. F. Pinkerton : Martin
Kate Pinkerton : Sparkes
Uncle-Priest : Ruysdael
Imperial Commissioner :
  Reschiglian

May 2 (mat.)
LOHENGRIN
Same as Mar. 17 except:
Elsa : Rappold

May 2
CAVALLERIA RUSTICANA
Hageman (c)
Santuzza : Gadski
Lola : Duchène
Turiddu : Cristalli
Alfio : Gilly
Lucia : Mattfeld

PAGLIACCI/Hageman (c)
Same as Jan. 27 except:
Nedda : Fornia
Tonio : Scotti

1 9 1 4 – 1 5

BROOKLYN
November 17
MANON LESCAUT/Polacco (c)
Manon : Bori
Lescaut : Scotti
Des Grieux : Martinelli
Geronte : De Segurola
Edmondo : Bada
Ballet Master : Reiss
Innkeeper : Ananian
Musician : Duchène

Sergeant : Reschiglian
Lamplighter : Audisio
Captain : Rossi

PHILADELPHIA
November 24
TOSCA/Toscanini (c)
Tosca : Farrar
Cavaradossi : Martinelli
Scarpia : Scotti
Angelotti : Rossi
Sacristan : Ananian
Spoletta : Bada
Sciarrone : Bégué
Jailer : Reschiglian
Shepherd : Braslau

BROOKLYN
November 28
CAVALLERIA RUSTICANA
Polacco (c)
Santuzza : Gadski
Lola : Duchène
Turiddu : Botta
Alfio : Tegani
Lucia : Mattfeld

PAGLIACCI/Polacco (c)
Nedda : Bori
Canio : Martinelli
Tonio : Scotti
Beppe : Audisio
Silvio : Tegani

PHILADELPHIA
December 1
LA GIOCONDA/Polacco (c)
La Gioconda : Destinn
Laura : Matzenauer
Alvise : De Segurola
La Cieca : Duchène
Enzo : Caruso
Barnaba : Amato
Zuane : Bégué
Singer : Reschiglian
Isepo : Audisio

BROOKLYN
December 5
LOHENGRIN/Hertz (c)
King Henry : Ruysdael
Lohengrin : Urlus
Elsa : Gadski
Telramund : Goritz
Ortrud : Matzenauer (for
  Ober)
Herald : Middleton

PHILADELPHIA
December 8
LOHENGRIN
Same as Dec. 5 except:
Telramund : Weil

1914–15

December 15
AIDA/Polacco (c)
King : Rossi
Amneris : Duchène
Aida : Rappold (for
Destinn)
Radames : Caruso
Amonasro : Amato
Ramfis : Didur
Messenger : Audisio
Priestess : Borniggia (t)

BROOKLYN
December 19
LA BOHÈME/Polacco (c)
Rodolfo : Botta
Marcello : Tegani
Schaunard : Didur
Colline : De Segurola
Mimi : Farrar
Musetta : Sparkes (for
Schumann)
Benoit : Ananian
Parpignol : Audisio
Alcindoro : Leonhardt
Sergeant : Reschiglian

PHILADELPHIA
December 22
DIE ZAUBERFLÖTE/Hertz (c)
Sarastro : Braun
Tamino : Urlus
High Priest : Schlegel
Two Priests : Bloch, Bayer
Queen of the Night : Hempel
Pamina : Gadski
Three Ladies : Curtis, Fornia,
Robeson
Papageno : Goritz
Papagena : Case (for
Schumann)
Monostatos : Reiss
Three Genii : Sparkes, Cox,
Mattfeld

BROOKLYN
December 26
DIE ZAUBERFLÖTE
Same as Dec. 22 except:
Sarastro : Witherspoon
Tamino : Sembach
Priest : Althouse
Pamina : Destinn
Papagena : Schumann
Monostatos : Bloch

PHILADELPHIA
December 29
MADAMA BUTTERFLY
Toscanini (c)
Cio-Cio-San : Farrar
B. F. Pinkerton : Martinelli
Sharpless : Tegani

Suzuki : Fornia
Kate Pinkerton : Egener
Goro : Bada
Yamadori : Audisio
Uncle-Priest : Bégué
Imperial Commissioner :
Reschiglian

BROOKLYN
January 5
LA TRAVIATA/Polacco (c)
Violetta : Hempel
Alfredo : Botta
Germont : Tegani (for
Amato)
Flora : Egener
Annina : Mattfeld
Gastone : Bada
Baron Douphol : Reschiglian
Marquis d'Obigny : Bégué
Doctor Grenvil : Ananian

PHILADELPHIA
January 12
CAVALLERIA RUSTICANA
Same as Nov. 28 except:
Santuzza : Destinn

PAGLIACCI
Same as Nov. 28 except:
Canio : Caruso
Tonio : Amato

BROOKLYN
January 19
EURYANTHE/Toscanini (c)
King Ludwig : Middleton
Adolar : Sembach
Lysiart : Weil
Euryanthe : Hempel
Eglantine : Ober
Rudolph : Bloch
Bertha : Garrison

PHILADELPHIA
January 26
BORIS GODUNOV/Polacco (c)
Boris Godunov : Didur
Fyodor : Delaunois
Xenia : Cox
Nurse : Duchène
Shuiski : Bada
Shchelkalov : Reschiglian
Pimen : Rothier
Grigori : Althouse
Varlaam : De Segurola
Missail : Audisio
Innkeeper : Mattfeld
Officer : Rossi
Simpleton : Reiss
Lavitski : Reschiglian
Chernikovski : Schlegel
Boyar : Mariani

BROOKLYN
February 2
CARMEN/Toscanini (c)
Carmen : Farrar
Don José : Caruso
Micaela : Alda
Escamillo : Amato
Zuniga : Rothier
Morales : Defrère
Frasquita : Sparkes
Mercedes : Braslau
Dancaire : Leonhardt
Remendado : Bada
(100th performance by
Metropolitan Opera at
Brooklyn Academy)

PHILADELPHIA
February 9
DIE WALKÜRE/Hertz (c)
Wotan : Weil
Fricka : Matzenauer
Brünnhilde : Kurt
Siegmund : Urlus
Sieglinde : Gadski
Hunding : Ruysdael
Helmwige : Sparkes
Gerhilde : Schumann
Ortlinde : Curtis
Rossweisse : Fornia
Grimgerde : Robeson
Waltraute : Mulford
Siegrune : Mattfeld
Schwertleite : Duchène

BROOKLYN
February 16
FIDELIO/Hertz (c)
Don Fernando : Middleton
Don Pizarro : Weil
Florestan : Urlus
Leonore : Matzenauer
Rocco : Braun
Marzelline : Schumann
Jaquino : Reiss
Prisoners : Bloch, Leonhardt

PHILADELPHIA
February 23
MADAME SANS-GÊNE
Toscanini (c)
Caterina : Farrar
Tonietta : Sparkes
Giulia : Fornia
La Rossa : Mattfeld
Lefebvre : Martinelli
Fouché : De Segurola
Vinaigre : Bloch
Count Neipperg : Althouse
Queen Carolina : Curtis
Princess Elisa : Egener
Despreaux : Bada
Gelsomine : Tegani

270

Leroy : Leonhardt
De Brigode : Reschiglian
Napoleone : Amato
Roustan : Bégué

BROOKLYN
March 2
MADAME SANS-GÊNE
Same as Feb. 23 except:
La Rossa : Braslau

March 9
TOSCA/Polacco (c)
Same as Nov. 24 except:
Cavaradossi : Botta
Sacristan : Leonhardt

March 16
AIDA
Same as Dec. 15 except:
Amneris : Ober
Aida : Destinn
Radames : Martin
Amonasro : Tegani
Priestess : Sparkes

PHILADELPHIA
March 23
L'AMORE DEI TRE RE
Toscanini (c)
Archibaldo : Didur
Manfredo : Amato
Avito : Ferrari-Fontana
Flaminio : Bada
A Youth : Audisio
Fiora : Bori
A Maid : Egener
A Young Woman : Braslau
An Old Woman : Duchène

BROOKLYN
March 30
TANNHÄUSER/Hertz (c)
Hermann : Witherspoon
Tannhäuser : Urlus
Wolfram : Goritz
Walther : Althouse
Biterolf : Schlegel
Heinrich : Bayer
Reinmar : Ruysdael
Elisabeth : Gadski
Venus : Matzenauer
Shepherd : Sparkes

April 6
MADAMA BUTTERFLY
Polacco (c)
Same as Dec. 29 except:
B. F. Pinkerton : Botta
Imperial Commissioner :
Rossi

April 13
L'ORACOLO/Hageman (c)
Win-Shee : Didur

Chim-Fen : Scotti
Hoo-Tsin : Rossi
Win-San-Luy : Botta
Hoo-Chee : Bakos
Ah-Yoe : Bori
Hua-Quee : Braslau
Fortune Teller : Audisio

HÄNSEL UND GRETEL
Hageman (c)
Hänsel : Mattfeld
Gretel : Schumann
Witch : Reiss
Gertrude : Robeson
Peter : Goritz
Sandman : Braslau
Dewman : Garrison

PHILADELPHIA
April 20
CARMEN/Polacco (c)
Same as Feb. 2 except:
Don José : Martinelli

ATLANTA
April 26
LES HUGUENOTS/Polacco (c)
Marguerite : Hempel
St. Bris : Rothier
Valentine : Kurt
Nevers : Scotti
Cossé : Audisio
Tavannes : Bada
Meru : Ananian
Retz : Bégué
Raoul : Martinelli
Marcel : Didur
Urbain : Garrison
Maurevert : Rossi
Bois Rosé : Bada
Lady of Honor : Mattfeld
Night Watchman :
Reschiglian

April 27 (mat.)
LES CONTES D'HOFFMANN
Hageman (c)
(Not given in New York)
Olympia : Case
Giulietta : Fornia
Antonia : Bori
Hoffmann : Martin
Nicklausse : Delaunois
Lindorf : Ruysdael
Coppelius : Didur
Dapertutto : Rothier
Miracle : Rothier
Cochenille : Reiss
Franz : Reiss
Pitichinaccio : Bada
Luther : Bégué
Nathaniel : Audisio
Hermann : Ananian

Spalanzani : De Segurola
Schlemil : De Segurola
Crespel : Rossi
The Voice : Duchène

April 28
CARMEN/Polacco (c)
Same as Feb. 2 except:
Don José : Martin
Escamillo : Whitehill
Morales : Tegani

April 29
RIGOLETTO/Papi (c—t—for
Polacco)
(Not given in New York)
Duke : Botta
Rigoletto : Amato
Gilda : Hempel
Sparafucile : De Segurola
Maddalena : Braslau
Giovanna : Mattfeld
Monterone : Rossi
Marullo : Bégué
Borsa : Audisio
Ceprano : Reschiglian
Countess : Egener
Page : Borniggia

April 30
L'AMORE DEI TRE RE
Polacco (c)
Same as Mar. 23 except:
Avito : Botta

May 1 (mat.)
DIE ZAUBERFLÖTE
Hageman (c)
Same as Dec. 22 except:
Sarastro : Ruysdael
Tamino : Sembach
Priests : Gries (t),
Burgstaller (for Leonhardt)
Pamina : Kurt
Papagena : Schumann

May 1
MADAME SANS-GÊNE/Papi (c)
Same as Feb. 23 except:
Giulia : Mattfeld
La Rossa : Braslau

1 9 1 5 – 1 6

BROOKLYN
November 16
IL TROVATORE/Polacco (c)
Leonora : Rappold
Manrico : Martinelli
Count di Luna : Amato
Azucena : Ober
Inez : Mattfeld

1915–16

Ferrando : Rothier
Ruiz : Audisio
Gypsy : Reschiglian

PHILADELPHIA
November 23
IL TROVATORE
Same as Nov. 16

BROOKLYN
November 27
BORIS GODUNOV/Polacco (c)
Boris Godunov : Didur
Fyodor : Delaunois
Xenia : Sparkes
Nurse : Duchène
Shuiski : Bada
Pimen : Rothier
Grigori : Althouse
Marina : Ober
Varlaam : De Segurola
Innkeeper : Mattfeld
Simpleton : Bloch

PHILADELPHIA
November 30
MANON/Polacco (c)
Manon : Alda
Lescaut : Scotti
Des Grieux : Caruso
Count des Grieux : Rothier
Poussette : Sparkes
Javotte : Braslau
Rosette : Duchène
Guillot : Reiss
De Brétigny : De Segurola
Innkeeper : Leonhardt
Guards : Bégué, Reschiglian
Servant : Savage

BROOKLYN
December 4
DIE ZAUBERFLÖTE
Bodanzky (c)
Sarastro : Scott
Tamino : Sembach
High Priest : Schlegel
Two Priests : Bloch, Bayer
Queen of the Night : Hempel
Pamina : Kurt (for Zarska)
Three Ladies : Curtis,
Heinrich, Robeson
Papageno : Goritz
Papagena : Mason
Monostatos : Reiss
Three Genii : Sparkes, Cox,
Mattfeld
Guards : Althouse, Ruysdael

PHILADELPHIA
December 7
LOHENGRIN/Bodanzky (c)
King Henry : Braun

Lohengrin : Urlus
Elsa : Rappold
Telramund : Weil
Ortrud : Matzenauer
Herald : Schlegel

December 14
DER ROSENKAVALIER
Bodanzky (c)
Princess von Werdenberg :
Hempel
Baron Ochs : Goritz
Octavian : Ober
Von Faninal : Weil
Sophie : Mason
Marianne : Fornia
Valzacchi : Reiss
Annina : Mattfeld
Police Commissioner :
Schlegel
Majordomo of Princess :
Audisio
Majordomo of Von Faninal :
Bloch
Notary : Ruysdael
Innkeeper : Bayer
Singer : Althouse
Orphans : Cox, Van Dyck,
Barton
Milliner : Martin
Leopold : Burgstaller
Animal Vendor : Sappio
Negro Boy : Dobbins

BROOKLYN
December 18
LA BOHÈME/Bavagnoli (c)
Rodolfo : Damacco (for
Botta)
Marcello : Scotti
Schaunard : Tegani
Colline : De Segurola
Mimi : Alda
Musetta : Cajatti
Benoit : Malatesta
Parpignol : Audisio
Alcindoro : Leonhardt
Sergeant : Reschiglian

PHILADELPHIA
December 21
UN BALLO IN MASCHERA
Polacco (c)
Riccardo : Caruso
Renato : Amato
Amelia : Kurt
Ulrica : Duchène
Oscar : Mason
Silvano : Reschiglian
Samuel : De Segurola
Tom : Rothier
Judge : Bada
Servant : Audisio

BROOKLYN
December 25
IL BARBIERE DI SIVIGLIA
Bavagnoli (c)
Almaviva : Damacco
Dr. Bartolo : Malatesta
Rosina : Nielsen (t—for
Hempel)
Figaro : De Luca
Don Basilio : Didur
Berta : Mattfeld
Fiorello : Reschiglian
Sergeant : Audisio

PHILADELPHIA
December 28
TOSCA/Bavagnoli (c)
Tosca : Destinn
Cavaradossi : Martinelli
Scarpia : De Luca
Angelotti : Rossi
Sacristan : Malatesta
Spoletta : Bada
Sciarrone : Bégué
Jailer : Reschiglian
Shepherd : Braslau

BROOKLYN
January 4
AIDA/Bavagnoli (c)
King : Rossi
Amneris : Ober
Aida : Rappold
Radames : Caruso
Amonasro : Tegani (for
Amato)
Ramfis : Scott
Messenger : Audisio
Priestess : Sparkes

PHILADELPHIA
January 11
DIE ZAUBERFLÖTE
Same (?) as Dec. 4 except:
Tamino : Urlus
Pamina : Rappold
Priest : Bloch

BROOKLYN
January 18
TRISTAN UND ISOLDE
Bodanzky (c)
Tristan : Urlus
Isolde : Kurt
King Marke : Scott
Kurvenal : Weil
Brangaene : Ober
Melot : Schlegel
Steersman : Bayer
Shepherd : Bloch
Sailor's Voice : Bloch

272

PHILADELPHIA
January 25
LA BOHÈME
Same as Dec. 18 except:
Rodolfo : Caruso

BROOKLYN
February 1
MANON
Same as Nov. 30 except:
Lescaut : De Luca (for
  Scotti)

PHILADELPHIA
February 8
LUCIA DI LAMMERMOOR
  Bavagnoli (c)
Lucia : Barrientos
Alisa : Egener
Edgardo : Martinelli
Ashton : Amato
Raimondo : Rothier
Arturo : Bada
Normanno : Audisio

BROOKLYN
February 15
DIE MEISTERSINGER
  Bodanzky (c)
Hans Sachs : Weil
Pogner : Braun
Eva : Hempel (for Gadski)
Magdalene : Mattfeld
Walther : Urlus
Beckmesser : Goritz
Kothner : Schlegel
Vogelgesang : Bloch
Nachtigall : Leonhardt
Zorn : Bayer
Eisslinger : Garden
Moser : Audisio
Ortel : Tegani
Schwarz : Fuhrmann
Foltz : Ruysdael
David : Reiss
Night Watchman : Leonhardt

February 22
LUCIA DI LAMMERMOOR
Same as Feb. 8

PHILADELPHIA
February 29
MADAME SANS-GÊNE
  Polacco (c)
Caterina : Farrar
Tonietta : Sparkes
Giulia : Fornia
La Rossa : Mattfeld
Lefebvre : Martinelli
Fouché : De Segurola
Vinaigre : Bloch
Count Neipperg : Althouse

Queen Carolina : Curtis
Princess Elisa : Egener
Despreaux : Bada
Gelsomine : Tegani
Leroy : Leonhardt
De Brigode : Reschiglian
Napoleone : Amato
Roustan : Bégué

March 7
TRISTAN UND ISOLDE
Same as Jan. 18 except:
Isolde : Gadski
King Marke : Braun
Brangaene : Homer

March 14
HÄNSEL UND GRETEL
  Hageman (c)
Hänsel : Mattfeld
Gretel : Mason
Witch : Reiss
Gertrude : Robeson
Peter : Goritz
Sandman : Sparkes
Dewman : Warrum

PAGLIACCI/Bavagnoli (c)
Nedda : Cajatti
Canio : Caruso
Tonio : De Luca
Beppe : Audisio
Silvio : Tegani

March 21
IL BARBIERE DI SIVIGLIA
Same as Dec. 25 except:
Rosina : Barrientos

March 28
DIE MEISTERSINGER
Same as Feb. 15 except:
Pogner : Witherspoon
Eva : Gadski

BOSTON
April 3
BORIS GODUNOV
Same (?) as Nov. 27 except:
Fyodor : Braslau
Shchelkalov : Reschiglian
Missail : Audisio
Officer : Rossi
Lavitski : Reschiglian
Chernikovski : Schlegel

April 4
LA BOHÈME
Same as Dec. 18 except:
Rodolfo : Caruso
Marcello : De Luca

April 5 (mat.)
CARMEN/Polacco (c)
Carmen : Farrar

Don José : Martinelli
Micaela : Mason
Escamillo : Amato
Zuniga : Rothier
Morales : Laurenti
Frasquita : Sparkes
Mercedes : Braslau
Dancaire : Leonhardt
Remendado : Bada

April 5
TRISTAN UND ISOLDE
Same as Jan. 18 except:
King Marke : Braun
Brangaene : Homer
Shepherd : Reiss

April 6
LUCIA DI LAMMERMOOR
Same as Feb. 8 except:
Ashton : De Luca

April 7
AIDA
Same as Jan. 4 except:
Amneris : Homer
Amonasro : Amato

April 8 (mat.)
MADAMA BUTTERFLY
  Polacco (c)
Cio-Cio-San : Farrar
B. F. Pinkerton : Botta
Sharpless : Scotti
Suzuki : Fornia
Kate Pinkerton : Egener
Goro : Bada
Yamadori : Audisio
Uncle-Priest : Ruysdael
Yakuside : Cerri
Imperial Commissioner :
  Reschiglian

April 8
LOHENGRIN/Bodanzky (c)
Same as Dec. 7 except:
Lohengrin : Sembach
Elsa : Gadski
Ortrud : Ober

April 10
DER ROSENKAVALIER
Same as Dec. 14

April 11
TOSCA/Polacco (c)
Same as Dec. 28 except:
Tosca : Farrar
Cavaradossi : Botta
Scarpia : Scotti
Sciarrone : Reschiglian
Jailer : Laurenti

April 12 (mat.)
RIGOLETTO/Polacco (c)
Duke : Caruso

273

Rigoletto : De Luca
Gilda : Barrientos
Sparafucile : Didur
Maddalena : Perini
Marullo : Bégué
Borsa : Bada
Ceprano : Reschiglian
Countess : Egener
Page : Borniggia

April 12
IL TROVATORE/Bavagnoli (c)
Same as Nov. 16 except:
Azucena : Homer
Gypsy : Cottino (t)

April 13
DER WIDERSPENSTIGEN
ZÄHMUNG/Bodanzky (c)
Baptista : Goritz
Katharina : Ober
Bianca : Rappold
Hortensio : Leonhardt
Lucentio : Sembach
Petruchio : Whitehill
Grumio : Ruysdael
Tailor : Reiss
Majordomo : Bloch
Housekeeper : Mattfeld

April 14
CARMEN
Same as Apr. 5 except:
Escamillo : De Luca
Frasquita : Garrison

April 15 (mat.)
HÄNSEL UND GRETEL
Same as Mar. 14 except:
Witch : Homer
Sandman : Braslau
Dewman : Garrison

PAGLIACCI
Same as Mar. 14 except:
Tonio : Amato
Beppe : Bada

April 15
LA SONNAMBULA/Polacco (c)
Amina : Barrientos
Teresa : Perini
Count Rodolfo : Didur
Elvino : Damacco
Lisa : Sparkes
Alessio : Rossi
Notary : Audisio

BALLET DIVERTISSEMENT :
Galli and Bonfiglio

April 17
MADAME SANS-GÊNE
Same as Feb. 29 except:
La Rossa : Braslau

274

April 18
UN BALLO IN MASCHERA
Same as Dec. 21 except:
Amelia : Gadski
Oscar : Garrison

April 19 (mat.)
DER ROSENKAVALIER
Same as Dec. 14 except:
Princess von Werdenberg :
Kurt
Von Faninal : Leonhardt

April 19
IL BARBIERE DI SIVIGLIA
Same as Dec. 25 except:
Rosina : Barrientos

April 20
LA BOHÈME (for *Butterfly*)
Same as Dec. 18 except:
Rodolfo : Botta
Colline : Didur
Musetta : Sparkes

April 21 (mat.)
PARSIFAL/Bodanzky (c)
Amfortas : Whitehill
Titurel : Ruysdael
Gurnemanz : Braun
Parsifal : Sembach
Klingsor : Goritz
Kundry : Kurt
A Voice : Braslau
Knights of the Grail :
Bayer, Ruysdael
Esquires : Sparkes, Mattfeld,
Reiss, Bloch
Flower Maidens : Mason,
Garrison, Cox, Sparkes,
Curtis, Mattfeld

April 21
MARTHA/Bavagnoli (c)
Harriet : Barrientos
Nancy : Perini
Lionel : Caruso
Plunkett : De Luca
Tristan : Malatesta
Sheriff : Tegani
Servant : Reschiglian

April 22 (mat.)
DIE MEISTERSINGER
Same as Feb. 15 except:
Eva : Gadski
Walther : Sembach

April 22
AIDA
Same as Jan. 4 except:
Amneris : Homer
Radames : Martinelli
Amonasro : Amato

ATLANTA
April 24
SAMSON ET DALILA
Polacco (c)
Dalila : Ober
Samson : Caruso
High Priest : Amato
Abimelech : Schlegel
Old Hebrew : Rothier
Philistine Messenger : Bloch
Philistines : Audisio,
Reschiglian

April 25 (mat.)
LUCIA DI LAMMERMOOR
Same as Feb. 8 except:
Alisa : Mattfeld

April 26
LA SONNAMBULA
Same as Apr. 15 except:
Lisa : Mason

April 27
AIDA
Same as Jan. 4 except:
King : Ruysdael
Aida : Alda
Radames : Martinelli
Amonasro : Amato

April 28
MARTHA
Same as Apr. 21

April 29 (mat.)
DIE MEISTERSINGER
Same as Feb. 15 except:
Eva : Gadski
Walther : Sembach

April 29
LA BOHÈME/Polacco (c)
Same as Dec. 18 except:
Rodolfo : Caruso
Schaunard : Didur
Marcello : Amato
Colline : Rothier
Musetta : Sparkes

1 9 1 6 – 1 7

BROOKLYN
November 14
BORIS GODUNOV/Polacco (c)
Boris Godunov : Didur
Fyodor : Delaunois
Xenia : Sparkes
Nurse : Howard
Shuiski : Bada
Shchelkalov : Reschiglian
Pimen : Rothier

Grigori : Althouse
Marina : Ober
Varlaam : De Segurola
Missail : Audisio
Innkeeper : Mattfeld
Officer : Rossi
Simpleton : Bloch
Chernikovski : Schlegel

PHILADELPHIA
November 21
PRINCE IGOR/Polacco (c)
Igor : Amato
Jaroslavna : Alda
Vladimir : Althouse
Galitzky : Didur
Kontchak : Didur
Kontchakovna : Perini
Ovlour : Audisio
Skoula : De Segurola
Erochka . Bada
Nurse : Egener
Young Girl : Delaunois

BROOKLYN
November 25
LA BOHÈME/Papi
Rodolfo : Botta
Marcello : Scotti
Schaunard : Tegani
Colline : De Segurola
Mimi : Alda
Musetta : Mason
Benoit : Malatesta
Parpignol : Audisio
Alcindoro : Malatesta
Sergeant : Reschiglian

PHILADELPHIA
November 28
SAMSON ET DALILA
Polacco (c)
Dalila : Homer
Samson : Caruso
High Priest : De Luca
Abimelech : Schlegel
Old Hebrew : Rothier
Philistine Messenger : Bloch
Philistines : Audisio,
Reschiglian

BROOKLYN
December 2
CAVALLERIA RUSTICANA
Papi (c)
Santuzza : Kurt
Lola : Perini
Turiddu : Botta
Alfio : Tegani
Lucia : Mattfeld

PAGLIACCI/Papi (c)
Nedda : Mason

Canio : Martinelli
Tonio : Amato
Beppe : Bada
Silvio : Tegani

PHILADELPHIA
December 5
LOHENGRIN/Bodanzky (c)
King Henry : Braun
Lohengrin : Urlus
Elsa : Rappold
Telramund : Goritz
Ortrud : Ober
Herald : Leonhardt

December 12
IL TROVATORE/Polacco (c)
Leonora : Rappold
(for Muzio)
Manrico : Martinelli
Count di Luna : Amato
Azucena : Homer
Inez : Mattfeld
Ferrando : Rothier
Ruiz : Audisio
Gypsy : Reschiglian

BROOKLYN
December 16
LOHEHGRIN
Same as Dec. 5 except:
King Henry : Ruysdael
Telramund : Weil
Ortrud : Homer

PHILADELPHIA
December 19
MARTHA/Papi (c)
Harriet : Hempel
Nancy : Ober
Lionel : Caruso
Plunkett : De Luca
Tristan : Malatesta
Sheriff : Tegani
Servant : Reschiglian

BROOKLYN
December 23
TOSCA/Polacco (c)
Tosca : Muzio
Cavaradossi : Botta
Scarpia : Scotti
Angelotti : Rossi
Sacristan : Malatesta
Spoletta : Bada
Sciarrone : Bégué
Jailer : Reschiglian
Shepherd : Perini

PHILADELPHIA
December 26
SIEGFRIED/Eisler (c)
Siegfried : Urlus

Mime : Reiss
Wanderer : Braun
Alberich : Goritz
Fafner : Ruysdael
Erda : Homer
Brünnhilde : Kurt
Forest Bird : Sparkes

BROOKLYN
January 2
AIDA/Papi (c)
King : Rossi
Amneris : Homer
Aida : Rappold
Radames : Caruso
Amonasro : De Luca
Ramfis : Rothier
Messenger : Audisio
Priestess : Curtis

PHILADELPHIA
January 10
CARMEN/Polacco (c)
Carmen : Matzenauer
(for Farrar)
Don José : Martinelli
Micaela : Mason
Escamillo : De Luca
Zuniga : Rothier
Morales : Laurenti
Frasquita : Garrison
Mercedes : Braslau
Dancaire : Leonhardt
Remendado : Bada

BROOKLYN
January 16
CARMEN
Same as Jan. 10 except:
Micaela : Case

PHILADELPHIA
January 23
LA BOHÈME/Papi (c)
Same as Nov. 25 except:
Rodolfo : Caruso
Marcello : Amato

BROOKLYN
January 30
TRISTAN UND ISOLDE
Bodanzky (c)
Tristan : Urlus
Isolde : Gadski
King Marke : Ruysdael
Kurvenal : Goritz
Brangaene : Ober
Melot : Schlegel (?)
Steersman : Bayer (?)
Shepherd : Reiss
Sailor's Voice : Bloch (?)

1916–17

PHILADELPHIA
February 6
AIDA

Same as Jan. 2 except:
King : Ruysdael (for Rossi)
Amneris : Ober
Aida : Gadski
Radames : Martinelli
Amonasro : Tegani
Ramfis : Didur
Priestess : Egener

BROOKLYN
February 13
LUCIA DI LAMMERMOOR
Papi (c)
Lucia : Barrientos
Alisa : Egener
Edgardo : Martinelli
Ashton : De Luca
Raimondo : Rothier
Arturo : Bada
Normanno : Audisio

PHILADELPHIA
February 20
FRANCESCA DA RIMINI
Polacco (c)
Francesca : Alda
Samaritana : Mason
Ostasio : Tegani
Giovanni : Amato
Paolo : Martinelli
Malatestino : Bada
Biancofiore : Garrison
Garsenda : Sparkes
Altichiara : Braslau
Donella : Delaunois
Maid of Honor : Smith
Slave : Perini
Notary : Audisio
Jester : Malatesta
Archer : Bloch
Tower Warden : Reschiglian

BROOKLYN
February 27
MARTHA

Same as Dec. 19 except:
Harriet : Barrientos
Nancy : Perini
Plunkett : Didur

PHILADELPHIA
March 6
RIGOLETTO/Polacco (c)
Duke : Caruso
Rigoletto : De Luca
Gilda : Barrientos
Sparafucile : De Segurola
Maddalena : Perini
Giovanna : Mattfeld
Monterone : Rossi

Marullo : Bégué
Borsa : Bada
Ceprano : Reschiglian
Countess : Egener
Page : Borniggia

BROOKLYN
March 13
THAIS/Polacco (c)
Thais : Farrar
Nicias : Botta
Athanael : Amato
Palemon : Rothier
Crobyle : Sparkes
Myrtale : Delaunois
Albine : Howard
Servant : Bégué

PHILADELPHIA
March 20
THE CANTERBURY PILGRIMS
Bodanzky (c)
Chaucer : Sembach
Knight : Leonhardt
Squire : Althouse
Friar : Bloch
Miller : Ruysdael
Cook : Malatesta
Shipman : Laurenti
Summoner : Schlegel
Pardoner : Bayer
Host : Rossi
Man of Law : Leonhardt
Joannes : Audisio
King Richard : Reiss
Herald : Tegani
Alisoun : Ober
Prioress : Mason
Johanna : Sundelius
Girls : Tiffany, Egener

March 27
DIE WALKÜRE/Bodanzky (c)
Wotan : Whitehill
Fricka : Robeson
Brünnhilde : Matzenauer
Siegmund : Urlus
Sieglinde : Gadski
Hunding : Ruysdael
Helmwige : Sparkes
Gerhilde : Sundelius
Ortlinde : Curtis
Rossweisse : Perini
Grimgerde : Mulford
Waltraute : Robeson
Siegrune : Mattfeld
Schwertleite : Howard

April 3
TOSCA

Same as Dec. 23 except:
Tosca : Farrar
Shepherd : Braslau

April 10
L'ORACOLO/Polacco (c)
Win-Shee : Didur
Chim-Fen : Scotti
Hoo-Tsin : Rossi
Win-San-Luy : Botta
Hoo-Chee : Bakos
Ah-Yoe : Mason
Hua-Quee : Braslau
Fortune Teller : Audisio

PAGLIACCI

Same as Dec. 2 except:
Nedda : Muzio
Canio : Caruso

April 17
BORIS GODUNOV
Same as Nov. 14

ATLANTA
April 23
L'ELISIR D'AMORE/Papi (c)
Adina : Barrientos
Nemorino : Caruso
Belcore : Scotti
Dulcamara : Didur
Giannetta : Sparkes

April 24 (mat.)
IL TROVATORE

Same as Dec. 12 except:
Leonora : Muzio
Azucena : Ober

April 25
FRANCESCA DA RIMINI

Same as Feb. 20 except:
Ostasio : Laurenti
Biancofiore : Sparkes
Garsenda : Egener
Altichiara : Mattfeld

April 26 (mat.)
TOSCA

Same as Dec. 23 except:
Cavaradossi : Caruso
Sciarrone : Reschiglian
Jailer : Laurenti

April 27
BORIS GODUNOV

Same as Nov. 14 except:
Grigori : Botta
Chernikovski : Laurenti

April 28 (mat.)
SIEGFRIED/Bodanzky (c)

Same as Dec. 26 except:
Siegfried : Sembach
Alberich : Leonhardt
Erda : Howard
Brünnhilde : Gadski
Forest Bird : Mason

276

April 28
RIGOLETTO/Papi (c)
Same as Mar. 6 except:
Sparafucile : Rothier
Marullo : Laurenti

1 9 1 7 – 1 8

BROOKLYN
November 13
TOSCA/Moranzoni (c)
Tosca : Farrar
Cavaradossi : Althouse (for
Martin)
Scarpia : Scotti
Angelotti : Rossi
Sacristan : Malatesta
Spoletta : Bada
Colarone : D'Angelo
Jailer : Reschiglian
Shepherd : Braslau

PHILADELPHIA
November 20
AIDA/Papi (c)
King : Ruysdael
Amneris : Matzenauer
Aida : Muzio
Radames : Martinelli
Amonasro : Amato
Ramfis : Mardones
Messenger : Audisio
Priestess : Sundelius

BROOKLYN
November 24
LE NOZZE DI FIGARO
Bodanzky (c)
Almaviva : Didur
Countess : Matzenauer
Susanna : Hempel
Figaro : De Luca
Cherubino : Delaunois
Marcellina : Howard
Bartolo : Malatesta
Basilio : Reiss
Don Curzio : Bloch
Antonio : Leonhardt
Barbarina : Kanders
Peasant Girls : White,
Mazza (t)

PHILADELPHIA
November 27
MANON LESCAUT/Papi (c)
Manon : Alda
Lescaut : Amato
Des Grieux : Caruso
Geronte : De Segurola
Edmondo : Bada
Ballet Master : Reiss
Innkeeper : Laurenti

Musician : Perini
Sergeant : Reschiglian
Lamplighter : Audisio
Captain : D'Angelo

December 4
FAUST/Monteux (c)
Faust : Martinelli
Marguerite : Farrar
Méphistophélès : Whitehill
Valentin : Laurenti
Siébel : Delaunois
Marthe : Howard
Wagner : D'Angelo

BROOKLYN
December 8
IL TROVATORE/Papi (c)
Leonora : Muzio
Manrico : Kingston
Count di Luna : De Luca
Azucena : Homer
Inez : Egener
Ferrando : Rothier
Ruiz : Audisio
Gypsy : Reschiglian

PHILADELPHIA
December 11
LA FILLE DU RÉGIMENT
Papi (c)
Marie : Hempel
Marquise : Mattfeld
Sulpice : Scotti
Tonio : Carpi
Hortentius : Reschiglian
Corporal : D'Angelo
Peasant : Audisio
Duchesse de Crakentorp :
Savage
Notary : Alexander

December 18
CAVALLERIA RUSTICANA
Moranzoni (c)
Santuzza : Easton
Lola : Perini
Turiddu : Althouse
Alfio : Chalmers
Lucia : Mattfeld

PAGLIACCI/Moranzoni (c)
Nedda : Muzio
Canio : Caruso
Tonio : Amato
Beppe : Audisio
Silvio : Laurenti

BROOKLYN
December 25
LA FILLE DU RÉGIMENT
Same as Dec. 11

January 1
AIDA/Moranzoni (c)
Same as Nov. 20 except:
Amneris : Homer

PHILADELPHIA
January 8
SAINT ELIZABETH
Bodanzky (c)
Saint Elizabeth : Easton
Landgrave Ludwig :
Whitehill
Landgrave Hermann :
Schlegel
Landgravine Sophie :
Matzenauer
Seneschal : Leonhardt
Hungarian Magnate :
Ruysdael
Elizabeth (child) : Bitterl
Ludwig (child) : Belleri

BROOKLYN
January 15
RIGOLETTO/Moranzoni (c)
Duke : Caruso
Rigoletto : De Luca
Gilda : Conde
Sparafucile : Mardones
Maddalena : Perini
Giovanna : Mattfeld
Monterone : Rossi
Marullo : Laurenti
Borsa : Audisio
Ceprano : Reschiglian
Countess : Egener
Page : Borniggia

January 29
CAVALLERIA RUSTICANA
Papi (c)
Same as Dec. 18

PAGLIACCI/Papi (c)
Same as Dec. 18 except:
Canio : Kingston

PHILADELPHIA
February 5
LA TRAVIATA/Papi (c—for
Moranzoni)
Violetta : Hempel
Alfredo : Carpi
Germont : De Luca
Flora : Egener
Annina : Mattfeld
Gastone : Bada
Baron Douphol : Reschiglian
Marquis d'Obigny : Laurenti
Doctor Grenvil : Rossi

277

BROOKLYN
February 12
LA BOHÈME/Papi (c)
Rodolfo : Carpi
Marcello : Scotti
Schaunard : D'Angelo
Colline : Didur
Mimi : Alda
Musetta : Miller
Benoit : Malatesta
Parpignol : Audisio
Alcindoro : Malatesta
Sergeant : Reschiglian

PHILADELPHIA
February 19
LODOLETTA/Moranzoni (c)
Lodoletta : Easton
Flammen : Caruso
Franz : Malatesta
Gianetto : Amato
Antonio : Didur
Mad Woman : Robeson
Vannard : Arden
Maud : Egener
Voice : Bloch
Letter Carrier : Mandelli
Old Violinist : Burgstaller

BROOKLYN
February 26
THAÏS/Monteux (c)
Thaïs : Farrar
Nicias : Diaz
Athanael : Whitehill
Palemon : Rossi
Crobyle : Sparkes
Myrtale : Egener
Albine : Howard
Servant : Reschiglian

PHILADELPHIA
March 5
MADAMA BUTTERFLY
Moranzoni (c)
Cio-Cio-San : Farrar
B. F. Pinkerton : Althouse
Sharpless : Chalmers
Suzuki : Fornia
Kate Pinkerton : Egener
Goro : Reiss
Yamadori : Audisio
Uncle-Priest : Ruysdael
Imperial Commissioner :
  D'Angelo

BROOKLYN
March 9
I PURITANI/Moranzoni (c)
Lord Walton : Rossi
Sir George : Mardones
Elvira : Barrientos
Henrietta : Perini

Lord Arthur : Lazaro
Sir Richard : De Luca
Sir Bruno : Bada

PHILADELPHIA
March 12
RIGOLETTO/Papi (c)
Same as Jan. 15 except:
Duke : Lazaro
Gilda : Barrientos
Maddalena : Braslau
Borsa : Bada

March 19
L'AMORE DEI TRE RE
Moranzoni (c)
Archibaldo : Mardones
Manfredo : Amato
Avito : Caruso
Flaminio : Bada
Youth : Audisio
Fiora : Muzio
Maid : Kanders
Young Woman : Tiffany
Old Woman : Robeson
Shepherd : Arden

BROOKLYN
March 23
CARMEN/Monteux (c)
Carmen : Farrar
Don José : Martinelli
Micaela : Sundelius
Escamillo : Whitehill
Zuniga : Rothier
Morales : Laurenti
Frasquita : Sparkes
Mercedes : Fornia
Dancaire : Reiss
Remendado : Bada

PHILADELPHIA
March 26
CARMEN
Same as Mar. 23 except:
Mercedes : Perini

April 2
LA BOHÈME
Same as Feb. 12 except:
Rodolfo : Martinelli
Marcello : Chalmers
Colline : Scott
Alcindoro : Leonhardt

April 9
SAMSON ET DALILA
Monteux (c)
Dalila : Matzenauer
Samson : Caruso
High Priest : Whitehill
Abimelech : Schlegel
Old Hebrew : Rothier

Philistine Messenger : Bloch
Philistines : Audisio,
  Reschiglian

April 16 (mat.)
IL TROVATORE
Same as Dec. 8 except:
Manrico : Martinelli
Azucena : Matzenauer
Inez : Mattfeld

April 16
L'ORACOLO/Moranzoni (c)
Win-Shee : Didur
Chim-Fen : Scotti
Hoo-Tsin : Rossi
Win-San-Luy : Althouse
Hoo-Chee : Bakos
Ah-Yoe : Easton
Hua-Quee : Mattfeld
Fortune Teller : Audisio

LE COQ D'OR/Monteux (c)
Queen : Barrientos
King Dodon : Didur
Amelfa : Robeson
Astrologer : Diaz
Prince Guidon : Audisio
General Polkan : Ruysdael
Prince Afron : Reschiglian
Golden Cockerel : Sundelius
Pantomimists
Queen : Galli
King Dodon : Bolm
Amelfa : Smith
Astrologer : Bonfiglio
Prince Guidon : Hall
General Polkan : Bartik
Prince Afron : Ioucelli

BOSTON
April 22
LE PROPHÈTE/Bodanzky (c)
John of Leyden : Caruso
Fidès : Matzenauer
Bertha : Muzio
Jonas : Diaz
Mathisen : D'Angelo
Zacharias : Mardones
Oberthal : Rothier
Anabaptist : Laurenti
Officer : Audisio
Captain : Ruysdael
Peasant : Reschiglian

April 23
TOSCA
Same as Nov. 13 except:
Cavaradossi : McCormack
Shepherd : Arden

April 24 (mat.)
AÏDA/Moranzoni (c)
Same as Nov. 20 except:
Priestess : Sparkes

April 24
RIGOLETTO/Papi (c)
Same as Jan. 15 except:
Duke : Lazaro
Gilda : Barrientos
Sparafucile : Rothier
Maddalena : Howard
Borsa : Bada

April 25
L'ORACOLO
Same as Apr. 16

PAGLIACCI
Same as Dec. 18 except:
Beppe : Bada

April 26 (mat.)
LE COQ D'OR
Same as Apr. 16 except:
Queen : Garrison
Amelfa : Howard
Voice : Sparkes

PLACE CONGO (Ballet)
Monteux (c)
Aurore : Galli
Remon : Bonfiglio
Numa : Bartik

April 26
MADAMA BUTTERFLY/Papi (c)
Same (?) as Mar. 5 except:
B. F. Pinkerton : Carpi
Sharpless : Scotti
Goro : Bada
Yakuside : Cerri

April 27 (mat.)
SAMSON ET DALILA
Same as Apr. 9 except:
Dalila : Claussen
High Priest : Chalmers
Abimelech : D'Angelo

April 27
I PURITANI
Same as Mar. 9 except:
Sir Bruno : Audisio

1 9 1 8 – 1 9

BROOKLYN
November 12
MADAMA BUTTERFLY
Moranzoni (c)
Cio-Cio-San : Farrar
B. F. Pinkerton : Althouse
Sharpless : De Luca
Suzuki : Fornia
Kate Pinkerton : Egener
Goro : Bada

Yamadori : Audisio
Uncle-Priest : Schlegel
Yakuside : Cerri
Imperial Commissioner :
  Reschiglian

PHILADELPHIA
November 19
MAROUF/Monteux (c)
Marouf : De Luca
Princess : Alda
Sultan : Rothier
Fatimah : Howard
Vizier : De Segurola
Ali : Laurenti
Pastry Cook : Ananian
Fellah : Bada
Chief Sailor : Reiss
Merchants : Bada, Malatesta
Cadi : Rossi
Muezzins : Paltrinieri, Bada
Donkey Driver : Audisio

BROOKLYN
November 23
LA TRAVIATA/Moranzoni (c)
Violetta : Hempel
Alfredo : Carpi
Germont : Montesanto (d)
Flora : Egener
Annina : Mattfeld
Gastone : Bada
Baron Douphol : Reschiglian
Marquis d'Obigny : D'Angelo
Doctor Grenvil : Rossi

PHILADELPHIA
November 26
L'ELISIR D'AMORE/Papi (c)
Adina : Hempel
Nemorino : Caruso
Belcore : De Luca
Dulcamara : Didur
Giannetta : Sparkes

December 3
TOSCA/Moranzoni (c)
Tosca : Muzio
Cavaradossi : Crimi
Scarpia : Scotti
Angelotti : Rossi
Sacristan : Malatesta
Spoletta : Paltrinieri
Sciarrone : Reschiglian
Jailer : Laurenti
Shepherd : Arden

BROOKLYN
December 7
MAROUF
Same as Nov. 19 except:
Ali : Chalmers
Fellah : Diaz

Merchants : Paltrinieri,
  Rossi
Muezzins : Diaz, Paltrinieri

PHILADELPHIA
December 10
CAVALLERIA RUSTICANA
Papi (c)
Santuzza : Ponselle
Lola : Braslau
Turiddu : Althouse
Alfio : Laurenti
Lucia : Mattfeld

PAGLIACCI/Papi (c)
Nedda : Easton
Canio : Caruso
Tonio : Montesanto
Beppe : Reiss (for Audisio)
Silvio : Laurenti

December 17
IL TABARRO/Moranzoni (c)
Michele : Montesanto
Luigi : Crimi
Tinca : Bada
Talpa : Didur
Giorgetta : Muzio
Frugola : Gentle
Song Peddler : Audisio
Lovers : Tiffany, Reiss

SUOR ANGELICA
Moranzoni (c)
Angelica : Farrar
Princess : Perini
Abbess : Fornia
Alms Collector : Sundelius
Mistress of Novices : Arden
Genovieffa : Ellis
Osmina : Dalleri
Dolcina : Mattfeld
Aspirant Sisters : Beale,
  Egener
Nursing Sisters : Tiffany,
  Warwick
Novice : White

GIANNI SCHICCHI
Moranzoni (c)
Gianni Schicchi : De Luca
Lauretta : Easton
La Vecchia : Howard
Rinuccio : Crimi
Gherardo : Bada
Nella : Tiffany
Gherardino : Malatesta
Betto : Ananian
Simone : Didur
Marco : D'Angelo
Ciesca : Sundelius
Spinelloccio : Malatesta
Nicolao : De Segurola
Pinellino : Reschiglian
Guccio : Schlegel

1918–19

BROOKLYN

December 24
AIDA/Moranzoni (c)
King : Rossi
Amneris : Homer
Aida : Rappold
Radames : Kingston
Amonasro : Couzinou
Ramfis : Mardones
Messenger : Audisio
Priestess : Sparkes

December 31
FAUST/Monteux (c)
Faust : Martinelli
Marguerite : Alda
Méphistophélès : Rothier
Valentin : Couzinou
Siébel : Delaunois
Marthe : Howard
Wagner : Ananian

PHILADELPHIA

January 7
AIDA
Same as Dec. 24 except:
Aida : Muzio
Radames : Crimi
Amonasro : De Luca
Ramfis : Scott

BROOKLYN

January 14
THAIS/Monteux (c)
Thais : Farrar
Nicias : Diaz
Athanael : Couzinou
Palemon : Rothier
Crobyle : Delaunois
Myrtale : Sparkes (for
 Egener)
Albine : Braslau
Servant : Reschiglian

PHILADELPHIA

January 21
SAMSON ET DALILA
 Setti (c—for Monteux)
Dalila : Matzenauer
Samson : Caruso
High Priest : Couzinou
Abimelech : Ananian
Old Hebrew : Mardones
Philistine Messenger : Reiss
Philistines : Audisio,
 Reschiglian

BROOKLYN

January 28
CRISPINO E LA COMARE
 Papi (c)
Crispino : Scotti
Annetta : Hempel

280

Dr. Fabrizio : Chalmers
Mirabolano : De Segurola
Count del Fiore : Paltrinieri
Don Asdrubale : Ananian
Comare : Braslau
Bartolo : Audisio

PHILADELPHIA

February 4
IL BARBIERE DI SIVIGLIA
 Papi (c)
Almaviva : Hackett
Dr. Bartolo : Malatesta
Rosina : Hempel
Figaro : De Luca
Don Basilio : Mardones
Berta : Mattfeld
Fiorello : Reschiglian
Sergeant : Audisio

BROOKLYN

February 11
CAVALLERIA RUSTICANA
 Moranzoni (c)
Same as Dec. 10 except:
Santuzza : Easton
Lola : Perini
Turiddu : Crimi
Alfio : Montesanto

LE COQ D'OR/Monteux (c)
Queen : Barrientos
King Dodon : Didur
Amelfa : Robeson
Astrologer : Diaz
Prince Guidon : Audisio
General Polkan : Ananian
Prince Afron : Reschiglian
Golden Cockerel : Sundelius
 Pantomimists
Queen : Galli
King Dodon : Bolm
Amelfa : Smith
Astrologer : Bonfiglio
Prince Guidon : Agnini
General Polkan : Bartik
Prince Afron : Ioucelli

PHILADELPHIA

February 18
MADAMA BUTTERFLY
Same as Nov. 12 except:
B. F. Pinkerton : Lazaro
Sharpless : Montesanto
Yamadori : D'Angelo

BROOKLYN

February 25
BORIS GODUNOV/Papi (c)
Boris Godunov : Didur
Fyodor : Delaunois
Xenia : Mellish
Nurse : Perini

Shuiski : Bada
Shchelkalov : Reschiglian
 (for Laurenti)
Pimen : Rothier
Grigori : Althouse
Marina : Matzenauer
Varlaam : Ananian
Missail : Audisio
Innkeeper : Mattfeld
Officer : Rossi
Simpleton : Paltrinieri
Lavitski : Reschiglian
Chernikovski : Schlegel
Boyar : Paltrinieri

PHILADELPHIA

March 4
IL TROVATORE/Papi (c)
Leonora : Muzio
Manrico : Crimi
Count di Luna : De Luca
Azucena : Matzenauer
Inez : Egener
Ferrando : Rothier
Ruiz : Audisio
Gypsy : Reschiglian

BROOKLYN

March 8
LA FORZA DEL DESTINO
 Papi (c)
Marquis : D'Angelo (for
 Rossi)
Leonora : Ponselle
Don Carlo : Montesanto
Don Alvaro : Caruso
Padre Guardiano : Mardones
Fra Melitone : Chalmers
Preziosilla : Gentle
Curra : Mattfeld
Trabucco : Paltrinieri
Surgeon : Reschiglian
Alcade : Ananian (for
 D'Angelo)

PHILADELPHIA

March 11
LA BOHÈME/Papi (c)
Rodolfo : Caruso
Marcello : Montesanto
Schaunard : D'Angelo
Colline : De Segurola
Mimi : Muzio
Musetta : Sparkes
Benoit : Ananian
Parpignol : Audisio
Alcindoro : Ananian
Sergeant : Reschiglian

March 18
LA REINE FIAMMETTE
 Monteux (c)
Orlanda : Farrar
Agramente : Howard

Angioletta : Ellis
Chiarina : Mattfeld
Pantasille : Perini
Michela : Sparkes
Pomone : Tiffany
Viola : Ellis
Violette : Sparkes
Violine : Beale
Youths : Mellish, Arden
Danielo : Lazaro
Sforza : Rothier
Giorgio d'Ast : Didur
Luc Agnolo : Laurenti
Castiglione : Bada
Cortez : Reiss
Cesano : Paltrinieri
Vasari : Audisio
Prosecutor : Ananian
Novices : Warwick, White

March 25
LA FORZA DEL DESTINO
Same as Mar. 8 except:
Don Carlo : De Luca
Preziosilla : Delaunois

April 1
L'AMORE DEI TRE RE
Moranzoni (c)
Archibaldo : Didur
Manfredo : Chalmers
Avito : Martinelli
Flaminio : Bada
A Youth : Audisio
Fiora : Muzio
A Maid : Egener
A Young Woman : Tiffany
An Old Woman : Mattfeld

April 8
RIGOLETTO/Moranzoni (c)
Duke : Lazaro
Rigoletto : De Luca
Gilda : Barrientos
Sparafucile : De Segurola
Maddalena : Braslau
Giovanna : Mattfeld
Monterone : Rossi
Marullo : Laurenti
Borsa : Bada
Ceprano : Reschiglian
Countess : Egener
Page : Puglioli (for White)

April 15
FAUST
Same as Dec. 31 except:
Marguerite : Easton
Valentin : Chalmers
Siébel : Ellis (for Delaunois)
Wagner : D'Angelo (for
  Ananian)

ATLANTA
April 21
LA FORZA DEL DESTINO
Same as Mar. 8 except:
Don Carlo : De Luca
Preziosilla : Delaunois
Fra Melitone : Malatesta
Trabucco : Bada

April 22 (mat.)
FAUST/Moranzoni (c)
Same as Dec. 31 except:
Valentin : Chalmers
Siébel : Sparkes
Marthe : Robeson

April 23
AIDA
Same as Dec. 24 except:
King : D'Angelo
Amneris : Matzenauer
Aida : Muzio
Radames : Lazaro
Amonasro : Chalmers
Messenger : Paltrinieri

April 24 (mat.)
MARTHA/Papi (c)
Harriet : Barrientos
Nancy : Howard
Lionel : Caruso
Plunkett : Didur
Tristan : Malatesta
Sheriff : D'Angelo
Servant : Reschiglian

April 25
LA BOHÈME
Same as Mar. 11 except:
Rodolfo : Martinelli
Marcello : Scotti
Schaunard : Didur
Colline : Rothier
Mimi : Alda
Parpignol : Paltrinieri

April 26 (mat.)
I PURITANI/Moranzoni (c)
(Not given in New York)
Lord Walton : D'Angelo
Sir George : Mardones
Elvira : Barrientos
Henrietta : Delaunois
Lord Arthur : Lazaro
Sir Richard : De Luca
Sir Bruno : Bada

April 26
CAVALLERIA RUSTICANA
Moranzoni (c)
Same as Dec. 10 except:
Santuzza : Ponselle
Lola : Delaunois
Alfio : Chalmers

PAGLIACCI/Moranzoni (c)
Same as Dec. 10 except:
Tonio : Scotti
Beppe : Paltrinieri

1919–20

BROOKLYN
November 18
LA BOHÈME/Papi (c)
Rodolfo : Harrold (d)
Marcello : Chalmers
Schaunard : Didur
Colline : De Segurola
Mimi : Alda
Musetta : Sundelius
Benoit : Ananian
Parpignol : Audisio
Alcindoro : Ananian
Sergeant : Reschiglian

PHILADELPHIA
November 25
AIDA/Moranzoni (c)
King : Ananian
Amneris : Besanzoni
Aida : Destinn
Radames : Martinelli
Amonasro : Couzinou (for
  Zanelli)
Ramfis : Martino
Messenger : Audisio
Priestess : Vosari

BROOKLYN
November 29
LUCIA DI LAMMERMOOR
Papi (c)
Lucia : Garrison
Alisa : Egener
Edgardo : Crimi
Ashton : De Luca
Raimondo : Martino
Arturo : Bada
Normanno : Dua

PHILADELPHIA
December 2
L'ELISIR D'AMORE/Papi (c)
Adina : Garrison
Nemorino : Caruso
Belcore : De Luca
Dulcamara : Malatesta
Giannetta : Ellis

BROOKLYN
December 6
CARMEN/Wolff (c)
Carmen : Farrar
Don José : Martinelli

Micaela : Kellogg
Escamillo : Couzinou
Zuniga : De Segurola
Morales : Picco
Frasquita : Tiffany
Mercedes : Ingram
Dancaire : Ananian
Remendado : Dua

PHILADELPHIA
December 9
Tosca/Moranzoni (c)
Tosca : Farrar
Cavaradossi : Hackett
Scarpia : Scotti
Angelotti : D'Angelo
Sacristan : Malatesta
Spoletta : Paltrinieri
Sciarrone : D'Angelo (for
  Laurenti)
Jailer : Reschiglian
Shepherd : Arden

December 19
La Bohème
Same as Nov. 18 except:
Marcello : Scotti
Schaunard : Picco
Colline : Martino
Musetta : Romaine
Benoit : Malatesta
Alcindoro : Malatesta

BROOKLYN
December 23
Martha/Bodanzky (c)
Harriet : Garrison
Nancy : Perini
Lionel : Caruso
Plunkett : De Luca
Tristan : Malatesta
Sheriff : D'Angelo
Servant : Reschiglian

December 30
Faust/Wolff (c)
Faust : Harrold
Marguerite : Farrar
Méphistophélès : Rothier
Valentin : Couzinou
Siébel : Delaunois
Marthe : Mattfeld
Wagner : Ananian (for
  D'Angelo)

PHILADELPHIA
January 6
La Juive/Bodanzky (c)
Rachel : Ponselle
Eleazar : Caruso
Brogni : Mardones
Princess : Scotney
Leopold : Harrold

Ruggiero : Chalmers
Albert : D'Angelo
Herald : Ananian
Majordomo : Ananian

BROOKLYN
January 13
L'Oracolo/Moranzoni (c)
Win-Shee : Didur
Chim-Fen : Scotti
Hoo-Tsin : D'Angelo
Win-San-Luy : Diaz
Hoo-Chee : Quintina
Ah-Yoe : Easton
Hua-Quee : Marsh
Fortune Teller : Audisio

Le Coq d'Or/Bodanzky (c)
Queen : Garrison
King Dodon : Didur
Amelfa : Bérat
Astrologer : Diaz
Prince Guidon : Audisio
General Polkan : Ananian
Prince Afron : Reschiglian
Golden Cockerel : Sundelius
Pantomimists
Queen : Galli
King Dodon : Bolm
Amelfa : Rudolph
Astrologer : Bonfiglio
Prince Guidon : Agnini
General Polkan : Bartik
Prince Afron : Cella

PHILADELPHIA
January 20
Rigoletto/Moranzoni (c)
Duke : Hackett
Rigoletto : De Luca
Gilda : Garrison
Sparafucile : Martino
Maddalena : Perini
Giovanna : Bérat
Monterone : D'Angelo
Marullo : Laurenti
Borsa : Bada
Ceprano : Reschiglian
Countess : Egener
Page : Borniggia

BROOKLYN
January 27
Il Trovatore/Papi (c)
Leonora : Muzio
Manrico : Kingston
Count di Luna : Amato
Azucena : Gordon
Inez : Egener
Ferrando : Martino
Ruiz : Audisio
Gypsy : Reschiglian

PHILADELPHIA
February 3
L'Oracolo
Same as Jan. 13 except:
Hua-Quee : Gordon

Cleopatra's Night/Papi (c)
Cleopatra : Alda
Meiamoun : Kingston
Mardion : Gordon
Iras : Tiffany
Eunuch : Picco
Roman Officer : D'Angelo
Mark Antony :
  Reschiglian (?)

BROOKLYN
February 10
Cleopatra's Night
Same as Feb. 3

Pagliacci/Papi (c)
Nedda : Muzio
Canio : Martinelli
Tonio : De Luca
Beppe : Bada
Silvio : Picco

PHILADELPHIA
February 17
Zaza/Moranzoni (c)
Zaza : Farrar
Anaide : Howard
Floriana : Ingram
Natalia : Egener
Mme. Dufresne : Tiffany
Milio Dufresne : Crimi
Cascart : Amato
Bussy : Picco
Malardot : Bada
Lartigon : Ananian
Duclou : Malatesta
Michelin : Laurenti
Courtois : Reschiglian
  (for D'Angelo)
Marco : Paltrinieri
Toto : Quintina
Auguste : Audisio
Claretta : White
Simona : Warwick

BROOKLYN
February 24
La Juive
Same as Jan. 6 except:
Brogni : Rothier
Leopold : Diaz
Ruggiero : Picco

PHILADELPHIA
March 2
Martha
Same as Dec. 23 except:
Harriet : Barrientos

Plunkett : Didur
Sheriff : Laurenti

BROOKLYN

March 6

AIDA

Same as Nov. 25 except:
King : D'Angelo
Amneris : Gordon
Aida : Ponselle
Radames : Crimi
Amonasro : Amato
Priestess : Curtis

PHILADELPHIA

March 9

MADAMA BUTTERFLY
Moranzoni (c)

Cio-Cio-San : Easton
B. F. Pinkerton : Hackett
Sharpless : Chalmers
Suzuki : Fornia
Kate Pinkerton : Kellogg
Goro : Paltrinieri
Yamadori : Audisio
Uncle-Priest : D'Angelo
(for Ananian)
Imperial Commissioner :
Reschiglian

March 16

IL TROVATORE

Same as Jan. 27 except:
Manrico : Crimi
Count di Luna : Zanelli
Azucena : Matzenauer

March 23

IL BARBIERE DI SIVIGLIA
Papi (c)

Almaviva : Hackett
Dr. Bartolo : Malatesta
Rosina : Barrientos
Figaro : Amato
Don Basilio : Mardones
Berta : Bérat
Fiorello : Reschiglian
Sergeant : Audisio

March 30

LA FORZA DEL DESTINO
Papi (c)

Marquis : D'Angelo
Leonora : Ponselle
Don Carlo : Amato
Don Alvaro : Caruso
Padre Guardiano : Mardones
Fra Melitone : Chalmers
Preziosilla : Gordon
Curra : Egener
Trabucco : Paltrinieri
Surgeon : Reschiglian

April 6

L'AMORE DEI TRE RE
Moranzoni (c)

Archibaldo : Didur
Manfredo : Amato
Avito : Martinelli
Flaminio : Bada
A Youth : Audisio
Fiora : Muzio
A Maid : Egener
A Young Woman : Tiffany
An Old Woman : Bérat

April 13

LUCIA DI LAMMERMOOR

Same as Nov. 29 except:
Lucia : Barrientos
Edgardo : Lazaro
Normanno : Audisio

April 20

EUGEN ONEGIN/Bodanzky (c)

Larina : Gordon
Tatiana : Muzio
Olga : Perini
Filipievna : Howard
Onegin : De Luca
Lenski : Martinelli
Prince Gremin : Didur
Triquet : Bada
Zaretski : Picco
Captain : D'Angelo
Guillot : Lellman

ATLANTA

April 26

SAMSON ET DALILA/Wolff (c)

Dalila : Matzenauer
Samson : Caruso
High Priest · Amato
Abimelech : Ananian
Old Hebrew : Mardones
Philistine Messenger : Bada
Philistines : Audisio,
Reschiglian

April 27

ZAZA

Same as Feb. 17 except:
Floriana : Tiffany (for
Gordon)
Milio Dufresne : Martinelli
Michelin : Reschiglian
Courtois : D'Angelo
Claretta : Manetti (for White)

April 28

LUCIA DI LAMMERMOOR

Same as Nov. 29 except:
Lucia : Barrientos
Edgardo : Harrold
Raimondo : Mardones
Normanno : Audisio

April 29

LA JUIVE/Wolff (c)

Same as Jan. 6 except:
Brogni : Rothier
Leopold : Diaz

April 30

MADAMA BUTTERFLY

Same as Mar. 9 except:
Cio-Cio-San : Farrar
B. F. Pinkerton : Harrold
Sharpless : Scotti
Suzuki : Gordon
Kate Pinkerton : Egener
Uncle-Priest : Ananian

May 1 (mat.)

IL TROVATORE

Same as Jan. 27 except:
Leonora : Easton
Manrico : Martinelli
Count di Luna : De Luca
Azucena : Matzenauer
Ferrando : Rothier

May 1

L'ELISIR D'AMORE

Same as Dec. 2 except:
Adina : Barrientos
Belcore : Scotti
Giannetta : Tiffany

1 9 2 0 – 2 1

BROOKLYN

November 16

FAUST/Wolff (c)

Faust : Harrold
Marguerite : Farrar
Méphistophélès : Whitehill
Valentin : Chalmers
Siébel : Delaunois
Marthe : Howard
Wagner : D'Angelo

November 23

AIDA/Moranzoni (c)

King : Gustafson
Amneris : Gordon
Aida : Destinn
Radames : Martinelli
Amonasro : Danise
Ramfis : Martino
Messenger : Audisio
Priestess : Harvard

PHILADELPHIA

November 30

LA JUIVE/Bodanzky (c)

Rachel : Ponselle
Eleazar : Caruso
Brogni : Rothier
Princess : Scotney

Leopold : Diaz
Ruggiero : Leonhardt
Albert : D'Angelo
Herald : Ananian
Majordomo : Ananian

December 7
CARMEN/Wolff (c)
Carmen : Farrar
Don José : Martinelli
Micaela : Miriam
Escamillo : Whitehill
Zuniga : Martino
Morales : Laurenti
Frasquita : Mellish
Mercedes : Ingram
Dancaire : Leonhardt
Remendado : Dua

BROOKLYN
December 11
L'ELISIR D'AMORE/Papi (c)
Adina : Scotney (for
  Garrison)
Nemorino : Caruso
Belcore : De Luca
Dulcamara : Malatesta
Giannetta : Tiffany
(*Caruso suffered a hemorrhage
  and the audience was dis-
  missed after first act. This
  was his final performance
  on tour*)

PHILADELPHIA
December 14
MEFISTOFELE/Moranzoni (c)
Marguerite : Alda
Helen of Troy : Easton
Martha : Easton
Pantalis : Perini
Mefistofele : Didur
Faust : Gigli
Wagner : Bada
Nereus : Paltrinieri

BROOKLYN
December 21
TRISTAN UND ISOLDE (*English*)
  Bodanzky (c)
Tristan : Sembach
Isolde : Easton
King Marke : Gustafson
Kurvenal : Whitehill
Brangaene : Gordon
Melot : Leonhardt
Steersman : D'Angelo
Shepherd : Dua
Sailor's Voice : Diaz

December 28
ZAZA/Moranzoni (c)
Zaza : Farrar
Anaide : Howard

Floriana : Ingram
Natalia : Egener
Mme. Dufresne : Arden
Milio Dufresne : Martinelli
Cascart : De Luca
Bussy : Picco
Malardot : Bada
Lartigon : Ananian
Duclou : Malatesta
Michelin : Laurenti
Courtois : D'Angelo
Marco : Paltrinieri
Toto : Quintina
Auguste : Audisio
Claretta : White
Simona : Warwick

PHILADELPHIA
January 4
LA BOHÈME/Papi (c)
Rodolfo : Gigli
Marcello : Scotti
Schaunard : Picco
Colline : Martino
Mimi : Alda
Musetta : Roselle
Benoit : Ananian
Parpignol : Audisio
Alcindoro : Ananian
Sergeant : Reschiglian

BROOKLYN
January 11
RIGOLETTO/Moranzoni (c)
Duke : Gigli
Rigoletto : Danise
Gilda : Garrison
Sparafucile : Rothier
Maddalena : Perini
Giovanna : Bérat
Monterone : Ananian
Marullo : Laurenti
Borsa : Paltrinieri
Ceprano : Reschiglian
Countess : Mellish
Page : Borniggia

January 15
TOSCA/Moranzoni (c)
Tosca : Easton
Cavaradossi : Chamlee
Scarpia : Scotti
Angelotti : Ananian
Sacristan : Malatesta
Spoletta : Bada
Sciarrone : D'Angelo
Jailer : Laurenti
Shepherd : Bada (for Arden)

PHILADELPHIA
January 18
TRISTAN UND ISOLDE (*English*)
Same as Dec. 21 except:

Isolde : Matzenauer
Kurvenal : Leonhardt
Melot : Laurenti
Shepherd : Diaz (for Dua)

January 25
DON CARLO/Papi (c)
Philip II : Didur
Don Carlo : Crimi
Rodrigo : De Luca
Grand Inquisitor : D'Angelo
Friar : Gustafson
Elizabeth : Ponselle
Princess Eboli : Gordon
Theobald : Dalossy
Count Lerma : Bada
Herald : Bada
Voice : Sundelius
Countess Aremberg : Savage

February 1
TOSCA
Same as Jan. 15 except:
Tosca : Muzio
Cavaradossi : Martinelli
Angelotti : D'Angelo
Spoletta : Paltrinieri
Sciarrone : Reschiglian
Jailer : D'Angelo
Shepherd : Arden

BROOKLYN
February 8
CAVALLERIA RUSTICANA
  Moranzoni (c)
Santuzza : Ponselle
Lola : Perini
Turiddu : Gigli
Alfio : Danise
Lucia : Bérat

LE COQ D'OR/Bamboschek (c)
Queen : Scotney
King Dodon : Didur
Amelfa : Bérat
Astrologer : Diaz
Prince Guidon : Audisio
General Polkan : Ananian
Prince Afron : Reschiglian
Pantomimists
Queen : Galli
King Dodon : Bolm
Amelfa : Rudolph
Astrologer : Bonfiglio
Prince Guidon : Agnini
General Polkan : Bartik
Prince Afron : Marks

PHILADELPHIA
February 15
MADAMA BUTTERFLY (for
  Louise) Moranzoni (c)
Cio-Cio-San : Easton
B. F. Pinkerton : Harrold

Sharpless : Chalmers
Suzuki : Leveroni
Kate Pinkerton : Egener
Goro : Bada
Yamadori : Audisio
Uncle-Priest : Ananian
Imperial Commissioner :
  Reschiglian
Yakuside : Cerri

BROOKLYN
February 19
SAMSON ET DALILA/Wolff (c)
Dalila : Matzenauer
Samson : Sembach
High Priest : Amato
Abimelech : Schlegel
Old Hebrew : Rothier
Philistine Messenger : Bada
Philistines : Audisio,
  Reschiglian

PHILADELPHIA
March 1
ANDREA CHÉNIER
  Moranzoni (c)
Andrea Chénier : Gigli
Maddalena : Peralta (for
  Muzio)
Countess di Coigny : Howard
Carlo Gérard : Danise
Bersi : Dalossy
Fléville : Laurenti
Abbé : Paltrinieri
Madelon : Perini
Mathieu : Ananian
Spy : Bada
Fouquier : Leonhardt
Dumas : D'Angelo
Roucher : Picco
Schmidt : Reschiglian
Majordomo : Reschiglian

BROOKLYN
March 5
LOHENGRIN (*English*)
  Bodanzky (c)
King Henry : Gustafson
Lohengrin : Harrold
Elsa : Easton
Telramund : Whitehill
Ortrud : Claussen
Herald : Leonhardt

PHILADELPHIA
March 8
LOUISE/Wolff (c)
Louise : Farrar
Julien : Harrold
Mother : Bérat
Father : Rothier
Irma : Dalossy
Camille : Egener
Gertrude : Perini

Apprentice : Ellis
Elise : Roselle
Blanche : Miriam
Suzanne : Tiffany
Forewoman : Axman
Marguerite : Mellish
Madeleine : Kellogg
Painter : Reschiglian
First Philosopher : Leonhardt
Second Philosopher : Audisio
Sculptor : Picco
Poet : Malatesta
Student : Paltrinieri
Song Writer : Laurenti
Street Sweeper : Axman
Newspaper Girl : Roselle
Young Rag Picker : Leveroni
Milk Woman : Egener
Coal Picker : Arden
Noctambulist : Diaz
King of the Fools : Diaz
First Policeman : Righi
Second Policeman : Sterzini
Rag Picker : Ananian
Junk Man : D'Angelo
Street Arab : Ellis
Old Clothes Man : Paltrinieri
Bird Food Vendor : Mellish
Artichoke Vendor : Tiffany
Chair Mender : Arden
Carrot Vendor : Audisio

March 15
RIGOLETTO
Same as Jan. 11 except:
Duke : Hackett
Rigoletto : De Luca
Gilda : Chase
Maddalena : Howard (for
  Perini)
Monterone : D'Angelo
Borsa : Bada
Page : Puglioli (t—for
  Borniggia)

BROOKLYN
March 19
L'AMORE DEI TRE RE
  Moranzoni (c)
Archibaldo : Didur
Manfredo : Danise
Avito : Gigli
Flaminio : Paltrinieri
A Youth : Audisio
Fiora : Muzio (for Bori)
A Maid : Harvard
Young Woman : Tiffany
Old Woman : Bérat
Shepherd : Arden

PHILADELPHIA
March 22
AIDA
Same as Nov. 23 except:

King : D'Angelo
Amneris : Claussen
Aida : Muzio
Radames : Crimi
Amonasro : Zanelli
Ramfis : Rothier

March 29
MANON/Wolff (c)
Manon : Bori
Lescaut : Chalmers
Des Grieux : Hackett
Count des Grieux : Rothier
Poussette : Tiffany
Javotte : Egener
Rosette : Arden
Guillot : Ananian
De Brétigny : Laurenti
Innkeeper : Leonhardt
Guards : Reschiglian,
  D'Angelo
Servant : Savage

April 5
CAVALLERIA RUSTICANA
Same as Feb. 8 except:
Santuzza : Peralta
Lola : Telva
Alfio : Picco
Lucia : Arden

IL SEGRETO DI SUSANNA
  Papi (c)
Count Gil : Chalmers
Countess Susanna : Bori
Sante : Paltrinieri

L'ORACOLO/Moranzoni (c)
Win-Shee : Didur
Chim-Fen : Scotti
Hoo-Tsin : Picco
Win-San Luy : Diaz
Hoo-Chee : Quintina
Ah-Yoe : Delaunois
Hua-Quee : Arden
Fortune Teller : Paltrinieri

April 12
FAUST/Wolff (c)
Faust : Martinelli
Marguerite : Easton
Méphistophélès : Rothier
Valentin : Danise
Siébel : Ellis
Marthe : Bérat
Wagner : Ananian

April 19
LOHENGRIN (*English*)
Same as Mar. 5

ATLANTA
April 25
ANDREA CHÉNIER
Same as Mar. 1 except:

285

Andrea Chénier : Crimi (for
  Gigli)
Maddalena : Ponselle
Mathieu : Didur
Roucher : Martino
Fouquier : Ananian
Schmidt : Malatesta

April 26 (mat.)
LA BOHÈME
Same as Jan. 4 except:
Rodolfo : Harrold
Schaunard : D'Angelo
Mimi : Bori
Benoit : Malatesta
Alcindoro : Leonhardt

April 27
MEFISTOFELE
Same as Dec. 14 except:
Marguerite : Easton
Helen of Troy : Peralta
Martha : Howard
Faust : Chamlee (for Gigli)

April 28 (mat.)
MANON/Bamboschek (c)
Same as Mar. 29 except:
Rosette : Telva

April 29
AIDA
Same as Nov. 23 except:
King : D'Angelo
Amneris : Claussen
Aida : Ponselle
Radames : Crimi
Priestess : Tiffany

April 30 (mat.)
RIGOLETTO/Papi (c)
Same as Jan. 11 except:
Duke : Chamlee
Rigoletto : De Luca
Gilda : Chase
Maddalena : Howard
Giovanna : Leveroni
Monterone : D'Angelo
Countess : Egener

April 30
TOSCA
Same as Jan. 15 except:
Cavaradossi : Hackett
Sciarrone : Reschiglian
Jailer : Leonhardt
Shepherd : Telva

1 9 2 1 – 2 2

BROOKLYN
November 15
CARMEN/Wolff (c)
Carmen : Farrar

286

Don José : Martinelli
Micaela : Sundelius
Escamillo : Mardones
Zuniga : Martino
Morales : Laurenti
Frasquita : Tiffany
Mercedes : Schaaf
Dancaire : Ananian
Remendado : Paltrinieri

November 22
AIDA/Moranzoni (c)
King : Gustafson
Amneris : Matzenauer
Aida : Ponselle
Radames : Crimi
Amonasro : De Luca
Ramfis : Didur
Messenger : Audisio
Priestess : Philo (d)

PHILADELPHIA
November 29
LUCIA DI LAMMERMOOR
  Papi (c)
Lucia : Galli-Curci
Alisa : Anthony
Edgardo : Martinelli
Ashton : Danise
Raimondo : Mardones
Arturo : Paltrinieri
Normanno : Audisio

December 6
LOUISE/Wolff (c)
Louise : Farrar
Julien : Pertile
Mother : Bérat
Father : Rothier
Irma : Delaunois
Camille : Dalossy
Gertrude : Perini
Apprentice : Ellis
Elise : Roselle
Blanche : Miriam
Suzanne : Tiffany
Forewoman : Axman
Marguerite : Mellish
Madeleine : Anthony
Painter : Reschiglian
First Philosopher : Leonhardt
Second Philosopher : Audisio
Sculptor : Picco
Poet : Malatesta
Student : Paltrinieri
Song Writer : Laurenti
Street Sweeper : Axman
Newspaper Girl : Ellis
Young Rag Picker : Schaaf
Milk Woman : Roselle
Coal Picker : Arden
Noctambulist : Meader
King of the Fools : Meader
First Policeman : Righi

Second Policeman : Sterzini
Rag Picker : Ananian
Junk Man : D'Angelo
Street Arab : Ellis
Old Clothes Man : Paltrinieri
Bird Food Vendor : Mellish
Artichoke Vendor : Schaaf
Chair Mender : Arden
Carrot Vendor : Paltrinieri
Rag Vendor : Laurenti

BROOKLYN
December 10
LA BOHÈME/Papi (c)
Rodolfo : Gigli
Marcello : Danise
Schaunard : Didur
Colline : Mardones
Mimi : Alda
Musetta : Roselle
Benoit : Ananian
Parpignol : Audisio
Alcindoro : Ananian
Sergeant : Reschiglian

PHILADELPHIA
December 13
ERNANI/Papi (c)
Ernani : Martinelli (for
  Crimi)
Don Carlos : Danise
Don Ruy Gomez : Mardones
Elvira : Ponselle
Giovanna : Anthony
Don Riccardo : Paltrinieri
Iago : Reschiglian

BROOKLYN
December 20
RIGOLETTO/Papi (c)
Duke : Chamlee
Rigoletto : De Luca
Gilda : Chase
Sparafucile : Rothier
Maddalena : Perini
Giovanna : Anthony
Monterone : Ananian
Marullo : Picco
Borsa : Bada
Ceprano : Reschiglian
Countess : Mellish
Page : Borniggia

PHILADELPHIA
December 27
LOHENGRIN (*English*)
  Bodanzky (c)
King Henry : Blass
Lohengrin : Harrold (for
  Sembach)
Elsa : Jeritza
Telramund : Whitehill
Ortrud : Matzenauer
Herald : Schlegel

BROOKLYN

January 3

DIE TOTE STADT
Bodanzky (c)
Paul : Harrold
Marietta : Jeritza
Apparition of Marie : Jeritza
Frank : Leonhardt
Brigitta : Telva
Juliette : Miriam
Lucienne : Anthony
Gaston : Agnini
Victorin : Diaz
Fritz : Laurenti
Count Albert : Bada

PHILADELPHIA

January 10

LE ROI D'YS/Wolff (c)
Mylio : Gigli
Karnac : Danise
King : Rothier
St. Corentin : Ananian
Jahel : Picco
Margared : Gordon
Rozenn : Alda

BROOKLYN

January 17

LOUISE
Same as Dec. 6 except:
Camille : Egener (for Dalossy)
Apprentice : Miriam
Blanche : Keener
Newspaper Girl : Miriam
Young Rag Picker : Arden
Milk Woman : Egener
Coal Picker : Schaaf
Noctambulist : Diaz
King of the Fools : Diaz
Street Arab : Miriam
Old Clothes Man : Bada
Artichoke Vendor : Sundelius
Chair Mender : Telva

PHILADELPHIA

January 24

BORIS GODUNOV/Papi (c)
Boris Godunov : Chaliapin
Fyodor : Delaunois
Xenia : Anthony (for Dalossy)
Nurse : Howard
Shuiski : Bada
Shchelkalov : Schlegel
Pimen : Mardones
Grigori : Diaz
Marina : Matzenauer
Varlaam : Ananian
Missail : Audisio
Innkeeper : Mattfeld

Officer : D'Angelo
Simpleton : Paltrinieri
Lavitski : Reschiglian
Chernikovski : Reschiglian
Boyar : Paltrinieri

BROOKLYN

January 31

IL BARBIERE DI SIVIGLIA
Papi (c)
Almaviva : Harrold
Dr. Bartolo : Ananian
Rosina : Galli-Curci
Figaro : Ruffo
Don Basilio : Didur
Berta : Bérat
Fiorello : Reschiglian
Sergeant : Audisio

PHILADELPHIA

February 7

DON CARLO/Papi (c)
Philip II : Didur
Don Carlo : Crimi
Rodrigo : De Luca
Grand Inquisitor : D'Angelo
Friar : Gustafson
Elizabeth : Ponselle
Princess Eboli : Matzenauer
Theobald : Roselle (for Dalossy)
Herald : Paltrinieri
Voice : Sundelius
Countess Aremberg : Savage

February 14

LA TRAVIATA/Moranzoni (c)
Violetta : Galli-Curci
Alfredo : Gigli
Germont : De Luca
Flora : Egener
Annina : Anthony
Gastone : Bada
Baron Douphol : Picco
Marquis d'Obigny : Laurenti
Doctor Grenvil : D'Angelo

BROOKLYN

February 21

MADAMA BUTTERFLY
Moranzoni (c)
Cio-Cio-San : Farrar
B. F. Pinkerton : Kingston
Sharpless : Chalmers (for Scotti)
Suzuki : Fornia
Kate Pinkerton : Egener
Goro : Paltrinieri
Yamadori : Audisio
Uncle-Priest : Gustafson
Yakuside : Quintina
Imperial Commissioner : Reschiglian

PHILADELPHIA

February 28

TOSCA/Bamboschek (c)
Tosca : Jeritza
Cavaradossi : Harrold
Scarpia : Scotti
Angelotti : D'Angelo
Sacristan : Malatesta
Spoletta : Bada
Sciarrone : Reschiglian
Jailer : D'Angelo
Shepherd : Bada

BROOKLYN

March 4

DIE WALKÜRE/Bodanzky (c)
Wotan : Whitehill
Fricka : Gordon
Brünnhilde : Claussen
Siegmund : Kingston
Sieglinde : Easton
Hunding : Gustafson
Helmwige : Mellish
Gerhilde : Tiffany
Ortlinde : Miriam
Rossweisse : Perini
Grimgerde : Telva
Waltraute : Wakefield
Siegrune : Anthony
Schwertleite : Howard

PHILADELPHIA

March 7

LA BOHÈME
Same as Dec. 10 except:
Rodolfo : Martinelli
Marcello : De Luca
Colline : Martino
Mimi : Bori
Musetta : Délaunois
Benoit : Malatesta
Alcindoro : Malatesta

March 14

DIE WALKÜRE
Same as Mar. 4 except:
Siegmund : Sembach
Helmwige : Sundelius
Grimgerde : Bradley

BROOKLYN

March 18

IL SEGRETO DI SUSANNA
Papi (c)
Count Gil : Scotti
Countess Susanna : Bori
Sante : Paltrinieri

PAGLIACCI/Moranzoni (c)
Nedda : Muzio
Canio : Salazar
Tonio : Caupolican
Beppe : Paltrinieri
Silvio : Picco

PHILADELPHIA
March 21
ANDREA CHÉNIER
Moranzoni (c)

Andrea Chénier : Gigli
Maddalena : Muzio
Countess di Coigny : Howard
Carlo Gérard : Danise
Bersi : Dalossy
Fléville : Reschiglian
Abbé : Paltrinieri
Madelon : Perini
Mathieu : Ananian
Spy : Bada
Fouquier : Leonhardt
Dumas : D'Angelo
Roucher : Picco
Schmidt : Malatesta
Majordomo : Malatesta

March 28
DIE TOTE STADT

Same as Jan. 3 except:
Fritz : Leonhardt

April 4
MADAMA BUTTERFLY

Same as Feb. 21 except:
B. F. Pinkerton : Chamlee
Sharpless : Scotti
Kate Pinkerton : Arden

April 11
PARSIFAL/Bodanzky (c)

Amfortas : Whitehill
Titurel : Gustafson
Gurnemanz : Blass
Parsifal : Sembach
Klingsor : Leonhardt
Kundry : Claussen
Voice : Telva
Knights of the Grail : Bada,
    D'Angelo
Esquires : Ellis, Schaaf,
    Meader, Audisio
Flower Maidens : Sundelius,
    Ellis, Delaunois, Mellish,
    Miriam, Telva

April 18
SAMSON ET DALILA
Hasselmans (c)

Dalila : Matzenauer (for
    Gordon)
Samson : Martinelli
High Priest : De Luca
Abimelech : Schlegel
Old Hebrew : Rothier
Philistine Messenger : Bada
Philistines : Paltrinieri,
    Reschiglian

288

ATLANTA
April 24
ERNANI

Same as Dec. 13 except:
Giovanna : Egener

April 25 (mat.)
CARMEN/Hasselmans (c)

Same as Nov. 15 except:
Carmen : Easton
Don José : Harrold
Micaela : Dalossy
Morales : Reschiglian
Frasquita : Anthony
Mercedes : Telva
Remendado : Bada

April 26
LORELEY/Moranzoni (c)

Rudolph : Martino
Anna : Delaunois
Walter : Gigli
Loreley : Muzio
Baron Hermann : Danise

April 27 (mat.)
IL SEGRETO DI SUSANNA

Same as Mar. 18

PAGLIACCI/Bamboschek (c)

Same as Mar. 18 except:
Tonio : De Luca
Beppe : Bada
Silvio : Reschiglian

April 28
LA TRAVIATA

Same as Feb. 14 except:
Gastone : Paltrinieri
Baron Douphol : D'Angelo
Marquis d'Obigny :
    Reschiglian
Doctor Grenvil : Ananian

April 29 (mat.)
FAUST/Hasselmans (c)

Faust : Harrold
Marguerite : Easton
Méphistophélès : Rothier
Valentin : Chalmers
Siébel : Miriam
Marthe : Telva
Wagner : D'Angelo

April 29
L'AMORE DEI TRE RE
Moranzoni (c)

Archibaldo : Mardones
Manfredo : Picco
Avito : Martinelli
Flaminio : Bada
Youth : Paltrinieri
Fiora : Bori
Maid : Egener

Young Woman : Anthony
Old Woman : Telva
Shepherd : Schaaf

1 9 2 2 – 2 3

BROOKLYN
November 14
LA TRAVIATA/Moranzoni (c)

Violetta : Bori
Alfredo : Gigli
Germont : De Luca
Flora : Egener
Annina : Anthony
Gastone : Bada
Baron Douphol : Reschiglian
    (for Picco)
Marquis d'Obigny : D'Angelo
Doctor Grenvil : Ananian

November 21
DER ROSENKAVALIER
Bodanzky (c)

Princess von Werdenberg :
    Easton
Baron Ochs : Bender
Octavian : Jeritza
Von Faninal : Schützendorf
Sophie : Sundelius
Marianne : Anthony
Valzacchi : Bada
Annina : Howard
Police Commissioner :
    Schlegel
Majordomo of Princess :
    Audisio
Majordomo of Von Faninal :
    Monti
Notary : Gustafson
Innkeeper : Meader
Singer : Harrold
Orphans : Robertson, Bradley,
    Wakefield
Milliner : Tindal
Leopold : Paltrinieri
Animal Vendor : Lipparini
Negro Boy : Gitchell

PHILADELPHIA
November 28
MEFISTOFELE/Moranzoni (c)

Marguerite : Alda
Helen of Troy : Peralta
Martha : Perini
Pantalis : Perini
Mefistofele : Chaliapin
Faust : Gigli
Wagner : Paltrinieri
Nereus : Paltrinieri

December 5
DER ROSENKAVALIER

Same as Nov. 21 except:

Sophie : Rethberg
Valzacchi : Meader
Innkeeper : Diaz
Singer : Diaz

BROOKLYN
December 9
MADAMA BUTTERFLY
Moranzoni (c)
Cio-Cio-San : Easton
B. F. Pinkerton : Chamlee
Sharpless : Scotti
Suzuki : Perini
Kate Pinkerton : Arden
Goro : Audisio
(for Paltrinieri)
Yamadori : Ananian (for
Audisio)
Uncle-Priest : Gustafson
Yakuside : Quintina
Imperial Commissioner :
Reschiglian

PHILADELPHIA
December 12
MADAMA BUTTERFLY
Same as Dec. 9 except:
Kate Pinkerton : Anthony
Goro : Paltrinieri
Yamadori : Audisio

BROOKLYN
December 19
CAVALLERIA RUSTICANA
Moranzoni (c)
Santuzza : Peralta
Lola : Perini
Turiddu : Tokatyan
Alfio : Picco
Lucia : Anthony

PAGLIACCI/Papi (c)
Nedda : Rethberg
Canio : Kingston
Tonio : Ruffo
Beppe : Bada
Silvio : Schützendorf

PHILADELPHIA
December 26
LORELEY/Moranzoni (c)
Rudolph : Mardones
Anna : Sundelius
Walter : Johnson
Loreley : Alda
Baron Hermann : Danise

BROOKLYN
January 2
ROMÉO ET JULIETTE
Hasselmans (c)
Juliette : Bori
Stephano : Delaunois

Gertrude : Wakefield
Roméo : Gigli
Tybalt : Bada
Benvolio : Paltrinieri
Mercutio : De Luca
Paris : Picco
Gregorio : Ananian
Capulet : Burke
Friar Laurence : Rothier
Duke of Verona : Gustafson

PHILADELPHIA
January 9
DIE WALKÜRE/Bodanzky (c)
Wotan : Whitehill
Fricka : Gordon
Brünnhilde : Matzenauer
Siegmund : Taucher
Sieglinde : Rethberg
Hunding : Bender
Helmwige : Mellish
Gerhilde : Ryan
Ortlinde : Robertson
Rossweisse : Schaaf (for
Perini)
Grimgerde : Bradley
Waltraute : Wakefield
Siegrune : Delaunois
Schwertleite : Howard

BROOKLYN
January 16
TRISTAN UND ISOLDE
Bodanzky (c)
Tristan : Taucher
Isolde : Matzenauer
King Marke : Bender
Kurvenal : Whitehill
Brangaene : Gordon
Melot : Schlegel
Steersman : D'Angelo
Shepherd : Meader
Sailor's Voice : Bada

PHILADELPHIA
January 23
ROMÉO ET JULIETTE
Same as Jan. 2 except:
Tybalt : Diaz
Capulet : Didur

BROOKLYN
January 30
GUILLAUME TELL/Papi (c)
Tell : Danise
Arnold : Martinelli
Walter Furst : Mardones
Melchthal : Picchi
Matilde : Ponselle
Jemmy : Dalossy
Hedwig : Perini
Fisherman : Bloch
Leutold : Picco

Gessler : Ananian
Rudolf : Bada

PHILADELPHIA
February 6
RIGOLETTO/Bamboschek (c—
for Papi)
Duke : Chamlee
Rigoletto : Danise
Gilda : Galli-Curci
Sparafucile : Mardones
Maddalena : Perini
Giovanna : Anthony
Monterone : Ananian
Marullo : Picco
Borsa : Bada
Ceprano : Reschiglian
Countess : Anthony (for
Schaaf)
Page : Grassi

BROOKLYN
February 13
LUCIA DI LAMMERMOOR
Papi (c)
Lucia : Galli-Curci
Alisa : Anthony
Edgardo : Chamlee
Ashton : De Luca
Raimondo : Mardones
Arturo : Bada
Normanno : Audisio

PHILADELPHIA
February 20
THAIS/Hasselmans (c)
Thais : Jeritza
Nicias : Tokatyan
Athanael : Whitehill
Palemon : Ananian
Crobyle : Ryan
Myrtale : Anthony
Albine : Telva
Servant : Reschiglian

February 27
LA BOHÈME/Papi (c)
Rodolfo : Martinelli
Marcello : Scotti
Schaunard : D'Angelo
Colline : Mardones
Mimi : Sabanieeva
Musetta : Sundelius
Benoit : Malatesta
Parpignol : Audisio
Alcindoro : Malatesta
Sergeant : Reschiglian

BROOKLYN
February 27
ANIMA ALLEGRA
Moranzoni (c)
Consuelo : Bori

289

Donna Sacramento : Howard
Coralito : Mario
Carmen : Anthony
Frasquita : Telva
Mariquita : Schaaf
Pedro : Lauri-Volpi
Don Eligio : Didur
Lucio : Tokatyan
Tonio : Bada
Diego : Picco
Ramirrez : Picchi
Singer : Diaz
Gypsy : Ananian

PHILADELPHIA

March 6
Mona Lisa/Bodanzky (c)
Tourist : Bohnen
Francesco : Bohnen
Wife : Kemp
Mona Fiordalisa : Kemp
Monk : Taucher
Giovanni : Taucher
Sandro : Gustafson
Pietro : Schlegel
Arrigo : Meader
Alessio : Bloch
Masolino : D'Angelo
Ginevra : Peralta
Dianora : Dalossy
Piccarda : Telva

March 13
CARMEN/Hasselmans (c)
Carmen : Bourskaya
Don José : Harrold
Micaela : Morgana
Escamillo : De Luca
Zuniga : Picchi
Morales : Picco
Frasquita : Ryan
Mercedes : Wakefield
Dancaire : D'Angelo
Remendado : Meader

BROOKLYN

March 13
La Bohème
Same as Feb. 27 except:
Rodolfo : Lauri-Volpi
Schaunard : Didur
Musetta : Anthony
Sergeant : Ananian

PHILADELPHIA

March 20
AIDA/Moranzoni (c)
King : Burke
Amneris : Claussen
Aida : Kemp
Radames : Kingston
Amonasro : Bohnen

Ramfis : Mardones
Messenger : Audisio
Priestess : Robertson

March 27 (mat.)
SNEGOUROTCHKA
Hasselmans (c)
Snegourotchka : Sabanieeva
Lel : Delaunois
Koupava : Anthony (for Ryan)
Fairy of Spring : Telva
Bobylicka : Howard
Faun : Paltrinieri
Czar : Harrold (for Diaz)
Mizguir : Burke
King Winter : Gustafson
Bobyl : Bada
Bermiate : Picco
Carnival : Meader
Court Jesters : Audisio, Reschiglian

March 27
SNEGOUROTCHKA
Same as Mar. 27 except:
Snegourotchka : Bori
Lel : Bourskaya
Koupava : Dalossy
Mizguir : Schützendorf
King Winter : Rothier
Bermiate : D'Angelo

April 3
LA TRAVIATA
Same as Nov. 14 except:
Alfredo : Lauri-Volpi
Annina : Wakefield
Gastone : Paltrinieri
Baron Douphol : Picco
Doctor Grenvil : Picchi

April 10
LOHENGRIN/Bodanzky (c)
King Henry : Bohnen
Lohengrin : Taucher
Elsa : Kemp
Telramund : Whitehill
Ortrud : Claussen
Herald : Schützendorf

April 17
L'AFRICAINE/Bodanzky (c)
Don Pedro : Didur
Don Diego : Ananian
Inez : Sundelius
Vasco da Gama : Gigli
Don Alvar : Paltrinieri
Nelusko : Danise
Selika : Ponselle
Grand Inquisitor : Rothier
Grand Brahmin : Rothier
Anna : Telva

Usher : Reschiglian
Officer : Audisio

ATLANTA

April 23
ROMÉO ET JULIETTE
Same as Jan. 2 except:
Stephano : Dalossy
Mercutio : Schützendorf
Capulet : Didur
Duke of Verona : D'Angelo

April 24 (mat.)
AIDA
Same as Mar. 20 except:
King : Picchi
Radames : Martinelli
Amonasro : Scotti

April 25
LUCIA DI LAMMERMOOR
Same as Feb. 13 except:
Alisa : Ryan
Edgardo : Gigli

April 26 (mat.)
DON CARLO/Papi (c)
Philip II : Chaliapin
Don Carlo : Martinelli
Rodrigo : De Luca
Grand Inquisitor : Rothier
Monk : Picchi
Elisabeth : Ponselle
Princess Eboli : Telva
Theobald : Ryan
Countess Aremberg : Savage
Herald : Paltrinieri (for Bada)
Voice : Robertson

April 27
L'AFRICAINE/Bamboschek (c)
Same as Apr. 17 except:
Inez : Mario
Don Alvar : Bada

April 28 (mat.)
LA BOHÈME/Moranzoni (c)
Same as Feb. 27 except:
Rodolfo : Harrold
Schaunard : Didur
Colline : Picchi
Mimi : Bori
Musetta : Mario

April 28
GUILLAUME TELL
Same as Jan. 30 except:
Melchthal : D'Angelo
Hedwig : Wakefield
Fisherman : Paltrinieri (for Diaz)

1 9 2 3 – 2 4

BROOKLYN
November 6
ANDREA CHÉNIER
Moranzoni (c)

Andrea Chénier : Gigli
Maddalena : Peralta
Countess di Coigny : Howard
Carlo Gérard : De Luca
Bersi : Dalossy
Fléville : Reschiglian
Abbé : Paltrinieri
Madelon : Telva
Mathieu : Didur
Spy : Bada
Fouquier : Ananian
Dumas : D'Angelo
Roucher : Picco
Schmidt : Malatesta
Majordomo : Malatesta

PHILADELPHIA
November 13
THAIS/Hasselmans (c)

Thais : Jeritza
Nicias : Tokatyan
Athanael : Whitehill
Palemon : Ananian
Crobyle : Guilford
Myrtale : Egener
Albine : Telva
Servant : Reschiglian

BROOKLYN
November 20
L'ORACOLO/Moranzoni (c)

Win-Shee : Didur
Chim-Fen : Scotti
Hoo-Tsin : D'Angelo
Win-San Luy . Harrold
Hoo-Chee : Quintina
Ah-Yoe : Delossy
Hua-Quee : Telva
Fortune Teller : Audisio

L'AMICO FRITZ
Moranzoni (c)

Suzel : Bori
Fritz : Fleta
Rabbi David : Danise
Beppe : Alcock
Hanezo : Malatesta
Federico : Paltrinieri
Caterina : Anthony

PHILADELPHIA
November 27
L'ORACOLO

Same as Nov. 20 except:
Win-San-Luy : Chamlee
Ah-Yoe : Mario (for
   Dalossy)

L'AMICO FRITZ
Same as Nov. 20

BROOKLYN
December 1
TOSCA/Moranzoni (c)

Tosca : Jeritza
Cavaradossi : Chamlee
Scarpia : Scotti
Angelotti : Ananian
Sacristan : Malatesta
Spoletta : Paltrinieri
Sciarrone : Reschiglian
Jailer : D'Angelo
Shepherd : Alcock

PHILADELPHIA
December 4
MEFISTOFELE/Moranzoni (c)

Marguerite : Alda
Helen of Troy : Peralta
Martha : Howard
Pantalis : Perini
Mefistofele : Chaliapin
Faust : Gigli
Wagner : Bada
Nereus : Bada

December 11
DIE MEISTERSINGER
Bodanzky (c)

Hans Sachs : Whitehill
Pogner : Rothier
Eva : Rethberg
Magdalene : Telva
Walther : Laubenthal
Beckmesser : Schützendorf
Kothner : Schlegel
Vogelgesang : Bloch
Nachtigall : D'Angelo
Zorn : Bada
Eisslinger : Paltrinieri
Moser : Audisio
Ortel : Ananian
Schwarz : Gustafson
Foltz : Wolfe
David : Meader
Night Watchman : Gabor

December 18
FEDORA/Papi (c)

Fedora : Jeritza
Olga : Mario
Loris Ipanov : Martinelli
De Siriex : Scotti
Dimitri : Dalossy
Désiré : Paltrinieri
Baron Rouvel : Bada
Cyril : Picchi
Borov : Picco
Grech : D'Angelo
Lorek : Ananian
Sergio : Mandelli (for
   Audisio)

Lasinski : Sebestyen
Savoyard : Alcock

BROOKLYN
December 18
ROMÉO ET JULIETTE
Hasselmans (c)

Juliette : Bori
Stephano : Delaunois
Gertrude : Wakefield
Roméo : Tokatyan
Tybalt : Diaz
Benvolio : Audisio
Mercutio : De Luca
Paris : Reschiglian
Gregorio : Gustafson
Capulet : Burke
Friar Laurence : Rothier
Duke of Verona : Wolfe

December 25
ERNANI/Papi (c)

Ernani : Martinelli
Don Carlos : Ruffo
Don Ruy Gomez : Mardones
Elvira : Ponselle
Giovanna : Egener
Don Riccardo : Bada
Iago : Reschiglian

January 1
FAUST/Hasselmans (c)

Faust : Martinelli
Marguerite : Mario
Méphistophélès : Rothier
Valentin : Tibbett
Siébel : Anthony
Marthe : Wakefield
Wagner : Wolfe

PHILADELPHIA
January 8
LOHENGRIN/Bodanzky (c)

King Henry : Bender
Lohengrin : Laubenthal
Elsa : Reinhardt
Telramund : Whitehill
Ortrud : Matzenauer
Herald : Tibbett

BROOKLYN
January 15
TANNHÄUSER/Bodanzky (c)

Hermann : Bender
Tannhäuser : Laubenthal
Wolfram : Whitehill
Walther : Meader
Biterolf : Schlegel
Heinrich : Bloch
Reinmar : Gustafson
Elisabeth : Reinhardt
Venus : Matzenauer
Shepherd : Delaunois

291

1923–24

PHILADELPHIA

January 22

L'AFRICAINE/Bodanzky (c)

Don Pedro : Wolfe
Don Diego : D'Angelo
Inez : Mario
Vasco da Gama : Gigli
Don Alvar : Bada
Nelusko : Danise
Selika : Ponselle
Grand Inquisitor : Rothier
Grand Brahmin : Rothier
Anna : Telva
Officer : Audisio
Usher : Reschiglian

BROOKLYN

January 29

RIGOLETTO/Papi (c)

Duke : Chamlee
Rigoletto : De Luca
Gilda : Galli-Curci
Sparafucile : Mardones
Maddalena : Perini
Giovanna : Wakefield
Monterone : Picchi
Marullo : Tibbett
Borsa : Bada
Ceprano : Reschiglian
Countess : Guilford
Page : Grassi

PHILADELPHIA

February 5

LUCIA DI LAMMERMOOR
Bamboschek (c)

Lucia : Galli-Curci
Alisa : Anthony
Edgardo : Harrold (for
Chamlee)
Ashton : De Luca
Raimondo : Mardones
Arturo : Bada
Normanno : Audisio

BROOKLYN

February 12

LA BOHÈME/Papi (c)

Rodolfo : Chamlee
Marcello : De Luca
Schaunard : Picco
Colline : Martino
Mimi : Alda
Musetta : Hunter
Benoit : Ananian
Parpignol : Audisio
Alcindoro : Malatesta
Sergeant : Reschiglian

PHILADELPHIA

February 19

MARTHA/Papi (c)

Harriet : Alda

Nancy : Howard
Lionel : Gigli
Plunkett : De Luca
Tristan : Malatesta
Sheriff : D'Angelo
Servant : Reschiglian

February 26

LA BOHÈME

Same as Feb. 12 except:
Marcello : Scotti
Colline : Didur
Mimi : Bori
Musetta : Guilford
Parpignol : Mandelli

BROOKLYN

February 26

AIDA/Moranzoni (c)

King : D'Angelo
Amneris : Gordon
Aida : Rethberg
Radames : Kingston
Amonasro : Danise
Ramfis : Mardones
Messenger : Audisio
Priestess : Wells

PHILADELPHIA

March 4

LA HABANERA/Hasselmans (c)

Ramon : Danise
Pedro : Tokatyan
Father : Rothier
Pilar : Delaunois
Young Girl : Wells
Comrades : Paltrinieri,
Audisio, Gabor, Gustafson
Blind Beggars : Ananian,
Bada, D'Angelo
Servant : Wolfe
Bride : Egener
Bridegroom : Audisio
Middle-Aged Man :
Reschiglian
Boy : Hunter

LE COQ D'OR/Bamboschek (c)

Queen : Sabanieeva
King Dodon : Didur
Amelfa : Howard (for
Alcock)
General Polkan : D'Angelo
Prince Guidon : Audisio
Prince Afron : Reschiglian
Astrologer : Diaz
Golden Cockerel : Guilford
Pantomimists
Queen : Galli
King Dodon : Kosloff
Amelfa : Rudolph
Astrologer : Bonfiglio
General Polkan : Bartik

Prince Guidon : Swee
Prince Afron : Da Re

March 11

DIE WALKÜRE/Bodanzky (c)

Wotan : Schorr
Fricka : Telva (for Gordon)
Brünnhilde : Branzell
Siegmund : Taucher
Sieglinde : Rethberg
Hunding : Gustafson
Helmwige : Mellish
Gerhilde : Wells
Ortlinde : Robertson
Rossweisse : Perini
Grimgerde : Telva
Waltraute : Wakefield
Siegrune : Anthony
Schwertleite : Howard

March 18

LE ROI DE LAHORE
Hasselmans (c)

Alim : Lauri-Volpi
Scindia : De Luca
Timur : Rothier
Indra : Mardones
Sita : Reinhardt
Kalad : Delaunois

March 25

GUILLAUME TELL/Papi (c)

Tell : Danise
Arnold : Martinelli
Walter Furst : Mardones
Melchthal : Picchi
Matilde : Peralta
Jemmy : Anthony
Hedwig : Perini
Fisherman : Bloch
Leutold : Picco
Gessler : Didur
Rudolf : Bada

April 1

LA TRAVIATA/Moranzoni (c)

Violetta : Bori
Alfredo : Lauri-Volpi
Germont : Danise
Flora : Anthony
Annina : Wakefield
Gastone : Paltrinieri
Baron Douphol : Picco
Marquis d'Obigny : D'Angelo
Doctor Grenvil : Picchi

April 8

DER FREISCHÜTZ
Bodanzky (c)

Ottokar : Schützendorf
Cuno : Schlegel
Agathe : Reinhardt
Aennchen : Sabanieeva (for
Mario)

Caspar : Bohnen
Max : Taucher
Samiel : Schützendorf (for Wolfe)
Hermit : Rothier
Kilian : Gabor

April 15
BORIS GODUNOV/Papi (c)
Boris Godunov : Chaliapin
Fyodor : Delaunois
Xenia : Dalossy
Nurse : Perini
Shuiski : Bada
Shchelkalov : Tibbett
Pimen : Mardones
Grigori : Diaz
Marina : Telva
Varlaam : Ananian
Missail : Audisio
Innkeeper : Wakefield
Officer : D'Angelo
Simpleton : Paltrinieri
Lavitski : Picco
Chernikovski : Reschiglian

ATLANTA
April 21
MARTHA
Same as Feb. 19 except:
Tristan : Ananian

April 22 (mat.)
IL TROVATORE
Moranzoni (c)
Leonora : Ponselle
Manrico : Martinelli
Count di Luna : Danise
Azucena : Telva
Inez : Guilford
Ferrando : Rothier
Ruiz : Audisio
Gypsy : Reschiglian

April 23
BORIS GODUNOV
Same as Apr. 15 except:
Fyodor : Hunter
Nurse : Howard
Shchelkalov : Picco
Grigori : Tokatyan
Lavitski : Tibbett

April 24 (mat.)
RIGOLETTO/Moranzoni (c)
Same as Jan. 29 except:
Duke : Gigli
Gilda : Bori
Sparafucile : Didur
Monterone : Ananian
Marullo : Picco
Borsa : Paltrinieri

April 25
FEDORA
Same as Dec. 18 except:
Fedora : Easton
Désiré : Bada
Sergio : Audisio (for Mandelli)
Savoyard : Wakefield

April 26 (mat.)
FAUST/Bamboschek (c)
Same as Jan. 1 except:
Faust : Tokatyan
Marguerite : Alda
Méphistophélès : Chaliapin
Siébel : Dalossy
Marthe : Howard
Wagner : D'Angelo

April 26
CAVALLERIA RUSTICANA
Moranzoni (c)
Santuzza : Ponselle
Lola : Telva
Turiddu : Gigli
Alfio : Picco
Lucia : Wakefield

PAGLIACCI/Moranzoni (c)
Nedda : Bori
Canio : Martinelli
Tonio : Danise
Beppe : Bada
Silvio : Reschiglian

CLEVELAND
April 28
AIDA
Same as Feb. 26 except:
Amneris : Claussen (for Branzell)
Aida : Ponselle
Radames : Martinelli
Messenger : Paltrinieri
Priestess : Guilford

April 29
CARMEN/Bamboschek (c)
Carmen : Easton
Don José : Johnson
Micaela : Mario
Escamillo : Mardones
Zuniga : Rothier
Morales : Tibbett
Frasquita : Anthony
Mercedes : Wakefield
Dancaire : D'Angelo
Remendado : Bada

April 30
RIGOLETTO/Moranzoni (c)
Same as Jan. 29 except:
Duke : Gigli

Gilda : Mario (for Bori)
Sparafucile : Didur
Maddalena : Telva
Monterone : Ananian
Borsa : Paltrinieri

May 1
FAUST/Bamboschek (c)
Same as Jan. 1 except:
Faust : Tokatyan (for Johnson)
Marguerite : Alda
Méphistophélès : Chaliapin
Siébel : Dalossy
Marthe : Howard
Wagner : D'Angelo

May 2
BORIS GODUNOV
Same as Apr. 15 except:
Fyodor : Hunter
Nurse : Howard
Shchelkalov : Picco
Grigori : Tokatyan
Lavitski : Tibbett

May 3 (mat.)
ROMÉO ET JULIETTE
Bamboschek (c)
Same as Dec. 18 except:
Stephano : Dalossy
Roméo : Gigli
Tybalt : Bada
Benvolio : Paltrinieri
Paris : Picco
Gregorio : Ananian
Capulet : Didur
Duke of Verona : D'Angelo

May 3
IL TROVATORE
Same as Apr. 22 except:
Inez : Anthony
Ferrando : Picchi

ROCHESTER
May 5
FAUST/Bamboschek (c)
Faust : Johnson
Marguerite : Alda
Méphistophélès : Chaliapin
Valentin : Danise
Siébel : Dalossy
Marthe : Howard
Wagner : D'Angelo

May 6
LA BOHÈME
Same as Feb. 12 except:
Rodolfo : Martinelli
Colline : Rothier
Mimi : Bori
Musetta : Guilford
Alcindoro : Ananian

293

Parpignol : Mandelli
Sergeant : Cottino (t—for
  Reschiglian)

1924 – 25

BROOKLYN
November 4
MARTHA/Papi (c)
Harriet : Alda
Nancy : Howard
Lionel : Gigli
Plunkett : Didur
Tristan : Malatesta
Sheriff : D'Angelo
Servant : Reschiglian

PHILADELPHIA
November 11
FAUST/Hasselmans (c)
Faust : Martinelli
Marguerite : Alda
Méphistophélès : Chaliapin
Valentin : Ballester (d)
Siébel : Dalossy
Marthe : Wakefield
Wagner : Ananian

BROOKLYN
November 18
LOHENGRIN/Bamboschek
  (c—for Bodanzky)
King Henry : Gustafson
Lohengrin : Laubenthal
Elsa : Jeritza
Telramund : Whitehill
Ortrud : Matzenauer
Herald : Schlegel

PHILADELPHIA
November 25
FEDORA/Papi (c)
Fedora : Jeritza
Olga : Guilford
Loris Ipanov : Martinelli
De Siriex : Scotti
Dimitri : Hunter
Désiré : Paltrinieri
Baron Rouvel : Bada
Cyril : Martino
Borov : Picco
Grech : D'Angelo
Lorek : Ananian
Lasinski : Pelletier
Sergio : Mandelli
Savoyard : Alcock

BROOKLYN
November 29
BORIS GODUNOV/Papi (c)
Boris Godunov : Chaliapin

294

Fyodor : Delaunois
Xenia : Anthony
Nurse : Alcock
Shuiski : Paltrinieri
Shchelkalov : Tibbett
Pimen : Mardones
Grigori : Tokatyan
Marina : Bourskaya
Varlaam : Martino
Missail : Altglass
Innkeeper : Wakefield
Officer : D'Angelo
Simpleton : Bloch
Lavitski : Schlegel
Chernikovski : Wolfe

PHILADELPHIA
December 2
LES CONTES D'HOFFMANN
  Hasselmans (c)
Olympia : Morgana
Giulietta : Bori
Antonia : Bori
Hoffmann : Fleta
Nicklausse : Howard
Lindorf : Schützendorf
Coppelius : De Luca
Dapertutto : De Luca
Miracle : De Luca
Andrès : Bada
Cochenille : Bada
Pitichinaccio : Bada
Franz : Bada
Luther : Picco
Nathaniel : Altglass
Hermann : Gustafson
Spalanzani : Ananian
Schlemil : Tibbett
Crespel : D'Angelo
Voice : Alcock

December 9
LA GIOCONDA/Serafin (c)
La Gioconda : Ponselle
Laura : Gordon
Alvise : Mardones
La Cieca : Alcock
Enzo : Gigli
Barnaba : Danise
Zuane : Reschiglian
Singer : Reschiglian
Isepo : Paltrinieri
Monk : D'Angelo
Steersman : D'Angelo

BROOKLYN
December 16
LES CONTES D'HOFFMANN
Same as Dec. 2 except:
Antonia : Mario
Nicklausse : Bourskaya

Spalanzani : Meader
Voice : Wakefield

PHILADELPHIA
December 16
JENUFA/Bodanzky (c)
Grandmother Buryja :
  Howard
Laca Klemen : Oehman
Stewa Buryja : Laubenthal
Sexton's Widow :
  Matzenauer
Jenufa : Jeritza
Mill Foreman : Gabor
Village Judge : Wolfe
His Wife : Robertson
Karolka : Dalossy
Maid : Anthony
Barena : Ryan
Aunt : Mattfeld

BROOKLYN
December 23
LA GIOCONDA
Same as Dec. 9 except:
La Gioconda : Easton
Barnaba : Ruffo
Steersman : Gabor

December 30
DIE MEISTERSINGER
  Bodanzky (c)
Hans Sachs : Whitehill
Pogner : Bender
Eva : Roeseler
Magdalene : Wakefield
Walther : Laubenthal
Beckmesser : Schützendorf
Kothner : Schlegel
Vogelgesang : Bloch
Nachtigall : D'Angelo
Zorn : Bada
Eisslinger : Paltrinieri
Moser : Altglass
Ortel : Ananian
Schwarz : Gustafson
Foltz : Wolfe
David : Meader
Night Watchman : Gabor

PHILADELPHIA
January 6
FALSTAFF/Serafin (c)
Sir John Falstaff : Scotti
Ford : Tibbett
Fenton : Tokatyan
Dr. Caius : Bada
Bardolph : Paltrinieri
Pistol : Didur
Mistress Ford : Bori
Anne : Alda
Dame Quickly : Telva
Mistress Page : Howard

January 13
MADAMA BUTTERFLY
Serafin (c)
Cio-Cio-San : Rethberg
  (for Easton)
B. F. Pinkerton : Chamlee
  (for Johnson)
Sharpless : De Luca
Suzuki : Bourskaya
Kate Pinkerton : Egener
  (for Wells)
Goro : Bada
Yamadori : D'Angelo
Uncle-Priest : Ananian
Yakuside : Quintina
Imperial Commissioner :
  Reschiglian

BROOKLYN
January 13
LA BOHÈME/Papi (c)
Rodolfo : Fleta
Marcello : Danise
Schaunard : Picco
Colline : Rothier
Mimi : Alda
Musetta : D'Arle
Benoit : Malatesta
Parpignol : Altglass
Alcindoro : Malatesta
Sergeant : Gabor

PHILADELPHIA
January 20
ANDREA CHÉNIER/Serafin (c)
Andrea Chénier : Fleta
Maddalena : Easton
Countess di Coigny :
  Bourskaya
Carlo Gérard : Danise
Bersi : Dalossy
Fléville : Tibbett
Abbé : Paltrinieri
Madelon : Bourskaya
Mathieu : Ananian
Spy : Paltrinieri
Fouquier : Gustafson
Dumas : Gabor (for
  D'Angelo)
Roucher : Picco
Schmidt : Reschiglian
Majordomo : Reschiglian

BROOKLYN
January 27
DIE WALKÜRE/Bodanzky (c)
Wotan : Bohnen
Fricka : Branzell
Brünnhilde : Branzell
  (for Claussen in Act III)
Siegmund : Taucher
Sieglinde : Müller
Hunding : Gustafson
Helmwige : Roeseler

Gerhilde : Wells
Ortlinde : Robertson
Rossweisse : Bourskaya
Grimgerde : Telva
Waltraute : Wakefield
Siegrune : Delaunois
Schwertleite : Howard

PHILADELPHIA
February 3
DINORAH/Papi (c)
Hoel : De Luca
Corentino : Tokatyan (for
  Meader)
Dinorah : Galli-Curci
Huntsman : D'Angelo
Harvester : Bada (for
  Altglass)
Goatherds : Ryan, Alcock

BROOKLYN
February 10
LUCIA DI LAMMERMOOR
  Papi (c)
Lucia : Galli-Curci
Alisa : Egener
Edgardo : Lauri-Volpi
Ashton : Danise
Raimondo : Mardones
Arturo : Bada
Normanno : Altglass

PHILADELPHIA
February 17
ROMÉO ET JULIETTE
  Hasselmans (c)
Juliette : Mario
Stephano : Delaunois
Gertrude : Wakefield
Roméo : Johnson
Tybalt : Meader
Benvolio : Altglass
Mercutio : De Luca
Paris : Picco
Gregorio : Ananian
Capulet : Gustafson
Friar Laurence : Rothier
Duke of Verona : D'Angelo

February 24
LA BOHÈME
Same as Jan. 13 except:
Rodolfo : Gigli
Colline : Martino
Mimi : Müller
Musetta : Hunter
Sergeant : Cottino

BROOKLYN
February 24
FALSTAFF
Same as Jan. 6 except:
Pistol : Gustafson
Anne : Mario

PHILADELPHIA
March 3
TRISTAN UND ISOLDE
  Bodanzky (c)
Tristan : Taucher
Isolde : Larsen-Todsen
King Marke : Bohnen
Kurvenal : Schorr
Brangaene : Telva
Melot : Gabor
Steersman : D'Angelo
Shepherd : Meader
Sailor's Voice : Meader

March 10
CARMEN/Hasselmans (c)
Carmen : Bourskaya
Don José : Johnson
Micaela : Mario
Escamillo : Whitehill
Zuniga : Martino
Morales : Reschiglian
Frasquita : Robertson
Mercedes : Wakefield
Dancaire : Ananian
Remendado : Paltrinieri

March 17
SIEGFRIED/Bodanzky (c)
Siegfried : Laubenthal
Mime : Meader
Wanderer : Schorr
Alberich : Schützendorf
Fafner : Gustafson
Erda : Branzell
Brünnhilde : Larsen-Todsen
Forest Bird : Sabanieeva

March 24
GIOVANNI GALLURESE
  Serafin (c)
Giovanni Gallurese :
  Lauri-Volpi
Maria : Müller
Nuvis : D'Angelo
Rivegas : Danise
Bastiano : Bada
Spanish Officer : Picco
José : Didur
Tropea : Reschiglian
Don Pasquale : Malatesta
Shepherd's Voice : Bonetti

March 31
DIE MEISTERSINGER
Same as Dec. 30 except:
Pogner : Rothier
Eva : Müller
Magdalene : Howard
Kothner : Tibbett

April 7
LA JUIVE/Hasselmans (c)
Rachel : Larsen-Todsen
Eleazar : Martinelli

Brogni : Mardones
Princess Eudoxia : Ryan
Leopold : Errolle
Ruggiero : Gabor
Albert : D'Angelo
Herald : Wolfe
Majordomo : Wolfe

April 14

AIDA/Serafin (c)

King : Ananian
Amneris : Branzell
Aida : Rethberg
Radames : Martinelli
Amonasro : Danise
Ramfis : Mardones
Messenger : Paltrinieri
Priestess : Ryan

ATLANTA

April 20

LA GIOCONDA

Same as Dec. 9 except:
La Cieca : Telva
Enzo : Lauri-Volpi

April 21

FALSTAFF

Same as Jan. 6

April 22

LA JUIVE

Same as Apr. 7 except:
Rachel : Easton (for
  Ponselle)
Brogni : Rothier
Princess Eudoxia : Mario
Ruggiero : Picco
Herald : Ananian
Majordomo : Reschiglian

April 23 (mat.)

LOHENGRIN

Same as Nov. 18 except:
King Henry : Bohnen
Lohengrin : Taucher
Elsa : Rethberg
Ortrud : Claussen
Herald : Tibbett

April 24

MEFISTOFELE/Serafin (c)

Marguerite : Alda
Helen of Troy : Peralta
Martha : Howard
Pantalis : Telva
Mefistofele : Chaliapin
Faust : Lauri-Volpi
Wagner : Bada
Nereus : Paltrinieri

April 25 (mat.)

LES CONTES D'HOFFMANN

Same as Dec. 2 except:
Olympia : Hunter
Hoffmann : Tokatyan

296

Lindorf : D'Angelo
Spalanzani : Meader
Voice : Wakefield

April 25

TOSCA/Papi (c)

Tosca : Easton
Cavaradossi : Martinelli
Scarpia : Scotti
Angelotti : D'Angelo
Sacristan : Ananian
Spoletta : Bada (for
  Paltrinieri)
Sciarrone : Reschiglian
Jailer : Gabor
Shepherd : Wakefield

CAVALLERIA RUSTICANA
Papi (c)

Santuzza : Ponselle
Lola : Telva
Turiddu : Tokatyan
Alfio : Picco
Lucia : Wakefield

CLEVELAND

April 27

L'AFRICAINE/Serafin (c)

Don Pedro : Didur
Don Diego : Ananian
Inez : Mario
Vasco da Gama : Lauri-Volpi
Don Alvar : Bada
Nelusko : Danise
Selika : Ponselle
Grand Inquisitor : Rothier
Grand Brahmin : Rothier
Anna : Wakefield
Usher : Reschiglian
Officer : Altglass

April 28

FAUST

Same as Nov. 11 except:
Faust : Tokatyan
Valentin : De Luca
Marthe : Howard
Wagner : D'Angelo

April 29

IL TROVATORE/Papi (c)

Leonora : Ponselle
Manrico : Martinelli
Count di Luna : Danise
Azucena : Telva (for
  Gordon)
Inez : Anthony
Ferrando : D'Angelo
Ruiz : Paltrinieri
Gypsy : Reschiglian

April 30

FALSTAFF

Same as Jan. 6 except:
Anne : Mario

May 1

PAGLIACCI/Papi (c)

Nedda : Rethberg
Canio : Martinelli
Tonio : Danise
Beppe : Bada
Silvio : Tibbett

LE COQ D'OR/Bamboschek (c)

Queen : Sabanieeva
King Dodon : Didur
Amelfa : Wakefield
Astrologer : Diaz
General Polkan : D'Angelo
Prince Guidon : Paltrinieri
Prince Afron : Reschiglian
Golden Cockerel : Guilford
Pantomimists
Queen : Galli
King Dodon : Kosloff
Amelfa : Rudolph
Astrologer : Bonfiglio
General Polkan : Bartik
Prince Guidon : Swee
Prince Afron : Da Re

May 2 (mat.)

PARSIFAL/Serafin (c)

Amfortas : Whitehill
Titurel : Gustafson
Gurnemanz : Bohnen
Parsifal : Laubenthal
Klingsor : Didur
Kundry : Easton
Voice : Telva
Knights of the Grail :
  Meader, D'Angelo
Esquires : Dalossy, Hunter,
  Altglass, Paltrinieri
Flower Maidens : Roeseler,
  Anthony (for Guilford),
  Dalossy, Robertson, Ryan,
  Telva

May 2

LA TRAVIATA/Bamboschek (c)

Violetta : Bori
Alfredo : Lauri-Volpi
Germont : De Luca
Flora : Wells
Annina : Wakefield
Gastone : Bada
Baron Douphol : Picco
Marquis d'Obigny : D'Angelo
Doctor Grenvil : Ananian

May 3 (mat.)

CONCERT/Papi, Bamboschek,
  Serafin, Hasselmans (c)

Rothier, Rethberg, Mario,
  Wells, Lauri-Volpi, Bada,
  Picco, Gustafson, Gordon,
  Tokatyan, Tibbett

May 4

LES CONTES D'HOFFMANN
Same as Dec. 2 except:
Olympia : Sabanieeva
Hoffmann : Tokatyan (for Errolle)
Lindorf : Ananian
Hermann : Gabor
Spalanzani : Meader
Voice : Wakefield

May 5

AIDA
Same as Apr. 14 except:
King : D'Angelo
Amneris : Claussen

ROCHESTER

May 6

FALSTAFF
Same as Jan. 6 except:
Anne : Mario

May 7

BORIS GODUNOV
Same as Nov. 29 except:
Fyodor : Hunter
Xenia : Dalossy
Nurse : Howard
Shuiski : Bada
Grigori : Errolle
Marina : Gordon
Varlaam : Ananian
Simpleton : Meader
Lavitski . Picco
Chernikovski : Reschiglian
Boyar : Paltrinieri

1 9 2 5 – 2 6

BROOKLYN

November 3

AIDA/Serafin (c)
King : Gustafson
Amneris : Matzenauer
Aida : Rethberg
Radames : Martinelli
Amonasro : Danise
Ramfis : Mardones
Messenger : Bada
Priestess : Wells

PHILADELPHIA

November 10

MARTHA/Papi (c)
Harriet : Alda
Nancy : Howard
Lionel : Gigli
Plunkett : De Luca
Tristan : Malatesta
Sheriff : Picco
Servant : Reschiglian

BROOKLYN

November 17

TOSCA/Serafin (c)
Tosca : Jeritza
Cavaradossi : Martinelli
Scarpia : Scotti
Angelotti : Ananian
Sacristan : Malatesta
Spoletta : Paltrinieri
Sciarrone : Reschiglian
Jailer : Picco
Shepherd : Bonetti

PHILADELPHIA

November 24

TOSCA
Same as Nov. 17 except:
Shepherd : Alcock (for Bonetti)

BROOKLYN

November 28

FAUST/Hasselmans (c)
Faust : Chamlee
Marguerite : Mario
Méphistolphélès : Chaliapin
Valentin : Danise
Siébel : Dalossy
Marthe : Howard
Wagner : D'Angelo

PHILADELPHIA

December 1

L'AFRICAINE/Serafin (c)
Don Pedro : Didur
Don Diego : Ananian
Inez : Mario
Vasco da Gama : Gigli
Don Alvar : Bada
Nelusko : Danise
Selika : Ponselle
Grand Inquisitor : Rothier
Grand Brahmin : Rothier
Anna : Wakefield
Usher : Reschiglian
Officer : Altglass

December 8

DER BARBIER VON BAGDAD
Bodanzky (c)
Caliph : Schützendorf
Kadi Baba Mustapha : Meader
Bostana : Bourskaya
Nureddin : Laubenthal
Barber : Bender
Soldiers-Muezzins : Gabor, Paltrinieri, Reschiglian, Altglass

L'HEURE ESPAGNOLE
Hasselmans (c)
Concépcion : Bori

Gonzalve : Errolle
Torquemada : Bada
Ramiro : Tibbett
Inigo : Didur

December 15

AIDA/Setti (c)
Same as Nov. 3 except:
Amneris : Gordon
Aida : Peralta (for Rethberg)
Messenger : Altglass
Priestess : Robertson

BROOKLYN

December 15

FEDORA/Papi (c)
Fedora : Jeritza
Olga : Guilford
Loris Ipanov : Johnson
De Siriex : Scotti
Dimitri : Dalossy
Désiré : Paltrinieri
Baron Rouvel : Bada
Cyril : Martino
Borov : Picco
Grech : D'Angelo
Lorek : Ananian
Lasinski : Pelletier
Sergio : Mandelli
Savoyard : Alcock

December 22

CAVALLERIA RUSTICANA
Papi (c)
Santuzza : Ponselle
Lola : Bourskaya
Turiddu : Tokatyan
Alfio : Basiola
Lucia : Anthony

L'HEURE ESPAGNOLE
Same as Dec. 8

December 29

RIGOLETTO/Serafin (c)
Duke : Gigli
Rigoletto : Basiola (for Danise)
Gilda : Mario
Sparafucile : Mardones
Maddalena : Telva
Giovanna : Wakefield
Monterone : Ananian
Marullo : Picco
Borsa : Bada
Ceprano : Reschiglian
Countess : Guilford
Page : Tomisani

PHILADELPHIA

December 29

THAIS/Hasselmans (c)
Thais : Jeritza
Nicias : Tokatyan

297

Athanael : Whitehill
Palemon : D'Angelo
Crobyle : Anthony
Myrtale : Egener
Albine : Howard
Servant : Gabor

January 5
LA CENA DELLE BEFFE
Serafin (c)

Giannetto Malespini : Gigli
Neri Chiaramantesi : Ruffo
Gabriello Chiaramantesi : Bada
Tornaquinci : D'Angelo
Calandra : Reschiglian
Fazio : Picco
Trinca : Paltrinieri
Doctor : Didur
Lapo : Altglass
Ginevra : Alda
Lisabetta : Dalossy
Laldomine : Alcock
Fiammetta : Anthony
Cintia : Wakefield

January 12
IL BARBIERE DI SIVIGLIA
Papi (c)

Almaviva : Tokatyan
Dr. Bartolo : Malatesta
Rosina : Galli-Curci
Figaro : Danise
Don Basilio : Mardones
Fiorello : Reschiglian
Berta : Wakefield
Sergeant : Paltrinieri

BROOKLYN
January 12
TANNHÄUSER/Bodanzky (c)
Hermann : Gustafson
Tannhäuser : Taucher
Wolfram : Schützendorf
Walther : Meader
Biterolf : Schlegel
Heinrich : Bloch
Reinmar : D'Angelo
Elisabeth : Rethberg
Venus : Peralta
Shepherd : Delaunois

PHILADELPHIA
January 19
I GIOJELLI DELLA MADONNA
Papi (c)
Gennaro : Martinelli
Carmela : Telva
Maliella : Jeritza
Rafaele : Danise
Biaso : Bada
Ciccillo : Paltrinieri
Rocco : Ananian
Stella : Anthony

Serena : Wakefield
Concetta : Ryan
Totonno : Altglass

BROOKLYN
January 26
IL BARBIERE DI SIVIGLIA
Bamboschek (c)

Same as Jan. 12 except:
Figaro : De Luca

PHILADELPHIA
February 2
TRISTAN UND ISOLDE
Bodanzky (c)
Tristan : Laubenthal
Isolde : Larsen-Todsen
King Marke : Bohnen
Kurvenal : Schorr
Brangaene : Branzell
Melot : Gabor
Steersman : Wolfe
Shepherd : Meader
Sailor's Voice : Meader (for Bloch)

BROOKLYN
February 9
LA BOHÈME/Papi (c)
Rodolfo : Johnson
Marcello : Scotti
Schaunard : Picco
Colline : Mardones
Mimi : Bori
Musetta : Kandt
Benoit : Malatesta
Parpignol : Altglass
Alcindoro : Malatesta
Sergeant : Gabor

PHILADELPHIA
February 16
LA JUIVE/Hasselmans (c)
Rachel : Larsen-Todsen
Eleazar : Martinelli
Brogni : Rothier
Princess Eudoxia : Morgana
Leopold : Errolle
Ruggiero : Gabor
Albert : D'Angelo
Herald : Ananian
Majordomo : Wolfe

February 23
DIE WALKÜRE/Bodanzky (c)
Wotan : Schorr
Fricka : Telva (for Claussen)
Brünnhilde : Larsen-Todsen
Siegmund : Melchior
Sieglinde : Müller
Hunding : Gustafson
Helmwige : Roeseler
Gerhilde : Wells

Ortlinde : Robertson
Rossweisse : Bourskaya
Grimgerde : Telva
Waltraute : Wakefield
Siegrune : Delaunois
Schwertleite : Howard

BROOKLYN
February 23
SAMSON ET DALILA
Hasselmans (c)
(Not given in New York)
Dalila : Branzell
Samson : Martinelli
High Priest : Danise
Abimelech : Ananian
Old Hebrew : Rothier
Philistine Messenger : Bada
Philistines : Paltrinieri, Reschiglian

PHILADELPHIA
March 2
TANNHÄUSER
Same as Jan. 12 except:
Tannhäuser : Laubenthal (for Melchior)
Wolfram : Schorr
Biterolf : Gabor
Heinrich : Paltrinieri
Elisabeth : Müller (for Easton)
Shepherd : Kandt

March 9
LA VIDA BREVE/Serafin (c)
Salud : Bori
Grandmother : Howard
Carmela : Alcock
Paco : Errolle (for Tokatyan)
Uncle Sarvaor : D'Angelo
Singer : Gabor (for Martino)
Manuel : Picco
Voices : Bada, Altglass, Ryan, Anthony

LE ROSSIGNOL/Serafin (c)
Nightingale : Talley
Cook : Bourskaya
Fisherman : Errolle
Emperor of China : Didur
Chamberlain : Schützendorf
Priest : Wolfe
Japanese Ambassadors : Altglass, Picco, Paltrinieri
Voices : Robertson, Altglass, Bonetti
Death : Wakefield

March 16
DIE MEISTERSINGER
Bodanzky (c)
Hans Sachs : Whitehill

Pogner : Rothier
Eva : Müller
Magdalene : Telva
Walther : Laubenthal
Beckmesser : Schützendorf
Kothner : Schlegel
Vogelgesang : Bloch
Nachtigall : D'Angelo
Zorn : Bada
Eisslinger : Paltrinieri
Moser : Altglass
Ortel : Ananian
Schwarz : Gustafson
Foltz : Wolfe
David : Meader
Night Watchman : Gabor

March 23
LA GIOCONDA/Serafin (c)
La Gioconda : Larsen-Todsen
Laura : Branzell
Alvise : Mardones
La Cieca : Alcock
Enzo : Gigli
Barnaba : Danise
Zuane : Reschiglian
Singer : Reschiglian
Isepo : Paltrinieri
Monk : Ananian
Steersman : Ananian

March 30
RIGOLETTO
Same as Dec. 29 except:
Duke : Lauri-Volpi
Gilda : Talley
Maddalena : Alcock
Countess : Wells

April 6
DON QUICHOTTE
Hasselmans (c)
Dulcinea : Easton
Don Quichotte : Chaliapin
Sancho : De Luca
Pedro : Anthony
Garcias : Egener
Rodriquez : Meader
Juan : Bada
Bandit Chief : Ananian
Servants : Reschiglian, Gabor
Bandits : D'Angelo, Wolfe

April 13
SAMSON ET DALILA
Same as Feb. 23 except:
High Priest : Whitehill
Old Hebrew : Mardones

PETROUCHKA (Ballet)
Serafin (c)
Ballerina : Rudolph
Petrouchka : Bolm

Moor : Bonfiglio
Old Showman : Bartik
Merchant : Agnini
Street Dancers : Friedenthal,
De Leporte
Gypsies : Ogden, Rogge,
Glover

ATLANTA
April 19
AIDA
Same as Nov. 3 except:
King : D'Angelo
Amneris : Claussen
Aida : Ponselle
Amonasro : Bohnen
Priestess : Robertson

April 20
DON QUICHOTTE
Same as Apr. 6 except:
Dulcinea : Telva
Bandit : Gabor

April 21
LA BOHÈME
Same as Feb. 9 except:
Rodolfo : Gigli
Schaunard : Didur
Musetta : Hunter
Benoit : Ananian
Alcindoro : Ananian
Sergeant : Reschiglian

PAGLIACCI/Bamboschek (c—
for Papi)
Nedda : Lewis
Canio : Tokatyan
Tonio : Tibbett
Beppe : Paltrinieri
Silvio : Picco

April 22 (mat.)
I GIOJELLI DELLA MADONNA
Same as Jan. 19 except:
Maliella : Easton
Rafaele : Basiola
Stella : Guilford
Concetta : Robertson

April 23
LUCIA DI LAMMERMOOR
Serafin (c)
Lucia : Talley
Alisa : Egener
Edgardo : Gigli
Ashton : De Luca
Raimondo : Rothier
Arturo : Bada
Normanno : Paltrinieri

April 24 (mat.)
TANNHÄUSER/Bamboschek (c)
Same as Jan. 12 except:

Hermann : Bohnen
Tannhäuser : Laubenthal
Wolfram : Tibbett
Biterolf : Gabor
Reinmar : Gustafson
Elisabeth : Easton

April 24
IL TROVATORE/Serafin (c)
Leonora : Ponselle
Manrico : Martinelli
Count di Luna : Basiola
Azucena : Telva
Inez : Robertson
Ferrando : Rothier
Ruiz : Paltrinieri
Gypsy : Reschiglian

CLEVELAND
April 26
LA CENA DELLE BEFFE
Same as Jan. 5 except:
Neri Chiaramantesi : Tibbett
Laldomine : Bonetti

PAGLIACCI/Papi (c)
Same as Apr. 21 except:
Nedda : Bori
Canio : Martinelli
Tonio : Basiola
Beppe : Meader

April 27
BORIS GODUNOV/Papi (c)
Boris Godunov : Chaliapin
Fyodor : Hunter
Xenia : Guilford
Nurse : Flexer
Shuiski : Bada
Shchelkalov : Picco
Pimen : Rothier
Grigori : Tokatyan
Marina : Telva
Varlaam : Ananian
Missail : Altglass
Innkeeper : Wakefield
Officer : D'Angelo
Simpleton : Bloch
Lavitski : Reschiglian
Chernikovski : Gabor

April 28
LA GIOCONDA
Same as Mar. 23 except:
La Gioconda : Ponselle
Laura : Telva
Enzo : Lauri-Volpi
Isepo : Altglass
Monk : D'Angelo
Steersman : Gabor

April 29
ROMÉO ET JULIETTE
Hasselmans (c)
Juliette : Bori

299

Stephano : Hunter
Gertrude : Wakefield
Roméo : Gigli
Tybalt : Bada
Benvolio : Altglass
Mercutio : Tibbett
Paris : Picco
Gregorio : Gustafson
Capulet : Didur
Friar Laurence : Rothier
Duke of Verona : D'Angelo

April 30
SAMSON ET DALILA
Same as Feb. 23 except:
Dalila : Claussen
First Philistine : Altglass

May 1 (mat.)
LUCIA DI LAMMERMOOR
Same as Apr. 23 except:
Alisa : Anthony (for Egener)
Edgardo : Lauri-Volpi
Raimondo : Mardones

May 1
LA BOHÈME
Same as Feb. 9 except:
Rodolfo : Gigli
Colline : Didur
Musetta : Hunter
Benoit : Ananian
Alcindoro : Ananian
Sergeant : Reschiglian

CAVALLERIA RUSTICANA
Bamboschek (c)
Same as Dec. 22 except:
Lola : Flexer
Lucia : Wakefield

May 3
RIGOLETTO
Same as Dec. 29 except:
Duke : Lauri-Volpi
Rigoletto : De Luca
Gilda : Galli-Curci
Sparafucile : Didur
Giovanna : Anthony
Countess : Robertson

May 4
DON QUICHOTTE
Same as Apr. 6 except:
Garcias : Bonetti

May 5
AIDA
Same as Nov. 3 except:
King : D'Angelo
Amneris : Claussen
Aida : Ponselle
Amonasro : Basiola

300

Messenger : Paltrinieri
Priestess : Robertson

ROCHESTER
May 6
RIGOLETTO
Same as Dec. 29 except:
Duke : Lauri-Volpi
Rigoletto : De Luca
Gilda : Talley
Giovanna : Anthony
Borsa : Paltrinieri
Countess : Robertson

May 7
TOSCA
Same as Nov. 17 except:
Tosca : Easton
Angelotti : D'Angelo
Sacristan : Picco
Spoletta : Bada
Shepherd : Wakefield

1926–27

BROOKLYN
November 2
LUCIA DI LAMMERMOOR
Bamboschek (c)
Lucia : Talley
Alisa : Anthony
Edgardo : Gigli
Ashton : Danise
Raimondo : Pinza
Arturo : Tedesco (d)
Normanno : Paltrinieri

PHILADELPHIA
November 2
TOSCA/Serafin (c)
Tosca : Jeritza
Cavaradossi : Martinelli
Scarpia : Scotti
Angelotti : D'Angelo
Sacristan : Malatesta
Spoletta : Bada
Sciarrone : Reschiglian
Jailer : Picco
Shepherd : Flexer

November 9
L'AFRICAINE/Serafin (c)
Don Pedro : Didur
Don Diego : Ananian
Inez : Guilford
Vasco da Gama : Gigli
Don Alvar : Bada
Nelusko : Danise
Selika : Ponselle
Grand Inquisitor : Rothier

Grand Brahmin : Rothier
Anna : Wakefield
Usher : Reschiglian
Officer : Altglass

November 23
DIE ZAUBERFLÖTE
Bodanzky (c)

Sarastro : Bender
Tamino : Meader
High Priest : Ludikar
Two Priests : Gabor,
Burgstaller
Queen of the Night : Talley
Pamina : Rethberg
Three Ladies : Roeseler
(for Fleischer), Wells,
Telva
Papageno : Schützendorf
Papagena : Hunter
Monostatos : Bloch
Three Genii : Ryan,
Anthony, Flexer
Guards : Bloch, Gustafson

BROOKLYN
November 27
LA CENA DELLE BEFFE
Serafin (c)

Giannetto Malespini : Gigli
Neri Chiaramantesi : Tibbett
Gabriello Chiaramantesi :
Bada
Tornaquinci : D'Angelo
Calandra : Reschiglian
Fazio : Picco
Trinca : Paltrinieri
Doctor : Didur
Lapo : Altglass
Ginevra : Alda
Lisabetta : Dalossy
Laldomine : Alcock
Fiammetta : Ryan (for
Anthony)
Cintia : Wakefield

PHILADELPHIA
November 30
TURANDOT/Serafin (c)
Princess Turandot : Jeritza
Emperor Altoum : Altglass
Timur : Ludikar
Calaf : Lauri-Volpi
Liu : Attwood
Ping : De Luca
Pang : Bada
Pong : Tedesco
Mandarin : Cehanovsky
Maids : Lerch, Flexer

BROOKLYN
December 7
DIE ZAUBERFLÖTE
Same as Nov. 23 except:
Sarastro : Ludikar
(for Bender)
Tamino : Laubenthal
High Priest : Cehanovsky
(for Ludikar)
Pamina : Fleischer
Monostatos : Meader
Guard : Altglass

PHILADELPHIA
December 7
LA BOHÈME/Bellezza (c)
Rodolfo : Gigli
Marcello : Scotti
Schaunard : Picco
Colline : Didur
Mimi : Alda
Musetta : Guilford
Benoit : Malatesta
Parpignol : Paltrinieri
Alcindoro : Malatesta
Sergeant : Cottino (t)

December 14
ANDREA CHÉNIER/Serafin (c)
Andrea Chénier : Lauri-Volpi
Maddalena : Rethberg
Countess di Coigny :
Bourskaya
Carlo Gérard : Ruffo
Bersi : Anthony
Fléville : Cehanovsky
Abbé : Tedesco
Madelon : Bourskaya
Mathieu : Didur
Spy : Bada
Fouquier : Gustafson
Dumas : Cehanovsky
Roucher : Picco
Schmidt : Reschiglian
Majordomo : Reschiglian

BROOKLYN
December 21
DON QUICHOTTE
Hasselmans (c)
Dulcinea : Telva
Don Quichotte : Chaliapin
Sancho : De Luca
Pedro : Anthony
Garcias : Egener
Rodriguez : Meader
Juan : Bada
Bandit Chief : Ananian
Servants : Reschiglian,
Gabor
Bandits : D'Angelo, Wolfe

December 28
CAVALLERIA RUSTICANA
Bellezza (c)
Santuzza : Jeritza
Lola : Flexer
Turiddu : Chamlee
Alfio : Basiola
Lucia : Mattfeld

PAGLIACCI/Bellezza (c)
Nedda : Mario
Canio : Fullin
Tonio : Tibbett
Beppe : Tedesco
Silvio : Cehanovsky

PHILADELPHIA
December 28
DIE WALKÜRE/Bodanzky (c)
Wotan : Whitehill
Fricka : Howard
Brünnhilde : Claussen
Siegmund : Taucher
Sieglinde : Easton
Hunding : Bender
Helmwige : Guilford (for
Roeseler)
Gerhilde : Ryan
Ortlinde : Fleischer
Rossweisse : Bourskaya
Grimgerde : Bonetti
Waltraute : Alcock
Siegrune : Anthony
Schwertleite : Howard

January 4
LA VESTALE/Serafin (c)
Licinio : Lauri-Volpi
Giulia : Ponselle
Cinna : Basiola
Pontifex Maximus : Pinza
High Priestess : Telva
Consul : D'Angelo

January 11
LA CENA DELLE BEFFE
Same as Nov. 27 except:
Neri Chiaramantesi : Ruffo

BROOKLYN
January 11
IL TROVATORE/Bellezza (c)
Leonora : Rethberg
Manrico : Martinelli
Count di Luna : Danise
Azucena : Gordon
Inez : Anthony
Ferrando : Rothier
Ruiz : Tedesco
Gypsy : Gabor

PHILADELPHIA
January 18
RIGOLETTO/Bellezza (c)
Duke : Lauri-Volpi
Rigoletto : Danise
Gilda : Galli-Curci
Sparafucile : Didur
Maddalena : Alcock
Giovanna : Anthony
Monterone : Ananian
Marullo : Reschiglian
Borsa : Paltrinieri
Ceprano : Cehanovsky
Countess : Egener
Page : Tomisani

January 25
L'AMORE DEI TRE RE
Serafin (c)
Archibaldo : Ludikar
Manfredo : Tibbett
Avito : Johnson
Flaminio : Bada
Youth : Bada
Fiora : Bori
Maid : Bonetti
Young Woman : Anthony
Old Woman : Flexer
Shepherd : Flexer

BROOKLYN
January 25
RIGOLETTO
Same as Jan. 18 except:
Sparafucile : Rothier
Giovanna : Mattfeld
Monterone : D'Angelo
Marullo : Picco
Ceprano : Reschiglian

PHILADELPHIA
February 1
LOHENGRIN/Bodanzky (c)
King Henry : Ludikar
Lohengrin : Kirchhoff
Elsa : Jeritza
Telramund : Schützendorf
Ortrud : Claussen
Herald : Cehanovsky

BROOKLYN
February 8
ROMÉO ET JULIETTE
Hasselmans (c)
Juliette : Bori
Stephano : Dalossy
Gertrude : Wakefield
Roméo : Tokatyan
Tybalt : Diaz

Benvolio : Altglass
Mercutio : De Luca
Paris : Picco
Gregorio : Ananian
Capulet : Didur
Friar Laurence : Rothier
Duke of Verona : D'Angelo

PHILADELPHIA
February 15
LA JUIVE/Hasselmans (c)
Rachel : Larsen-Todsen
Eleazar : Martinelli
Brogni : Pinza
Princess Eudoxia : Morgana
Leopold : Tedesco
Ruggiero : Picco
Albert : D'Angelo
Herald : Ananian
Majordomo : Ananian

BROOKLYN
February 22
SIEGFRIED/Bodanzky (c)
Siegfried : Kirchhoff
Mime : Meader
Wanderer : Schorr
Alberich : Schützendorf
Fafner : Gustafson
Erda : Telva
Brünnhilde : Larsen-Todsen
Forest Bird : Fleischer

PHILADELPHIA
March 1
SIEGFRIED
Same as Feb. 22 except:
Wanderer : Bohnen
Erda : Branzell
Brünnhilde : Easton

BROOKLYN
March 5
L'AFRICAINE
Same as Nov. 9 except:
Inez : Morgana
Nelusko : De Luca
Selika : Easton

PHILADELPHIA
March 8
MADAMA BUTTERFLY
Bellezza (c)
Cio-Cio-San : Easton
B. F. Pinkerton : Chamlee
Sharpless : Scotti
Suzuki : Bourskaya
Kate Pinkerton : Flexer

Goro : Bada
Yamadori : Malatesta
Uncle-Priest : Wolfe
Yakuside : Malatesta
Imperial Commissioner :
 Reschiglian

March 15
FALSTAFF/Serafin (c)
Sir John Falstaff : Scotti
Ford : Tibbett
Fenton : Tokatyan
Dr. Caius : Bada
Bardolph : Paltrinieri
Pistol : Didur
Mistress Ford : Fleischer
Anne : Mario
Dame Quickly : Telva
Mistress Page : Wakefield
Innkeeper : Burgstaller

BROOKLYN
March 15
LES CONTES D'HOFFMANN
Hasselmans (c)
Olympia : Talley
Giulietta : Lewis
Antonia : Sabanieeva
Hoffmann : Chamlee
Nicklausse : Bourskaya
 (for Howard)
Lindorf : Wolfe
Coppelius : Ludikar
Dapertutto : De Luca
Miracle : Rothier
Andrès : Tedesco
Cochenille : Tedesco
Pitichinaccio : Tedesco
Franz : Tedesco
Luther : Picco
Nathaniel : Altglass
Hermann : Gustafson
Spalanzani : Ananian
Schlemil : Cehanovsky
Crespel : D'Angelo
Voice : Alcock

PHILADELPHIA
March 22
TRISTAN UND ISOLDE
Bodanzky (c)
Tristan : Laubenthal
Isolde : Larsen-Todsen
King Marke : Ludikar
Kurvenal : Whitehill
Brangaene : Branzell
Melot : Gabor
Steersman : D'Angelo
Shepherd : Meader
Sailor's Voice : Meader

March 29
THE KING'S HENCHMAN
Serafin (c)
Eadgar : Tibbett
Aethelwold : Johnson
Aelfrida : Guilford
Ase : Alcock
Maccus : Gustafson
Dunstan : Meader
Ordgar : D'Angelo
Gunner : Altglass
Cynric : Cehanovsky
Brand : Macpherson
Wulfred : Picco
Oslac : Wolfe
Thored : Gabor
Hwita : Bloch
Blacksmith : Wolfe
Saddler : Ananian
Miller : Macpherson
Fisherman : Vajda
Old Man : Bloch
Hildeburh : Wakefield
Ostharu : Anthony
Godgyfu : Lerch
Leofsydu : Flexer
Blacksmith's Wife : Egener
Miller's Wife : Bonetti
Fisherman's Wife : Anthony
Woman Servant : Flexer
Young Girl : Lerch

April 5
BORIS GODUNOV/Bellezza (c)
Boris Godunov : Chaliapin
Fyodor : Anthony
Xenia : Ryan
Nurse : Howard
Shuiski : Bada
Shchelkalov : Cehanovsky
Pimen : Pinza
Grigori : Tokatyan
Marina : Telva
Varlaam : Ananian
Missail : Paltrinieri
Innkeeper : Bourskaya
Officer : D'Angelo
Simpleton : Tedesco
Lavitski : Cehanovsky
Chernikovski : Reschiglian

April 12
MIGNON/Hasselmans (c)
Mignon : Bori
Philine : Talley
Wilhelm Meister : Gigli
Lothario : Rothier
Laerte : Bada
Jarno : Wolfe
Frederic : Dalossy
Antonio : D'Angelo

BALTIMORE

April 18

TURANDOT

Same as Nov. 30 except:
Princess Turandot : Easton
Calaf : Johnson
Liu : Guilford

April 19

IL TROVATORE

Same as Jan. 11 except:
Leonora : Ponselle
Count di Luna : Basiola
Azucena : Claussen
Inez : Egener
Ruiz : Paltrinieri
Gypsy : Reschiglian

April 20

RIGOLETTO

Same as Jan. 18 except:
Duke : Gigli
Rigoletto : De Luca
Sparafucile : Pinza
Maddalena : Bourskaya
Monterone : D'Angelo
Marullo : Picco
Borsa : Bada
Ceprano : Reschiglian
Countess : Lerch

April 21

LA BOHÈME

Same as Dec. 7 except:
Rodolfo : Johnson
Schaunard : Didur
Colline : Rothier
Mimi : Bori
Musetta : Hunter
Benoit : Ananian
Parpignol : Altglass
Alcindoro : Ananian
Sergeant : Reschiglian

CAVALLERIA RUSTICANA
Bamboschek (c)

Santuzza : Ponselle
Lola : Bourskaya
Turiddu : Tokatyan
Alfio : Tibbett
Lucia : Wakefield

WASHINGTON

April 22

LA TRAVIATA/Serafin (c)

Violetta : Galli-Curci
Alfredo : Gigli
Germont : De Luca
Flora : Egener
Annina : Anthony

Gastone : Bada
Baron Douphol : Picco
Marquis d'Obigny :
  Reschiglian
Doctor Grenvil : Ananian

April 23 (mat.)

LA BOHÈME/Bellezza (c)

Rodolfo : Johnson
Marcello : Picco
Schaunard : Didur
Colline : Pinza
Mimi : Bori
Musetta : Hunter
Benoit : Ananian
Parpignol : Altglass
Alcindoro : Ananian
Sergeant : Reschiglian

CAVALLERIA RUSTICANA
Bamboschek (c)

Santuzza : Easton
Lola : Bourskaya
Turiddu : Tokatyan
Alfio : Tibbett
Lucia : Egener

April 23

IL TROVATORE/Serafin (c)

Same as Jan. 11 except:
Leonora : Ponselle
Count di Luna : Basiola
Azucena : Claussen
Ruiz : Paltrinieri

ATLANTA

April 25

LA TRAVIATA

Same as Apr. 22 except:
Germont : Tibbett
Gastone : Paltrinieri

April 26

GIANNI SCHICCHI/Bellezza (c)

Gianni Schicchi : De Luca
Lauretta : Hunter
La Vecchia : Bourskaya
Rinuccio : Tokatyan
Gherardo : Paltrinieri
  (for Bada)
Nella : Anthony
Betto : Ananian
Simone : Ludikar
Marco : D'Angelo
La Ciesca : Guilford
Spinelloccio : Picco
Nicolao : Gustafson
Pinellino : Reschiglian
Guccio : Gabor

L'AMORE DEI TRE RE

Same as Jan. 25 except:
Archibaldo : Pinza

Avito : Martinelli
Youth : Altglass
Fiora : Ponselle
Maid : Egener
Young Woman : Lerch
Old Woman : Wakefield

April 27

TURANDOT

Same as Nov. 30 except:
Princess Turandot : Easton
Calaf : Johnson
Liu : Guilford

April 28

MIGNON

Same as Apr. 12 except:
Frederic : Hunter

April 29 (mat.)

LOHENGRIN/Bamboschek (c)

Same as Feb. 1 except:
King Henry : Gustafson
Elsa : Easton
Telramund : Tibbett

April 29

LA FORZA DEL DESTINO
  Bellezza (c)

Marquis : D'Angelo
Leonora : Ponselle
Don Carlo : Basiola
Don Alvaro : Martinelli
Padre Guardiano · Pinza
Fra Melitone : Picco
Preziosilla : Bourskaya
Curra : Egener
Trabucco : Paltrinieri
Surgeon : Reschiglian
Alcade : Ananian

April 30 (mat.)

ROMÉO ET JULIETTE

Same as Feb. 8 except:
Stephano : Hunter
Roméo : Gigli
Tybalt : Bada
Benvolio : Paltrinieri
Mercutio : Cehanovsky
Capulet : Ludikar
Duke of Verona : Macpherson

April 30

MADAMA BUTTERFLY

Same as Mar. 8 except:
B. F. Pinkerton : Tokatyan
Kate Pinkerton : Lerch
Goro : Tedesco
Yamadori : Altglass
Uncle-Priest : Gustafson
Yakuside : Quintina

303

CLEVELAND

May 2

AIDA/Serafin (c)

King : Gustafson
Amneris : Claussen
Aida : Ponselle
Radames : Martinelli
Amonasro : De Luca
Ramfis : Pinza
Messenger : Tedesco
Priestess : Lerch

May 3

TURANDOT

Same as Nov. 30 except:
Princess Turandot : Easton
Calaf : Tokatyan
Liu : Guilford

May 4

LA TRAVIATA

Same as Apr. 22 except:
Germont : Tibbett
Gastone : Paltrinieri

May 5

LA FORZA DEL DESTINO

Same as Apr. 29

May 6 (mat.)

MIGNON

Same as Apr. 12 except:
Frederic : Egener

May 6

LOHENGRIN/Bamboschek (c)

Same as Feb. 1 except:
Elsa : Easton
Telramund : Tibbett

May 7 (mat.)

LA BOHÈME

Same as Dec. 7 except:
Colline : Rothier
Mimi : Bori
Benoit : Ananian
Parpignol : Altglass
Alcindoro : Ananian
Sergeant : Reschiglian

May 7

IL TROVATORE/Serafin (c)

Same as Jan. 11 except:
Leonora : Ponselle
Count di Luna : Basiola
Azucena : Claussen
Ferrando : D'Angelo
Ruiz : Paltrinieri

ROCHESTER

May 9

LA FORZA DEL DESTINO

Same as Apr. 29 except:

Don Carlo : De Luca
Padre Guardiano : Rothier

May 10

LES CONTES D'HOFFMANN

Same as Mar. 15 except:
Giulietta : Bori
Antonia : Bori
Hoffmann : Tokatyan
Dapertutto : Tibbett
Andrès : Bada
Cochenille : Bada
Pitichinaccio : Bada
Franz : Bada
Spalanzani : D'Angelo
Voice : Wakefield

1 9 2 7 – 2 8

PHILADELPHIA

November 1

LA GIOCONDA/Serafin (c)

La Gioconda : Ponselle
Laura : Telva
Alvise : Rothier
La Cieca : Alcock
Enzo : Gigli
Barnaba : Danise
Zuane : Reschiglian
Singer : Reschiglian
Isepo : Tedesco
Monk : D'Angelo
Steersman : D'Angelo

BROOKLYN

November 1

MADAMA BUTTERFLY
  Bellezza (c)

Cio-Cio-San : Easton
B. F. Pinkerton : Martinelli
Sharpless : Scotti
Suzuki : Bourskaya
Kate Pinkerton : Wells
Goro : Paltrinieri
Yamadori : Malatesta
Uncle-Priest : Gustafson
Imperial Commissioner :
  Picco
Yakuside : Quintina

November 8

DIE MEISTERSINGER
  Bodanzky (c)

Hans Sachs : Whitehill
Pogner : Mayr
Eva : Manski
Magdalene : Howard
Walther : Kirchhoff
Beckmesser : Schützendorf
Kothner : Gabor

Vogelgesang : Bloch
Nachtigall : D'Angelo
Zorn : Bada
Eisslinger : Paltrinieri
Moser : Altglass
Ortel : Ananian
Schwarz : Gustafson
Foltz : Wolfe
David : Meader
Night Watchman : Cehanovsky

PHILADELPHIA

November 15

VIOLANTA/Bodanzky (c)

Simone Trovai : Whitehill
Violanta : Jeritza
Alfonso : Kirchhoff
Giovanni Bracca : Bada
Bice : Guilford
Barbara : Wakefield
Matteo : Altglass
Soldiers : Paltrinieri,
  Wolfe
Maids : Ryan, Bonetti

HÄNSEL UND GRETEL
  Bodanzky (c)

Hänsel : Bourskaya
Gretel : Mario
Witch : Manski
Gertrude : Wakefield
Peter : Schützendorf
Sandman : Alcock
Dewman : Parisette

November 22

AIDA/Serafin (c)

King : Macpherson
Amneris : Telva
Aida : Stückgold
Radames : Martinelli
Amonasro : Danise
Ramfis : Ludikar
Messenger : Tedesco
Priestess : Ryan

BROOKLYN

November 26

NORMA/Serafin (c)

Oroveso : Rothier
Norma : Ponselle
Pollione : Lauri-Volpi
Adalgisa : Vettori
Clotilde : Egener
Flavio : Paltrinieri

PHILADELPHIA

November 29

LA BOHÈME/Bellezza (c)

Rodolfo : Gigli
Marcello : Danise (for
  Scotti)

Schaunard : Didur
Colline : Rothier
Mimi : Alda
Musetta : Fleischer
Benoit : Ananian
Parpignol : Altglass
Alcindoro : Ananian
Sergeant : Reschiglian

December 6
DER ROSENKAVALIER
Bodanzky (c)
Princess von Werdenberg :
Easton
Baron Ochs : Mayr
Octavian : Stückgold
Von Faninal : Schützendorf
Sophie : Fleischer
Marianne : Manski
Valzacchi : Bada
Annina : Howard
Police Commissioner : Wolfe
Majordomo of Princess :
Altglass
Majordomo of Von Faninal :
Ditello
Notary : Gustafson
Innkeeper : Meader
Singer : Tedesco
Orphans : Parisette, Bonetti,
Falco
Milliner : Wells
Hairdresser : Agnini
Leopold : Burgstaller
Animal Vendor : Lipparini
Negro Boy : Tawil

BROOKLYN
December 6
TOSCA/Bellezza (c)
Tosca : Jeritza
Cavaradossi : Jagel
Scarpia : Scotti
Angelotti : Ananian
Sacristan : Malatesta
Spoletta : Paltrinieri
Sciarrone : Reschiglian
Jailer : Picco
Shepherd : Flexer

PHILADELPHIA
December 13
MANON LESCAUT/Serafin (c)
Manon : Alda
Lescaut : Scotti
Des Grieux : Gigli
Geronte : Ludikar
Edmondo : Tedesco
Ballet Master : Bada
Innkeeper : Picco
Musician : Alcock
Sergeant : Reschiglian
Lamplighter : Altglass
Captain : Ananian

December 20
CAVALLERIA RUSTICANA
Bellezza (c)
Santuzza : Jeritza
Lola : Bourskaya
Turiddu : Jagel
Alfio : Basiola
Lucia : Falco

PAGLIACCI/Bellezza (c)
Nedda : Mario
Canio : Martinelli
Tonio : De Luca
Beppe : Bada
Silvio : Tibbett

December 27
NORMA
Same as Nov. 26 except:
Pollione : Jagel
Adalgisa : Telva
Clotilde : Falco

January 3
MADAMA BUTTERFLY
Same as Nov. 1 except:
Cio-Cio-San : Rethberg
Sharpless : De Luca
Suzuki : Telva (for
Bourskaya)
Imperial Commissioner :
Reschiglian

BROOKLYN
January 3
TURANDOT/Serafin (c)
Princess Turandot : Jeritza
Emperor Altoum : Meader
(for Altglass)
Timur : Ludikar
Calaf : Lauri-Volpi
Liu : Dalossy
Ping : Basiola
Pang : Bada
Pong : Tedesco
Mandarin : Cehanovsky
Maids : Parisette, Flexer

PHILADELPHIA
January 10
DIE MEISTERSINGER
Same as Nov. 8 except:
Hans Sachs : Schorr
Pogner : Ludikar
Eva : Stückgold
Walther : Laubenthal
Moser : Weisberg (for
Altglass)

January 17
FAUST/Hasselmans (c)
Faust : Lauri-Volpi
Marguerite : Alda
Méphistophélès : Chaliapin

Valentin : Danise
Siébel : Dalossy
Marthe : Falco
Wagner : Wolfe

BROOKLYN
January 17
LUCIA DI LAMMERMOOR
Bellezza (c)
Lucia : Galli-Curci
Alisa : Egener
Edgardo : Martinelli
Ashton : De Luca
Raimondo : Pinza
Arturo : Tedesco
Normanno : Paltrinieri

PHILADELPHIA
January 24
CARMEN/Pelletier
(c for Hasselmans)
Carmen : Jeritza
Don José : Martinelli
Micaela : Mario
Escamillo : Basiola
Zuniga : D'Angelo
Morales : Cehanovsky
Frasquita : Ryan
Mercedes : Alcock
Dancaire : Picco
Remendado : Bada

January 31
IL BARBIERE DI SIVIGLIA
Bellezza (c)
Almaviva : Tokatyan
Dr. Bartolo : Malatesta
Rosina : Galli-Curci
Figaro : De Luca
Don Basilio : Pinza
Berta : Wakefield
Fiorello : Cehanovsky
Sergeant : Paltrinieri

BROOKLYN
January 31
LA BOHÈME/Bamboschek (c)
Same as Nov. 29 except:
Rodolfo : Chamlee
Marcello : Scotti
Musetta : Guilford

February 7
HÄNSEL UND GRETEL
Same as Nov. 15 except:
Hänsel : Dalossy
Dewman : Ryan

PAGLIACCI
Same as Dec. 20 except:
Nedda : Bori
Canio : Tokatyan
Tonio : Danise
Beppe : Tedesco

PHILADELPHIA
February 14
Les Contes d'Hoffmann
Hasselmans (c)

Olympia : Talley
Giulietta : Corona
Antonia : Mario
Hoffmann : Chamlee
Nicklausse : Howard
Lindorf : Wolfe
Coppelius : Didur
Dapertutto : De Luca
Miracle : Rothier
Andrès : Paltrinieri
Cochenille : Paltrinieri
Pitichinaccio : Paltrinieri
Franz : Paltrinieri
Luther : Gustafson
Nathaniel : Tedesco
Hermann : Gabor
Spalanzani : Meader
Schlemil : Cehanovsky
Crespel : D'Angelo
Voice : Wakefield

February 21
L'Amore dei Tre Re
Serafin (c)

Archibaldo : Rothier
Manfredo : Tibbett
Avito : Johnson
Flaminio : Bada
Youth : Paltrinieri
Fiora : Easton
Maid : Bonetti
Young Woman : Parisette
Old Woman : Flexer
Shepherd : Flexer

BROOKLYN
February 21
Il Trovatore/Bellezza (c)

Leonora : Corona
Manrico : Martinelli
Count di Luna : Basiola
Azucena : Branzell
Inez : Falco
Ferrando : Wolfe
Ruiz : Tedesco
Gypsy : Gabor

PHILADELPHIA
February 28
Tristan und Isolde
Bodanzky (c)

Tristan : Laubenthal
Isolde : Kappel
King Marke : Ludikar
Kurvenal : Schorr
Brangaene : Claussen
Melot : Gabor
Steersman : D'Angelo
Shepherd : Meader
Sailor's Voice : Meader

BROOKLYN
March 3
The King's Henchman
Serafin (c)

Eadgar : Tibbett
Aethelwold : Johnson
Aelfrida : Easton
Ase : Alcock
Maccus : Gustafson
Dunstan : Meader
Ordgar : D'Angelo
Gunner : Altglass
Cynric : Cehanovsky
Brand : Marshall
Wulfred : Ananian
Oslac : Wolfe
Thored : Gabor
Hwita : Bloch
Blacksmith : Wolfe
Saddler : Ananian
Miller : Marshall
Fisherman : Vajda
Old Man : Bloch
Hildeburh : Bonetti
Ostharu : Ryan
Godgyfu : Parisette
Leofsydu : Flexer
Blacksmith's Wife :
  Cingolani (for Egener)
Saddler's Wife : Bonetti
Miller's Wife : Bonetti
Fisherman's Wife : Ryan
Woman Servant : Flexer
Young Girl : Parisette

PHILADELPHIA
March 6
Madonna Imperia/Serafin (c)

Madonna Imperia : Guilford
Balda : Falco
Fiorella : Ryan
Filippo Mala : Jagel
Chancellor of Ragusa : Pinza
Prince of Coira : Wolfe
Count of the Embassy :
  D'Angelo
Servant : Picco
Valet : Paltrinieri
Prelate of Bordeaux : Bada

Le Coq d'Or/Bamboschek (c)
Queen : Talley
King Dodon : Pinza
Amelfa : Alcock
Astrologer : Diaz
General Polkan : D'Angelo
Prince Guidon : Paltrinieri
Prince Afron : Reschiglian
Golden Cockerel : Guilford
Pantomimists
Queen : Galli
King Dodon : Kosloff
Amelfa : Leporte

Astrologer : Bonfiglio
General Polkan : Bartik
Prince Guidon : Swee
Prince Afron : Casanova

BROOKLYN
March 13
Mignon/Hasselmans (c)

Mignon : Bori
Philine : Talley
Wilhelm : Chamlee
Lothario : Whitehill
Laerte : Bada
Jarno : Wolfe
Frederic : Dalossy
Antonio : Cehanovsky

PHILADELPHIA
March 20
Rigoletto/Bellezza (c)

Duke : Gigli
Rigoletto : Danise
Gilda : Talley
Sparafucile : Rothier
Maddalena : Wakefield
Giovanna : Falco
Monterone : Patton
Marullo : Ananian
Borsa : Tedesco
Ceprano : Reschiglian
Countess : Egener
Page : Tomisani

March 27
Siegfried/Bodanzky (c)

Siegfried : Laubenthal
Mime : Bloch
Wanderer : Bohnen
Alberich : Schützendorf
Fafner : Gustafson
Erda : Branzell
Brünnhilde : Easton
Forest Bird : Fleischer

BROOKLYN
March 31
Faust

Same as Jan. 17 except:
Faust : Tokatyan
Marguerite : Guilford
Valentin : De Luca
Siébel : Parisette (for
  Dalossy)
Marthe : Wakefield

PHILADELPHIA
April 3 (mat.)
Parsifal/Bodanzky (c)

Amfortas : Schützendorf
Titurel : Gustafson
Gurnemanz : Bohnen
Parsifal : Kirchhoff
Klingsor : Gabor

Kundry : Kappel
Voice : Telva
Knights of the Grail :
  Bada, D'Angelo
Esquires : Dalossy, Parisette,
  Meader, Paltrinieri
Flower Maidens : Lerch,
  Guilford, Dalossy, Fleischer,
  Ryan, Telva

April 3
LA RONDINE/Bellezza (c)
Magda : Bori
Lisette : Fleischer
Ruggero : Gigli
Prunier : Tokatyan
Rambaldo : Ludikar
Perichauld : Picco
Gobin : Paltrinieri
Crebillon : Wolfe
Yvette : Ryan
Bianca : Falco
Suzy · Alcock

April 10
LE PROPHÈTE/Pelletier
  (c—for Bodanzky)
John of Leyden : Martinelli
Fidès : Branzell
Bertha : Fleischer
Jonas : Tedesco
Mathisen : D'Angelo
Zacharias : Pinza
Oberthal : Rothier
Anabaptist : Cehanovsky
Officer : Altglass
Captain : Cehanovsky
Citizen : Reschiglian
Peasant : Altglass

BALTIMORE
April 16
LA FORZA DEL DESTINO
  Bellezza (c)
Marquis : D'Angelo
Leonora : Ponselle
Don Carlo : De Luca
Don Alvaro : Martinelli
Padre Guardiano : Pinza
Fra Melitone : Malatesta
Preziosilla : Telva
Curra : Falco
Trabucco : Paltrinieri
Surgeon : Reschiglian
Alcade : Ananian

April 17
BORIS GODUNOV/Bellezza (c)
Boris Godunov : Chaliapin
Fyodor : Ryan
Xenia : Dalossy
Nurse : Bourskaya
Shuiski : Bada
Shchelkalov : Cehanovsky

Pimen : Pinza
Grigori : Tokatyan
Marina : Claussen
Varlaam : Ananian
Missail : Paltrinieri
Innkeeper : Wakefield
Officer : D'Angelo
Simpleton : Tedesco
Lavitski : Picco
Chernikovski : Reschiglian

WASHINGTON
April 18
NORMA/Bellezza (c)
Same as Nov. 26 except:
Pollione : Jagel
Adalgisa : Telva

April 19 (mat.)
BORIS GODUNOV
Same as Apr. 17

BALTIMORE
April 19
ROMÉO ET JULIETTE
  Hasselmans (c)
Juliette : Bori
Stephano : Fleischer
Gertrude : Wakefield
Roméo : Gigli
Tybalt : Bada
Benvolio : Paltrinieri
Mercutio : Tibbett
Paris : Picco
Gregorio : Ananian
Capulet · Ludikar
Friar Laurence : Rothier
Duke of Verona : Gustafson

April 20
DIE MEISTERSINGER
Same as Nov. 8 except:
Pogner : Rothier
Eva : Easton
Magdalene : Telva
Walther : Laubenthal

WASHINGTON
April 21 (mat.)
ROMÉO ET JULIETTE
Same as Apr. 19 except:
Stephano : Dalossy
Mercutio : De Luca

April 21
TANNHÄUSER/Bamboschek (c)
Hermann : Gustafson
Tannhäuser : Kirchhoff
Wolfram : Tibbett
Walther : Altglass
Biterolf : Gabor
Heinrich : Bloch
Reinmar : Wolfe

Elisabeth : Easton
Venus : Claussen
Shepherd : Fleischer

ATLANTA
April 23
L'AFRICAINE/Bamboschek (c)
Don Pedro : Ludikar
Don Diego : Ananian
Inez : Mario
Vasco da Gama : Gigli
Don Alvar : Bada
Nelusko : Basiola
Selika : Ponselle
Grand Inquisitor : Rothier
Grand Brahmin : Rothier
Anna : Wakefield
Usher : Reschiglian
Officer : Paltrinieri

April 24
IL BARBIERE DI SIVIGLIA
Same as Jan. 31 except:
Fiorello : Reschiglian

April 25 (mat.)
HÄNSEL UND GRETEL
  Bamboschek (c)
Same as Nov. 15 except:
Hänsel : Fleischer
Peter : Ludikar
Sandman : Flexer
Dewman : Ryan

PAGLIACCI/Bamboschek (c)
Same as Dec. 20 except:
Nedda : Bori
Tonio : Tibbett
Beppe : Tedesco
Silvio : Cehanovsky

April 26
RIGOLETTO
Same as Mar. 20 except:
Rigoletto : De Luca
Maddalena : Bourskaya
Monterone : Ananian
Marullo : Picco
Borsa : Bada

April 27 (mat.)
DIE WALKÜRE/Bamboschek (c)
Wotan : Whitehill
Fricka : Telva
Brünnhilde : Claussen
Siegmund : Kirchhoff
Sieglinde : Easton
Hunding : Ludikar
Helmwige : Manski
Gerhilde : Ryan
Ortlinde : Lerch
Rossweisse : Bourskaya
Grimgerde : Dalossy

Waltraute : Wakefield
Siegrune : Vettori
Schwertleite : Flexer

April 27
NORMA/Bellezza (c)
Same as Nov. 26 except:
Oroveso : Pinza
Pollione : Jagel
Adalgisa : Telva
Clotilde : Falco

April 28 (mat.)
CARMEN/Hasselmans (c)
Same as Jan. 24 except:
Carmen : Easton
Micaela : Moore
Escamillo : Tibbett
Mercedes : Wakefield

April 28
LA BOHÈME
Same as Nov. 29 except:
Marcello : Scotti
Schaunard : Picco
Mimi : Bori
Benoit : Malatesta
Parpignol : Paltrinieri

CLEVELAND
April 30
AIDA/Bellezza (c)
Same as Nov. 22 except:
King : D'Angelo
Amneris : Claussen
Aida : Ponselle
Amonasro : Tibbett
Ramfis : Pinza

May 1
MIGNON
Same as Mar. 13 except:
Wilhelm : Gigli
Lothario : Rothier
Jarno : Ananian
Antonio : D'Angelo

May 2
NORMA/Bellezza (c)
Same as Nov. 26 except:
Oroveso : Pinza
Pollione : Jagel
Adalgisa : Telva

May 3
RIGOLETTO
Same as Mar. 20 except:
Rigoletto : De Luca
Gilda : Galli-Curci
Maddalena : Bourskaya
Monterone : Ananian
Marullo : Picco
Borsa : Bada

May 4 (mat.)
HÄNSEL UND GRETEL
Bamboschek (c)
Same as Nov. 15 except:
Hänsel : Fleischer
Peter : Ludikar
Sandman : Flexer
Dewman : Ryan

PAGLIACCI
Same as Dec. 20 except:
Nedda : Bori
Tonio : Basiola
Beppe : Tedesco
Silvio : Cehanovsky

May 4
TANNHÄUSER
Same as Apr. 21 except:
Venus : Telva
Shepherd : Dalossy

May 5 (mat.)
LES CONTES D'HOFFMANN
Same as Feb. 14 except:
Giulietta : Bori
Antonia : Bori
Hoffmann : Tokatyan
Nicklausse : Bourskaya
Coppelius : De Luca
Andrès : Bada
Cochenille : Bada
Pitichinaccio : Bada
Franz : Bada
Luther : Picco
Nathaniel : Altglass
Hermann : Gustafson
Spalanzani : Ananian

May 5
IL TROVATORE
Same as Feb. 21 except:
Leonora : Ponselle
Azucena : Claussen
Inez : Egener
Ferrando : D'Angelo
Ruiz : Paltrinieri

ROCHESTER
May 7
LA BOHÈME
Same as Nov. 29 except:
Rodolfo : Martinelli
Marcello : De Luca
Schaunard : Picco
Colline : Ludikar
Mimi : Bori
Parpignol : Paltrinieri
Sergeant : D'Angelo

May 8
NORMA/Bellezza (c)
Same as Nov. 26 except:
Pollione : Jagel

Adalgisa : Telva
Clotilde : Falco

1928 – 29

PHILADELPHIA
October 30
ANDREA CHÉNIER/Serafin (c)
Andrea Chénier : Gigli
Maddalena : Rethberg
Countess di Coigny :
  Bourskaya
Carlo Gérard : Danise
Bersi : Dalossy
Fléville : Cehanovsky
Abbé : Tedesco
Madelon : Telva
Mathieu : Didur
Spy : Bada
Fouquier : Gustafson
Dumas : Gabor
Roucher : Telva
Schmidt : Malatesta
Majordomo : Malatesta

BROOKLYN
October 30
RIGOLETTO/Bellezza (c)
Duke : Lauri-Volpi
Rigoletto : De Luca
Gilda : Mario
Sparafucile : Rothier
Maddalena : Alcock
Giovanna : Falco
Monterone : Ananian
Marullo : D'Angelo
Borsa : Paltrinieri
Ceprano : Reschiglian
Countess : Egener
Page : Tomisani

November 6
MADAMA BUTTERFLY
Bellezza (c)
Cio-Cio-San : Rethberg
B. F. Pinkerton : Martinelli
Sharpless : Scotti
Suzuki : Wakefield
Kate Pinkerton : Egener
Goro : Bada
Yamadori : Malatesta
Uncle-Priest : Gustafson
Imperial Commissioner :
  Picco
Yakuside : Quintina

PHILADELPHIA
November 13
DIE AEGYPTISCHE HELENA
Bodanzky (c)
Helena : Jeritza
Menelas : Kirchhoff

Aithra : Fleischer
Altair : Schützendorf
Da-ud : Carroll
Aithra's Maids : Falco,
Bourskaya
Elves : Lerch, Ryan,
Bourskaya, Wakefield (for
Flexer)
Omniscient Shell : Telva

November 20
L'AFRICAINE/Serafin (c)
Don Pedro : Didur
Don Diego : Ananian
Inez : Lerch
Vasco da Gama : Gigli
Don Alvar : Bada
Nelusko : Basiola
Selika : Ponselle
Grand Inquisitor : Rothier
Grand Brahmin : Rothier
Anna ; Wakefield
Usher : Reschiglian
Officer : Altglass

BROOKLYN
November 24
NORMA/Serafin (c)
Oroveso : Rothier
Norma : Ponselle
Pollione : Jagel
Adalgisa : Vettori (for
Telva)
Clotilde : Egener
Flavio : Bada

PHILADELPHIA
November 27
DIE WALKÜRE/Bodanzky (c)
Wotan : Whitehill
Fricka : Matzenauer
Brünnhilde : Easton
Siegmund : Laubenthal
Sieglinde : Rethberg
Hunding : Mayr
Helmwige : Manski
Gerhilde : Ryan
Ortlinde : Parisette
Rossweisse : Bourskaya
Grimgerde : Telva
Waltraute : Alcock
Siegrune : Carroll
Schwertleite : Flexer

December 4
RIGOLETTO
Same as Oct. 30 except:
Sparafucile : Didur
Giovanna : Wakefield
Monterone : D'Angelo
Marullo : Picco
Countess : Wells

BROOKLYN
December 4
DIE AEGYPTISCHE HELENA
Same as Nov. 13 except:
Altair : Whitehill
Fourth Elf : Flexer

PHILADELPHIA
December 11
ERNANI/Bellezza (c)
Ernani : Martinelli
Don Carlos : Danise
Don Ruy Gomez : Pinza
Elvira : Ponselle
Giovanna : Falco
Don Riccardo : Paltrinieri
Iago : Reschiglian

December 18
HÄNSEL UND GRETEL
Bodanzky (c)
Hänsel : Fleischer
Gretel : Mario
Witch : Manski
Gertrude : Wakefield
Peter : Schützendorf
Sandman : Alcock
Dewman : Lerch

PAGLIACCI/Bellezza (c)
Nedda : Rethberg
Canio : Lauri-Volpi
Tonio : Danise
Beppe : Bada
Silvio . Cehanovsky

BROOKLYN
December 25
FAUST/Hasselmans (c)
Faust : Martinelli
Marguerite : Rethberg
Méphistophélès : Rothier
Valentin : Danise
Siébel : Besuner
Marthe : Wakefield
Wagner : Wolfe

PHILADELPHIA
January 1
MANON/Hasselmans (c)
Manon : Bori
Lescaut : De Luca
Des Grieux : Gigli
Count des Grieux : Rothier
Poussette : Lerch
Javotte : Parisette
Rosette : Flexer
Guillot : Bada
De Brétigny : Cehanovsky
Innkeeper : Ananian
Guards : Windheim, Gabor
Sergeant : Ananian
Archer : Cehanovsky
Servant : Gola

January 8
TANNHÄUSER/Bodanzky (c)
Hermann : Mayr
Tannhäuser : Kirchhoff
Wolfram : Schorr
Walther : Altglass
Biterolf : Gabor
Heinrich : Bloch
Reinmar : Wolfe
Elisabeth : Jeritza
Venus : Claussen
Shepherd : Lerch (for
Dalossy)

January 15
L'AMORE DEI TRE RE
Serafin (c)
Archibaldo : Didur
Manfredo : Tibbett
Avito : Johnson
Flaminio : Bada
Youth : Altglass
Fiora : Ponselle
Maid : Bonetti
Young Woman : Parisette
Old Woman : Flexer
Shepherd : Flexer

BROOKLYN
January 15
LA TRAVIATA/Bamboschek (c)
Violetta : Galli-Curci
Alfredo : Lauri-Volpi
Germont : De Luca
Flora : Wells
Annina : Falco
Gastone : Paltrinieri
Baron Douphol : Reschiglian
Marquis d'Obigny : Picco
Doctor Grenvil : Ananian

PHILADELPHIA
January 22
LOHENGRIN/Bodanzky (c)
King Henry : Bohnen
Lohengrin : Kirchhoff (for
Laubenthal)
Elsa : Easton (for Kappel)
Telramund : Schorr
Ortrud : Branzell
Herald : Tibbett

January 29
IL BARBIERE DI SIVIGLIA
Bamboschek (c)
Almaviva : Tokatyan
Dr. Bartolo : Malatesta
Rosina : Galli-Curci
Figaro : Ruffo
Don Basilio : Pinza
Berta : Wakefield
Fiorello : Reschiglian
Sergeant : Paltrinieri

1928-29

BROOKLYN
January 29
CARMEN/Hasselmans (c)
Carmen : Jeritza
Don José : Martinelli
Micaela : Morgana
Escamillo : Tibbett
Zuniga : D'Angelo
Morales : Cehanovsky
Frasquita : Ryan
Mercedes : Alcock
Dancaire : Picco
Remendado : Bada

February 5
TRISTAN UND ISOLDE
Bodanzky (c)
Tristan : Kirchhoff
Isolde : Kappel
King Marke : Bohnen
Kurvenal : Whitehill
Brangaene : Branzell
Melot : Gabor
Steersman : D'Angelo
Shepherd : Meader
Sailor's Voice : Bloch

PHILADELPHIA
February 5
MADAMA BUTTERFLY
Same as Nov. 6 except.
Cio-Cio-San : Müller
B. F. Pinkerton : Johnson
Suzuki : Bourskaya
Kate Pinkerton : Wells
Goro : Paltrinieri

February 12
AIDA/Serafin (c)
King : Gustafson
Amneris : Claussen
Aida : Müller
Radames : Jagel
Amonasro : Danise
Ramfis : Pinza
Messenger : Paltrinieri
Priestess : Doninelli

February 19
SIEGFRIED/Serafin (c)
Siegfried : Laubenthal
Mime : Meader
Wanderer : Schorr
Alberich : Schützendorf
Fafner : Gustafson
Erda : Branzell
Brünnhilde : Kappel
Forest Bird : Sabanieeva

BROOKLYN
February 19
IL TROVATORE/Bellezza (c)
Leonora : Corona
Manrico : Lauri-Volpi

Count di Luna : Danise
Azucena : Telva (for
  Claussen)
Inez : Egener
Ferrando : Pinza
Ruiz : Paltrinieri
Gypsy : Gabor

PHILADELPHIA
February 26
THE KING'S HENCHMAN
Serafin (c)
Eadgar : Tibbett
Aethelwold : Johnson
Aelfrida : Easton
Ase : Alcock
Maccus : Gustafson
Dunstan : Meader
Ordgar : D'Angelo
Gunner : Altglass
Cynric : Cehanovsky
Brand : Marshall
Wulfred : Ananian
Oslac : Wolfe
Thored : Gabor
Hwita : Windheim
Blacksmith : Wolfe
Saddler : Ananian
Miller : Marshall
Fisherman : Vajda
Old Man : Windheim
Hildeburh : Bonetti
Ostharu : Ryan
Godgyfu : Parisette
Leofsydu : Flexer
Blacksmith's Wife : Egener
Saddler's Wife : Bonetti
Fisherman's Wife : Ryan
Woman Servant : Flexer
Young Girl : Parisette

BROOKLYN
March 2
ROMÉO ET JULIETTE
Hasselmans (c)
Juliette : Bori
Stephano : Carroll
Gertrude : Wakefield
Roméo : Johnson
Tybalt : Bada
Benvolio : Altglass
Mercutio : Tibbett
Paris : Picco
Gregorio : Ananian
Capulet : D'Angelo
Friar Laurence : Rothier
Duke of Verona : Wolfe

PHILADELPHIA
March 5
TRISTAN UND ISOLDE
Same as Feb. 5 except:
Tristan : Melchior

Kurvenal : Schorr
Sailor's Voice : Meader

March 12
BORIS GODUNOV/Bellezza (c)
Boris Godunov : Chaliapin
Fyodor : Dalossy
Xenia : Ryan
Nurse : Flexer
Shuiski : Bada
Shchelkalov : Cehanovsky
Pimen : Rothier
Grigori : Tokatyan
Marina : Telva
Varlaam : Ananian
Missail : Paltrinieri
Innkeeper : Bourskaya
Officer : D'Angelo
Simpleton : Tedesco
Lavitski : Cehanovsky
Chernikovski : Reschiglian

BROOKLYN
March 12
LA BOHÈME/Bamboschek (c)
Rodolfo : Lauri-Volpi
Marcello : Tibbett
Schaunard : Picco
Colline : Ludikar
Mimi : Fleischer
Musetta : Sabanieeva
Benoit : Malatesta
Parpignol : Altglass
Alcindoro : Malatesta
Sergeant : Cottino

PHILADELPHIA
March 19
LA RONDINE/Bellezza (c)
Magda : Bori
Lisette : Fleischer
Ruggero : Gigli
Prunier : Tokatyan
Rambaldo : Ludikar
Perichauld : Picco
Gobin : Paltrinieri
Crebillon : Wolfe
Yvette : Ryan
Bianca : Falco
Suzy : Alcock

March 26 (mat.)
PARSIFAL/Bodanzky (c)
Amfortas : Schützendorf
Titurel : Gustafson
Gurnemanz : Bohnen
Parsifal : Melchior
Klingsor : Gabor
Kundry : Kappel
A Voice : Telva
Knights of the Grail : Bada,
  D'Angelo
Esquires : Dalossy, Falco,
  Meader, Altglass

310

Flower Maidens : Lerch,
Falco, Dalossy, Fleischer,
Ryan, Telva

March 26
LUCIA DI LAMMERMOOR
Bellezza (c)

Lucia : Talley
Alisa : Falco
Edgardo : Lauri-Volpi
Ashton : De Luca
Raimondo : Pinza
Arturo : Tedesco
Normanno : Paltrinieri

BROOKLYN
March 30
LA RONDINE
Same as Mar. 19

PHILADELPHIA
April 2
FRA GHERARDO/Serafin (c)

Gherardo : Johnson
Mariola : Müller
Gentleman : Marshall
Fair Woman : Doninelli
Notary : Paltrinieri
Squint-eye : D'Angelo
Blind Man : Ananian
Old Woman : Bourskaya
Angry Voice : Wakefield
Woman's Voice : Wells
Soldiers : Cehanovsky, Patton
Man : Reschiglian
Woman : Wells
Frate Putagio : Ludikar
Frate Simone : Bada
Young Friar : Windheim
Mothers : Claussen, Alcock
Old Man : Pinza
Unbeliever : Paltrinieri
Podesta : Pinza
Bishop : Basiola
Podesta's Assessor :
Cehanovsky
Red-haired Man : D'Angelo
Youth : Gabor
Guard : Reschiglian

April 9
MIGNON/Hasselmans (c)

Mignon : Bori
Philine : Talley
Wilhelm : Gigli
Lothario : Whitehill
Laerte : Bada
Jarno : Wolfe
Frederic : Dalossy
Antonio : Cehanovsky

BALTIMORE
April 15
L'AMORE DEI TRE RE
Same as Jan. 15 except:

Archibaldo : Pinza
Youth : Paltrinieri
Fiora : Bori
Maid : Egener
Young Woman : Falco

PAGLIACCI

Same as Dec. 18 except:
Nedda : Fleischer
Tonio : Basiola (for Danise)
Beppe : Tedesco

April 16
NORMA

Same as Nov. 24 except:
Oroveso : Pinza
Adalgisa : Telva
Flavio : Paltrinieri

WASHINGTON
April 17
MANON

Same as Jan. 1 except:
Poussette : Doninelli
Javotte : Egener
Guards : Reschiglian,
Paltrinieri
Archer : D'Angelo

April 18
CAVALLERIA RUSTICANA
Bellezza (c)

Santuzza : Ponselle
Lola : Telva
Turiddu : Tokatyan
Alfio : Tibbett
Lucia : Falco

PAGLIACCI

Same as Dec. 18 except:
Nedda : Fleischer
Canio : Johnson
Tonio : Basiola (for Danise)

BALTIMORE
April 19
MANON

Same as Jan. 1 except:
Poussette : Doninelli
Javotte : Egener
Guards : Reschiglian,
Paltrinieri
Archer : D'Angelo

WASHINGTON
April 20 (mat.)
AIDA

Same as Feb. 12 except:
King : D'Angelo
Amneris : Telva
Aida : Ponselle
Radames : Lauri-Volpi

BALTIMORE
April 20
FAUST

Same as Dec. 25 except:
Faust : Johnson
Marguerite : Mario
Valentin : Tibbett
Siébel : Egener
Wagner : Ananian

ATLANTA
April 22
LA RONDINE

Same as Mar. 19 except:
Crebillon : D'Angelo
Suzy : Flexer

April 23
AIDA

Same as Feb. 12 except:
King : Macpherson
Aida : Ponselle
Radames : Lauri-Volpi
Amonasro : Basiola
Messenger : Tedesco

April 24
MANON

Same as Jan. 1 except:
Poussette : Doninelli
Javotte : Egener
Rosette : Flexer
Guards : Reschiglian,
Paltrinieri
Archer : D'Angelo

April 25
LA GIOCONDA/Serafin (c)

La Gioconda : Ponselle
Laura : Telva
Alvise : Pinza
La Cieca : Wakefield
Enzo : Lauri-Volpi
Barnaba : Danise
Zuane : Reschiglian
Singers : Reschiglian,
Paltrinieri
Isepo : Paltrinieri
Monk : D'Angelo
Steersman : Picco

April 26
FAUST

Same as Dec. 25 except:
Faust : Johnson
Marguerite : Fleischer
Valentin : Tibbett
Siébel : Egener
Wagner : Cehanovsky

April 27 (mat.)
MARTHA/Serafin (c)
Harriet : Mario
Nancy : Bourskaya

311

Lionel : Gigli
Plunkett : De Luca
Tristan : D'Angelo
Sheriff : Picco
Servant : Reschiglian

April 27
LA TRAVIATA
Same as Jan. 15 except:
Violetta : Bori
Germont : Tibbett
Flora : Egener
Gastone : Bada

CLEVELAND
April 29
NORMA
Same as Nov. 24 except:
Adalgisa : Telva
Flavio : Paltrinieri

April 30
L'AMORE DEI TRE RE
Same as Jan. 15 except:
Archibaldo : Pinza
Youth : Paltrinieri
Fiora : Bori
Maid : Egener
Young Woman : Falco

CAVALLERIA RUSTICANA
Same as Apr. 18 except:
Santuzza : Aves
Lola : Bourskaya
Turiddu : Jagel (for
Tokatyan)
Alfio : Basiola

May 1
LA GIOCONDA
Same as Apr. 25

May 2
MANON
Same as Jan. 1 except:
Poussette : Doninelli
Javotte : Egener
Guards : Reschiglian,
Paltrinieri
Archer : D'Angelo

May 3 (mat.)
AIDA
Same as Feb. 12 except:
King : D'Angelo
Amneris : Telva
Aida : Corona
Radames : Lauri-Volpi
Messenger : Tedesco

May 3
LOHENGRIN/Bamboschek (c)
King Henry : Ludikar
Lohengrin : Johnson

Elsa : Manski (for Easton)
Telramund : Tibbett
Ortrud : Claussen
Herald : Cehanovsky

May 4 (mat.)
LA RONDINE
Same as Mar. 19 except:
Prunier : Tedesco (for
Tokatyan)
Crebillon : D'Angelo
Suzy : Flexer

May 4
LUCIA DI LAMMERMOOR
Same as Mar. 26 except:
Alisa : Egener
Edgardo : Jagel (for
Lauri-Volpi)
Ashton : Basiola
Normanno : Bada

ROCHESTER
May 6
HÄNSEL UND GRETEL
Bamboschek (c)
Same as Dec. 18 except:
Gertrude : Telva
Peter : Ludikar
Sandman : Flexer
Dewman : Ryan

PAGLIACCI
Same as Dec. 18 except:
Nedda : Vettori
Tonio : De Luca

May 7
MANON
Same as Jan. 1 except:
Lescaut : Basiola
Poussette : Doninelli
Javotte : Egener
Guards : Reschiglian,
Paltrinieri
Archer : D'Angelo

1 9 2 9 – 3 0

BROOKLYN
October 29
ANDREA CHÉNIER/Bellezza (c)
Andrea Chénier : Lauri-Volpi
Maddalena : Corona
(for Ponselle)
Countess di Coigny :
Bourskaya
Carlo Gérard : Basiola
Bersi : Dalossy
Fléville : Cehanovsky
Abbé : Windheim
Madelon : Flexer

Mathieu : Ananian
Spy : Bada
Fouquier : Gustafson
Dumas : Gabor
Roucher : Picco
Schmidt : Malatesta
Majordomo : Malatesta

PHILADELPHIA
October 29
LA CAMPANA SOMMERSA
Serafin (c)
Rautendelein : Rethberg
Magda : Manski
Witch : Claussen
Neighbor : Falco
Elves : Doninelli, Besuner,
Swarthout (d)
Heinrich : Martinelli
Nickelmann : De Luca
Faun : D'Angelo
Pastor : Pinza
Schoolmaster : Tedesco
Barber : Paltrinieri

BROOKLYN
November 5
MADAMA BUTTERFLY
Sturani (c—t)
Cio-Cio-San : Oltrabella
(for Rethberg)
B. F. Pinkerton : Jagel
Sharpless : Scotti
Suzuki : Bourskaya
Kate Pinkerton : Wells
Goro : Bada
Yamadori : D'Angelo
Uncle-Priest : Ananian
Imperial Commissioner :
Gandolfi

PHILADELPHIA
November 5
LA BOHÈME/Bellezza (c)
Rodolfo : Lauri-Volpi
Marcello : Tibbett
Schaunard : Picco
Colline : Pasero
Mimi : Bori
Musetta : Guilford
Benoit : Malatesta
Parpignol : Paltrinieri
Alcindoro : Malatesta
Sergeant : Cottino (t)

November 12
LOHENGRIN/Rosenstock (c)
King Henry : Mayr
Lohengrin : Kirchhoff
Elsa : Stückgold
Telramund : Schützendorf
Ortrud : Matzenauer
Herald : Marshall

November 19
LA FANCIULLA DEL WEST
Bellezza (c)

Minnie : Jeritza
Dick Johnson : Martinelli
Jack Rance : Tibbett
Nick : Tedesco
Ashby : Pasero
Sonora : Marshall
Trin : Bada
Sid : Gabor
Bello : Cehanovsky
Harry : Paltrinieri
Joe : Windheim
Happy : Malatesta
Larkens : Picco
Billy : Ananian
Wowkle : Besuner
Jake Wallace : Macpherson
Jose Castro : Ananian
Pony-Express Rider : Altglass

BROOKLYN
November 23
CAVALLERIA RUSTICANA
Bellezza (c)

Santuzza : Jeritza
Lola : La Mance
Turiddu : Tokatyan
Alfio : Tibbett
Lucia : Egener

PAGLIACCI/Bellezza (c)

Nedda : Biondo (d)
Canio : Martinelli
Tonio : De Luca
Peppe : Bada
Silvio : Cehanovsky

PHILADELPHIA
November 26
DIE WALKÜRE/Bodanzky (c)

Wotan : Whitehill
Fricka : Claussen
Brünnhilde : Manski
Siegmund : Laubenthal
Sieglinde : Stückgold
Hunding : Gustafson
Helmwige : Aves
Gerhilde : Wells
Ortlinde : Besuner
Rossweisse : Bourskaya
Grimgerde : Telva
Waltraute : Wakefield
Siegrune : Carroll
Schwertleite : Flexer

December 3
LA TRAVIATA/Serafin (c)

Violetta : Bori
Alfredo : Tokatyan (for
  Lauri-Volpi)
Germont : Basiola (for
  Danise)

Flora : Egener
Annina : Falco
Gastone : Paltrinieri
Baron Douphol : Gandolfi
Marquis d'Obigny : Picco
Doctor Grenvil : Wolfe

BROOKLYN
December 3
LA FANCIULLA DEL WEST
Same as Nov. 19 except:
Harry : Altglass
Larkens : D'Angelo
Pony-Express Rider : Belleri

PHILADELPHIA
December 10
TURANDOT/Serafin (c)

Princess Turandot : Jeritza
Emperor Altoum : Altglass
Timur : Ludikar
Calaf : Lauri-Volpi
Liu : Oltrabella
Ping : Basiola
Pang : Bada
Pong : Tedesco
Mandarin : Cehanovsky
Maids : Ryan, Flexer

December 17
DIE MEISTERSINGER
Bodanzky (c)

Hans Sachs : Whitehill
Pogner : Rothier
Eva : Rethberg
Magdalene : Wakefield
Walther : Laubenthal
Beckmesser : Schützendorf
Kothner : Gabor
Vogelgesang : Bloch
Nachtigall : D'Angelo
Zorn : Bada
Eisslinger : Paltrinieri
Moser : Altglass
Ortel : Ananian
Schwarz : Gustafson
Foltz : Wolfe
David : Windheim
Night Watchman : Cehanovsky

BROOKLYN
December 24
AIDA/Serafin (c)

King : Macpherson
Amneris : Telva
Aida : Stückgold
Radames : Lauri-Volpi
Amonasro : Danise
Ramfis : Pasero
Messenger : Tedesco
Priestess : Ryan

December 31
DIE WALKÜRE
Same as Nov. 26 except:

Wotan : Schorr
Siegmund : Kirchhoff
Ortlinde : Fleischer
Grimgerde : Falco (for
  Telva)

PHILADELPHIA
January 7
LUCIA DI LAMMERMOOR
Bellezza (c)
(Not given in New York)

Lucia : Galli-Curci
Alisa : Egener
Edgardo : Martinelli
Ashton : Danise
Raimondo : Pasero
Arturo : Tedesco
Normanno : Paltrinieri

January 14
LUISA MILLER/Serafin (c)

Count Walter : Pasero
Rodolfo : Lauri-Volpi
Federica : Swarthout
Wurm : Ludikar
Miller : De Luca
Luisa : Ponselle
Laura : Doninelli
Peasant : Windheim (for
  Paltrinieri)

BROOKLYN
January 14
IL BARBIERE DI SIVIGLIA
Bellezza (c)

Almaviva : Tokatyan
Dr. Bartolo : Malatesta
Rosina : Galli-Curci
Figaro : Danise
Don Basilio : Pinza
Berta : Wakefield
Fiorello : Gandolfi
Sergeant : Paltrinieri

PHILADELPHIA
January 21
TANNHÄUSER/Bodanzky (c)

Hermann : Bohnen
Tannhäuser : Kirchhoff
Wolfram : Schorr
Walther : Windheim
Biterolf : Gabor
Heinrich : Bloch
Reinmar : Wolfe
Elisabeth : Kappel
Venus : Ohms
Shepherd : Lerch

January 28
ROMÉO ET JULIETTE
Hasselmans (c)

Juliette : Moore
Stephano : Swarthout
Gertrude : Wakefield

1929–30

Roméo : Johnson
Tybalt : Bada
Benvolio : Altglass
Mercutio : De Luca
Paris : Picco
Gregorio : Ananian
Capulet : Ludikar
Friar Laurence : Rothier
Duke of Verona : Macpherson

BROOKLYN
January 28
Tosca/Bellezza (c)

Tosca : Jeritza
Cavaradossi : Jagel
Scarpia : Scotti
Angelotti : D'Angelo
Sacristan : Malatesta
Spoletta : Paltrinieri
Sciarrone : Gandolfi
Jailer : Malatesta
Shepherd : Flexer

PHILADELPHIA
February 4
Tosca

Same as Jan. 28

February 11
Tristan und Isolde
Bodanzky (c)

Tristan : Laubenthal
Isolde : Ohms
King Marke : Bohnen
Kurvenal : Whitehill
Brangaene : Branzell
Melot : Gabor
Steersman : Wolfe
Shepherd : Bloch
Sailor's Voice : Bloch

BROOKLYN
February 11
Les Contes d'Hoffmann
Hasselmans (c)

Olympia : Morgana
Giulietta : Bori
Antonia : Mario
Hoffmann : Tokatyan
Nicklausse : Bourskaya
Lindorf : Gandolfi
Coppelius : Didur
Dapertutto : Basiola
Miracle : Rothier
Andrès : Bada
Cochenille : Bada
Pitichinaccio : Bada
Franz : Bada
Luther : Picco
Nathaniel : Altglass
Hermann : Gustafson
Spalanzani : Meader
Schlemil : Cehanovsky

Crespel : D'Angelo
Voice : Wakefield

PHILADELPHIA
February 18
Faust/Hasselmans (c)

Faust : Tokatyan
(for Trantoul)
Marguerite : Moore
Méphistophélès : Rothier
Valentin : De Luca
Siébel : Swarthout
Marthe : Wakefield
Wagner : Ananian

February 25
Sadko/Serafin (c)

Foma Nazaritch : Altglass
Luka Zinovitch : Macpherson
Sadko : Johnson
Lioubava : Claussen
Niejata : Swarthout
Douda : D'Angelo
Sopiel : Bada
Jesters : Falco, Besuner
Norseman : Gustafson
Hindu : Tedesco
Venetian : Basiola
Ocean : Wolfe (for Ludikar)
Volkhova : Fleischer
Apparition : Cehanovsky

BROOKLYN
March 1
Tannhäuser

Same as Jan. 21 except:
Hermann : Gustafson
Tannhäuser : Laubenthal
Walther : Altglass
Elisabeth : Müller
Venus : Kappel

PHILADELPHIA
March 4
Madama Butterfly

Same as Nov. 5 except:
Cio-Cio-San : Müller
B. F. Pinkerton : Tokatyan
Sharpless : Basiola
Yakuside : Quintina

BROOKLYN
March 11
Sadko

Same as Feb. 25 except:
Ocean : Ludikar

PHILADELPHIA
March 18
Fidelio/Bodanzky (c)

Don Fernando : Cehanovsky
Don Pizarro : Schützendorf
Florestan : Laubenthal
Leonore : Kappel
Rocco : Ludikar

Marzelline : Mario
Jaquino : Meader
Prisoners : Altglass, Gabor

March 25
L'Elisir d'Amore/Serafin (c)

Adina : Morgana
Nemorino : Gigli
Belcore : De Luca
Dulcamara : Pinza
Giannetta : Falco

BROOKLYN
March 29
Manon/Hasselmans (c)

Manon : Bori
Lescaut : Basiola
Des Grieux : Gigli
Count des Grieux : Ludikar
Poussette : Doninelli
Javotte : Egener
Rosette : Flexer
Guillot : Bada
De Brétigny : Cehanovsky
Innkeeper : Ananian
Guards : Windheim, Gandolfi
Servant : Gola
Sergeant : Ananian
Archer : Cehanovsky

PHILADELPHIA
April 1
Aida

Same as Dec. 24 except:
King : D'Angelo
Amneris : Branzell
Aida : Müller
Radames : Jagel
Ramfis : Pinza
Messenger : Paltrinieri
Priestess : Doninelli

April 8
Hänsel und Gretel
Bodanzky (c)

Hänsel : Fleischer
Gretel : Mario
Witch : Wakefield
Gertrude : Telva
Peter : Schützendorf
Sandman : Flexer
Dewman : Lerch

Pagliacci

Same as Nov. 23 except:
Nedda : Guilford
Canio : Johnson
Tonio : Danise
Beppe : Paltrinieri

April 15 (mat.)
Parsifal/Serafin (c)

Amfortas : Schützendorf
Titurel : Gustafson
Gurnemanz : Tappolet

314

Parsifal : Melchior
Klingsor : Didur
Kundry : Kappel
A Voice : Telva
Knights of the Grail : Bada,
    D'Angelo
Esquires : Dalossy, Falco,
    Meader, Altglass
Flower Maidens : Lerch,
    Doninelli, Dalossy,
    Fleischer, Besuner, Telva

April 15
LOUISE/Hasselmans (c)

Louise : Bori
Julien : Trantoul
Mother : Bourskaya
Father : Rothier
Irma : Doninelli
Camille : Ryan
Gertrude : Flexer
Apprentice : Sabanieeva
Elise : Egener
Blanche : Wells
Suzanne : Besuner
Forewoman : Savage
Marguerite : Parisette
Madeleine : Falco
Painter : Gandolfi
First Philosopher : Ananian
Second Philosopher :
    Gustafson
Sculptor : Picco
Poet : Windheim
Student : Paltrinieri
Song Writer : Cehanovsky
Street Sweeper : Parisette
Newspaper Girl : Besuner
Young Rag Picker :
    Swarthout
Milk Woman : Egener
Coal Picker : Divine
Noctambulist : Tedesco
King of the Fools : Tedesco
First Policeman : Belleri
Second Policeman : Coscia
Rag Picker : D'Angelo
Junk Man : Ananian
Street Arab : Sabanieeva
Old Clothes Man : Bloch
Bird Food Vendor : Ryan
Artichoke Vendor : Doninelli
Watercress Vendor : Divine
Chair Mender : Flexer
Carrot Vendor : Windheim
Rag Vendor : Paltrinieri
Green Peas Vendor :
    Paltrinieri

BALTIMORE
April 21
AIDA/Bellezza (c—for
    Serafin)

King : D'Angelo

Amneris : Claussen
Aida : Ponselle
Radames : Martinelli
Amonasro : Tibbett
Ramfis : Pinza
Messenger : Paltrinieri
Priestess : Doninelli

April 22
LOUISE

Same as Apr. 15 except:
Gertrude : Wakefield
Second Philosopher : Sterzini
    (t)
Coal Picker : Wakefield
Old Clothes Man : Bada
Watercress Vendor :
    Swarthout
Chair Mender : Wakefield

WASHINGTON
April 23
LA BOHÈME

Same as Nov. 5 except:
Rodolfo : Gigli
Colline : Pinza
Musetta : Fleischer
    (for Guilford)
Benoit : Ananian
Parpignol : Altglass
Sergeant : Gandolfi

April 24
ANDREA CHÉNIER/Serafin (c)

Same as Oct. 29 except:
Andrea Chénier : Martinelli
Maddalena : Ponselle
Carlo Gérard : De Luca
Bersi : Swarthout
Abbé : Tedesco
Madelon : Wakefield
Mathieu : Ludikar
Fouquier : D'Angelo
Dumas : Ananian

April 25
LA TRAVIATA/Bellezza (c)

Same as Dec. 3 except:
Germont : Tibbett
Doctor Grenvil : Ananian

BALTIMORE
April 25
L'ELISIR D'AMORE

Same as Mar. 25 except:
Adina : Fleischer

April 26
LA JUIVE/Hasselmans (c)

Rachel : Ponselle
Eleazar : Martinelli
Brogni : Rothier
Princess Eudoxia : Mario
Leopold : Tedesco

Ruggiero : Picco
Albert : D'Angelo
Herald : Ananian
Majordomo : Ananian

RICHMOND
April 28
LA TRAVIATA/Bellezza (c)

Same as Dec. 3 except:
Alfredo : Gigli
Germont : De Luca
Gastone : Bada
Doctor Grenvil : Ananian

April 29
AIDA/Bellezza (c—for Serafin)

Same as Dec. 24 except:
Amneris : Claussen
Aida : Ponselle
Radames : Martinelli
Amonasro : Danise
Ramfis : Pinza
Messenger : Paltrinieri
Priestess : Doninelli

April 30 (mat.)
LES CONTES D'HOFFMANN

Same as Feb. 11 except:
Olympia : Doninelli
Giulietta : Corona
Hoffmann : Trantoul
Nicklausse : Swarthout
Coppelius : Ludikar
Dapertutto : Tibbett
Nathaniel : Tedesco
Hermann : Ananian
Spalanzani : D'Angelo

April 30
L'ELISIR D'AMORE

Same as Mar. 25 except:
Adina : Fleischer
Belcore : Basiola

ATLANTA
May 1
LOUISE

Same as Apr. 15 except:
Gertrude : Wakefield
Second Philosopher :
    ? (for Sterzini)
Young Rag Picker : Belleri
    (for Swarthout)
Coal Picker : Wakefield
Old Clothes Man : Bada
Watercress Vendor :
    Swarthout
Chair Mender : Wakefield

May 2
IL TROVATORE/Serafin (c)

Leonora : Ponselle
Manrico : Martinelli
Count di Luna : Danise

Azucena : Claussen
Inez : Egener
Ferrando : Ludikar
Ruiz : Paltrinieri
Gypsy : Gandolfi

May 3 (mat.)
LA BOHÈME

Same as Nov. 5 except:
Rodolfo : Gigli
Marcello : De Luca
Colline : Pinza
Musetta : Fleischer
Benoit : Ananian
Sergeant : Gandolfi

May 3
CAVALLERIA RUSTICANA

Same as Nov. 23 except:
Santuzza : Corona
Lola : Swarthout
Alfio : Basiola
Lucia : Falco

PAGLIACCI

Same as Nov. 23 except:
Nedda : Mario
Tonio : Tibbett

CLEVELAND
May 5
LA GIOCONDA/Serafin (c)

La Gioconda : Ponselle
Laura : Claussen
Alvise : Pinza
La Cieca : Swarthout
Enzo : Gigli
Barnaba : Danise
Zuane : Gandolfi
First Singer : Gandolfi
Second Singer : Paltrinieri
Isepo : Paltrinieri
Monk : D'Angelo
Steersman : Picco

May 6
LOUISE

Same as Apr. 15 except:
Gertrude : Wakefield
Second Philosopher :
   Macpherson
Coal Picker : Wakefield
Second Policeman :
   Grimard (t—for Coscia)
Old Clothes Man : Bada
Watercress Vendor :
   Swarthout
Chair Mender : Wakefield

May 7
CAVALLERIA RUSTICANA
Bellezza (c)

Santuzza : Ponselle
Lola : Swarthout

316

Turiddu : Gigli
Alfio : Basiola
Lucia : Falco

PAGLIACCI

Same as Nov. 23 except:
Nedda : Mario (for Fleischer)

May 8
LA BOHÈME

Same as Nov. 5 except:
Rodolfo : Martinelli
Marcello : De Luca
Colline : Pinza
Musetta : Fleischer (for
   Guilford)
Benoit : Ananian
Sergeant : Gandolfi

May 9 (mat.)
CARMEN/Hasselmans (c)

Carmen : Bourskaya
Don José : Trantoul
Micaela : Mario
Escamillo : Pinza
Zuniga : D'Angelo
Morales : Cehanovsky
Frasquita : Doninelli
Mercedes : Wakefield
Dancaire : Picco
Remendado : Windheim

May 9
SADKO

Same as Feb. 25 except:
Foma Nazaritch : Paltrinieri
Luka Zinovitch : Gandolfi
Sadko : Jagel
Norseman : Macpherson
Ocean : Ludikar

May 10 (mat.)
LA TRAVIATA

Same as Dec. 3 except:
Germont : Tibbett
Gastone : Bada
Doctor Grenvil : Ananian

May 10
IL TROVATORE

Same as May 2 except:
Leonora : Corona
Gypsy : Malatesta

ROCHESTER
May 12
LOUISE

Same as Apr. 15 except:
Gertrude : Wakefield
Second Philosopher :
   Macpherson
Coal Picker : Wakefield
Second Policeman : Grimard
   (for Coscia)

Old Clothes Man : Bada
Watercress Vendor :
   Swarthout
Chair Mender : Wakefield

May 13
LA FANCIULLA DEL WEST
Serafin (c)

Same as Nov. 19 except:
Minnie : Corona
Jack Rance : Danise
Ashby : D'Angelo (for
   Ludikar)
Sonora : Gandolfi
Sid : Picco
Larkens : Ananian
Pony-Express Rider : Belleri

1 9 3 0 – 3 1

BROOKLYN
October 28
LA BOHÈME/Bellezza (c)

Rodolfo : Johnson
Marcello : Scotti
Schaunard : Picco
Colline : Rothier
Mimi : Bori
Musetta : Guilford
Benoit : Ananian
Parpignol : Windheim
Alcindoro : Malatesta
Sergeant : Coscia

PHILADELPHIA
October 28
LA GIOCONDA/Serafin (c)

La Gioconda : Ponselle
Laura : Claussen
Alvise : Pinza
La Cieca : Swarthout
Enzo : Gigli
Barnaba : Danise
Zuane : Gandolfi
First Singer : Gandolfi
Second Singer : Paltrinieri
Isepo : Paltrinieri
Monk : D'Angelo
Steersman : Gabor

November 4
LA FANCIULLA DEL WEST
Bellezza (c)

Minnie : Jeritza
Dick Johnson : Johnson
Jack Rance : Danise
Nick : Tedesco
Ashby : D'Angelo
Sonora : Gandolfi
Trin : Bada
Sid : Gabor
Bello : Cehanovsky
Harry : Paltrinieri

Joe : Windheim
Happy : Malatesta
Larkens : Picco
Billy : Ananian
Wowkle : Besuner
Jake Wallace : Macpherson
Jose Castro : Ananian
Pony-Express Rider : Belleri

November 11
DIE WALKÜRE/Bodanzky (c)

Wotan : Schorr
Fricka : Branzell
Brünnhilde : Kappel
Siegmund : Laubenthal
Sieglinde : Müller
Hunding : Andresen
Helmwige : Manski
Gerhilde : Wells
Ortlinde : Besuner
Rossweisse : Bourskaya
Grimgerde : Telva
Waltraute : Wakefield
Siegrune : Divine
Schwertleite : Flexer

BROOKLYN
November 11
MIGNON/Hasselmans (c)

Mignon : Bori
Philine : Sabanieeva
Wilhelm : Gigli
Lothario : Rothier
Laerte : Bada
Jarno : Ananian
Frederic . Swarthout
Antonio : D'Angelo

PHILADELPHIA
November 18
HÄNSEL UND GRETEL
Bodanzky (c)

Hänsel : Fleischer
Gretel : Mario
Witch : Manski
Gertrude : Wakefield
Peter : Schützendorf
Sandman : Flexer
Dewman : Belkin

PAGLIACCI/Bellezza (c)

Nedda : Bori
Canio : Martinelli
Tonio : De Luca
Beppe : Bada
Silvio : Frigerio

November 25
ANDREA CHÉNIER
Sturani (c—t)

Andrea Chénier : Gigli
Maddalena : Ponselle
Countess di Coigny :
  Bourskaya

Carlo Gérard : Basiola
Bersi : Swarthout
Fléville : Cehanovsky
Abbé : Windheim
Madelon : Bourskaya
Mathieu : Ludikar
Spy : Bada
Fouquier : Gustafson
Dumas : Ananian
Roucher : Picco
Schmidt : Gandolfi
Majordomo : Gandolfi

HARTFORD
November 25
TOSCA/Bellezza (c)

Tosca : Jeritza
Cavaradossi : Martinelli
Scarpia : Scotti
Angelotti : D'Angelo
Sacristan : Malatesta
Spoletta : Paltrinieri
Sciarrone : D'Angelo
  (for Gandolfi)
Jailer : Malatesta
Shepherd : Flexer

PHILADELPHIA
December 2
DER FLIEGENDE HOLLÄNDER
Bodanzky (c)

Senta : Jeritza
Mary : Telva
Dutchman : Schorr
Erik · Kirchhoff
Daland : Andresen
Steersman : Clemens

WHITE PLAINS
December 2
LA BOHÈME

Same as Oct. 28 except:
Rodolfo : Gigli
Colline : Pinza

BROOKLYN
December 6
DER FLIEGENDE HOLLÄNDER

Same as Dec. 2 except:
Erik : Laubenthal
Daland : Ludikar

PHILADELPHIA
December 9
DON GIOVANNI/Serafin (c)

Don Giovanni : Pinza
Donna Anna : Ponselle
Donna Elvira : Müller
Zerlina : Fleischer
Commendatore : Rothier
Don Ottavio : Gigli
Leporello : Ludikar
Masetto : D'Angelo

December 16
LA BOHÈME/Sturani (c)

Same as Oct. 28 except:
Rodolfo : Martinelli
Marcello : Basiola
Colline : Pasero
Musetta : Sabanieeva
Alcindoro : Ananian

WHITE PLAINS
December 16
TOSCA

Same as Nov. 25 except:
Cavaradossi : Lauri-Volpi
Sciarrone : Gandolfi

BROOKLYN
December 23
CARMEN/Hasselmans (c)

Carmen : Jeritza
Don José : Tokatyan (for
  Martinelli)
Micaela : Doninelli
Escamillo : Basiola
Zuniga : D'Angelo
Morales : Cehanovsky
Frasquita : Ryan
Mercedes : Flexer
Dancaire : Picco
Remendado : Bada

December 30
LOHENGRIN/Riedel (c)

King Henry : Andresen
Lohengrin : Laubenthal
Elsa : Kappel
Telramund : Schorr
Ortrud : Branzell
Herald : Cehanovsky

PHILADELPHIA
January 6
BOCCACCIO/Bodanzky (c)

Boccaccio : Jeritza
Pietro : Kirchhoff
Scalza : Meader
Beatrice : Morgana
Lotteringhi : Windheim
Isabella : Manski
Lambertuccio : Schützendorf
Peronella : Telva
Fiammetta : Fleischer
Leonetto : Clemens
Tofano : Altglass
Majordomo : Wolfe
Bookseller : Gandolfi
Checco : Gabor
Filippa : Flexer
Pantalone : Schützendorf
Colombina : Morgana
Pulcinella : Burgstaller
Arlecchino : Meader
Narcisino : Clemens

1930–31

January 13
SIEGFRIED/Bodanzky (c)
Siegfried : Laubenthal
Mime : Meader
Wanderer : Schorr
Alberich : Schützendorf
Fafner : Tappolet
Erda : Branzell
Brünnhilde : Ohms
Forest Bird : Sabanieeva

BROOKLYN
January 13
RIGOLETTO/Bellezza (c)
Duke : Lauri-Volpi
Rigoletto : De Luca
Gilda : Pons
Sparafucile : Pinza
Maddalena : Bourskaya
Giovanna : Falco
Monterone : D'Angelo
Marullo : Picco
Borsa : Paltrinieri
Ceprano : Gandolfi
Countess : Egener
Page : Tomisani

PHILADELPHIA
January 20
TOSCA
Same as Nov. 25 except:
Cavaradossi : Tokatyan
Sciarrone : Gandolfi

January 27
IL BARBIERE DI SIVIGLIA
Bellezza (c)
Almaviva : Tedesco
Dr. Bartolo : Malatesta
Rosina : Pons
Figaro : De Luca
Don Basilio : Pinza
Berta : Falco
Fiorello : Gandolfi
Sergeant : Paltrinieri

BROOKLYN
January 27
BOCCACCIO
Same as Jan. 6 except:
Bookseller : Cehanovsky

PHILADELPHIA
February 3
FAUST/Hasselmans (c)
Faust : Martinelli
Marguerite : Fleischer
Méphistophélès : Rothier
Valentin : Basiola
Siébel : Besuner
Marthe : Wakefield
Wagner : Ananian

February 10
GÖTTERDÄMMERUNG
Bodanzky (c)
Siegfried : Laubenthal
Gunther : Schorr
Hagen : Bohnen
Brünnhilde : Kappel
Gutrune : Manski
Woglinde : Fleischer
Wellgunde : Wells
Flosshilde : Telva
(Norn, Alberich, Waltraute
scenes omitted)

BROOKLYN
February 14
MADAMA BUTTERFLY
Bellezza (c)
Cio-Cio-San : Rethberg
B. F. Pinkerton : Martinelli
Sharpless : De Luca
Suzuki : Petrova
Kate Pinkerton : Wells
Goro : Paltrinieri
Yamadori : Malatesta
Uncle-Priest : Ananian
Imperial Commissioner :
Gandolfi

PHILADELPHIA
February 17
MADAMA BUTTERFLY
Sturani (c)
Same as Feb. 14 except:
B. F. Pinkerton : Tokatyan
Sharpless : Scotti
Goro : Windheim
Yakuside : Quintina

February 24
AIDA/Serafin (c)
King : D'Angelo
Amneris : Branzell
Aida : Corona
Radames : Martinelli
Amonasro : Tibbett
Ramfis : Pinza
Messenger : Paltrinieri
Priestess : Doninelli

March 3
PETER IBBETSON/Serafin (c)
Peter Ibbetson : Johnson
Colonel Ibbetson : Tibbett
Mary : Bori
Mrs. Deane : Telva
Mrs. Glyn : Bourskaya
Achille : Bada
Major Duquesnois : Rothier
Chaplain : D'Angelo
Charlie Plunkett : Paltrinieri
Guy Mainwaring : Picco
Footman : Windheim

Diana Vivash : Wells
Madge Plunkett : Divine
Victorine : Falco
Sister of Charity : Egener
Manservant : Gandolfi
Prison Governor :
Cehanovsky
Turnkey : Gandolfi
Pasquier de la Marière :
Cehanovsky
Marie Pasquier : Biondo
Mme. Seraskier : Doninelli

BROOKLYN
March 7
IL BARBIERE DI SIVIGLIA
Same as Jan. 27 except:
Figaro : Danise
Berta : Wakefield
Fiorello : Gandolfi

PHILADELPHIA
March 10
TRISTAN UND ISOLDE
Bodanzky (c)
Tristan : Melchior
Isolde : Kappel
King Marke : Bohnen
Kurvenal : Whitehill
Brangaene : Ranzow
Melot : Gabor
Steersman : Wolfe
Shepherd : Meader
Sailor's Voice : Clemens

March 17
PELLÉAS ET MÉLISANDE
Hasselmans (c)
Mélisande : Bori
Geneviève : Bourskaya
Little Yniold : Dalossy
Pelléas : Johnson
Golaud : Whitehill
Arkel : Rothier
Physician : Ananian

March 24
MANON/Hasselmans (c)
Manon : Moore
Lescaut : De Luca
Des Grieux : Gigli
Count des Grieux : Ludikar
Poussette : Doninelli
Javotte : Egener
Rosette : Flexer
Guillot : Meader
De Brétigny : Picco
Innkeeper : Ananian
Guards : Altglass, Gabor
Servant : Gola
Sergeant : Ananian
Archer : Picco

318

BROOKLYN
March 24

PETER IBBETSON

Same as Mar. 3 except:
Guy Mainwaring : Cehanovsky
Sister of Charity : Lerch
Mme. Seraskier : Lerch

PHILADELPHIA
March 31 (mat.)

PARSIFAL/Bodanzky (c)

Amfortas : Schützendorf
Titurel : Tappolet
Gurnemanz : Bohnen
Parsifal : Laubenthal
Klingsor : Gabor
Kundry : Ohms
A Voice : Telva
Knights of the Grail : Bada,
  D'Angelo
Esquires : Dalossy, Falco,
  Meader, Altglass
Flower Maidens : Lerch,
  Falco, Dalossy, Fleischer,
  Ryan, Telva

March 31

LUCIA DI LAMMERMOOR
  Bellezza (c)

Lucia : Pons
Alisa : Egener
Edgardo : Lauri-Volpi
Ashton : Basiola
Raimondo : Pinza
Arturo · Tedesco
Normanno : Paltrinieri

April 7

GUILLAUME TELL/Serafin (c)

Tell : Danise
Arnold : Lauri-Volpi
Walter Furst : Rothier
Melchthal : D'Angelo
Matilde : Fleischer
Jemmy : Doninelli
Hedwig : Petrova
Fisherman : Tedesco
Leutold : Cehanovsky
Gessler : Ludikar
Rudolf : Bada

BALTIMORE
April 13

MIGNON

Same as Nov. 11 except:
Philine : Pons
Lothario : Pinza
Antonio : Cehanovsky

WASHINGTON
April 14

TOSCA

Same as Nov. 25 except:
Cavaradossi : Lauri-Volpi

Scarpia : Tibbett
Angelotti : Cehanovsky
Sacristan : D'Angelo
Jailer : Picco

April 15 (mat.)

MIGNON

Same as Nov. 11 except:
Philine : Pons
Antonio : Cehanovsky

BALTIMORE
April 15

TOSCA

Same as Nov. 25 except:
Cavaradossi : Thill
Scarpia : Tibbett
Angelotti : Cehanovsky
Sacristan : D'Angelo
Jailer : Picco

WASHINGTON
April 16

PETER IBBETSON

Same as Mar. 3 except:
Diana Vivash : Lerch
Madge Plunkett : Flexer
Marie Pasquier : Flexer

BALTIMORE
April 17

LUCIA DI LAMMERMOOR

Same as Mar. 31 except:
Edgardo : Tokatyan
Ashton : Danise
Arturo : Bada

April 18

LA TRAVIATA/Serafin (c)

Violetta : Ponselle
Alfredo : Lauri-Volpi
Germont : Tibbett
Flora : Egener
Annina : Falco
Gastone : Bada
Baron Douphol : Gandolfi
Marquis d'Obigny : Picco
Doctor Grenvil : Ananian

WHITE PLAINS
April 20

LA TRAVIATA

Same as Apr. 18

April 25 (mat.)

LUCIA DI LAMMERMOOR

Same as Mar. 31 except:
Ashton : Danise
Arturo : Bada

CLEVELAND
April 27

LA TRAVIATA

Same as Apr. 18 except:
Gastone : Paltrinieri

April 28

TOSCA

Same as Nov. 25 except:
Cavaradossi : Thill
Scarpia : Tibbett
Angelotti : Cehanovsky
Sacristan : D'Angelo
Jailer : Picco

April 29

MIGNON

Same as Nov. 11 except:
Philine : Pons
Lothario : Pinza
Antonio : Cehanovsky

April 30

CARMEN

Same as Dec. 23 except:
Don José : Thill
Micaela : Moore
Escamillo : Pinza
Frasquita : Doninelli
Remendado : Windheim

May 1 (mat.)

RIGOLETTO

Same as Jan. 13 except:
Duke : Gigli
Rigoletto : Basiola
Sparafucile : Ludikar
Monterone : Ananian
Borsa : Bada

May 1

NORMA/Serafin (c)

Oroveso : Rothier
Norma : Ponselle
Pollione : Tokatyan
Adalgisa : Swarthout
Clotilde : Egener
Flavio : Paltrinieri

May 2 (mat.)

PETER IBBETSON

Same as Mar. 3 except:
Mrs. Deane : Swarthout
Major Duquesnois : D'Angelo
Diana Vivash : Lerch
Madge Plunkett : Flexer
Marie Pasquier : Flexer

May 2

LUCIA DI LAMMERMOOR

Same as Mar. 31 except:
Alisa : Falco
Edgardo : Gigli
Ashton : Danise
Raimondo : Rothier
Arturo : Windheim

ROCHESTER
May 4

LA TRAVIATA

Same as Apr. 18 except:

Violetta : Bori
Alfredo : Gigli
Germont : Danise
Flora : Falco
Gastone : Paltrinieri

1 9 3 1 – 3 2

BROOKLYN
November 3
HÄNSEL UND GRETEL
Riedel (c)
Hänsel : Bourskaya
Gretel : Mario
Witch : Manski
Gertrude : Wakefield
Peter : Ludikar
Sandman : Flexer
Dewman : Besuner

PAGLIACCI/Bellezza (c)
Nedda : Fleischer
Canio : Martinelli
Tonio : Danise
Beppe : Tedesco
Silvio : Frigerio

PHILADELPHIA
November 3
MANON/Hasselmans (c)
Manon : Bori
Lescaut : Basiola
Des Grieux : Gigli
Count des Grieux : Rothier
Poussette : Doninelli
Javotte : Egener
Rosette : Divine
Guillot : Bada
De Brétigny : Cehanovsky
Innkeeper : Ananian
Guards : Altglass, Gabor
Servant : Gola
Sergeant : Ananian
Archer : Cehanovsky

November 10
SCHWANDA,
DER DUDELSACKPFEIFER
Bodanzky (c)
Schwanda : Schorr
Dorota : Müller
Babinsky : Laubenthal
Queen : Branzell
Sorcerer : Andresen
Judge : Paltrinieri
Executioner : Windheim
Devil : Schützendorf
Devil's Disciple : Windheim
Devil's Captain : Altglass
First Halberdier : Altglass
Second Halberdier : Wolfe

WHITE PLAINS
November 13
MADAMA BUTTERFLY
Sturani (c)
Cio-Cio-San : Müller
B. F. Pinkerton : Gigli
Sharpless : De Luca
Suzuki : Bourskaya
Kate Pinkerton : Wells
Goro : Bada
Yamadori : D'Angelo
Uncle-Priest : Ananian
Yakuside : Quintina
Imperial Commissioner :
Picco

PHILADELPHIA
November 17
TOSCA/Bellezza (c)
Tosca : Jeritza
Cavaradossi : Martinelli
Scarpia : Scotti
Angelotti : Cehanovsky
Sacristan : Malatesta
Spoletta : Bada
Sciarrone : Cehanovsky
(for Picco)
Jailer : Malatesta
Shepherd : Flexer

BROOKLYN
November 17
LA GIOCONDA/Serafin (c)
La Gioconda : Ponselle
Laura : Claussen
Alvise : Pinza
La Cieca : Petrova
Enzo : Gigli
Barnaba : Basiola
Zuane : Picco (for Gandolfi)
First Singer : Picco (for
Gandolfi)
Second Singer : Paltrinieri
Isepo : Paltrinieri
Monk : D'Angelo
Steersman : Gabor

HARTFORD
November 24
LA TRAVIATA/Serafin (c)
Violetta : Ponselle
Alfredo : Gigli
Germont : De Luca
Flora : Egener
Annina : Falco
Gastone : Bada
Baron Douphol : Gandolfi
Marquis d'Obigny : Picco
Doctor Grenvil : Ananian

PHILADELPHIA
November 24
DIE WALKÜRE/Bodanzky (c)
Wotan : Schorr

Fricka : Branzell
Brünnhilde : Ohms
Siegmund : Lorenz
Sieglinde : Müller
Hunding : Gauld
Helmwige : Manski
Gerhilde : Wells
Ortlinde : Besuner
Rossweisse : Bourskaya
Grimgerde : Von Essen
Waltraute : Wakefield
Siegrune : Divine
Schwertleite : Flexer

December 1
LA TRAVIATA
Same as Nov. 24 except:
Violetta : Bori

BROOKLYN
December 5
TOSCA
Same as Nov. 17 except:
Cavaradossi : Jagel
Spoletta : Windheim

PHILADELPHIA
December 8
L'ORACOLO/Bellezza (c)
Win-Shee : Pasero
Chim-Fen : Scotti
Hoo-Tsin : D'Angelo
Win-San-Luy : Tokatyan
Hoo-Chee : Rosenthal
Ah-Yoe : Guilford
Hua-Quee : Wakefield
Fortune Teller : Paltrinieri

PAGLIACCI
Same as Nov. 3 except:
Beppe : Paltrinieri

December 15
DER FLIEGENDE HOLLÄNDER
Bodanzky (c)
Senta : Jeritza
Mary : Claussen
Dutchman : Schorr
Erik : Lorenz
Daland : Ludikar
Steersman : Clemens

BROOKLYN
December 22
SCHWANDA,
DER DUDELSACKPFEIFER
Same as Nov. 10 except:
Dorota : Manski
Babinsky : Lorenz

December 29
LA TRAVIATA
Same as Nov. 24 except:
Violetta : Bori
Alfredo : Lauri-Volpi

PHILADELPHIA
January 5
DONNA JUANITA/Bodanzky (c)
Rene du Faure : Jeritza
Don Pomponio : Windheim
Donna Olympia : Manski
Sir Douglas : D'Angelo
Gaston du Faure : Clemens
Riego Manrique : Laubenthal
Gil Polo : Schützendorf
Petrita : Fleischer
Picador : Cehanovsky
Tepa : Besuner
Marco : Flexer
Pichegru : Gabor
Eusebio : Altglass

January 12
HÄNSEL UND GRETEL
Riedel (c)
Hänsel : Bourskaya
Gretel : Mario
Witch : Manski
Gertrude : Wakefield
Peter : Ludikar
Sandman : Flexer
Dewman : Besuner

LA NOTTE DI ZORAIMA
Serafin (c)
Zoraima : Ponselle
Manuela : Biondo
Muscar : Jagel
Pedrito : Basiola
Lyoval : D'Angelo
First Inca Insurgent : Gabor
Second Inca Insurgent : Wolfe
Inca Prisoner : Paltrinieri
A Voice : Tedesco

January 19
RIGOLETTO/Bellezza (c)
Duke : Lauri-Volpi
Rigoletto : De Luca
Gilda : Pons
Sparafucile : Rothier
Maddalena : Bourskaya
(for Swarthout)
Giovanna : Falco
Monterone : Gandolfi
Marullo : Picco
Borsa : Bada
Ceprano : Ananian
Countess : Egener
Page : Tomisani

BROOKLYN
January 19
DONNA JUANITA
Same as Jan. 5

PHILADELPHIA
January 26
TRISTAN UND ISOLDE
Bodanzky (c)
Tristan : Melchior

Isolde : Kappel
King Marke : Andresen
Kurvenal : Schorr
Brangaene : Branzell
Melot : Gabor
Steersman : Wolfe
Shepherd : Clemens
Sailor's Voice : Clemens

February 2
LA BOHÈME/Bellezza (c)
Rodolfo : Martinelli
Marcello : De Luca
Schaunard : Didur
Colline : Pinza
Mimi : Rethberg
Musetta : Guilford
Benoit : Ananian
Parpignol : Altglass
Alcindoro : Malatesta
Sergeant : Coscia

HARTFORD
February 2
MIGNON/Hasselmans (c)
Mignon : Bori
Philine : Pons
Wilhelm : Tedesco
(for Tokatyan)
Lothario : Rothier
Laerte : Bada
Jarno : Wolfe
Frederic : Swarthout
Antonio : Wolfe

PHILADELPHIA
February 9
SIEGFRIED/Bodanzky (c)
Siegfried : Melchior
Mime : Clemens
Wanderer : Bohnen
Alberich : Schützendorf
Fafner : Tappolet
Erda : Doe
Brünnhilde : Kappel
Forest Bird : Sabanieeva

BROOKLYN
February 9
LA BOHÈME
Same as Feb. 2 except:
Colline : Pasero

PHILADELPHIA
February 16
SIMON BOCCANEGRA
Serafin (c)
Simon Boccanegra : Tibbett
Maria Boccanegra : Rethberg
Jacopo Fiesco : Pinza
Gabriele : Martinelli
Paolo Albiani : Frigerio
Pietro : Ananian
Captain : Paltrinieri
Maidservant : Besuner

February 23
TANNHÄUSER/Bodanzky (c)
Hermann : Tappolet
Tannhäuser : Melchior
Wolfram : Schorr
Walther : Clemens
Biterolf : Gabor
Heinrich : Paltrinieri
Reinmar : Wolfe
Elisabeth : Kappel
Venus : Manski
Shepherd : Fleischer

BROOKLYN
February 27
DIE WALKÜRE
Same as Nov. 24 except:
Fricka : Claussen (for Doe)
Brünnhilde : Ljungberg
Siegmund : Melchior
Sieglinde : Kappel
Hunding : Tappolet
Gerhilde : Ryan (for Wells)

PHILADELPHIA
March 1
PETER IBBETSON/Serafin (c)
Peter Ibbetson : Johnson
Colonel Ibbetson : Tibbett
Mary : Bori
Mrs. Deane : Swarthout
Mrs. Glyn : Bourskaya
Achille : Bada
Major Duquesnois : Rothier
Chaplain : D'Angelo
Charlie Plunkett : Paltrinieri
Guy Mainwaring : Picco
Footman : Windheim
Diana Vivash : Wells
Madge Plunkett : Divine
Victorine : Falco
Sister of Charity : Egener
Manservant : Gandolfi
Prison Governor : Cehanovsky
Turnkey : Gandolfi
Pasquier de la Marière :
Cehanovsky
Marie Pasquier : Biondo
Mme. Seraskier : Doninelli

March 8
AIDA/Serafin (c)
King : Macpherson
Amneris : Petrova
Aida : Rethberg
Radames : Merli
Amonasro : Tibbett
Ramfis : Pinza
Messenger : Paltrinieri
Priestess : Doninelli

BROOKLYN
March 12
L'AFRICAINE/Serafin (c)
Don Pedro : Pasero

Don Diego : Ananian
Inez : Morgana
Vasco da Gama : Gigli
Don Alvar : Paltrinieri
Nelusko : Borgioli
Selika : Rethberg
Grand Inquisitor : Rothier
Grand Brahmin : Rothier
Anna : Wakefield
Usher : Gandolfi
Officer : Windheim

PHILADELPHIA

March 15
SADKO/Serafin (c)
Foma Nazaritch : Altglass
Luka Zinovitch : Gandolfi
Sadko : Thill
Lioubava : Bourskaya
Niejata : Petrova
Douda : D'Angelo
Sopiel : Bada
Jesters : Falco, Besuner
Norseman : Macpherson
Hindu : Tedesco
Venetian : Basiola
Ocean : Ludikar
Volkhova : Fleischer
Apparition : Cehanovsky

March 22
IL BARBIERE DI SIVIGLIA
Bellezza (c)
Almaviva : Tokatyan
Dr. Bartolo : Malatesta
Rosina : Pons
Figaro : De Luca
Don Basilio : Pinza
Berta : Wakefield
Fiorello : Gandolfi
Sergeant : Paltrinieri

March 29
ROMÉO ET JULIETTE
Hasselmans (c)
Juliette : Bori (for Moore)
Stephano : Swarthout
Gertrude : Wakefield
Roméo : Johnson
Tybalt : Bada
Benvolio : Altglass
Mercutio : Tibbett
Paris : Picco
Gregorio : Ananian
Capulet : D'Angelo
Friar Laurence : Rothier
Duke of Verona : Wolfe

BROOKLYN

March 29
LUCIA DI LAMMERMOOR
Bellezza (c)
Lucia : Pons
Alisa : Egener

Edgardo : Merli
Ashton : Basiola
Raimondo : Pinza
Arturo : Tedesco
Normanno : Paltrinieri

PHILADELPHIA

April 5
GÖTTERDÄMMERUNG
Bodanzky (c)
Siegfried : Laubenthal
Gunther : Whitehill
Hagen : Bohnen
Brünnhilde : Ljungberg
Gutrune : Manski
Woglinde : Fleischer
Wellgunde : Wells
Flosshilde : Von Essen
Vassals : Altglass, Gabor
(Norn, Alberich, Waltraute
scenes omitted)

WHITE PLAINS

April 8
LES CONTES D'HOFFMANN
Hasselmans (c)
Hoffmann : Jagel
Olympia : Pons
Giulietta : Moore
Antonia : Mario
Nicklausse : Swarthout
Lindorf : Wolfe
Coppelius : Ludikar
Dappertutto : Tibbett
Dr. Miracle : Rothier
Spalanzani : D'Angelo
Schlemil : Cehanovsky
Crespel : D'Angelo
Voice : Wakefield
Andrès : Bada
Cochenille : Bada
Pitichinaccio : Bada
Frantz : Bada
Luther : Picco
Nathanael : Altglass
Hermann : Ananian

PHILADELPHIA

April 12
L'AFRICAINE
Same as Mar. 12 except:
Don Pedro : Ludikar
Don Alvar : Bada
Grand Inquisitor : Pinza
Grand Brahmin : Pinza

BALTIMORE

April 18
LES CONTES D'HOFFMANN
Same as Apr. 8 except:
Antonia : Bori
Lindorf : Gandolfi
Dappertutto : De Luca
Luther : Cehanovsky

Nathanael : Paltrinieri
Hermann : Cehanovsky

April 19
TANNHÄUSER
Same as Feb. 23 except:
Hermann : Pinza
Tannhäuser : Laubenthal
Wolfram : Tibbett
Walther : Clemens
Biterolf : Cehanovsky
Reinmar : D'Angelo
Elisabeth : Ljungberg
Venus : Claussen
Shepherd : Doninelli

April 20
L'AFRICAINE
Same as Mar. 12 except:
Don Pedro : Ludikar
Inez : Doninelli
Don Alvar : Bada
Nelusko : Basiola
Selika : Ponselle

CLEVELAND

April 21
LAKMÉ/Hasselmans (c)
Lakmé : Pons
Mallika : Swarthout
Ellen : Doninelli
Rose : Flexer
Mrs. Benson : Egener
Gerald : Jagel
Nilakantha : Pinza
Frederic : De Luca
Hadji : Paltrinieri
Fortune Teller : Bada
Chinese Merchant : Windheim
Thief : Ananian

April 22
MANON
Same as Nov. 3 except:
Rosette : Flexer
Guards : Windheim, Gandolfi

April 23 (mat.)
LES CONTES D'HOFFMANN
Same as Apr. 8 except:
Hoffmann : Tokatyan
Giulietta : Corona (for
Moore)
Voice : Flexer
Nathanael : Windheim

April 23
LA GIOCONDA
Same as Nov. 17 except:
Laura : Carmela Ponselle
La Cieca : Wakefield
Enzo : Martinelli
Zuane : Gandolfi
First Singer : Gandolfi
Steersman : Coscia

ROCHESTER
April 25
LUCIA DI LAMMERMOOR
Same as Mar. 29 except:
Alisa : Falco
Edgardo : Gigli
Arturo : Bada

1 9 3 2 – 3 3

PHILADELPHIA
November 22
LA GIOCONDA/Sturani
(c—for Serafin)

La Gioconda : Ponselle
Laura : Bampton (d)
Alvise : Pasero
La Cieca : Petrova
Enzo : Lauri-Volpi
Barnaba : Borgioli
Zuane : Gandolfi
First Singer : Gandolfi
Second Singer : Paltrinieri
Isepo : Paltrinieri
Monk : D'Angelo
Steersman : Gabor

November 29
IL BARBIERE DI SIVIGLIA
Bellezza (c)
(Not given in New York)
Almaviva : Schipa
Dr. Bartolo : Malatesta
Rosina : Pons
Figaro : Bonelli (d)
Don Basilio : Pinza
Berta : Wakefield
Fiorello : Paltrinieri
Sergeant : Paltrinieri

HARTFORD
November 29
LOHENGRIN/Bodanzky (c)
King Henry : Hofmann
Lohengrin : Laubenthal
Elsa : Ljungberg
Telramund : Schorr
Ortrud : Branzell
Herald : Cehanovsky

BROOKLYN
December 6
LA TRAVIATA/Serafin (c)
Violetta : Ponselle
Alfredo : Schipa
Germont : Tibbett
Flora : Egener
Annina : Wakefield
Gastone : Bada
Baron Douphol : Gandolfi
Marquis d'Obigny : Picco
Doctor Grenvil : Ananian

PHILADELPHIA
December 6
DIE WALKÜRE/Bodanzky (c)
Wotan : Hofmann
Fricka : Doe
Brünnhilde : Ljungberg
Siegmund : De Loor
Sieglinde : Stückgold
  (for Kappel)
Hunding : Tappolet
Helmwige : Manski
Gerhilde : Wells
Ortlinde : Besuner
Rossweisse : Bourskaya
Grimgerde : Falco
Waltraute : Bampton
Siegrune : Vettori
Schwertleite : Doe

WHITE PLAINS
December 9
LAKMÉ/Hasselmans (c)
Lakmé : Pons
Mallika : Swarthout
Ellen : Doninelli
Rose : Falco
Mrs. Benson : Egener
Gerald : Martinelli
Nilakantha : Rothier
Frederic : Cehanovsky
Hadji : Paltrinieri
Fortune Teller : Altglass
Chinese Merchant : Bada
Thief : Ananian

PHILADELPHIA
December 13
SIMON BOCCANEGRA
Serafin (c)
Simon Boccanegra : Tibbett
Maria Boccanegra : Müller
Jacopo Fiesco : Pasero
Gabriele : Martinelli
Paolo Albiani : Frigerio
Pietro : Ananian
Captain : Paltrinieri
Maidservant : Besuner

BROOKLYN
December 17
LOHENGRIN
Same as Nov. 29 except:
King Henry : Tappolet
Lohengrin : De Loor

PHILADELPHIA
December 20
TANNHÄUSER/Bodanzky (c)
Hermann : Tappolet
Tannhäuser : Laubenthal
Wolfram : Tibbett
Walther : Clemens
Biterolf : Gabor
Heinrich : Paltrinieri

Reinmar : Wolfe
Elisabeth : Rethberg
Venus : Halstead
Shepherd : Doninelli

December 27
LA TRAVIATA
Same as Dec. 6 except:
Violetta : Bori
Germont : Bonelli
Flora : Vettori (for Egener)
Annina : Falco

BROOKLYN
December 27
LA BOHÈME/Bellezza (c)
Rodolfo : Lauri-Volpi
Marcello : Borgioli
Schaunard : Frigerio
Colline : Pasero
Mimi : Müller
Musetta : Morgana
Benoit : Malatesta
  (for Ananian)
Parpignol : Altglass
Alcindoro : Malatesta
Sergeant : Coscia

WHITE PLAINS
December 30
HÄNSEL UND GRETEL
Riedel (c)
Hänsel : Fleischer
Gretel : Mario
Witch : Wakefield
Gertrude : Doe
Peter : Schützendorf
Sandman : Bampton
Dewman : Besuner

PAGLIACCI/Sturani (c)
Nedda : Bori
Canio : Martinelli
Tonio : Bonelli
Beppe : Tedesco
Silvio : Frigerio

PHILADELPHIA
January 3
AIDA/Serafin (c)
King : Anderson
Amneris : Carmela Ponselle
Aida : Rethberg
Radames : Lauri-Volpi
Amonasro : Borgioli
Ramfis : Pasero
Messenger : Paltrinieri
Priestess : Doninelli

January 10
THE EMPEROR JONES
Serafin (c)
Brutus Jones : Tibbett
Henry Smithers : Windheim

323

Old Native Woman : Besuner
Congo Witch-Doctor :
  Winfield

PAGLIACCI/Cimara
  (c—for Bellezza)

Same as Dec. 30 except:
Nedda : Morgana
Canio : Tokatyan
  (for Martinelli)

January 17
SIEGFRIED/Bodanzky (c)

Siegfried : Laubenthal
Mime : Windheim
Wanderer : Hofmann
Alberich : Schützendorf
Fafner : Tappolet
Erda : Doe
Brünnhilde : Kappel
Forest Bird : Fleischer

BROOKLYN
January 17
MANON/Hasselmans (c)
Manon : Bori
Lescaut : De Luca
Des Grieux : Tokatyan
  (for Lauri-Volpi)
Count des Grieux : Rothier
Poussette : Doninelli
Javotte : Falco
Rosette : Flexer
Guillot : Bada
De Brétigny : Cehanovsky
Innkeeper : Ananian
Guards : Altglass, Gabor
Servant : Gola
Sergeant : Ananian
Archer : Cehanovsky

January 24
IL SIGNOR BRUSCHINO
  Serafin (c)

Gaudenzio : Pinza
Sofia : Fleischer
Bruschino (father) : De Luca
Bruschino (son) : Windheim
Florville : Tedesco
Commissary of Police :
  D'Angelo
Filiberto : Gandolfi
Marianna : Vettori

THE EMPEROR JONES
Same as Jan. 10

PHILADELPHIA
January 24
LA BOHÈME
Same as Dec. 27 except:
Rodolfo : Martinelli
Mimi : Rethberg
Musetta : Doninelli

January 31
PELLÉAS ET MÉLISANDE
  Hasselmans (c)

Mélisande : Bori
Geneviève : Bourskaya
Little Yniold : Dalossy
Pelléas : Johnson
Golaud : Pinza
Arkel : Rothier
Physician : Ananian

February 7
RIGOLETTO/Bellezza (c)

Duke : Lauri-Volpi
Rigoletto : De Luca
Gilda : Pons
Sparafucile : Rothier
  (for Pasero)
Maddalena : Swarthout
Giovanna : Falco
Monterone : Gandolfi
Marullo : Picco
Borsa : Bada
Ceprano : Ananian
Countess : Vettori
Page : Tomisani

HARTFORD
February 7
AIDA
Same as Jan. 3 except:
Radames : Martinelli
Amonasro : Tibbett
Ramfis : Pinza

WHITE PLAINS
February 10
LOHENGRIN/Riedel
  (c—for Bodanzky)
Same as Dec. 17 except:
King Henry : Tappolet
Ortrud : Doe

PHILADELPHIA
February 14
DIE VERKAUFTE BRAUT
  Bodanzky (c)
Kruschina : Schützendorf
Kathinka : Bourskaya
  (for Manski)
Marie : Rethberg
  (for Fleischer)
Micha : Tappolet
Agnes : Falco (for Petrova)
Wenzel : Windheim
Hans : Laubenthal
Kezal : Hofmann
Springer : Gandolfi
Esmeralda : Gleason
Muff : Wolfe

February 21
L'AMORE DEI TRE RE
  Serafin (c)
Archibaldo : Pasero

Manfredo : Borgioli
Avito : Martinelli
Flaminio : Bada
Youth : Tedesco
Fiora : Bori
Maid : Vettori
Young Woman : Gleason
Old Woman : Flexer
Shepherd : Flexer

BROOKLYN
February 21
LAKMÉ
Same as Dec. 9 except:
Rose : Wakefield
Mrs. Benson : Falco
Gerald : Jagel
Frederic : De Luca
Fortune Teller : Windheim
Chinese Merchant : Bada

PHILADELPHIA
February 28
TRISTAN UND ISOLDE
  Riedel (c)
Tristan : Melchior
Isolde : Leider
King Marke : Tappolet
Kurvenal : Schorr
Brangaene : Doe
Melot : Gabor
Steersman : Wolfe
Shepherd : Clemens
Sailor's Voice : Clemens

March 7
MANON
Same as Jan. 17 except:
Des Grieux : Crooks

BALTIMORE
March 13
RIGOLETTO
Same as Feb. 7 except:
Rigoletto : Bonelli
Sparafucile : Pinza
Marullo : D'Angelo
Ceprano : Cehanovsky
Countess : Falco

March 14
PAGLIACCI/Bellezza (c)
Same as Dec. 30 except:
Canio : Lauri-Volpi
Tonio : Borgioli
Beppe : Bada
Silvio : Cehanovsky

THE EMPEROR JONES
Same as Jan. 10

March 15
TRISTAN UND ISOLDE
Same as Feb. 28 except:
Brangaene : Olszewska

Melot : Cehanovsky
Steersman : D'Angelo
Shepherd : Windheim
Sailor's Voice : Windheim

1933 – 34

PHILADELPHIA
December 19
LAKMÉ/Hasselmans (c)
Lakmé : Pons
Mallika : Swarthout
Ellen : Gleason
Rose : Flexer
Mrs. Benson : Falco
Gerald : Martinelli
Nilakantha : Rothier
Frederic : Cehanovsky
Hadji : Paltrinieri
Fortune Teller : Windheim
Chinese Merchant : Altglass
Thief : Ananian

January 2
DIE WALKÜRE/Bodanzky (c)
Wotan : Schorr
Fricka : Branzell
Brünnhilde : Ljungberg
Siegmund : Lorenz
Sieglinde : Kappel
Hunding : List
Helmwige : Manski
Gerhilde : Wells
Ortlinde : Halstead
Rossweisse : Bourskaya
Grimgerde : Falco
Waltraute : Doe
Siegrune : Vettori
Schwertleite : Petina

BROOKLYN
January 2
RIGOLETTO/Bellezza (c)
Duke : Martini
Rigoletto : De Luca
Gilda : Pons
Sparafucile : Lazzari
Maddalena : Swarthout
Giovanna : Wakefield
Monterone : Gandolfi
Marullo : Picco
Borsa : Bada
Ceprano : Ananian
Countess : Clark
Page : Tomisani

PHILADELPHIA
January 9
MIGNON/Hasselmans (c)
Mignon : Bori
Philine : Pons
Wilhelm : Schipa
Lothario : Pinza

Laerte : Bada
Jarno : Wolfe
Frederic : Swarthout
Antonio : Wolfe

January 16
LA TRAVIATA/Serafin (c)
Violetta : Muzio
Alfredo : Schipa
Germont : Bonelli
Flora : Vettori
Annina : Falco
Gastone : Bada
Baron Douphol : Gandolfi
Marquis d'Obigny : Picco
Doctor Grenvil : Ananian

BROOKLYN
January 16
TRISTAN UND ISOLDE
  Riedel (c)
Tristan : Melchior
Isolde : Kappel
King Marke : List
Kurvenal : Schützendorf
Brangaene : Bampton
Melot : Gabor
Steersman : Wolfe
Shepherd : Clemens
Sailor's Voice : Clemens

PHILADELPHIA
January 23
GIANNI SCHICCHI/Bellezza (c)
Gianni Schicchi : De Luca
Lauretta : Fleischer
La Vecchia : Bourskaya
Rinuccio : Jagel
Gherardo : Paltrinieri
Nella : Clark
Gherardino : Castino
Betto : Ananian
Simone : Pinza
Marco : D'Angelo
Ciesca : Vettori
Spinelloccio : Malatesta
Nicolao : Gandolfi
Pinellino : Wolfe
Guccio : Gabor

SALOME/Bodanzky (c)
Herod : Lorenz
Herodias : Manski
Salome : Ljungberg
Jokanaan : Schorr
Narraboth : Clemens
Page : Doe
First Nazarene : Anderson
Second Nazarene : Clemens
First Jew : Windheim
Second Jew : Paltrinieri
Third Jew : Bada
Fourth Jew : Altglass
Fifth Jew : Wolfe
First Soldier : D'Angelo

Second Soldier : Gabor
Cappadocian : Gandolfi
Slave : Clark

January 30
MANON/Hasselmans (c)
Manon : Bori
Lescaut : De Luca
Des Grieux : Schipa
Count des Grieux : Rothier
Poussette : Gleason
Javotte : Clark
Rosette : Petina
Guillot : Bada
De Brétigny : Cehanovsky
Innkeeper : Ananian
Guards : Altglass, Gabor
Servant : Gola
Sergeant : Ananian
Archer : Cehanovsky

HARTFORD
January 30
CAVALLERIA RUSTICANA
  Bellezza (c)
Santuzza : Ponselle
Lola : Swarthout
Turiddu : Jagel
Alfio : Borgioli
Lucia : Falco

THE EMPEROR JONES
  Serafin (c)
Brutus Jones : Tibbett
Henry Smithers : Windheim
Old Native Woman : Besuner
Congo Witch-Doctor : Barros

PHILADELPHIA
February 6
TRISTAN UND ISOLDE
  Riedel (c—for Bodanzky,
  Act III)
Same as Jan. 16 except:
Isolde : Leider
Kurvenal : Schorr
Brangaene : Branzell

BROOKLYN
February 6
FAUST/Hasselmans (c)
Faust : Martinelli
Marguerite : Rethberg
Méphistophélès : Pinza
Valentin : Bonelli
Siébel : Swarthout
Marthe : Wakefield
Wagner : Ananian

PHILADELPHIA
February 13
MERRY MOUNT/Serafin (c)
Faint-not-Tinker : Gabor
Samoset : Wolfe

1933–34

Desire Annable : Petina
Jonathan Banks : Paltrinieri
Wrestling Bradford : Tibbett
Plentiful Tewke : Swarthout
Praise-God-Tewke : D'Angelo
Myles Brodrib : Gandolfi
Peregrine Brodrib : Gleason
Love Brewster : Clark
Bridget Crackston : Wakefield
Jack Prence : Windheim
Lady Marigold Sandys :
  Corona
Thomas Morton : Cehanovsky
Sir Gower Lackland :
  Johnson
Jewel Scrooby : Picco
Puritans : Altglass,
  Malatesta

February 20
ROMÉO ET JULIETTE
  Hasselmans (c)
Juliette : Norena
Stephano : Swarthout
Gertrude : Falco (for
  Wakefield)
Roméo : Hackett
Tybalt : Bada
Benvolio : Altglass
Mercutio : De Luca
Paris : Picco
Gregorio : Ananian
Capulet : D'Angelo
Friar Laurence : Rothier
Duke of Verona : Anderson

BROOKLYN
February 20
LA TRAVIATA
Same as Jan. 16 except:
Violetta : Bori
Alfredo : Jagel
Germont : Tibbett
Annina : Wakefield (for
  Falco)
Gastone : Paltrinieri
Baron Douphol : ? (for
  Gandolfi)
Marquis d'Obigny :
  Cehanovsky
Doctor Grenvil : Wolfe

PHILADELPHIA
February 27
LA BOHÈME/Bellezza (c)
Rodolfo : Jagel
Marcello : Borgioli
Schaunard : Picco
Colline : Lazzari
Mimi : Bori
Musetta : Morgana
Benoit : Malatesta
Parpignol : Altglass

Alcindoro : Malatesta
Sergeant : Coscia

March 6
LUCIA DI LAMMERMOOR
  Bellezza (c)
Lucia : Pons
Alisa : Vettori
Edgardo : Martinelli
Ashton : Bonelli
Raimondo : Rothier
Arturo : Tedesco
Normanno : Bada

BROOKLYN
March 6
MERRY MOUNT
Same as Feb. 13 except:
Desire Annable : Besuner
Plentiful Tewke : Petina

HARTFORD
March 13
FAUST
Same as Feb. 6 except:
Wagner : Cehanovsky
  (for Ananian)

PHILADELPHIA
March 13
DIE MEISTERSINGER
  Bodanzky (c)
Hans Sachs : Hofmann
Pogner : List
Eva : Fleischer
Magdalene : Doe
Walther : Lorenz
Beckmesser : Schützendorf
Kothner : Gabor
Vogelgesang : Windheim
Nachtigall : D'Angelo
Zorn : Bada
Eisslinger : Paltrinieri
Moser : Altglass
Ortel : Ananian
Schwarz : Anderson
Foltz : Wolfe
David : Clemens
Night Watchman : Gabor

March 20
MADAMA BUTTERFLY
  Bellezza (c)
Cio-Cio-San : Rethberg
B. F. Pinkerton : Althouse
Sharpless : Borgioli
Suzuki : Bourskaya
Kate Pinkerton : Wells
Goro : Paltrinieri
Yamadori : Picco
Uncle-Priest : Ananian
Yakuside : Quintina
Imperial Commissioner : Picco

BROOKLYN
March 20
LINDA DI CHAMOUNIX
  Serafin (c)
Linda : Pons
Pierotto : Swarthout
Maddalena : Vettori
Charles : Crooks
Antonio : De Luca
Prefect : Lazzari
Marquis de Boisfleury :
  Malatesta
Intendant : Bada

PHILADELPHIA
March 27
AIDA/Serafin (c)
King : Anderson
Amneris : Olszewska
Aida : Rethberg
Radames : Martinelli
Amonasro : Bonelli
Ramfis : Lazzari
Messenger : Paltrinieri
Priestess : Clark

BOSTON
April 2
AIDA
Same as Mar. 27 except:
King : D'Angelo
Amonasro : Borgioli
Ramfis : Pinza

April 3
MANON
Same as Jan. 30 except:
Des Grieux : Crooks
Poussette : Besuner
Rosette : Falco
Innkeeper : D'Angelo
Guards : Windheim, Gandolfi
Sergeant : D'Angelo

April 4 (mat.)
TANNHÄUSER/Bodanzky (c)
Hermann : List
Tannhäuser : Melchior
Wolfram : Schorr
Walther : Windheim
Biterolf : Cehanovsky
Heinrich : Paltrinieri
Reinmar : D'Angelo
Elisabeth : Rethberg
Venus : Leider
Shepherd : Fleischer

April 4
LUCIA DI LAMMERMOOR
Same as Mar. 6 except:
Edgardo : Martini
Ashton : Borgioli
Raimondo : Lazzari (for
  Pinza)

Arturo : Bada
Normanno : Paltrinieri

April 5
PAGLIACCI/Bellezza (c)
Nedda : Fleischer
Canio : Martinelli
Tonio : Tibbett
Beppe : Paltrinieri
Silvio : Cehanovsky

THE EMPEROR JONES
Same as Jan. 30

April 6
GÖTTERDÄMMERUNG
Bodanzky (c)
Siegfried : Melchior
Gunther : Schorr
Hagen : List
Brünnhilde : Leider
Gutrune : Manski
Waltraute : Olszewska
Woglinde : Fleischer
Wellgunde : Wells
Flosshilde : Petina
First Norn : Petina
Second Norn : Wells
Third Norn : Manski
Vassals : Windheim,
Cehanovsky

April 7 (mat.)
PELLÉAS ET MÉLISANDE
Hasselmans (c)
Mélisande · Bori
Geneviève : Bourskaya
Little Yniold : Dalossy
Pelléas : Johnson
Golaud : Pinza
Arkel : Rothier
Physician : D'Angelo

April 7
RIGOLETTO
Same as Jan. 2 except:
Duke : Hackett
Sparafucile : D'Angelo
Maddalena : Bourskaya
Giovanna : Falco
Marullo : Cehanovsky
Ceprano : Coscia
Countess : Vettori

BALTIMORE
April 9
MADAMA BUTTERFLY
Same as Mar. 20 except:
B. F. Pinkerton : Martinelli
Sharpless : Cehanovsky
Kate Pinkerton : Vettori
Goro : Bada
Yamadori : Malatesta
Uncle-Priest : D'Angelo

April 10
GIANNI SCHICCHI
Same as Jan. 23 except:
Rinuccio : Martini
Betto : Picco

SALOME
Same as Jan. 23 except:
Herod : Jagel
Page : Bourskaya
First Nazarene : List

April 11
LA TRAVIATA
Same as Jan. 16 except:
Violetta : Bori
Alfredo : Crooks
Germont : Tibbett
Annina : Vettori
Gastone : Paltrinieri
Doctor Grenvil : Wolfe

ROCHESTER
April 12
MERRY MOUNT
Same as Feb. 13 except:
Bridget Crackston : Vettori

1 9 3 4 – 3 5

BROOKLYN
January 8
LA GIOCONDA/Panizza (c)
La Gioconda : Ponselle
Laura : Carmela Ponselle
Alvise : Pinza
La Cieca : Leonard (d)
Enzo : Martinelli
Barnaba : A. Borgioli
Zuane : Gandolfi
First Singer : Gandolfi
Second Singer : Paltrinieri
Isepo : Paltrinieri
Monk : D'Angelo
Steersman : Malatesta

HARTFORD
January 15
LA BOHÈME/Bellezza (c)
Rodolfo : Martini
Marcello : Tibbett
Schaunard : Picco
Colline : Lazzari
Mimi : Bori
Musetta : Morgana
Benoit : Malatesta
Parpignol : Altglass
Alcindoro : Malatesta
Sergeant : Coscia

BROOKLYN
January 22
TANNHÄUSER/Bodanzky (c)
Hermann : List

Tannhäuser : Melchior
Wolfram : Bonelli
Walther : Clemens
Biterolf : Gabor
Heinrich : Paltrinieri
Reinmar : Wolfe
Elisabeth : Rethberg
Venus : Konetzni
Shepherd : Clark

January 29
AIDA/Panizza (c)
King : D'Angelo
Amneris : Bampton
Aida : Müller
Radames : Jagel
Amonasro : Bonelli
Ramfis : Pinza
Messenger : Paltrinieri
Priestess : Vettori (for
Clark)

NEWARK
January 29
LA BOHÈME
Same as Jan. 15 except:
Marcello : De Luca

BROOKLYN
February 5
IL TROVATORE/Bellezza (c)
Leonora : Rethberg
Manrico : Martinelli
Count di Luna : A. Borgioli
Azucena : Olszewska
Inez : Vettori
Ferrando : Lazzari
Ruiz : Paltrinieri
Gypsy : Malatesta

February 12
FAUST/Hasselmans (c)
Faust : Martinelli
Marguerite : Norena
Méphistophélès : Rothier
Valentin : De Luca
Siébel : Besuner
Marthe : Wakefield
Wagner : Ananian

February 26
LUCIA DI LAMMERMOOR
Bellezza (c)
Lucia : Pons
Alisa : Vettori
Edgardo : Schipa
Ashton : De Luca
Raimondo : Lazzari
Arturo : Tedesco
Normanno : Altglass

March 5
LOHENGRIN/Bodanzky (c)
King Henry : Hofmann
Lohengrin : Melchior

Elsa : Flagstad
Telramund : Schützendorf
Ortrud : Branzell
Herald : Cehanovsky

BALTIMORE
March 12
DIE WALKÜRE/Bodanzky (c)
Wotan : Schorr
Fricka : Doe
Brünnhilde : Flagstad
Siegmund : Althouse
Sieglinde : Kappel
Hunding : List
Helmwige : Manski
Gerhilde : Wells
Ortlinde : Besuner
Rossweisse : Bourskaya
Grimgerde : Falco
Waltraute : Doe
Siegrune : Vettori
Schwertleite : Petina

BROOKLYN
March 26
MANON/Hasselmans (c)
Manon : Mario
Lescaut : De Luca
Des Grieux : Hackett
Count des Grieux : Rothier
Poussette : Clark
Javotte : Falco
Rosette : Petina
Guillot : Bada
De Brétigny : Cehanovsky
Innkeeper : Ananian
Guards : Altglass, Gabor
Servant : Gola
Sergeant : Ananian
Archer : Cehanovsky

NEWARK
March 28
LUCIA DI LAMMERMOOR
Panizza (c)
Same as Feb. 26 except:
Alisa : Falco
Edgardo : Martinelli
Ashton : Bonelli

BOSTON
April 1
DIE WALKÜRE
Same as Mar. 12 except:
Fricka : Branzell
Siegmund : Melchior
Sieglinde : Rethberg

April 2
LA TRAVIATA/Panizza (c)
Violetta : Mason (t)
Alfredo : Hackett
Germont : Tibbett
Flora : Vettori

328

Annina : Falco
Gastone : Bada
Baron Douphol : Cehanovsky
Marquis d'Obigny : Picco
Doctor Grenvil : Wolfe

April 3 (mat.)
LOHENGRIN
Same as Mar. 5 except:
King Henry : List

April 3
LAKMÉ/Hasselmans (c)
Lakmé : Pons
Mallika : Swarthout
Ellen : Besuner
Rose : Petina
Mrs. Benson : Falco
Gerald : Martinelli
Nilakantha : Pinza
Frederic : De Luca
Hadji : Paltrinieri
Fortune Teller : Windheim
Chinese Merchant : Bada
Thief : D'Angelo

April 4
PETER IBBETSON/Pelletier (c)
Peter Ibbetson : Johnson
Colonel Ibbetson : Tibbett
Mary : Mario
Mrs. Deane : Swarthout
Mrs. Glyn : Bourskaya
Achille : Bada
Major Duquesnois : D'Angelo
Chaplain : D'Angelo
Charlie Plunkett : Paltrinieri
Guy Mainwaring : Picco
Footman : Altglass
Diana Vivash : Wells
Madge Plunkett : Petina
Victorine : Falco
Sister of Charity : Vettori
Manservant : Picco
Prison Governor : Cehanovsky
Turnkey : Picco
Pasquier de la Marière :
Cehanovsky
Marie Pasquier : Besuner
Mme. Seraskier : Petina

April 5
DIE MEISTERSINGER
Bodanzky (c)
Hans Sachs : Schorr
Pogner : List
Eva : Fleischer
Magdalene : Doe
Walther : Althouse
Beckmesser : Schützendorf
Kothner : Gabor
Vogelgesang : Altglass
Nachtigall : D'Angelo
Zorn : Bada
Eisslinger : Paltrinieri

Moser : Weisberg
Ortel : Ananian
Schwarz : Anderson
Foltz : Wolfe
David : Windheim
Night Watchman : Cehanovsky

April 6 (mat.)
FAUST
Same as Feb. 12 except:
Marguerite : Rethberg
Méphistophélès : Pinza
Valentin : Tibbett
Siébel : Swarthout
Marthe : Falco
Wagner : Defrère (t—for
Wolfe)

April 6
LUCIA DI LAMMERMOOR
Panizza (c)
Same as Feb. 26 except:
Edgardo : Martini
Raimondo : D'Angelo
Arturo : Bada
Normanno : Paltrinieri

BALTIMORE
April 9
AIDA
Same as Jan. 29 except:
Aida : Rethberg
Radames : Martinelli
Amonasro : Tibbett
Priestess : Clark

ROCHESTER
April 10
TANNHÄUSER
Same as Jan. 22 except:
Wolfram : Tibbett
Walther : Windheim
Biterolf : Cehanovsky
Reinmar : D'Angelo
Elisabeth : Flagstad
Venus : Manski

1 9 3 5 – 3 6

Edward Johnson, *Manager*

PHILADELPHIA
December 17
TOSCA/Papi (c)
Tosca : Lehmann
Cavaradossi : Crooks
Scarpia : Thomas
Angelotti : Cehanovsky
Sacristan : D'Angelo
Spoletta : Paltrinieri
Sciarrone : Cehanovsky
Jailer : Gabor
Shepherd : Flexer (for
Petina)

HARTFORD
January 14
CARMEN/Hasselmans (c)

Carmen : Ponselle
Don José : Kullman
Micaela : Burke
Escamillo : Pinza
Zuniga : D'Angelo
Morales : Cehanovsky
Frasquita : Votipka
Mercedes : Olheim
Dancaire : Bada
Remendado : Windheim

NEWARK
January 21
MADAMA BUTTERFLY/Papi (c)

Cio-Cio-San : Fisher
B. F. Pinkerton : Crooks
Sharpless : Bonelli
Suzuki : Bourskaya
Kate Pinkerton : Flexer
Goro : Paltrinieri
Yamadori : Altglass
Uncle-Priest : D'Angelo
Yakuside : Gili
Imperial Commissioner :
  Marwick

BROOKLYN
January 21
LA TRAVIATA/Panizza (c)

Violetta : Mason
Alfredo : Martini
Germont : Thomas
Flora : Votipka
Annina : Besuner
Gastone : Bada
Baron Douphol : Gandolfi
Marquis d'Obigny :
  Cehanovsky
Doctor Grenvil : Wolfe

PHILADELPHIA
January 28
CARMEN

Same as Jan. 14 except:
Don José : Martinelli
Micaela : Bori

BROOKLYN
February 11
LUCIA DI LAMMERMOOR
  Papi (c)

Lucia : Pons
Alisa : Symons
Edgardo : Bentonelli
Ashton : Morelli
Raimondo : Lazzari
Arturo : Bada
Normanno : Paltrinieri

PHILADELPHIA
February 18
AIDA/Panizza (c)

King : D'Angelo
Amneris : Bampton
Aida : Rethberg
Radames : Jagel
Amonasro : Tibbett
Ramfis : Pinza
Messenger : Paltrinieri
Priestess : Votipka

BROOKLYN
February 25
CARMEN

Same as Jan. 14 except:
Don José : Maison
Micaela : Fisher

PHILADELPHIA
March 3
TRISTAN UND ISOLDE
  Bodanzky (c)

Tristan : Melchior
Isolde : Flagstad
King Marke : List
Kurvenal : Schorr
Brangaene : Branzell
Melot : Gabor
Steersman : Wolfe
Shepherd : Clemens
Sailor's Voice : Clemens

HARTFORD
March 10
TRISTAN UND ISOLDE

Same as Mar. 3 except:
Kurvenal : Huehn
Shepherd : Windheim
Sailor's Voice : Windheim

BROOKLYN
March 17
AIDA

Same as Feb. 18 except:
Amneris : Castagna
Aida : Giannini
Amonasro : Thomas
Ramfis : Baromeo
Messenger : Windheim
  (for Paltrinieri)

BOSTON
March 23
TANNHÄUSER/Bodanzky (c)

Hermann : List
Tannhäuser : Melchior
Wolfram : Tibbett
Walther : Windheim
Biterolf : Gabor
Heinrich : Paltrinieri
Reinmar : Wolfe
Elisabeth : Lehmann

Venus : Branzell
Shepherd : Symons

March 24
AIDA

Same as Feb. 18 except:
Amneris : Castagna
Radames : Martinelli
Amonasro : Morelli

March 25 (mat.)
MADAMA BUTTERFLY
  Panizza (c)

Same as Jan. 21 except:
B. F. Pinkerton : Bentonelli
Sharpless : Huehn
Suzuki : Petina
Kate Pinkerton : Flexer
Goro : Bada
Yamadori : Cehanovsky
Imperial Commissioner :
  Cehanovsky

March 25
TRISTAN UND ISOLDE

Same as Mar. 3 except:
Shepherd : Windheim
Sailor's Voice : Windheim

March 26
MIGNON/Hasselmans (c)

Mignon : Bori
Philine : Antoine
Wilhelm : Crooks
Lothario : Pinza
Laerte : Bada
Jarno : Wolfe
Frederic : Olheim
Antonio : Wolfe

March 27
FIDELIO/Bodanzky (c)

Don Fernando : Huehn
Don Pizarro : Schorr
Florestan : Maison
Leonore : Flagstad
Rocco : List
Marzelline : Mario
Jaquino : Windheim
First Prisoner : Paltrinieri
Second Prisoner : Gabor

March 28 (mat.)
CARMEN

Same as Jan. 14 except:
Don José : Maison

March 28
RIGOLETTO/Panizza (c)

Duke : Jagel
Rigoletto : Tibbett
Gilda : Antoine
Sparafucile : Pinza
Maddalena : Petina
Giovanna : Votipka

Monterone : D'Angelo
Marullo : Cehanovsky
Borsa : Bada (for
  Paltrinieri)
Ceprano : Wolfe
Countess : Symons
Page : Tomisani

ROCHESTER
March 30
TRISTAN UND ISOLDE

Same as Mar. 3 except:
Kurvenal : Huehn
Shepherd : Windheim
Sailor's Voice : Windheim

NEWARK
April 1
RIGOLETTO

Same as Mar. 28 except:
Duke : Bentonelli
Sparafucile : Baromeo
Maddalena : Olheim
Giovanna : Symons
  (for Votipka)

BALTIMORE
April 2
LA BOHÈME/Papi (c)

Rodolfo : Martini
Marcello : Tibbett
Schaunard : Cehanovsky
Colline : Pinza
Mimi : Bori
Musetta : Gleason
Benoit : D'Angelo
Parpignol : Bada
Alcindoro : D'Angelo
Sergeant : Coscia

April 3
TRISTAN UND ISOLDE

Same as Mar. 3 except:
Kurvenal : Huehn
Shepherd : Windheim
Sailor's Voice : Windheim

April 4
CARMEN

Same as Jan. 14 except:
Don José : Maison
Escamillo : Huehn

1 9 3 6 – 3 7

PHILADELPHIA
December 22
DIE VERKAUFTE BRAUT
  (English) Pelletier (c)
Kruschina : Engelman (d)
Kathinka : Browning (d)
Marie : Dickson (d)
Micha : Gurney (d)

330

Agnes : Kaskas
Wenzel : Rasely (d)
Hans : Chamlee
Kezal : D'Angelo
Springer : Cordon (d)
Esmeralda : Bodanya (d)
Muff : Burgstaller

BROOKLYN
December 29
DIE WALKÜRE/Bodanzky (c)

Wotan : Schorr
Fricka : Thorborg
Brünnhilde : Flagstad
Siegmund : Melchior
Sieglinde : Rethberg
Hunding : List
Helmwige : Manski
Gerhilde : Votipka
Ortlinde : Jessner
Rossweisse : Bourskaya
Grimgerde : Petina
Waltraute : Doe
Siegrune : Olheim
Schwertleite : Kaskas

PHILADELPHIA
January 5
SAMSON ET DALILA
  Abravanel (c)

Dalila : Wettergren
Samson : Maison
High Priest : Pinza
Abimelech : Gurney
Old Hebrew : List
Philistine Messenger : Bada
Philistines : Altglass,
  Engelman

BROOKLYN
January 12
SAMSON ET DALILA

Same as Jan. 5 except:
Old Hebrew : Baromeo

HARTFORD
January 19
RIGOLETTO/Panizza (c)

Duke : Kullman
Rigoletto : Tibbett
Gilda : Pons
Sparafucile : Lazzari
Maddalena : Kaskas
Giovanna : Votipka
Monterone : Cordon
Marullo : Cehanovsky
Borsa : Paltrinieri
Ceprano : Engelman
Countess : Symons
Page : Browning

PHILADELPHIA
January 26
DIE WALKÜRE

Same as Dec. 29 except:

Brünnhilde : Lawrence
Sieglinde : Flagstad

NEWARK
January 26
LA TRAVIATA/Panizza (c)

Violetta : Bovy
Alfredo : Martini
Germont : Tibbett
Flora : Symons
Annina : Browning
Gastone : Bada
Baron Douphol : Engelman
Marquis d'Obigny :
  Cehanovsky
Doctor Grenvil : Cordon

BROOKLYN
February 2
IL TROVATORE/Papi (c)

Leonora : Rethberg
Manrico : Martinelli
Count di Luna : Morelli
Azucena : Castagna
Inez : Votipka
Ferrando : Lazzari
Ruiz : Paltrinieri
Gypsy : Gabor

PHILADELPHIA
February 16
LAKMÉ/Abravanel (c)

Lakmé : Pons
Mallika : Petina
Ellen : Bodanya
Rose : Browning
Mrs. Benson : Bourskaya
Gerald : Jagel
Nilakantha : Baromeo
Frederic : Cehanovsky
Hadji : Paltrinieri
Fortune Teller : Altglass
Chinese Merchant : Bada
Thief : Cordon

BROOKLYN
February 23
CAVALLERIA RUSTICANA
  Papi (c)

Santuzza : Ponselle
Lola : Olheim
Turiddu : Jagel (for Rayner)
Alfio : Royer
Lucia : Kaskas

PAGLIACCI/Papi (c)
Nedda : Burke
Canio : Carron
Tonio : Tibbett
Beppe : Paltrinieri
Silvio : Cehanovsky

PHILADELPHIA
March 9
LA BOHÈME/Papi (c)
Rodolfo : Kullman
Marcello : Brownlee
Schaunard : Cehanovsky
Colline : Lazzari
Mimi : Sayao
Musetta : Andreva
Benoit : D'Angelo
Parpignol : Altglass
Alcindoro : D'Angelo
Sergeant : Coscia

BROOKLYN
March 16
LA BOHÈME
Same as Mar. 9 except:
Mimi : Somigli

HARTFORD
March 16
DIE WALKÜRE
Same as Dec. 29 except:
Fricka : Branzell
Hunding : Hofmann

PHILADELPHIA
March 23
LOHENGRIN/Abravanel (c)
King Henry : Hofmann
Lohengrin : Melchior
Elsa : Flagstad
Telramund : Huehn
Ortrud : Ruenger
Herald : Cehanovsky

BALTIMORE
March 29
LOHENGRIN
Same as Mar. 23 except:
King Henry : List
Ortrud : Branzell
Herald : Gabor (for
  Cehanovsky)

March 31
CAVALLERIA RUSTICANA
Papi (c)
Same as Feb. 23 except:
Lola : Petina
Turiddu : Rayner
Alfio : Morelli

PAGLIACCI
Same as Feb. 23 except:
Canio : Martinelli

BOSTON
April 1
TRISTAN UND ISOLDE
Bodanzky (c)
Tristan : Melchior
Isolde : Flagstad

King Marke : List
Kurvenal : Huehn
Brangaene : Branzell
Melot : Gabor
Steersman : Wolfe
Shepherd : Laufkoetter
Sailor's Voice : Clemens

April 2
LE COQ D'OR/Papi (c)
Queen : Pons
King Dodon : Pinza
Amelfa : Doe
Astrologer : Massue
Prince Guidon : Paltrinieri
General Polkan : Cordon
Prince Afron : Engelman
Golden Cockerel : Votipka

PAGLIACCI
Same as Feb. 23

April 3 (mat.)
DAS RHEINGOLD/Bodanzky (c)
Wotan : Schorr
Donner : Huehn
Froh : Clemens
Loge : Maison
Alberich : Habich
Mime : Laufkoetter
Fasolt : Cordon
Fafner : List
Fricka : Branzell
Freia : Manski
Erda : Doe
Woglinde : Andreva
Wellgunde : Petina
Flosshilde : Doe

April 3
IL TROVATORE
Same as Feb. 2 except:
Ferrando : Pinza
Ruiz : Bada

April 5
DIE WALKÜRE
Same as Dec. 29 except:
Fricka : Branzell

April 6
LA TRAVIATA
Same as Jan. 26 except:
Violetta : Sayao
Alfredo : Jagel (for Crooks)
Flora : Votipka

April 7
SIEGFRIED/Bodanzky (c)
Siegfried : Melchior
Mime : Laufkoetter
Wanderer : Schorr
Alberich : Habich
Fafner : List
Erda : Doe (for Branzell)

Brünnhilde : Flagstad
Forest Bird : Andreva

April 8 (mat.)
LES CONTES D'HOFFMANN
Abravanel (c)
Hoffmann : Maison
Olympia : Andreva
Giulietta : Swarthout
Antonia : Burke
Nicklausse : Petina
Lindorf : Tibbett
Coppelius : Tibbett
Dappertutto : Tibbett
Dr. Miracle : Tibbett
Spalanzani : D'Angelo
Schlemil : Cordon
Crespel : D'Angelo
Voice : Kaskas
Andrès : Bada
Cochenille : Bada
Pitichinaccio : Bada
Frantz : Bada
Luther : Gabor
Nathanael : Rasely
Hermann : Engelman
Stella : Walsingham

April 8
LUCIA DI LAMMERMOOR
Papi (c)
Lucia : Pons
Alisa : Votipka
Edgardo : Jagel
Ashton : Morelli
Raimondo : Cordon
Arturo : Massue
Normanno : Paltrinieri

April 9
GÖTTERDÄMMERUNG
Bodanzky (c)
Siegfried : Melchior
Gunther : Schorr
Hagen : List
Alberich : Habich
Brünnhilde : Flagstad
Gutrune : Manski
Waltraute : Branzell
Woglinde : Andreva
Wellgunde : Petina
Flosshilde : Doe
First Norn : Doe
Second Norn : Petina
Third Norn : Manski
Vassals : Laufkoetter, Gabor

April 10 (mat.)
HÄNSEL UND GRETEL
Riedel (c)
Hänsel : Jessner
Gretel : Mario
Witch : Manski
Gertrude : Doe
Peter : Gabor

Sandman : Browning
Dewman : Andreva

CAVALLERIA RUSTICANA

Same as Feb. 23 except:
Santuzza : Rethberg
 (for Ponselle)
Lola : Petina
Turiddu : Rayner
Alfio : Morelli

April 10

FAUST/Pelletier (c)

Faust : Crooks
Marguerite : Jepson
Méphistophélès : Pinza
Valentin : Cehanovsky
Siébel : Olheim
Marthe : Bourskaya
Wagner : Engelman

CLEVELAND

April 12

LE COQ D'OR

Same as Apr. 2

CAVALLERIA RUSTICANA

Same as Feb. 23 except:
Lola : Petina
Turiddu : Rayner
Alfio : Morelli
Lucia : Browning

April 13

TRISTAN UND ISOLDE

Same as Apr. 1 except:
Melot : Cehanovsky
Steersman : D'Angelo
Sailor's Voice : Laufkoetter

April 14

FAUST

Same as Apr. 10 except:
Valentin : Bonelli
Marthe : Votipka

April 15

AIDA/Panizza (c)

King : Cordon
Amneris : Castagna
Aida : Rethberg
Radames : Jagel
Amonasro : Morelli
Ramfis : Baromeo
Messenger : Paltrinieri
Priestess : Votipka

April 16 (mat.)

LOHENGRIN

Same as Mar. 23 except:
King Henry : List
Ortrud : Branzell

April 16

MIGNON/Pelletier (c)

Mignon : Swarthout

332

Philine : Antoine
Wilhelm : Crooks
Lothario : Pinza
Laerte : Paltrinieri
Jarno : Cordon
Frederic : Olheim
Antonio : Cordon

April 17 (mat.)

CARMEN/Papi (c)

Carmen : Ponselle
Don José : Maison
Micaela : Burke
Escamillo : Huehn
Zuniga : D'Angelo
Morales : Engelman
Frasquita : Votipka
Mercedes : Olheim
Dancaire : Cehanovsky
Remendado : Paltrinieri

April 17

IL TROVATORE

Same as Feb. 2 except:
Manrico : Carron
Ferrando : Baromeo

ROCHESTER

April 19

LOHENGRIN

Same as Mar. 23 except:
King Henry : List
Ortrud : Branzell

1 9 3 7 – 3 8

PHILADELPHIA

November 30

NORMA/Panizza (c)

Oroveso : Pinza
Norma : Cigna
Pollione : Martinelli
Adalgisa : Castagna
Clotilde : Votipka
Flavio : Paltrinieri

HARTFORD

December 7

IL TROVATORE/Papi (c)

Leonora : Cigna
Manrico : Martinelli
Count di Luna : Bonelli
Azucena : Kaskas
Inez : Votipka
Ferrando : Lazzari
Ruiz : Paltrinieri
Gypsy : Coscia

PHILADELPHIA

December 14

LA TRAVIATA/Panizza (c)

Violetta : Bovy
Alfredo : Martini

Germont : Thomas
Flora : Votipka
Annina : Browning
Gastone : Bada
Baron Douphol : Engelman
Marquis d'Obigny :
 Cehanovsky
Doctor Grenvil : Cordon

December 21

TRISTAN UND ISOLDE
Bodanzky (c)

Tristan : Melchior
Isolde : Flagstad
King Marke : Hofmann
Kurvenal : Huehn
Brangaene : Wettergren
Melot : Gabor
Steersman : D'Angelo
Shepherd : Clemens
Sailor's Voice : Laufkoetter

January 11

OTELLO/Panizza (c)

Otello : Martinelli
Desdemona : Jessner (for
 Cigna)
Iago : Tibbett
Emilia : Votipka
Cassio : Massue
Roderigo : Paltrinieri
Lodovico : Moscona
Montano : Cehanovsky
Herald : Engelman

NEWARK

January 18

IL TROVATORE

Same as Dec. 7 except:
Leonora : Rethberg
Count di Luna : Tagliabue
Azucena : Castagna

PHILADELPHIA

January 25

GIANNI SCHICCHI/Papi (c)

Gianni Schicchi : Huehn
Lauretta : Burke
La Vecchia : Doe
Rinuccio : Kullman
Gherardo : Rasely
Nella : Symons
Gherardino : Demers
Betto : Cehanovsky
Simone : Baromeo
Marco : D'Angelo
La Ciesca : Votipka
Spinelloccio : Malatesta
Nicolao : Engelman
Pinellino : Wolfe
Guccio : Gabor

ELEKTRA/Bodanzky (c)

Klytaemnestra : Thorborg
Elektra : Pauly

Chrysothemis : Jessner
Aegisth : Althouse
Orest : Schorr
Guardian of Orest : Cordon
Confidante : Kaskas
Trainbearer : Petina
Young Servant : Laufkoetter
Old Servant : Gabor
Overseer of Servants :
  Manski
Serving Women : Doe,
  Olheim, Browning,
  Votipka, Fisher

HARTFORD
February 8
TANNHÄUSER/Abravanel (c)
Hermann : List
Tannhäuser : Melchior
Wolfram : Tibbett
Walther : Clemens
Biterolf : Gabor
Heinrich : Altglass
Reinmar : Wolfe
Elisabeth : Flagstad
Venus : Thorborg
Shepherd : Farell

PHILADELPHIA
February 15
SIEGFRIED/Bodanzky (c)
Siegfried : Melchior
Mime : Laufkoetter
Wanderer : Hofmann
Alberich : Vogel
Fafner : List
Erda : Kaskas
Brünnhilde : Flagstad
Forest Bird : Bodanya

March 8
AMELIA GOES TO THE BALL
  Panizza (c)
Amelia : Dickson
Husband : Brownlee
Lover : Chamlee
Friend : Olheim
Chief of Police : Cordon
Cook : Browning
Maid : Symons

SALOME/Panizza (c)
Herod : Maison
Herodias : Manski
Salome : Lawrence
Jokanaan : Huehn
Narraboth : Laufkoetter
Page : Browning
First Nazarene : Cordon
Second Nazarene : Massue
First Jew : Laufkoetter
Second Jew : Paltrinieri
Third Jew : Bada
Fourth Jew : Altglass
Fifth Jew : Wolfe

First Soldier : D'Angelo
Second Soldier : Gabor
Cappadocian : Engelman
Slave : Symons

March 15
DON GIOVANNI/Panizza (c)
Don Giovanni : Pinza
Donna Anna : Giannini
Donna Elvira : Jessner
Zerlina : Farell
Commendatore : List
Don Ottavio : Crooks
Leporello : Lazzari
Masetto : D'Angelo

BALTIMORE
March 21
TANNHÄUSER/Leinsdorf (c)
Same as Feb. 8 except:
Wolfram : Huehn
Walther : Laufkoetter
Heinrich : Paltrinieri
Reinmar : D'Angelo
Venus : Branzell

March 22
OTELLO
Same as Jan. 11 except:
Desdemona : Rethberg
Iago : Tagliabue
  (for Tibbett)
Lodovico : Cordon

March 23
FAUST/Pelletier (c)
Faust : Crooks
Marguerite : Jepson
Méphistophélès : Pinza
Valentin : Brownlee
Siébel : Olheim
Marthe : Votipka
Wagner : Engelman

BOSTON
March 24
OTELLO
Same as Jan. 11 except:
Desdemona : Rethberg
Lodovico : Cordon

March 25
TRISTAN UND ISOLDE
Same as Dec. 21 except:
King Marke : List
Brangaene : Branzell
Steersman : Cordon
Shepherd : Laufkoetter
Sailor's Voice : Laufkoetter

March 26 (mat.)
DON GIOVANNI
Same as Mar. 15

March 26
CARMEN/Papi (c)
Carmen : Castagna
Don José : Kiepura
Micaela : Burke
Escamillo : Brownlee
Zuniga : Cordon
Morales : Engelman
Frasquita : Votipka
Mercedes : Olheim
Dancaire : Cehanovsky
Remendado : Paltrinieri

March 28
PARSIFAL/Bodanzky (c)
Amfortas : Schorr
Titurel : Cordon
Gurnemanz : List
Parsifal : Melchior
Klingsor : Gabor
Kundry : Flagstad
A Voice : Doe
Knights of the Grail :
  Bada, D'Angelo
Esquires : Bodanya, Olheim,
  Laufkoetter, Paltrinieri
Flower Maidens : Fisher,
  Petina, Olheim, Burke,
  Votipka, Doe

March 29
LA BOHÈME/Papi (c)
Rodolfo : Kiepura
Marcello : Tagliabue
Schaunard : Cehanovsky
Colline : Cordon
Mimi : Sayao
Musetta : Bodanya
Benoit : D'Angelo
Parpignol : Paltrinieri
Alcindoro : D'Angelo
Sergeant : Coscia

March 30 (mat.)
DIE WALKÜRE/Bodanzky (c)
Wotan : Schorr
Fricka : Branzell
Brünnhilde : Flagstad
Siegmund : Melchior
Sieglinde : Rethberg
Hunding : List
Helmwige : Manski
Gerhilde : Votipka
Ortlinde : Jessner
Rossweisse : Browning
Grimgerde : Petina
Waltraute : Doe
Siegrune : Olheim
Schwertleite : Kaskas

March 30
IL BARBIERE DI SIVIGLIA
  Papi (c)
Almaviva : Chamlee
Dr. Bartolo : D'Angelo

333

Rosina : Pons
Figaro : Brownlee
Don Basilio : Pinza
Berta : Petina
Fiorello : Engelman
Sergeant : Paltrinieri

March 31
DER ROSENKAVALIER
  Bodanzky (c)

Princess von Werdenberg :
  Lehmann
Baron Ochs : List
Octavian : Stückgold (t)
Von Faninal : Huehn
Sophie : Farell
Marianne : Manski
Valzacchi : Bada
Annina : Doe
Police Commissioner : Cordon
Majordomo of Princess :
  Laufkoetter
Majordomo of Von Faninal :
  Laufkoetter
Notary : Gabor
Innkeeper : Laufkoetter
Singer : Massue
Orphans : Bodanya,
  Browning, Kaskas
Milliner : Votipka
Hairdresser : Temoff
Leopold : Burgstaller
Animal Vendor : Paltrinieri
Negro Boy : Leweck

April 1
ROMÉO ET JULIETTE
  Pelletier (c)

Juliette : Sayao
Stephano : Browning
Gertrude : Doe
Roméo : Crooks
Tybalt : Bada
Benvolio : Paltrinieri
Mercutio : Brownlee
Paris : Massue
Gregorio : Engelman
Capulet : Cordon
Friar Laurence : Pinza
Duke of Verona : D'Angelo

April 2 (mat.)
LOHENGRIN/Leinsdorf (c)

King Henry : List
Lohengrin : Melchior
Elsa : Flagstad
Telramund : Huehn
Ortrud : Branzell
Herald : Cehanovsky

April 2
AIDA/Panizza (c)

King : Cordon
Amneris : Castagna
Aida : Rethberg

Radames : Martinelli
Amonasro : Tagliabue
Ramfis : Pinza
Messenger : Bada
Priestess : Votipka

CLEVELAND
April 4
LA TRAVIATA

Same as Dec. 14 except:
Violetta : Jepson

April 5
TRISTAN UND ISOLDE

Same as Dec. 21 except:
King Marke : List
Brangaene : Branzell
Shepherd : Laufkoetter
Sailor's Voice : Laufkoetter

April 6
CAVALLERIA RUSTICANA
  Papi (c)

Santuzza : Giannini
Lola : Kaskas
Turiddu : Rayner
Alfio : Tagliabue
Lucia : Browning

DIE FLEDERMAUS (Ballet)
  Pelletier (c)

PAGLIACCI/Papi (c)
Nedda : Burke
Canio : Martinelli
Tonio : Bonelli
Beppe : Paltrinieri
Silvio : Dickson

April 7
RIGOLETTO/Panizza (c)

Duke : Kiepura
Rigoletto : Tagliabue
Gilda : Galli-Campi (t)
Sparafucile : Cordon
  (for Pinza)
Maddalena : Petina
Giovanna : Votipka
Monterone : D'Angelo
  (for Cordon)
Marullo : Cehanovsky
Borsa : Bada
Ceprano : Engelman
Countess : Votipka
Page : Browning

April 8 (mat.)
TANNHÄUSER/Leinsdorf (c)

Same as Feb. 8 except:
Wolfram : Huehn
Walther : Laufkoetter
Heinrich : Paltrinieri
Venus : Branzell

April 8
DIE VERKAUFTE BRAUT
  (English) Pelletier (c)
  (Not given in New York)
Kruschina : Engelman
Kathinka : Browning
Marie : Burke
Micha : Wolfe
Agnes : Kaskas
Wenzel : Rasely
Hans : Chamlee
Kezal : D'Angelo
Springer : Cordon
Esmeralda : Bodanya
Muff : Burgstaller

April 9 (mat.)
LA BOHÈME

Same as Mar. 29 except:
Mimi : Moore

April 9
AIDA

Same as Apr. 2 except:
Amonasro : Bonelli

ROCHESTER
April 11
AIDA

Same as Apr. 2 except:
Aida : Giannini
Amonasro : Bonelli
Messenger : Paltrinieri

1938 – 39

PHILADELPHIA
November 22
DER ROSENKAVALIER
  Bodanzky (c)

Princess von Werdenberg :
  Lehmann
Baron Ochs : List
Octavian : Stevens (d)
Von Faninal : Schorr
Sophie : Farell
Marianne : Manski
Valzacchi : Laufkoetter
Annina : Doe
Police Commissioner :
  Cordon
Majordomo of Princess :
  Witte (d)
Majordomo of Von Faninal :
  Witte
Notary : Gabor
Innkeeper : Witte
Singer : Massue
Orphans : Bodanya,
  Browning, Kaskas
Milliner : Besuner
Hairdresser : Casanova
Leopold : Burgstaller

Animal Vendor : Paltrinieri
Negro Boy : Montague

November 29
AIDA/Panizza (c)
King : Gurney
Amneris : Castagna
Aida : Caniglia
Radames : Martinelli
Amonasro : Tibbett
Ramfis : Moscona
Messenger : Paltrinieri
Priestess : Browning

HARTFORD
December 6
OTELLO/Panizza (c)
Otello : Martinelli
Desdemona : Caniglia
Iago : Tibbett
Emilia : Votipka
Cassio : Massue
Roderigo : Paltrinieri
Lodovico : Moscona
Montano : Engelman
Herald : Engelman

PHILADELPHIA
December 13
MANON/Pelletier (c)
Manon : Sayao
Lescaut : Brownlee
Des Grieux : Crooks
Count des Grieux : Moscona
Poussette : Bodanya
Javotte : Stellman
Rosette : Browning
Guillot : De Paolis
De Brétigny : Cehanovsky
Innkeeper : D'Angelo
Guards : Altglass, Gabor
Servant : Gola

December 27
TOSCA/Papi (c)
Tosca : Lawrence
Cavaradossi : Masini
Scarpia : Bonelli
Angelotti : Cordon
Sacristan : D'Angelo
Spoletta : De Paolis
Sciarrone : Engelman
Jailer : Gabor
Shepherd : Petina

January 3
DAS RHEINGOLD/Bodanzky (c)
Wotan : Nissen
Donner : Huehn
Froh : Witte
Loge : Maison
Alberich : Vogel
Mime : Laufkoetter
Fasolt : Cordon
Fafner : List

Fricka : Thorborg
Freia : Manski
Erda : Szantho (t)
Woglinde : Votipka
Wellgunde : Browning
Flosshilde : Doe

January 10
DIE WALKÜRE/Leinsdorf (c)
Wotan : Nissen
Fricka : Thorborg
Brünnhilde : Flagstad
Siegmund : Melchior
Sieglinde : Rethberg
Hunding : List
Helmwige : Manski
Gerhilde : Votipka
Ortlinde : Besuner
Rossweisse : Browning
Grimgerde : Petina
Waltraute : Doe
Siegrune : Olheim
Schwertleite : Kaskas

January 24
SIEGFRIED/Leinsdorf (c)
Siegfried : Melchior
Mime : Witte
Wanderer : Janssen (d)
Alberich : Vogel
Fafner : Alsen
Erda : Branzell
Brünnhilde : Flagstad
Forest Bird : Bodanya

January 31
GÖTTERDÄMMERUNG
Bodanzky (c)
Siegfried : Melchior
Gunther : Janssen
Hagen : List
Alberich : Vogel
Brünnhilde : Lawrence
Gutrune : Manski
Waltraute : Branzell
Woglinde : Votipka
Wellgunde : Petina
Flosshilde : Doe
First Norn : Doe
Second Norn : Browning
Third Norn : Manski
Vassals : Altglass, Gabor

HARTFORD
February 7
DIE MEISTERSINGER
Bodanzky (c)
Hans Sachs : Schorr
Pogner : List (for Alsen)
Eva : Rethberg
Magdalene : Branzell
Walther : Kullman
Beckmesser : Vogel
Kothner : Huehn
Vogelgesang : Witte

Nachtigall : D'Angelo
Zorn : Massue
Eisslinger : Paltrinieri
Moser : Altglass
Ortel : Gabor
Schwarz : Gurney
Foltz : Wolfe
David : Laufkoetter
Night Watchman : Cehanovsky

NEWARK
February 7
IL BARBIERE DI SIVIGLIA
Papi (c)
Almaviva : Martini
Dr. Bartolo : Lazzari
Rosina : Sayao
Figaro : Thomas (for Bonelli)
Don Basilio : Pinza
Berta : Petina
Fiorello : Engelman
Sergeant : Engelman

PHILADELPHIA
February 14
LOUISE/Panizza (c)
Louise : Moore
Julien : Kullman
Mother : Doe
Father : Pinza
Irma : Morel
Camille : Votipka
Gertrude : Petina
Apprentice : Bodanya
Elise : Besuner
Blanche : Olheim
Suzanne : Browning
Forewoman : Savage
Marguerite : Stellman
Madeleine : Kaskas
Painter : Engelman
First Philosopher : Cordon
Second Philosopher : D'Angelo
Sculptor : Cehanovsky
Poet : Rasely
Student : Paltrinieri
Song Writer : Massue
Street Sweeper : Savage
Newspaper Girl : Browning
Young Rag Picker : Besuner
Milk Woman : Stellman
Coal Picker : Kaskas
Noctambulist : De Paolis
King of the Fools : De Paolis
First Policeman : Altglass
Second Policeman : Coscia
Rag Picker : Gurney
Junk Man : D'Angelo
Street Arab : Bodanya
Old Clothes Man : Rasely
Bird Food Vendor : Demers
Artichoke Vendor : Morel

1938–39

Watercress Vendor : Kaskas
Chair Mender : Kaskas
Carrot Vendor : De Paolis
Rag Vendor : Cehanovsky
Green Peas Vendor : Massue

February 28
IL BARBIERE DI SIVIGLIA
Same as Feb. 7 except:
Rosina : Pons
Sergeant : Paltrinieri

BALTIMORE
March 13
TOSCA
Same as Dec. 27 except:
Tosca : Jessner (for
Lawrence)
Cavaradossi : Martinelli
Scarpia : Tibbett

March 14
DIE WALKÜRE
Same as Jan. 10 except:
Wotan : Schorr
Ortlinde : Jessner

March 15
THAIS/Pelletier (c)
Athanael : Thomas
Nicias : Tokatyan
Palemon : Cordon
Servant : Engelman
Thais : Jepson
Crobyle : Farell
Myrtale : Browning
Albine : Kaskas
Enchantress : Morel
Cenobites : Massue, Altglass,
Engelman, Gabor

BOSTON
March 16
FALSTAFF/Panizza (c)
Sir John Falstaff : Tibbett
Ford : Brownlee
Fenton : Kullman
Dr. Caius : Paltrinieri
Bardolph : De Paolis
Pistol : Cordon
Mistress Ford : Jessner
Anne : Morel
Dame Quickly : Castagna
Mistress Page : Petina
Innkeeper : Burgstaller

March 17
TRISTAN UND ISOLDE
Bodanzky (c)
Tristan : Melchior
Isolde : Flagstad
King Marke : List
Kurvenal : Janssen
Brangaene : Thorborg

Melot : Gabor
Steersman : D'Angelo
Shepherd : Witte
Sailor's Voice : Witte

March 18 (mat.)
LA BOHÈME/Papi (c)
Rodolfo : Kiepura
Marcello : Brownlee
Schaunard : Cehanovsky
Colline : Pinza
Mimi : Moore
Musetta : Morel
Benoit : D'Angelo
Parpignol : Paltrinieri
Alcindoro : D'Angelo
Sergeant : Coscia

March 18
LOHENGRIN/Leinsdorf (c)
King Henry : List
Lohengrin : Maison
Elsa : Flagstad
Telramund : Janssen
Ortrud : Thorborg
Herald : Gabor

March 20
DIE WALKÜRE
Same as Jan. 10 except:
Wotan : Schorr
Ortlinde : Jessner

March 21
LOUISE
Same as Feb. 14 except:
Julien : Maison
Elise : Votipka
Young Rag Picker : Votipka
Artichoke Vendor : Votipka
Green Peas Vendor :
De Paolis

March 22 (mat.)
TRISTAN UND ISOLDE
Same as Mar. 17 except:
Shepherd : Laufkoetter

March 22
AIDA
Same as Nov. 29 except:
King : Cordon
Aida : Rethberg
Amonasro : Thomas
Ramfis : Pinza
Priestess : Votipka

March 23
DIE MEISTERSINGER
Same as Feb. 7 except:
Magdalene : Thorborg
Beckmesser : Gabor
Kothner : Janssen
Vogelgesang : Laufkoetter
(for Witte)

Ortel : Cehanovsky
David : Witte (for
Laufkoetter)

March 24
THAIS
Same as Mar. 15 except:
Thais : Lawrence

March 25 (mat.)
TANNHÄUSER/Leinsdorf (c)
Hermann : List
Tannhäuser : Melchior
Wolfram : Janssen
Walther : Witte
Biterolf : Gabor
Heinrich : Altglass
Reinmar : D'Angelo
Elisabeth : Flagstad
Venus : Thorborg
Shepherd : Farell

March 25
RIGOLETTO/Papi (c)
Duke : Kiepura
Rigoletto : Brownlee
(for Tibbett)
Gilda : Pons
Sparafucile : Pinza
Maddalena : Petina
Giovanna : Votipka
Monterone : Cordon
Marullo : Cehanovsky
Borsa : Paltrinieri
Ceprano : Engelman
Countess : Votipka
Page : Browning

CLEVELAND
March 27
OTELLO
Same as Dec. 6 except:
Desdemona : Jepson
Iago : Brownlee (for
Tibbett)
Cassio : De Paolis
Lodovico : Cordon
Montano : Cehanovsky

March 28
LOUISE
Same as Feb. 14 except:
Elise : Votipka
Marguerite : ? (for
Stellman)
Young Rag Picker : Votipka
Milk Woman : ? (for
Stellman)
Artichoke Vendor : Votipka
Green Peas Vendor :
De Paolis

March 29
DIE WALKÜRE
Same as Jan. 10 except:

336

Wotan : Schorr
Brünnhilde : Lawrence
Sieglinde : Flagstad
Ortlinde : Jessner

March 30

THAIS

Same as Mar. 15

March 31 (mat.)

MANON

Same as Dec. 13 except:
Manon : Moore
Des Grieux : Kiepura
Count des Grieux : Cordon
Second Guard : Engelman

March 31

LOHENGRIN

Same as Mar. 18 except:
Lohengrin : Melchior

April 1 (mat.)

TOSCA

Same as Dec. 27 except:
Cavaradossi : Kiepura
Scarpia : Tibbett

April 1

LUCIA DI LAMMERMOOR
Papi (c)

Lucia : Aimaro (for Pons)
Alisa : Votipka
Edgardo : Martinelli
Ashton : Brownlee
Raimondo : Pinza
Arturo : Massue
Normanno : Paltrinieri

ROCHESTER

April 3

MANON

Same as Dec. 13 except:
Manon : Moore
Des Grieux : Kiepura
Count des Grieux : Cordon
Rosette : Petina

DALLAS

April 10

MANON

Same as Dec. 13 except:
Manon : Moore
Des Grieux : Kiepura
Count des Grieux : Pinza
Rosette : Petina
Guillot : Defrère (t)

April 11

OTELLO/Cimara (c)

Same as Dec. 6 except:
Desdemona : Jessner
Lodovico : Cordon
Montano : Cehanovsky

April 12 (mat.)

TANNHÄUSER

Same as Mar. 25 except:
Hermann : Cordon
Elisabeth : Rethberg
Shepherd : Stellman

April 12

CARMEN (*Act IV Prelude, Ballet*)/Papi (c)

LA BOHÈME

Same as Mar. 18 except:
Rodolfo : Kullman
Musetta : Bodanya

NEW ORLEANS

April 13

AIDA/Papi (c)

Same as Nov. 29 except:
King : Cordon
Aida : Rethberg
Ramfis : Pinza
Priestess : Votipka

April 14

LA BOHÈME

Same as Mar. 18 except:
Rodolfo : Martini
Musetta : Bodanya
Parpignol : Altglass

April 15 (mat.)

CARMEN/Papi (c)

Carmen : Castagna
Don José : Kullman
Micaela : Burke
Escamillo : Brownlee
Zuniga : D'Angelo
Morales : Engelman
Frasquita : Votipka
Mercedes : Olheim
Dancaire : Cehanovsky
Remendado : Paltrinieri

April 15

LOHENGRIN

Same as Mar. 18 except:
King Henry : Cordon
Lohengrin : Melchior
Elsa : Rethberg

1 9 3 9 – 4 0

PHILADELPHIA

November 28

BORIS GODUNOV/Panizza (c)

Boris Godunov : Pinza
Fyodor : Petina
Xenia : Farell
Nurse : Kaskas
Shuiski : De Paolis
Shchelkalov : Cehanovsky
Pimen : Moscona

Grigori : Kullman
Marina : Thorborg
Rangoni : Warren
Varlaam : Cordon
Missail : Paltrinieri
Innkeeper : Doe
Officer : Gurney
Simpleton : Massue
Lavitski : Engelman
Chernikovski : Gabor
Boyar : Massue

December 12

ORFEO ED EURIDICE
Leinsdorf (c)

Orfeo : Thorborg
Euridice : Jessner
Amor : Farell
A Happy Shade : Dickey

NEWARK

December 19

TOSCA/Papi (c)

Tosca : Giannini
Cavaradossi : Kullman
Scarpia : Tibbett
Angelotti : Cehanovsky
Sacristan : D'Angelo
Spoletta : De Paolis
Sciarrone : Engelman
Jailer : Gabor
Shepherd : Kaskas (for Petina)

PHILADELPHIA

December 26

TRISTAN UND ISOLDE
Leinsdorf (c)

Tristan : Melchior
Isolde : Flagstad
King Marke : List
Kurvenal : Huehn
Brangaene : Thorborg
Melot : Cehanovsky
Steersman : Gurney
Shepherd : Laufkoetter
Sailor's Voice : Marlowe (d)

January 2

FAUST/Pelletier (c)

Faust : Bjoerling
Marguerite : Jepson
Méphistophélès : Pinza
Valentin : Brownlee
Siébel : Browning
Marthe : Votipka
Wagner : Engelman

January 9

DIE MEISTERSINGER
Leinsdorf (c)

Hans Sachs : Schorr
Pogner : Cordon
Eva : Rethberg
Magdalene : Branzell

Walther : Maison
(for Kullman)
Beckmesser : Olitzki
Kothner : Huehn
Vogelgesang : Altglass
Nachtigall : D'Angelo
Zorn : Massue
Eisslinger : Paltrinieri
Moser : Oliviero
Ortel : Cehanovsky
Schwarz : Gurney
Foltz : Beattie
David : Marlowe (for
Laufkoetter)
Night Watchman : Cehanovsky

January 23
LA GIOCONDA/Panizza (c)
La Gioconda : Milanov
Laura : Castagna
Alvise : Pinza
La Cieca : Kaskas
Enzo : Jagel (for Martinelli)
Barnaba : Morelli
Zuane : Engelman
First Singer : Engelman
Second Singer : Paltrinieri
Isepo : Paltrinieri
Monk : D'Angelo
Steersman : Coscia

January 30
LAKMÉ/Pelletier (c)
Lakmé : Pons
Mallika : Petina
Ellen : Dickey
Rose : Browning
Mrs. Benson : Olheim
Gerald : Tokatyan
Nilakantha : Pinza
Frederic : Cehanovsky
Hadji : Massue
Fortune Teller : Oliviero
Chinese Merchant : Belleri
Thief : Engelman

HARTFORD
February 6
SIEGFRIED/Leinsdorf (c)
Siegfried : Melchior
Mime : Laufkoetter
Wanderer : Schorr
Alberich : Olitzki
Fafner : List
Erda : Branzell
Brünnhilde : Flagstad
Forest Bird : Bodanya

PHILADELPHIA
February 13
LA BOHÈME/Papi (c)
Rodolfo : Kullman
Marcello : De Luca
Schaunard : Cehanovsky

Colline : Lazzari
Mimi : Sayao
Musetta : Dickey
Benoit : D'Angelo
Parpignol : Oliviero
Alcindoro : D'Angelo
Sergeant : Coscia

February 27
LA TRAVIATA/Panizza (c)
Violetta : Novotna
Alfredo : Crooks
Germont : De Luca
Flora : Votipka
Annina : Browning
Gastone : De Paolis
Baron Douphol : Engelman
Marquis d'Obigny :
Cehanovsky
Doctor Grenvil : D'Angelo

HARTFORD
March 5
IL BARBIERE DI SIVIGLIA
Papi (c)
Almaviva : Martini
Dr. Bartolo : D'Angelo
Rosina : Pons
Figaro : Thomas
Don Basilio : Lazzari
Berta : Petina
Fiorello : Engelman
Sergeant : Paltrinieri

PHILADELPHIA
March 19
PARSIFAL/Leinsdorf (c)
Amfortas : Janssen
Titurel : Cordon
Gurnemanz : Kipnis
Parsifal : Melchior
Klingsor : Olitzki
Kundry : Flagstad
A Voice : Doe
Knights of the Grail :
Cehanovsky, D'Angelo
Esquires : Bodanya, Olheim,
Laufkoetter, Oliviero
Flower Maidens : Jessner,
Petina, Olheim, Burke,
Votipka, Doe

ROCHESTER
March 25
DIE WALKÜRE/Leinsdorf (c)
Wotan : Schorr
Fricka : Thorborg
Brünnhilde : Lawrence
Siegmund : Melchior
Sieglinde : Traubel
Hunding : Cordon
Helmwige : Manski
Gerhilde : Votipka
Ortlinde : Jessner

Rossweisse : Browning
Grimgerde : Heidt
Waltraute : Stellman
Siegrune : Olheim
Schwertleite : Doe

BALTIMORE
March 25
IL BARBIERE DI SIVIGLIA
Same as Mar. 5 except:
Rosina : Sayao
Don Basilio : Pinza

March 26
DER ROSENKAVALIER
Leinsdorf (c)
Princess von Werdenberg :
Lehmann
Baron Ochs : List
Octavian : Stevens
Von Faninal : Huehn
Sophie : Farell
Marianne : Manski
Valzacchi : Laufkoetter
Annina : Doe
Police Commissioner :
Cordon
Majordomo of Princess :
Marlowe
Majordomo of Von Faninal :
Marlowe
Notary : Gabor
Innkeeper : Marlowe
Singer : Carter
Orphans : Stellman,
Browning, Kaskas
Milliner : Votipka
Hairdresser : Casanova
Leopold : Burgstaller
Animal Vendor : Paltrinieri
Negro Boy : Montague

March 27
LAKMÉ
Same as Jan. 30 except:
Rose : Stellman
Hadji : Carter
Fortune Teller : Paltrinieri
Chinese Merchant : Gabor

BOSTON
March 28
DER ROSENKAVALIER
Same as Mar. 26 except:
Baron Ochs : Kipnis

March 29
LAKMÉ
Same as Jan. 30 except:
Rose : Stellman
Hadji : Carter
Fortune Teller : Paltrinieri
Chinese Merchant : Gabor

March 30 (mat.)
DIE WALKÜRE
Same as Mar. 25 except:
Sieglinde : Lehmann
Hunding : List

March 30
LA TRAVIATA
Same as Feb. 27 except:
Violetta : Jepson
Annina : Olheim

April 1
TRISTAN UND ISOLDE
McArthur (c—t)
Same as Dec. 26 except:
King Marke : Kipnis
Kurvenal : Janssen
Shepherd : Marlowe

April 2
LA GIOCONDA
Same as Jan. 23 except:
Alvise : Moscona
Enzo : Martinelli
Barnaba : Warren

April 3 (mat.)
LOHENGRIN/Leinsdorf (c)
King Henry : List
Lohengrin : Melchior
Elsa : Flagstad
Telramund : Huehn
Ortrud : Branzell
Herald : Warren

April 3
MANON/Pelletier (c)
Manon : Moore
Lescaut : Brownlee
Des Grieux : Crooks
Count des Grieux : Moscona
Poussette : Dickey
Javotte : Stellman
Rosette : Olheim
Guillot : De Paolis
De Brétigny : Cehanovsky
Innkeeper : D'Angelo
Guards : Marlowe, Gabor
Servant : Gola

April 4
BORIS GODUNOV
Same as Nov. 28 except:
Simpleton : Marlowe
Boyar : Marlowe

April 5
GÖTTERDÄMMERUNG
Leinsdorf (c)
Siegfried : Melchior
Gunther : Schorr
Hagen : List
Alberich : Olitzki
Brünnhilde : Flagstad

Gutrune : Jessner
Waltraute : Branzell
Woglinde : Votipka
Wellgunde : Herlick (for Petina)
Flosshilde : Olheim
First Norn : Kaskas
Second Norn : Petina
Third Norn : Votipka
Vassals : Marlowe, Engelman

April 6 (mat.)
FAUST
Same as Jan. 2 except:
Faust : Crooks
Valentin : Warren
Siébel : Olheim

April 6
TOSCA
Same as Dec. 19 except:
Scarpia : Brownlee
Angelotti : Cordon

CLEVELAND

April 8
AIDA/Panizza (c)
King : Cordon
Amneris : Castagna
Aida : Bampton
Radames : Martinelli
Amonasro : Warren
Ramfis : Pinza
Messenger : Paltrinieri
Priestess : Votipka

April 9
TANNHÄUSER/Leinsdorf (c)
Hermann : Kipnis
Tannhäuser : Melchior
Wolfram : Janssen (for Tibbett)
Walther : Carter
Biterolf : Gabor
Heinrich : Marlowe
Reinmar : Gurney
Elisabeth : Flagstad
Venus : Thorborg
Shepherd : Stellman

April 10
LA BOHÈME
Same as Feb. 13 except:
Colline : Cordon
Mimi : Albanese (for Moore)
Parpignol : Paltrinieri
Sergeant : Gabor

April 11
CARMEN/Pelletier (c)
Carmen : Swarthout
Don José : Tokatyan
Micaela : Albanese

Escamillo : Pinza
Zuniga : Cordon
Morales : Engelman
Frasquita : Votipka
Mercedes : Olheim
Dancaire : Cehanovsky
Remendado : De Paolis

April 12 (mat.)
MADAMA BUTTERFLY/Papi (c)
Cio-Cio-San : Burke
B. F. Pinkerton : Kullman
Sharpless : Brownlee
Suzuki : Petina
Kate Pinkerton : Stellman
Goro : De Paolis
Yamadori : Cehanovsky
Uncle-Priest : Cordon
Imperial Commissioner : Engelman

April 12
TRISTAN UND ISOLDE
Same as Dec. 26 except:
King Marke : Kipnis
Melot : Gabor
Shepherd : Marlowe

April 13 (mat.)
LA TRAVIATA
Same as Feb. 27 except:
Violetta : Jepson
Germont : Brownlee (for Tibbett)
Annina : Olheim
Doctor Grenvil : Cordon

April 13
LA GIOCONDA
Same as Jan. 23 except:
La Cieca : Swarthout
Enzo : Martinelli
Barnaba : Warren

DALLAS

April 15
LAKMÉ
Same as Jan. 30 except:
Rose : Stellman
Hadji : Carter
Fortune Teller : Paltrinieri
Chinese Merchant : Gabor

April 16
DIE WALKÜRE
Same as Mar. 25 except:
Wotan : Huehn
Sieglinde : Lehmann
Rosseweisse : Herlick
Grimgerde : Petina

April 17 (mat.)
FAUST
Same as Jan. 2 except:
Faust : Crooks

Valentin : Warren (for
  Brownlee)
Siébel : Olheim

April 17
LA TRAVIATA/Papi (c)
Same as Feb. 27 except:
Alfredo : Martini
Germont : Brownlee
  (for Tibbett)
Annina : Olheim

NEW ORLEANS
April 18
RIGOLETTO/Papi (c)
Duke : Kullman
Rigoletto : De Luca (for
  Tibbett)
Gilda : Pons
Sparafucile : Cordon
Maddalena : Olheim
Giovanna : Votipka
Monterone : D'Angelo
Marullo : Cehanovsky
Borsa : Paltrinieri
Ceprano : Engelman
Countess : Stellman
Page : Herlick

April 19
TANNHÄUSER
Same as Apr. 9 except:
Hermann : Cordon
Wolfram : Huehn
Elisabeth : Lehmann

April 20 (mat.)
FAUST
Same as Jan. 2 except:
Faust : Crooks
Valentin : Warren
Siébel : Olheim

April 20
TOSCA
Same as Dec. 19 except:
Scarpia : Brownlee
Angelotti : Cordon
Shepherd : Olheim

ATLANTA
April 22
LA TRAVIATA/Papi (c)
Same as Feb. 27 except:
Violetta : Jepson
Annina : Olheim

April 23
LA BOHÈME
Same as Feb. 13 except:
Rodolfo : Martini
Marcello : Brownlee
Colline : Pinza
Mimi : Moore
Parpignol : Paltrinieri
Sergeant : Gabor

340

April 24
TANNHÄUSER
Same as Apr. 9 except:
Hermann : Cordon
Wolfram : Huehn (for
  Tibbett)
Elisabeth : Lehmann

1 9 4 0 – 4 1

PHILADELPHIA
December 3
LE NOZZE DI FIGARO
  Panizza (c)
Almaviva : Brownlee
Countess : Rethberg
Susanna : Albanese
Figaro : Pinza
Cherubino : Novotna
Marcellina : Petina
Bartolo : Baccaloni (d)
Basilio : De Paolis
Don Curzio : Rasely
Antonio : D'Angelo
Barbarina : Farell
Peasant Girls : Olheim,
  Besuner (for Stellman)

December 10
DIE WALKÜRE/Leinsdorf (c)
Wotan : Huehn
Fricka : Branzell
Brünnhilde : Flagstad
Siegmund : Melchior
Sieglinde : Traubel
Hunding : List
Helmwige : Stellman
Gerhilde : Votipka
Ortlinde : Jessner
Rossweisse : Doe
Grimgerde : Petina
Waltraute : Besuner
Siegrune : Olheim
Schwertleite : Kaskas

December 17
UN BALLO IN MASCHERA
  Papi (c—for Panizza)
Riccardo : Bjoerling
Renato : Sved
Amelia : Milanov
Ulrica : Thorborg
Oscar : Andreva
Silvano : Kent
Samuel : Cordon
Tom : Moscona
Judge : Carter
Servant : Oliviero

January 7
LOUISE/Panizza (c)
Louise : Moore
Julien : Maison

Mother : Doe
Father : Pinza
Irma : Stellman
Camille : Votipka
Gertrude : Petina
Apprentice : Bodanya
Elise : Dickey
Blanche : Olheim
Suzanne : Besuner
Forewoman : Savage
Marguerite : Herlick
Madeleine : Kaskas
Painter : Engelman
First Philosopher : Cordon
Second Philosopher :
  D'Angelo
Sculptor : Cehanovsky
Poet : Rasely
Student : Dudley
Song Writer : Massue
Street Sweeper : Savage
Newspaper Girl : Dickey
Young Rag Picker : Besuner
Milk Woman : Stellman
Coal Picker : Kaskas
Noctambulist : De Paolis
King of the Fools :
  De Paolis
First Policeman : Darcy
Second Policeman : Kent
Rag Picker : Gurney
Junk Man : D'Angelo
Street Arab : Bodanya
Old Clothes Man : Rasely
Bird Food Vendors :
  Mabilli, Santoro
Artichoke Vendor : Votipka
Watercress Vendor : Kaskas
Chair Mender : Kaskas
Carrot Vendor : De Paolis
Rag Vendor : Cehanovsky
Green Peas Vendor : Massue

January 14
DER ROSENKAVALIER
  Leinsdorf (c)
Princess von Werdenberg :
  Lehmann
Baron Ochs : List
Octavian : Bokor (t—
  for Stevens)
Von Faninal : Olitzki
Sophie : Steber
Marianne : Votipka
Valzacchi : Laufkoetter
Annina : Doe
Police Commissioner :
  Cordon
Majordomo of Princess :
  Darcy
Majordomo of Von Faninal :
  Oliviero
Notary : Gabor
Innkeeper : Dudley
Singer : Carter

Orphans : Bodanya, Besuner, Kaskas
Milliner : Dickey
Hairdresser : Casanova
Leopold : Burgstaller
Animal Vendor : Oliviero
Negro Boy : Montague

January 21
LA FILLE DU RÉGIMENT
Papi (c)
Marie : Pons
Marquise : Petina
Sulpice : Baccaloni
Tonio : Jobin
Hortentius : D'Angelo
Corporal : Engelman
Peasant : Oliviero
Duchesse de Crakentorp : Savage
Le Petit Duc : Kosloff (t)
Notary : Fisher (t)

February 4
TRISTAN UND ISOLDE
Leinsdorf (c)
Tristan : Melchior
Isolde : Flagstad
King Marke : List
Kurvenal : Huehn
Brangaene : Thorborg (for Branzell)
Melot : Darcy
Steersman : Gurney
Shepherd : Laufkoetter
Sailor's Voice : Darcy

HARTFORD
February 11
LOUISE
Same as Jan. 7 except:
Julien : Kullman
Suzanne : Browning
Young Rag Picker : Browning
Bird Food Vendor : Petina

PHILADELPHIA
February 18
OTELLO/Panizza (c)
Otello : Martinelli
Desdemona : Roman
Iago : Tibbett
Emilia : Votipka
Cassio : De Paolis
Roderigo : Dudley
Lodovico : Moscona
Montano : Cehanovsky
Herald : Engelman

March 4
MADAMA BUTTERFLY/Papi (c)
Cio-Cio-San : Albanese
B. F. Pinkerton : Tokatyan (for Kullman)

Sharpless : Brownlee
Suzuki : Browning
Kate Pinkerton : Stellman
Goro : De Paolis
Yamadori : Cehanovsky
Uncle-Priest : Gurney
Imperial Commissioner : Engelman

HARTFORD
March 11
CARMEN/Pelletier (c)
Carmen : Castagna
Don José : Martinelli
Micaela : Albanese
Escamillo : Bonelli
Zuniga : Cordon
Morales : Engelman
Frasquita : Votipka
Mercedes : Olheim
Dancaire : Cehanovsky
Remendado : De Paolis

PHILADELPHIA
March 18
DON GIOVANNI/Walter (c)
Don Giovanni : Pinza
Donna Anna : Milanov
Donna Elvira : Novotna
Zerlina : Sayao
Commendatore : Cordon
Don Ottavio : Schipa
Leporello : Baccaloni
Masetto : Kent

BALTIMORE
March 24
LE NOZZE DI FIGARO
Same as Dec. 3 except:
Cherubino : Stevens
Second Peasant Girl : Stellman

March 25
IL TROVATORE/Panizza (c)
Leonora : Milanov
Manrico : Carron
Count di Luna : Valentino (for Bonelli)
Azucena : Castagna
Inez : Stellman
Ferrando : Moscona
Ruiz : Oliviero
Gypsy : Kent

March 26
DIE VERKAUFTE BRAUT (English) Walter (c)
Kruschina : Kent
Kathinka (Ludmila) : Votipka
Marie : Novotna
Micha : Gurney
Agnes (Hata) : Petina

Wenzel (Vashek) : Laufkoetter
Hans (Jenik) : Kullman
Kezal : Cordon
Springer (Ringmaster) : Dudley
Esmeralda : Bodanya
Muff (Murru) : Burgstaller

BOSTON
March 27
LE NOZZE DI FIGARO
Same as Dec. 3 except:
Countess : Jessner
Cherubino : Stevens
Second Peasant Girl : Stellman

March 28
TANNHÄUSER/Leinsdorf (c)
Hermann : List
Tannhäuser : Melchior
Wolfram : Huehn (for Janssen)
Walther : Dudley
Biterolf : Harrell
Heinrich : Darcy
Reinmar : Gurney
Elisabeth : Lehmann
Venus : Thorborg
Shepherd : Stellman

March 29 (mat.)
MADAMA BUTTERFLY
Panizza (c)
Same as Mar. 4 except:
B. F. Pinkerton : Kullman
Kate Pinkerton : Votipka

March 29
CAVALLERIA RUSTICANA
Papi (c)
Santuzza : Roman
Lola : Kaskas
Turiddu : Jagel
Alfio : Warren
Lucia : Doe

PAGLIACCI/Papi (c)
Nedda : Jepson
Canio : Martinelli
Tonio : Valentino (for Bonelli)
Beppe : Dudley
Silvio : Cehanovsky (for Valentino)

March 31
DON GIOVANNI
Same as Mar. 18 except:
Zerlina : Farell

April 1
LA FILLE DU RÉGIMENT
Same as Jan. 21

341

1940–41

April 2 (mat.)
TRISTAN UND ISOLDE
McArthur (c)
Same as Feb. 4 except:
King Marke : Kipnis

April 2
RIGOLETTO/Papi (c)
Duke : Landi
Rigoletto : Tibbett
Gilda : Tuminia
Sparafucile : Moscona
Maddalena : Castagna
Giovanna : Votipka
Monterone : Cordon
Marullo : Cehanovsky
Borsa : De Paolis
Ceprano : Engelman
Countess : Stellman
Page : Herlick

April 3
L'AMORE DEI TRE RE
Montemezzi (c)
Archibaldo : Pinza
Manfredo : Bonelli
Avito : Kullman
Flaminio : De Paolis
Youth : Massue
Fiora : Moore
Maid : Browning
Young Woman : Stellman
Old Woman : Kaskas
Shepherd's Voice : ? (for Mabilli)

April 4
LOHENGRIN/Leinsdorf (c)
King Henry : Cordon
Lohengrin : Melchior
Elsa : Flagstad
Telramund : Huehn
Ortrud : Thorborg
Herald : Warren

April 5 (mat.)
IL BARBIERE DI SIVIGLIA
Papi (c)
Almaviva : Schipa
Dr. Bartolo : Baccaloni
Rosina : Tuminia
Figaro : Thomas
Don Basilio : Pinza
Berta : Petina
Fiorello : Engelman
Sergeant : Dudley

April 5
IL TROVATORE
Same as Mar. 25 except:
Leonora : Roman
Inez : Votipka

342

CLEVELAND
April 14
LE NOZZE DI FIGARO
Same as Dec. 3 except:
Susanna : Sayao
Cherubino : Stevens
Second Peasant Girl : Stellman

April 15
TRISTAN UND ISOLDE
McArthur (c)
Same as Feb. 4 except:
King Marke : Kipnis

April 16
LA FILLE DU RÉGIMENT
Same as Jan. 21 except:
Corporal : Kent

April 17
DIE WALKÜRE
Same as Dec. 10 except:
Fricka : Thorborg
Sieglinde : Bampton
Rossweisse : Browning
Waltraute : Doe

April 18 (mat.)
CAVALLERIA RUSTICANA
Same as Mar. 29 except:
Santuzza : Milanov

PAGLIACCI
Same as Mar. 29 except:
Nedda : Burke
Tonio : Bonelli
Beppe : De Paolis
Silvio : Valentino

April 18
IL BARBIERE DI SIVIGLIA
Same as Apr. 5 except:
Rosina : Sayao
Figaro : Brownlee
Don Basilio : Cordon

April 19 (mat.)
FAUST/Pelletier (c)
Faust : Kullman
Marguerite : Jepson
Méphistophélès : Pinza
Valentin : Bonelli
Siébel : Browning
Marthe : Votipka
Wagner : Kent

April 19
RIGOLETTO/Panizza (c)
Same as Apr. 2 except:
Sparafucile : Cordon
Monterone : Gurney

NEW ORLEANS
April 21
L'ARLESIENNE (Ballet Excerpts)/Pelletier (c)

MADAMA BUTTERFLY
Panizza (c)
Same as Mar. 4 except:
B. F. Pinkerton : Kullman
Sharpless : Bonelli
Suzuki : Petina
Kate Pinkerton : Votipka

April 22
MANON/Pelletier (c)
Manon : Novotna
Lescaut : Brownlee
Des Grieux : Jobin (for Crooks)
Count des Grieux : Pinza
Poussette : Dickey
Javotte : Stellman
Rosette : Olheim
Guillot : De Paolis
De Brétigny : Cehanovsky
Innkeeper : D'Angelo
Guards : Dudley, Kent
Servant : Savage

April 23
CAVALLERIA RUSTICANA
Same as Mar. 29 except:
Turiddu : Tokatyan
Lucia : Votipka

PAGLIACCI
Same as Mar. 29 except:
Tonio : Tibbett
Beppe : De Paolis
Silvio : Valentino

DALLAS
April 24
IL TROVATORE
Same as Mar. 25 except:
Leonora : Roman
Count di Luna : Bonelli
Inez : Votipka
Ferrando : Cordon

April 25
LE NOZZE DI FIGARO
Same as Dec. 3 except:
Susanna : Sayao
Barbarina : Dickey
Second Peasant Girl : Stellman

April 26 (mat.)
LA FILLE DU RÉGIMENT
Same as Jan. 21 except:
Corporal : Kent

April 26

RIGOLETTO
Same as Apr. 2 except:
Duke : Kullman
Sparafucile : Cordon
Monterone : Gurney

ATLANTA

April 28

CAVALLERIA RUSTICANA
Same as Mar. 29 except:
Lucia : Votipka

L'ARLESIENNE (Ballet
Excerpts)/Pelletier (c)

PAGLIACCI
Same as Mar. 29 except:
Nedda : Albanese
Tonio : Tibbett
Beppe : De Paolis
Silvio : Valentino

April 29

FAUST
Same as Apr. 19 except:
Siébel : Olheim

April 30

LOHENGRIN
Same as Apr. 4 except:
Elsa : Rethberg
Telramund : Janssen

RICHMOND

May 1

LA BOHÈME/Papi (c)
Rodolfo : Kullman
Marcello : Bonelli
Schaunard : Cehanovsky
Colline : Cordon
Mimi : Moore
Musetta : Dickey
Benoit : Baccaloni
Parpignol : Oliviero
Alcindoro : Baccaloni
Sergeant : Kent

May 2

LE NOZZE DI FIGARO
Same as Dec. 3 except:
Barbarina : Dickey
Second Peasant Girl :
Stellman

ROCHESTER

May 5

CARMEN
Same as Mar. 11 except:
Carmen : Swarthout
Zuniga : D'Angelo
Morales : Kent

ALBANY

May 6

LA BOHÈME
Same as May 1 except:
Colline : Moscona
Mimi : Novotna
Parpignol : Dreeben (t)

1941 – 42

PHILADELPHIA

November 25

TANNHÄUSER/Leinsdorf (c)
Hermann : Kipnis
Tannhäuser : Melchior
Wolfram : Huehn
Walther : Carter
Biterolf : Harrell
Heinrich : Darcy
Reinmar : Gurney
Elisabeth : Traubel
Venus : Branzell
Shepherd : Stellman

HARTFORD

December 2

DON GIOVANNI/Walter (c)
Don Giovanni : Pinza
Donna Anna : Bampton
Donna Elvira : Novotna
Zerlina : Sayao
Commendatore : Cordon
Don Ottavio : Kullman
Leporello : Baccaloni
Masetto : Kent

PHILADELPHIA

December 9

SAMSON ET DALILA
Pelletier (c)
Dalila : Stevens
Samson : Maison
High Priest : Warren
Abimelech : Cordon
Old Hebrew : Moscona
Philistine Messenger : Darcy
Philistines : Dudley, Kent

December 16

L'ELISIR D'AMORE
Panizza (c)
Adina : Sayao
Nemorino : Landi
Belcore : Valentino
Dulcamara : Baccaloni
Giannetta : Paulee

December 23

LAKMÉ/Pelletier (c)
Lakmé : Pons
Mallika : Petina
Ellen : Dickey
Rose : Browning

Mrs. Benson : Doe
Gerald : Tokatyan (for
Jobin)
Nilakantha : Pinza
Frederic : Cehanovsky
Hadji : Carter
Fortune Teller : Oliviero
Chinese Merchant : Dudley
Thief : Engelman

January 6

DIE ZAUBERFLÖTE (English)
Walter (c)
Sarastro : Kipnis
Tamino : Kullman
High Priest : Schorr
Two Priests : Dudley,
D'Angelo
Queen of the Night : Bok
Pamina : Conner
Three Ladies : Steber,
Stellman, Kaskas
Papageno : Harrell
Papagena : Andreva
Monostatos : Laufkoetter
Three Genii : Farell,
Paulee, Olheim
Guards : Darcy, Gurney

January 20

PHOEBUS AND PAN/Beecham (c)
Momus : Andreva
Mercurius : Kaskas
Tmolus : Jagel
Midas : Carron
Phoebus : Darcy
Pan : Brownlee

LE COQ D'OR/Beecham (c)
Queen : Antoine
King Dodon : Pinza
General Polkan : Cordon
Prince Guidon : Darcy
Prince Afron : Kent
Amelfa : Doe
Astrologer : De Paolis
Golden Cockerel : Votipka
Skhomoroh : Arshansky

February 3

LOHENGRIN/Leinsdorf (c)
King Henry : List
Lohengrin : Maison
Elsa : Varnay
Telramund : Huehn
Ortrud : Thorborg
Herald : Warren

February 17

GÖTTERDÄMMERUNG
Leinsdorf (c)
Siegfried : Melchior
Gunther : Janssen
Hagen : Kipnis
Alberich : Olitzki

343

Brünnhilde : Traubel
Gutrune : Jessner
Waltraute : Thorborg
Woglinde : Steber
Wellgunde : Petina
Flosshilde : Olheim
First Norn : Van Kirk
Second Norn : Browning
Third Norn : Votipka
Vassals : Dudley, Engelman

March 3
CARMEN/Beecham (c)
Carmen : Djanel
Don José : Jobin
Micaela : Albanese
Escamillo : Warren
Zuniga : D'Angelo
Morales : Engelman
Frasquita : Dickey (for
  Votipka)
Mercedes : Olheim
Dancaire : Cehanovsky
Remendado : De Paolis

March 10
THE ISLAND GOD/Panizza (c)
Ilo : Warren
Telea : Varnay
Luca : Jobin
Greek God : Cordon
Voice of Fisherman : Carter

LA BOHÈME/Breisach (c)
Rodolfo : Kiepura
Marcello : Valentino
Schaunard : Cehanovsky
Colline : Pinza
Mimi : Albanese
Musetta : Dickey
Benoit : Pechner
Parpignol : Oliviero
Alcindoro : Pechner
Sergeant : Engelman

BALTIMORE
March 16
DIE ZAUBERFLÖTE
Same as Jan. 6 except:
Pamina : Novotna
Papageno : Brownlee

March 17
CARMEN
Same as Mar. 3 except:
Zuniga : Cordon
Frasquita : Votipka

March 18
LA TRAVIATA/Panizza (c)
Violetta : Sayao
Alfredo : Landi (for Crooks)
Germont : Bonelli
Flora : Votipka
Annina : Olheim

Gastone : De Paolis
Baron Douphol : Engelman
Marquis d'Obigny :
  Cehanovsky
Doctor Grenvil : D'Angelo

BOSTON
March 19
LOHENGRIN
Same as Feb. 3 except:
King Henry : Cordon
Lohengrin : Melchior
Elsa : Stellman (for Varnay
  —Act III)

March 20
DIE ZAUBERFLÖTE
Same as Jan. 6

March 21 (mat.)
LA TRAVIATA
Same as Mar. 18 except:
Violetta : Novotna
Alfredo : Peerce
Germont : Warren

March 21
IL BARBIERE DI SIVIGLIA
  St. Leger (c)
Almaviva : Landi
Dr. Bartolo : Baccaloni
Rosina : Sayao
Figaro : Brownlee
Don Basilio : Cordon
  (for Pinza)
Berta : Petina
Fiorello : Harrell
Sergeant : Dudley

March 23
ORFEO ED EURIDICE
  Walter (c)
Orfeo : Thorborg
Euridice : Novotna
Amor : Farell
A Happy Shade : Dickey

March 24
DIE WALKÜRE/Leinsdorf (c)
Wotan : Schorr
Fricka : Thorborg
Brünnhilde : Varnay
Siegmund : Melchior
Sieglinde : Lehmann
Hunding : List
Helmwige : Van Delden
Gerhilde : Votipka
Ortlinde : Stellman
Rossweisse : Browning
Grimgerde : Van Kirk
Waltraute : Doe
Siegrune : Olheim
Schwertleite : Kaskas

March 25 (mat.)
CARMEN
Same as Mar. 3 except:
Zuniga : Cordon
Frasquita : Votipka

March 25
LA BOHÈME
Same as Mar. 10 except:
Rodolfo : Kullman
Marcello : Brownlee
Colline : Moscona (for
  Pinza)
Mimi : Sayao
Benoit : Baccaloni
Alcindoro : Baccaloni
Sergeant : Gurney

March 26
AIDA/Pelletier (c)
King : Gurney
Amneris : Castagna
Aida : Roman
Radames : Martinelli
Amonasro : Warren
Ramfis : Cordon
Messenger : Dudley
Priestess : Votipka

March 27
DER ROSENKAVALIER
  Leinsdorf (c)
Princess von Werdenberg :
  Lehmann
Baron Ochs : List
Octavian : Novotna
Von Faninal : Huehn
Sophie : Steber
Marianne : Votipka
Valzacchi : De Paolis
Annina : Petina
Police Commissioner :
  Gurney
Majordomo of Princess :
  Darcy
Majordomo of Von Faninal :
  Dudley
Notary : Pechner
Innkeeper : Dudley
Singer : Carter
Orphans : Stellman,
  Browning, Van Kirk
Milliner : Dickey
Hairdresser : Arshansky
Leopold : Burgstaller
Animal Vendor : Oliviero
Coachman : Gurney
Musician : Engelman
Negro Boy : Montague

March 28 (mat.)
FAUST/Beecham (c)
Faust : Crooks
Marguerite : Albanese

Méphistophélès : Cordon
  (for Pinza)
Valentin : Warren
Siébel : Browning
Marthe : Votipka
Wagner : Engelman

March 28
RIGOLETTO/Panizza (c)
Duke : Peerce
Rigoletto : Weede
Gilda : Sayao
Sparafucile : Moscona
  (for Cordon)
Maddalena : Castagna
Giovanna : Olheim
Monterone : Gurney
Marullo : Pechner
Borsa : De Paolis
Ceprano : Cehanovsky
Countess : Stellman
Page : Herlick

CLEVELAND
April 6
DON GIOVANNI
Same as Dec. 2 except:
Don Giovanni : Brownlee
Don Ottavio : Crooks
Masetto : Harrell

April 7
LOHENGRIN
Same as Feb. 3 except:
King Henry : Cordon
Lohengrin : Melchior

April 8
CARMEN
Same as Mar. 3 except:
Zuniga : Gurney (for
  D'Angelo)
Frasquita : Votipka

April 9
DER ROSENKAVALIER
Same as Mar. 27 except:
Animal Vendor : Dreeben (t)

April 10 (mat.)
DIE ZAUBERFLÖTE
  Breisach (c)
Same as Jan. 6 except:
High Priest : Cordon
Papageno : Brownlee
Monostatos : Garris

April 10
LA TRAVIATA
Same as Mar. 18 except:
Violetta : Jepson
Alfredo : Peerce
Germont : Thomas
Annina : Browning
Doctor Grenvil : Harrell

April 11 (mat.)
TOSCA/Panizza (c)
Tosca : Jessner (for Moore)
Cavaradossi : Kullman
Scarpia : Sved
Angelotti : Cordon
Sacristan : Baccaloni
Spoletta : De Paolis
Sciarrone : Engelman
Jailer : Gurney
Shepherd : Petina

April 11
AIDA
Same as Mar. 26 except:
King : Hatfield
Radames : Carron (for
  Martinelli)
Amonasro : Thomas
Ramfis : Moscona

BLOOMINGTON
April 13
AIDA
Same as Mar. 26 except:
Aida : Bampton
Radames : Carron

DALLAS
April 15
LUCIA DI LAMMERMOOR
  Cimara (c)
(Not given in New York)
Lucia : Pons
Alisa : Votipka
Edgardo : Peerce
Ashton : Brownlee
Raimondo : Cordon
Arturo : Carter
Normanno : Dudley

April 16
DON GIOVANNI/Breisach (c)
Same as Dec. 2 except:
Don Giovanni : Brownlee
  (for Pinza)
Zerlina : Antoine
Masetto : Harrell

April 17
CARMEN/Pelletier (c)
Same as Mar. 3 except:
Frasquita : Votipka

April 18 (mat.)
AIDA/Cleva (c)
Same as Mar. 26 except:
Radames : Carron
Ramfis : Moscona (for
  Cordon)
Messenger : Carter
Priestess : Stellman

April 18
IL BARBIERE DI SIVIGLIA
Same as Mar. 21 except:
Figaro : Thomas
Fiorello : Engelman

BIRMINGHAM
April 20
LA TRAVIATA/Cimara (c)
Same as Mar. 18 except:
Violetta : Jepson
Alfredo : Peerce

ATLANTA
April 21
CARMEN
Same as Mar. 3 except:
Don José : Kullman
Escamillo : Bonelli
Zuniga : Cordon
Frasquita : Votipka

April 22
IL BARBIERE DI SIVIGLIA
Same as Mar. 21 except:
Fiorello : Engelman

April 23
LA FILLE DU RÉGIMENT
  St. Leger (c)
Marie : Pons
Marquise : Petina
Sulpice : Baccaloni
Tonio : Jobin
Hortentius : D'Angelo
Corporal : Engelman
Peasant : Dudley
Duchesse de Crakentorp :
  Savage
Le Petit Duc : Kosloff
Notary : Fisher

RICHMOND
April 24
CARMEN/Pelletier (c)
Same as Mar. 3 except:
Don José : Kullman
Escamillo : Brownlee
Zuniga : Cordon
Frasquita : Votipka

April 25
LA FILLE DU RÉGIMENT
Same as Apr. 23

1942 – 43

PHILADELPHIA
November 24
DON GIOVANNI/Walter (c)
Don Giovanni : Pinza
Donna Anna : Milanov
Donna Elvira : Novotna

1942–43

Zerlina : Farell
Commendatore : Cordon
Don Ottavio : Kullman
Leporello : Baccaloni
Masetto : Harrell

December 8
TRISTAN UND ISOLDE
Leinsdorf (c)

Tristan : Melchior
Isolde : Traubel
King Marke : Kipnis
Kurvenal : Huehn
Brangaene : Thorborg
Melot : Darcy
Steersman : Gurney
Shepherd : Laufkoetter
Sailor's Voice : Garris

December 15
TOSCA/Sodero (c)

Tosca : Moore
Cavaradossi : Kullman
Scarpia : Tibbett
Angelotti : Olitzki
Sacristan : Baccaloni
Spoletta : De Paolis
Sciarrone : Engelman
(for Cehanovsky)
Jailer : Engelman
Shepherd : Desana (t)

December 29
LUCIA DI LAMMERMOOR
St. Leger (c)

Lucia : Pons
Alisa : Votipka
Edgardo : Peerce
Ashton : Warren
Raimondo : Cordon
Arturo : De Paolis
Normanno : Dudley

January 5
DER ROSENKAVALIER
Leinsdorf (c)

Princess von Werdenbreg :
Jessner (for Lehmann)
Baron Ochs : List
Octavian : Stevens
Von Faninal : Olitzki
Sophie : Farell
Marianne : Votipka
Valzacchi : Garris
Annina : Olheim
Police Commissioner :
Gurney
Majordomo of Princess :
Darcy
Majordomo of Von Fainal :
Dudley
Notary : Pechner
Innkeeper : Dudley
Singer : Gary (d)
Orphans : Stellman, Paulee,
Van Kirk

Milliner : Raymondi
Hairdresser : Arshansky
Leopold : Burgstaller
Animal Vendor : Oliviero
Coachman : Gurney
Musician : Engelman
Negro Boy : Duse

January 19
BORIS GODUNOV/Szell (c)

Boris Godunov : Kipnis
Fyodor : Petina
Xenia : Farell
Nurse : Kaskas
Shuiski : De Paolis
Shchelkalov : Harrell
Pimen : Moscona
Grigori : Maison
Marina : Thorborg
Rangoni : Warren
Varlaam : Baccaloni
Missail : Dudley
Innkeeper : Doe
Officer : Gurney
Simpleton : Garris
Boyar : Hawkins
Lavitski : Hatfield
Chernikovski : Alvary
Marina's Companions :
Stellman, Olheim

February 2
LA TRAVIATA/Sodero (c)

Violetta : Sayao
Alfredo : Peerce
Germont : Thomas
Flora : Stellman
Annina : Paulee
Gastone : De Paolis
Baron Douphol : Cehanovsky
Marquis d'Obigny : D'Angelo
Doctor Grenvil : Alvary

CHICAGO

March 22
LE NOZZE DI FIGARO
Walter (c)

Almaviva : Brownlee
Countess : Steber
Susanna : Sayao
Figaro : Pinza
Cherubino : Novotna
Marcellina : Petina
Bartolo : Baccaloni
Basilio : De Paolis
Don Curzio : Garris
Antonio : D'Angelo
Barbarina : Farell
Peasant Girls : Paulee,
Raymondi

March 23
FAUST/Beecham (c)

Faust : Jobin
Marguerite : Steber
(for Albanese)

Méphistophélès : Cordon
Valentin : Bonelli
Siébel : Browning
Marthe : Votipka
Wagner : Engelman (for
Harrell)

March 24
LA FORZA DEL DESTINO
Walter (c)

Marquis : D'Angelo
Leonora : Roman
Don Carlo : Tibbett
Don Alvaro : Baum
Padre Guardiano : Pinza
Fra Melitone : Baccaloni
Preziosilla : Petina
Curra : Votipka
Trabucco : De Paolis
Surgeon : Gurney
Alcade : Alvary

March 25
LA TRAVIATA

Same as Feb. 2 except:
Violetta : Jepson
Alfredo : Melton
Germont : Warren
Annina : Olheim

March 26
DIE ZAUBERFLÖTE (English)
Walter (c)

Sarastro : Pinza
Tamino : Kullman
High Priest : Cordon
Two Priests : Dudley,
D'Angelo
Queen of the Night :
Antoine
Pamina : Novotna
Three Ladies : Steber,
Stellman, Kaskas
Papageno : Brownlee
Papagena : Raymondi
Monostatos : Garris
Three Genii : Farell, Paulee,
Olheim
Guards : Darcy, Gurney

March 27 (mat.)
CARMEN/Beecham (c)

Carmen : Djanel
Don José : Jobin
Micaela : Albanese
Escamillo : Warren
Zuniga : Alvary
Morales : Harrell
Frasquita : Votipka
Mercedes : Olheim
Dancaire : Cehanovsky
Remendado : De Paolis

March 27
IL TROVATORE/Sodero (c)

Leonora : Milanov

Manrico : Martinelli
Count di Luna : Valentino
Azucena : Castagna
Inez : Stellman
Ferrando : Moscona
Ruiz : Oliviero
Gypsy : Engelman

March 29
TANNHÄUSER/Szell (c)
Hermann : Cordon
Tannhäuser : Melchior
Wolfram : Tibbett
Walther : Garris
Biterolf : Hawkins
Heinrich : Darcy
Reinmar : Gurney
Elisabeth : Bampton
Venus : Lawrence
Shepherd : Stellman

March 30
IL BARBIERE DI SIVIGLIA
St. Leger (c)
Almaviva : Martini
Dr. Bartolo : Baccaloni
Rosina : Sayao
Figaro : Brownlee
Don Basilio : Pinza
Berta : Petina
Fiorello : Harrell
Sergeant : Dudley

March 31
TRISTAN UND ISOLDE
Same as Dec. 8 except:
Shepherd : Garris
Sailor's Voice : Darcy

April 1
AIDA/Pelletier (c)
King : Alvary
Amneris : Castagna
Aida : Roman
Radames : Jagel
Amonasro : Bonelli
Ramfis : Moscona
Messenger : Oliviero
Priestess : Votipka

April 2
BORIS GODUNOV
Same as Jan. 19 except:
Grigori : Kullman
Lavitski : Pechner

April 3 (mat.)
DON GIOVANNI/Breisach
(c—for Walter)
Same as Nov. 24 except:
Zerlina : Sayao
Don Ottavio : Melton

April 3
LA TRAVIATA
Same as Feb. 2 except:
Violetta : Albanese

Alfredo : Kullman
Germont : Tibbett
Flora : Votipka
Annina : Olheim

CLEVELAND

April 5
LA FORZA DEL DESTINO
Sodero (c)
Same as Mar. 24 except:
Leonora : Milanov

April 6
FAUST
Same as Mar. 23 except:
Faust : Kullman
Marguerite : Jepson
Méphistophélès : Pinza
(for Cordon)
Valentin : Thomas

April 7
LA TRAVIATA
Same as Feb. 2 except:
Violetta : Albanese
Alfredo : Melton
Germont : Tibbett
Flora : Votipka
Annina : Olheim

April 8
CARMEN
Same as Mar. 27 except:
Carmen : Petina (for
Swarthout)
Morales : Engelman

April 9 (mat.)
LA BOHÈME/Sodero (c)
Rodolfo : Kullman
Marcello : Brownlee
Schaunard : Cehanovsky
Colline : Pinza
Mimi : Sayao
Musetta : Greer
Benoit : Baccaloni
Parpignol : Oliviero
Alcindoro : Baccaloni
Sergeant : Engelman

LA GIOCONDA—*Dance of the*
Hours (Ballet)/Sodero (c)

April 9
AIDA
Same as Apr. 1 except:
King : Gurney
Radames : Baum
Amonasro : Tibbett
Ramfis : Cordon
Messenger : Dudley
Priestess : Stellman

April 10 (mat.)
IL BARBIERE DI SIVIGLIA
Same as Mar. 30

April 10
IL TROVATORE
Same as Mar. 27 except:
Leonora : Bampton
Count di Luna : Warren

ROCHESTER

April 12
LA BOHÈME
Same as Apr. 9

PHILADELPHIA

April 20
PARSIFAL/Leinsdorf (c)
Amfortas : Huehn
Titurel : Moscona
Gurnemanz : List
Parsifal : Melchior
Klingsor : Olitzki
Kundry : Thorborg
A Voice : Van Kirk
Knights of the Grail : Darcy,
Hawkins
Esquires : Farell, Olheim,
Garris, Dudley
Flower Maidens : Steber,
Jessner, Olheim, Farell,
Stellman, Browning

1 9 4 3 – 4 4

PHILADELPHIA

November 23
CARMEN/Beecham (c)
Carmen : Djanel
Don José : Jobin
Micaela : Conner
Escamillo : Sved
Zuniga : Alvary
Morales : Baker (d)
Frasquita : Votipka
Mercedes : Browning
Dancaire : Cehanovsky
Remendado : De Paolis

December 7
DIE WALKÜRE/Szell (c)
Wotan : Janssen
Fricka : Thorborg
Brünnhilde : Traubel
Siegmund : Melchior
Sieglinde : Varnay (for
Bampton)
Hunding : List
Helmwige : Doree
Gerhilde : Votipka
Ortlinde : Stellman
Rossweisse : Browning
Grimgerde : Johnson (d)
Waltraute : Doe
Siegrune : Paulee
Schwertleite : Harshaw

347

December 14
RIGOLETTO/Sodero (c)

Duke : Kullman
Rigoletto : Tibbett
Gilda : Pons
Sparafucile : Moscona
Maddalena : Kaskas
Giovanna : Altman
Monterone : Hawkins
Marullo : Cehanovsky
Borsa : De Paolis
Ceprano : Cassel
Countess : Stellman
Page : Herlick

December 21
LES CONTES D'HOFFMANN
Beecham (c)

Hoffmann : Jobin
Olympia : Munsel
Giulietta : Djanel
Antonia : Novotna
Nicklausse : Glaz
Lindorf : Harrell
Coppelius : Pinza
Dappertutto : Singher
Dr. Miracle : Pinza
Spalanzani : De Paolis
Schlemil : Gurney
Crespel : Moscona
Voice : Harshaw
Andrès : Oliviero
Cochenille : Oliviero
Pitichinaccio : De Paolis
Frantz : De Paolis
Luther : Pechner
Nathanael : Dudley
Hermann : Cassel
Stella : Youchkevich

January 4
UN BALLO IN MASCHERA
Walter (c)

Riccardo : Peerce
Renato : Warren
Amelia : Milanov
Ulrica : Thorborg
Oscar : Greer
Silvano : Cehanovsky
Samuel : Cordon
Tom : Moscona
Judge : Dudley
Servant : Oliviero

January 18
SALOME/Szell (c)

Herod : Jagel
Herodias : Branzell
Salome : Djanel
Jokanaan : Huehn
(for Janssen)
Narraboth : Garris
Page : Glaz
First Nazarene : Cordon
Second Nazarene : Darcy

First Jew : Laufkoetter
Second Jew : Oliviero
Third Jew : De Paolis
Fourth Jew : Dudley
Fifth Jew : Pechner
First Soldier : Harrell
Second Soldier : Gurney
Cappadocian : Hawkins
Slave : Paulee

GIANNI SCHICCHI/Sodero (c)

Gianni Schicchi : Baccaloni
Lauretta : Conner
(for Albanese)
La Vecchia : Kaskas
Rinuccio : De Paolis
(for Martini)
Gherardo : Oliviero
(for De Paolis)
Nella : Greer
Betto : Cehanovsky
Simone : Lazzari
Marco : Pechner
La Ciesca : Votipka
Spinelloccio : D'Angelo
Nicolao : Alvary
Pinellino : Gurney
Guccio : Baker
Gherardino : Statile

February 1
NORMA/Sodero (c)

Oroveso : Lazzari
Norma : Milanov
Pollione : Jagel
Adalgisa : Castagna
Clotilde : Votipka
Flavio : De Paolis

March 7
AIDA/Pelletier (c)

King : Alvary
Amneris : Castagna
Aida : Milanov (for Roman)
Radames : Baum
Amonasro : Warren
Ramfis : Moscona
Messenger : Dudley
Priestess : Votipka

March 21
PELLÉAS ET MÉLISANDE
Cooper (c)

Mélisande : Sayao
Geneviève : Harshaw
Little Yniold : Raymondi
Pelléas : Jobin (for Singher)
Golaud : Brownlee
Arkel : Kipnis
Physician : D'Angelo

April 4
PARSIFAL/Cooper (c)

Amfortas : Singher
Titurel : Moscona

Gurnemanz : List
Parsifal : Melchior
Klingsor : Olitzki
Kundry : Thorborg
A Voice : Harshaw
Knights of the Grail : Darcy,
Hawkins
Esquires : Farell, Browning,
Garris, Dudley
Flower Maidens : Jessner
(for Munsel), Carroll,
Paulee, Farell, Stellman,
Browning

BOSTON

April 10
UN BALLO IN MASCHERA

Same as Jan. 4 except:
Silvano : Baker
Samuel : Lazzari

April 11
DIE ZAUBERFLÖTE (English)
Walter (c)

Sarastro : Pinza
Tamino : Kullman
High Priest : Moscona
Two Priests : Dudley,
D'Angelo
Queen of the Night :
Bowman
Pamina : Conner
Three Ladies : Steber,
Stellman, Kaskas
Papageno : Brownlee
Papagena : Raymondi
Monostatos : Garris
Three Genii : Farell,
Paulee, Glaz
Guards : Darcy, Gurney

April 12 (mat.)
LA BOHÈME/Sodero (c)

Rodolfo : Martini
Marcello : Valentino
Schaunard : Cehanovsky
Colline : Lazzari
Mimi : Novotna
Musetta : Carroll
Benoit : Pechner
Parpignol : Oliviero
Alcindoro : D'Angelo
Sergeant : Coscia

April 12
CARMEN

Same as Nov. 23 except:
Micaela : Albanese
Escamillo : Singher

April 13
LE NOZZE DI FIGARO
Walter (c)

Almaviva : Brownlee
Countess : Steber

Susanna : Greer
Figaro : Pinza
Cherubino : Novotna
Marcellina : Glaz
Bartolo : Lazzari
Basilio : De Paolis
Don Curzio : Garris
Antonio : D'Angelo
Barbarina : Farell
Peasant Girls : Paulee,
Raymondi

April 14
AIDA

Same as Mar. 7 except:
King : Gurney
Amneris : Thorborg
Amonasro : Sved
Priestess : Stellman

April 15 (mat.)
FAUST/Beecham (c)

Faust : Jobin
Marguerite : Albanese
Méphistophélès : Pinza
Valentin : Singher
Siébel : Browning
Marthe : Votipka
Wagner : Baker

April 15
LA TRAVIATA/Sodero (c)

Violetta : Steber
Alfredo : Peerce
Germont : Warren
Flora : Stellman
Annina : Paulee
Gastone : De Paolis
Baron Douphol : Cehanovsky
Marquis d'Obigny : D'Angelo
Doctor Grenvil : Alvary

CHICAGO
April 17
TRISTAN UND ISOLDE
Beecham (c)

Tristan : Melchior
Isolde : Lawrence
King Marke : List
Kurvenal : Janssen
Brangaene : Thorborg
Melot : Darcy
Steersman : Gurney
Shepherd : Garris
Sailor's Voice : Garris

April 18
LA TRAVIATA/Cimara (c)

Same as Apr. 15 except:
Violetta : Albanese
Alfredo : Tokatyan
Flora : Votipka
Marquis d'Obigny : Baker

April 19
DIE ZAUBERFLÖTE

Same as Apr. 11 except:
Sarastro : Moscona (for
Pinza)
High Priest : Janssen

MILWAUKEE
April 20
TANNHÄUSER/Breisach (c)

Hermann : List
Tannhäuser : Melchior
Wolfram : Singher
Walther : Garris
Biterolf : Hawkins
Heinrich : Darcy
Reinmar : Gurney
Elisabeth : Bampton
Venus : Lawrence
Shepherd : Stellman

CHICAGO
April 21
MIGNON/Beecham (c)

Mignon : Tourel
Philine : Munsel
Wilhelm : Melton
Lothario : Pinza
Laerte : Dame
Jarno : Gurney
Frederic : Browning

April 22 (mat.)
UN BALLO IN MASCHERA

Same as Jan. 4 except:
Silvano : Baker
Samuel : Lazzari

April 22
CARMEN

Same as Nov. 23 except:
Micaela : Albanese

April 24
TOSCA/Sodero (c)

Tosca : Moore
Cavaradossi : Kullman
Scarpia : Sved
Angelotti : Alvary
Sacristan : Pechner
Spoletta : De Paolis
Sciarrone : Cehanovsky
Jailer : Baker
Shepherd : Paulee

April 25
PARSIFAL

Same as Apr. 4 except:
Amfortas : Janssen
Gurnemanz : Kipnis
First Flower Maiden :
Jessner (for Munsel)

April 26
LES CONTES D'HOFFMANN

Same as Dec. 21 except:
Olympia : Antoine
(for Munsel)
Antonia : Steber
Nicklausse : Petina
Lindorf : Cehanovsky
Hermann : Baker
Muse : Djanel

April 27
AIDA

Same as Mar. 7 except:
Amneris : Harshaw
Ramfis : Lazzari

April 28
TANNHÄUSER

Same as Apr. 20 except:
Hermann : Kipnis

April 29 (mat.)
LA BOHÈME

Same as Apr. 12 except:
Rodolfo : Kullman
Marcello : Brownlee
Colline : Pinza
Mimi : Albanese
Musetta : Greer
Sergeant : Schubel

April 29
RIGOLETTO/Cimara (c)

Same as Dec. 14 except:
Duke : Tokatyan
Gilda : Antoine (for Munsel)
Sparafucile : Lazzari
Maddalena : Petina
Giovanna : Paulee
Borsa : Dudley
Ceprano : Baker
Page : Gentile (t—for
Herlick)

CLEVELAND
May 1
LES CONTES D'HOFFMANN

Same as Dec. 21 except:
Giulietta : Jepson (t)
Antonia : Steber
Nicklausse : Browning
Hermann : Baker
Muse : Jepson

May 2
LA TRAVIATA

Same as Apr. 15 except:
Violetta : Albanese
Alfredo : Kullman
Germont : Tibbett
Flora : Votipka
Gastone : Dudley
Marquis d'Obigny : Baker
Doctor Grenvil : D'Angelo

349

1943–44

May 3
LE NOZZE DI FIGARO
Breisach (c)
Same as Apr. 13 except:
Susanna : Sayao
Cherubino : Greer
Marcellina : Petina
Barbarina : Carroll
Second Peasant Girl :
Stellman

May 4
MIGNON
Same as Apr. 21 except:
Lothario : Moscona

May 5 (mat.)
TANNHÄUSER
Same as Apr. 20 except:
Hermann : Kipnis
Biterolf : Harrell

May 5
LUCIA DI LAMMERMOOR
Sodero (c)
Lucia : Pons
Alisa : Votipka
Edgardo : Peerce
Ashton : Warren
Raimondo : Moscona
Arturo : De Paolis
Normanno : Dudley

May 6 (mat.)
CARMEN/Pelletier (c)
Same as Nov. 23 except:
Micaela : Albanese
Escamillo : Valentino

May 6
RIGOLETTO/Cimara (c)
Same as Dec. 14 except:
Duke : Tokatyan
Gilda : Munsel
Sparafucile : Lazzari
Maddalena : Petina
Giovanna : Paulee
Marullo : Pechner
Borsa : Dudley
Ceprano : Baker
Page : Gentile (for Herlick)

ROCHESTER
May 8
RIGOLETTO/Cimara (c)
Same as Dec. 14 except:
Duke : Peerce
Gilda : Munsel
Sparafucile : Lazzari
Maddalena : Petina
Giovanna : Browning
Borsa : Dudley
Ceprano : Baker
Page : Gentile (for Herlick)

350

1944–45

PHILADELPHIA
November 28
TRISTAN UND ISOLDE
Leinsdorf (c)
Tristan : Melchior
Isolde : Traubel
King Marke : Kipnis
Kurvenal : Janssen
Brangaene : Thebom (d)
Melot : Darcy
Steersman : Pechner
Shepherd : Garris
Sailor's Voice : Garris

December 5
FAUST/Pelletier (c)
Faust : Kullman (for Jobin)
Marguerite : Albanese
Méphistophélès : Pinza
Valentin : Singher
Siébel : Lipton
Marthe : Votipka
Wagner : Baker

December 19
LA TRAVIATA/Cimara (c)
Violetta : Sayao
Alfredo : Melton
Germont : Warren
Flora : Votipka
Annina : Paulee
Gastone : De Paolis
Baron Douphol : Cehanovsky
Marquis d'Obigny : D'Angelo
Doctor Grenvil : Harrell
(for Alvary)

January 2
LOHENGRIN/Leinsdorf (c)
King Henry : Cordon
Lohengrin : Melchior
Elsa : Bampton
Telramund : Sved
Ortrud : Thorborg
Herald : Harrell

January 16
LA BOHÈME/Sodero (c)
Rodolfo : Peerce
Marcello : Brownlee
Schaunard : Thompson
Colline : Moscona
Mimi : Albanese
Musetta : Greer
Benoit : Baccaloni
Parpignol : Oliviero
Alcindoro : Baccaloni
Sergeant : Baker

January 30
DIE MEISTERSINGER/Szell (c)
Hans Sachs : Janssen

Pogner : List
Eva : Steber
Magdalene : Thorborg
Walther : Kullman
Beckmesser : Pechner
Kothner : Harrell
Vogelgesang : Bowe
Nachtigall : Thompson
Zorn : Manning
Eisslinger : Darcy
(for Laufkoetter)
Moser : Oliviero
Ortel : Hawkins
Schwarz : Gurney
Foltz : Hargrave
David : Laufkoetter
(for Garris)
Night Watchman : D'Angelo

February 27
MIGNON/Pelletier (c)
Mignon : Stevens
Philine : Antoine
Wilhelm : Gerard
Lothario : Pinza
Laerte : Dame
Jarno : Gurney
Frederic : Paulee
Antonio : Hawkins

March 13
LA GIOCONDA/Cooper (c)
La Gioconda : Roman
Laura : Castagna
Alvise : Lazzari (for
Moscona)
La Cieca : Harshaw
Enzo : Jagel
Barnaba : Warren
Zuane : Gurney
First Singer : Hawkins
Second Singer : Manning
Isepo : Oliviero
Monk : Hargrave
Steersman : Baker

March 20
DON GIOVANNI/Walter (c)
Don Giovanni : Pinza
Donna Anna : Kirk
Donna Elvira : Steber
Zerlina : Conner
Commendatore : Moscona
Don Ottavio : Kullman
Leporello : Baccaloni
Masetto : Harrell

March 27
GÖTTERDÄMMERUNG/Szell (c)
Siegfried : Melchior
Gunther : Janssen
Hagen : List
Alberich : Lechner
Brünnhilde : Traubel
Gutrune : Jessner

Waltraute : Thebom
Woglinde : Votipka
Wellgunde : Browning
Flosshilde : Glaz
First Norn : Harshaw
Second Norn : Lipton
Third Norn : Palmer
Vassals : Manning, Hawkins

BALTIMORE

April 2

AIDA/Cooper (c)

King : Hawkins
Amneris : Harshaw
Aida : Milanov
Radames : Carron
Amonasro : Warren
Ramfis : Cordon
Messenger : Manning
Priestess : Votipka

April 3

TRISTAN UND ISOLDE

Same as Nov. 28 except:
King Marke : List
Brangaene : Thorborg

BOSTON

April 5

NORMA/Sodero (c)

Oroveso : Cordon
Norma : Milanov
Pollione : Jagel
Adalgisa : Tourel
Clotilde : Votipka
Flavio : De Paolis

April 6

TRISTAN UND ISOLDE

Same as Nov. 28 except:
Tristan : Carron
Kurvenal : Hawkins
(for Janssen)
Brangaene : Thorborg

April 7 (mat.)

LUCIA DI LAMMERMOOR
Sodero (c)

Lucia : Munsel
Alisa : Votipka
Edgardo : Peerce
Ashton : Warren
Raimondo : Moscona
Arturo : Garris
Normanno : Oliviero

April 7

IL TROVATORE/Cimara (c)

Leonora : Roman
Manrico : Baum
Count di Luna : Valentino
Azucena : Harshaw
Inez : Stellman

Ferrando : Lazzari
Ruiz : Oliviero
Gypsy : Baker

April 9

DON GIOVANNI

Same as Mar. 20 except:
Commendatore : Cordon

April 10

PARSIFAL/Cooper (c)

Amfortas : Singher
(for Janssen)
Titurel : Moscona
Gurnemanz : Kipnis
Parsifal : Darcy
Klingsor : Olitzki
Kundry : Thorborg
A Voice : Harshaw
Knights of the Grail :
Cehanovsky, Hawkins
Esquires : Farell, Browning,
Garris, Marlowe
Flower Maidens : Benzell,
Carroll, Glaz, Farell,
Stellman, Browning

April 11 (mat.)

AIDA/Sodero (c)

Same as Apr. 2 except:
Priestess : Stellman

April 11

IL BARBIERE DI SIVIGLIA
Pelletier (c)

Almaviva : Landi
Dr. Bartolo : Baccaloni
Rosina : Munsel
Figaro : Valentino
Don Basilio : Lazzari
Berta : Altman
Fiorello : Baker
Sergeant : Oliviero

April 12

PELLÉAS ET MÉLISANDE

Mélisande : Sayao
Geneviève : Harshaw
Little Yniold : Raymondi
Pelléas : Singher
Golaud : Tibbett
Arkel : Kipnis
Physician : Alvary

April 13

DIE MEISTERSINGER
Breisach (c—for Szell)

Same as Jan. 30 except:
Hans Sachs : Gynrod
(for Janssen)
Vogelgesang : Marlowe
Eisslinger : Laufkoetter
Foltz : Alvary
David : Garris

April 14 (mat.)

MIGNON

Same as Feb. 27 except:
Philine : Benzell (for Munsel)
Wilhelm : Melton
Frederic : Browning

April 14

RIGOLETTO/Sodero (c)

Duke : Peerce
Rigoletto : Warren
Gilda : Antoine
Sparafucile : Moscona
Maddalena : Castagna
Giovanna : Altman
Monterone : Hargrave
Marullo : Cehanovsky
Borsa : De Paolis
Ceprano : Baker
Countess : Stellman
Page : Altman

CLEVELAND

April 16

FAUST

Same as Dec. 5 except:
Faust : Jobin
Valentin : Warren
Siébel : Browning

April 17

DIE MEISTERSINGER
Breisach (c—for Szell)

Same as Jan. 30 except:
Hans Sachs : Gynrod
(for Janssen)
Vogelgesang : Marlowe
Eisslinger : Laufkoetter
David : Garris

April 18

AIDA/Breisach (c)

Same as Apr. 2 except:
Aida : Bampton
Radames : Baum
Amonasro : Tibbett
Messenger : Oliviero
Priestess : Stellman

April 19

LA BOHÈME

Same as Jan. 16 except:
Schaunard : Cehanovsky
Colline : Pinza
Mimi : Sayao

April 20 (mat.)

LE COQ D'OR (English)
Cooper (c)

Queen : Munsel
King Dodon : Cordon
General Polkan : Gurney
Prince Guidon : Manning
Prince Afron : Thompson

Amelfa : Harshaw
Astrologer : Marlowe
Golden Cockerel : Votipka

April 20
LUCIA DI LAMMERMOOR
Same as Apr. 7 except:
Lucia : Pons (t)
Edgardo : Melton
Ashton : Valentino
Arturo : Dame

April 21 (mat.)
LE NOZZE DI FIGARO
Leinsdorf (c)

Almaviva : Brownlee
Countess : Steber
Susanna : Sayao
Figaro : Pinza
Cherubino : Novotna
Marcellina : Glaz
Bartolo : Baccaloni
Basilio : De Paolis
Don Curzio : Garris
Antonio : D'Angelo
Barbarina : Benzell
Peasant Girls : Altman,
  Stellman

April 21
LA GIOCONDA
Same as Mar. 13 except:
Laura : Thebom
Alvise : Moscona

LAFAYETTE
April 23
IL BARBIERE DI SIVIGLIA
Same as Apr. 11 except:
Don Basilio : Pinza
Berta : Doe
Sergeant : Manning

MILWAUKEE
April 24
TRISTAN UND ISOLDE
Same as Nov. 28 except:
Tristan : Carron
Isolde : Varnay (for Traubel)
King Marke : List
Brangaene : Thorborg
Melot : Thompson

MINNEAPOLIS
April 26
LUCIA DI LAMMERMOOR
  Cimara (c)
Same as Apr. 7 except:
Edgardo : Melton

April 27
DIE WALKÜRE/Breisach (c)
Wotan : Hawkins
Fricka : Thebom

352

Brünnhilde : Traubel
Siegmund : Darcy
Sieglinde : Varnay
Hunding : List
Helmwige : Stellman
Gerhilde : Votipka
Ortlinde : Jessner
Rossweisse : Browning
Grimgerde : Doe
Waltraute : Palmer
Siegrune : Altman
Schwertleite : Harshaw

April 28 (mat.)
DON GIOVANNI
Same as Mar. 20 except:
Donna Anna : Milanov

April 28
CARMEN/Pelletier (c)
Carmen : Tourel
Don José : Tokatyan
Micaela : Benzell
Escamillo : Valentino
Zuniga : D'Angelo
Morales : Baker
Frasquita : Votipka
Mercedes : Browning
Dancaire : Cehanovsky
Remendado : De Paolis

MILWAUKEE
April 29
DIE WALKÜRE
Same as Apr. 27 except:
Wotan : Janssen

CHICAGO
April 30
LUCIA DI LAMMERMOOR
Same as Apr. 7 except:
Lucia : Pons

May 1
LOHENGRIN
Same as Jan. 2 except:
King Henry : Moscona
Lohengrin : Baum
Elsa : Traubel
Herald : Thompson

May 2
DON GIOVANNI
Same as Mar. 20 except:
Donna Anna : Milanov

May 3
LE COQ D'OR
Same as Apr. 20 except:
King Dodon : Harrell

May 4
DIE MEISTERSINGER
  Breisach (c—for Szell)
Same as Jan. 30 except:

Vogelgesang : Marlowe
Foltz : Alvary
David : Garris

May 5 (mat.)
NORMA
Same as Apr. 5 except:
Oroveso : Moscona

May 5
LA BOHÈME
Same as Jan. 16 except:
Marcello : Valentino
Schaunard : Cehanovsky
Colline : Lazzari
Musetta : Benzell
Benoit : Pechner
Alcindoro : D'Angelo

ROCHESTER
May 7
LUCIA DI LAMMERMOOR
Same as Apr. 7 except:
Ashton : Valentino
Raimondo : Lazzari

1945 – 46

PHILADELPHIA
November 27
DER ROSENKAVALIER/Szell (c)
Princess von Werdenberg :
  Jessner
Baron Ochs : List
Octavian : Novotna (for
  Stevens)
Von Faninal : Lechner
Sophie : Steber
Marianne : Votipka
Valzacchi : De Paolis
Annina : Glaz
Police Commissioner : Alvary
Majordomo of Princess :
  Laufkoetter
Majordomo of Von Faninal :
  Marlowe
Notary : Pechner
Innkeeper : Oliviero
Singer : Baum (for Hayward)
Orphans : Stellman, Paulee,
  Kaskas (for Altman)
Milliner : Raymondi
Hairdresser : Caton
Leopold : Burgstaller
Animal Vendor : Oliviero
Negro Boy : Smithers

December 11
ROMÉO ET JULIETTE
  Cooper (c)
Juliette : Munsel
Stephano : Greer
Gertrude : Kaskas

Roméo : Jobin
Tybalt : Hayward
Benvolio : Manning
Mercutio : Singher
Paris : Cehanovsky
Gregorio : D'Angelo
Capulet : Valentino
Friar Laurence : Moscona
Duke of Verona : Hawkins

December 18
TANNHÄUSER/Busch (c)
Hermann : Cordon
Tannhäuser : Ralf (for
 Melchior)
Wolfram : Sved (for
 Janssen)
Walther : Garris
Biterolf : Hawkins
Heinrich : Laufkoetter
Reinmar : Ezekiel
Elisabeth : Varnay (for
 Traubel)
Venus : Thebom
Shepherd : Stellman

January 8
TOSCA/Sodero (c)
Tosca : Resnik
Cavaradossi : Bjoerling
Scarpia : Tibbett
Angelotti : Alvary
Sacristan : Baccaloni
Spoletta : Marlowe
 (for De Paolis)
Sciarrone : Cehanovsky
Jailer : Baker
Shepherd : Paulee

January 22
IL TABARRO/Cimara (c)
Michele : Sved
Luigi : Jagel
Tinca : De Paolis
Talpa : Lazzari
Giorgetta : Albanese
La Frugola : Harshaw
Song Vendor : Marlowe
Lovers : Stellman, Hayward

DON PASQUALE/Busch (c)
Don Pasquale : Baccaloni
Ernesto : Landi
Norina : Sayao
Dr. Malatesta : Brownlee
Notary : De Paolis

February 5
DIE WALKÜRE/Breisach (c)
Wotan : Berglund
Fricka : Thorborg
Brünnhilde : Traubel
Siegmund : Melchior
Sieglinde : Varnay

Hunding : Kipnis
Helmwige : Hober
Gerhilde : Votipka
Ortlinde : Jessner
Rossweisse : Browning
Grimgerde : Lipton
Waltraute : Palmer
Siegrune : Altman
Schwertleite : Harshaw

February 19
FIDELIO/Walter (c)
Don Fernando : Hawkins
Don Pizarro : Schon
Florestan : Carron
Leonore : Resnik
Rocco : Alvary
Marzelline : Benzell
Jaquino : Garris
First Prisoner : Manning
Second Prisoner : D'Angelo

March 5
RIGOLETTO/Sodero (c)
Duke : Peerce
Rigoletto : Warren
Gilda : Munsel
Sparafucile : Vaghi
Maddalena : Lipton
Giovanna : Altman
Monterone : Hawkins
Marullo : Cehanovsky
Borsa : De Paolis
Ceprano : Kent
Countess : Stellman
Page : Altman

March 19
OTELLO/Szell (c)
Otello : Ralf
Desdemona : Roman
Iago : Warren
Emilia : Lipton
Cassio : De Paolis
Roderigo : Marlowe
Lodovico : Moscona
Montano : Hargrave
Herald : Ezekiel

March 26
DIE MEISTERSINGER
 Breisach (c)
Hans Sachs : Berglund
Pogner : List
Eva : Steber
Magdalene : Thorborg
Walther : Ralf
Beckmesser : Pechner
Kothner : Harrell (t)
Vogelgesang : Marlowe
Nachtigall : Thompson
Zorn : Manning
Eisslinger : Darcy

Moser : Oliviero
Ortel : Hawkins
Schwarz : Ezekiel
Foltz : Alvary
David : Garris
Night Watchman : D'Angelo

BALTIMORE
April 1
LA GIOCONDA/Cooper (c)
La Gioconda : Milanov
Laura : Stevens
Alvise : Pinza
La Cieca : Harshaw
Enzo : Tucker
Barnaba : Warren
Zuane : Hawkins
First Singer : Ezekiel
Second Singer : Manning
Isepo : Oliviero
Monk : Hargrave
Steersman : Baker

April 2
TANNHÄUSER
Same as Dec. 18 except:
Wolfram : Singher (for
 Janssen)
Heinrich : Darcy
Venus : Thorborg

BOSTON
April 4
TANNHÄUSER
Same as Dec. 18 except:
Wolfram : Janssen
Heinrich : Darcy
Elisabeth : Traubel

April 5
DER ROSENKAVALIER
Same as Nov. 27 except:
Octavian : Stevens
Von Faninal : Olitzki
Sophie : Conner
Majordomo of Princess :
 Darcy
Singer : Hayward
Third Orphan : Altman

April 6 (mat.)
ROMÉO ET JULIETTE
Same as Dec. 11 except:
Friar Laurence : Pinza

April 6
LA TRAVIATA/Sodero (c)
Violetta : Steber
Alfredo : Tucker
Germont : Warren
Flora : Votipka
Annina : Paulee
Gastone : De Paolis

1945–46

Baron Douphol : Cehanovsky
Marquis d'Obigny : Hargrave
Doctor Grenvil : Alvary

April 8
DIE ZAUBERFLÖTE (English)
Walter (c)
Sarastro : Pinza
Tamino : Melton
High Priest : Ezekiel
Two Priests : Manning,
D'Angelo
Queen of the Night : Benzell
Pamina : Conner
Three Ladies : Resnik,
Stellman, Kaskas
Papageno : Brownlee
Papagena : Raymondi
Monostatos : Garris
Three Genii : Farell, Paulee,
Altman
Guards : Darcy, Hargrave

April 9
DIE MEISTERSINGER/Szell (c)
Same as Mar. 26 except:
Hans Sachs : Janssen
Kothner : Schon

April 10 (mat.)
CARMEN/Pelletier (c)
Carmen : Stevens
Don José : Jobin
Micaela : Albanese
Escamillo : Singher
Zuniga : D'Angelo
Morales : Baker
Frasquita : Votipka
Mercedes : Browning
Dancaire : Cehanovsky
Remendado : De Paolis

April 10
LA BOHÈME/Sodero (c)
Rodolfo : Kullman (for
Bjoerling)
Marcello : Brownlee
Schaunard : Thompson
Colline : Cordon
Mimi : Sayao
Musetta : Greer
Benoit : Baccaloni
Parpignol : Oliviero
Alcindoro : Baccaloni
Sergeant : Baker

April 11
UN BALLO IN MASCHERA
Walter (c)
Riccardo : Peerce
Renato : Warren
Amelia : Milanov
Ulrica : Thorborg
Oscar : Alarie
Silvano : Baker

Samuel : Cordon
Tom : Alvary
Judge : Manning
Sergeant : Oliviero

April 12
DIE WALKÜRE
Same as Feb. 5 except:
Wotan : Janssen
Siegmund : Ralf
Hunding : List
Siegrune : Glaz

April 13 (mat.)
MADAMA BUTTERFLY
Sodero (c)
Cio-Cio-San : Albanese
B. F. Pinkerton : Melton
Sharpless : Valentino
Suzuki : Browning
Kate Pinkerton : Stellman
Goro : De Paolis
Yamadori : Cehanovsky
Uncle-Priest : Hawkins
Imperial Commissioner :
Baker

April 13
IL BARBIERE DI SIVIGLIA
Cimara (c)
Almaviva : Landi
Dr. Bartolo : Baccaloni
Rosina : Sayao
Figaro : Brownlee
Don Basilio : Pinza
Berta : Altman
Fiorello : Oliviero
Sergeant : Marlowe

PHILADELPHIA

April 16
PARSIFAL/Cooper (c)
Amfortas : Singher
Titurel : Moscona
Gurnemanz : Kipnis
Parsifal : Ralf
Klingsor : Pechner
Kundry : Thorborg
A Voice : Harshaw
Knights of the Grail :
Darcy, Hawkins
Esquires : Farell, Browning,
Garris, Marlowe
Flower Maidens : Jessner,
Quartararo, Paulee, Farell,
Stellman, Browning

ROCHESTER

April 20
IL BARBIERE DI SIVIGLIA
Same as Apr. 13 except:
Almaviva : Martini (for
Landi)
Rosina : Munsel
Sergeant : Manning

CLEVELAND

April 22
CARMEN
Same as Apr. 10 except:
Micaela : Steber
Escamillo : Sved
Zuniga : Alvary

April 23
TANNHÄUSER
Same as Dec. 18 except:
Hermann : Kipnis
Wolfram : Singher
(for Janssen)
Heinrich : Darcy
Elisabeth : Traubel
Venus : Thorborg

April 24
DIE ZAUBERFLÖTE
Same as Apr. 8 except:
Tamino : Kullman
Pamina : Novotna
Papageno : Thompson

April 25
MADAMA BUTTERFLY
Same as Apr. 13 except:
Sharpless : Brownlee

April 26 (mat.)
ROMÉO ET JULIETTE
Same as Dec. 11 except:
Tybalt : Garris
Friar Laurence : Pinza
Duke of Verona : Hargrave

April 26
DER ROSENKAVALIER
Same as Nov. 27 except:
Von Faninal : Olitzki
Majordomo of Princess :
Darcy
Singer : Hayward
Third Orphan : Altman

April 27 (mat.)
UN BALLO IN MASCHERA
Same as Apr. 11 except:
Ulrica : Harshaw

April 27
IL BARBIERE DI SIVIGLIA
Same as Apr. 13 except:
Rosina : Antoine

April 28 (mat.)
LA BOHÈME
Same as Apr. 10 except:
Rodolfo : Bjoerling
Marcello : Valentino
Schaunard : Cehanovsky
Mimi : Albanese
Benoit : Pechner
Alcindoro : D'Angelo

354

BLOOMINGTON
April 29
TANNHÄUSER
Same as Dec. 18 except:
Heinrich : Darcy
Elisabeth : Traubel
Venus : Thorborg

April 30
LA BOHÈME
Same as Apr. 10 except:
Rodolfo : Peerce
Colline : Pinza
Mimi : Albanese

MINNEAPOLIS
May 2
TANNHÄUSER
Same as Dec. 18 except:
Heinrich : Darcy
Elisabeth : Traubel
Venus : Thorborg

May 3
LA TRAVIATA
Same as Apr. 6 except:
Alfredo : Peerce
Marquis d'Obigny : Baker

May 4 (mat.)
DIE ZAUBERFLÖTE
Same as Apr. 8 except:
Tamino : Kullman
Pamina : Novotna
Third Lady : Harshaw
Papageno : Thompson

May 4
LA BOHÈME
Same as Apr. 10 except:
Rodolfo : Bjoerling
Schaunard : Cehanovsky
Mimi : Kirsten
Benoit : Pechner
Alcindoro : Pechner

MILWAUKEE
May 5
MADAMA BUTTERFLY
Same as Apr. 13 except:
B. F. Pinkerton : Kullman
Sharpless : Brownlee

CHICAGO
May 6
TANNHÄUSER
Same as Dec. 18 except:
Hermann : Kipnis
Wolfram : Singher
(for Janssen)
Heinrich : Darcy
Elisabeth : Traubel
Venus : Thorborg

May 7
LA TRAVIATA
Same as Apr. 6 except:
Violetta : Albanese
Alfredo : Peerce
Germont : Merrill
Marquis d'Obigny : Baker

May 8
LA GIOCONDA
Same as Apr. 1

May 9
DIE ZAUBERFLÖTE
Same as Apr. 8 except:
Tamino : Kullman
Pamina : Novotna
Third Lady : Harshaw

May 10
DIE WALKÜRE
Same as Feb. 5 except:
Wotan : Hawkins
(for Janssen)
Siegmund : Ralf
Hunding : Cordon
Helmwige : Resnik
Ortlinde : Stellman

May 11 (mat.)
DER ROSENKAVALIER
Same as Nov. 27 except:
Octavian : Stevens
Von Faninal : Thompson
Annina : Lipton
Majordomo of Princess :
Manning
Singer : Hayward
Third Orphan : Altman

May 11
UN BALLO IN MASCHERA
Same as Apr. 11 except:
Ulrica : Harshaw

ST. LOUIS
May 13
TANNHÄUSER
Same as Dec. 18 except:
Wolfram : Singher
Heinrich : Manning
Elisabeth : Traubel
Venus : Thorborg

May 14
CARMEN
Same as Apr. 10 except:
Escamillo : Thompson
(for Merrill)
Zuniga : Alvary

May 15
RIGOLETTO
Same as Mar. 5 except:

Sparafucile : Pinza
Borsa : Manning
Ceprano : Baker

DALLAS
May 17
DER ROSENKAVALIER
Rudolf (c)
Same as Nov. 27 except:
Octavian : Stevens
Von Faninal : Thompson
Annina : Lipton
Majordomo of Princess :
Manning
Singer : Hayward
Second Orphan : Browning
(for Paulee)
Third Orphan : Altman
Milliner : Greer

May 18 (mat.)
RIGOLETTO
Same as Mar. 5 except:
Gilda : Antoine
Sparafucile : Cordon
Monterone : Hargrave
Ceprano : Baker

May 18
ROMÉO ET JULIETTE
Same as Dec. 11 except:
Juliette : Kirsten
Gertrude : Altman
Friar Laurence : Pinza

May 19 (mat.)
MADAMA BUTTERFLY
Same as Apr. 13 except:
B. F. Pinkerton : Kullman
Sharpless : Brownlee

MEMPHIS
May 20
CARMEN
Same as Apr. 10 except:
Micaela : Kirsten
Escamillo : Valentino
Zuniga : Alvary

May 21
MADAMA BUTTERFLY
Same as Apr. 13 except:
B. F. Pinkerton : Kullman
Sharpless : Brownlee

CHATTANOOGA
May 22
RIGOLETTO
Same as Mar. 5 except:
Sparafucile : Pinza
Maddalena : Browning
Borsa : Manning
Ceprano : Baker

1 9 4 6 – 4 7

PHILADELPHIA

November 12
AIDA/Sodero (c)
King : Kinsman (d)
Amneris : Thebom
Aida : Milanov
Radames : Vinay
Amonasro : Warren
Ramfis : Moscona
Messenger : Oliviero
Priestess : Votipka

November 26
MADAMA BUTTERFLY
Sodero (c)
Cio-Cio-San : Albanese
B. F. Pinkerton : Melton
Sharpless : Valentino
Suzuki : Altman
Kate Pinkerton : Stellman
Goro : De Paolis
Yamadori : Cehanovsky
Uncle-Priest : Hawkins
Imperial Commissioner :
  Baker

December 3
LE NOZZE DI FIGARO
Busch (c)
Almaviva : Valentino
Countess : Steber
Susanna : Sayao
Figaro : Pinza
Cherubino : Novotna
Marcellina : Glaz
Bartolo : Baccaloni
Basilio : De Paolis
Don Curzio : Chabay
Antonio : Alvary
Barbarina : Benzell
Peasant Girls : Altman,
  Raymondi

December 17
LAKMÉ/Fourestier (c)
Lakmé : Pons
Mallika : Jordan
Ellen : Farell
Rose : Stellman
Mrs. Benson : Votipka
Gerald : Jobin
Nilakantha : Vaghi
Frederic : Singher
Hadji : Carter
Fortune Teller : Oliviero
Chinese Merchant : Marlowe
Thief : Hargrave

January 7
SIEGFRIED/Stiedry (c)
Siegfried : Svanholm
Mime : Garris

356

Wanderer : Berglund
Alberich : Lechner
Fafner : Ernster
Erda : Harshaw
Brünnhilde : Varnay
Forest Bird : Benzell

January 21
DER ROSENKAVALIER/Busch (c)
Princess von Werdenberg :
  Jessner
Baron Ochs : Ernster
Octavian : Novotna
Von Faninal : Thompson
Sophie : Conner
Marianne : Votipka
Valzacchi : De Paolis
Annina : Lipton
Police Commissioner : Alvary
Majordomo of Princess :
  Darcy
Majordomo of Von Faninal :
  Marlowe
Notary : Pechner
Innkeeper : Chabay
Singer : Hayward
Orphans : Stellman, Jordan,
  Altman
Milliner : Greer
Hairdresser : Caton
Leopold : Burgstaller
Animal Vendor : Oliviero
Negro Boy : Smithers

February 4
THE ABDUCTION FROM THE
SERAGLIO
Cooper (c)
Selim : Hargrave
Constanza : Steber
Blonda : Benzell
Belmonte : Kullman
Pedrillo : Garris
Osmin : Ernster
Mute : Burgstaller

February 18
LA BOHÈME/Cimara (c)
Rodolfo : Tagliavini
Marcello : Valentino
Schaunard : Thompson
Colline : Vaghi
Mimi : Kirsten
Musetta : Greer
Benoit : Pechner
  (for Baccaloni)
Parpignol : Oliviero
Alcindoro : Pechner
  (for Baccaloni)
Sergeant : Baker

March 4
TRISTAN UND ISOLDE/Busch (c)
Tristan : Ralf
Isolde : Traubel

King Marke : Ernster
Kurvenal : Janssen
Brangaene : Harshaw
Melot : Darcy
Steersman : Pechner
Shepherd : Chabay
Sailor's Voice : Darcy

March 11
BORIS GODUNOV/Cooper (c)
Boris Godunov : Pinza
Fyodor : Jordan
Xenia : Benzell
Nurse : Altman
Shuiski : Garris
Shchelkalov : Thompson
Pimen : Moscona
Grigori : Kullman
Marina : Lipton
Rangoni : Valentino
Varlaam : Baccaloni
Missail : Oliviero
Innkeeper : Turner
Officer : Hines
Simpleton : Marlowe
Nikitich : Hawkins
Lavitski : Baker
Chernikovski : Cehanovsky
Boyar : Darcy
Kruschov : Chabay

BALTIMORE

March 17
BORIS GODUNOV
Same as Mar. 11 except:
Shuiski : De Paolis
Shchelkalov : Merrill
Grigori : Tucker
Lavitski : Thompson

March 18
DER ROSENKAVALIER
Same as Jan. 21 except:
Octavian : Stevens
Valzacchi : Garris
Annina : Glaz
Milliner : Benzell
Negro Boy : Buonamassa
  (t—for Smithers)

BOSTON

March 20
CARMEN/Fourestier (c)
Carmen : Stevens
Don José : Jobin (for Vinay)
Micaela : Conner
Escamillo : Singher
Zuniga : Alvary
Morales : Baker
Frasquita : Votipka
Mercedes : Lipton
Dancaire : Cehanovsky
Remendado : De Paolis

March 21
MADAMA BUTTERFLY
Same as Nov. 26 except:
Cio-Cio-San : Kirsten
(for Albanese)
B. F. Pinkerton : Tucker
Suzuki : Browning

March 22 (mat.)
HÄNSEL UND GRETEL
(English) Stiedry (c)
Hänsel : Stevens
Gretel : Conner
Witch : Votipka
Gertrude : Harshaw
Peter : Brownlee
Sandman : Stellman
Dewman : Raymondi

VALPURGIS NIGHT (Ballet)
Kritz (c)

March 22
AIDA
Same as Nov. 12 except:
Radames : Svanholm
Amonasro : Merrill

March 24
BORIS GODUNOV
Same as Mar. 11 except:
Xenia : Greer
Nurse : Lipton
Shuiski : De Paolis
Shchelkalov : Merrill
Grigori : Tucker
Marina : Thebom
(for Stevens)
Lavitski : Thompson

March 25
RIGOLETTO/Sodero (c)
Duke : Peerce
Rigoletto : Warren
Gilda : Munsel
Sparafucile : Vaghi
Maddalena : Lipton
Giovanna : Altman
Monterone : Hawkins
Marullo : Cehanovsky
Borsa : Chabay
Ceprano : Baker
Countess : Stellman
Page : Jordan

March 26 (mat.)
LA BOHÈME/Sodero (c)
Same as Feb. 18 except:
Marcello : Brownlee
Colline : Moscona
Benoit : Baccaloni
Alcindoro : Baccaloni

March 26
LOHENGRIN/Busch (c)
King Henry : Ernster

Lohengrin : Svanholm
Elsa : Traubel
Telramund : Janssen
Ortrud : Harshaw
Herald : Harrell

March 27
LAKMÉ
Same as Dec. 17 except:
Ellen : Greer
Frederic : Harrell
Hadji : Garris

March 28
OTELLO/Busch (c)
Otello : Ralf
Desdemona : Ilitsch
Iago : Warren
Emilia : Lipton
Cassio : De Paolis
Roderigo : Hayward
Lodovico : Moscona
Montano : Hargrave
Herald : Kinsman

March 29 (mat.)
IL BARBIERE DI SIVIGLIA
Sodero (c)
Almaviva : Tagliavini
Dr. Bartolo : Baccaloni
Rosina : Munsel
Figaro : Brownlee
Don Basilio : Vaghi
Berta : Altman
Fiorello : Baker
Sergeant : Marlowe
Ambrogio : Burgstaller

March 29
FAUST/Fourestier (c)
Faust : Kullman
Marguerite : Kirsten
Méphistophélès : Pinza
Valentin : Singher
Siébel : Lipton
Marthe : Turner
Wagner : Cehanovsky

CLEVELAND

April 7
LAKMÉ
Same as Dec. 17 except:
Hadji : Garris

April 8
LOHENGRIN
Same as Mar. 26 except:
Telramund : Hawkins (for
Janssen)
Herald : Thompson

April 9
FAUST/Pelletier (c)
Same as Mar. 29 except:
Valentin : Merrill
Siébel : Stellman

April 10
LA TRAVIATA/Cimara (c)
Violetta : Steber
Alfredo : Peerce
Germont : Warren
Flora : Votipka
Annina : Altman
Gastone : Chabay
Baron Douphol : Cehanovsky
Marquis d'Obigny :
Hargrave (for Baker)
Doctor Grenvil : Alvary

April 11 (mat.)
HÄNSEL UND GRETEL
Same as Mar. 22

VALPURGIS NIGHT (Ballet)
Same as Mar. 22

April 11
BORIS GODUNOV
Same as Mar. 11 except:
Xenia : Greer
Nurse : Lipton
Shchelkalov : Harrell
Grigori : Tucker
Marina : Thebom
Lavitski : Thompson

April 12 (mat.)
MADAMA BUTTERFLY
Same as Nov. 26 except:
Cio-Cio-San : Kirsten
B. F. Pinkerton : Kullman
(for Tagliavini)
Sharpless : Brownlee
Suzuki : Browning
Imperial Commissioner :
Hargrave (for Baker)

April 12
AIDA/Rudolf (c)
Same as Nov. 12 except:
Aida : Ilitsch
Radames : Baum
Ramfis : Vaghi

BLOOMINGTON

April 14
FAUST/Pelletier (c)
Same as Mar. 29 except:
Siébel : Stellman
Marthe : Votipka
Wagner : Baker

April 15
MADAMA BUTTERFLY
Same as Nov. 26 except:
Cio-Cio-San : Ilitsch
B. F. Pinkerton : Tagliavini
Sharpless : Brownlee
Suzuki : Browning
Kate Pinkerton : Jordan

357

1946–47

MINNEAPOLIS

April 17

LE NOZZE DI FIGARO

Same as Dec. 3 except:
Almaviva : Brownlee
Countess : Quartararo
Susanna : Greer
Cherubino : Stevens
Don Curzio : Garris
Barbarina : Farell
Second Peasant Girl :
  Stellman

April 18

LOHENGRIN

Same as Mar. 26 except:
Lohengrin : Ralf
Herald : Thompson

April 19 (mat.)

FAUST/Pelletier (c)

Same as Mar. 29 except:
Méphistophélès : Moscona
Siébel : Stellman
Marthe : Votipka
Wagner : Baker

April 19

MADAMA BUTTERFLY

Same as Nov. 26 except:
Cio-Cio-San : Ilitsch
B. F. Pinkerton : Tagliavini
Suzuki : Browning
Kate Pinkerton : Jordan

CHICAGO

April 21

BORIS GODUNOV

Same as Mar. 11 except:
Xenia : Greer
Nurse : Lipton
Shchelkalov : Merrill
Pimen : Lazzari
Grigori : Tucker
Marina : Stevens
Lavitski : Thompson

April 22

MADAMA BUTTERFLY
  Cimara (c)

Cio-Cio-San : Kirsten
B. F. Pinkerton : Kullman
Suzuki : Browning

April 23

LUCIA DI LAMMERMOOR
  Cimara (c—for Sodero)

Lucia : Munsel
Alisa : Votipka
Edgardo : Tagliavini
Ashton : Merrill
Raimondo : Vaghi
Arturo : Chabay
Normanno : Oliviero

358

April 24

LE NOZZE DI FIGARO

Same as Dec. 3 except:
Almaviva : Brownlee
Countess : Quartararo
Susanna : Greer
Cherubino : Stevens
Don Curzio : Garris
Barbarina : Farell
Second Peasant Girl :
  Stellman

April 25

AIDA

Same as Nov. 12 except:
Aida : Ilitsch
Radames : Baum
Ramfis : Lazzari (for Vaghi)

April 26 (mat.)

LA BOHÈME/Sodero (c)

Same as Feb. 18 except:
Rodolfo : Peerce
Colline : Lazzari
Mimi : Sayao
Benoit : Baccaloni
Alcindoro : Baccaloni

April 26

FAUST/Pelletier (c)

Same as Mar. 29 except:
Faust : Berini
Méphistophélès : Hines
Siébel : Stellman
Wagner : Baker

ATLANTA

April 28

LE NOZZE DI FIGARO

Same as Dec. 3 except:
Almaviva : Brownlee
Countess : Quartararo
Cherubino : Stevens
Marcellina : Turner
Don Curzio : Garris
Barbarina : Farell
Second Peasant Girl :
  Stellman

April 29 (mat.)

MADAMA BUTTERFLY
  Cimara (c)

Same as Nov. 26 except:
Cio-Cio-San : Kirsten
B. F. Pinkerton : Tagliavini
Suzuki : Browning
Kate Pinkerton : Jordan

April 29

AIDA

Same as Nov. 12 except:
Aida : Kirk (for Ilitsch)
Radames : Baum

DALLAS

May 1

LAKMÉ/Pelletier (c)

Same as Dec. 17 except:
Ellen : Greer
Gerald : Knight
Hadji : Garris

May 2

LOHENGRIN

Same as Mar. 26 except:
Lohengrin : Ralf
Herald : Thompson

May 3 (mat.)

BORIS GODUNOV

Same as Mar. 11 except:
Xenia : Farell
Nurse : Lipton
Shuiski : De Paolis
Grigori : Tucker
Marina : Stevens
Boyar : Chabay

May 4 (mat.)

LA BOHÈME/Sodero (c)

Same as Feb. 18 except:
Marcello : Brownlee
Schaunard : Cehanovsky
Mimi : Sayao
Benoit : Baccaloni
Alcindoro : Baccaloni

May 4

CONCERT *(Benefit Texas City
  Disaster Victims)*

Busch, Kritz, Rudolf,
  Pelletier, Sodero (c)
Ilitsch, Kirsten, Quartararo,
  Stellman, Harshaw, Lipton,
  Baum, Berini, Singher,
  Baccaloni, Valentino,
  Moscona, Pinza

SAN ANTONIO

May 5

LE NOZZE DI FIGARO

Same as Dec. 3 except:
Almaviva : Brownlee
Cherubino : Stevens
Don Curzio : Garris
Barbarina : Farell
Second Peasant Girl :
  Stellman

HOUSTON

May 6

AIDA

Same as Nov. 12 except:
Aida : Kirk (for Ilitsch)
  Acts II-IV)
Radames : Baum
Amonasro : Merrill

May 7
MADAMA BUTTERFLY

Same as Nov. 26 except:
Cio-Cio-San : Kirsten
B. F. Pinkerton : Tagliavini
Suzuki : Browning
Kate Pinkerton : Jordan

NEW ORLEANS
May 8
LE NOZZE DI FIGARO

Same as Dec. 3 except:
Almaviva : Brownlee
Susanna : Greer
Cherubino : Stevens
Don Curzio : Garris
Barbarina : Farell
Second Peasant Girl :
    Stellman

May 9
LA TRAVIATA/Sodero (c)

Same as Apr. 10 except:
Violetta : Sayao
Alfredo : Tagliavini
Germont : Valentino
Flora : Jordan
Marquis d'Obigny : Baker
Doctor Grenvil : Hargrave

May 10
LUCIA DI LAMMERMOOR

Same as Apr. 23 except:
Alisa : Stellman
Edgardo : Peerce
Raimondo : Moscona
Arturo : Chabay

MEMPHIS
May 12
AIDA

Same as Nov. 12 except:
Aida : Kirk (for Ilitsch)
Radames : Baum
Amonasro : Merrill
Ramfis : Vaghi

May 13
LE NOZZE DI FIGARO

Same as Dec. 3 except:
Almaviva : Brownlee
Cherubino : Stevens
Don Curzio : Garris
Barbarina : Farell
Second Peasant Girl :
    Stellman

ST. LOUIS
May 14
LOHENGRIN

Same as Mar. 26 except:
Lohengrin : Ralf
Herald : Thompson

May 15
AIDA

Same as Nov. 12 except:
Aida : Kirk (for Ilitsch)
Radames : Baum
Amonasro : Merrill
Ramfis : Vaghi

May 16
BORIS GODUNOV

Same as Mar. 11 except:
Xenia : Greer
Grigori : Berini
Marina : Stevens
Boyar : Chabay

May 17 (mat.)
MADAMA BUTTERFLY

Same as Nov. 26 except:
Cio Cio San : Ilitsch
B. F. Pinkerton : Tucker
Sharpless : Brownlee
Suzuki : Browning
Kate Pinkerton : Jordan

May 17
FAUST/Pelletier (c)

Same as Mar. 29 except:
Méphistophélès : Moscona
Valentin : Merrill
Siébel : Stellman
Marthe : Votipka
Wagner : Baker

ROCHESTER
May 19
LE NOZZE DI FIGARO

Same as Dec. 3 except:
Almaviva : Brownlee
Cherubino : Stevens
Barbarina : Farell
Second Peasant Girl :
    Stellman

1947 – 48

PHILADELPHIA
November 11
DON GIOVANNI/Rudolf (c)

Don Giovanni : Pinza
Donna Anna : Resnik
Donna Elvira : Stoska
Zerlina : Conner
Commendatore : Hines
Don Ottavio : Kullman
Leporello : Baccaloni
Masetto : Harrell

November 25
DIE MEISTERSINGER/Martin (c)

Hans Sachs : Janssen
Pogner : Ernster
Eva : Stoska

Magdalene : Harshaw
Walther : Ralf
Beckmesser : Pechner
Kothner : Harrell
Vogelgesang : Hayward
Nachtigall : Thompson
Zorn : Chabay
Eisslinger : Darcy
Moser : Oliviero
Ortel : Cehanovsky (for
    Hawkins)
Schwarz : Hines
Foltz : Alvary
David : Garris
Night Watchman : Kinsman

December 9
MANON/Fourestier (c)

Manon : Dosia
Lescaut : Singher
Des Grieux : Kullman
Count des Grieux : Moscona
Poussette : Greer
Javotte : Stellman
Rosette : Turner
Guillot : De Paolis
De Brétigny : Cehanovsky
Innkeeper : Luise
Guards : Marlowe, Baker
Servant : Savage

December 23
TOSCA/Antonicelli (c)

Tosca : Tassinari (d)
Cavaradossi : Tagliavini
Scarpia : Sved
Angelotti : Alvary
Sacristan : Luise
Spoletta : De Paolis
Sciarrone : Cehanovsky
Jailer : Davidson
Shepherd : Jordan

January 6
LOUISE/Fourestier (c)

Louise : Kirsten
Julien : Jobin
Mother : Harshaw
Father : Brownlee
Irma : Stellman
Camille : Votipka
Gertrude : Glaz
Apprentice : Raymondi
Elise : Manski
Blanche : Jordan
Suzanne : Lipton
Forewoman : Savage
Marguerite : Sachs
Madeleine : Lenchner
Painter : Cehanovsky
First Philosopher : Hines
Second Philosopher :
    Hawkins
Sculptor : Harvuot

1947–48

Poet : Marlowe
Student : Oliviero
Song Writer : Thompson
Street Sweeper : Sachs
Newspaper Girl : Lenchner
Young Rag Picker : Lipton
Milk Woman : Manski
Coal Picker : Altman
Noctambulist : Hayward
King of the Fools : De Paolis
First Policeman : Darcy
Second Policeman : Davidson
Rag Picker : Moscona
Junk Man : Kinsman
Street Arab : Raymondi
Old Clothes Man : Chabay
Bird Food Vendor : Lenchner
Artichoke Vendor : Votipka
Watercress Vendor : Altman
Chair Mender : Sachs
Carrot Vendor : Oliviero
Rag Vendor : Cehanovsky
Green Peas Vendor : Darcy

January 20
IL BARBIERE DI SIVIGLIA
Cimara (c)
Almaviva : Knight
Dr. Bartolo : Baccaloni
Rosina : Garcia (d)
Figaro : Valdengo
Don Basilio : Pinza
Berta : Altman
Fiorello : Baker
Sergeant : Oliviero
Ambrogio : Burgstaller

February 3
LA GIOCONDA/Cooper (c)
La Gioconda : Ilitsch
Laura : Stevens
Alvise : Moscona
La Cieca : Harshaw
Enzo : Tucker
Barnaba : Valentino
Zuane : Hawkins
First Singer : Davidson
Second Singer : Chabay
Isepo : Oliviero
Monk : Kinsman
Steersman : Baker

February 17
PETER GRIMES/Cooper (c)
Peter Grimes : Jagel
Ellen Orford : Resnik
Captain Balstrode : Brownlee
Auntie : Turner
Two Nieces : Lenchner,
   Stellman
Bob Boles : Hayward
Swallow : Hines
Mrs. (Nabob) Sedley : Lipton
Rev. Horace Adams : Garris
Ned Keene : Thompson

360

Hobson : Kinsman
Lawyer : Oliviero
Fisherwoman : Altman
Fisherman : Davidson
Dr. Thorp : Hill
Boy (John) : Smithers

March 2
DIE WALKÜRE/Stiedry (c)
Wotan : Berglund
Fricka : Thorborg
Brünnhilde : Traubel
Siegmund : Lorenz (for
   Melchior)
Sieglinde : Stoska
Hunding : Szekely
Helmwige : Stellman
Gerhilde : Votipka
Ortlinde : Jessner
Rossweisse : Browning
Grimgerde : Lipton
Waltraute : Palmer
Siegrune : Glaz
Schwertleite : Sachs

BALTIMORE

March 9
RIGOLETTO/Cimara (c)
Duke : Di Stefano (for
   Peerce)
Rigoletto : Warren
Gilda : Gracia
Sparafucile : Vaghi
Maddalena : Elmo
Giovanna : Sachs
Monterone : Hawkins
Marullo : Cehanovsky
Borsa : Chabay
Ceprano : Baker
Countess : Stellman
Page : Manski

BOSTON

March 15
DER ROSENKAVALIER/Busch (c)
Princess von Werdenberg :
   Jessner
Baron Ochs : Ernster
Octavian : Stevens
Von Faninal : Thompson
Sophie : Steber
Marianne : Votipka
Valzacchi : De Paolis
Annina : Lipton
Police Commissioner : Alvary
Majordomo of Princess :
   Darcy
Majordomo of Von Faninal :
   Marlowe
Notary : Pechner
Innkeeper : Chabay
Singer : Baum
Orphans : Altman, **Lenchner**,
   Stellman

Milliner : Manski
Hairdresser : Caton
Leopold : Burgstaller
Animal Vendor : Chabay
Negro Boy : Smithers

March 16
LA BOHÈME/Antonicelli (c)
Rodolfo : Tagliavini
Marcello : Brownlee
Schaunard : Cehanovsky
Colline : Vaghi
Mimi : Albanese
Musetta : Benzell
Benoit : Luise
Parpignol : Marlowe
Alcindoro : Luise
Sergeant : Davidson

March 17 (mat.)
RIGOLETTO
Same as Mar. 9 except:
Duke : Peerce
Rigoletto : Valentino (for
   Warren)
Gilda : Munsel
Sparafucile : Szekely
Monterone : Schon
Marullo : Pechner
Ceprano : Harvuot

March 17
MANON
Same as Dec. 9 except:
Manon : Sayao
Des Grieux : Di Stefano

March 18
DON GIOVANNI/Busch (c)
Same as Nov. 11 except:
Donna Anna : Bampton
Zerlina : Greer

March 19
SIEGFRIED/Stiedry (c)
Siegfried : Svanholm
Mime : Garris
Wanderer : Berglund
Alberich : Pechner
Fafner : Ernster
Erda : Thorborg
Brünnhilde : Traubel
Forest Bird : Lenchner

March 20 (mat.)
LOUISE
Same as Jan. 6 except:
Julien : Vinay
Blanche : Altman
First Philosopher : Alvary
Poet : Garris
Student : De Paolis
Carrot Vendor : De Paolis

March 20
LA TRAVIATA/Antonicelli (c)
Violetta : Albanese
Alfredo : Tucker
Germont : Warren
Flora : Manski
Annina : Altman
Gastone : Chabay
Baron Douphol : Cehanovsky
Marquis d'Obigny : Baker
Doctor Grenvil : Alvary

March 21 (mat.)
LUCIA DI LAMMERMOOR
Cimara (c)
Lucia : Pons
Alisa : Votipka
Edgardo : Peerce
Ashton : Valentino (for
Valdengo)
Raimondo : Vaghi
Arturo : Knight
Normanno : Marlowe

PHILADELPHIA
March 23
PARSIFAL/Stiedry (c)
Amfortas : Janssen
Titurel : Moscona (for
Ernster)
Gurnemanz : Berglund
Parsifal : Melchior
Klingsor : Pechner
Kundry : Thorborg
A Voice : Harshaw
Knights of the Grail :
Knight, Hawkins
Esquires : Greer, Browning,
Garris, Chabay
Flower Maidens : Greer,
Stellman (for Manski),
Lipton, Lenchner, Sachs,
(for Stellman), Browning

BALTIMORE
March 29
DON GIOVANNI/Busch (c)
Same as Nov. 11 except:
Donna Anna : Bampton
Zerlina : Sayao
Don Ottavio : Melton
Masetto : Alvary

March 30
LA BOHÈME
Same as Mar. 16 except:
Rodolfo : Bjoerling
Colline : Moscona
Musetta : Greer
Sergeant : Baker

RICHMOND
March 31
LA TRAVIATA
Same as Mar. 20 except:

Violetta : Steber
Alfredo : Peerce
Baron Douphol : Harvuot
Marquis d'Obigny : Hawkins

ATLANTA
April 1
CARMEN/Pelletier (c)
Carmen : Stevens
Don José : Baum
Micaela : Albanese (for
Pinza)
Escamillo : Singher
Zuniga : Kinsman
Morales : Baker
Frasquita : Votipka
Mercedes : Browning
Dancaire : Cehanovsky
Remendado : De Paolis

April 2
LUCIA DI LAMMERMOOR
Same as Mar. 21 except:
Alisa : Manski
Edgardo : Melton
Ashton : Warren
Raimondo : Moscona
Arturo : Hayward

April 3 (mat.)
DER ROSENKAVALIER
Same as Mar. 15 except:
Octavian : Novotna
Valzacchi : Garris
Annina : Glaz
Majordomo of Princess :
Chabay
Animal Vendor : Marlowe

April 3
LA BOHÈME
Same as Mar. 16 except:
Rodolfo : Bjoerling
Musetta : Greer

CHATTANOOGA
April 5
AIDA/Cooper (c)
King : Kinsman
Amneris : Thebom
Aida : Ilitsch
Radames : Baum
Amonasro : Warren
Ramfis : Moscona
Messenger : Chabay
Priestess : Stellman

MEMPHIS
April 6
DER ROSENKAVALIER
Same as Mar. 15 except:
Baron Ochs : List
Octavian : Novotna
Sophie : Conner

Valzacchi : Garris
Annina : Glaz
Majordomo of Princess :
Chabay
Singer : Hayward
Animal Vendor : Marlowe

April 7
LA TRAVIATA
Same as Mar. 20 except:
Violetta : Kirsten
Alfredo : Peerce
Germont : Valentino
Flora : Votipka
Gastone : De Paolis
Marquis d'Obigny : Hawkins
Doctor Grenvil : Harvuot

DALLAS
April 8
UN BALLO IN MASCHERA
Busch (c)
Riccardo : Bjoerling
Renato : Warren
Amelia : Ilitsch
Ulrica : Elmo
Oscar : Manski
Silvano : Baker
Samuel : Vaghi
Tom : Alvary
Judge : Chabay
Servant : Marlowe

April 9
MANON/Pelletier (c)
Same as Dec. 9 except:
Manon : Sayao
Des Grieux : Di Stefano
Count des Grieux : Pinza
Innkeeper : Pechner

April 10 (mat.)
LA TRAVIATA/Cimara (c)
Same as Mar. 20 except:
Alfredo : Peerce
Germont : Valentino
Flora : Votipka
Annina : Browning
Gastone : De Paolis
Marquis d'Obigny : Hawkins
Doctor Grenvil : Harvuot

April 10
CAVALLERIA RUSTICANA
Antonicelli (c)
Santuzza : Resnik
Lola : Lipton
Turiddu : Berini (for Jagel)
Alfio : Brownlee
Lucia : Turner

PAGLIACCI/Antonicelli (c)
Nedda : Kirsten (for
Quartararo)

Canio : Jagel (for Baum)
Tonio : Warren
Beppe : Chabay
Silvio : Thompson

LOS ANGELES

April 13
CARMEN

Same as Apr. 1 except:
Don José : Vinay
Micaela : Conner
Mercedes : Lipton

April 14
DIE WALKÜRE

Same as Mar. 2 except:
Fricka : Thebom
Siegmund : Melchior
Sieglinde : Bampton
Hunding : Ernster
Helmwige : Resnik
Schwertleite : Harshaw

April 15
PETER GRIMES

Same as Feb. 17 except:
Ellen Orford : Stoska
Lawyer : Marlowe

April 16
IL TROVATORE/Cooper (c)

Leonora : Resnik
Manrico : Bjoerling
Count di Luna : Warren
Azucena : Elmo
Inez : Manski
Ferrando : Hines
Ruiz : Chabay
Gypsy : Baker

April 17 (mat.)
DER ROSENKAVALIER

Same as Mar. 15 except:
Baron Ochs : List
Sophie : Conner
Annina : Glaz
Police Commissioner :
Hawkins
Majordomo of Princess :
Chabay
Animal Vendor : Marlowe

April 17
LA BOHÈME

Same as Mar. 16 except:
Rodolfo : Peerce
Mimi : Kirsten
Musetta : Greer
Benoit : Baccaloni
Parpignol : Tortolero (t)
Alcindoro : Baccaloni

April 18 (mat.)
AIDA

Same as Apr. 5 except:

Amneris : Harshaw
Radames : Vinay (for Baum)
Messenger : Marlowe

April 19
TRISTAN UND ISOLDE/Busch (c)

Tristan : Melchior
Isolde : Traubel
King Marke : Szekely
Kurvenal : Berglund
Brangaene : Thebom
Melot : Darcy
Steersman : Kinsman
Shepherd : Chabay
Sailor's Voice : Garris

April 20
MANON/Pelletier (c)

Same as Dec. 9 except:
Manon : Sayao
Des Grieux : Di Stefano
Count des Grieux : Pinza
Innkeeper : Pechner

April 21 (mat.)
MADAMA BUTTERFLY
Antonicelli (c)

Cio-Cio-San : Kirsten
B. F. Pinkerton : Tucker
Sharpless : Brownlee
Suzuki : Browning
Kate Pinkerton : Stellman
Goro : De Paolis
Yamadori : Cehanovsky
Uncle-Priest : Hawkins
Imperial Commissioner :
Baker

April 21
UN BALLO IN MASCHERA

Same as Apr. 8 except:
Amelia : Roman
Silvano : Harvuot

April 22
CAVALLERIA RUSTICANA

Same as Apr. 10 except:
Turiddu : Jagel
Alfio : Valentino

PAGLIACCI

Same as Apr. 10 except:
Nedda : Quartararo
Canio : Vinay
Tonio : Valdengo

April 23
DIE ZAUBERFLÖTE (English)
Stiedry (c)

Sarastro : Pinza
Tamino : Kullman
High Priest : Hines
Two Priests : Hayward,
Harvuot

Queen of the Night : Benzell
Pamina : Stoska
Three Ladies : Jessner,
Stellman, Lipton
Papageno : Brownlee
Papagena : Greer
Monostatos : Garris
Three Genii : Lenchner,
Manski, Glaz
Guards : Darcy, Davidson

April 24 (mat.)
LA TRAVIATA

Same as Mar. 20 except:
Violetta : Sayao
Alfredo : Peerce
Flora : Votipka
Gastone : De Paolis
Marquis d'Obigny : Hawkins
Doctor Grenvil : Harvuot

DENVER

April 26
AIDA

Same as Apr. 5 except:
Aida : Roman
Ramfis : Hines
Messenger : Marlowe

April 27 (mat.)
LA BOHÈME

Same as Mar. 16 except:
Rodolfo : Peerce
Marcello : Valentino
Schaunard : Thompson
Colline : Moscona
Musetta : Greer
Benoit : Baccaloni
Alcindoro : Baccaloni

April 27
CARMEN

Same as Apr. 1 except:
Don José : Vinay
Micaela : Pinza
Zuniga : Alvary

LINCOLN

April 28
TOSCA

Same as Dec. 23 except:
Tosca : Resnik
Cavaradossi : Bjoerling
Scarpia : Brownlee
Sacristan : Baccaloni
Shepherd : Altman

ST. LOUIS

April 29
DER ROSENKAVALIER
Rudolf (c)

Same as Mar. 15 except:
Baron Ochs : List
Sophie : Conner

Valzacchi : Garris
Majordomo of Princess :
  Chabay
Milliner : Greer
Animal Vendor : Marlowe

April 30
CAVALLERIA RUSTICANA
Same as Apr. 10 except:
Santuzza : Roman
Turiddu : Bjoerling

PAGLIACCI
Same as Apr. 10 except:
Nedda : Quartararo
Canio : Vinay
Tonio : Valdengo

May 1
LA TRAVIATA
Same as Mar. 20 except:
Violetta · Kirsten
Alfredo : Peerce
Germont : Valentino
Flora : Votipka
Gastone : De Paolis
Marquis d'Obigny : Hawkins

BLOOMINGTON
May 3
DER ROSENKAVALIER
  Rudolf (c)
Same as Mar. 15 except:
Baron Ochs : List
Sophie · Conner
Valzacchi : Garris
Majordomo of Princess :
  Chabay
Animal Vendor : Marlowe

May 4
DON GIOVANNI
Same as Nov. 11 except:
Donna Elvira : Quartararo
Zerlina : Greer
Masetto : Alvary

LAFAYETTE
May 5
LA TRAVIATA
Same as Mar. 20 except:
Violetta : Kirsten
Alfredo : Peerce
Germont : Valentino
Flora : Stellman
Annina : Browning
Gastone : De Paolis
Doctor Grenvil : Hawkins

MINNEAPOLIS
May 6
DER ROSENKAVALIER
  Rudolf (c)
Same as Mar. 15 except:

Baron Ochs : List
Sophie : Conner
Valzacchi : Garris
Majordomo of Princess :
  Chabay
Animal Vendor : Marlowe

May 7
DON GIOVANNI
Same as Nov. 11 except:
Donna Anna : Kirk
Donna Elvira : Quartararo
Zerlina : Sayao
Masetto : Alvary

May 8 (mat.)
IL TROVATORE
Same as Apr. 16 except:
Ferrando : Moscona

May 8
TOSCA
Same as Dec. 23 except:
Tosca : Roman
Cavaradossi : Peerce
Scarpia : Brownlee
Angelotti : Thompson
Shepherd : Altman

CLEVELAND
May 10
MANON/Pelletier (c)
Same as Dec. 9 except:
Manon : Sayao
Des Grieux : Di Stefano
  (for Melton)
Count des Grieux : Pinza

May 11
DIE MEISTERSINGER/Busch (c)
Same as Nov. 25 except:
Eva : Jessner (for Stoska)
Walther : Kullman
Kothner : Schon
Moser : Marlowe
Ortel : Hawkins

May 12
LA BOHÈME
Same as Mar. 16 except:
Rodolfo : Peerce
Schaunard : Thompson
Colline : Moscona
Mimi : Kirsten
Musetta : Greer
Benoit : Baccaloni
Alcindoro : Baccaloni

May 13
IL TROVATORE
Same as Apr. 16 except:
Leonora : Roman
Count di Luna : Merrill

May 14 (mat.)
CAVALLERIA RUSTICANA
  Cimara (c)
Same as Apr. 10 except:
Lola : Altman (for Lipton)
Turiddu : Tucker

PAGLIACCI/Cimara (c)
Same as Apr. 10 except:
Nedda : Quartararo
Canio : Baum
Tonio : Valdengo

May 14
DON GIOVANNI
Same as Nov. 11 except:
Donna Anna : Bampton
Zerlina : Sayao
Masetto : Alvary

May 15
UN BALLO IN MASCHERA
Same as Apr. 8 except:
Renato : Valentino
Oscar : Greer
Samuel : Moscona

ROCHESTER
May 17
DER ROSENKAVALIER
Same as Mar. 15 except:
Baron Ochs : List
Valzacchi : Garris
Majordomo of Princess :
  Chabay
Milliner : Greer
Animal Vendor : Marlowe

1 9 4 8 – 4 9

PHILADELPHIA
December 7
GÖTTERDÄMMERUNG
  Stiedry (c)
Siegfried : Melchior
Gunther : Janssen
Hagen : Ernster
Alberich : Pechner
Brünnhilde : Traubel
Gutrune : Stoska
Waltraute : Harshaw
Woglinde : Manski
Wellgunde : Stellman
Flosshilde : Glaz
First Norn : Madeira
Second Norn : Lipton
Third Norn : Palmer
Vassals : Darcy, Hawkins

December 21
IL TROVATORE/Cooper (c)
Leonora : Roman
Manrico : Bjoerling

1948–49

Count di Luna : **Valentino**
Azucena : Elmo
Inez : Manski
Ferrando : Hines
Ruiz : Marlowe
Gypsy : Davidson

January 4
Mignon/Pelletier (c)

Mignon : Stevens
Philine : Munsel
Wilhelm : Melton
Lothario : Hines
Laerte : De Paolis
Jarno : Hawkins
Frederic : Madeira
Antonio : Davidson

January 18
Le Nozze di Figaro/Busch (c)

Almaviva : Brownlee
Countess : Steber
Susanna : Sayao
Figaro : Tajo
Cherubino : Novotna
Marcellina : Glaz
Bartolo : Baccaloni
Basilio : De Paolis
Don Curzio : Chabay
Antonio : Alvary
Barbarina : Bollinger
Peasant Girls : Altman,
Raymondi

February 1
Siegfried/Stiedry (c)

Siegfried : Svanholm
Mime : Garris
Wanderer : Berglund
Alberich : Pechner
Fafner : Vichegonov
Erda : Harshaw
Brünnhilde : Traubel
Forest Bird : Lenchner

February 15
L'Elisir d'Amore
Antonicelli (c)

Adina : Sayao
Nemorino : Tagliavini
Belcore : Valdengo
Dulcamara : Baccaloni
Giannetta : Lenchner

March 1
Gianni Schicchi
Antonicelli (c)

Gianni Schicchi : Tajo
Lauretta : Albanese
La Vecchia : Elmo
Rinuccio : Di Stefano
Gherardo : De Paolis
Nella : Lenchner
Betto : Cehanovsky
Simone : Moscona

364

Marco : Pechner
La Ciesca : Votipka
Spinelloccio : Luise
Nicolao : Alvary
Pinellino : Hawkins
Guccio : Baker
Gherardino : R. Tonry, Jr.

Salome/Reiner (c)

Herod : Jagel
Herodias : Thorborg
Salome : Welitch
Jokanaan : Janssen
Narraboth : Garris
Page : Glaz
First Nazarene : Ernster
Second Nazarene : Darcy
First Jew : Chabay
Second Jew : Hayward
Third Jew : De Paolis
Fourth Jew : Franke
Fifth Jew : Pechner
First Soldier : Hines
Second Soldier : Kinsman
Cappadocian : Hawkins
Slave : Manski

March 15
La Traviata/Antonicelli (c)

Violetta : Albanese (for
Kirsten)
Alfredo : Peerce
Germont : Warren
Flora : Votipka
Annina : Altman
Gastone : Chabay
Baron Douphol : Cehanovsky
Marquis d'Obigny : Baker
Doctor Grenvil : Alvary

BALTIMORE
March 21
Otello/Cellini (c—t)

Otello : Vinay
Desdemona : Albanese
Iago : Warren
Emilia : Lipton
Cassio : Garris
Roderigo : Chabay
(for Hayward)
Lodovico : Moscona
Montano : Harvuot
Herald : Kinsman

March 22
Le Nozze di Figaro

Same as Jan. 18 except:
Almaviva : Valentino
Cherubino : Stevens
Second Peasant Girl :
Stellman

BOSTON
March 23
La Traviata

Same as Mar. 15 except:

Germont : Merrill
Doctor Grenvil : Hawkins

March 24
Gianni Schicchi

Same as Mar. 1 except:
Gianni Schicchi : Baccaloni
Lauretta : Conner
Gherardino : Smithers

Salome

Same as Mar. 1 except:
Jokanaan : Berglund
Narraboth : Sullivan
Second Nazarene : Baker
Second Jew : Murray (for
Hayward)

March 25
Le Nozze di Figaro
Reiner (c)

Same as Jan. 18 except:
Cherubino : Bollinger
Barbarina : Lenchner
Second Peasant Girl :
Stellman

March 26 (mat.)
Mignon

Same as Jan. 4 except:
Philine : Benzell (for
Munsel)
Wilhelm : Di Stefano
Laerte : Garris

March 26
Aida/Cooper (c)

King : Kinsman
Amneris : Harshaw
Aida : Ribla
Radames : Baum
Amonasro : Valentino
Ramfis : Moscona
Messenger : Franke
Priestess : Votipka

March 28
Madama Butterfly
Antonicelli (c)

Cio-Cio-San : Kirsten
B. F. Pinkerton : Kullman
Sharpless : Brownlee
Suzuki : Browning
Kate Pinkerton : Manski
Goro : De Paolis
Yamadori : Cehanovsky
Uncle-Priest : Luise
Imperial Commissioner :
Baker

March 29
Il Trovatore

Same as Dec. 21 except:
Azucena : Harshaw (for
Elmo)
Inez : Stellman

March 30 (mat.)
CARMEN/Pelletier (c)
Carmen : Stevens
Don José : Vinay
Micaela : Bollinger (for
Pinza)
Escamillo : Merrill
Zuniga : Kinsman
Morales : Baker
Frasquita : Votipka
Mercedes : Lipton
Dancaire : Cehanovsky
Remendado : De Paolis

March 30
LA BOHÈME/Antonicelli (c)
Rodolfo : Tagliavini
Marcello : Valentino
Schaunard : Thompson
Colline : Moscona
Mimi : Sayao
Musetta : Benzell
Benoit : Luise
Parpignol : Marlowe
Alcindoro : Luise
Sergeant : Davidson

March 31
PETER GRIMES/Cooper (c)
Peter Grimes : Sullivan
Ellen Orford : Stoska
Captain Balstrode : Brownlee
Auntie : Madeira
Nieces : Lenchner, Stellman
Bob Boles : Chabay (for
Hayward)
Swallow : Hines
Mrs. (Nabob) Sedley : Lipton
Rev. Horace Adams : Garris
Ned Keene : Thompson
Hobson : Kinsman
Lawyer : Marlowe
Fisherwoman : Altman
Fisherman : Davidson
Dr. Thorp : Vittucci
Boy (John) : Smithers

April 1
TRISTAN UND ISOLDE
Rudolf (c)
Tristan : Svanholm
Isolde : Traubel
King Marke : Ernster
Kurvenal : Janssen
Brangaene : Thebom
Melot : Darcy
Steersman : Kinsman
Shepherd : Chabay
Sailor's Voice : Garris

April 2 (mat.)
OTELLO
Same as Mar. 21

April 2
IL BARBIERE DI SIVIGLIA
Cimara (c)
Almaviva : Knight
Dr. Bartolo : Baccaloni
Rosina : Munsel
Figaro : Merrill
Don Basilio : Tajo
Berta : Turner
Fiorello : Baker
Sergeant : Franke
Ambrogio : Burgstaller

CLEVELAND
April 4
LUCIA DI LAMMERMOOR
Cimara (c)
Lucia : Pons
Alisa : Votipka
Edgardo : Tagliavini
Ashton : Valentino
Raimondo : Moscona
Arturo : Chabay (for
Hayward)
Normanno : Franke

April 5
MIGNON
Same as Jan. 4 except:
Wilhelm : Di Stefano
Laerte : Garris

April 6
LA TRAVIATA
Same as Mar. 15 except:
Germont : Merrill
Gastone : De Paolis
Marquis d'Obigny : Davidson

April 7
RIGOLETTO/Cimara (c)
Duke : Bjoerling
Rigoletto : Warren
Gilda : Pons
Sparafucile : Moscona
Maddalena : Lipton (for
Elmo)
Giovanna : Altman
Monterone : Harvuot
Marullo : Cehanovsky
Borsa : Chabay
Ceprano : Baker
Countess : Stellman
Page : Altman

April 8 (mat.)
MADAMA BUTTERFLY
Rudolf (c)
Same as Mar. 28 except:
Kate Pinkerton : Stellman
Uncle-Priest : Hawkins

April 8
L'ELISIR D'AMORE
Same as Feb. 15 except:
Giannetta : Manski

April 9 (mat.)
IL BARBIERE DI SIVIGLIA
Cellini (c)
Same as Apr. 2 except:
Figaro : Valentino
Berta : Altman

April 9
OTELLO/Busch (c)
Same as Mar. 21

ROCHESTER
April 11
MADAMA BUTTERFLY
Same as Mar. 28 except:
Suzuki : Altman
Kate Pinkerton : Stellman
Uncle-Priest : Hawkins

ATLANTA
April 18
OTELLO/Busch(c)
Same as Mar. 21

April 19
MIGNON
Same as Jan. 4 except:
Wilhelm : Di Stefano
Laerte : Garris
*(Garris was found murdered
on April 21)*

April 20 (mat.)
LA TRAVIATA/Cimara (c)
Same as Mar. 15 except:
Violetta : Kirsten
Alfredo : Kullman
Germont : Merrill
Gastone : De Paolis

April 20
L'ELISIR D'AMORE
Same as Feb. 15 except:
Belcore : Brownlee
Giannetta : Manski

MEMPHIS
April 21
LUCIA DI LAMMERMOOR
Same as Apr. 4 except:
Lucia : Munsel
Alisa : Stellman
Ashton : Valdengo
Raimondo : Hines
Arturo : Hayward

DALLAS
April 22
OTELLO/Busch (c)
Same as Mar. 21 except:
Cassio : De Paolis (for
Garris)

1948–49

April 23 (mat.)
MIGNON
Same as Jan. 4 except:
Wilhelm : Di Stefano
Laerte : Chabay (for Garris)

April 23
LE NOZZE DI FIGARO
Same as Jan. 18 except:
Cherubino : Bollinger
Barbarina : Lenchner
Second Peasant Girl :
Stellman

April 24 (mat.)
AIDA
Same as Mar. 26 except:
Aida : Roman
Radames : Svanholm

LOS ANGELES
April 26
RIGOLETTO
Same as Apr. 7 except:
Duke : Peerce
Gilda : Conner
Sparafucile : Hines
Countess : Manski

April 27
LE NOZZE DI FIGARO
Same as Jan. 18 except:
Second Peasant Girl :
Stellman

April 28
LUCIA DI LAMMERMOOR
Same as Apr. 4 except:
Lucia : Munsel
Edgardo : Tucker
Ashton : Merrill
Arturo : Hayward

April 29
CARMEN
Same as Mar. 30 except:
Micaela : Quartararo
Escamillo : Guarrera
Zuniga : Alvary
Morales : Harvuot
Mercedes : Browning

April 30 (mat.)
LA TRAVIATA
Same as Mar. 15 except:
Violetta : Sayao
Alfredo : Melton
Germont : Valentino
Annina : Madeira
Marquis d'Obigny : Davidson
Doctor Grenvil : Hawkins

April 30
IL BARBIERE DI SIVIGLIA
Same as Apr. 2 except:
Figaro : Valdengo
Berta : Altman

366

May 1 (mat.)
LA BOHÈME
Same as Mar. 30 except:
Rodolfo : Di Stefano
Marcello : Brownlee
Mimi : Albanese
Benoit : Alvary
Parpignol : Franke
Alcindoro : Alvary

May 2
AIDA
Same as Mar. 26 except:
Amneris : Thebom
Aida : Roman
Amonasro : Guarrera

May 3
PETER GRIMES
Same as Mar. 31 except:
Bob Boles : Hayward
Rev. Horace Adams : Franke
(for Garris)
Lawyer : Franke

May 4
MIGNON
Same as Jan. 4 except:
Philine : Cotlow
Laerte : Chabay (for Garris)

May 5
LA BOHÈME
Same as Mar. 30 except:
Rodolfo : Peerce
Schaunard : Cehanovsky
Colline : Tajo
Mimi : Kirsten
Benoit : Baccaloni
Parpignol : Franke
Alcindoro : Baccaloni
Sergeant : Baker

May 6
L'ELISIR D'AMORE
Same as Feb. 15 except:
Nemorino : Di Stefano
Dulcamara : Tajo

May 7 (mat.)
CARMEN
Same as Mar. 30 except:
Don José : Baum
Micaela : Albanese
Escamillo : Guarrera
Zuniga : Alvary
Mercedes : Browning

May 7
LA TRAVIATA
Same as Mar. 15 except:
Violetta : Kirsten
Alfredo : Tucker
Germont : Valdengo
Flora : Stellman

Baron Douphol : Harvuot
(for Thompson)
Marquis d'Obigny : Davidson
Doctor Grenvil : Hawkins

DENVER
May 9
OTELLO/Busch (c)
Same as Mar. 21 except:
Iago : Valdengo
Cassio : Chabay
Roderigo : Hayward

May 10 (mat.)
LUCIA DI LAMMERMOOR
Same as Apr. 4 except:
Lucia : Munsel
Edgardo : Peerce
Ashton : Guarrera

May 10
MIGNON
Same as Jan. 4 except:
Philine : Cotlow
Wilhelm : Di Stefano

DES MOINES
May 11
LA BOHÈME
Same as Mar. 30 except:
Rodolfo : Tucker
Marcello : Valdengo
Schaunard : Cehanovsky
Colline : Tajo
Benoit : Baccaloni
Parpignol : Franke
Alcindoro : Baccaloni
Sergeant : Baker

MINNEAPOLIS
May 12
OTELLO/Busch (c)
Same as Mar. 21 except:
Cassio : Chabay
Roderigo : Hayward

May 13
MIGNON
Same as Jan. 4 except:
Philine : Cotlow

May 14 (mat.)
IL BARBIERE DI SIVIGLIA
Same as Apr. 2 except:
Figaro : Valdengo
Berta : Altman

May 14
LA BOHÈME
Same as Mar. 30 except:
Rodolfo : Tucker
Schaunard : Cehanovsky
Benoit : Alvary
Parpignol : Tortolero (t)
Alcindoro : Alvary

BLOOMINGTON
May 16
LUCIA DI LAMMERMOOR
Same as Apr. 4 except:
Lucia : Munsel
Alisa : Manski
Edgardo : Peerce
Ashton : Valdengo
Arturo : Hayward

May 17
CARMEN
Same as Mar. 30 except:
Escamillo : Guarrera
Zuniga : Alvary
Morales : Harvuot
Mercedes : Madeira

LAFAYETTE
May 18
MIGNON
Same as Jan. 4 except:
Mignon : Thebom
Philine : Cotlow
Wilhelm : Di Stefano
Laerte : Chabay

ST. LOUIS
May 19
LUCIA DI LAMMERMOOR
Same as Apr. 4 except:
Lucia : Munsel
Alisa : Manski
Edgardo : Peerce
Ashton : Merrill
Arturo : Hayward

May 20
CARMEN
Same as Mar. 30 except:
Micaela : Quartararo
Escamillo : Guarrera
Zuniga : Alvary
Morales : Harvuot

May 21
LA BOHÈME
Same as Mar. 30 except:
Rodolfo : Di Stefano
Schaunard : Cehanovsky
Benoit : Alvary
Parpignol : Franke
Alcindoro : Alvary
Sergeant : Baker

1949 – 50

PHILADELPHIA
November 29
MANON LESCAUT
Antonicelli (c)
Manon : Kirsten
Lescaut : Valdengo
Des Grieux : Bjoerling

Geronte : Baccaloni
Edmondo : Hayward
Ballet Master : De Paolis
Innkeeper : Cehanovsky
Musician : Madeira
Sergeant : Harvuot
Lamplighter : Franke
Captain : Hawkins

December 6
TRISTAN UND ISOLDE
Perlea (c)
Tristan : Melchior
Isolde : Traubel
King Marke : Szekely
Kurvenal : Janssen
Brangaene : Thebom
Melot : Darcy
Steersman : Harbour
Shepherd : Klein
Sailor's Voice : Chabay

December 20
LA BOHÈME/Antonicelli (c)
Rodolfo : Tagliavini
Marcello : Brownlee
Schaunard : Thompson
Colline : Moscona
Mimi : Sayao
Musetta : Hunt
Benoit : Luise
Parpignol : Franke
Alcindoro : Luise
Sergeant : Baker

January 3
SIMON BOCCANEGRA
Stiedry (c)
Simon Boccanegra : Warren
Jacopo Fiesco : Szekely
Paolo : Valdengo
Pietro : Alvary
Maria : Varnay
Gabriele : Tucker
Captain : Franke
Maidservant : Altman

January 17
DER ROSENKAVALIER
Reiner (c)
Princess von Werdenberg :
Steber
Baron Ochs : List
Octavian : Novotna
Von Faninal : Thompson
Sophie : Berger
Marianne : Votipka
Valzacchi : Klein
Annina : Glaz
Police Commissioner : Alvary
Majordomo of Princess :
Darcy
Majordomo of Von Faninal :
Franke
Notary : Pechner

Innkeeper : Chabay
Singer : Baum
Orphans : Lenchner,
Stellman, Altman
Milliner : Hunt
Hairdresser : Vittucci
Leopold : Burgstaller
Animal Vendor : Chabay
Negro Boy : Smithers

January 31
DIE MEISTERSINGER
Reiner (c)
Hans Sachs : Janssen
Pogner : Ernster
Eva : Varnay
Magdalene : Thorborg
Walther : Svanholm
Beckmesser : Pechner
Kothner : Schon
Vogelgesang : Franke
Nachtigall : Thompson
Zorn : De Paolis
Eisslinger : Darcy
Moser : Chabay
Ortel : Hawkins
Schwarz : Davidson
Foltz : Alvary
David : Klein
Night Watchman : Harvuot

February 14
DON GIOVANNI/Reiner (c)
Don Giovanni : Schoeffler
Donna Anna : Welitch
Donna Elvira : Resnik
Zerlina : Munsel
Commendatore : Moscona
Don Ottavio : Peerce
Leporello : Baccaloni
Masetto : Harrell

March 7
FAUST/Pelletier (c)
Faust : Conley
Marguerite : Kirsten
Méphistophélès : Tajo
Valentin : Guarrera
Siébel : Bollinger
Marthe : Turner
Wagner : Harbour

BALTIMORE
March 14
TOSCA/Antonicelli (c)
Tosca : Welitch
Cavaradossi : Peerce
Scarpia : Schoeffler
Angelotti : Alvary
Sacristan : Pechner
Spoletta : Chabay
Sciarrone : Cehanovsky
Jailer : Davidson
Shepherd : Altman

367

March 15
LOHENGRIN/Stiedry (c)

King Henry : Moscona
Lohengrin : Lorenz
Elsa : Traubel
Telramund : Janssen
Ortrud : Varnay
Herald : Guarrera

BOSTON
March 27
MANON LESCAUT

Same as Nov. 29 except:
Des Grieux : Tucker

March 28
FAUST

Same as Mar. 7 except:
Faust : Di Stefano
Marguerite : Albanese
Siébel : Manski
Wagner : Baker

March 29 (mat.)
RIGOLETTO/Perlea (c)

Duke : Peerce
Rigoletto : Warren
Gilda : Conner (for Munsel)
Sparafucile : Moscona
Maddalena : Lipton
Giovanna : Altman
Monterone : Harvuot
Marullo : Cehanovsky
Borsa : Chabay
Ceprano : Baker
Countess : Bollinger
Page : Altman

March 29
DIE WALKÜRE/Stiedry (c)

Wotan : Janssen
Fricka : Thebom
Brünnhilde : Traubel
Siegmund : Svanholm
Sieglinde : Bampton
Hunding : Vichegonov
Helmwige : Stellman
Gerhilde : Votipka
Ortlinde : Jessner
Rossweisse : Browning
Grimgerde : Turner
Waltraute : Palmer
Siegrune : Glaz
Schwertleite : Madeira

March 30
TOSCA

Same as Mar. 14 except:
Cavaradossi : Bjoerling
Angelotti : Thompson
Spoletta : De Paolis
Jailer : Baker

March 31
SIMON BOCCANEGRA

Same as Jan. 3 except:
Jacopo Fiesco : Vichegonov
Paolo : Thompson
Maria : Roman

April 1 (mat.)
DER ROSENKAVALIER

Same as Jan. 17 except:
Octavian : Stevens
Sophie : Conner
Valzacchi : De Paolis
Annina : Lipton
Milliner : Manski

April 1
AIDA/Cooper (c)

King : Kinsman
Amneris : Thebom
Aida : Roman
Radames : Vinay
Amonasro : Valentino
Ramfis : Moscona
Messenger : Franke
Priestess : Votipka

April 2 (mat.)
LOHENGRIN

Same as Mar. 15 except:
King Henry : Ernster
Lohengrin : Svanholm
Telramund : Sved
Ortrud : Harshaw

CLEVELAND
April 10
SAMSON ET DALILA/Cooper (c)

Dalila : Stevens
Samson : Vinay
High Priest : Merrill
Abimelech : Hawkins
Old Hebrew : Hines
Philistine Messenger : Darcy
Philistines : Franke (for
  Chabay), Harvuot

April 11
LA BOHÈME/Cimara (c)

Same as Dec. 20 except:
Rodolfo : Peerce
Schaunard : Cehanovsky
Benoit : Pechner
Alcindoro : Pechner

April 12
FAUST

Same as Mar. 7 except:
Faust : Di Stefano
Marguerite : Albanese
Valentin : Warren
Wagner : Baker

April 13
LOHENGRIN

Same as Mar. 15 except:
King Henry : Ernster
Lohengrin : Svanholm
Ortrud : Harshaw
Herald : Thompson

April 14 (mat.)
AIDA/Rudolf (c)

Same as Apr. 1 except:
Radames : Baum
Amonasro : Merrill
Priestess : Bollinger

April 14
TOSCA

Same as Mar. 14 except:
Cavaradossi : Tagliavini
Scarpia : Sved
Angelotti : Thompson
Spoletta : De Paolis

April 15 (mat.)
CARMEN/Perlea (c)

Carmen : Stevens
Don José : Kullman
Micaela : Conner
Escamillo : Guarrera
Zuniga : Alvary
Morales : Baker
Frasquita : Manski
Mercedes : Browning
Dancaire : Cehanovsky
Remendado : De Paolis (for
  Chabay)

April 15
MANON LESCAUT

Same as Nov. 29 except:
Innkeeper : Davidson

BLOOMINGTON
April 17
LOHENGRIN

Same as Mar. 15 except:
King Henry : Ernster
Lohengrin : Svanholm
Elsa : Bampton
Ortrud : Harshaw
Herald : Thompson

April 18
SAMSON ET DALILA

Same as Apr. 10 except:
Old Hebrew : Moscona

LAFAYETTE
April 19
AIDA

Same as Apr. 1 except:
Radames : Baum
Amonasro : Guarrera
Ramfis : Hines
Priestess : Bollinger

ST. LOUIS

April 20

DIE MEISTERSINGER

Same as Jan. 31 except:
Hans Sachs : Schoeffler
Eva : Stoska
Magdalene : Harshaw
Vogelgesang : Hayward
Moser : Franke
David : Laufkoetter (t)

April 21

TOSCA

Same as Mar. 14 except:
Cavaradossi : Tagliavini
Scarpia : Sved
Spoletta : De Paolis

April 22 (mat.)

RIGOLETTO

Same as Mar. 29 except:
Duke : Di Stefano
Gilda : Munsel
Sparafucile : Hines
Maddalena : Madeira
Monterone : Schon
Borso : De Paolis
Countess : Manski

April 22

SAMSON ET DALILA

Same as Apr. 10 except:
Samson : Baum
Old Hebrew : Moscona

ATLANTA

April 24

TOSCA

Same as Mar. 14 except:
Cavaradossi : Tagliavini
Scarpia : Brownlee
Spoletta : De Paolis

April 25

LOHENGRIN

Same as Mar. 15 except:
King Henry : Ernster
Lohengrin : Svanholm
Elsa : Varnay
Ortrud : Thebom

April 26 (mat.)

FAUST

Same as Mar. 7 except:
Faust : Di Stefano
Marguerite : Albanese
Valentin : Merrill
Siébel : Manski
Wagner : Baker

April 26

RIGOLETTO

Same as Mar. 29 except:
Duke : Tucker

Gilda : Munsel
Sparafucile : Hines
Maddalena : Madeira
Monterone : Hawkins
Borsa : De Paolis
Ceprano : Harvuot

MEMPHIS

April 27

LA BOHÈME

Same as Dec. 20 except:
Rodolfo : Di Stefano
(for Peerce)
Schaunard : Harvuot
Mimi : Albanese
Benoit : Pechner
Alcindoro : Pechner

DALLAS

April 28

L'ELISIR D'AMORE
Antonicelli (c)

Adina : Sayao
Nemorino : Tagliavini
Belcore : Valdengo
Dulcamara : Tajo
Giannetta : Lenchner

April 29 (mat.)

FAUST

Same as Mar. 7 except:
Faust : Di Stefano
Marguerite : Conner
Méphistophélès : Hines
Valentin : Warren
Siébel : Manski
Wagner : Baker

April 29

TOSCA

Same as Mar. 14 except:
Cavaradossi : Tucker
Scarpia : Sved
Spoletta : De Paolis

April 30 (mat.)

SAMSON ET DALILA

Same as Apr. 10 except:
Old Hebrew : Moscona
Philistine Messenger :
De Paolis (for Darcy)

HOUSTON

May 1

LA TRAVIATA/Perlea (c)

Violetta : Albanese
Alfredo : Peerce
Germont : Merrill
Flora : Manski
Annina : Altman
Gastone : De Paolis
Baron Douphol : Cehanovsky
Marquis d'Obigny : Baker
Doctor Grenvil : Alvary

May 2

LOHENGRIN

Same as Mar. 15 except:
King Henry : Ernster
Lohengrin : Svanholm
Elsa : Varnay
Ortrud : Thebom

OKLAHOMA CITY

May 3

CARMEN

Same as Apr. 15 except:
Don José : Vinay
Escamillo : Merrill
Zuniga : Kinsman
Morales : Harvuot
Frasquita : Bollinger
Mercedes : Madeira

DES MOINES

May 4

FAUST

Same as Mar. 7 except:
Faust : Kullman
Marguerite : Albanese
Méphistophélès : Hines
(for Tajo)
Siébel : Manski
Wagner : Baker

MINNEAPOLIS

May 5

DIE MEISTERSINGER

Same as Jan. 31 except:
Magdalene : Harshaw
Vogelgesang : Hayward
Nachtigall : Baker
Moser : Franke
David : Laufkoetter

May 6 (mat.)

AIDA

Same as Apr. 1 except:
Aida : Ribla
Radames : Baum
Amonasro : Guarrera
Ramfis : Hines
Priestess : Bollinger

May 6

L'ELISIR D'AMORE

Same as Apr. 28 except:
Adina : Munsel
Belcore : Valentino

May 7 (mat.)

CARMEN

Same as Apr. 15 except:
Don José : Vinay
Escamillo : Merrill
Morales : Harvuot
Frasquita : Bollinger
Mercedes : Madeira

369

CHICAGO
May 8

TOSCA

Same as Mar. 14 except:
Cavaradossi : Bjoerling
Scarpia : Sved
Spoletta : De Paolis
Sciarrone : Harvuot

May 9

CARMEN

Same as Apr. 15 except:
Don José : Vinay
Escamillo : Merrill
Morales : Harvuot
Frasquita : Bollinger
Mercedes : Madeira

May 10

LA TRAVIATA

Same as May 1 except:
Alfredo : Di Stefano
Germont : Warren
Gastone : Franke
Marquis d'Obigny : Davidson
Doctor Grenvil : Hawkins

May 11

DIE MEISTERSINGER

Same as Jan. 31 except:
Magdalene : Harshaw
Vogelgesang : Hayward
Nachtigall : Baker
Moser : Franke
David : Laufkoetter

May 12

RIGOLETTO

Same as Mar. 29 except:
Duke : Bjoerling
Gilda : Munsel
Sparafucile : Hines
Maddalena : Madeira
Monterone : Schon
Borsa : De Paolis
Countess : Manski

May 13 (mat.)

AIDA

Same as Apr. 1 except:
Amneris : Harshaw
Radames : Baum
Amonasro : Merrill
Ramfis : Hines
Priestess : Bollinger

May 13

LA BOHÈME

Same as Dec. 20 except:
Marcello : Valentino
Schaunard : Cehanovsky
Colline : Alvary (for Tajo)
Mimi : Kirsten
Benoit : Pechner
Alcindoro : Pechner

370

ROCHESTER
May 15

FAUST

Same as Mar. 7 except:
Faust : Di Stefano
Marguerite : Conner
Méphistophélès : Vichegonov
Valentin : Merrill
Marthe : Altman
Wagner : Baker

1950 – 51

Rudolf Bing, *General Manager*

PHILADELPHIA
November 28

DON CARLO/Stiedry (c)

Philip II : Siepi
Don Carlo : Bjoerling
Rodrigo : Merrill
Grand Inquisitor : Hotter
Friar : Vichegonov
Elizabeth : Rigal
Princess Eboli : Barbieri
Theobald : Bollinger
Count Lerma : Franke
Herald : Darcy
Voice : Amara
Countess Aremberg : Morse

January 9

DER ROSENKAVALIER
Reiner (c)

Princess von Werdenberg :
Traubel
Baron Ochs : Krenn
Octavian : Novotna
(for Stevens)
Von Faninal : Brownlee
Sophie : Berger
Marianne : Votipka
Valzacchi : De Paolis
Annina : Glaz
Police Commissioner : Alvary
Majordomo of Princess :
Darcy
Majordomo of Von Faninal :
Franke
Notary : Davidson
Innkeeper : Chabay
Singer : Baum
Orphans : Troxell, Lenchner,
Roggero
Milliner : Warner
Hairdresser : Barone
Leopold : Burgstaller
Animal Vendor : Chabay
Negro Boy : Smithers

February 20

CAVALLERIA RUSTICANA
Erede (c)

Santuzza : Milanov

Lola : Lipton
Turiddu : Tucker
Alfio : Harvuot
Lucia : Madeira

PAGLIACCI/Erede (c)

Nedda : Rigal
Canio : Vinay
Tonio : Warren
Beppe : Hayward
Silvio : Guarrera

BALTIMORE
March 27

FAUST/Cleva (c)

Faust : Di Stefano
Marguerite : De Los Angeles
Méphistophélès : Siepi
Valentin : Guarrera
Siébel : Roggero
Marthe : Votipka
Wagner : Davidson

March 28

FLEDERMAUS (English)
Ormandy (c)

Eisenstein : Sullivan
Rosalinda : Piazza
Adele : Munsel
Ida : Gollner
Alfred : Tucker
Orlofsky : Novotna
Dr. Falke : Brownlee
Frank : Thompson
Dr. Blind : Franke
Frosch : Gilford (actor)

PHILADELPHIA
April 2

LA BOHÈME/Cleva (c)

Rodolfo : Tucker
Marcello : Valdengo
Schaunard : Cehanovsky
Colline : Siepi
Mimi : De Los Angeles
Musetta : Hunt
Benoit : Baccaloni
Parpignol : Franke
Alcindoro : Baccaloni
Sergeant : Davidson

April 3

FLEDERMAUS

Same as Mar. 28 except:
Eisenstein : Kullman
Rosalinda : Resnik (for
Piazza)
Alfred : Sullivan

BOSTON
April 9

LA TRAVIATA/Erede (c)

Violetta : Rigal
Alfredo : Di Stefano

Germont : Valdengo (for
Merrill)
Flora : Browning
Annina : Roggero
Gastone : De Paolis
Baron Douphol : Cehanovsky
Marquis d'Obigny : Davidson
Doctor Grenvil : Harvuot

April 10
DIE ZAUBERFLÖTE (English)
Stiedry (c)
Sarastro : Hines
Tamino : Tucker
High Priest : Schoeffler
Two Priests : Hayward,
Harvuot
Queen of the Night : Berger
Pamina : Steber
Three Ladies : Amara,
Votipka, Harshaw
Papageno : Brownlee
Papagena : Raymondi
Monostatos : Chabay
Three Genii : Peters,
Lenchner, Glaz
Guards : Darcy, Davidson

April 11 (mat.)
LA BOHÈME

Same as Apr. 2 except:
Rodolfo : Di Stefano
Marcello : Valentino
Colline : Moscona
Benoit : Alvary
Alcindoro : Davidson
Sergeant : Tomanelli

April 11
IL BARBIERE DI SIVIGLIA
Erede (c)
Almaviva : Conley
Dr. Bartolo : Baccaloni
Rosina : Pons
Figaro : Valdengo
Don Basilio : Siepi
Berta : Madeira
Fiorello : Harvuot
Sergeant : De Paolis
Ambrogio : Burgstaller

April 12
FLEDERMAUS/Kozma (c)

Same as Mar. 28 except:
Eisenstein : Kullman
Ida : Ames
Alfred : Sullivan

April 13
DON CARLO

Same as Nov. 28 except:
Don Carlo : Tucker
Rodrigo : Valentino
(for Merrill)
Grand Inquisitor : Hines
Princess Eboli : Thebom

April 14 (mat.)
MADAMA BUTTERFLY/Erede (c)
Cio-Cio-San : Kirsten
B. F. Pinkerton : Conley
Sharpless : Valdengo
Suzuki : Browning
Kate Pinkerton : Amara
Goro : De Paolis
Yamadori : Cehanovsky
Uncle-Priest : Alvary
Imperial Commissioner :
Harvuot

April 14
FAUST

Same as Mar. 27 except:
Méphistophélès : Hines

April 15 (mat.)
TRISTAN UND ISOLDE
Reiner (c)
Tristan : Svanholm
Isolde : Varnay
King Marke : Ernster
Kurvenal : Schoeffler
Brangaene : Harshaw
Melot : Thompson
Steersman : Davidson
Shepherd : Chabay
Sailor's Voice : Hayward

CLEVELAND

April 16
DON CARLO

Same as Nov. 28 except:
Don Carlo : Tucker
Rodrigo : Valentino
Grand Inquisitor : Hines
Princess Eboli : Thebom

April 17
LA TRAVIATA/Cleva (c)

Same as Apr. 9 except:
Violetta : Kirsten
Alfredo : Conley
Germont : Warren
Flora : Votipka

April 18
FLEDERMAUS

Same as Mar. 28 except:
Eisenstein : Kullman
Ida : Ames
Alfred : Sullivan

April 19
IL BARBIERE DI SIVIGLIA

Same as Apr. 11 except:
Berta : Glaz
Fiorello : Cehanovsky

April 20 (mat.)
IL TROVATORE/Erede (c)
Leonora : Rigal (for
Milanov)

Manrico : Baum
Count di Luna : Valentino
Azucena : Harshaw
Inez : Amara
Ferrando : Moscona
Ruiz : Hayward
Gypsy : Cehanovsky
Messenger : Franke

April 20
TRISTAN UND ISOLDE

Same as Apr. 15 except:
Isolde : Traubel
Kurvenal : Janssen
Brangaene : Thebom
Sailor's Voice : Darcy

April 21 (mat.)
CAVALLERIA RUSTICANA

Same as Feb. 20 except:
Santuzza : Varnay
Lola : Roggero
Alfio : Valentino
Lucia : Votipka

PAGLIACCI

Same as Feb. 20 except:
Tonio : Valdengo

April 21
DON GIOVANNI/Reiner (c)

Don Giovanni : Brownlee
(for Schoeffler)
Donna Anna : Milanov
Donna Elvira : Steber
Zerlina : Munsel
Commendatore : Hines
Don Ottavio : Peerce
Leporello : Baccaloni
Masetto : Alvary

ATLANTA

April 23
IL TROVATORE

Same as Apr. 20 except:
Leonora : Milanov
Azucena : Thebom
Gypsy : Davidson

April 24
FLEDERMAUS/Kozma (c)

Same as Mar. 28 except:
Eisenstein : Kullman
Ida : Morse
Alfred : Sullivan

April 25 (mat.)
CAVALLERIA RUSTICANA

Same as Feb. 20 except:
Santuzza : Resnik
Lola : Glaz
Lucia : Votipka

PAGLIACCI

Same as Feb. 20 except:
Tonio : Valdengo

April 25

IL BARBIERE DI SIVIGLIA

Same as Apr. 11 except:
Rosina : Peters
Figaro : Brownlee
Don Basilio : Hines
Fiorello : Cehanovsky

MEMPHIS
April 26

FAUST

Same as Mar. 27 except:
Marguerite : Steber

DALLAS
April 27

FLEDERMAUS/Kozma (c)

Same as Mar. 28 except:
Eisenstein : Kullman
Ida : Morse
Alfred : Sullivan

April 28 (mat.)

DON CARLO

Same as Nov. 28 except:
Don Carlo : Tucker
Rodrigo : Valentino
   (for Merrill)
Grand Inquisitor : Hines
Friar : Moscona
Princess Eboli : Thebom
Herald : Hayward

April 28

MADAMA BUTTERFLY

Same as Apr. 14 except:
Cio-Cio-San : De Los Angeles
Suzuki : Glaz
Kate Pinkerton : Hunt
Imperial Commissioner :
   Davidson

April 29 (mat.)

IL BARBIERE DI SIVIGLIA

Same as Apr. 11 except:
Almaviva : Di Stefano
Rosina : Berger
Figaro : Guarrera
   (for Valdengo)
Don Basilio : Hines
Fiorello : Cehanovsky

HOUSTON
April 30

IL TROVATORE

Same as Apr. 20 except:
Azucena : Thebom
Ruiz : Chabay (for
   Hayward)

May 1

FAUST

Same as Mar. 27

372

OKLAHOMA CITY
May 2

LA TRAVIATA

Same as Apr. 9 except:
Violetta : Kirsten
Alfredo : Tucker
Germont : Warren
Gastone : Chabay

DES MOINES
May 3

FLEDERMAUS/Kozma (c)

Same as Mar. 28 except:
Adele : Hunt
Ida : Ames
Alfred : Kullman

MINNEAPOLIS
May 4

FLEDERMAUS

Same as Mar. 28 except:
Rosalinda : Resnik (for
   Piazza)
Adele : Hunt (for Munsel)
Ida : Ames
Alfred : Conley

May 5 (mat.)

CAVALLERIA RUSTICANA

Same as Feb. 20 except:
Lola : Roggero
Turiddu : Baum
Alfio : Valentino

PAGLIACCI

Same as Feb. 20

May 5

DIE ZAUBERFLÖTE

Same as Apr. 10 except:
High Priest : Moscona
Queen of the Night : Peters
Third Lady : Lipton
Papagena : Hunt
First Genie : Warner
First Guard : Hayward

May 6 (mat.)

FAUST

Same as Mar. 27 except:
Siébel : Bollinger

BLOOMINGTON
May 7

FLEDERMAUS/Kozma (c)

Same as Mar. 28 except:
Rosalinda : Resnik (for
   Piazza)
Adele : Hunt (for Munsel)
Ida : Morse
Alfred : Sullivan

May 8

DON CARLO

Same as Nov. 28 except:

Don Carlo : Tucker
Rodrigo : Valentino
Grand Inquisitor : Hines
Friar : Moscona
Princess Eboli : Thebom
Herald : Hayward

LAFAYETTE
May 9

FAUST

Same as Mar. 27 except:
Méphistophélès : Hines

CHICAGO
May 10

FLEDERMAUS/Kozma (c)

Same as Mar. 28 except:
Eisenstein : Kullman
Rosalinda : Resnik
Ida : Morse

May 11

LA TRAVIATA

Same as Apr. 9 except:
Violetta : Kirsten
Alfredo : Peerce
Gastone : Chabay

May 12 (mat.)

FLEDERMAUS/Kozma (c)

Same as Mar. 28 except:
Eisenstein : Kullman
Rosalinda : Resnik
   (for Piazza)
Ida : Ames
Alfred : Conley

May 12

LA BOHÈME

Same as Apr. 2 except:
Rodolfo : Tagliavini
Benoit : Alvary
Parpignol : D'Elia
Alcindoro : Davidson
Sergeant : Tomanelli

ROCHESTER
May 14

FLEDERMAUS/Kozma (c)

Same as Mar. 28 except:
Eisenstein : Kullman
Rosalinda : Resnik
Ida : Ames
Alfred : Conley

1951 – 52

PHILADELPHIA
November 20

AIDA/Cleva (c)

King : Vichegonov
Amneris : Nikolaidi
Aida : Milanov

Radames : Del Monaco
Amonasro : London
Ramfis : Hines
Messenger : Hayward
Priestess : Amara

December 4
RIGOLETTO/Erede (c)
Duke : Tucker
Rigoletto : Warren
Gilda : Gueden
Sparafucile : Pernerstorfer
Maddalena : Madeira
Giovanna : Votipka
Monterone : Scott
Marullo : Harvuot
Borsa : Franke
Ceprano : Davidson
Countess : Bollinger
Page : Roggero
Guard : Brazis

January 15
GIANNI SCHICCHI/Erede (c)
Gianni Schicchi : Baccaloni
Lauretta : Peters
La Vecchia : Madeira
Rinuccio : Hayward
Gherardo : De Paolis
Nella : Lenchner
Betto : Cehanovsky
Simone : Alvary
Marco : Harvuot
La Ciesca : Votipka
Spinelloccio : Pechner
Nicolao : Davidson
Pinellino : Hawkins
Guccio : Scott
Gherardino : E. Tonry

SALOME/Reiner (c)
Herod : Svanholm
Herodias : Hoengen
Salome : Welitch
Jokanaan : Hotter
Narraboth : Sullivan
Page : Glaz
First Nazarene : Darcy
First Jew : Carelli
Second Jew : Hayward
Third Jew : De Paolis
Fourth Jew : Franke
Fifth Jew : Pechner
First Soldier : Scott
Second Soldier : Vichegonov
Cappadocian : Hawkins
Slave : Lenchner

February 12
CARMEN/Reiner (c)
Carmen : Stevens
Don José : Tucker
Micaela : Conner
Escamillo : Silveri

Zuniga : Hawkins
Morales : Harvuot
Frasquita : Amara
Mercedes : Roggero
Dancaire : Cehanovsky
Remendado : De Paolis

March 18
LE NOZZE DI FIGARO
Reiner (c)
Almaviva : Valdengo
Countess : De Los Angeles
Susanna : Conner
Figaro : Siepi
Cherubino : Miller
Marcellina : Madeira
Bartolo : Pechner
Basilio : De Paolis
Don Curzio : Carelli
Antonio : Alvary
Barbarina : Warner
Peasant Girls : Lenchner,
Roggero

BALTIMORE
March 25
CARMEN
Same as Feb. 12 except:
Don José : Del Monaco
Micaela : Gueden
Escamillo : Guarrera
Zuniga : Scott
Frasquita : Lenchner

March 26
IL TROVATORE/Erede (c)
Leonora : Milanov
Manrico : Baum
Count di Luna : Warren
Azucena : Barbieri
Inez : Amara
Ferrando : Moscona
Ruiz : Hayward
Gypsy : Tomanelli
Messenger : Franke

PHILADELPHIA
April 8
PARSIFAL/Stiedry (c)
Amfortas : Schoeffler
Titurel : Vichegonov
Gurnemanz : Ernster
Parsifal : Hopf
Klingsor : Pernerstorfer
Kundry : Harshaw
A Voice : Madeira
Knights of the Grail : Darcy,
Hawkins
Esquires : Warner, Miller,
Franke, Carelli
Flower Maidens : Amara,
Hunt, Glaz, Bollinger,
Lenchner, Roggero

CLEVELAND
April 14
AIDA
Same as Nov. 20 except:
Amneris : Thebom
Amonasro : Warren

April 15
MADAMA BUTTERFLY/Cleva (c)
Cio-Cio-San : De Los Angeles
(for Albanese)
B. F. Pinkerton : Kullman
Sharpless : Valentino
Suzuki : Miller
Kate Pinkerton : Amara
Goro : De Paolis
Yamadori : Cehanovsky
Uncle-Priest : Alvary
Imperial Commissioner :
Brazis

April 16
RIGOLETTO
Same as Dec. 4 except:
Sparafucile : Moscona
Countess : Amara

April 17
CARMEN
Same as Feb. 12 except:
Escamillo : Merrill

April 18 (mat.)
LA BOHÈME/Erede (c)
Rodolfo : Di Stefano
Marcello : Guarrera
Schaunard : Harvuot
Colline : Hines
Mimi : De Los Angeles
Musetta : Gueden
Benoit : Davidson
Parpignol : Franke
Alcindoro : Alvary
Sergeant : Tomanelli

April 18
GIANNI SCHICCHI
Same as Jan. 15 except:
Gherardino : Lyons (t)

SALOME
Same as Jan. 15 except:
Herodias : Harshaw
Salome : Varnay
Jokanaan : Schoeffler
First Nazarene : Moscona

April 19 (mat.)
LA TRAVIATA/Cleva (c)
Violetta : Steber (for
Albanese)
Alfredo : Peerce
Germont : Merrill
Flora : Votipka
Annina : Roggero

373

1951–52

Gastone : Franke
Baron Douphol : Cehanovsky
Marquis d'Obigny : Brazis
Doctor Grenvil : Hawkins

April 19
LE NOZZE DI FIGARO
Rudolf (c)
Same as Mar. 18 except:
Countess : Rigal (for Steber)
Marcellina : Glaz
Bartolo : Baccaloni
Antonio : Davidson
Barbarina : Peters

BOSTON
April 21
AIDA
Same as Nov. 20 except:
Amneris : Thebom
Amonasro : Warren
Messenger : Franke

April 22
GIANNI SCHICCHI
Same as Jan. 15 except:
Gherardino : Lyons

SALOME
Same as Jan. 15 except:
Herodias : Harshaw
Salome : Varnay
Jokanaan : Schoeffler
First Nazarene : Moscona

April 23 (mat.)
CARMEN
Same as Feb. 12 except:
Micaela : Gueden
Escamillo : Guarrera
Mercedes : Glaz

April 23
MANON/Cleva (c)
Manon : Sayao
Lescaut : Singher
Des Grieux : Di Stefano
Count des Grieux : Hines
Poussette : Lenchner
Javotte : Roggero
Rosette : Miller
Guillot : Carelli
De Brétigny : Cehanovsky
Innkeeper : Davidson
Guards : Franke, Brazis
Servant : Savage

April 24
IL TROVATORE
Same as Mar. 26 except:
Count di Luna : Merrill
Azucena : Harshaw
Gypsy : Brazis
Messenger : De Paolis

April 25
DIE MEISTERSINGER/Reiner (c)
Hans Sachs : Schoeffler
Pogner : Ernster
Eva : Steber
Magdalene : Glaz
Walther : Svanholm
Beckmesser : Pechner
Kothner : Janssen
Vogelgesang : Hayward
Nachtigall : Brazis
Zorn : De Paolis
Eisslinger : Darcy
Moser : Carelli
Ortel : Hawkins
Schwarz : Davidson
Foltz : Alvary
David : Franke
Night Watchman : Harvuot

April 26 (mat.)
RIGOLETTO
Same as Dec. 4 except:
Sparafucile : Hines
Marullo : Cehanovsky
Borsa : Carelli

April 26
CAVALLERIA RUSTICANA
Erede (c)
Santuzza : Resnik
Lola : Miller
Turiddu : Del Monaco
Alfio : Valentino
Lucia : Votipka

PAGLIACCI/Erede (c)
Nedda : Rigal
Canio : Baum (for Vinay)
Tonio : Valdengo
Beppe : Hayward
Silvio : Guarrera

April 27 (mat.)
LA BOHÈME
Same as Apr. 18 except:
Marcello : Valentino
Colline : Moscona
Mimi : Steber
Musetta : Munsel
Benoit : Baccaloni
Alcindoro : Baccaloni

WASHINGTON
April 28
AIDA
Same as Nov. 20 except:
King : Scott
Amneris : Thebom
Amonasro : Warren

April 29 (mat.)
MADAMA BUTTERFLY
Same as Apr. 15 except:
Cio-Cio-San : Kirsten

B. F. Pinkerton : Sullivan
Kate Pinkerton : Lenchner
(for Bollinger)
Goro : Franke
Yamadori : Brazis
Imperial Commissioner :
Davidson

April 29
CARMEN
Same as Feb. 12 except:
Micaela : Gueden
Escamillo : Merrill
Mercedes : Glaz

RICHMOND
April 30
AIDA
Same as Nov. 20 except:
King : Scott
Amneris : Thebom
Aida : Rigal
Radames : Baum
Amonasro : Guarrera
Ramfis : Moscona
Priestess : Bollinger

ATLANTA
May 1
LA TRAVIATA
Same as Apr. 19 except:
Violetta : Kirsten
Alfredo : Di Stefano
Flora : Lenchner
Annina : Amara
Gastone : Carelli

May 2
CARMEN
Same as Feb. 12 except:
Micaela : Gueden
Escamillo : Merrill
Mercedes : Glaz

May 3 (mat.)
LA BOHÈME
Same as Apr. 18 except:
Rodolfo : Conley
Colline : Siepi
Mimi : Kirsten

May 3
AIDA
Same as Nov. 20 except:
King : Scott
Amneris : Thebom
Amonasro : Warren
Priestess : Bollinger

BIRMINGHAM
May 5
LUCIA DI LAMMERMOOR
Cleva (c)
Lucia : Pons

374

Alisa : Votipka
Edgardo : Peerce
Ashton : Merrill
Raimondo : Scott
Arturo : Hayward
Normanno : Franke

May 6

MADAMA BUTTERFLY
Same as Apr. 15 except:
Cio-Cio-San : Kirsten
B. F. Pinkerton : Di Stefano
Suzuki : Glaz
Kate Pinkerton : Bollinger

MEMPHIS

May 7

CARMEN
Same as Feb. 12 except:
Don José : Del Monaco
Escamillo : Guarrera
Mercedes : Glaz

May 8

RIGOLETTO
Same as Dec. 4 except:
Sparafucile : Moscona
Page : Lenchner

DALLAS

May 9

AIDA
Same as Nov. 20 except:
King : Scott
Amneris : Thebom
Amonasro : Merrill

May 10 (mat.)

LA BOHÈME
Same as Apr. 18 except:
Marcello : Valentino
Colline : Moscona
Mimi : Kirsten
Alcindoro : De Paolis

May 10

COSI FAN TUTTE/Stiedry (c)
Fiordiligi : Steber
Dorabella : Miller
Despina : Munsel
Ferrando : Tucker
Guglielmo : Guarrera
Don Alfonso : Alvary

May 11 (mat.)

CARMEN
Same as Feb. 12 except:
Don José : Baum
Escamillo : Guarrera
Mercedes : Glaz

HOUSTON

May 12

CAVALLERIA RUSTICANA
Same as Apr. 26 except:
Santuzza : Milanov

PAGLIACCI
Same as Apr. 26 except:
Canio : Vinay
Tonio : Merrill

May 13

RIGOLETTO
Same as Dec. 4 except:
Gilda : Warner (for Munsel)
Sparafucile : Moscona
Marullo : Cehanovsky
Page : Lenchner

OKLAHOMA CITY

May 14

AIDA
Same as Nov. 20 except:
King : Scott
Amneris : Thebom
Aida : Rigal
Amonasro : Merrill

DES MOINES

May 15

CARMEN/Adler (c)
Same as Feb. 12 except:
Don José : Baum
Escamillo : Guarrera
Mercedes : Glaz

MINNEAPOLIS

May 16

RIGOLETTO
Same as Dec. 4 except:
Duke : Di Stefano
Gilda : Peters
Sparafucile : Hines
Page : Lenchner

May 17 (mat.)

CARMEN
Same as Feb. 12 except:
Don José : Vinay
Escamillo : Merrill
Mercedes : Glaz

May 17

COSI FAN TUTTE
Same as May 10 except:
Dorabella : Thebom

May 18 (mat.)

MADAMA BUTTERFLY
Same as Apr. 15 except:
Cio-Cio-San : Kanazawa (t)
B. F. Pinkerton : Sullivan
Kate Pinkerton : Bollinger
Uncle-Priest : Scott

BLOOMINGTON

May 19

AIDA
Same as Nov. 20 except:
King : Scott

Amneris : Thebom
Aida : Rigal
Amonasro : Merrill
Priestess : Bollinger

May 20

COSI FAN TUTTE
Same as May 10

LAFAYETTE

May 21

CARMEN
Same as Feb. 12 except:
Don José : Vinay
Escamillo : Guarrera
Mercedes : Glaz

ST. LOUIS

May 22

AIDA
Same as Nov. 20 except:
King : Scott
Amneris : Thebom
Amonasro : Merrill

May 23

CARMEN
Same as Feb. 12 except:
Don José : Vinay
Escamillo : Guarrera
Frasquita : Lenchner
Mercedes : Glaz

May 24 (mat.)

LA BOHÈME
Same as Apr. 18 except:
Rodolfo : Tucker
Marcello : Valentino
Colline : Moscona
Mimi : Steber
Musetta : Bollinger
Alcindoro : De Paolis

May 24

LA TRAVIATA
Same as Apr. 19 except:
Violetta : Kirsten
Germont : Warren
Flora : Lenchner
Annina : Amara

TORONTO

May 26

AIDA
Same as Nov. 20 except:
King : Scott
Amneris : Thebom
Amonasro : Merrill

May 27

LA BOHÈME
Same as Apr. 18 except:
Rodolfo : Peerce

Marcello : Valentino
Colline : Moscona
Mimi : Steber
Musetta : Munsel

May 28
CARMEN

Same as Feb. 12 except:
Don José : Vinay
Escamillo : Merrill
Mercedes : Glaz

May 29
RIGOLETTO

Same as Dec. 4 except:
Gilda : Munsel
Sparafucile : Moscona
Maddalena : Glaz
Marullo : Cehanovsky
Page : Lenchner

MONTREAL
May 30
AIDA

Same as Nov. 20 except:
King : Scott
Amneris : Thebom
Radames : Baum
Amonasro : Merrill
Priestess : Bollinger

May 31 (mat.)
CARMEN

Same as Feb. 12 except:
Escamillo : Guarrera
Zuniga : Scott
Mercedes : Glaz

May 31
LA TRAVIATA

Same as Apr. 19 except:
Germont : Warren
Flora : Lenchner
Annina : Madeira
Gastone : Carelli
Baron Douphol : Davidson

1 9 5 2 – 5 3

PHILADELPHIA
November 18
LA FORZA DEL DESTINO
Stiedry (c)

Marquis : Vichegonov
Leonora : Milanov
Don Carlo : Warren
Don Alvaro : Tucker
Padre Guardiano : Hines
Fra Melitone : Pechner
Preziosilla : Miller
Curra : Castellano
Surgeon : Brazis

376

December 9
TOSCA/Cleva (c)

Tosca : Kirsten
Cavaradossi : Tagliavini
Scarpia : Weede
Angelotti : Alvary
Sacristan : Davidson
Spoletta : De Paolis
Sciarrone : Cehanovsky
Jailer : Brazis
Shepherd : Roggero

January 27
COSI FAN TUTTE/Stiedry (c)

Fiordiligi : Steber
Dorabella : Thebom
Despina : Peters
Ferrando : Tucker
Guglielmo : Guarrera
Don Alfonso : Brownlee

February 24
THE RAKE'S PROGRESS
Reiner (c)

Trulove : Scott
Anne : Gueden
Tom Rakewell : Conley
Nick Shadow : Harrell
Mother Goose : Lipton
Baba the Turk : Thebom
Sellem : Franke
Keeper of Madhouse :
  Davidson

March 17
BORIS GODUNOV/Stiedry (c)

Boris Godunov : London
Fyodor : Miller
Xenia : Warner
Nurse : Madeira
Shuiski : Franke
Shchelkalov : Harvuot
Pimen : Scott
Grigori : Sullivan
Marina : Rankin
Rangoni : S. Bjoerling
Varlaam : Baccaloni
Missail : Hayward
Innkeeper : Lipton
Officer : Hawkins
Simpleton : Carelli
Nikitich : Davidson
Lavitski : Hawkins
Chernikovski : Davidson
Boyar : Carelli
A Woman : Votipka
Mityukh : Brazis
Marina's Companions :
  Lenchner, Castellano, Glaz,
  Roggero

BALTIMORE
March 24
LA FORZA DEL DESTINO
Same as Nov. 18 except:

Don Carlo : Silveri
Don Alvaro : Del Monaco
Padre Guardiano : Siepi
Surgeon : Cehanovsky

March 25
LA BOHÈME/Erede (c)

Rodolfo : Conley
Marcello : Merrill
Schaunard : Harvuot
Colline : Hines
Mimi : Conner
Musetta : Resnik
Benoit : Davidson
Parpignol : Franke
Alcindoro : De Paolis
Sergeant : Brazis

PHILADELPHIA
April 7
DIE MEISTERSINGER/Reiner (c)

Hans Sachs : Schoeffler
Pogner : Hotter
Eva : Steber
Magdalene : Glaz
Walther : Svanholm
Beckmesser : Pechner
Kothner : Harrell
Vogelgesang : Hayward
Nachtigall : Brazis
Zorn : De Paolis
Eisslinger : Darcy
Moser : Carelli
Ortel : Hawkins
Schwarz : Davidson
Foltz : Alvary
David : Franke
Night Watchman : Harvuot

CLEVELAND
April 13
RIGOLETTO/Erede (c)

Duke : Conley
Rigoletto : Merrill
Gilda : Pons
Sparafucile : Hines
Maddalena : Madeira
Giovanna : Votipka
Monterone : Scott
Marullo : Harvuot
Borsa : Franke
Ceprano : Davidson
Countess : Lenchner
Page : Roggero
Guard : Brazis

April 14
LA GIOCONDA/Cleva (c)

La Gioconda : Milanov
Laura : Thebom
Alvise : Siepi
La Cieca : Madeira
Enzo : Tucker
Barnaba : Warren
Zuane : Cehanovsky

First Singer : Carelli
Second Singer : Davidson
Isepo : De Paolis
Monk : Scott
Steersman : Tomanelli

April 15
CARMEN/Reiner (c)

Carmen : Stevens
Don José : Del Monaco
Micaela : Gueden
Escamillo : Merrill
Zuniga : Hawkins
Morales : Harvuot
Frasquita : Amara
Mercedes : Roggero
Dancaire : Cehanovsky
Remendado : De Paolis

April 16
BORIS GODUNOV

Same as Mar. 17 except:
Marina : Thebom
First Companion : Amara
Third Companion :
  Holiday (t)

April 17 (mat.)
TOSCA

Same as Dec. 9 except:
Cavaradossi : Conley
Angelotti : Harvuot

April 17
LA FORZA DEL DESTINO

Same as Nov. 18 except:
Curra : Votipka

April 18 (mat.)
DER ROSENKAVALIER
  Reiner (c)

Princess von Werdenberg :
  Varnay
Baron Ochs : Alvary
Octavian : Stevens
Von Faninal : Brownlee
Sophie : Gueden
Marianne : Votipka
Valzacchi : De Paolis
Annina : Lipton
Police Commissioner :
  Hawkins
Majordomo of Princess :
  Darcy
Majordomo of Von Faninal :
  Franke
Notary : Pechner
Innkeeper : Franke
Singer : Baum
Orphans : Castellano,
  Lenchner, Roggero
Milliner : Warner
Hairdresser : Palomanos
Leopold : Mayreder
Animal Vendor : Carelli
Negro Boy : Lyons

April 18
DON GIOVANNI/Rudolf (c)

Don Giovanni : Siepi
Donna Anna : Harshaw
Donna Elvira : Resnik
Zerlina : Conner
Commendatore : Ernster
Don Ottavio : Peerce
Leporello : Baccaloni
Masetto : Davidson

BOSTON

April 20
LA FORZA DEL DESTINO

Same as Nov. 18 except:
Padre Guardiano : Siepi

April 21
CARMEN

Same as Apr. 15 except:
Micaela : Conner
Escamillo : Guarrera
Zuniga : Scott

April 22 (mat.)
AIDA/Cellini (c)

King : Vichegonov
Amneris : Thebom
Aida : Rigal
Radames : Baum
Amonasro : Merrill
Ramfis : Moscona
Messenger : Franke
Priestess : Amara

April 22
TOSCA

Same as Dec. 9 except:
Cavaradossi : Conley
Scarpia : London
Angelotti : Harvuot
Sacristan : Baccaloni

April 23
DER ROSENKAVALIER

Same as Apr. 18 except:
Octavian : Miller (for
  Stevens)
Notary : Davidson
Singer : Gari

April 24
COSI FAN TUTTE
Same as Jan. 27

April 25 (mat.)
MADAMA BUTTERFLY/Cleva (c)

Cio-Cio-San : Kirsten
B. F. Pinkerton : Conley
Sharpless : Valentino
Suzuki : Miller
Kate Pinkerton : Castellano
Goro : De Paolis
Yamadori : Cehanovsky

Uncle-Priest : Hawkins
Imperial Commissioner :
  Brazis

April 25
RIGOLETTO

Same as Apr. 13 except:
Duke : Peerce
Rigoletto : Warren
Gilda : Gueden
Borsa : Carelli
Guard : Tomanelli

April 26 (mat.)
LOHENGRIN/Stiedry (c)

King Henry : Ernster
Lohengrin : Sullivan
Elsa : Steber
Telramund : S. Bjoerling
Ortrud : Harshaw
Herald : Guarrera
Nobles : Franke, Carelli,
  Brazis, Scott

WASHINGTON

April 27
LA BOHÈME

Same as Mar. 25 except:
Marcello : Guarrera
Colline : Siepi
Mimi : Gueden

April 28 (mat.)
RIGOLETTO

Same as Apr. 13 except:
Rigoletto : Warren
Gilda : Peters
Marullo : Cehanovsky
Borsa : Carelli

April 28
CAVALLERIA RUSTICANA
  Erede (c)

Santuzza : Milanov
Lola : Miller
Turiddu : Tucker
Alfio : Valentino
Lucia : Votipka

PAGLIACCI/Erede (c)

Nedda : Rigal
Canio : Del Monaco
Tonio : Merrill
Beppe : Hayward
Silvio : Guarrera

April 29
SAMSON ET DALILA/Cleva (c)

Dalila : Stevens
Samson : Baum
High Priest : S. Bjoerling
Abimelech : Scott
Old Hebrew : Ernster
Philistine Messenger : Darcy
Philistines : Franke, Harvuot

1952–53

ATLANTA

April 30

RIGOLETTO
Same as Apr. 13 except:
Duke : Tucker
Rigoletto : Warren
Gilda : Gueden
Marullo : Cehanovsky

May 1

SAMSON ET DALILA
Same as Apr. 29

May 2 (mat.)

COSÌ FAN TUTTE
Same as Jan. 27 except:
Ferrando : Sullivan

May 2

TOSCA
Same as Dec. 9 except:
Tosca : Rigal
Cavaradossi : Del Monaco
Scarpia : London
Sacristan : Pechner

BIRMINGHAM

May 4

CARMEN
Same as Apr. 15 except:
Don José : Tucker
Escamillo : London

May 5

AIDA/Cleva (c)
Same as Apr. 22 except:
King : Scott
Aida : Milanov
Radames : Del Monaco
Amonasro : Warren

MEMPHIS

May 6

SAMSON ET DALILA
Same as Apr. 29 except:
Samson : Vinay
Philistines : Carelli,
Cehanovsky

May 7

AIDA/Cleva (c)
Same as Apr. 22 except:
Aida : Milanov
Radames : Del Monaco

DALLAS

May 8

DON GIOVANNI/Reiner (c)
Same as Apr. 18 except:
Donna Anna : Resnik
Donna Elvira : Rigal
Zerlina : Warner
Commendatore : Scott
Don Ottavio : Conley

May 9 (mat.)

RIGOLETTO
Same as Apr. 13 except:
Duke : Tucker
Gilda : Peters
Sparafucile : Moscona
Borsa : Carelli

May 9

DER ROSENKAVALIER
Rudolf (c)
Same as Apr. 18 except:
Notary : Davidson
Second Orphan : Amara

May 10 (mat.)

TRISTAN UND ISOLDE
Stiedry (c)
Tristan : Vinay
Isolde : Harshaw
King Marke : Ernster
Kurvenal : S. Bjoerling
Brangaene : Thebom
Melot : Cehanovsky
Steersman : Brazis
Shepherd : Franke
Sailor's Voice : Darcy

HOUSTON

May 11

CARMEN
Same as Apr. 15

May 12

TOSCA
Same as Dec. 9 except:
Cavaradossi : Peerce
Scarpia : London
Angelotti : Harvuot

OKLAHOMA CITY

May 13

LA BOHÈME
Same as Mar. 25 except:
Colline : Scott
Alcindoro : Alvary

DES MOINES

May 14

AIDA/Cleva (c)
Same as Apr. 22 except:
Aida : Milanov
Amonasro : Warren

MINNEAPOLIS

May 15

DER ROSENKAVALIER
Same as Apr. 18 except:
Notary : Davidson
Singer : Gari

May 16 (mat.)

LA BOHÈME
Same as Mar. 25 except:

Rodolfo : Sullivan (for
Tucker)
Marcello : Guarrera
Colline : Scott

May 16

SAMSON ET DALILA
Same as Apr. 29 except:
Dalila : Thebom
Samson : Vinay
Abimelech : Hawkins
Old Hebrew : Moscona
Philistines : Carelli,
Cehanovsky

May 17 (mat.)

DON GIOVANNI/Reiner (c)
Same as Apr. 18 except:
Don Giovanni : London
Zerlina : Peters
Don Ottavio : Conley

BLOOMINGTON

May 18

RIGOLETTO
Same as Apr. 13 except:
Rigoletto : Warren
Gilda : Gueden
Sparafucile : Siepi
Borsa : Carelli
Guard : Tomanelli

May 19

TRISTAN UND ISOLDE
Same as May 10 except:
Melot : Darcy

LAFAYETTE

May 20

LA BOHÈME
Same as Mar. 25 except:
Rodolfo : Tucker
Marcello : Guarrera
(for Merrill)
Colline : Scott

ROCHESTER

May 21

TOSCA
Same as Dec. 9 except:
Cavaradossi : Del Monaco
Scarpia : London
Angelotti : Harvuot
Sacristan : Alvary
Jailer : Tomanelli

MONTREAL

May 22

RIGOLETTO
Same as Apr. 13 except:
Duke : Tucker
Rigoletto : Warren
Gilda : Peters
Sparafucile : Vichegonov

Marullo : Cehanovsky
Borsa : Carelli

May 23 (mat.)
LA BOHÈME

Same as Mar. 25 except:
Rodolfo : Peerce
Marcello : Guarrera
Colline : Siepi
Mimi : Gueden

May 23
SAMSON ET DALILA

Same as Apr. 29 except:
Samson : Vinay
Old Hebrew : Moscona
Philistines : Carelli,
  Cehanovsky

May 24
TOSCA

Same as Dec. 9 except:
Cavaradossi : Del Monaco
Scarpia : London
Jailer : Tomanelli

TORONTO

May 25
LA FORZA DEL DESTINO

Same as Nov. 18 except:
Padre Guardiano : Siepi

May 26
CARMEN

Same as Apr. 15 except:
Don José : Vinay
Micaela : Conner
Escamillo : Guarrera

May 27
TOSCA

Same as Dec. 9 except:
Cavaradossi : Peerce
Scarpia : London
Angelotti : Harvuot
Sacristan : Pechner

May 28
LOHENGRIN

Same as Apr. 26

May 29
RIGOLETTO

Same as Apr. 13 except:
Rigoletto : Warren
Gilda : Gueden
Sparafucile : Vichegonov
Maddalena : Lipton

May 30
SAMSON ET DALILA

Same as Apr. 29 except:
Dalila : Thebom
Old Hebrew : Moscona
Philistine Messenger :
  Carelli

1 9 5 3 – 5 4

PHILADELPHIA
December 1
PELLÉAS ET MÉLISANDE
  Monteux (c)

Mélisande : Conner
Geneviève : Lipton
Little Yniold : Georgiou
Pelléas : Uppman
Golaud : Singher
Arkel : Hines
Physician : Vichegonov

December 15
FAUST/Monteux (c)

Faust : Conley (for
  Bjoerling)
Marguerite : De Los Angeles
Méphistophélès :
  Rossi-Lemeni
Valentin : Merrill
Siébel : Roggero
Marthe : Votipka
Wagner : Davidson

January 19
DON GIOVANNI/Rudolf (c)

Don Giovanni : Siepi
Donna Anna : Harshaw
Donna Elvira : Steber
Zerlina : Peters
Commendatore : Vichegonov
Don Ottavio : Valletti
Leporello : Kunz
Masetto : Alvary

February 9
IL TROVATORE/Cleva (c)

Leonora : Milanov
Manrico : Penno (d)
Count di Luna : Warren
Azucena : Barbieri
Inez : Leone
Ferrando : Moscona
Ruiz : Hayward
Gypsy : Brazis
Messenger : McCracken

March 16
IL BARBIERE DI SIVIGLIA
  Erede (c)

Almaviva : Valletti
Dr. Bartolo : Corena
Rosina : Peters
Figaro : Guarrera
Don Basilio : Siepi
Berta : Madeira
Fiorello : Cehanovsky
Sergeant : De Paolis
Ambrogio : Mayreder

BALTIMORE
March 29
NORMA/Cleva (c)

Oroveso : Siepi

Norma : Milanov
Pollione : Penno
Adalgisa : Thebom
Clotilde : Leone
Flavio : Franke

March 30
IL BARBIERE DI SIVIGLIA

Same as Mar. 16 except:
Figaro : Merrill
Don Basilio : Hines
Berta : Votipka

PHILADELPHIA
April 6
TANNHÄUSER/Rudolf (c)

Hermann : Hines
Tannhäuser : Vinay
Wolfram : London
Walther : Sullivan
Biterolf : Harvuot
Heinrich : Franke
Reinmar : Scott
Elisabeth : Harshaw
Venus : Varnay
Shepherd : Krall

CLEVELAND
April 19
LUCIA DI LAMMERMOOR
  Cleva (c)

Lucia : Pons
Alisa : Votipka
Edgardo : Peerce
Ashton : Warren
Raimondo : Scott
Arturo : Hayward
Normanno : McCracken

April 20
TANNHÄUSER

Same as Apr. 6 except:
Elisabeth : Varnay (for
  Harshaw)
Venus : Resnik (for Varnay)

April 21 (mat.)
CARMEN/Kozma (c)

Carmen : Thebom
Don José : Tucker
Micaela : Amara
Escamillo : Guarrera
Zuniga : Hawkins
Morales : Harvuot
Frasquita : Krall
Mercedes : Roggero
Dancaire : Cehanovsky
Remendado : De Paolis

April 21
FAUST/Adler (c)

Same as Dec. 15 except:
Méphistophélès : Siepi
Siébel : Miller

1953–54

April 22
AIDA/Cleva (c)
King : Vichegonov
Amneris : Thebom
Aida : Milanov
Radames : Baum (for Penno)
Amonasro : London
Ramfis : Hines (for
   Moscona)
Messenger : Franke
Priestess : Roggero

April 23
LA BOHÈME/Adler
   (c—for Erede)
Rodolfo : Peerce
Marcello : Valentino
Schaunard : Harvuot
Colline : Hines
Mimi : Albanese
Musetta : Fenn
Benoit : Davidson
Parpignol : McCracken
Alcindoro : De Paolis
Sergeant : Brazis

April 24 (mat.)
IL BARBIERE DI SIVIGLIA
   Cimara (c—for Erede)
Same as Mar. 16 except:
Figaro : Merrill
Berta : Votipka

April 24
IL TROVATORE
Same as Feb. 9 except:
Manrico : Baum (for Penno)
Azucena : Nikolaidi
Ferrando : Scott (for
   Moscona)

BOSTON
April 26
DON GIOVANNI
Same as Jan. 19 except:
Don Giovanni : London
Zerlina : Conner
Commendatore : Scott (for
   Vichegonov)
Leporello : Corena

April 27
FAUST/Adler (c)
Same as Dec. 15 except:
Méphistophélès : Hines
Siébel : Miller

April 28 (mat.)
CARMEN
Same as Apr. 21 except:
Escamillo : London

April 28
LA BOHÈME
Same as Apr. 23 except:

380

Marcello : Guarrera
Colline : Siepi
Mimi : Amara (for Gueden)
Alcindoro : Alvary

April 29
IL TROVATORE
Same as Feb. 9 except:
Leonora : Nelli (for
   Milanov)
Manrico : Baum
Azucena : Madeira

April 30
TANNHÄUSER
Same as Apr. 6 except:
Hermann : Vichegonov
   (for Hines)

May 1 (mat.)
IL BARBIERE DI SIVIGLIA
   Cimara (c—for Erede)
Same as Mar. 16 except:
Figaro : Merrill
Berta : Votipka

May 1
LA TRAVIATA/Cleva (c)
Violetta : Albanese
Alfredo : Tucker
Germont : Warren
Flora : Roggero
Annina : Leone
Gastone : Carelli
Baron Douphol : Davidson
Marquis d'Obigny : Brazis
Doctor Grenvil : Hawkins

ATLANTA
May 3
DON GIOVANNI
Same as Jan. 19 except:
Don Giovanni : London
Leporello : Corena

May 4 (mat.)
FAUST/Adler (c)
Same as Dec. 15 except:
Méphistophélès : Hines
Valentin : Guarrera (for
   Merrill)

May 4
LUCIA DI LAMMERMOOR
Same as Apr. 19 except:
Ashton : Valentino
Raimondo : Moscona
Normanno : Franke

May 5
LA FORZA DEL DESTINO
   Stiedry (c)
Marquis : Vichegonov
Leonora : Milanov

Don Carlo : Warren
Don Alvaro : Tucker
Padre Guardiano : Siepi
Fra Melitone : Pechner
Preziosilla : Roggero
Curra : Votipka
Trabucco : De Paolis
Surgeon : Cehanovsky

BIRMINGHAM
May 6 (mat.)
LA TRAVIATA
Same as May 1 except:
Alfredo : Peerce
Flora : Krall
Baron Douphol : Cehanovsky

May 6
LA BOHÈME
Same as Apr. 23 except:
Rodolfo : Conley
Marcello : Guarrera
Mimi : De Los Angeles
Parpignol : D'Elia

MEMPHIS
May 7
DON GIOVANNI
Same as Jan. 19 except:
Zerlina : Warner (for
   Peters)
Leporello : Corena
Masetto : Davidson

DALLAS
May 8
LUCIA DI LAMMERMOOR
Same as Apr. 19 except:
Edgardo : Valentino
Raimondo : Moscona
Arturo : Carelli
Normanno : Franke

May 9 (mat.)
LA TRAVIATA
Same as May 1 except:
Violetta : Steber
Flora : Krall
Gastone : Franke
Baron Douphol : Cehanovsky

May 9
LE NOZZE DI FIGARO
   Stiedry (c)
Almaviva : Guarrera
Countess : De Los Angeles
Susanna : Peters
Figaro : Siepi
Cherubino : Roggero
Marcellina : Glaz
Bartolo : Pechner
Basilio : De Paolis
Don Curzio : Carelli
Antonio : Alvary
Barbarina : Warner

Peasant Girls : Leone,
Warfield

May 10

FAUST/Adler (c)
Same as Dec. 15 except:
Faust : Hayward
Marguerite : Conner
Méphistophélès : Hines

OKLAHOMA CITY

May 11

RIGOLETTO/Erede (c)
Duke : Peerce
Rigoletto : Merrill (for
Warren).
Gilda : Peters
Sparafucile : Moscona
Maddalena : Glaz
Giovanna : Votipka
Monterone : Scott
Marullo : Harvuot
Borsa : Franke
Ceprano : Cehanovsky
Countess : Leone
Page : Warfield
Guard : Brazis

ST. LOUIS

May 12

FAUST/Adler (c)
Same as Dec. 15 except:
Méphistophélès : Siepi
Valentin : Guarrera

DES MOINES

May 13

LA TRAVIATA
Same as May 1 except:
Alfredo : Peerce
Germont : Merrill
Flora : Krall
Baron Douphol : Cehanovsky
Doctor Grenvil : Harvuot

MINNEAPOLIS

May 14

LA FORZA DEL DESTINO
Same as May 5 except:
Padre Guardiano : Moscona
Preziosilla : Madeira
Curra : Krall
Trabucco : Franke

May 15 (mat.)

LUCIA DI LAMMERMOOR
Same as Apr. 19 except:
Edgardo : Sullivan
Ashton : Valentino
Arturo : Carelli
Normanno : Franke

May 15

LE NOZZE DI FIGARO
Rudolf (c)
Same as May 9 except:

Countess : Steber
Susanna : Conner
Bartolo : Baccaloni
Antonio : Davidson

May 16 (mat.)

FAUST/Adler (c)
Same as Dec. 15 except:
Méphistophélès : Hines

BLOOMINGTON

May 17

IL BARBIERE DI SIVIGLIA
Same as Mar. 16 except:
Almaviva : Anthony
Dr. Bartolo : Baccaloni
Figaro : Merrill

May 18

FAUST/Adler (c)
Same as Dec. 15 except:
Marguerite : Conner
Méphistophélès : Hines
Valentin : Guarrera

LAFAYETTE

May 19

RIGOLETTO
Same as May 11 except:
Rigoletto : Warren
Maddalena : Madeira
Marullo : Cehanovsky
Borsa : Carelli
Ceprano : Davidson

CHICAGO

May 20

FAUST/Adler (c)
Same as Dec. 15 except:
Faust : Tucker
Marguerite : Conner
Méphistophélès : Hines
(for Siepi)

May 21

AIDA
Same as Apr. 22 except:
Amonasro : Warren
Ramfis : Moscona

May 22 (mat.)

LUCIA DI LAMMERMOOR
Same as Apr. 19 except:
Ashton : Valentino
Normanno : Franke

May 22

LA BOHÈME/Erede (c)
Same as Apr. 23 except:
Rodolfo : Tucker
Marcello : Guarrera
Mimi : Amara
Parpignol : D'Elia

May 23 (mat.)

RIGOLETTO
Same as May 11 except:
Duke : Conley
Rigoletto : Warren
Sparafucile : Vichegonov
Maddalena : Madeira
Ceprano : Davidson

May 23

LA TRAVIATA
Same as May 1 except:
Alfredo : Peerce
Germont : Merrill
Gastone : De Paolis (for
Carelli)
Baron Douphol : Cehanovsky
Doctor Grenvil : Harvuot

TORONTO

May 24

LUCIA DI LAMMERMOOR
Same as Apr. 19 except:
Edgardo : Tucker
Ashton : Valentino
Normanno : Franke

May 25

AIDA
Same as Apr. 22 except:
Escamillo : Guarrera
Ramfis : Moscona
Priestess : Krall

May 26

IL BARBIERE DI SIVIGLIA
Same as Mar. 16 except:
Almaviva : Conley
Dr. Bartolo : Baccaloni
Figaro : Merrill
Don Basilio : Hines

May 27

LA TRAVIATA/Cimara
(c—for Cleva)
Same as May 1 except:
Alfredo : Peerce
Baron Douphol : Cehanovsky
Doctor Grenvil : Harvuot

May 28

FAUST/Adler (c)
Same as Dec. 15 except:
Marguerite : Conner
Méphistophélès : Hines
Valentin : Guarrera
(for Merrill)

May 29

RIGOLETTO
Same as May 11 except:
Duke : Tucker
Rigoletto : Warren
Maddalena : Madeira
Ceprano : Davidson

1 9 5 4 – 5 5

PHILADELPHIA
November 23
ANDREA CHÉNIER/Cleva (c)
Andrea Chénier : Del Monaco
Maddalena : Milanov
Countess di Coigny : Glaz
Carlo Gérard : Warren
Bersi : Elias
Fléville : Cehanovsky
Abbé : Carelli
Madelon : Rankin
Mathieu : Alvary
Spy : De Paolis
Fouquier : Scott
Dumas : Hawkins
Roucher : Valentino
Schmidt : Davidson
Majordomo : Sgarro

December 21
MANON/Monteux (c)
Manon : De Los Angeles
Lescaut : Corena
Des Grieux : Valletti
Count des Grieux : Hines
Poussette : Vartenissian
Javotte : Roggero
Rosette : Elias
Guillot : Carelli
De Brétigny : Cehanovsky
Innkeeper : Davidson
Guards : McCracken, Marsh
Servant : Savage

January 11
UN BALLO IN MASCHERA
Mitropoulos (c)
Riccardo : Tucker
Renato : Warren
Amelia : Nelli (for
Milanov)
Ulrica : Anderson
Oscar : Peters
Silvano : Marsh
Samuel : Moscona
Tom : Scott
Judge : McCracken
Servant : Anthony

February 15
ARABELLA/Kempe (c)
Count Waldner : Herbert
Adelaide : Thebom
Arabella : Steber
Zdenka : Gueden
Mandryka : London
Matteo : Sullivan
Count Elemer : Carelli
Count Dominik : Harvuot
Count Lamoral : Davidson
Fiakermilli : Peters
Fortune Teller : Votipka

Welko : Wilkes
Djura : Farruggio
Jankel : Marko
Waiter : Mayreder

March 15
TRISTAN UND ISOLDE
Kempe (c)
Tristan : Svanholm
Isolde : Varnay
King Marke : Hines
Kurvenal : Metternich
Brangaene : Lipton
Melot : McCracken
Steersman : Marsh
Shepherd : Franke
Sailor's Voice : Da Costa

BALTIMORE
March 28
ANDREA CHÉNIER
Same as Nov. 23 except:
Madelon : Warfield
Fouquier : Sgarro

March 29
MANON
Same as Dec. 21 except:
Des Grieux : Campora
Guillot : De Paolis

PHILADELPHIA
April 5
LA BOHÈME/Cleva (c)
Rodolfo : Campora
Marcello : Bastianini
Schaunard : Cehanovsky
Colline : Hines
Mimi : Amara
Musetta : Fenn
Benoit : Davidson
Parpignol : McCracken
Alcindoro : De Paolis
Sergeant : Marsh

CLEVELAND
April 11
CARMEN/Rudolf (c)
Carmen : Stevens
Don José : Baum (for
Tucker)
Micaela : Amara
Escamillo : Merrill
Zuniga : Scott
Morales : Harvuot
Frasquita : Krall
Mercedes : Roggero
Dancaire : Cehanovsky
Remendado : De Paolis

April 12
LA TRAVIATA/Cimara (c)
Violetta : Kirsten
Alfredo : Peerce

Germont : Bastianini
Flora : Krall
Annina : Leone
Gastone : Carelli
Baron Douphol : Davidson
Marquis d'Obigny : Marsh
Doctor Grenvil : Hawkins

April 13 (mat.)
CAVALLERIA RUSTICANA
Adler (c)
Santuzza : Nelli
Lola : Glaz (for Miller)
Turiddu : Conley
Alfio : Valentino
Lucia : Votipka

PAGLIACCI/Kozma (c)
Nedda : Amara
Canio : Gari (for Baum)
Tonio : Merrill
Beppe : Anthony
Silvio : Guarrera

April 13
LA GIOCONDA/Cleva (c)
La Gioconda : Milanov
Laura : Thebom
Alvise : Moscona
La Cieca : Warfield
Enzo : Campora
Barnaba : Warren
Zuane : Hawkins
First Singer : McCracken
Second Singer : Marsh
Isepo : De Paolis
Monk : Scott
Steersman : Sgarro

April 14
MADAMA BUTTERFLY
Cimara (c)
Cio-Cio-San : Albanese
B. F. Pinkerton : Sullivan
Sharpless : Valentino
Suzuki : Roggero (for
Miller)
Kate Pinkerton : Leone
Goro : De Paolis
Yamadori : Cehanovsky
Uncle-Priest : Scott
Imperial Commissioner :
Marsh

April 15
ANDREA CHÉNIER
Same as Nov. 23 except:
Andrea Chénier : Baum
Madelon : Warfield
Mathieu : Baccaloni
Spy : Anthony

April 16 (mat.)
LE NOZZE DI FIGARO
Stiedry (c)
Almaviva : Guarrera

Countess : Steber
Susanna : Peters
Figaro : Siepi
Cherubino : Roggero (for
  Miller)
Marcellina : Glaz
Bartolo : Corena
Basilio : De Paolis
Don Curzio : Carelli
Antonio : Davidson
Barbarina : Georgiou
Peasant Girls : Leone,
  Warfield

April 16

Tosca/Cleva (c)
Tosca : Kirsten
Cavaradossi : Tucker
Scarpia : Cassel
Angelotti : Harvuot
Sacristan : Pechner
Spoletta : Franke
Sciarrone : Cehanovsky
Jailer : Marsh
Shepherd : Elias

BOSTON

April 18

ANDREA CHÉNIER
Same as Nov. 23 except:
Andrea Chénier : Tucker
Madelon : Warfield

April 19

TOSCA
Same as Apr. 16 except:
Tosca : Albanese
Cavaradossi : Conley
Angelotti : Alvary
Sacristan : Corena
Spoletta : De Paolis

April 20 (mat.)

CAVALLERIA RUSTICANA
Same as Apr. 13 except:
Santuzza : Milanov
Turiddu : Gari

PAGLIACCI
Same as Apr. 13 except:
Canio : Baum
Tonio : Warren (for Merrill)

April 20

MANON/Rich (c)
Same as Dec. 21 except:
Manon : Steber
Des Grieux : Campora
Count des Grieux : Moscona
Guillot : De Paolis

April 21

FAUST/Adler (c)
Faust : Conley
Marguerite : Kirsten

Méphistophélès : Hines
Valentin : Guarrera (for
  Merrill)
Siébel : Elias (for Roggero)
Marthe : Votipka
Wagner : Davidson

April 22

OTELLO/Stiedry (c)
Otello : Svanholm
Desdemona : Amara
Iago : Warren
Emilia : Lipton
Cassio : Franke
Roderigo : McCracken
Lodovico : Moscona
Montano : Harvuot
Herald : Sgarro

April 23 (mat.)

LA TRAVIATA
Same as Apr. 12 except:
Violetta : Albanese
Annina : Elias
Gastone : Franke
Baron Douphol : Cehanovsky

April 23

LE NOZZE DI FIGARO
Same as Apr. 16

April 24 (mat.)

MADAMA BUTTERFLY
Same as Apr. 14 except:
Cio-Cio-San : Kirsten
Kate Pinkerton : Krall
Goro : Franke
Yamadori : Harvuot

WASHINGTON

April 25

LA TRAVIATA/Cleva (c)
Same as Apr. 12 except:
Violetta : Albanese
Alfredo : Tucker
Germont : Warren
Flora : Roggero

April 26

FAUST
Same as Apr. 21 except:
Faust : Campora
Valentin : Merrill
Siébel : Miller

ATLANTA

April 27

CARMEN
Same as Apr. 11 except:
Carmen : Thebom
Don José : Tucker
Escamillo : Guarrera

April 28

MANON/Rich (c)
Same as Dec. 21 except:

Manon : Albanese
Des Grieux : Campora
Count des Grieux : Moscona
Guillot : De Paolis
First Guard : Anthony

April 29

ANDREA CHÉNIER
Same as Nov. 23 except:
Andrea Chénier : Baum
Maddalena : Nelli (for
  Milanov)
Madelon : Warfield

April 30 (mat.)

IL BARBIERE DI SIVIGLIA
Cimara (c)
Almaviva : Conley
Dr. Bartolo : Corena
Rosina : Peters
Figaro : Merrill
Don Basilio : Hines
Berta : Votipka
Fiorello : Cehanovsky
Sergeant : De Paolis
Ambrogio : Mayreder

April 30

MADAMA BUTTERFLY
Cleva (c)
Same as Apr. 14 except:
Cio-Cio-San : Kirsten
B. F. Pinkerton : Gari
Sharpless : Guarrera
Suzuki : Miller
Goro : Franke
Yamadori : Harvuot
Uncle-Priest : Hawkins

BIRMINGHAM

May 2

FAUST
Same as Apr. 21 except:
Faust : Peerce
Valentin : Merrill
Siébel : Miller

May 3

TOSCA
Same as Apr. 16 except:
Tosca : Milanov
Cavaradossi : Campora
Angelotti : Alvary
Sciarrone : Harvuot

MEMPHIS

May 4

IL BARBIERE DI SIVIGLIA
Same as Apr. 30 except:
Rosina : Pons
Berta : Warfield

May 5

LA BOHÈME
Same as Apr. 5 except:

1954–55

Rodolfo : Peerce
Marcello : Guarrera
Schaunard : Harvuot
Colline : Moscona
Musetta : Hurley
Parpignol : D'Elia (t)
Alcindoro : Alvary

DALLAS
May 6
PAGLIACCI

Same as Apr. 13 except:
Canio : Baum
Tonio : Warren

CAVALLERIA RUSTICANA

Same as Apr. 13 except:
Lola : Miller
Turiddu : Gari

May 7 (mat.)
IL BARBIERE DI SIVIGLIA

Same as Apr. 30

May 7
ANDREA CHÉNIER

Same as Nov. 23 except:
Andrea Chénier : Tucker
Carlo Gérard : Bastianini
Fléville : Harvuot
Madelon : Warfield
Mathieu : Pechner
Spy : Anthony

May 8 (mat.)
MANON/Rich (c)

Same as Dec. 21 except:
Manon : Albanese
Lescaut : Valentino
Des Grieux : Campora
Count des Grieux : Moscona
Guillot : De Paolis
First Guard : Anthony

HOUSTON
May 9
LA TRAVIATA

Same as Apr. 12 except:
Alfredo : Conley (for
  Campora)
Germont : Warren
Gastone : Franke

May 10
LA BOHÈME

Same as Apr. 5 except:
Rodolfo : Peerce
Schaunard : Harvuot
Mimi : Albanese
Musetta : Hurley
Parpignol : D'Elia
Alcindoro : Alvary

OKLAHOMA CITY
May 11
CAVALLERIA RUSTICANA

Same as Apr. 13 except:
Santuzza : Milanov
Lola : Roggero

PAGLIACCI

Same as Apr. 13 except:
Canio : Baum

DES MOINES
May 12
MADAMA BUTTERFLY/Cleva (c)

Same as Apr. 14 except:
Cio-Cio-San : Kirsten
B. F. Pinkerton : Conley
Sharpless : Guarrera
Suzuki : Miller
Kate Pinkerton : Krall
Imperial Commissioner :
  Davidson

MINNEAPOLIS
May 13
ANDREA CHÉNIER

Same as Nov. 23 except:
Andrea Chénier : Tucker
Madelon : Warfield
Spy : Anthony
Schmidt : Marsh

May 14 (mat.)
CARMEN

Same as Apr. 11 except:
Carmen : Thebom
Escamillo : Guarrera
Zuniga : Hawkins

May 14
IL BARBIERE DI SIVIGLIA

Same as Apr. 30 except:
Dr. Bartolo : Baccaloni
  (for Corena)
Berta : Warfield

May 15 (mat.)
TOSCA

Same as Apr. 16 except:
Cavaradossi : Peerce
Angelotti : Alvary
Spoletta : De Paolis
Sciarrone : Harvuot

BLOOMINGTON
May 16
ANDREA CHÉNIER

Same as Nov. 23 except:
Andrea Chénier : Baum
Countess di Coigny : Elias
  (for Glaz)
Bersi : Roggero (for Elias—
  Act I)
Madelon : Warfield

Spy : Anthony
Schmidt : Marsh

May 17
LA BOHÈME/Kozma (c)

Same as Apr. 5 except:
Marcello : Guarrera
Schaunard : Harvuot
Musetta : Hurley
Parpignol : D'Elia
Sergeant : Tomanelli

LAFAYETTE
May 18
TOSCA

Same as Apr. 16 except:
Tosca : Albanese
Cavaradossi : Peerce
Angelotti : Alvary
Sciarrone : Harvuot
Jailer : Sgarro

CHICAGO
May 19
ANDREA CHÉNIER

Same as Nov. 23 except:
Andrea Chénier : Tucker
Madelon : Warfield
Schmidt : Marsh

May 20
MANON/Rich (c)

Same as Dec. 21 except:
Manon : Kirsten
Des Grieux : Campora
Count des Grieux : Moscona
First Guard : Anthony

May 21 (mat.)
LA BOHÈME

Same as Apr. 5 except:
Rodolfo : Peerce
Marcello : Guarrera
Schaunard : Harvuot
Colline : Scott
Mimi : Albanese
Musetta : Hurley
Parpignol : D'Elia
Alcindoro : Alvary
Sergeant : Tomanelli

May 21
IL BARBIERE DI SIVIGLIA

Same as Apr. 30 except:
Berta : Warfield

May 22 (mat.)
CARMEN

Same as Apr. 11 except:
Don José : Tucker
Escamillo : Guarrera

May 22
LA TRAVIATA

Same as Apr. 12 except:
Germont : Warren

384

TORONTO
May 23
MADAMA BUTTERFLY/Cleva (c)
Same as Apr. 14 except:
Sharpless : Guarrera
Suzuki : Miller
Kate Pinkerton : Krall
Imperial Commissioner :
  Davidson
May 24
CAVALLERIA RUSTICANA
Same as Apr. 13 except:
Santuzza : Milanov
Lola : Miller
Turiddu : Tucker

PAGLIACCI
Same as Apr. 13 except:
Canio : Baum
Tonio : Warren
May 25
LA TRAVIATA
Same as Apr. 12 except:
Germont : Merrill
Flora : Roggero
May 26
TOSCA
Same as Apr. 16 except:
Tosca : Albanese
Cavaradossi : Campora
  (for Peerce)
Angelotti : Alvary
Sacristan : Corena
Sciarrone : Harvuot
May 27
ANDREA CHÉNIER
Same as Nov. 23 except:
Andrea Chénier : Tucker
Madelon : Warfield
May 28
CARMEN
Same as Apr. 11 except:
Carmen : Thebom
Escamillo : Guarrera
Morales : Marsh

MONTREAL
May 30
MANON/Rich (c)
Same as Dec. 21 except:
Manon : Albanese
Des Grieux : Campora
Count des Grieux : Alvary
Guillot : De Paolis
First Guard : Anthony
May 31
FAUST
Same as Apr. 21 except:
Faust : Peerce

Marguerite : Conner
  (for Kirsten)
Valentin : Merrill
Siébel : Miller
June 1
LA TRAVIATA/Cleva (c)
Same as Apr. 12 except:
Violetta : Albanese
Alfredo : Conley
Germont : Warren
Baron Douphol : Cehanovsky
Doctor Grenvil : Harvuot

1955 – 56

PHILADELPHIA
November 22
AIDA/Cleva (c)
King : Sgarro
Amneris : Nikolaidi
Aida : Tebaldi
Radames : Ortica
Amonasro : Bastianini
Ramfis : Tozzi
Messenger : McCracken
Priestess : Vartenissian
December 20
LES CONTES D'HOFFMANN
  Monteux (c)
Hoffmann : Tucker
Olympia : Peters
Giulietta : Stevens
Antonia : Amara
Nicklausse : Miller
Lindorf : Singher
Coppelius : Singher
Dappertutto : Singher
Dr. Miracle : Singher
Spalanzani : Franke
Schlemil : Harvuot
Crespel : Scott
Voice : Warfield
Andrès : De Paolis
Cochenille : De Paolis
Pitichinaccio : De Paolis
Frantz : De Paolis
Luther : Davidson
Nathanael : McCracken
Hermann : Marsh
Stella : Kelepovska
January 24
TOSCA/Mitropoulos (c)
Tosca : Tebaldi
Cavaradossi : Di Stefano
Scarpia : Schoeffler
Angelotti : Harvuot
Sacristan : Pechner
Spoletta : De Paolis
Sciarrone : Cehanovsky
Jailer : Sgarro
Shepherd : Mark

February 14
DIE MEISTERSINGER/Kempe (c)
Hans Sachs : Edelmann
Pogner : Tozzi
Eva : Della Casa
Magdalene : Glaz
Walther : Da Costa
Beckmesser : Davidson
Kothner : Brownlee
Vogelgesang : Hayward
Nachtigall : Marsh
Zorn : De Paolis
Eisslinger : McCracken
Moser : Carelli
Ortel : Hawkins
Schwarz : Scott
Foltz : Alvary
David : Franke
Night Watchman : Harvuot
March 13
DIE ZAUBERFLÖTE (English)
  Walter (c)
Sarastro : Hines
Tamino : Sullivan
High Priest : Schoeffler
Two Priests : McCracken,
  Hawkins
Queen of the Night : Peters
Pamina : Amara
Three Ladies : Krall,
  Chambers, Warfield
Papageno : Uppman
Papagena : Hurley
Monostatos : Franke
Three Genii : Cundari, Elias,
  Roggero
Guards : Da Costa, Sgarro
March 27
SOIREE (Ballet) Schippers (c)
Moylan, Briansky, Black,
  Vitale

DON PASQUALE/Schippers (c)
Don Pasquale : Corena
Ernesto : Valletti
Norina : Gueden
Dr. Malatesta : Guarrera
Notary : De Paolis

BALTIMORE
April 9
DON PASQUALE
Same as Mar. 27 except:
Dr. Malatesta : Merrill
April 10
TOSCA
Same as Jan. 24 except:
Tosca : Milanov
Cavaradossi : Bjoerling
Scarpia : Warren
Spoletta : Franke

385

1955–56

Jailer : Marsh
Shepherd : Elias

BOSTON

April 16
DIE ZAUBERFLÖTE/Stiedry (c)
Same as Mar. 13 except:
Sarastro : Scott (for Hines)
High Priest : Harvuot

April 17
UN BALLO IN MASCHERA
Kozma (c)
Riccardo : Bjoerling
Renato : Warren
Amelia : Nelli (for Milanov)
Ulrica : Anderson
Oscar : Wilson
Silvano : Cehanovsky
Samuel : Moscona
Tom : Scott
Judge : McCracken
Servant : Anthony

April 18
DIE MEISTERSINGER
Stiedry (c)
Same as Feb. 14 except:
Eva : Steber
Beckmesser : Pechner
Vogelgesang : Anthony
Schwarz : Davidson

April 19 (mat.)
LES CONTES D'HOFFMANN
Schippers (c)
Same as Dec. 20 except:
Hoffmann : Campora
Giulietta : Thebom
Andrès : Anthony
Cochenille : Anthony
Pitichinaccio : Anthony
Frantz : Anthony

April 19
CARMEN/Rudolf (c)
Carmen : Stevens
Don José : Tucker
Micaela : Conner
Escamillo : Guarrera
Zuniga : Hawkins
Morales : Marsh
Frasquita : Krall
Mercedes : Roggero
Dancaire : Cehanovsky
Remendado : De Paolis

April 20
BORIS GODUNOV/Kozma (c)
Boris Godunov : Siepi
Fyodor : Miller
Xenia : Cundari
Nurse : Warfield
Shuiski : Kullman
Shchelkalov : Budney

Pimen : Tozzi
Grigori : Gari
Marina : Lipton
Rangoni : Harvuot
Varlaam : Alvary
Missail : McCracken
Innkeeper : Glaz
Officer : Hawkins
Simpleton : Franke
Nikitich : Davidson
Boyar : Carelli
Woman : Votipka
Mityukh : Sgarro
Krushchov : Carelli

April 21 (mat.)
AIDA
Same as Nov. 22 except:
Amneris : Thebom
Aida : Milanov
Radames : Baum
Amonasro : McFerrin
Ramfis : Moscona

April 21
SOIREE (Ballet)
Same as Mar. 27 except:
Solov (The Boy)

DON PASQUALE
Same as Mar. 27 except:
Dr. Malatesta : Merrill

April 22 (mat.)
LA BOHÈME/Cleva (c)
Rodolfo : Peerce
Marcello : Valentino
Schaunard : Cehanovsky
Colline : Hines
Mimi : Amara
Musetta : Hurley
Benoit : Davidson
Parpignol : Anthony
Alcindoro : Alvary
Sergeant : Marsh

CLEVELAND

April 23
LES CONTES D'HOFFMANN
Schippers (c)
Same as Dec. 20 except:
Giulietta : Lipton
(for Stevens)

April 24
UN BALLO IN MASCHERA
Same as April 17 except:
Amelia : Milanov

April 25 (mat.)
FAUST/Adler (c)
Faust : Campora
Marguerite : Conner
Méphistophélès : Siepi
Valentin : Merrill

Siébel : Miller
Marthe : Votipka
Wagner : Davidson

April 25
FLEDERMAUS/Kozma (c)
Eisenstein : Kullman
Rosalinda : Steber
Adele : Munsel
Ida : Moylan
Alfred : Sullivan
Orlofsky : Thebom
Dr. Falke : Brownlee
Frank : Harvuot
Dr. Blind : Franke
Frosch : Mann (actor)

April 26
LA BOHÈME
Same as Apr. 22 except:
Marcello : Guarrera
Schaunard : Harvuot
Colline : Moscona
Mimi : Albanese

April 27
RIGOLETTO/Cleva (c)
Duke : Bjoerling
Rigoletto : Warren
Gilda : Peters
Sparafucile : Tozzi
Maddalena : Elias
Giovanna : Votipka
Monterone : Scott
Marullo : Cehanovsky
Borsa : Carelli
Ceprano : Marsh
Countess : Leone
Page : Georgiou
Guard : Sgarro

April 28 (mat.)
DER ROSENKAVALIER
Rudolf (c)
Princess von Werdenberg :
  Steber
Baron Ochs : Edelmann
Octavian : Stevens
Von Faninal : Brownlee
Sophie : Conner
Marianne : Votipka
Valzacchi : De Paolis
Annina : Lipton
Police Commissioner :
  Hawkins
Majordomo of Princess :
  McCracken
Majordomo of Von Faninal :
  Anthony
Notary : Pechner
Innkeeper : Franke
Singer : Da Costa
Orphans : Georgiou,
  Vartenissian, Warfield

386

Milliner : Cundari
Hairdresser : Vitale
Leopold : Mayreder
Animal Vendor : Carelli
Negro Boy : Nevins

April 28
AIDA

Same as Nov. 22 except:
Amneris : Thebom
Aida : Milanov
Radames : Baum
Amonasro : Merrill
Priestess : Krall

WASHINGTON
April 30
LE NOZZE DI FIGARO
Rudolf (c)

Almaviva : Guarrera
Countess : Steber
Susanna : Conner
Figaro : Siepi
Cherubino : Miller
Marcellina : Warfield
Bartolo : Corena
Basilio : De Paolis
Don Curzio : Carelli
Antonio : Davidson
Barbarina : Cundari
Peasant Girls : Leone, Elias

RICHMOND
May 1
TOSCA

Same as Jan. 24 except:
Tosca : Milanov
Cavaradossi : Campora
Scarpia : Cassel
Spoletta : Franke
Shepherd : Elias

ATLANTA
May 2
LES CONTES D'HOFFMANN
Schippers (c)
Same as Dec. 20

May 3
DIE MEISTERSINGER
Stiedry (c)
Same as Feb. 14 except:
Eva : Steber
Beckmesser : Pechner
Vogelgesang : Anthony
Schwarz : Davidson

May 4
BORIS GODUNOV
Mitropoulos (c)
Same as Apr. 20 except:
Boris Godunov : Hines
Pimen : Scott
Marina : Thebom

Innkeeper : Lipton
Simpleton : Anthony

May 5 (mat.)
DON PASQUALE
Same as Mar. 27 except:
Dr. Malatesta : Merrill

SOIREE (Ballet)
Same as Mar. 27 except:
Solov (The Boy)

May 5
TOSCA
Same as Jan. 24 except:
Tosca : Milanov
Cavaradossi : Campora
Scarpia : Cassel
Angelotti : Alvary
Spoletta : Franke
Shepherd : Elias

BIRMINGHAM
May 7
LE NOZZE DI FIGARO
Same as Apr. 30 except:
Susanna : Wilson
Antonio : Alvary

May 8
RIGOLETTO
Same as Apr. 27 except:
Duke : Conley
Marullo : Harvuot
Page : Cundari

MEMPHIS
May 9
LES CONTES D'HOFFMANN
Schippers (c)
Same as Dec. 20 except:
Olympia : Hurley
Giulietta : Thebom

May 10
TOSCA
Same as Jan. 24 except:
Tosca : Albanese
(for Milanov)
Cavaradossi : Peerce
Scarpia : Cassel
Angelotti : Alvary
Sacristan : Corena
Spoletta : Franke
Shepherd : Elias

DALLAS
May 11
LES CONTES D'HOFFMANN
Schippers (c)
Same as Dec. 20 except:
Olympia : Hurley
Giulietta : Thebom

May 12 (mat.)
DON PASQUALE
Same as Mar. 27 except:
Ernesto : Anthony
Norina : Peters
Dr. Malatesta : Merrill

SOIREE (Ballet)
Same as Mar. 27 except:
Solov (The Boy)

May 12
TOSCA
Same as Jan. 24 except:
Tosca : Milanov
Cavaradossi : Campora
Scarpia : Warren
Angelotti : Alvary
Spoletta : Franke
Shepherd : Elias

May 13 (mat.)
DIE MEISTERSINGER
Stiedry (c)
Same as Feb. 14 except:
Eva : Steber
Beckmesser : Pechner
Vogelgesang : Anthony
Schwarz : Davidson

HOUSTON
May 14
LUCIA DI LAMMERMOOR
Cleva (c)
Lucia : Pons
Alisa : Votipka
Edgardo : Campora
Ashton : Valentino
Raimondo : Moscona
Arturo : Franke
Normanno : McCracken

May 15
LE NOZZE DI FIGARO
Same as Apr. 30 except:
Susanna : Peters

OKLAHOMA CITY
May 16
TOSCA
Same as Jan. 24 except:
Tosca : Milanov
Cavaradossi : Campora
Scarpia : Warren
Angelotti : Alvary
Shepherd : Elias

DES MOINES
May 17
LES CONTES D'HOFFMANN
Schippers (c)
Same as Dec. 20 except:
Olympia : Hurley (for
Peters)
Giulietta : Thebom

1955–56

MINNEAPOLIS
May 18

BORIS GODUNOV
Mitropolous (c)
Same as Apr. 20 except:
Boris Godunov : Hines
Pimen : Scott
Grigori : Da Costa

May 19 (mat.)
RIGOLETTO/Cimara
(c—for Cleva)
Same as Apr. 27 except:
Duke : Peerce
Marullo : Harvuot
Ceprano : Cehanovsky
Page : Cundari
Guard : Marsh

May 19
AIDA
Same as Nov. 22 except:
Amneris : Thebom
Aida : Milanov
Radames : Baum
Amonasro : McFerrin
Ramfis : Moscona
Priestess : Krall

May 20 (mat.)
DIE MEISTERSINGER
Stiedry (c)
Same as Feb. 14 except:
Eva : Steber
Vogelgesang : Anthony
Moser : Folmer (t)

BLOOMINGTON
May 21
DON PASQUALE
Same as Mar. 27 except:
Ernesto : Carelli
Norina : Peters

SOIREE (Ballet)
Same as Mar. 27 except:
Solov (The Boy)

May 22
BORIS GODUNOV
Mitropoulos (c)
Same as Apr. 20 except:

Rangoni : Valentino
Varlaam : Davidson
Simpleton : Anthony
Nikitich : Hawkins

LAFAYETTE
May 23
LES CONTES D'HOFFMANN
Schippers (c)
Same as Dec. 20 except:
Olympia : Hurley
Giulietta : Thebom

CHICAGO
May 24
BORIS GODUNOV
Mitropoulos (c)
Same as Apr. 20 except:
Krushchov : Anthony

May 25
AIDA
Same as Nov. 22 except:
Amneris : Thebom
Aida : Milanov
Radames : Baum
Amonasro : Merrill
Ramfis : Hines
Priestess : Krall

May 26
DIE MEISTERSINGER
Stiedry (c)
Same as Feb. 14 except:
Eva : Steber (for Amara)
Vogelgesang : Anthony
Moser : Folmer (for Carelli)

May 27 (mat.)
FLEDERMAUS
Same as Apr. 25 except:
Adele : Peters
Alfred : Carelli (for
Hayward)

May 27
CARMEN
Same as Apr. 19 except:
Escamillo : Valentino
(for Guarrera—Acts III,
IV)

Zuniga : Scott

TORONTO
May 28
AIDA
Same as Nov. 22 except:
Amneris : Thebom
Aida : Nelli (for Milanov)
Radames : Baum
Amonasro : Merrill
Priestess : Roggero

May 29
FAUST
Same as Apr. 25 except:
Méphistophélès : Hines

May 30
CARMEN
Same as Apr. 19 except:
Micaela : Amara
Escamillo : Valentino
(for Guarrera)
Zuniga : Scott

May 31
FLEDERMAUS
Same as Apr. 25 except:
Adele : Peters

June 1
LA BOHÈME/Kozma (c)
Same as Apr. 22 except:
Marcello : Guarrera
Schaunard : Harvuot
Colline : Moscona
Parpignol : McCracken
Alcindoro : De Paolis

June 2
RIGOLETTO/Cimara (c)
Same as Apr. 27 except:
Duke : Tucker
Marullo : Harvuot
Borsa : Franke
Page : Cundari

*(3738 Metropolitan Opera
performances on tour,
1883-1956)*

TOUR CHRONOLOGY BY CITIES

Figures in parentheses indicate number of cities in each tour and number of performances.

Key to abbreviations: Al—Albany At—Atlanta Ba—Baltimore Bir—Birmingham Bl—Bloomington Bo—Boston Br—Brooklyn Bu—Buffalo Cha—Chattanooga Chi—Chicago Ci—Cincinnati Cl—Cleveland Da—Dallas Den—Denver Des—Des Moines Det—Detroit Ha—Hartford Hou—Houston In—Indianapolis KC—Kansas City Laf—Lafayette Li—Lincoln LA—Los Angeles Lou—Louisville Mem—Memphis Mex—Mexico Mil—Milwaukee Mo—Montreal Na—Nashville NH—New Haven NO—New Orleans Nrk—Newark Ok—Oklahoma City Om—Omaha Par—Paris Ph—Philadelphia Pi—Pittsburgh Po—Portland Pr—Providence Ri—Richmond Ro—Rochester SA—San Antonio SF—San Francisco SL—St. Louis SLak—Salt Lake City SP—St. Paul Spr—Springfield Sy—Syracuse Tol—Toledo Tor—Toronto Tr—Troy U—Utica Wa—Washington WP—White Plains

1883-84—Bo Br Ph Chi SL Ci Wa Ba (8-80)
1884-85—Chi Ci Bo (3-42)
1885-86—Ph Chi SL Ci Cl (5-41)
1888-89—Ph Bo Mil Chi SL (5-42)
1889-90A (Abbey)—Chi Mex SF Den Om Lou Bo Ph (8-84)
1889-90 (Damrosch)—Bo Chi (2-30)
1891-92—Chi Lou Br Al Tr Ph Bo (7-53)
1893-94—Ph Di Do Chi SL (5-60)
1894-95—Ph Br Ba Wa Bo Chi SL (7-81)
1895-96—Br Bo Ba Wa Ph Bu Det Chi SL (9-71)
1896-97—Br NH Ha Chi SL Lou Ci Bo (8-53)
1898-99—Chi Br Ph Bo Ba Wa Pi (7-63)
1899-00—NH Sp Al U Sy Mo Tor Det Cl KC SL In Lou Ci Chi Mil Bo Po Ph Br Pi Wa Ba (23-112)
1900-01—LA SF Den KC Li Min Ph Br Bo Pi Ci Chi (12-95)
1901-02—Al Mo Tor Ro Sy Bu Lou Na Mem At Bir NO Hou SA LA SF KC SL In Ci Cl Ph Bo Chi Pi Ba Br (27-145)
1902-03—Ph Wa Bo Chi Ci Pi (6-60)
1903-04—Ph Wa Bu Chi Ci Pi Bo Pr Ha Spr NH (11-60)
1904-05—Ph Bo Pi Ci Chi Min Om KC SLak SF LA Da Hou NO At Bir Na (17-66)
1905-06—Ph Ba Wa Pi Chi SL KC SF (8-46)
1906-07—Ph Ba Wa Bo Chi Ci SL KC Om SP Min Mil (12-59)

1907-08—Ph Bo Ba Wa Chi Pi (6-44)
1908-09—Br Ph Ba Chi Pi (5-67)
1909-10—Br Ph Ba Bo Chi Pi Cl Tol Det Mil SP SL In Lou At Par (16-163)
1910-11—Al Br Ph Mo Cl Ci At (7-38)
1911-12—Br Ph Bo Ba At (5-39)
1912-13—Al Br Ph At (4-33)
1913-14—Al Br Ph At (4-31)
1914-15—Br Ph At (3-34)
1915-16—Br Ph Bo At (4-56)
1916-17—Br Ph At (3-34)
1917-18—Br Ph Bo (3-36)
1918-19—Br Ph At (3-33)
1919-20—Br Ph At (3-33)
1920-21—Br Ph At (3-34)
1921-22—Br Ph At (3-33)
1922-23—Br Ph At (3-34)
1923-24—Br Ph At Cl Ro (5-43)
1924-25—Br Ph At Cl Ro (5-47)
1925-26—Br Ph At Cl Ro (5-48)
1926-27—Br Ph Ba Wa At Cl Ro (7-56)
1927-28—Ph Br Ba Wa At Cl Ro (7-60)
1928-29—Ph Br Ba Wa At Cl Ro (7-59)
1929-30—Br Ph Ba Wa Ri At Cl Ro (8-60)
1930-31—Br Ph Ha WP Ba Wa Cl Ro (8-54)
1931-32—Br Ph WP Ha Ba Cl Ro (7-44)
1932-33—Ph Ha Br WP Ba (5-30)
1933-34—Ph Br Ha Bo Ba Ro (6-34)
1934-35—Br Ha Nrk Ba Bo Ro (6-22)
1935-36—Ph Ha Nrk Br Bo Ro Ba (7-24)
1936-37—Ph Br Ha Nrk Ba Bo Cl Ro (8-37)

389

1937-38—Ph Ha Nrk Ba Bo Cl Ro (7-35)
1938-39—Ph Ha Nrk Ba Bo Cl Ro Da
NO At (10-45)
1939-40—Ph New Ha Ro Ba Bo Cl Da
NO At (10-48)
1940-41—Ph Ha Ba Bo Cl NO Da At Ri
Ro Al (10-49)
1941-42—Ph Ha Ba Bo Cl Bl Da Bir At
Ri (10-46)
1942-43—Ph Chi Cl Ro (4-31)
1943-44—Ph Bo Chi Mil Cl Ro (6-41)
1944-45—Ph Ba Bo Cl Laf Mil Min Chi
Ro (9-47)
1945-46—Ph Ba Bo Ro Cl Bl Min Mil Chi
SL Da Mem Cha (13-59)
1946-47—Ph Ba Bo Cl Bl Min Chi At Da
SA Hou NO Mem SL Ro (15-67)
1947-48—Ph Ba Bo Ri At Cha Mem Da
LA Den Li SL Bl Laf Min Cl Ro (17-
70)

1948-49—Ph Ba Bo Cl Ro At Mem Da
LA Den Des Min Bl Laf SL (15-69)
1949-50—Ph Ba Bo Cl Bl Laf SL At Mem
Da Hou Ok Des Min Chi Ro (16-59)
1950-51—Ph Ba Bo Cl At Mem Da Hou
Ok Des Min Bl Laf Chi Ro (15-49)
1951-52—Ph Ba Cl Bo Wa Ri At Bir
Mem Da Hou Ok Des Min Bl Laf SL
Tor Mo (19-63)
1952-53—Ph Ba Cl Bo Wa At Bir Mem
Da Hou Ok Des Min Bl Laf Ro Mo
Tor (18-63)
1953-54—Ph Ba Cl Bo At Bir Mem Da
Ok SL Des Min Bl Laf Chi Tor (16-57)
1954-55—Ph Ba Cl Bo Wa At Bir Mem
Da Hou Ok Des Min Bl Laf Chi Tor
Mo (18-66)
1955-56—Ph Ba Bo Cl Wa Ri At Bir Mem
Da Hou Ok Des Min Bl Laf Chi Tor
(18-62)

1956-57—Ph Ba Bo Cl Wa Ri At Bir Mem Da Hou Ok Des Min Bl Laf Chi
Tor Mo (19-66) (based on advance information and subject to change)

ERRATA IN TOUR CASTS

1885-86. Substitute Edmond C. Stanton for Hermann Grau as manager at the beginning.
Insert Hermann Grau before CHICAGO.

1889-90A. Mexico. Delete (?) on Nordica appearances, and insert Nordica under *Aida*
Jan. 14 and *L'Africaine* Jan. 28 verified by Ira Glackens, Nordica's biographer (*Yankee Diva*).

1893-94. Insert Henry E. Abbey as manager.

1899-1900. Chicago, Nov. 24, *Walküre:* Add (t) to Bach as Grimgerde. Philadelphia, Jan. 9,
Fliegende Holländer: delete (t) after Breuer as Steersman.

1900-01. Chicago, April 27, *Il Trovatore:* After Gauthier (Manrico) delete (d), substitute (t).

1901-02. Toronto, Oct. 10, State Concert: Correct spelling is Gilibert. Add to Perello: (d).

1905-06. Philadelphia, Jan. 4 matinee: Abarbanell is correct spelling.

1907-08. Pittsburgh, April 29, *Walküre:* insert Same as Feb. 11 except:

1908-09. Philadelphia, Jan. 26, *Nozze di Figaro:* Add (t) to Maestri (Curzio). Chicago,
April 16, *Walküre:* Substitute Destinn for Sparkes as Gerhilde.

1929-30. Boston. Add on March 25, Young People's Special Matinee. *Faust*, with Richard
Crooks, Ezio Pinza, John Brownlee, Wilfred Engelman, Susanne Fisher, Lucielle Browning,
Thelma Votipka; Wilfred Pelletier conducting.

1944-45. Boston, April 12, *Pelléas et Mélisande:* conductor probably Cooper.

TOUR CHRONOLOGY BY CITIES: Insert Minn (eapolis)

INDEX

394

397

399